Setting the Stage for Modernity

Trendsetter der Moderne

jovis

Setting the Stage for Modernity

Trendsetter der Moderne

Cafés
Hotels
Restaurants

Places of Pleasure and Leisure

Orte des Genusses und der Freizeit

Franziska Bollerey

jovis

Dank dem „Wohlgelehrten und Durchleuchtigen"

Foreword

Over the course of the modern era, cafés, hotels, and restaurants can be said to have developed into true trendsetters of modernity. From the eighteenth century onwards, these public spaces provided the newly emerging social classes in particular with opportunities to meet and interact. The technological and scientific innovations collected under the heading of the 'Industrial Revolution'—as well as the theories and ideas collectively known as 'the Enlightenment'—led to truly revolutionary upheavals. They led to a critical distancing from the old powers, namely from the privileged, hereditary nobility on the one hand and monarchist absolutism on the other. A newly emerging middle class began to grow in importance, as described by Franco Moretti in his book *The Bourgeois: Between History and Literature*. The figure of the bourgeois now stood in the centre of changes in society—and at the same time became the audience, beneficiary, and underwriter of the institutions discussed in this book. Cafés, hotels, and restaurants provided and continue to provide the ideal framework for the customs which, in English, came to be known as sociability. On entering the premises, the anonymous public sphere of the outside world was transformed into an increasingly familiar environment, becoming more comfortable the longer one remained. Even now, in an age of widespread electronic connectivity, these surroundings represent an unparalleled guarantee of civilised, high-quality human interaction.

Cafés

Like hotels and restaurants, cafés acted—and still act—as stages for social display, particularly in the metropolises. In doing so, they fulfil a deep-rooted societal need. Customers and staff become actors. Every visitor is placed individually in the scene: they arrive, look around in the expectation of being greeted, and finally

Vorwort

Cafés, Hotels und Restaurants haben sich im Laufe der Neuzeit zu wahren Trendsettern der Moderne entwickelt. Seit dem 18. Jahrhundert boten sich an diesen öffentlichen Orten vor allem den neu entstehenden gesellschaftlichen Schichten Möglichkeiten des Zusammentreffens. Die unter dem Begriff „Industrielle Revolution" subsumierten materiellen Innovationen haben – ebenso wie die unter „Aufklärung" firmierenden Theorien und Gedanken – zu wahrhaft revolutionären Umbrüchen geführt. Diese führten zu einem kritischen Abstand von den alten Mächten, dem privilegierten Geburtsadel und dem monarchischen Absolutismus. Eine neu entstehende Mittelschicht gewann nun an Raum, wie es Franco Moretti in seinem Buch *Der Bourgeois. Eine Schlüsselfigur der Moderne* beschreibt. Der Bürger ist nun der zentrale Protagonist gesellschaftlicher Veränderungen. Gleichzeitig wurde er zum Adressaten, Nutznießer und Garanten der in diesem Buch behandelten Institutionen. Cafés, Hotels und Restaurants boten den perfekten Rahmen für den im Englischen als Sociability bezeichneten Entfaltungsraum: Die anonyme Öffentlichkeit der Außenwelt verwandelt sich nach dem Betreten der jeweiligen Räumlichkeiten und in verstärktem Maße nach einer längeren Verweilzeit in eine zunehmend vertrauter werdende Umgebung, die auch im Zeitalter hochgradiger elektronischer Vernetzung einen konkurrenzlosen Garanten kultivierter und qualitätvoller menschlicher Kontaktnahme darstellt.

Cafés

Cafés, ebenso wie Hotels und Restaurants, waren und sind dabei vor allem in den Metropolen auch Bühnen einer Zurschaustellung, die einem tiefverwurzelten gesellschaftlichen Bedürfnis entspricht. Klienten und Personal werden zu Akteuren. Auftritt, Suchblick in Erwartung persönlicher Begrüßung wie auch Abgang

depart. Particularly in the case of public figures, this can amount to the celebration of a veritable 'holding court' in these spaces. The philosopher and writer Jean-Paul Sartre may serve as an example here; Simone de Beauvoir wrote of the Café de Flore in Paris, where she and Sartre held court, that 'we worked there from nine in the morning until midday, when we went out to eat. At two we returned and conversed with acquaintances until four, after which we again worked until eight. After dinner we kept appointments with all sorts of people.'

The café thus became not only a venue for intellectual debates, but the setting for literary and journalistic work. *The Guardian*, still a major British newspaper today, was founded in 'Button's Coffee House' in London at the start of the eighteenth century. The section 'A Hub for Artists and Writers' illustrates the role of coffee houses as sites of creative inspiration: we find early English coffee houses referred to as 'penny universities' or 'cradles of public opinion', and the Paris cafés 'Coupole' und 'Dôme' were sometimes called 'trottoir academies' in the 1920s. Stefan Zweig called these locations 'our best teaching establishments' and Siegfried Kracauer proposed 'café seminars'. Their remarks point to the character of the café as a site of creative inspiration.

Coffee and coffee house both act as stimulant and venue. The beverage and surroundings productively complemented one another and promoted bourgeois emancipation. As Wolfgang Schivelbusch succinctly puts it, 'coffee as a productive force for the bourgeoisie.' Another aspect of coffee house culture is the 'global march of a stimulant' and its close relationship with colonialism. This facet underlies the contemporary fascination with the Orient, which is closely bound up with the history of coffee and the coffee house; long before the world's fairs began to promote globalisation in 1851, the transfer of cultures was taking place in these spaces. The dialectic found in the coffee house—of restraint and freedom on the one hand, and idleness and bustle on the other—also characterises the hotel.

setzen noch immer jeden Besucher individuell in Szene bis hin zur Zelebrierung einer veritablen „Hofhaltung", wie dies vor allem auf Personen der Öffentlichkeit zutrifft. Der Philosoph und Schriftsteller Jean-Paul Sartre mag hier als Beispiel dienen. Über den Ort von Sartres und Simone de Beauvoirs gemeinsamer Hofhaltung, das Pariser Café de Flore, notiert die Letztere: „Von neun Uhr morgens bis Mittags, wo wir zum Essen gingen. Um Zwei kamen wir zurück und unterhielten uns mit Bekannten bis Vier, worauf wir wieder arbeiteten bis Acht. Nach dem Abendessen trafen wir Verabredungen mit allen möglichen Leuten."

Das Café wird also nicht nur zum Schauplatz intellektueller Debatten sondern auch Rahmen für die schriftstellerische und journalistische Arbeit. So wird die noch heute bestehende englische Tageszeitung *The Guardian* Anfang des 18. Jahrhunderts im Londoner Kaffeehaus Button's aus der Taufe gehoben. Sowohl Bezeichnungen wie „Penny Universities" oder „cradles of public opinion" für die frühen englischen Kaffeehäuser, oder in den 1920er Jahren „Trottoirakademien" für das Pariser „Coupole" und „Dôme", als auch Stefan Zweigs Bemerkung von „unserer besten Bildungsstätte" oder Siegfried Kracauers Aussage vom „Seminar im Café" verweisen darüberhinaus auf den Charakter des Kaffeehauses als einem Ort der schöpferischen Inspiration – illustriert im Folgenden im Unterkapitel „Ein Treffpunkt für Künstler und Schriftsteller".

Kaffee und Kaffeehaus – Stimulans und Aufenthaltsort gleichermaßen. Getränk und Örtlichkeit ergänzen sich auf produktive Weise und fördern die bürgerliche Emanzipation. Wolfgang Schivelbusch bringt es auf einen Nenner: „Der Kaffee als bürgerliche Produktivkraft". Ein weiterer Aspekt des Phänomens Kaffeehaus liegt auch in dem eng mit der Kolonialgeschichte verbundenen „global march of a stimulant", hinter dem auch die mit Kaffee und Kaffeehaus verquickte Faszination vom Orient steht. Lange vor den Weltausstellungen als Beförderern der Globalisierung ab 1851 findet hier ein Kulturtransfer statt. Die im Kaffeehaus anzutreffende Dialektik von Gebundenheit und Ungebundenheit einerseits und Müßiggang und Betriebsamkeit andererseits charakterisiert auch das Hotel.

Hotels

Following on the heels of the grand tours previously reserved for the aristocracy, travel developed—and so, necessarily, did the hotel industry. In the wake of the world's fairs, the hotel industry became a fixed part of modern life. From the beginning of the nineteenth century it began to offer levels of entertainment and comfort that went beyond accommodation and board. In 1809, for example, the 'Badische Hof' hotel in Baden-Baden already boasted ballrooms, theatres, a library, and reading and writing rooms.

Completely divorced from the culture of everyday life, the hotel provided an unconstrained 'home away from home' of a non-committing nature, a complete novelty in association with the available leisure activities. The Grand Hotels, in particular, tried to outbid one another with the attractions they offered: dining halls overflowing with champagne, performances of the Milan Scala opera house, and so on. Most notably, the hotelier César Ritz, a leading light in the luxury hotel industry, was particularly adept at attracting a wealthy clientele. Brilliantly, he combined comfort, cuisine, and service; it is said, not without reason, that 'Ritz was one of the great civilising influences of his time'. Even as an individual, he came to be a trendsetter of modernity.

Amongst other features, bathrooms were among the civilised advancements of the modern age. Long before they became a standard part of domestic architecture, they began to appear in hotels—initially one by one, but soon as an essential part of hotel complexes. Architects were instructed to ensure the frictionless removal of waste from these mighty machineries of accommodation. The building of hotels became a lucrative construction assignment, both in cases of complete new builds and in those where existing facilities were to be expanded—such as the 'Engadiner Kulm' hotel in St. Moritz or the 'Montreux Palace', the latter for many years the home of the author Vladimir Nabokov. In places that were particularly beloved by travellers, such as Venice, old palaces were converted while Grand Hotels were erected on the Lido. Along with train stations and department stores, hotels were among the biggest and most prominent construction projects in the metropolises. The 'Grand Hotel' in Paris, built in 1861/62, comprised an area of 10,000 square metres; the 'Stevens Hotel' in Chicago contained 3,000 rooms.

Hotels

In Nachfolge der dem Adel vorbehalten gewesenen „Grand Tour" entwickelt sich das Reisen und dadurch bedingt auch die Hotellerie im Gefolge der Weltausstellungen zu einem festen Bestandteil modernen Lebens. Damit einher geht auch ein über die Beherbergung und Beköstigung hinausgehendes Angebot an Unterhaltung und Komfort, das bereits zu Anfang des 19. Jahrhunderts einsetzt. So verfügte zum Beispiel der Badische Hof in Baden-Baden bereits ab 1809 über Ballsäle, Theater, eine Bibliothek sowie Lese- und Schreibzimmer.

Der Alltagskultur vollständig enthoben, bot das Hotel als Rahmen von Unverbindlichkeit dennoch „a home away from home", was in Zusammenhang mit den Freizeitangeboten eine absolute Novität war. Insbesondere die Grand Hotels überboten sich mit Attraktionen: champagnergeflutete Speisesäle, Auftritte der Mailänder Scala et cetera. Vor allem der für das Luxus-Hotelwesen wegweisende César Ritz wusste die zahlungskräftige Klientel an sich zu binden. Auf geniale Weise kombinierte er Komfort, Cuisine und Service. Nicht zu Unrecht heißt es über ihn: „Ritz was one of the great civilizing influences of his time". Er wird damit auch als Person zu einem Trendsetter der Moderne.

Zu den zivilisatorischen Errungenschaften der Neuzeit gehörten unter anderem auch die Badezimmer, die – lange bevor sie eine Standardausstattung im Wohnungsbau darstellten – erst vereinzelt, dann aber mehr und mehr zu einem zugehörigen Teil von Hotelkomplexen wurden. Dem Architekten oblag es dabei, den reibungslosen Ablauf innerhalb dieser gewaltigen Beherbergungsmaschinerien zu gewährleisten. Der Hotelbau wurde zu einer lukrativen Bauaufgabe, sei es als kompletter Neubau oder als Erweiterung bestehender Einrichtungen wie im Fall des Engadiner Kulm in St. Moritz oder des Montreux Palace, dem langjährigen Domizil des Schriftstellers Vladimir Nabokov. In den Stätten besonderer Reisesehnsucht wie beispielsweise Venedig wurden alte Paläste umgebaut, aber auch auf dem Lido moderne Grand Hotels errichtet. In den Metropolen gehörten neben den Bahnhöfen und Warenhäusern vor allem die Hotels zu den prominentesten und größten Bauprojekten. Das Grand Hotel in Paris von 1861/62 umfasste 10.000 Quadratmeter Fläche, das Stevens in Chicago zählte 3000 Räume.

An army of attendants was employed to keep the entire hotel apparatus running smoothly. With this, the hotel also became a theatre of social disparity; this is discussed in the chapter 'On and Behind the Stage'. The heading 'From Purpose-Oriented Travel to Tourism: The Urbanization of the Countryside' deals with the impact of hotel-building around the turn of the twentieth century. The construction of hotels at a scale disproportionate to their surroundings eventually reached its climax in the huge hotel-castles built to serve mass tourism in both summer and winter. Spa resorts and scenic locations near the sea, large lakes, and in the mountains were prime locations for the construction of new hotels. Due to their number, concentration in specific locations, and frequently excessive size, hotels contributed to the urbanisation and drastic transformation of the original settlements. 'I am going to start a spa .... Stop, look at that village, that poor village! I will make a town of it, yes, I will, a lovely town full of big hotels which will be filled with visitors—with elevators, with servants, with carriages...' cries Guy de Maupassant's protagonist in his novel *Mont Oriol*.

As businesses, hotels depend on making a return on their investment. Here, too, efforts were made early on to ensure success, and from around 1830 the reputations of hotels were made known in travel guides. The names of prominent guests also served as advertising. This was also the case for cafés and restaurants, which promoted themselves through the presence of famous personalities.

With a few exceptions, the Ritz triad of 'comfort, cuisine, and service' has now degenerated, with a few exceptions which are discussed in the chapter 'Surface Culture'. Instead, accessories such as mini bars, TV-screen greetings, Wi-Fi, or full-body air dryers are intended to contribute to guests' wellbeing. 'The rage for mechanical devices may be the ruin of a once-good hotel, for the basis of righteousness in a hotel is not mechanical devices but personal human contacts', wrote Norman S. Hayner in 1936. The superficial culture examined in this chapter also plays an increasingly dominant role in restaurants.

Um diesen gesamten Hotelorganismus in Betrieb zu halten, stand ein Heer von Bediensteten zur Verfügung. Damit wird das Hotel auch Schauplatz sozialer Disparitäten, auf die im Unterkapitel „Vor und Hinter den Kulissen" eingangen wird. Im Unterkapitel „Von der Zweckreise zum Tourismus. Die Verstädterung der Landschaft" wird der um die Wende zum 20. Jahrhundert einsetzende, den Maßstab des landschaftlichen Kontextes durchbrechende Hotelbau behandelt, der in den Bettenburgen des Sommer- wie Winter-Massentourismus seinen Höhepunkt findet. Bevorzugt ausersehen für den Bau von Hotels waren Kurorte und landschaftlich herausragende Gegenden am Meer, an größeren Seen und im Gebirge. Durch ihre Konzentration an einem Ort und die häufige Überdimensionierung trugen Hotels zu einer Verstädterung und einer drastischen Veränderung der ursprünglichen Siedlungen bei. „Ich will eine Bäderstadt lancieren ... Sieh das Dorf hier, dieses arme Dorf! Eine Stadt werde ich daraus machen, eine weiße Stadt voller Grand Hotels, die voller Gäste sind, Hotels mit Lift, Personal und Wagen", läßt Guy de Maupassant in seinem Roman *Mont Oriol* den Protagonisten Andermatt ausrufen.

Als Investitionsobjekt ist das Hotel abhängig von seiner Rendite. Auch hier wurden die Weichen bereits in der Geschichte gestellt. Die dafür zuträgliche Propagierung der Reputation übernehmen ab circa 1830 Reiseführer. Propagandamittel waren auch die Namen prominenter Gäste. Dies gilt auch für Cafés und Restaurants, die mit der Präsenz berühmter Persönlichkeiten für sich werben.

Die Ritz'sche Trias von „Comfort, Cuisine und Service" ist in der heutigen Zeit mit Ausnahme einiger unter dem Titel „Surface Culture" abgehandelter Luxusherbergen ganz generell einer Degeneration anheimgefallen. Stattdessen sollen heute Accessoires wie Minibar, Bildschirmbegrüßung, Wi-Fi oder Ganzkörperfön zum Wohlbefinden des Gastes beitragen. „The rage for mechanical devices may be the ruin of a once good hotel, for the basis of righteousness in a hotel is not mechanical devices but personal human contacts", schrieb bereits 1936 Norman S. Hayner. Diese hier kritisierte Oberflächenkultur spielt auch eine immer dominantere Rolle beim Besuch von Restaurants.

Restaurants

Nowadays, a visit to a restaurant by René Redzepi, Ferran Adrià, or any of the other contemporary 'kitchen gods' is more about prestige than culinary enjoyment. From the creation of dishes to their presentation, this chapter deals with the culinary arts in detail. It discusses what is considered edible and what norms are observed for the preparation of dishes and their presentation. Ideas of moderation and gluttony, or necessity and luxury, are dependent on the prevailing societal and cultural frameworks. Above all, Western society and its gastronomic culture are discussed. Famous protagonists of the culinary arts and of the physiology of taste—among them the gastrosophers and gastronomers of early modernity, such as Jean Anthelme Brillat-Savarin and Alexandre Grimod de la Reynière—have their say. The refinement and stylisation of cooking is closely bound up with prevailing table customs and the way they are made visible.

For example, Ludwig XIV was frequently to be seen publicly en famille at the grand couvert. This courtly culture came to an abrupt end with the French Revolution. However, it would be incorrect to assume that the cooks, formerly beholden to the courtly food culture and suddenly unemployed, would usher in the birth of the restaurant. At this point, eating establishments which—unlike the predetermined offerings of the *table d'hôte system*—provided menus with a choice of dishes had already existed for some time. The terminology still used today is of interest here: *restaurant* originally meant a hearty meat broth, a *soupe de santé*. From the second half of the eighteenth century, the eateries which offered this healthy soup were referred to as restaurants themselves, as shown in the chapter 'The Birth of the Restaurant'.

If the restaurant is defined as a place of culinary enjoyment in a refined environment, with sophisticated, individual service alongside a multitude of elaborate dishes, the space in which all this takes place—as an architectural composition—should also be considered. Further chapters of the restaurant section of this book introduce the designs of renowned architects and examine these spaces in detail.

Features of the fast food industry, as well as the selling and eating of street food, are also discussed. Finally, new formats and trends in gastronomy are assessed with reference to the historical context.

Restaurants

Ein Aufenthalt in den Restaurants von René Redzepi, Ferran Adrià oder anderen zeitgenössischen Küchengöttern dient heute mehr der Prestigevermehrung als dem kulinarischen Genuß. Ausführlich wird in diesem Kapitel auf die Kulinarik eingegangen: die Kreation von Speisen und ihre Inszenierung. Es wird erläutert, was als essbar gilt, welche Normen der Zubereitung gelten, welche Regeln beim Verzehr. Dabei sind Maß und Maßlosigkeit, Notwendigkeit und Luxus von den jeweiligen gesellschaftlichen und kulturellen Rahmenbedingungen abhängig. Behandelt wird vor allem die westliche Gesellschaft und ihre Gastro-Kultur. Berühmte Protagonisten der Kochkunst und der Physiologie des Geschmacks, unter ihnen in der Neuzeit Gastrosophen und Gastronomiekritiker wie Jean Anthelme Brillat-Savarin und Alexandre Grimod de la Reynière kommen zu Wort. Die Verfeinerung und Stilisierung des Kochens ist eng mit den vorherrschenden Tafelsitten und deren Zur-Schau-Stellung verbunden.

So war ein Ludwig XIV. „en famille" beim „grand couvert" regelmäßig öffentlich zu besichtigen. Die höfische Kultur fand mit der Französischen Revolution ihr abruptes Ende. Fälschlich jedoch wäre die Annahme, dass die ehemals der höfischen Eßkultur verpflichteten und mit ihrem Verschwinden dann arbeitslosen Köche die Geburtsstunde des Restaurants eingeläutet hätten. Gaststätten, die auf Menukarten – im Unterschied zum vorgegebenen Angebot des *table-d'hôte-Systems* – auszuwählende Gerichte anboten, hatten sich schon eine geraume Weile vorher etabliert. Ein Kuriosum dabei ist deren bis heute gültige Namensgebung: *Restaurant* war ursprünglich eine kräftigende Fleischbrühe, eine *soupe de santé*. Ab der zweiten Hälfte des 18. Jahrhunderts nannte man dann die Speisegaststätten, in denen die Gesundheitsbouillon angeboten wurde, Restaurant, wie im Kapitel „Die Geburt des Restaurants" ausgeführt wird.

Wenn man das Restaurant als einen Ort kulinarischen Genusses in gepflegtem Ambiente und mit gehobenem, individuellen Service nebst einer Vielzahl elaborierter Speisen definiert, so muß man doch auch dem Raum selbst, in dem all dies stattfindet, als architektonischer Aufgabe Aufmerksamkeit schenken. Dies behandeln ausführlich weitere Kapitel des Restaurant-Teiles im Buch, wo Entwürfe renommierter Architekten vorgestellt werden.

Overall, this work unfolds a broad spectrum of cultural, architectural, and socio-historical analyses based on the premise that these public spaces—café, hotel, and restaurant—present as in a concave mirror an exemplary microcosm of the societal development of the last two hundred years. It is precisely in these spaces that society made the transition into the modern period. In a very modern way, they were the stages on which contemporary society-defining trends appeared—and they continue to fulfil this role today.

Ebenfalls erörtert werden auch die Aspekte des Fast-Food-Wesens sowie das an Bedeutung stets zunehmende Phänomen des Straßenverkaufs und -verzehrs von Speisen. Abschließend werden neue Formen und Tendenzen der Gastronomie an ihren historischen Gegebenheiten gemessen.

Insgesamt tut sich ein breit gefächertes Spektrum kultur-, architektur- und sozialhistorischer Betrachtung auf – unter der Prämisse, dass sich die gesellschaftliche Entwicklung der letzten zweihundert Jahre vorzüglich und wie in einem Brennspiegel an den öffentlichen Orten Café, Hotel und Restaurant ablesen und darstellen läßt. Gerade hier vollzog sich der Übergang einer Gesellschaft in die Moderne und in ebendiesem modernen Sinn bildeten und bilden sie die Bühne für den Auftritt der jeweils gesellschaftsbestimmenden Tendenzen.

Genius Loci: The Coffee House

Genius Loci: Das Kaffeehaus

Coffee and coffeehouse: luxury and location. Both, productively complementing each other, promoted civic emancipation. English authors speak of coffeehouses as 'Cradles of Public Opinion'. Pubs and inns as places to convene away from home have existed since antiquity. Consumption of alcoholic beverages acts on people's social behaviour in a specific way. Induced by the stimulating effects of coffee the meeting of people in a coffeehouse is of an entirely different character.

> 'Consumed hot, coffee acts stimulating on the central nervous system … accordingly coffee furthers mental activity making reflection and work easier … the perception of external impressions and their assimilation is facilitated … a certain urge towards procreation is generated, a drifting of thoughts and conceptions, a mobility and ardour in wishes and ideals',[1]

lexicographic articles subsume the matter. The coffee house becomes a shelter for the *genius loci* of critical and creative protagonists. In the following our topic will be coffee as an *agens* from its global spread and its capitalization as economic plant up to its global marketing as an everyday mass product. Parallel we will consider the steps of development and facets of coffeehouse culture.[2]

'Java-Jargon'

'Our aim is to see more people drinking coffee than eating Hamburgers',[3] thus Starbuck's stated intention. Here we speak of sales, of market shares. Here the multitude of worldwide corporate-design-levellers is augmented with one more brand, even more furthering the replaceable character of individual urban scenes. This definitely is not coffee or coffeehouse culture. It does not help that Starbucks takes refuge to a literary figure, namely that of the first mate from Herman Melville's *Moby Dick*.[4] A very vague trace of a formerly highly differentiated culture may be detected in the number of coffee varieties the Starbucks chain offers. It was and is Italians and Viennese[5] who created innumerable variants. 'Espresso' and 'Cappuccino' today form part of everyday clients' orders and only real connoisseurs still discern the origin of the coffee beans or the processes of their improvement. The customers patronizing chain coffee shops today, however, have long reduced their connoisseurship to the 'latte-language' or the 'java-jargon'.[6] With studied casualness they give order for a 'latte macchiato'.

Kaffee und Kaffeehaus: ein Genussmittel und ein Ort. Beide sich auf produktive Weise ergänzend und die bürgerliche Emanzipation fördernd. Englische Autoren sprechen von den „cradles of public opinion". Gasthäuser und Schenken, um sich außerhalb des Hauses zu begegnen, gibt es seit der Antike. Der Konsum von alkoholischen Getränken kennzeichnet das soziale Verhalten in letzteren. Entsprechend der belebenden Wirkung des Kaffees hatte das Aufeinandertreffen der Gäste im Kaffeehaus einen vollkommen anderen Charakter.

> „Heiß getrunken wirkt der Kaffee anregend auf das zentrale Nervensystem … Dabei regt der Kaffee die geistigen Fähigkeiten an, sodass man leichter denkt und arbeitet … Die Auffassung äußerer Eindrücke und ihre Verarbeitung wird erleichtert … Es entsteht ein gewisser Drang zur Produktivität, ein Treiben der Gedanken und Vorstellungen, eine Beweglichkeit und Glut in den Wünschen und Idealen",[1]

so bringen es lexikalische Eintragungen auf einen Nenner. Das Kaffeehaus entwickelt sich zu einem *genius loci* für kritische und schöpferische Geister. Im Folgenden soll die Rede sein von dem *Agens* Kaffee – von seiner globalen Verbreitung und Kapitalisierung als Nutzpflanze bis zu seiner globalen Vermarktung als Massenartikel. Auch soll die Rede sein von den Etappen und Facetten der Kaffeehauskultur.[2]

Hier spricht man Java-Jargon

„Our aim is to see more people drinking coffee than eating Hamburgers",[3] so die erklärte Intention von Starbucks. Hier geht es um Absatz, um Marktanteile. Hier wird der Vielzahl der weltweiten Corporate-Design-Egalisierer eine weitere Marke hinzugefügt und damit die Tendenz zu verwechselbaren Stadtbildern weiter verstärkt. Von Kaffee- oder gar Kaffeehauskultur kann man hier nicht reden. Da hilft auch nicht, dass man sich bei der Namensgebung einer literarischen Figur bediente, des Ersten Maats aus Herman Melvilles *Moby Dick*.[4] Ein vager Hauch der ehemals so diversifizierten Kaffeekultur lässt sich vielleicht noch an der Fächerung des Angebots ablesen. Hier waren und sind es die Italiener und die Wiener[5], die unzählige Varianten kreierten. Espresso und Cappuccino gehören inzwischen zum Wortschatz alltäglicher Bestellungen, wirkliche Kenner legen auch Wert auf die Herkunft der Kaffeebohnen und den Prozess der

What most do not know: the combination of coffee and milk is an age-old recipe. 'Le café au lait' Madame de Sévigné (1626–1696) wrote in 1690, is 'la plus jolie chose du monde'.[7] The addition of cloves or cinnamon or mixing coffee with chocolate—called 'Mochaccino' in the Java-jargon—also go back to the seventeenth century. And Louis-Sébastien Mercier (1740–1814), who around the middle of the eighteenth century unfolds all facets of the everyday life of Parisians, reports that milk coffee, presented by 'women with huge milk cans, made from tinplate on their backs, conquered a big following amongst the workers'.[8] This serves as proof that the consumption of coffee—and that was true already since the sixteenth century in the Ottoman Empire—was common in all strata of society. Whereas working class people, no matter whether in London, Paris[9] or Berlin, had their coffee in the streets, presented by ambulant vendors or at stalls, nobility made use of salons or, since the middle of the seventeenth century, of the first coffee houses.

There were differences, too, in the quality of the raw product as well as in the refinement of preparing it for consumption. From the nineteenth century on surrogates were offered to the working population due to the price of coffee that was speculatively driven upwards by the commodity exchanges. At the same time the rich consumed refined creations of coffee or *confisérie* goods.

Chain coffee stores such as the one mentioned above and 'Coffee Republic, 'Caffè Nero' or 'Costa Coffee' in Britain, 'Coffee Company' in the Netherlands and 'Balzac Coffee' in Germany, may well serve the revival of the historic public consumption of coffee—but what does this mean for coffeehouse culture? Unquestionably, places that allow the application of the term 'genius loci' are not created in this way, for 'branding' for most brands and store-chains means a worldwide interchangeable and uniformly recognizable appearance that next to the identical logo includes a standardized set of interior decorations. The Italian-style British 'Caffè Nero' branch houses try to achieve a certain differentiation. The Dutch 'Coffee Company' uses a trademark central table to individualize their places. A still more striking exception from this is the café of the brothers Costes in Paris who, in 1984, opened their first place in Paris' 'Halles' quarter. Philippe Starck (b. 1949), then in the first stages of his career, gave a certain modernist-minimalist character to the venue. Meanwhile however, the Costes brothers since the 1990s have subscribed to the retro-styles of Jacques Garcia:

Veredelung. Wer jedoch in Kettencafés ein- und ausgeht, dessen Kenntnisse sind zumeist auf die „latte language" oder den „Java-Jargon" reduziert.[6] Betont lässig gibt man seine „latte macchiato"-Bestellung auf.

Dabei ist die Kombination von Milch und Kaffee wahrlich keine Novität. „Le café au lait", schrieb Madame de Sévigné 1690, sei „la plus jolie chose du monde."[7] Und Louis-Sébastien Mercier, der um die Mitte des 18. Jahrhunderts alle Facetten des Pariser Alltagslebens aufblättert, berichtet, dass der Milchkaffee, ausgeschenkt von „Frauen mit großen Kannen aus Weißblech auf dem Rücken, sich unter den Arbeitern eine große Anhängerschaft erobert hat".[8] Dies ist ein Indiz dafür, dass Kaffeetrinken – und dies war seit dem 16. Jahrhundert schon im Osmanischen Reich der Fall – in allen sozialen Schichten üblich war. Während die unteren Gesellschaftsschichten den Kaffee – gleich ob in London, Paris[9] oder Berlin – vorerst auf der Straße, wo er von ambulanten Verkäufern feilgehalten wurde, oder auch an Buden tranken, standen dem Adel und den oberen Schichten Salons und ab der Mitte des 17. Jahrhunderts die ersten Kaffeehäuser zur Verfügung.

Differenzen gab es auch in der Qualität des Produkts und der Raffinesse der Zubereitung. Im 19. Jahrhundert werden wegen der an den Börsen spekulativ in die Höhe getriebenen Kaffeepreise für die Arbeiter auch Surrogate angeboten, während die Vermögenden raffinierte Kaffee- und Confiseriekreationen genossen. Das Hinzufügen von Nelken und Zimt oder das Mischen mit Schokolade – im Java-Jargon „Mochaccino" genannt – gehen bereits auf das 17. Jahrhundert zurück.

Caféketten wie die bereits genannte oder Coffee Republic, Caffè Nero, Costa Coffee und andere tragen zwar zur Wiederbelebung historischer Kaffeegenüsse bei; aber was bedeutet dies für die Kaffeehauskultur? Unverwechselbare Orte, bei denen man von einem *genius loci* sprechen könnte, werden so jedenfalls nicht geschaffen. Denn zum Branding der meisten Marken und Ketten gehört ein weltweit einheitliches Erscheinungsbild, das neben dem Logo auch die Inneneinrichtung einschließt. Eine Ausnahme von dieser Regel stellen in Paris die Brüder Costes dar. 1984 eröffnen sie im Quartier des Halles ihr erstes Café. Philippe Starck, am Anfang seiner Karriere, verleiht dem Ort einen modernistisch-minimalistischen Charakter. Seit den 1990er Jahren haben die Costes sich den Retrostilen von Jacques Garcia verschrieben: venezianische Glasleuchter, Leder, Plüsch und Samt. Eklektizismus und Neohisto-

Venetian glass chandeliers, leather, plush and velvet. Eclecticism and Neo-Historicism—in short modern 'historic neo-authenticity'—are very much in favour. One example from Paris may be mentioned here: 'Le Fumoir'[10] is an amalgam of English Colonial Style, Casablanca-appeal and historical Parisian Café elements. The 'Le Fumoir' however, similar to the former Berlin restaurant 'Theodor Tucher' on Pariser Platz in the immediate vicinity of the Brandenburg Gate, merits being mentioned here because of another reason: following the example of so many famous historical Cafés, the presence of books in both places attracts immediate attention. Whether the atmospheric effects that were part of the quality of historic coffee places can thus be recreated, or if this was intended at all, remains, however, an open question.

One thing strikes the reader of all recent publications that deal with historic coffee houses: here we hear of personalities, literary and political discourses. Books on contemporary coffee houses in contrast exclusively give information on the interior design, the number of branch shops in the different chains or the yearly profit the chain makes. No recent publication can do without mentioning 'Cyber-Cafés'. Here coffee is dealt from automats into plastic or waxed-paper beakers (which you can see people carry away drinking while walking back to their computer) and the screen-conveyed communication necessarily leads to an atomization of any feeling of community of those present. Here the damnable reduction of experience comes to light, a lack of awareness for an all-encompassing sensitivity. Without disputing the usefulness of such places: coffee houses they are not. The inspiring power of the coffee house as dwelling place sprang from the physical proximity of neighbouring visitors, from the sounds, smells and delights present, and last not least from an excellent and expertly served coffee.

The Global March of a Stimulant

'Noir comme le diable
Chaud comme l'enfer
Pur comme un ange
Doux comme l'amour.'

Presumably this ode of Charles Maurice de Talleyrand's (1754–1838) goes back to an Arabic text.[11] Indeed it was the Arabs who cultivated coffee as a luxury good and bestowed on it the nobility of an object of sensual

rismus – kurz die historische Neoauthentizität – erfreuen sich großer Beliebtheit. Ein Beispiel aus Paris sei hier genannt: Das Fumoir[10] ist ein Amalgam aus englischem Kolonialstil, Casablanca-Bar und historischem Pariser Café. Es verdient ähnlich wie ehemals das Tucher in Berlin am Pariser Platz jedoch aus einem anderen Grund eine Erwähnung: Nach dem Vorbild so vieler berühmter historischer Cafés springt hier die Anwesenheit von Büchern ins Auge. Ob sich so Atmosphären aus der Taufe heben lassen, wie sie den historischen Orten eigen waren, und ob dieses überhaupt intendiert ist, bleibt offen. Auffällig ist, dass in allen jüngeren Publikationen, deren Thematik das Kaffeehaus ist, bei der Behandlung historischer Cafés die Rede von Persönlichkeiten sowie literarischen und politischen Diskursen ist, bei der Abhandlung neuerer Cafés jedoch ausschließlich von deren Einrichtung, der Vermehrung der Filialen und von deren Absatz gesprochen wird. Keine der neueren Publikationen verzichtet auf die Erwähnung von Cyber-Cafés. Hier läuft der Kaffee aus Automaten in Plastik- oder gewachste Pappbecher und die über den Bildschirm stattfindende Kommunikation führt notwendigerweise zu einer Vereinzelung der Anwesenden. Hier zeigt sich die erbärmliche Reduktion ganzheitlicher Erfahrungen, das mangelnde Bewusstsein für eine allumfassende Sinnlichkeit. Ohne die notwendige Existenz dieser elektronischen Schreibstuben negieren zu wollen: Kaffeehäuser sind solche oben erwähnten Orte nicht. Denn die inspirierende Kraft des Verweilortes Kaffeehaus wird von dem physischen Neben- und Miteinander der Besucher, den Geräuschen, Gerüchen und Genüssen und eben auch einem qualitätvollen und virtuos servierten Kaffee bestimmt.

Kreuzzug eines Genussmittels

„Noir comme le diable,
Chaud comme l'enfer,
Pur comme un ange,
Doux comme l'amour."

Anzunehmen ist, dass diese Ode Charles Maurice de Talleyrands (1754–1838) auf einen arabischen Text zurückgeht.[11] Es sind in der Tat die Araber, die den Kaffee als Genussmittel kultivieren, ihm den Adel eines Gegenstands sinnlicher Wahrnehmung verleihen. Fälschlicherweise und für lange Zeit – und hierzu hat auch der

perception. Wrongly—and to this the Swedish naturalist Carl von Linné (1707–1777) has contributed with his specification of the plant as 'caffea arabicus'[12] (fig. 1)—its origin was supposed to be Arabia (Saudi Arabia).

As a matter of fact however, the plant originated in Abessinia (Ethiopia) and in the hill region north of Lake Victoria. A centre of its occurrence was the 'Kaffa' region in Southeast Ethiopia, probably the reason the beverage later was called 'Qawha'[13] in the Turkish and Arabian language area. Another etymological derivation is the designation 'Bunn' for the present noun for the coffee 'bean'. 'Bunn' was the word for the fruit of the coffee shrub used by the African tribe of Habaschi. Similar to betel nut or coca the raw beans were, according to the Scottish merchant James Bruce,[14] chewed or eaten pulverized and mixed with butter or tallow and rolled into balls. In Vienna to the present day 'Hof-Conditorei Ch. Demel's Sons' sell roasted coffee beans coated in chocolate.

Probably the Ethiopians already brought coffee to Yemen as early as the thirteenth or fourteenth century. From here via the harbours of Aden and Mocha (then Al Mukha)—another term that was to become part of the coffee lore—it reached Mecca and Suez, from there Aleppo (Haleb) and ultimately Cairo. The latter developed into an important storage and trading post[15] and—next to Mecca—into a centre of public coffee consumption. A great number of historic sources[16] deals with the effects and spread of this luxury commodity and hands down to posterity the long-term controversy about psycho-physiological advantages and disadvantages of drinking coffee. Early proof of the anabolic effects of caffeine is given by the Sufis. According to a first-time Mocha information, it is said of them, that they kept themselves awake night by night by intensive consummation of coffee to serve their emphatic religious rites.[17] There are two gates of entry for the colonization of Europe by coffee—it has also been called the crusade of a luxury good. From Alexandria it was brought as an export commodity by sea to Venice, Marseille, the Netherlands, England, and Germany in the course of the seventeenth century. A second route takes its course from Syria to Constantinople and from there to Central Europe. Since Osman I (1299–1326), the Ottoman empire was in permanent expansion: from Anatolia via Asia Minor to Africa and Europe (in 1529 and 1683 Turkish armies besieged Vienna; Budapest for more than 140 years was under Turkish reign) and thus became the first territory for the spread of coffee (fig. 2).

schwedische Naturforscher Carl von Linné (1707–1777) mit seiner Artenbezeichnung „caffea arabicus“[12] beigetragen (Abb. 1) – wird auch sein Ursprung in Arabien (Saudi-Arabien) angenommen.

Tatsächlich aber war die Pflanze in Abessinien (Äthiopien) und in den nördlich des Victoriasees liegenden Gebirgszügen beheimatet. Ein Zentrum des Vorkommens war die im Südosten Äthiopiens gelegene Region Kaffa, wohl die Namenspatin des später im arabischen und türkischen Sprachraum als „Qawha“[13] bekannten Getränkes. Eine andere etymologische Herleitung ist die Bezeichnung „Bunn“ für das heutige Wort Kaffeebohne. „Bunn“ benannte der afrikanische Stamm der Habaschi die Frucht des Kaffeestrauches. Ähnlich wie Betel oder Koka wurden die rohen Bohnen gekaut oder zerstoßen und mit Talg oder Butter vermengt zu Kugeln gerollt verzehrt, so berichtet es der schottische Kaufmann James Bruce.[14] In Wien verkauft noch heute die Hofkonditorei Ch. Demel's Söhne mit Schokolade überzogene geröstete Kaffeebohnen.

Wahrscheinlich hatten die Äthiopier den Kaffee bereits im 13. und 14. Jahrhundert in den Jemen gebracht. Von dort gelangte er ab dem 16. Jahrhundert über die Hafenstädte Aden und Mocha (Al Mukha) (ebenfalls ein Name, der in die Kaffeenomenklatur eingeht) nach Mekka und Suez und von dort nach Aleppo (Haleb) und nach Kairo. Kairo wurde zu einem wichtigen Lager und Handelsplatz[15] und neben Mekka zu einem Zentrum öffentlichen Kaffeeausschanks. Eine Vielzahl historischer Quellen[16] setzt sich mit der Wirkung und Verbreitung dieses Genussartikels auseinander und führt der Nachwelt auch den langwährenden Streit um die psycho-physiologischen Vor- und Nachteile des Kaffeegenusses vor Augen. Einen frühen Beweis der anabolischen Auswirkung des Koffeins lieferten die Sufi. Ihnen wird – zum ersten Mal aus Mocha überliefert – nachgesagt, dass sie sich nach dem intensiven Genuss von Kaffee in einer Art Trance nächtelang wachhielten, um ihren emphatischen religiösen Handlungen zu obliegen.[17] Die Kolonialisierung Europas durch den Kaffee – man spricht auch vom Kreuzzug eines Genussmittels – kennt zwei Einfallstore. Von Alexandria aus gelangte er als Exportgut im 17. Jahrhundert auf dem Wasserweg nach Venedig, Marseille, in die Niederlande und nach England und Deutschland. Eine zweite Route verläuft über Syrien nach Konstantinopel und von dort nach Zentraleuropa. Das seit den Zeiten Osmans I. (1299–1326) von Anato-

Around 1600 coffee as everyday beverage was common in the whole empire. In its geographic centre however, coffee could not be cultivated. This took place in its region of origin, Ethiopia and especially on plantations in Yemen and Arabia, until in the second half of the seventeenth and in the eigthteenth century European colonial powers organized cultivation more universally.

It was the Dutch who—experienced in speculation and the creation of an added value gained by the cultivation of tulips—organized global coffee growing over the so-called 'coffee belt'. In 1614 a Dutch delegation composed of merchants and agrarian experts was staying in Aden to spy on Arabic methods of coffee growing and processing. In 1616 they succeeded in gaining possession of seeds and plants.

Coffee shoots were then grown in domestic Botanic Gardens. The East Indian Company VOC, founded in 1602, as well as the West Indian Company WIC of 1621 formed the structural backbone of exporting plants to the Dutch colonies and re-importing coffee harvests. In 1658 coffee growing started in Ceylon (Sri Lanka) that had recently been taken over from the Portuguese.[18] On the same island the Dutch unscrupulously controlled the growing of cinnamon and secured a world monopoly.[19] In 1699 they succeeded in establishing the coffee plant on the island of Java in the immediate vicinity of their trading post of Batavia (Jakarta) founded in 1595. From here the Dutch organized the systematic spread across their islands of Sumatra, Bali, Timor and later Celebes. Allegedly it was the shoot of a coffee plant from Java, cultivated in the Amsterdam Botanic Garden in 1706 that made history as the ancestor of the entire Central American coffee culture. Nicolaas Witsen, the then burgomaster of Amsterdam donated a (Java) coffee plant to Louis XIV, whom he ardently admired.

Gabriel Mathieu Clieu (1688–1774), a French naval officer, was successful in 1721 in transporting a shoot of this plant, now from the Paris Botanical Gardens 'Jardin des Plantes', to Martinique, from where cultivation spread: in 1727 to Haiti, in 1728 to Jamaica—Jamaica 'Blue Mountain Coffee' today is the most expensive brand of coffee—in 1748 to Cuba, from there to Puerto Rico, Trinidad, Venezuela and so on. It was the Dutch again who did the first step in introducing coffee to Surinam in 1718. From here the Portuguese merchant Francisco della Melo Palheta smuggled a plant into the Brazilian province of Pará. Brazil at the beginning of the twentieth century

lien aus und vor allem seit dem Fall von Konstantinopel 1453 in Kleinasien, Afrika und Europa (1529 und 1683 stehen die osmanischen Heere vor Wien; Budapest ist circa 140 Jahre lang unter türkischer Herrschaft) ständig expandierende Reich wurde zum ersten Verbreitungsterritorium des Kaffees (Abb. 2). Um 1600 war der Kaffee als Getränk im gesamten Osmanischen Reich allgemein verbreitet. Im Kernland konnte der Kaffee als Nutzpflanze nicht kultiviert werden. Das geschah im Kaffeeursprungsland Äthiopien und im Besonderen in Plantagen im Jemen und in Arabien, bis die europäischen Kolonialmächte ab der zweiten Hälfte des 17. Jahrhunderts und im 18. Jahrhundert den Anbau weltweit organisierten.

Die Niederländer, die in Zusammenhang mit der Tulpenzucht Erfahrungen in der Spekulation und der Abschöpfung des Mehrwertes von Naturgütern erworben hatten, waren es, die den globalen Anbau im sogenannten Kaffeegürtel initiierten. 1614 hatte sich eine niederländische Delegation, bestehend aus Kaufleuten und Agrarexperten, in Aden aufgehalten, um den arabischen Kaffeeanbau und seine Weiterverarbeitung auszuspionieren. 1616 gelang es ihnen auch, in den Besitz von Samen und Pflanzen zu kommen.

Kaffeeschösslinge wurden dann in den heimischen Botanischen Gärten gezüchtet. Die 1602 gegründete Ostindische Kompanie (VOC) sowie die seit 1621 bestehende Westindische Kompanie (WIC) waren das strukturelle Rückgrat für den Export der Pflanzen in die niederländischen Kolonien sowie den Rücktransport der Ernten. 1658 begann in dem gerade von den Portugiesen eroberten Ceylon (Sri Lanka) der Kaffeeanbau.[18] Auf dieser Insel kontrollierten die Niederländer auch skrupellos den Zimtanbau und verschafften sich das Weltmonopol.[19] 1699 gelang ihnen die Ansiedlung der Kaffeepflanze auf Java in unmittelbarer Nähe ihres 1595 gegründeten Handelsstützpunktes Batavia (Jakarta). Von dort aus organisierten sie die systematische Ausbreitung auf ihren Inseln: Sumatra, Bali, Timor und später Celebes. Angeblich war es der Schössling einer Pflanze aus Java, der 1706 im Amsterdamer Botanischen Garten weitergezüchtet wurde und als Ahne der gesamten mittelamerikanischen Kaffeekultur in die Geschichte eingehen sollte. Der damalige Amsterdamer Bürgermeister Nicolaas Witsen, ein glühender Verehrer Ludwigs XIV. machte diesem 1714 eine (Java-)Kaffeepflanze zum Geschenk.

Dem französischen Marineoffizier Gabriel Mathieu Clieu (1688–1774) gelang es 1721, einen Ableger dieser

1

Ibriq ou Pot Pour Faire cuire le Café
Plante du Café
Instrument Pour Torrefier le Café
Feves de Café

2

Pontus Euxinus Hodie Mare Nigrum
Cara Denghis Turcis Zorno More Russis
Czarno Morze Polonis Mauro Thalassa Graecis
et das Schwartze Meer Germanis
Mare Caspium al. Hircanum
Mare Mediterraneum
Mare Arabicum
Imperium Turcicum in Europa, Asia et Africa

3

4

grew eighty percent of the world production of raw coffee. After an initial period of coffee consumption, tea-drinking England only in 1840 started large-scale coffee cultivation in India, in 1878 in central Africa and later East Africa. Australia was reached in 1876.[20]

Global migration of this—compared to tea, which looks back on a history of more than one thousand five hundred years—very young luxury is accompanied by the history of its consummation. Knowledge of this beverage, 'black as ink', is brought to Europe by merchants and travellers to the Orient in the seventeeth and eighteenth century. Coffee beans as well as implements needed for their preparation only very infrequently come to the European continent as in the case of the Frenchman Jean de la Roque, who brought them from Istanbul to Marseille. One of the first known European consumers of coffee is William Harvey (1578–1658) physician and discoverer of the circulation of blood (1628)—consummation and discovery here are to be seen in direct connection.

Spread of consumption is equally furthered by various representatives of the Osman Empire itself, who in

1
Coffee plant and grinder beneath an Osman coffee drinker with an 'Ibriq' coffee pot (Sylvestre Dufour, 1671)

Kaffeepflanze und -mühle sowie osmanischer Kaffeetrinker mit dem „Ibriq" (Sylvestre Dufour, 1671).

2
Map of the Osman Empire, or 'Imperium Turcicum', 1685

Karte des Osmanischen Reiches „Imperium Turcicum", 1685.

3
In the eighteenth century, elaborate serving systems evolved, such as this pivoting table that served three rooms at the same time ● This coffee house, situated at Tophane Square in Constantinople, features lavish furnishings (copperplate engraving by Antoine Melling, 1819)

Im 18. Jahrhundert entstanden raffinierte Serviersysteme wie dieser drehbare, drei Zimmer gleichzeitig bedienende Tisch. ● Eine uxuriöse Ausstattung zeigt dieses am Tophaneplatz in Konstantinopel gelegene Kaffeehaus (Kupferstich von Antoine Melling, 1819).

4
This view of the terrace of a simple Constantinople coffee house (copperplate engraving by William Bartlett, 1839) with a view of the Valens aqueduct and Hagia Sophia suggests the appearance of the first coffee houses ● The interior of this Tatar coffeehouse, too (copperplate engraving from around 1800) shows typical characteristics: raised dais, conversation, the playing of games, the conveying of news, and the performances by a storyteller. The garments convey a whiff of the exotic. This oriental fashion spilled over to Europe

Die Ansicht (Kupferstich von William Bartlett, 1839) der Terrasse dieses einfacheren Kaffeehauses in Konstantinopel mit Blick auf den Valens-Aquädukt und die Hagia Sophia lässt Rückschlüsse auf das Aussehen der ersten Kaffeehäuser zu. ● Auch die Innenansicht dieses tartarischen Kaffeehauses (Kupferstich um 1800) zeigt die typischen Charakteristiken: erhöhte Sitznischen, Diskurs, Disput, Spiel, Nachrichtenübermittlung bzw. den Auftritt eines Erzählers. Die Kleidung vermittelt einen Hauch Exotik und die Orient-Mode schwappt nach Europa.

Pflanze aus nun wiederum dem Pariser Botanischen Garten, dem Jardin des Plantes, nach Martinique zu bringen, von wo aus die Kultivierung sich fortsetzte: 1727 Haiti, 1728 Jamaika – der Jamaica Blue Mountain ist heute die teuerste Kaffeesorte –, 1748 Kuba, von dort nach Puerto Rico, Trinidad, Venezuela usw. Doch auch hier hatten die Niederländer mit der Anpflanzung von Kaffee in Surinam 1718 schon den ersten Schritt gemacht. Von hier aus schmuggelt 1727 der portugiesische Kaufmann Francisco de Melo Palheta eine Pflanze in die brasilianische Provinz Pará. Brasilien produziert Anfang des 20. Jahrhunderts 80 Prozent der gesamten Welterzeugung an Rohkaffee. Die Tee trinkende Nation England hatte erst 1840 mit der Großkultivierung des Kaffees in Indien, 1878 in Zentralafrika und danach in Ostafrika begonnen. Australien erreichte der Kaffeeanbau 1876.[20]

Die globale Wanderung dieser im Vergleich zum Tee mit seiner 1500-jährigen Geschichte jungen Nutzpflanze als Genussmittel wird begleitet von der Geschichte seines Konsums. Die Kenntnis vom Genuss dieses Getränkes – schwarz wie Tinte – bringen Kaufleute und Orientreisende im 16. und 17. Jahrhundert nach Europa. Vereinzelt gelangen auch Bohnen und die für die Zubereitung des Kaffees notwendigen Geräte auf den europäischen Kontinent, wie zum Beispiel 1644 durch den Franzosen Jean de la Roque aus Istanbul nach Marseille. Als einer der ersten regelmäßig Kaffee konsumierenden Europäer ist der Arzt und Entdecker des Blutkreislaufs (1628) – sein Konsum und die medizinische Entdeckung stehen in ursächlichem Zusammenhang – William Harvey (1578–1658) bekannt.

Die Verbreitung des Konsums beförderten aber auch die unterschiedlichsten Vertreter des Osmanischen Reiches selbst, die in den europäischen Hafen- und Handelszentren und in den europäischen Garnisonen nicht auf das ihnen vertraute Getränk verzichten wollten. Es ist bekannt, dass man in Venedig bereits in den 1610er Jahren Kaffee trank. Höhepunkte und Multiplikatoren der Kaffeefaszination waren mehrmonatige Aufenthalte osmanischer Gesandter 1665 in Wien und 1669 in Paris.[21] Zum Gefolge der Diplomaten gehörten Kaffeeköche, zum kulturpolitischen Programm für die Wiener und Pariser gehörte das Verkosten von Kaffee. Interessanterweise sind es diese beiden Städte, deren Namen sich in einer Art Typologisierung weltweit wiederfinden lassen: Wiener Kaffeehaus und Pariser Café. Der Konsum von

the European harbour and trading centres or in their European military posts as well as at European Universities did not like to do without their habitual beverage. It is a matter of record that in Venice around 1610 coffee was consumed. Peaks and multiplying effect at the same time were the sojourn of Ottoman envoys in Vienna in 1665 and in Paris in 1669.[21] Part of the diplomat's entourage was a number of coffee cooks and part of the cultural entertainment programme was a tasting ceremony of coffee for people in Paris or Vienna. Remarkably these two cities lend their names to the typology of places of coffee consumption world wide: the 'Wiener Kaffeehaus' and the Paris 'Café'. Drinking coffee consequently was not a novelty any more when around the middle of the seventeenth century the first coffee houses entered the stage of public life in Venice, Oxford, or London.

The Fascination of the Unknown: The Birth of Modern Cultural Transfer

It is the process of becoming familiar with the consumption of luxury goods such as tea, coffee, or chocolate that more than that of any other previously traded goods widens the horizon of Europeans. Together with Panoramas[22] and intensified by the presentation of non-European cultures during World Exhibitions they instigate a yearning for the unknown and the exotic and thus can be regarded as initiators of modern mass tourism.

What initially can be read off the eighteenth century architectural and interior decoration fashions of royalty and nobility (Chinoiseries, Oriental fashions, Egyptomania)—a very late example for this is John Nash's (1757–1835) Royal Pavilion of 1815–1822—soon was to become part of the knowledge of the enlightened bourgeoisie.[23] Coffee house owners of foreign origin play an important role of mediators here. According to the provenance and early use of coffee it was Syrians, Lebanese, Egyptians, Greeks, Armenians and later Dutch, English or Italian citizens who obtained concessions to roast, brew and distribute coffee.

The growing consumption of coffee during the fifteenth and sixteenth centuries led to a 'hitherto unknown social institution', the coffee house.[24] This aspect is completely disregarded in North-American and Europe-centred literature even under inclusion of sociological and philosophical works like those by Jürgen Habermas[25], to give only one example.

Kaffee war also keine Novität mehr, als um die Mitte des 16. Jahrhunderts die ersten Kaffeehäuser in Venedig, Oxford und London auf der Bühne des öffentlichen Lebens erscheinen.

Die Faszination des Fremden – die Geburtsstunde des modernen Kulturtransfers

Es sind die Kenntnis und der Konsum von Genussmitteln wie Kaffee, Schokolade und Tee, die mehr als der Umgang mit allen zuvor gehandelten Gütern den Horizont der Europäer erweitern. Sie schüren die Sehnsucht nach dem Fremden, dem Exotischen und können neben den Panoramen[22] und verstärkt durch die Zurschaustellung außereuropäischer Kulturen auf den Weltausstellungen als Initiatoren eines modernen Massentourismus interpretiert werden.

Was sich zunächst an den architektonischen und innenarchitektonischen Moden der Könige und des Adels (Chinese Style, Oriental Mode, Egyptomania – ein später Spross dieser Tendenz ist 1815–1822 der Royal Pavillon von John Nash (1757–1835)) ablesen lässt, gehört bald zum aufgeklärten Wissen des Bürgertums.[23] Eine wichtige Vermittlerrolle spielen hier ausländische Kaffeewirte. Entsprechend der Herkunft und frühen Verbreitung des Kaffees waren es Syrer, Libanesen, Ägypter, Griechen, Armenier, dann Holländer, auch Engländer und Italiener, die Konzessionen zum Brennen, Sieden und Ausschenken von Kaffee erwarben.

Der wachsende Konsum von Kaffee im 15. und 16. Jahrhundert führte zu einer „hitherto unknown social institution", dem Kaffeehaus.[24] Ein Aspekt, der in der Nordamerika- und Europa-zentrierten Literatur – eingeschlossen philosophische Abhandlungen über die bürgerliche Kultur, wie die von Jürgen Habermas[25] – vollkommen außer Acht gelassen wird.

In ihr beginnt die Kaffeehausgeschichte 1555 in Konstantinopel. Zwei Syrer, Hakm und Shams, betreiben mit großem ökonomischen Erfolg eine Kaffeeschenke am Bosporus (Abb. 3, 4). 1645 wird dann in Venedig von einem Kaffeehaus gesprochen.[26] Getrunken wurde der Kaffee dort jedoch schon früher. Die diplomatischen und wirtschaftlichen Kontakte der Republik Venedig mit dem Osmanischen Reich hatten auch zu einem Transfer dieses Genussmittels geführt. Dass die Osmanen eine gewichtige Rolle in der Lagunenstadt spielten, zeigen

The history of the coffee house commences in Constantinople in the year 1555. Two Syrians, Hakm and Shams, were running a very successful coffee place on the Bosporus (fig. 3, 4). In 1645, a coffee house is mentioned for Venice.[26] Coffee, however, had been consumed here earlier than that. Diplomatic and economic contacts between the Republic of Venice and the Ottoman Empire had led to a transfer of this luxury good as well. Albrecht Dürer's paintings clearly show the important role of Ottoman merchants in the lagoon city.[27] In 1585 the Venetian Gianfrancesco Morosini reports from Constantinople on the effects of coffee and its public consumption in coffee houses.[28] (fig. 5)

How far-reaching the fascination with the foreign was with the Venetians, who loved masquerades at any rate, reveals itself not only through the adaptation and imitation of oriental coffee table ware but also by the fashionable habit of wearing Turkish costumes for visiting the coffee houses.[29] (fig. 6)

In England it was the Greek who as representatives of the multi-ethnic Ottoman Empire, indulged in the consumption of coffee. No lesser person than the architect John Evelyn (1620–1706) who after the great fire supplied a competing design to Christopher Wren's (1632–1723) reconstruction plan for London, as early as 1673 noted in his diary 'there came in my time to the College [Balliol College, Oxford] one Nathaniel Canopius, out of Greece … he was the first I ever saw drink coffee.'[30]

In the same way the aforementioned physician William Harvey obtained his knowledge from an oriental fellow student at the University of Padua. The first place for drinking coffee in public however was opened by the Syrian Cirques Jobson in Oxford in 1650.

In London the strange drink was offered, as is recorded, in 1652 by the Greek citizen Pasqua Rosée who came to England as staff of the British Levant merchant Daniel Edwards. 'His coffee-making abilities were allied with a gift for publicity.'[31] On handbills he praised 'the vertue of the coffee-drink'. His immense success caused the envy of the beer brewers and led to his discrimination, eventually even deportation. The seed, however, germinated. Numerous coffee houses or renamed taverns or inns offered coffee now. To attract customers, names such as 'Smyrna', 'Sultaness' or 'The Turk's Head' purposefully played on associations with the exotic. The origin of its founder is betrayed by the name 'Grecian' for the coffee house that mainly was patronized by members of

unter anderem die Darstellungen Albrecht Dürers.[27] 1585 berichtet der Venezianer Gianfrancesco Morosini aus Konstantinopel über die Wirkung des Kaffees und seinen öffentlichen Genuss in Kaffeeschänken.[28] (Abb. 5)

Wie weit die Faszination des Fremden bei den ohnehin zur Maskerade neigenden Venezianern ging, beweist nicht nur die Übernahme und Imitation des orientalischen Kaffeegeschirrs, sondern auch die in Mode kommende türkische Kostümierung für den Besuch im Kaffeehaus.[29] (Abb.6)

In England sind es als Repräsentanten des osmanischen Vielvölkerstaates Griechen, die die ersten Kaffeehäuser gründen. Kein geringerer als der Architekt John Evelyn (1620–1706), der nach dem großen Brand von London 1666 für den Wiederaufbau einen Konkurrenzentwurf zu demjenigen von Christopher Wren (1632–1723) geliefert hatte, notiert bereits 1637 in seinem Tagebuch: „There came in my time to the College [Balliol College, Oxford] one Nathaniel Canopius, out of Greece … he was the first I ever saw drink coffee."[30]

Auch der bereits genannte Mediziner William Harvey hatte seine Kenntnis von einem orientalischen Kommilitonen an der Universität Padua. Zum öffentlichen Ausschank kommt es in Oxford erst 1650 durch den Syrer Circues Jobson.

In London wird das fremdartige Getränk nachweislich wiederum von einem Griechen, Pasqua Rosée, der in der Gefolgschaft des britischen Levante-Kaufmanns Daniel Edwards nach England gekommen war, 1652 ausgeschenkt. „His coffee-making abilities were allied with a gift for publicity."[31] Auf Handzetteln pries er „The vertue of the coffee-drink" an. Sein immenser Erfolg rief die Neider aus den Reihen der Bierbrauer auf den Plan und führte zu seiner Diskreditierung, ja Verbannung. Die Saat aber war aufgegangen. Unzählige Kaffeehäuser oder auch nur als solche umbenannte Tavernen und Schenken boten den Kaffee an. Namen wie Smyrna, Sultaness, The Turk's Head et cetera spielten, um Kunden anzulocken, bewusst mit der Assoziation des Exotischen. Auf die Herkunft seines Begründers verweist das Grecian, das vor allem von Mitgliedern der in unmittelbarer Nähe gelegenen Royal Society wie zum Beispiel Isaac Newton, Hans Sloane oder Edmond Halley frequentiert wurde. „For many years its name was synonymous with intellectual debate."[32]

Auch auf dem europäischen Festland sind es in der zweiten Hälfte des 17. Jahrhunderts vorerst Griechen und

the nearby Royal Society such as Isaac Newton (1642–1727), Hans Sloane (1660–1753) or Edmond Halley (1656–1742). 'For many years its name was synonymous with intellectual debate.'[32]

On the continent in the second half of the seventeenth century it was also Greeks and Armenians, who managed semi-permanent coffee stalls for example during the annual trade fairs of Saint-Germain in Paris or the Leipzig fair. Two Armenians dispensed coffee in Vienna from 1666 from a permanent location. Erroneously, the birth date of the Vienna coffee house frequently is connected with Gregorius Kolscycki, a citizen of the southern Hungarian city of Zombor. In return for his services as scout in 1683 after the defeat of the Turkish army besieging Vienna he obtained some coffee sacks left behind by the Ottomans as well as a licence from emperor Leopold I to brew coffee. There can be no doubt about the Ottoman origins of the highly developed coffee house culture of the Austro-Hungarian Empire. In Brno again it was a Turk, in Prague a Syrian, who in 1702 and 1714 respectively established coffee houses. Likewise it was a Greek who in 1760 founded the famous 'Caffè Greco' in Rome's Via dei Condotti. The illustrious guest list of this still existing coffee house constitutes a veritable encyclopaedia. There was not a single prominent and cultured visitor of the eternal city who was not a guest in this establishment. Mainly here a cultural transfer takes place between the representatives of different nations. In the immediate neighbourhood the 'Caffè degli Inglesi' was opened in Piazza di Spagna. Giovanni Battista Piranesi (1720–1776) was commissioned with the interior decoration. Piranesi enjoyed a great reputation as corresponding member of the London Society of Antiquaries. Architects as well as architectural theoreticians including the brothers Adam, John Soane and other influential British connoisseurs of the art as well were eager to meet Piranesi during their 'Grand Tour' and to converse with him. The 'Inglesi' became a trade centre of antiquities. Here Piranesi confronted guests with Egyptian culture.[33] 'In its interior, this coffee house is decorated in the Egyptian style after a drawing of the famous Piranesi. A wealth of Egyptian pagan idols, miraculously combined, appear in the different colours of granite and of other dark varieties of stone'[34], a traveller reports (fig. 7). Later, in 1838–1842, the Caffè Pedrocchi in Padova is to take up an Egyptian décor as part of the decoration canon of its suite of rooms.

Armenier, die unter anderem in Paris während der jährlichen Messe von Saint-Germain und auf der Leipziger Messe in Deutschland ihre semipermanenten Kaffeebuden betreiben. In Wien sind es ab 1666 zwei Armenier, die an einem festen Ort Kaffee ausschenken. Fälschlicherweise wird die Geburtsstunde des Wiener Kaffeehauses mit dem aus dem südungarischen Zombor stammenden Gregorius Kolscycki in Verbindung gebracht. Als Dank für seine Kundschaftertätigkeit hatte er 1683 nach der Vertreibung der türkischen Belagerer einige von den Osmanen zurückgelassene Säcke Kaffee sowie von Leopold I. die Lizenz zum Sieden erhalten. Zweifelsohne geht die so hoch kultivierte Kaffeekultur des k.u.k. Reiches auf den osmanischen Einfluss zurück. In Brünn etwa ist es 1702 ein Türke, in Prag 1714 ein Syrer, die Kaffeehäuser gründen. Die Gründung eines Griechen ist seit 1760 in Rom das Caffè Greco in der Via dei Condotti. Das heute noch existierende Café könnte mit seiner bedeutenden Gästeliste ein Lexikon füllen. Es gibt wohl kaum einen gebildeten Rombesucher, der hier nicht Gast war. Vor allem an diesem Ort findet ein Kulturtransfer auch zwischen den Vertretern der unterschiedlichsten Nationen statt. In unmittelbarer Nähe des Greco öffnet an der Piazza di Spagna das Caffè degli Inglesi. Den Auftrag zur Ausgestaltung erhält Giovanni Battista Piranesi, der als korrespondierendes Mitglied der Londoner Society of Antiquaries eine große Reputation genoss. Architekten und Architekturtheoretiker wie James Stuart, Nicholas Revette, Colen Campbell, Richard Boyle, der 3rd Earl of Burlington sowie Mäzene waren erpicht darauf, auf ihrer *grand tour* Piranesi zu begegnen und sich mit ihm auszutauschen. Das Inglesi wurde zu einem Zentrum des Antiquitätenhandels. Und hier konfrontierte Piranesi die Gäste mit der ägyptischen Kultur.[33] „Es ist dieses Kaffeehaus nach … einer Zeichnung des berühmten Piranesi im Egyptischen Styl inwendig ausgemalt. Eine Menge Egyptischer Götzenbilder [!] wunderbar zusammengestellt, erscheinen hier in verschiedenen Farben des Granits und anderer dunkler Steinarten",[34] berichtet ein Reisender (Abb. 7). Das Caffè Pedrocchi in Padua nimmt dann später, 1838–1842, im Stilkanon seiner Räume das Thema Ägypten wieder auf.

Indem die Ausländer neben dem fremdartigen Getränk in ihrem Tenue, aber auch der Inneneinrichtung ihrer Schankstätten fremde Kulturen thematisierten, setzten sie den Beginn eines internationalen Kulturtransfers. Die europäischen Kaffeehausbesitzer kultivieren

5

Coffeehouses also enabled easy contact between artists and impresarios, and served as points of sale for art. Here, Francesco Guardi (1712-1793) offers his Venetian veduti for sale in 'Caffè Florian' ● 'Florian' (lithograph by Giovanni Pividor, first half of the nineteenth century) was, besides 'Quadri' and 'Lavena', the most fashionable place in Venice

Kaffeehäuser dienten auch dem Kontakt zwischen Künstler und Impresario und waren Absatzmärkte für Kunst. Hier bietet Francesco Guardi (1712–1793) im „Caffè Florian" seine venezianischen Veduten an. ● Das Florian (Lithographie von Giovanni Pividor, 1. Hälfte 19. Jahrhundert) ist neben dem „Quadri" und dem „Lavena" das Kaffeehaus Venedigs schlechthin.

6

Coffee is served in Batavia, present-day Jakarta (Le Brun, 1718) ● A travelling coffee vendor (Jean Baptiste van Moor, 1714) ● Venetian in Oriental garments drinking coffee

Kaffee serviert in Batavia, dem heutigen Jakarta (Le Brun, 1718). ● Fliegender Kaffeeverkäufer (Jean Baptiste van Moor, 1714). ● Kaffee trinkender Venezianer in Orienttenue.

7

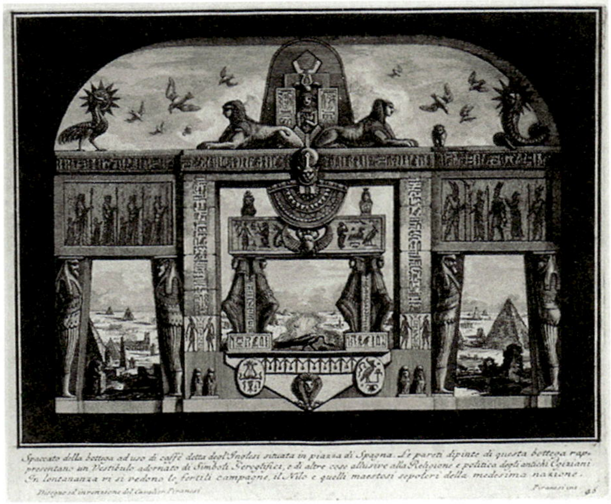

Spaccato della bottega ad uso di caffè detta degl'Inglesi situata in piazza di Spagna. Le pareti dipinte di questa bottega rap-
presentano un Vestibulo adornato di Simboli Geroglifici, e di altre cose allusive alla Religione e politica degli antichi Egiziani
In lontananza vi si vedono le fertili campagne, il Nilo e quelli maestosi sepolcri della medesima nazione.

8

9

Caffe du Jardin des Tuileries.

By making exotic cultures a topic of their *tenue* as well as of the interior of their coffee dispensing localities, these foreigners initiated an international process of cultural transfer. European coffee house owners subsequently were cultivating this tendency. Around 1780 the 'Café Turc' opened its doors in Paris on the Boulevard du Temple (fig. 8). Next to the orientalizing architectural language of the entire building, it was the characteristic element of a canopy that spans the space above the pavement, which clearly imitated the appearance of an Ottoman coffee house, anticipating the modern type of today's coffee houses. Likewise the coffee tents and coffee kiosks (from the Turkish: 'kösk'), appearing in Vienna's Prater gardens, in Berlin's 'Tiergarten' or in Paris[35], go back to oriental patterns (fig. 9). The beginnings of a coffee house culture in the emerging Prussian metropolis of Berlin date back to a North African by the name of Olivier. Berlin gave asylum to a great number of French Huguenots, who fled their country after the annulment of the edict of Nantes in 1683. Together with them, Olivier, who obviously was skilled in brewing coffee, came to Berlin and obtained a concession from Friedrich I in 1711. The royal wash house near the Lustgarten was converted to a 'Café Royal'. Later it moved to Berlin's boulevard of flaneurs, 'Unter den Linden' (Under the Lime Trees), where it

in der Folge diese Tendenz. In Paris eröffnet um 1780 das Café Turc auf dem Boulevard du Temple (Abb. 8). Charakterisierendes Element ist neben der orientalischen Formensprache des Gebäudes das den Bürgersteig überspannende Vordach, das deutlich auf das Erscheinungsbild osmanischer Kaffeehäuser zurückgreift und das bis heute existierende Straßencafé vorwegnimmt. Auch die vor allem in Wien im Prater und in Berlin im Tiergarten und in Paris[35] errichteten Kaffeezelte und Kaffeekioske (türkisch: köşk) sind dem orientalischen Einfluss zu verdanken (Abb. 9). Am Beginn der Kaffeehauskultur der jungen preußischen Metropole steht ein Nordafrikaner namens Olivier. Berlin hatte einer großen Zahl der nach der Aufhebung des Edikts von Nantes 1683 aus Frankreich geflohenen Hugenotten Asyl geboten. Mit ihnen war auch der offensichtlich im Kaffeesieden bewanderte Olivier, dem Friedrich I. eine Konzession verlieh, in die Stadt gekommen. Das königliche Waschhaus am Lustgarten wurde zum Café Royal umgenutzt. Es folgt ein Umzug an den Flanierboulevard Unter den Linden, wo das Café bis 1765 bestand. So wird in Berlin ein erster Grund gelegt für eine sich erst im 19. Jahrhundert voll entfaltende metropolitane Kaffeehauskultur.

Die Verspätete unter den europäischen Metropolen, Berlin, hatte, als die ersten Engadiner Zuckerbäcker in die Stadt kamen, einen noch beinahe kleinstädtischen Charakter. Der Kulturtransfer dieser bereits in Italien und vor allem in Venedig erfolgreich tätigen Virtuosen der Konditoreikunst bringt ähnlich wie in Wien, aber im Kontrast zu London und Paris, einen besonderen Typus des Kaffeehauses hervor: die Kaffeekonditorei. Wenn man sich heute ein Bild dieser frühen, biedermeierlich geprägten Etablissements machen will, sollte man das Café Ruszwurm in Budapest besuchen. Als Senior der Ladiner Kuchenbäcker hatte Josty zu Ende des 18. Jahrhunderts in Berlin an der Stechbahn Nummer 1 sein erstes Kaffeehaus eröffnet. 1865 verlegte er sein Geschäft an die Schlossfreiheit, später an den Potsdamer Platz.

> „Bis in sein hohes Alter kehrte Adolph von Menzel spätabends bei Josty ein. Gewöhnlich erschien er gegen halb zwölf Uhr, nachdem er vorher in dem nahegelegenen Lokal von Frederich reichlich gespeist hatte. Er setzte sich auf den für ihn reservierten Platz und konnte der Bedienung gegenüber, wenn nicht alles nach Wunsch ging, recht ungemütlich werden. Bis gegen ein Uhr vertiefte er sich bei einer Tasse Kaffee in die ausliegenden Journale,

7
Since the days of Johann Joachim Winckelmann, the German cultural elite in Rome preferred the 'Caffè Greco'. As coffee houses frequently served as postal addresses, the 'Greco' became the 'German's Post Box' (watercolour by Ludwig Johann Passini, 1856, Kunsthalle Hamburg) ● The English frequented the nearby 'Caffè degli Inglesi,' for which Giovanni Battista Piranesi designed the interior in the Egyptian style in 1769

Im „Caffè Greco" in Rom verkehrte seit Johann Joachim Winckelmann die deutsche Kulturelite. Da Cafés oft als Postadresse fungierten, war dieses die „Postbüchse der Deutschen" (Aquarell von Ludwig Johann Passini, 1856, Kunsthalle Hamburg). ● Die Engländer verkehrten im nahe gelegenen „Caffè degli Inglesi" für das Giovanni Battista Piranesi 1769 die ägyptisierende Inneneinrichtung entworfen hatte.

8
In 1780 'Café Turc' was opened on the Paris Boulevard du Temple ● In the nineteenth century, the fashion for Orientalism had developed to the extent, that, in 1850, real odalisques were displayed in 'Café Mauresque'

1780 eröffnet in Paris auf dem Boulevard du Temple das „Café Turc". ● Im 19. Jahrhundert geht der Orientalismus soweit, 1850 im „Café Mauresque" Odalisken zur Schau zu stellen.

9
Summer blinds and tent architectures inspired by luxurious Turkish marquees appeared in the European metropolises of the eighteenth century: in Berlin's 'Tiergarten' ● In Paris's 'Tuileries' around 1800 ● In London's Covent Garden

Von den türkischen Prachtzelten inspirierte sommerliche Markisen und Zeltarchitekturen erscheinen im 18. Jahrhundert in den europäischen Metropolen: Im Tiergarten in Berlin. ● In den Tuilerien in Paris um 1800. ● Im Covent Garden in London.

survived until 1765. Thus in Berlin the foundation was laid for a metropolitan coffee house culture that was fully to develop only in the nineteenth century.

Berlin, this latecomer amongst European metropolises was, when the first pastry makers from the Engadin region in Switzerland reached the city, still rather small-town in character. The cultural transfer brought by these virtuosi, who already had been successful in Italy and especially in Venice, generated, in contrast to London and Paris, a different type of coffee houses: the coffee-cum-pastry shop. Who today wants to evoke the image of those early, *Biedermeier*-style establishments, would have to visit Budapest's 'Café Ruszwurm'. In Berlin, the senior of all Engadine pastry makers, Josty, opened his first coffee-cum-pastry shop at Stechbahn 1. In 1865 he transferred it to the 'Schlossfreiheit', the area around the chateau, still later to Potsdamer Platz.

> 'Until his old age, Adolph von Menzel (1815–1905) used to stop at Josty late in the evening. Usually, he appeared around half past eleven after a rich dinner in the nearby restaurant Frederich. He occupied his reserved seat and was known to become rather unpleasant, when something did not go according to his wishes. Until one o'clock he absorbed himself in the laid-out journals, now and then murmuring under his breath, or sometimes taking out his sketch book and a giant carpenter's pencil to commit one of his sudden inspirations to paper.'[36]

The real type of Berlin pastry shop (*Konditorei*), a certain Andrea Giovanoli is said to have established in 1818 in Charlottenstrasse. This pattern was followed by his compatriots Stehely (fig. 10), Spargnapani and Stoppany, who all came from Engadine between 1820 and 1825 without any means[37] and went back to their native country as rich men.[38] Regular customers of Stehely's were amongst others the writer E.T.A. Hoffmann (1776–1822), the philosopher Max Stirner (1806–1856)[39] and the writer and poet Willibald Alexis (1798–1871).

> 'The sun goes down, evening is coming. Out of the pastry shops of Messrs. Stehely, Sparpagnani, Giovanoli, Josty, Courtin and whatever the names of all these free Swiss citizens may be, who bring us cakes instead of freedom the famous Berlin political correspondents step into the street. Their face is serene, they have baked exactly such

> gelegentlich vor sich hinbrummend, zuweilen auch sein Skizzenbuch und einen riesigen Zimmermannsbleistift hervorziehend, um einen seiner plötzlichen Einfälle zu Papier zu bringen."[36]

Den eigentlichen Typ der Berliner Konditorei soll Andrea Giovanoli 1818 in der Charlottenstraße geschaffen haben. Seinem Vorbild folgten seine Landsleute Stehely (Abb. 10), Spargnapani und Stoppany, die alle 1820 und 1825 mittellos aus dem Engadin gekommen waren[37] und mit ansehnlichem Vermögen in ihre Heimat zurückkehrten.[38] Zu den Stammgästen bei Stehely gehörten unter anderen E. T. A. Hoffmann (1776–1822), Max Stirner (1806–1856)[39] und Willibald Alexis (1798–1871).

> „Die Sonne geht unter, es wird Abend. Aus den Konditoreien der Herren Stehely, Sparpagnani, Giovanoli, Josty, Courtin und wie die freien Schweizer alle heißen mögen, welche uns statt der Freiheit Kuchen bringen, treten die berühmten politischen Korrespondenten Berlins. Ihr Gesicht ist heiter, sie haben just soviel Neues zusammenkonditort, um einen Artikel mit diplomatisch versteckten Angriffen zimmern zu können."[40] (Abb. 11)

Zuckerbäcker war ebenfalls der aus Österreich stammende Johann Georg Kranzler. Auch sein Café wurde zu einer Institution im spätbiedermeierlichen Berlin und lebte als solche im West-Berlin der Wirtschaftswunderzeit am Kurfürstendamm wieder auf.

Die Niederländer spielten nicht nur als koloniale Verbreiter der Nutzpflanze und Händler mit Kaffee eine Rolle, sondern auch als Promotoren des Getränks. 1673 stellt der Niederländer Jan Jantz van Huesden an den Rat der Stadt Bremen einen Antrag, Kaffee, Schokolade und „Potasi", eine auf Grundlage von getrockneten Kräutern hergestellte Gemüsesuppe, feilhalten zu dürfen.[41] Im Laufe der folgenden 300 Jahre wird Bremen die Kaffeestadt Deutschlands. Auch im zweiten bedeutenden Kaffeeumschlagplatz Hamburg soll ein Niederländer, Cornelius Decker oder auch Bontekoe aus Alkmaar, der erste Betreiber eines Kaffeehauses gewesen sein.[42] In den 1670er Jahren ist Bontekoe am Berliner Hof Leibarzt von Friedrich Wilhelm, dem Großen Kurfürsten.[43] Es ist anzunehmen, dass diese Kaffeehäuser weniger orientalischen Flair hatten. Sie können wohl eher als Repliken von Interieurs, wie sie uns die Maler des „gouden eeuw" überliefert haben, angesehen werden.

10

11

12

10
With its three-room-enfilade 'Stehely' is a typical coffee house of the Berlin 'Biedermeier' period (oil painting by Gustav Taubert, 1832)

Das „Stehely“ mit seiner Enfilade von drei Räumen ist ein typisches Café des Berliner Biedermeier (Gemälde von Gustav Taubert, 1832).

11
One of the most renowned coffee houses was Berlin's 'Café Josty', both at its first address (lithograph by C. Schmidt, 1845) and later at Potsdamer Platz (oil painting by Paul Hoeniger, 1880)

Eine der renommiertesten Kaffeehausadressen in Berlin war das „Café Josty“ an seinem ersten Standort (Lithographie von C. Schmidt, 1845) und dann am Potsdamer Platz (Gemälde von Paul Hoeniger, 1880).

12
Interior of a Dutch coffee house: 'Het Coffy-Huys' (copperplate engraving by Jan Luyken, 1694)

Interieur eines niederländischen Kaffeehauses: „Het Coffy-Huys“ (Kupferstich von Jan Luyken, 1694).

an amount of news, as suffices to construct an article full of diplomatically hidden attacks'.[40] (fig. 11)

The Austrian Johann Georg Kranzler (1795–1866) was pastry maker too. His café likewise became an institution in late-Biedermeier Berlin. In the post-war period of 'Wirtschaftswunder' (economic miracle) it had a second spring on West Berlin's Kurfürstendamm in the 1950s.

In other parts of Germany the Dutch not only played an important role as colonial distributors of the coffee plant and coffee merchants, but also as promoters of the beverage itself. In 1673 the Dutchman Jan Jantz van Huesden filed an application with the council of the city state of Bremen for the permission to sell coffee, hot chocolate and 'Potasi', a vegetable soup based on dried herbs.[41] In the course of the next three hundred years, Bremen became the leading city of coffee for Germany. In the country's second important trading place for coffee, Hamburg, another Dutchman, Cornelius Decker or Bontekoe from Alkmaar is said to have set up the first coffee house in town.[42] In the 1670s Bontekoe became resident doctor at the Berlin court of Friedrich Wilhelm, the Great Elector.[43] It is to be assumed, that these coffee houses were of less oriental character. They probably can be regarded as a kind of replica of the interiors that had been painted by the seventeenth century Dutch artists. Jan Luyken, most prominent exponent of the copperplate engraving after Rembrandt, in 1694 depicts a 'coffy huys'.[44] (fig. 12) In this way, the citizens of Bremen and Hamburg may have achieved knowledge of the solid wealth of the Dutch: heavy curtaining, decorously gilded mirrors, costly carpets on the tables—still today found in the Netherlands—and chandeliers.

Fighting for customers, which was typical even in the early days of consumer capitalism, as is demonstrated by the handbills of a Pasqua Rosée, the coffee house owners tried to outdo each other. Where the personality of the landlord or the notoriety of the guests were not the *causa movens* for a visit, other attractions were asked for: the interior decoration, later the attraction of gas or electric lighting, leisure time opportunities (board or card games, later billiards and reading matter, music or cabaret performances) and carefully selected personnel were the means in the fight for customers.

'Many of the Coffeamen [keep] beautiful boys, who serve as stales to procure them customers',[45] George Sandys (1577–1644) notes as early as 1644 in Istanbul.

Jan Luyken, wichtigster Vertreter des holländischen Kupferstichs nach Rembrandt, porträtiert 1694 ein „Coffy-Huys".[44] (Abb. 12) So mögen die Bremer und Hamburger Kenntnis vom behäbigen Wohlstand der Niederländer erhalten haben: schwere Vorhänge, dekorativ vergoldete Spiegel, kostbare Tischteppiche – heute noch in den Niederlanden an einigen Orten zu finden – und Kandelaber.

Im Kampf um Kunden, der bereits in der Frühphase des Konsumkapitalismus zu beobachten ist – erinnert sei hier an die Handzettel Pasqua Rosées – überschlagen sich die Cafétiers. Wo nicht der Charakter des Wirts oder berühmte Gäste die causa movens des Besuchs sind, muss man auf andere Attraktionen sinnen: Inneneinrichtung, Freizeitangebot (Brett- und Kartenspiele, später Billard und Lektüre, Musik- und Kabarettdarbietungen) sowie ausgewähltes Personal.

„Many of the Coffeaman [keep] beautiful boys, who serve as stales to procure them customers",[45] notiert bereits 1610 aus Istanbul George Sandys (1577–1644). Der Sizilianer Procopio dei Coltelli lässt 1684 in seinem Pariser Café Procope (Abb. 13) – wie in seiner italienischen Heimat üblich – acht- bis zwölfjährige Knaben bedienen.[46] Einen „Garçon" ruft man noch heute, wenn man in Frankreich der Bedienung bedarf. Zum Personal, das sich in Kleidung und Funktion immer weiter diffenzierte (Zahlkellner oder Marqueur, Kellner, Piccolo in Wien, *chausseur* und *limonadier* in Paris etc.) gehörte auch die Sitzkassiererin. Englische Darstellungen vom Beginn des 19. Jahrhunderts zeigen sie in einer Art Alkoven-Altar thronend und surveillierend. Im Wiener Kaffeehaus der Biedermeierzeit sieht man sie umlagert von Verehrern.

Auch Procopio hatte neben seinen Garçons eine „belle limonadière" (Abb. 14), denn zu Procopios Attraktionen gehörten – und das sah die ihm verliehene Konzession ausdrücklich vor – neben dem Ausschank von Kaffee auch raffinierte Limonaden und Destillate – berühmt ist noch heute der „Rosée du Soleil" auf der Basis von Fenchel, Anis, Koriander, Dill und zerstoßenem Kümmel[47] – sowie Sorbets, Halbgefrorenes und Eisvariationen. So findet mit dem Kaffee auch das Speiseeis seine Verbreitung. Und der Inbegriff von Qualität ist auch heute noch das *gelato* vom individuellen italienischen Eismacher. In der französischen Metropole hatte Procopio die Lust auf diese neuartigen Genüsse, die in der Öffentlichkeit des Kaffeehauses[48] vorerst nur

Procopio dei Coltelli had eight to twelve year-old boys serve in his Paris café 'Procope' (fig. 13), as was customary in his Italian homeland.[46] He reused the original interior of a former Turkish bath house for his establishment. Still today, one calls for a 'garçon' (boy), asking for service in a French restaurant. Another member of staff, that in apparel and function more and more diversified over time (head-waiter or *marqueur*, waiter, *Piccolo* in Vienna, *chausseur* or *limonadier* in Paris, and so on) was the female sitting head cashier. English representations from the beginning of the nineteenth century show her enthroned in a kind of alcove-altar surveying the premises. The Vienna coffee house of the early nineteenth century has her surrounded by admirers.

The café 'Procope' had besides its garçons a *belle limonadière* (fig. 14), for part of the Procope's attractions, next to selling coffee, was the offer of refined lemonades and distilled beverages. Famous to the present day is Procope's 'Rosée du soleil', based on fennel, aniseed, coriander, dill and crushed caraway[47] as well as sorbets, sherbets and variations of ice creams. Still today the very concept of quality is embodied by a *gelato* manufactured by an individual Italian ice cream producer. It was Procopio who in the French capital aroused curiosity for these novel pleasures that in the public sphere of the coffee houses remained a privilege of the male part of the population.[48] Ladies were served in their waiting carriages before they were allowed entry to the coffee houses. Furthermore the coffee house served the process of transporting the consumption of luxury goods formerly reserved to court and nobility into the bourgeois sphere.

The fascination with things oriental[49] for a long time remained a factor in the marketing of coffee houses. Around 1850 the opening of the 'Café des Mauresques' in Paris' Boulevard Saint Denis caused a rejuvenation of the 'oriental mode'. Showing the same arrogance that led to the presentation of non-European tribal people during the World Exhibitions, the 'Mauresques' 'exhibited' four odalisques smoking water pipes on a divan (fig. 8). More harmless but still mirroring the colonial power of the British Empire is J. Lyons & Company's contribution to the 1887 Newcastle Jubilee Exhibition celebrating Queen Victoria's fifty years jubilee on the throne. In its Indo-Chinese pavilion-café Lyons impressed media and public with its enormous range of coffee, tea, cake and pastry. In 1894 London's first Lyons' teashop opened in 213 Picadilly. It is not a question to be answered here, why tea

den Männern vorbehalten waren, geschürt. Den Frauen brachte man, bevor auch sie Zutritt zu den Kaffeehäusern hatten, Bestellungen an die wartenden Kutschen. Die Cafés boten darüberhinaus auch ein Forum für die Verbürgerlichung der ehemals dem Hof und dem Adel vorbehaltenen Genussmittel.

Das Faszinosum Orient[49] blieb ein Faktor für die Vermarktung. Um 1850 sorgt in Paris die Eröffnung des Café des Mauresques am Boulevard Saint Denis für eine Neubelebung der „oriental mode“. Entsprechend der kolonialen Arroganz, mit der man auch auf den Weltausstellungen fremde Ethnien zur Schau stellt, werden im Mauresques vier Odalisken Wasserpfeife rauchend auf einem Divan „ausgestellt“. (Abb. 8) Harmloser, aber doch auch die Kolonialmacht des British Empire widerspiegelnd ist der Beitrag von J. Lyons & Company Incorporated auf der Newcastle Jubilee Exhibition anlässlich des 50-jährigen Thronjubiläums von Queen Victoria 1887. In einem indo-chinesischen Pavillon-Café beeindruckt Lyons mit ihrem Kaffee-, Tee-, Kuchen- und Pastetenangebot das Publikum und die Medien. 1894 wird in London am Picadilly 213 der erste Lyons' Teashop eröffnet. Warum Tee die Gemüter, die Trinkgewohnheiten und den Kommerz anders berührt hat als der Kaffee – obwohl bereits ab dem frühen 14. Jahrhundert der Venezianer Marco Polo (1254–1324) in seiner weit verbreiteten Schrift *Il Millione*[50] die Kenntnis von der chinesischen Kultur nach Europa gebracht hatte – kann hier nicht beantwortet werden. Tatsache ist, dass nach anfänglicher Blüte der Kaffee- und Kaffeehauskultur im 17. und 18. Jahrhundert der Tee in England die absolute Oberhand gewinnt. „Teatime“ wird wie in den deutschsprachigen Ländern zum Synonym für die vierte Stunde des Nachmittags. Obwohl als Kette nach dem amerikanischen Typus des Schnellrestaurants für die hastenden *big city dwellers* konzipiert, war der Tee bei Lyons im Kännchen oder in der Tasse immer frisch aufgebrüht. In den 1920er Jahren gab es bereits 260 Lyons-Filialen. Das 1909 eröffnete Coventry Street Corner House am Strand wird 1922 auf eine Kapazität von 4500 Gästen erweitert. Die legendären Corner Houses am Strand (1915)[51] und an der Oxford Street (1928) konnten 2500 Gäste fassen.[52] Funktional optimiert und auf Umsatz ausgerichtet, stand in den Lyons-Filialen die Vermarktung der Kulturen der Hauptanbauländer des Tees, Indien und China, nicht zur Diskussion. Überseeische wie europäische und nordamerikanische Sphären erleben hingegen in Berlin

13

14

15

influenced minds, habits of consummation and commerce differently from coffee, although the Venetian Marco Polo (1254–1324) in his *Il Millione*[50] and other widespread writings brought the knowledge of the Chinese culture to Europe in the early fourteenth century. It is a fact though, that tea won the upper hand in England after an initial flourishing of coffee and coffee houses in the seventeenth and eighteenth century. The term 'teatime' now becomes, as on the continent, a synonym for the fifth hour of the afternoon. Although the tea rooms were part of a retail-chain and conceived as a restaurant catering to the hurrying city dweller, tea at Lyons whether in cup or pot always was freshly brewed. In the 1920s there were already more than 260 Lyons shops. In 1922 the Coventry Street Corner House, opened in the Strand in 1909, was enlarged to cater to 4,500 guests. The legendary Corner Houses in the Strand (1915)[51] and in Oxford Street (1928) held 2,500 clients.[52] In their functional character, aimed at maximum sales, the marketing of the culture of the main growing regions of tea, India and China was not part of Lyons strategy. Other overseas, European or North American references appear in the styling of cafés in Berlin in the 1920s, 30s and 40s. In 1911/1912 the renowned Berlin architect Heinrich Schwechten (1841–1924) built a multi-purpose house (offices, cinema, restaurants) at Potsdamer Platz. The main attraction here was the 2,500 seat 'Café Pica-

13

A central figure of this scene is the waiter boy—'garçon'—the 'Café Procope' of the Ancien Régime ● Another is to be seen in a Venetian 'bottega del caffè' in an etching by Giovanni Volpato (1735–1803)

Im Zentrum dieser Szene im „Café Procope" aus dem Ancien Régime der servierende Knabe, der „garçon". ● Ein solcher findet sich auch in einer venezianischen „bottega del caffè" auf einem Stich von Giovanni Volpato (1735–1803).

14

The lovely lady at the cash register acted as a magnet for many coffee houses, and was strategically employed as such In Vienna's ‚Silbernem Kaffeehaus' (J.A. Krafft and J.H. Nepomuk, ca. 1820) ● The proprietress of ‚Café de Mille Colonne', known as ‚la belle limonadière (copper plate engraving, 1814, sketch by Thomas Rowlandson) ● In the Paris ‚Cafè du Bosquet' admirers crowd behind the window panes

Die schöne Kassiererin wird zum Magneten so manchen Kaffeehauses und wird als solcher auch bewusst eingesetzt. In Wiens ‚Silbernem Kaffeehaus' (J. A. Krafft und J. H. Nepomuk, ca. 1820). ● Die Besitzerin des ‚Café de Mille Colonne', als ‚la belle limonadière' bekannt (Kupferstich, 1814, Zeichnung von Thomas Rowlandson). ● Im Pariser ‚Café du Bosquet' drängen die Bewunderer sich hinter der Scheibe.

15

Turkish coffee house, part of 'Haus Vaterland' in Berlin around 1930 (postcard by Klaus Lindow, Berlin)

Türkisches Café im „Haus Vaterland", um 1930 (Postkarte Klaus Lindow, Berlin).

in den 1920er, 30er und 40er Jahren noch einmal eine Hochzeit. 1911/12 wird von dem renommierten Berliner Architekten Heinrich Schwechten (1841–1924) am Potsdamer Platz ein Mehrzweckbau (Büros, Kino, Restauration) errichtet. Die Sensation war das seinerzeit in Europa größte, 2500 Personen aufnehmende Café Picadilly.[53] Dass derartige Quantitäten wie viele andere Entwicklungen der Massengesellschaft nur durch die Mechanisierung der Fertigungsprozesse möglich waren, ist spätestens seit Sigfried Giedions *Mechanization Takes Command*[54] Bestandteil bürgerlichen Wissens. Von einer Mechanisierung in der Kaffeebereitung kann frühestens seit Loysels „Percolateur" die Rede sein, der auf der Pariser Weltausstellung 1855 2000 Tassen stündlich lieferte.[55] Mit Ausbruch des Ersten Weltkriegs wird das Picadilly in Café Vaterland umbenannt. Aus dem Café Vaterland wird 1928 das Haus Vaterland, auf 4500 Quadratmetern der größte Tempel der Erlebnisgastronomie. Neben vielen Attraktionen wie einer spanischen Bodega, Grinzinger Weinstuben und einer Wildwestbar gibt es unter anderem auch ein türkisches Café (Abb. 15). Ein türkisches Café in einem Etablissement wie dem eben genannten ist eine Etappe auf dem Weg von der Begegnung mit authentischen Vertretern des osmanischen Vielvölkerstaates und dem individuellen Kaffeehaus hin zur dekorativen Pseudo-Authentizität und zum gedankenlosen Konsum. In dem Maße, wie Kultur zu einer Ware degradiert wird, verliert sie ihren emanzipatorischen Charakter. Dient ein solcher Kulturtransfer noch der Erweiterung des eigenen Horizonts, der Relativierung des eigenen Standortes oder beugt er sich nicht allzu oft den Gesetzen des Marktes?

Handel, Presse, Politik und das Kaffeehaus

Um sich die innovative Rolle des Kaffeehauses im 17. und 18. Jahrhundert vorzustellen, muss man sich die historische Situation vor Augen führen. Außer relativ primitiven Schänken und Gast- und Beherbergungshäusern, die in Zusammenhang mit den Routen und Endpunkten des Kutschverkehrs standen, gab es für die normale Bevölkerung kaum Orte wettergeschützten Zusammentreffens. Soziale Kontakte wurden in der Kirche – man denke an die Interieurgemälde niederländischer Kirchen im 17. Jahrhundert –, auf den Messen, an Börsen,[56] auf Jahrmärkten, auf der Straße und auf städtischen Plätzen geknüpft. Auf letzteren mischten

dilly', Europe's largest.[53] Sigfried Giedion's book *Mechanization Takes Command* made the informed part of the population familiar with the fact, that quantities such as these—like many other developments of a mass consumer society—were only possible through strict mechanization of the production process.[54] Of a 'mechanization' of the brewing of coffee one can talk at the earliest since Loysel's 'Percolateur', that provided two thousand cups of coffee per hour during the Paris World Exhibition in 1855.[55] At the outbreak of World War I the Berlin 'Picadilly' was renamed as 'Café Vaterland'—'Café Fatherland'. In 1928 'Café Vaterland' became 'Haus Vaterland', with 4,500 square metres the largest temple of event gastronomy. Besides attractions such as a Spanish Bodega, Viennese 'Grinzinger Weinstuben' and a Wild West Bar there was, among others, a Turkish Coffee House, too (fig. 15). A Turkish Café in an establishment as described constitutes a step on the way from an encounter with authentic representatives of the multi-national Ottoman Empire and the individual coffee house down to a pseudo-authentic and mindless consumerism. Inasmuch as culture degenerates into mere merchandise, it looses its emancipating character. Does cultural transfer like that, made possible by such a coffee house culture, still serves the widening of one's horizon, or the relativity of one's point of view, or does it all too often bow to the conditions of the market?

Trade, Media, Politics, and the Coffee House

To grasp the innovative role of the coffee house during the seventeenth and eighteenth centuries it is necessary to reflect on the historical situation. Except rather primitive pubs or inns and guesthouses along travel routes or at destinations of coach traffic, there were no other sheltered meeting places for the congregation of ordinary people. Social contacts were established in churches,—as one can see in the paintings of Netherlands church interiors of the seventeenth century—at trade fairs, exchanges,[56] fairs, in the street or in public squares. In the latter merchants and buyers mingled with inhabitants, showmen, sutlers, market criers, ambulant vendors, medicasters etc. As early as in the fourteenth century the intricate and vivacious urban life is depicted by Ambrosio Lorenzetti (1290–1348)[57]. But it was only in the seventeenth century that the togetherness he illustrated found shelter under the roof of a coffee house. The patrons of these establishments

sich Händler und Käufer mit Einheimischen, Schaustellern, Marketenderinnen, Marktschreiern, ambulanten Verkäufern, Quacksalbern et cetera. Bereits im 14. Jahrhundert illustriert Ambrosio Lorenzetti (1290–1348)[57] die Vielschichtigkeit und Lebendigkeit städtischen Lebens. Aber erst im 17. Jahrhundert findet das bei ihm abgebildete Neben- und Miteinander im Kaffeehaus ein Zuhause. Für viele der bis dahin auf die Straße angewiesene Aktivitäten öffnen die Kaffeewirte ihre Häuser. Darüber hinaus tragen sie dazu bei, dem unvollständigen Netzwerk der Nachrichtenermittlung und -vermittlung eine systematische Strukturierung zu ermöglichen. Sie übernahmen auch die Funktion von Postanlaufstellen und wurden so über die an die jeweiligen Briefempfänger mitgeteilten Nachrichten zum Sammelbecken für Neuigkeiten. Indem sie ihre Etablissements für Vorträge und Lesungen öffneten, demokratisierten sie Ausbildung und Bildung, die bislang das Privileg der weltlichen und kirchlichen Oberschicht war. Das Kaffeehaus tritt somit an, Strukturen zu verbessern; vor allem aber tritt es an, ein informeller Versammlungsort der unterschiedlichsten Repräsentanten (Händler, Bankiers, Politiker, Schriftsteller und Künstler, Wissenschaftler et cetera) des sich konstituierenden Bürgertums zu werden. Der Charakter dieser urbanen Biotope wurde durch die *clientèle* bestimmt und deren Zusammensetzung wiederum durch die Lage in der Stadt. Semipermanente Kaffeebuden befanden sich vorerst an den Zollschranken der Ausfallstraßen, auf Messen und in Häfen. Feste Standorte wählten sich die Kaffeehausbesitzer dann an „fashionablen" Plätzen und Straßen (Piazza San Marco, Venedig; Covent Garden Piazza, London; Palais Royal, Paris; die Pariser Boulevards; die Berliner Flaniermeile Unter den Linden; teilweise die Wiener Ringstraße). Ein interessantes Phänomen, ein sogenannter Synergieeffekt, ist hier zu beobachten: Cafés siedeln sich oft in großer Vielzahl nebeneinander oder vis-à-vis an. Weitere Ansiedelungsschwerpunkte waren künstlerische und wissenschaftliche Einrichtungen und Börsen. So siedelt sich bereits 1671 in unmittelbarer Nähe der Marseiller Börse ein Kaffeehaus an. Das Crown in New York, das De la Bourse in Brüssel seien hier aus einer Vielzahl genannt.

So befanden sich in London in den Straßen um Cornhill sowie um die königliche Börse herum vor allem Kaffeehäuser, die dem Handel verpflichtet waren wie das von Thomas Garraway 1670 in der Exchange Alley eröffnete Garraway's. Felle der Hudson Compa-

gave a home to these manifold activities so far carried out under the open sky. Furthermore they greatly improved the heretofore rather patchy network of exchanging news giving it a more systematic and localized structure. By obtaining the function of postal stations the coffee houses became a collecting place of information via the messages sent to the respective recipients of letters. Opening their premises to lectures and readings the coffee houses put teaching and education on a more democratic footing, which had been so far a privilege of the secular and ecclesiastical upper classes. The coffee house thus takes over the function to improve structures; mainly it serves as a provider of informal meeting places of the most different representatives of the evolving bourgeoisie such as merchants, bankers, politicians, writers, artists and scientists. The character of this urban biotope was determined by the clientele, whose composition on the other hand was predetermined by the topographical position of the coffee house in the different parts of the city. Semi-permanent coffee shops at first were to be found at custom barriers in the arterial roads, at trade fairs or in harbour areas. Coffee house owners later chose permanent locations in fashionable streets and places (Piazza San Marco, Venice; the 'Piazza' at Covent Garden, London; Palais Royal, Paris; the Paris Boulevards, Berlin's 'Unter den Linden'). An interesting phenomenon, quasi a sort of synergy effect, can be observed here: Coffee houses frequently took their abodes next to each other or vis-à-vis in a street. Another gravitation point was the neighbourhood of scientific institutions or stock exchanges. As soon as 1671 a coffee house opened next to the Marseille exchange. The 'Crown' in New York or the 'de la Bourse' in Brussels are examples of the same phenomenon.

In London's streets around Cornhill and in the vicinity of the Royal Exchange were to be found coffee houses that above all other purposes served trade activities, such as 'Garraway's', opened by Thomas Garraway in Exchange Alley in 1670. By candlelight Hudson Company furs were traded here in the same way as sugar, indigo, textiles or spices. This enables us to speak of a liberalization in trade, equally important for the function of coffee houses as its attributed role as promoter of free speech. At 'Garraway's', retail tea trade was introduced, too. Whole shiploads were auctioned here, coffee houses now competed with exchange trade, so far exclusively under royal control. Edward Lloyd enters business in 1686/87 in a lively thoroughfare towards Wapping. His clientele

ny wurden hier bei Kerzenlicht ebenso verhandelt wie Zucker, Indigo, Textilien und Gewürze. Man kann von einer Liberalisierung der Wirtschaft reden, die sicherlich ein ebenso relevanter Fakt ist wie die dem Kaffeehaus zugeschriebene Rolle, Promotor der freien Meinungsäußerung zu sein. Im Garraway's wird auch der Retailhandel mit Tee begründet. Hier werden ganze Schiffsladungen versteigert. Kaffeehäuser treten hier in Konkurrenz zum ausschließlich von der Krone kontrollierten Börsenhandel auf. Edward Lloyd beginnt sein Unternehmen 1686/1687 an einer belebten Durchgangsstraße nach Wapping. Seine Kunden rekrutierten sich aus Seefahrern und Kapitänen. Auch er versteigert Schiffsladungen. Durch sein ausgefeiltes System, Nachrichten über Art und Beschaffenheit von Ladungen, Schiffsrouten, Häfen in Griechenland, der Türkei und Ägypten zu sammeln und *on the premises*, zunächst mündlich und ab 1796 zwei- bis dreimal wöchentlich in „Lloyd's News" publiziert, verbreiten zu lassen, wurde der Besuch in seinem Kaffeehaus zu einem Muss für alle im Seehandel tätigen Kaufleute. Die freistehenden, bestuhlten langen Tische wurden bald durch Nischen ergänzt, in die sich die Gäste für diskretere Gespräche zurückziehen konnten (Abb. 16). „A staff of five distributed coffee, tea or sherbet[58], as well as paper and ink for business minded clients."[59] Bald werden hier Schiffsladungen versichert und Lloyd's wird Namensgeber für einen der bekanntesten Versicherungskonzerne der Welt.

Eine vollkommen andere *clientèle* frequentierte die Kaffeehäuser um den Covent Garden Market. 1631 hatte Inigo Jones (1573–1597) den Platz zu einer Piazza nach italienischem Vorbild im Stil des Neopalladianismus umgestaltet. Die Attraktion, sich hier mit seinem Kaffeehaus anzusiedeln, wurde noch durch die Eröffnung des 1674 von Christopher Wren entworfenen King's Drury Lane Theatre verstärkt. Bereits 1664 berichtet der berühmte Londoner Chronist Samuel Pepys (1633–1703)[60] über einen Besuch bei Will's, einer Kaffeehausgründung von William Urwin: „Where I met Drayden [John Dryden (1631–1700)] the poet I knew at Cambridge [Magdalen College] and all the wits of the town."[61] Zwei Phänomene sind hier zu beobachten. Erstens: Die Absolventen von Cambridge und Oxford verlagern ihr Bedürfnis, ihre Meinungen im Kaffeehaus auszutauschen in die Metropole. Über Arthur Tillyards 1655 in Oxford eröffnetes Kaffeehaus heißt es:

16

Will's Best Coffee Powder at
Manwarings Coffee House in
Falcon Court over against St
Dunstans Church in Fleet Street

17

Gäste in alter und neuer Zeit
CAFÉ PROCOPE
ICI
PROCOPIO DEI COLTELLI
FONDA EN 1686
LE PLUS ANCIEN CAFÉ DU MONDE
ET LE PLUS CÉLÈBRE CENTRE
DE LA VIE LITTÉRAIRE ET PHILOSOPHIQUE
AU 18E ET AU 19E SIÈCLES.
IL FUT FRÉQUENTÉ PAR
LA FONTAINE, VOLTAIRE,
LES ENCYCLOPÉDISTES
BENJAMIN FRANKLIN, DANTON, MARAT,
ROBESPIERRE, NAPOLÉON BONAPARTE,
BALZAC, VICTOR HUGO,
GAMBETTA, VERLAINE,
ET ANATOLE FRANCE.

18

was mainly composed of sailors and ship's captains. He, too auctions shiploads and develops an elaborate system of collecting news about ship cargoes, routes and harbours in Greece, Turkey and Egypt. These were distributed by word of mouth on the premises' and from 1796 three times a week printed in 'Lloyd's News', so that visiting their coffee house became a must for all sea traders. Soon the freestanding tables and chairs were complemented by niches where customers could cluster for more private discussions (fig. 16). 'A staff of five distributed coffee, tea or sherbet[58], as well as paper and ink for business minded clients.'[59] Soon cargoes are insured here and Lloyds gives his name to what was to become one of the most renowned insurance companies worldwide.

A totally different clientele crowded the coffee houses around Covent Garden Market. In 1631 Inigo Jones (1573–1597) reshaped the area into a piazza following Italian examples in the Neo-Palladian style. The attraction to open a coffee house here was still further intensified by the opening of the 'King's Drury Lane Theatre' designed by Christopher Wren in 1674. As early as 1664 Samuel Pepys (1633–1703)[60], the famous London chronicler reports a visit at 'Will's', a coffee house undertaking

16

This seating arrangement is superseded by the introduction of sitting niches for more intimate conversations (and better ways of listening in) (woodcut, ca. 1760) ● Gathering of coffee house clientele at a long table in 'Manwaring's Coffee House'

Sitznischen für intimere Diskussionen und deren Belauschung (Holzstich um 1760). ● Das Zusammentreffen der Kaffeehausklientel an einem langen Tisch (Manwaring's Coffee House).

17

Famous habitués benefited the reputation of establishments. Here we see the Paris café 'Procope' surrounded by medaillons of, amongst others, regulars George Louis Leclerc, Comte du Buffon, Denis Diderot, Jean-Jacques Rousseau, and François-Marie Arouet (Voltaire). Later, the list of celebrities grew considerably longer, including Benjamin Franklin, Napoleon Bonaparte, Honoré de Balzac, Victor Hugo, Paul Verlaine, and Anatole France ● The most illustrious clients of the Leipzig coffee house 'Zum arabischen Kaffeebaum' were Saxonian king August The Strong, August von Kotzebue, Franz Liszt, and Richard Wagner

Berühmte Stammgäste dienten der Reputation. Hier das Pariser „Café Procope" im 18. Jahrhundert gerahmt von Medaillons von u.a. George Louis Leclerc, Comte de Buffon, Denis Diderot, Jean-Jaques Rousseau, François-Marie Arouet (Voltaire). Inzwischen ist die Liste um viele Berühmtheiten gewachsen, Benjamin Franklin, Napoleon Bonaparte, Honoré Balzac, Victor Hugo, Paul Verlaine, Anatole France. ● Zu den herausragendsten Gästen des Kaffeehauses „Zum Arabischen Kaffeebaum" in Leipzig zählten der sächsische König August der Starke, Kotzebue, Franz Liszt, Richard Wagner.

18

John Dryden, Alexander Pope, Richard Steele and Joseph Addison were central figures in London's 'Will's' and 'Button's' in the early eighteenth century

Die Zentralfiguren von 'Will's" und „Button's" in London waren Anfang des 18. Jahrhunderts: John Dryden, Alexander Pope, Richard Steele und Joseph Addison.

„The discussions on scientific and philosophical subjects that took place in this coffee house are believed to have inspired the formation of the Royal Society, many of whose members would later frequent the coffee houses of London in order to attend similar debates and to give public demonstrations."[62]

Ein zweites Phänomen ist das einer Art von Hofhaltung. Über Dryden wird berichtet, dass die Besucher kamen „to bow the Laureate" und seine Meinung zu hören, gleich ob sie über Jean Racines (1639–1699) letzte Tragödie oder ein anderes Produkt der Literatur geäußert wurde. Andere Habituées bei Will's waren Jonathan Swift (1667–1745) und der junge Alexander Pope (1688–1744). Figuren wie Dryden, dem in kalten Jahreszeiten ein bequemer Sessel vor das Kaminfeuer gestellt wurde, hielten Hof. Sie wurden im wahrsten Sinne des Wortes vom Wirt und vom Kellner hofiert.

Hier findet sich ein erstes Beispiel von Hofhaltung in einem Kaffeehaus, das über die Vertreter der Aufklärung in Paris, die Literaten um 1900 in Wien oder in den 1920er Jahren auch in Berlin und über Jean Paul Sartre (1905–1980) in den 1950er Jahren in Paris bis in die Gegenwart reicht. Die Berühmtheiten fungierten als Kundenfänger: Indem sie sich in Kaffeehäusern aufhielten oder über sie schrieben, trugen sie zu deren Reputation bei (Abb. 17). Noch heute wird das „Hier verkehrte…", „hier saß…", „hier wohnte…" (zum Beispiel Agatha Christie im Pera Palace in Istanbul oder der Schauspieler Otto Sander in der Paris Bar in Berlin) werbewirksam eingesetzt. So gehörte die sich immer mehr kultisch steigernde Behandlung von Celebrities (Stammplätze für sie zu reservieren, sie mit dem ihnen Gewohnten zu verwöhnen, aber auch mit Novitäten zu überraschen) zum Kalkül der Kaffeehausbetreiber. Bei Will's in London wird eine soziale Norm kreiert, die noch heute Geltung hat: sich durch die persönliche Begrüßung durch den Wirt aus der Menge der Besucher hervorzuheben. In London trafen sich Anfang des 18. Jahrhunderts in der Gegend von Pall Mall die Tories in Ozinda's und die Whigs im Cacao Tree. Die Rolle als Treffpunkt der *established wits* übernimmt dann ab 1712/13 das von Daniel Button in der Russell Street, Covent Garden, eröffnete Haus. Spiritus Rector des Button's war Joseph Addison (1672–1719). An seine und die Person Richard Steeles (1672–1729) knüpft die Geschichtsschreibung die Geburtsstunde des modernen Journalismus. 1709 gibt Steele die periodisch

by William Urwin: 'Where I met Drayden [John Dryden (1631–1700)] the poet I knew at Cambridge [Magdalen College] and all the wits of the town.'[61] Two phenomena can be observed here at the same time: for one the graduates of Oxford and Cambridge transfer their need to exchange opinions in a coffee house to the metropolis.

About Arthur Tillyard's Oxford coffee house, opened in 1655, one can read:

> 'The discussions on scientific and philosophical subjects that took place in this coffee house are believed to have inspired the formation of the Royal Society, many of whose members would later frequent the coffee houses of London in order to attend similar debates and to give public demonstrations.'[62]

A second phenomenon is to be seen in the act of 'holding court'. Of Dryden it is said that visitors came 'to bow to the laureate' and to get his opinion, no matter if it related to Jean Racine's (1639–1699) latest tragedy or to another work of literature. Other habitués at 'Will's' were Jonathan Swift (1667–1745) or the young Alexander Pope (1688–1744). Characters such as Dryden, who in winter got a chair positioned in front of the fire place, held court in 'their' coffee house, they were literally 'courted' by landlord and waiters alike.

Here we have a first example of holding court in a coffee house, which will be continued by representatives of the Enlightenment in Paris, the 1900 literary world of Vienna or of the 1920s in Berlin, as well as by celebrities like Jean Paul Sartre (1905–1980) in the Paris of the 1950s right up to the present day. The famous became propagators of the coffee houses they frequented, about which they wrote and to whose fame they thus contributed. Famous clients that the coffee house owner sought to turn into habitués, are useful tools of attraction (fig. 17). While they are alive, one comes to see them. When they are dead, commemorative plaques at their former chairs keep their memory alive. Still today one exploits the 'Here frequented…', or 'here sat…', or 'here spent the night…' (proof of this habit can be found in Agatha Christie's 'Pera Palace' in Istanbul or actor Otto Sander's 'Paris Bar' in Berlin). Thus it became part of the commercial calculation of coffee house landlords, to more and more cultivate the treatment of celebrities by reserving their accustomed seats for them, treat them to their habitual foods and beverages, or to surprise them with choice novelties. The

erscheinende Kaffeehauszeitung *Tatler* heraus, ihr folgt der bei Button's herausgegebene *Spectator* 1710/11 und der von Addison und Steele editierte *Guardian* (Abb. 18).

Diesem Beispiel folgend und schon im Titel auf die Funktion des Kaffeehauses verweisend, veröffentlichen 1764/65 der bei Maria Theresia hoch angesehene Nationalökonom Pietro Verri und der Staatsrechtler Cesare Beccaria in Brescia *Il Caffè: Ossia brevi e vari discorsi …* Von Venedig und Mailand aus wird das Organ zum Sprachrohr der italienischen Aufklärung. Der Maler und erklärte Propagandist aufklärerischen Gedankenguts Johann Heinrich Füssli (1741–1825) hatte wahrscheinlich in Rom beim Zusammentreffen mit Johann Joachim Winkelmann (1717–1768) und Angelika Kauffmann im Caffè Greco die Wochenzeitschrift kennengelernt. Begeistert von den provokativen Inhalten übersetzt er eine Auswahl der Artikel, die 1769 unter dem Titel *Das Caffee oder vermischte Abhandlungen…* in Zürich erscheint[63] – ein treffliches Beispiel für den Multiplikatoreffekt des Kaffeehauses (Abb. 19). Zum „redaktionellen Treiben" des Kaffeehauses gehörten – und dies bereits bei Button's – vielfältige Aktivitäten. Neben dem Verfassen von Artikeln, den Redaktionssitzungen und der Organisation von Lesungen und Vorträgen – ein Angebot, welches den Kaffeehäusern den Beinamen „Penny-Universities"[64] einbrachte – hatte Addison den Leserbrief erfunden. In *The Guardian* wies er 1713 darauf hin, dass ein Briefkasten in Form eines Löwenkopfes, „a proper emblem of knowledge and action, being all head and paws", die Korrespondenz aufnehme. „It opens its mouth at all hours for the reception of such intelligence as shall be thrown on" und erklärte: „whatever the lion swallows I shall digest it for the use of the public."[65] "In imitation of the antique Aegyptian lion",[66] war der Löwenkopf (Abb. 20) nach Entwürfen von William Hogarth (1697–1764), des berühmten gesellschaftskritischen Malers und Zeichners, angefertigt und 1713 an der Westseite von Button's angebracht worden. Er trug die Martial (40–104) entlehnte Inschrift: „Servantur magnis isti cervibus ungues: Non nisi delecta pascitur ille fera."[67] Die Assoziation zum römischen – heute touristisch vermarkteten – *Bocca della Verità*, einem an der frühchristlichen Kirche Sta. Maria in Cosmedin angebrachten marmornen antiken Kanaldeckel, der dem Einwurf von Bittschriften diente wie auch den der Denunziation dienenden venezianischen *Boche de Leon*, sei hier gestattet.

personal greeting of a guest elevates the special visitor out of the crowd, a habit that had its beginnings in 'Will's' coffee house in London in the seventeenth century where it created a social norm. Here the role of the 'meeting place' of the 'established wits' changed from 1712/1713 to the house founded by Daniel Button in Russell Street, Covent Garden, that bore his name. The political meeting points were situated in the Pall Mall part of the city, where Tories frequented 'Ozinda's' and Whigs the 'Cacao Tree' coffee houses. Spiritus Rector at 'Button's' was Joseph Addison (1672–1719). With him and with Richard Steele (1672–1729) historical writing associates the beginnings of modern journalism. In 1709 Steele edits the periodic coffee house gazette *Tatler*, followed in 1710/11 by *Spectator* edited at Button's and *The Guardian* (fig. 18) edited jointly by Addison and Steele.

After their model and in its title referring to this function of the coffee house, political economist Pietro Verri and public law specialist Cesare Beccaria, both in high esteem with empress Maria Theresia, in 1764/1765 in Brescia publish *Il Caffè: Ossia brevi e vari discorsi....* Dispersed from Venice and Milan, this weekly becomes the mouthpiece of Italian enlightenment. Painter and dedicated follower of the enlightenment Johann Heinrich Füssli (1741–1825) probably learned of this publication in Rome's 'Caffè Greco', where he met Johann Joachim Winckelmann (1717–1768) and Swiss painter Angelica Kauffmann (1741–1807). Enthusiastic about the provocative content, Füssli translated a selection of the articles, that appeared in 1769 under the title *Das Caffee oder vermischte Abhandlungen...* ('The Coffee House or miscellaneous treatises...') in Zurich.[63] This constitutes an outstanding example for the multiplication effect that is linked to the existence of coffee houses (fig. 19). But there was more to the editing activities that took place in these institutions since the days of 'Button's'. Above the invention of writing articles, holding editorial meetings and organizing lectures and readings—an offer that gave coffee houses the by-name of 'penny universities'[64], Addison introduced the 'letter to the editor'. In *The Guardian* he pointed out in 1713, that a letter box in the shape of a lion's head—'a proper emblem of knowledge and action, being all head and paws' received the correspondence. 'It opens its mouth at all hours for the reception of such intelligence as shall be thrown into' and he claimed 'whatever the lion swallows, I shall digest it for the use of the public.'[65] 'In imitation of the antique Egyptian lion',[66] the

Im Laufe der Jahrhunderte wird das Kaffeehaus, sieht man von den dort schreibenden Literaten ab, immer mehr vom Produktions- zum reinen Verbreitungsort. Zeitungen zu abonnieren wird für die Kaffeehausbetreiber ab der zweiten Hälfte des 19. Jahrhunderts verbindlich; ja, sie werben mit den bei ihnen ausliegenden in- und ausländischen Zeitungen. Die Anzahl und das Spektrum waren beträchtlich und der Aktualitätsgrad hoch. Die meisten von ihnen erschienen in Morgen-, Mittags- und Abendausgaben. Die *Neue Zürcher Zeitung* hatte 1913 sechs tägliche Ausgaben. ‚Aber unsere beste Bildungsstätte für alles Neue bleibt das Kaffeehaus. Es ist eigentlich eine Art demokratischer, jedem für eine billige Schale Kaffee zugänglicher Klub, wo jeder Gast für diesen kleinen Obolus stundenlang sitzen, diskutieren, schreiben, Karten spielen, seine Post empfangen und vor allem eine unbegrenzte Zahl von Zeitungen und Zeitschriften konsumieren kann", schreibt Stefan Zweig 1942.[68]

Noch heute sind Kaffeehäuser Multiplikatoren tagespolitischer Druckerzeugnisse und provozieren so manche Diskussion. Ein aktueller, über 100 Kaffeehäuser in Wien beschreibender Führer erwähnt in einer ersten Rubrik nach Adresse und Öffnungszeiten die ausliegenden Zeitungen.[69] Wohl auch zum Schutz gegen unerlaubte Mitnahme hängen sie in Wien in Lesebügeln an ihren Zeitungsständern (Abb. 21). Das Kaffeehaus ist seit seinen Anfängen ein von Machthabern argwöhnisch beobachteter Ort, die dort zusammentreffenden und verbreiteten Nachrichten stimulieren, angefacht durch die Wirkung des Kaffees, auch hitzige politische Diskussionen. Bereits 1511 in Mekka[70] und 1539 und 1544 in Kairo ergehen Verbote, Kaffee zu trinken. „To draw too sharp a line between political and religious concerns is perhaps a mistake", schreibt Ralph S. Hattox.[71] Beide Motive haben beim Versuch, den Genuss von Kaffee und Kaffeehäusern zu verbieten, eine Rolle gespielt. Letztendlich setzte sich aber die Haltung durch, dass, wer Kaffee trinkt, nicht den Gesetzen der Scharia zuwiderhandelt, obwohl 1568 noch einmal „an die Kadis von Istanbul und Galata ... die Weisung [ergeht, weil dort] Laster und Liederlichkeit herrschen ... die Weinschenken und Kaffeehäuser zu schließen."[72] Ausschließlich politisch sind die Versuche, Kaffeehäuser zu schließen oder auf jeden Fall die Gespräche in ihnen zu bespitzeln. „Certainly they have been linked with the spread of dissent and new political ideas such as the theories

19

IL CAFFÈ
OSSIA
BREVI E VARJ DISCORSI
DISTRIBUITI IN FOGLJ PERIODICI
Dal Giugno 1764.
a tutto Maggio 1765.
TOMO I.

IN BRESCIA. MDCCLXV.
DALLE STAMPE DI GIAMMARIA RIZZARDI
CON LICENZA DE' SUPERIORI.
Si vende in Milano da GIUSEPPE GALEAZZI
Stampatore e Libraro.

Das
Caffee.
Oder
Vermischte Abhandlungen.
Eine Wochenschrift.
Aus dem Italiänischen übersezt.
Erster Band.

Zürich,
bey Füeßlin und Compagnie, 1769.

20

21

19

In 1764/1765 in Italy, the cultural-political explanatory gazette 'Il Caffè' appeared, published by Johann Heinrich Füssli in 1769 in Zurich in German

1764/65 erschien in Italien das kulturpolitisch-aufklärerische Organ „Il Caffè", das Johann Heinrich Füssli 1769 in deutscher Sprache in Zürich edierte.

20

In London's 'Button' one could find a collector of letters to the editor in the shape of a lion's head, inviting associations with the Roman 'Bocca della Verità' and the Venetian 'Boche de Leon' serving denunciations

Im Button's in London hing ein Nachrichtensammler in Form eines Löwenkopfs, der die Assoziation an den römischen Bocca della Verità wie auch an die Denunziationen dienenden Boche de Leon in Venedig aufkommen lässt.

21

Newspaper racks and holding brackets are typical atttributes of a Vienna coffee house

Zeitungsständer und Zeitungen in Lesebügeln gehören zu den typischen Ausstattungsgegenständen der Wiener Kaffeehäuser.

lion's head was made after the design of William Hogarth (1697–1764), the famous painter and graphic artist critical of society (fig. 20). Fixed to the west wall of Button's in 1713, it showed an inscription adopted from Martial (40–104): 'Servantur magnis isti cervibus ungues: Non nisi delecta pascitur ille fera.'[67] We may be allowed here the association with the Venetian 'Boche de Leon' serving denunciations as well as the 'Bocca della Verità', today touristically exploited, that in Rome was fixed to the wall of the early Christian church of 'Sta. Maria in Cosmedin', to serve as receptacle for petitions by the population. In fact the sculpted piece of stone was a former antique canalization-manhole-cover.

In the course of the centuries the coffee house more and more changes its character from a place of literary production—except in the case of writers actually still writing there—to that of a distribution centre. The subscription of journals and newspapers becomes in the course of the second half of the nineteenth century a must for the managers of coffee houses. The number of outlying national and international editions becomes part of the advertising strategy. The number and range of these publications was considerable, their grade of daily up-to-datedness very high. Most journals appeared in the morning, at noon and in the evening. *Neue Züricher Zeitung* in 1913 had no less than six editions a day. 'But our best place of education in everything new remains the coffee house. It is in fact a sort of democratic club, accessible for everybody for a cheap bowl of coffee, where each guest may remain for a small obolus for hours, may discuss, write, play cards, receive his mail and above all where he can consume any amount of newspapers and magazines' Stefan Zweig (1881–1942) writes as late as 1942.[68]

Up to the present day, coffee houses serve as multiplicators of daily print media and provoke more than one discussion. A recent Vienna coffee house guide that comprises more than a hundred places, mentions besides the address and hours of opening in the next following rubrication the number of outlying newspapers.[69] As a device against theft, the newspapers in Vienna and other places are inserted into a backbone-like wooden device (fig. 21). From its beginnings, the coffee house is a locality under close and mistrustful observation by those in power. Made more ardent by the stimulating effect of coffee, the news that are gathered and distributed here, tend to make political discussion more animated than in other places. As soon as in 1511, Mecca[70] and in 1539 and again 1544 Cairo

of Thomas Hobbes[73] (1588–1679) … and constituted centres of opposition to the Crown."[74] Wie ernst die Herrschenden diese Gefahr nahmen, zeigt die Proklamation Charles' II. vom 29. Dezember 1675 zum Verbot der Kaffeehäuser.[75] Kaffehäuser spielten bei der öffentlichen Meinungsbildung eine wichtige Rolle. Aus diesem Grunde waren sie Orte, an denen Regierungen ihre Spione einschleusten, um sich so Informationen über politisch Andersdenkende zu verschaffen. Dies sei am Beispiel der Stadt Yarmouth, einer Stadt in der eine beträchtliche Anzahl nonkonformistischer Protestanten lebte, verdeutlicht. Kurz nach der Restauration (Wiedereinführung der absoluten Monarchie und des Katholizismus als Staatsreligion durch Charles II.) wurde ein gewisser Bower als Agent der politischen Spionage eingesetzt. Um 1667 richtet Bower seiner Frau ein Kaffeehaus ein. Die Gespräche an den Tischen belauschend, verschaffte sie sich Kenntnis über stadtpolitische Bewegungen wie auch dem Schiffsverkehr mit Holland.[76] Kaffeehäuser ermutigten zum vielstimmigen öffentlichen Gespräch, was die Machthaber als Bedrohung ihrer Stellung empfanden. Doch das Kaffeehaus war nicht der einzige Akteur; es nahm eine Rolle in einem Netzwerk ein. Dies zeigte sich in Frankreich vor und während der Französischen Revolution ebenso wie 1830 und vor allem 1848 überall in Europa oder später in Italien zur Zeit Giuseppe Garibaldis (1807–1882).

Eines der wichtigsten Vehikel politischer Emanzipation in diesem Netzwerk ist die Aufklärungsliteratur. In Frankreich sind es unter anderem die Arbeiten der Encyclopédisten Denis Diderot (1713–1784), Jean-Baptiste le Rond, genannt d'Alembert, eines François-Marie Arouet (Voltaire, 1694–1778) – wegen einer ihm zugeschriebenen Satire hatte er 1717 elf Monate in der Bastille verbracht – und die des Naturphilosophen Jean-Jacques Rousseau – alle regelmäßige Gäste im Café Procope. Auf fruchtbaren Boden fielen sie vor allem bei den sogenannten proletarischen Intellektuellen, die der Druck der wirtschaftlichen Depression aus der Provinz nach Paris vertrieben hatte. Es waren stellungslose Advokaten, Ärzte, Künstler, Literaten, Studenten.[77] Sie liefern sich in den Cafés und Kaffeegärten des Palais Royal vehemente Redeschlachten. „Im Palais Royal", schreibt einer der zugewanderten Advokaten, Camille Desmoulins (1760–1794) – auch Voltaire ist ausgebildeter Jurist –, „lösen sich jeden Abend diejenigen ab, die Stentors Stimme haben. Sie steigen auf einen Tisch, man sammelt sich um sie … Sie lesen

were cities, where bans were issued against the consummation of coffee. 'To draw a sharp line between religious and political concerns is perhaps a mistake' Ralph S. Hattox writes.[71] Both aspects played a role in the attempts to prohibit coffee consumption and coffee houses. In the end the perspective prevails that who drinks coffee does not act contrary to the laws of the Sharia, although in 1568 once again there is an order addressed to the 'kadis of Istanbul and Galata … to close all wine taverns and coffee houses, because vice and looseness prevail there.'[72] In most cases attempts to close down coffee houses have a political background, in all cases however this is the case with attempts to spy on conversations hold there. It was said about coffee houses: 'Certainly they have been linked with the spread of dissent and new political ideas such as the theories of Thomas Hobbes (1588–1679)[73] … and constituted centres of opposition to the crown.'[74] So seriously did the authorities interpret the danger that on 29 December 1675 Charles II issued a 'proclamation for the suppression of Coffee Houses.'[75] These places played a vital role as cradles of public opinion and therefore were places where the government infiltrated spies to gain authentic insight into the political feelings of dissenters. This is exemplified by the case of Yarmouth—a town in which a dense concentration of Nonconformist protestants existed. Soon after the 'Restoration' (reinstallment of Catholicism and absolute monarchy by Charles II) a certain Bower was employed as intelligencer for the secretary of State to describe the political situation. Around 1667 Bower established his wife in a coffee house. By listening over the tables she gained confidential knowledge of town politics and ship movements to Holland. This was duly reported by letter to Secretary of State Williamson.[76]

Coffee houses had encouraged in public a polyphony of conversations, which threatened the power by usurping the prerogative of the crown respectively the political power. But the coffee house was not the only actor, it played its role as part of a network. This was the case in France before and during the French Revolution and again in 1830 and especially in 1848 all over Europe or later in Italy during the time of Giuseppe Garibaldi (1807–1882).

One of the most potent tools in this network of political emancipation is the literature of the Enlightenment. Here you find amongst others the works of the encyclopaedists Denis Diderot (1713–1784), Jean-Baptiste le Rond, called d'Alembert, and of a François-Marie Arouet, called Voltaire (1694–1778), who in 1716 spent

das Stärkste vor, was über die Tagesereignisse gedruckt worden ist."[78] Am 12. Juli 1789 steht Camille Desmoulins selbst auf einem Tisch im Café de Foy im Palais Royal und ruft nach dem Bekanntwerden der Entlassung des reformengagierten Finanzministers Jacques Necker (1732–1804)[79] zur Ergreifung der Waffen, zum Sturm auf die Bastille auf (Abb. 22).

Zu den Berühmtheiten des Café de Foy gehörte auch die immer und immer wieder porträtierte sogenannte „Amazone der Revolution", die schöne Théroigne de Méricourt (Anne Josèphe Terwagne), eine Abenteurerin flämischer Nationalität. Selbst zum Schauplatz blutiger Aktivitäten wurden die Cafés des Palais Royal. Im Café du Caveau wurden die Prämien verteilt auf die Köpfe, die überbracht wurden von denjenigen, die das Volksgericht verurteilt hatte (Abb. 23). Aus der Revolutionszeit gehen das Café de Foy und das Café Corazza ebenfalls im Palais Royal in die napoleonische Ära über. Letzeres hatte Napoleon I. (1769–1821) als Agent Provocateur in eigener Sache genutzt und Paul François Graf von Barras (1755–1829) unterhielt hier während des Direktoriums ein ausgedehntes Spionagenest. In seiner Nachfolge baut Joseph Fouché (1759–1820) die erste moderne Geheimpolizei auf. Die Vertreter seines feingeknüpften Spitzelnetzes hatten in den Kaffeehäusern reiche Beute. So wird das Kaffeehaus als Ort der freien Meinungsäußerung, als Ort der bürgerlichen Emanzipation auch Stammzelle der Bespitzelung. Die noch bis zum Ende des Zweiten Weltkriegs üblichen Methoden des Mit- und Abhörens – hinzu kommt mit dem neuen Medium des Telefons auch die Kontrolle der Telefongespräche – sind heute durch global agierende Nachrichtendienste abgelöst.

Ein Treffpunkt für Künstler und Schriftsteller

Noch heute kommen in Paris Gäste ins Café Procope, um an Voltaires angestammtem Platz zu sitzen. Indem sie sich in ihm aufgehalten haben, in ihm und über es geschrieben haben, tragen die Repräsentanten der Literatur, Malerei und später auch des Films – wie schon angedeutet – zum Ruhm eines Kaffeehauses bei. Den Kaffeehauswirten war – wie bereits in Zusammenhang mit den englischen Kaffeehäusern erwähnt – daran gelegen, diese Kundenmagnete an ihr Haus zu binden. Denn zu der zahlenden Kundschaft der als Prominentencafé ausgewiesenen Häuser gehört komplementär die

22

23

22

Coffee houses also served as stages for politicizing and agitation. In 1789, Camille Desmoulins calls for a storm on the Bastille in 'Café de Foy' ● In 1848, critical contemporaries gather in Vienna (etching by K. Gunther, 1848) ● "In den Zelten" in Berlin (woodcut, 1849)

Kaffeehäuser waren auch Bühnen des Politisierens und Agitierens. 1789 ruft Camille Desmoulins im Pariser Café de Foy zum Sturm auf die Bastille auf. ● 1848 sammeln sich die kritischen Geister in Wien (Stich von K. Gunther, 1848). ● „In den Zelten" in Berlin (Holzstich, 1849).

23

The 'Café du Caveau', a glamorous place during the *Ancien Régime* (colour engraving, eighteenth century), turned into a bloody place in the French Revolution: ● Here premiums for severed heads were distributed (copper-plate engraving, by Pierre Nolhac, 1902)

Das Café du Caveau, ein mondäner Ort zur Zeit des *Ancien Régime* (kolorierter Stich, 18. Jahrhundert) wird in den Revolutionsjahren zu einem blutigen Schauplatz. ● Hier wurden die Kopfgelder für abgeschlagene Köpfe verteilt (Kupferstich von Pierre Nolhac, 1902).

eleven month in the Bastille because of a piece of satirical writing attributed to him, and of natural philosopher Jean-Jacques Rousseau (1712–1778)—all of them regular customers at the 'Procope' coffee house. These places were ideal echo-rooms for the writings and teachings of this group of people. Fertile ground they found mainly with the so-called proletarian intellectuals, who under the pressure of financial difficulties had fled the provinces for Paris. They were advocates, physicians, artists, teachers or students without work.[77] They waged fierce battles of speech in the coffee houses and gardens of the 'Palais Royal'. 'In the Palais Royal', one of these immigrant advocates, Camille Desmoulins (1760–1794) (like Voltaire a fully trained jurist) wrote, 'those take turns every evening, who have Stentor's voice. They mount a table, people gather around … they read to them the strongest stuff that was printed on the same day about things going on.'[78] On 12 July of the year 1789, Camille Desmoulins himself stands on such a table in the 'Café de Foy' and calls everybody to arms to storm the Bastille, after it became known that Jacques Necker (1732–1804)[79] the reform-friendly minister of finances had been sacked (fig. 22).

One of the celebrities of the 'Café de Foy' was also beautiful Théroigne de Méricourt (Anne Josèphe Terwagne, 1762–1817) who as so-called 'Amazone of the Revolution' was of Flemish peasant origins and has been portrayed innumerable times. The cafés of the 'Palais Royal' also became the scene for bloody activities. In the 'Café du Caveau' rewards were distributed to those who delivered the severed heads of persons damned to capital punishment by the people's tribunal (fig. 23). From revolutionary times 'Café de Foy' and 'Café Corazza', also situated in the 'Palais Royal', pass on into the Napoleonic era. The latter was used by Napoleon I (1769–1821) himself as agent provocateur in his own interest. During the time of the Directory, Paul François, Count of Barras (1755–1829) ran an elaborated nucleus of spies here. In his wake, Joseph Fouché (1759–1820) organizes the first modern secret police system. Representatives of his far flung informant's network held rich harvests in the coffee houses. Thus the place of unimpeded free speech and of bourgeois emancipation at the same time also becomes the stem cell of organized spying by the state. This system of overhearing or listening in, practiced till the end of the Second World War and later in addition the control of telephone conversations is superseded by globally acting

Clientèle derer, die sich in den Strahlen der Prominenz sonnen wollen. Sie bilden die Folie für die Auftritte der im Rampenlicht Stehenden, das ihresgleichen, aber auch dem gemeinen Kaffeehauspublikum galt. Treffend charakterisiert Joseph Roth in *Zipper und sein Vater* im Finanzbeamten Arnold eine solche Figur.

> „Für alle Künste interessierte er sich. Jenen, die sie ausübten, nahe zu sein gehörte zu seinen bescheidenen Freuden. Sicherlich beneidete er sie. Denn sie allein, so schien es ihm, hatten einen Sinn in ihrem Leben gefunden und besaßen ein Recht, dazusein. … Erst wenn Arnold dieses Kaffeehaus betrat, war er seinem Tag endgültig entronnen. Hier erst begann seine Freiheit. … Diese Welt hatte nichts mit der bitteren und nüchternen des Tages zu tun."[80]

Die nahezu sublime Atmosphäre des aus dem quirlenden metropolitanen Tagesgeschehen herausgehobenen Ortes, den spezifischen „l'esprit du lieux" beschreibt folgende Schilderung des Café Procope:

> „An atmosphere of refined and elegant suppression pervades the place; … Here all is peace and tranquillity, and that is why the haunt of many earnest and aspiring poets and authors; for hither they may bring their portofolios in peace and security, and here they may work upon their manuscripts, knowing that their neighbours are similarly engrossed … And then, too are they not sitting on the same chairs and writing at the same tables that have been occupied by some of the greatest men in all the brilliant history of France … Are not there ancient walls the same that echoed the wit, badinage, and laughter of the masters?"[81]

Für beinahe ein Jahrhundert war das Schicksal des Café Procope eng mit dem der *Comédiens français* (Ancienne Comédie) verknüpft. Diese benutzten bis zu ihrem Umzug 1770 eine in unmittelbarer Nähe gelegene ehemalige „jeu de paume"-Halle für ihre Aufführungen. Es waren die schauspielenden und Theaterstücke schreibenden Persönlichkeiten, die den Grundstein zum nachhaltigen Ruhm legten. Das Café Procope nahm als Literatencafé des 18. Jahrhunderts eine herausgehobene Stellung ein. „Von hier aus wurde das gesamte öffentliche Leben Frankreichs einer Kritik unterzogen, Epigramme geschmiedet und die Meinung über die neuesten

secret services that substitute real people by electronic spying.

A Hub for Artists and Writers

Even today, people come into 'Café Procope' in Paris to sit at Voltaire's table: By dwelling in them, writing inside and about them, the representatives of literature, painting and later filmmaking contribute to the fame of coffee houses. Their owners, as was mentioned in connection with English coffee houses, strove to attach these customer magnets to their establishments, for part of the body of paying guests was the clientèle of those eager to warm themselves in the sun rays of prominence. They form a backdrop for the appearance of those in the limelight, who played to their equals but also to the common folk. Appropriately Joseph Roth (1894–1939) in his revenue clerk Arnold in 'Zipper und sein Vater', portrays such a type.

> 'He was interested in art. Being near to those who practiced it, was part of his modest satisfactions. He certainly envied them. For only they it seemed to him had found a meaning in life and had a right to exist. It was only when Arnold entered the café that he had the feeling of finally escaping his daily life. His freedom began … This world had nothing to do with the bitter and prosaic world of everyday.'[80]

The nearly sublime atmosphere of a place apart from whirling metropolitan daily life, its specific 'esprit du lieux' is to be found in the following sketch of the 'Café Procope':

> 'An atmosphere of refined and elegant suppression pervades the place: … Here all is peace and tranquillity, and that is why it is the haunt of many earnest and aspiring poets and authors: for hither they may bring their portfolios in peace and security, and there they may work upon their manuscripts, knowing that their neighbours are similarly engrossed … And then, too are they not sitting on the same chairs and writing at the same tables that have been occupied by some of the greatest men in all the brilliant history of France … Are not these ancient walls the same that echoed the wit, badinage, and laughter of the masters?'[81]

Schauspiele und Opern festgelegt. Es stand im Ruf einer wahren Zeitung von Paris …“[82] Von Voltaire wird berichtet, dass er sich als Geistlicher verkleidet in das Café Procope begab, um unerkannt die Meinungen über sein Theaterstück zu hören. Nach einem Dornröschenschlaf im 19. Jahrhundert erfährt das Café Procope um 1900 eine Neubelebung. Paul Verlaine war einer derjenigen, die sich in Reaktion auf die modischen Boulevardcafés, die vor allem Orte bürgerlicher Schau- und Konsumlust waren, nach einer alternativen Rückzugsmöglichkeit umsahen. „He would sit in his favourite place in the little rear salon at Voltaire's table.“[83] (Abb. 24)

In der zweiten Hälfte des 19. Jahrhunderts sind es neben den mondänen, viele Gäste fassenden, aufwendig ausgestatteten Cafés an den Boulevards, den Pariser Flaniermeilen, vor allem die Künstlercafés am Montmartre, die den Ruf der Kulturmetropole Paris festigen. Im Café Guerbois an der Grande rue des Batignolles (heute Avenue de Clichy) treffen sich die Impressionisten. Hier versammelt Édouard Manet (1823–1883) seine Freunde um sich. Gleich am Eingang waren zwei Tische für ihn reserviert. In der Folge wird in unmittelbarer Nähe der Ateliers von Edgar Degas (1834–1917) und Auguste Renoir (1841–1919) am Place Pigalle das Café de la Nouvelle Athènes (Abb. 25) der wichtigste Treffpunkt der Künstler. Der irische Autor George Moore nennt es die „véritable Académie française“[84]. Montmartre-Abtrünnige wie Claude Monet (1840–1926), Frédéric Bazille und andere siedeln in die Closerie des Lilas in Montparnasse über. Paul Fort (1872–1960) organisiert Dichterlesungen, Alfred Jarry (1873–1907), Chefredakteur der literarischen Zeitschrift *La Plume* trifft hier 1905 den jungen Pablo Picasso. Die Troubadoure des Fauvismus und Kubismus bevölkern ab 1905 das Dôme. Ilja Ehrenburg (1891–1967), Leo Trotzki (1879–1940), Wladimir Iljitsch Uljanow Lenin lesen hier die frisch aus St. Petersburg eingetroffenen Zeitungen. Das Renommee des Dôme führt 1911 zur Gründung von La Rotonde (Abb. 26). Als dritter Part des Dreigestirns erscheint 1927 La Coupole, das zum Zentrum des Nachtlebens der *Années folles* wird. Den gastronomischen Rahmen all dieser Orte bilden, kombiniert mit dem Café, die Brasserie und das Restaurant[85], zu denen in den 1920er Jahren noch die Bar Americain hinzukommt. Josephine Baker, Jean Cocteau, Fernand Léger, Blaise Cendrars, Alfred Jarry und viele andere extravagante Berühmtheiten ziehen die Gäste an wie Motten das Licht.

For more than a century the fate of the 'Procope' was intricately linked to that of the *Comédiens Français* (Ancienne Comédie). Until their removal in 1770 they utilized a former 'jeu-de-paume' hall for their performances. It was the performers and playwrights who laid the foundation stone for the 'Procope's' everlasting fame. As a café for artists and literates of the eighteenth century it occupied an elevated position. 'From here, the entire public life of France was critically commented, epigrams were formulated and the judgment over the latest plays and operas cast. It had the reputation of a true newspaper of Paris…'[82] Of Voltaire it was said that he went to the 'Café Procope' in the disguise of a clergyman to listen incognito to the opinions on his latest play 'Semiramis'. After a long Sleeping-Beauties-rest during the nineteenth century it experienced a revival around 1900. Paul Verlaine (1844–1896) was one of the fugitives from fashionable boulevard coffee houses as places of bourgeois hunger for consumption and attractions, who looked for alternative places of retreat. 'He would sit in his favourite place in the little rear salon at Voltaire's table.'[83] (fig. 24)

In the second half of the nineteenth century it is mainly the artist's cafés in Montmartre that helped strengthening the fame of Paris as a cultural metropole besides those mundane, elaborately furnished cafés along the boulevards, those flaneur runways, that held hundreds of customers. The 'Café Guerbois' in the Grande Rue des Batignolles (today Avenue de Clichy) was the meeting place of the impressionists. Here Édouard Manet (1823–1883) gathers his friends around him. Next to the entrance, two tables were reserved for him. Later the 'Café de la Nouvelle Athènes' (fig. 25) at Place Pigalle in the immediate neighbourhood of Edgar Degas' (1834–1917) and Auguste Renoir's (1841–1919) ateliers becomes the most important meeting place for artists. The Irish author George Moore (1852–1933) calls it the 'veritable Académie française'.[84] Fugitives from Montmartre such as Claude Monet (1840–1926), Frédéric Bazille and others move to the 'Closerie des Lilas' in Montparnasse. Paul Fort (1872–1960) organizes literary lectures, Alfred Jarry (1873–1907), playwright and editor-in-chief of the literary periodical *La Plume* meets here young Pablo Picasso (1881–1973). From 1905 on, the 'Dôme' is populated by the troubadours of fauvism and cubism. Here Ilja Ehrenburg (1891–1967), Leo Trotzki (1879–1924) and Wladimir Iljitsch Uljanov Lenin (1870–1924) read the newspapers freshly delivered from St. Petersburg. The

> „Jeder obskure Poet oder Maler, der in Bukarest oder Sevilla den Erfolg sucht, muss beim aktuellen Stand auf dem alten Kontinent notwendigerweise ein wenig Militärdienst im ‚Rotonde' oder im ‚Coupole' abgeleistet haben, jenen zwei Trottoirakademien [man denke an die Londoner Bezeichnung Penny Universities], an denen das Bohèmeleben, die Geringschätzung des Bürgertums, der Humor und das Saufen gelehrt wird."[86]

Obwohl sich in den Seitenstraßen des Boulevard Montparnasse, vor allem in der Rue Campagne première die Ateliers drängen – auch der renommierte Eugène Atget (1857– 1927)[87] betreibt hier sein Fotostudio – wandert die Künstler- und Intellektuellenschar weiter. Sie wandert nach Saint-Germain-des-Prés. Hier, wo Procopio dei Coltelli das Kaffeehausleben aus der Wiege gehoben hat, bestimmt seit den 1930er Jahren das magische Dreieck mit dem Café de Flore ab 1885, dem Les Deux Magots ab 1891 und der Brasserie Lipp [88] das intellektuelle Leben in Paris. Léon-Paul Fargue, der in seinem *Le piéton de Paris* den Facettenreichtum der Pariser Cafés aufblättert, ist Stammgast im Lipp.

> „Ohne wenigstens einen Abend pro Woche im Lipp verbracht zu haben, wüsste man nicht dreißig Zeilen in einer Pariser Zeitung zu schreiben, ein Bild zu malen oder deutlich seine Meinung auf dem Gebiet der Politik zu bekunden."[89]

24
Paul Verlaine occupies Voltaire's former habitual seat in 'Procope'

Paul Verlaine nistet sich an Voltaires ehemaligem Stammplatz im Procope ein.

25
The coffee house 'De la nouvelle Athène' of Montmartre became, due to the men of letters and artists who frequented it in the course of the nineteenth cenutry, a veritable 'Académie française'

Das Café „De la Nouvelle Athène" in Montmartre wurde wegen der in ihm verkehrenden Literaten und Künstler im 19. Jahrhundert zur veritablen „Académie française".

26
The following phase plays out in Saint-Germain, where Picasso meets Dora Maar. Here, a joint drawing of both on a serviette ● The coffee-house life of artists migrates to Montparnasse in the beginning of the twentieth century. Jean Cocteau, in 1916, takes photographs of Amedeo Modigliani, Pablo Picasso, and André Salmon in front of 'La Rotonde'

Die folgende Etappe spielt sich in Saint-Germain ab, wo Picasso Dora Maar kennenlernt, hier eine gemeinsame Serviettenskizze von Künstler und Muse. ● Das Kaffeehausleben der Künstler verlagert sich Anfang des 20. Jahrhunderts nach Montparnasse. Hier fotografiert Jean Cocteau 1916 Amedeo Modigliani, Pablo Picasso und André Salmon vor La Rotonde.

24

25

26

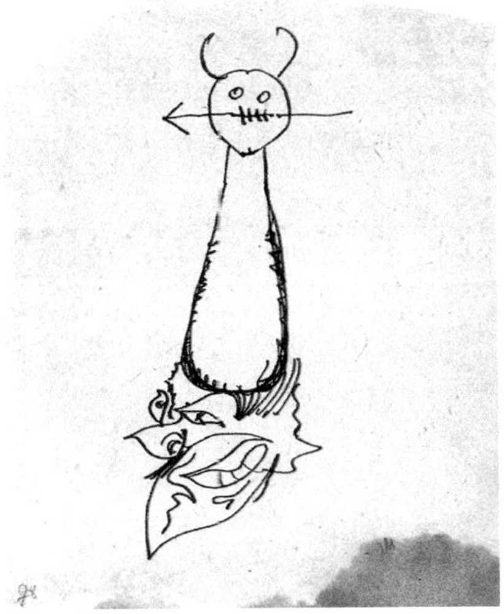

'Dôme's' reputation in 1911 leads to the opening of 'La Rotonde' (fig. 26) an establishment of similar character. As a third star in this constellation 'La Coupole' appears in 1927, which will become the centre of the night life of 'les Années folles'. The gastronomic framework of all these places is formed by the combination of brasserie, restaurant and café [85] which since the 1920s is augmented by the 'Bar Americain'. Josephine Baker (1906–1975), Jean Cocteau (1889–1963), Fernand Léger (1881–1955), Blaise Cendrars (Frederic-Louis Sauser, 1887–1961), Alfred Jarry and the many other extravagant celebrities draw clients like candlelight attract moths.

> 'Each and every obscure poet or painter who wants to be successful in Bucharest or Seville, according to the actual situation on the old continent has to do a little military service in 'La Rotonde' or 'Coupole', those two pedestrian academies [here one is reminded of the London designation 'Penny Universities'] that teach Bohème lifestyle, contempt for the bourgeois, sense of humour and heavy drinking.'[86]

Although the ateliers crowded the bystreets of Boulevard Montparnasse, mainly Rue Campagne Première—renowned Eugène Atget (1857–1927)[87] runs his photographical studio here—the congregation of artists and intellectuals moves on. It aims for Saint-Germain-des-Prés. Here, at the cradle of coffee house activity founded by Procopio dei Coltelli, since the 1930s the magical triangle of 'Café Flore' since 1885, the 'Deux Magots' since 1891 and 'Brasserie Lipp' (under this name since 1920)[88] dominate intellectual life in Paris. Lèon-Paul Fargue, who in 1939 unfolds in his *Le pièton de Paris* the multifaceted life of Paris coffee houses, is a regular customer at Lipp's. 'If I did not at least spend one night per week at 'Lipp's', it would be impossible to write even thirty lines in a Paris newspaper, to create a painting or distinctly contribute ones opinion in the field of politics.'[89]

Here, Lèon-Paul Fargue once again clearly characterizes the give-and-take activities in the coffee houses. Creative productive energies are nourished here and those inspired here, in turn elevate the place they frequent to fame by their presence and by their works. Deputies of parliament—who remain faithful to the 'Lipp' after 1945—or students of the Ecole des Beaux Arts coexist here alongside representatives of the theatre, the film business, literature and the fine arts. Amongst the guests

Hier charakterisiert Léon-Paul Fargue noch einmal deutlich das Geben und Nehmen im Kaffeehaus. Die schöpferische Produktivkraft erhält Nahrung und die im Café Inspirierten verhelfen im Gegenzug dem von ihnen frequentierten Ort durch ihre Anwesenheit und ihre Werke zum Ruhm. Politisierte Deputierte – die dem Lipp auch nach 1945 treu bleiben – oder Studenten der École des Beaux-Arts koexistierten im Lipp mit Vertretern des Theaters, des Films, der Literatur und Künstlern. Zu den Gästen zählten unter anderem Pablo Picasso, Colette und André Gide. 1935 wird der nach dem Besitzer Marcellin Cazes benannte, aus der Welt der Literatur nicht mehr wegzudenkende „Prix Cazes" gestiftet. Zur Legendenbildung trägt auch Ernest Hemingway, ein vielgesehener Gast der Pariser Kaffeehäuser, in seinem posthum 1965 erschienenen *Paris – ein Fest fürs Leben* bei.[90] Literarische Hochburg bleibt das Lipp auch nach dem Zweiten Weltkrieg. Hier verkehrt Michel Butor, neben Nathalie Sarraute und Alain Robbe-Grillet der wichtigste Vertreter der französischen Literaturströmung des „Nouveau roman". Das Deux Magots richtet sich in den Räumen eines ehemaligen Modegeschäfts ein. Zur ursprünglichen Ausstattung gehörten zwei hölzerne Holzfiguren chinesischer Mandarine. Sie werden die emblematischen Namensgeber. Im Deux Magots[91] findet sich André Breton, der das Charivari am Montparnasse hasste, mit einem sorgfältig erwählten Kreis von Surrealisten ein. Antoine de Saint-Exupéry verkehrt hier zu der Zeit, als er an seinem *Courrier Sud* arbeitet. Pablo Picasso lernt hier Dora Maar (Abb. 26) kennen.

Die Ausländer warfen sich ohne Vorbehalte in dieses geistige und künstlerische Getümmel. James Joyce versammelt hier seine Jünger um sich.

An dieser Stelle sei ein Exkurs nach Triest gestattet, wo Joyce seine *Dubliners* beendet und an *A Portrait of the Artist as a Young Man* und am *Ulysses* arbeitet. Während seiner Aufenthalte 1904 bis 1915 sowie 1919 bis 1920 gehören zu den von ihm frequentierten Plätzen das Caffè Stella Polare und die Pasticceria Pirona. Triest, bis zum Ende des Ersten Weltkriegs Vorposten des k.u.k.-Reiches am Meer, hat noch heute eine reiche Kaffeehauskultur.[92] Das Tommaseo, das Tergesteo, das Fabris, das Garibaldi, das Rosetti, das Degli Specchi und vor allem das San Marco sind verbunden mit Schriftstellern wie Italo Svevo (1861–1928), Umberto Saba (1883–1957)[93] und in der jüngeren Vergangenheit mit Namen wie Giorgio Voghera, Claudio Magris und Fulvio Tomizza.

are Pablo Picasso, Colette (1873–1954) or André Gide (1869–1957).

In 1935 the literary award 'Prix Cazes', named after 'Lipp's' owner Marcellin Cazes, is donated, an established feature of literary life. A contributor to the wealth of legends is also Ernest Hemingway (1899–1961), a frequent guest of Paris coffee houses, by his posthumous book *Paris. A Moveable Feast.*[90] 'Lipp' remains a literary fortress after World War II. It is visited by Michel Butor (1926–2016), besides Nathalie Sarraute (1900–1999) and Alain Robbe-Grillet (1922-2008) the most important exponent of the French literary current of the 'Nouveau roman'. The 'Deux Magots' settles on the premises of a former fashion store. Part of the original furnishings were two wooden sculptures of Chinese mandarins. They become the enigmatic giver of the establishment's name. In 'Deux Magots'[91] André Breton (1896–1966) who hated the Charivari on Montparnasse, meets a carefully selected circle of surrealists. Antoine de Saint-Exupéry (1900–1944) is a guest here during the time he works on his *Courrier Sud*. Pablo Picasso meets Dora Maar (1907–1997) here (fig. 26). Foreign guests throw themselves without restraint into this intellectual and artistic turmoil. James Joyce (1882–1941) gathers his apostles around himself here. An excursion may be in order here to Trieste, where Joyce finishes his *Dubliners*, commences work on *A Portrait of the Artist as a Young* man and goes on writing *Ulysses*. During his stays in Trieste 1904–1915 and again 1919–1920 'Caffè Stella Polare' and 'Pasticceria Pirona' are both places he frequents. The city, former Austrian Empire's door to the Mediterranean Sea until today has a remarkable coffee house culture with numerous, partly not very aptly restored places:[92] 'Tommaseo', 'Tergesteo', 'Fabris', 'Garibaldi', 'Rosetti', 'Degli Specchi' and above all others 'San Marco' are linked with writers such as Italo Svevo (1861–1928), Umberto Saba (1883–1957)[93] and in more recent times Giorgio Voghera (1908–1999), Claudio Magris (b.1939) and Fulvio Tomizza (1935–1999).

Joyce himself, who spent materially poor but creatively rich years in Trieste, we find back in Paris in 'Deux Magots' surrounded by Bertold Brecht (1898–1956), Alfred Döblin (1878–1957), Heinrich Mann (1871–1950) Joseph Roth and the permanently travelling, 'raving reporter' Egon Erwin Kisch (1885–1948).[94] Mainly in the years after 1933 and until the occupation of Paris by German troops in 1940, coffee houses develop into the most important meeting places of the many exiles. What

Der Joyce, für den die Triester Zeiten hart, aber auch fruchtbar waren, findet sich dann im Deux Magots umgeben von Bertolt Brecht, Alfred Döblin, Heinrich Mann, Joseph Roth und dem reisenden „rasenden Reporter" Egon Erwin Kisch wieder.[94] Vor allem nach 1933 werden bis zum Einmarsch der Deutschen 1940 in Paris die Cafés zu den wichtigsten Treffpunkten ihrer exilierten Existenz. Was in Friedenszeiten seit dem 18. Jahrhundert eine kommunikative Annehmlichkeit ist, Bekanntschaften – auch international – unter Gleichgesinnten zu schließen, wird für Emigranten eine existentielle Notwendigkeit.

> "In exile, the coffee house becomes house and home, church and parliament, desert and pilgrim's aim, a cradle of illusions and a cemetery. Exile makes you lonely and kills. In exile the coffee house is the only continuous locality. I have been sitting in cafés in a dozen exile countries and it was like I always sat in the same café, at the seaside, between mountains, in London, in Paris, next to Amsterdam's canals, between the monasteries of Bruges. I sat in the coffee house named exile and wrote."[95]

Das dritte Café im mythischen Trio in Saint-Germain ist das Café de Flore. Hier finden wir Raymond Queneau, den Autor des von Louis Malle verfilmten Buches *Zazie dans le métro*, George Bataille, Albert Camus, Alberto und Giovanni Giacometti, Jean Louis Barrault, dessen Rolle in *Les enfants du paradis* diesen Film zu einem Kultfilm gemacht hat. Zu den Aficionados zählen aus der Welt des Films Schauspielerinnen und Schauspieler wie Simone Signoret, Gérard Philippe, Brigitte Bardot und Regisseure wie Roman Polanski, Jean Rouch, Joseph Losey.[96] Jacques Lacan erschien jeden Tag, ebenso Roland Barthes für einige Zeit am Morgen. Pablo Picasso saß hier abends vis-á-vis vom Eingang, umgeben von spanischen Freunden, sozusagen als Fortsetzung seiner Aufenthalte im Barceloneser Café Els Quatre Gats, wo er als 16-jähriger seine ersten Bilder ausgestellt hatte.[97]

Die intellektuell explosive, stimulierende Atmosphäre sorgte dafür, dass Schriftsteller und Künstler Skizzen und Notizen anfertigten. Allerdings wurden nicht alle Kaffeehäuser unbedingt zu Schreibstuben. Im Café de Flore ist dies jedoch der Fall. Jean Paul Sartre (1905–1980), der ein paar Häuser weiter in der Rue du Seine im Hotel La Louisiane wohnte, benutzte das Café als Arbeitszimmer. „Als Lehrer mit nur wenig Geld

in the more peaceful times of the eighteenth century was a communicative amenity, namely to make the acquaintance on an international level of likely minded people (Benjamin Franklin [1706–1790] for example meets Isaac Newton [1643–1727] in 1725 in 'Bathon's Coffee House' in London; the 'Greco' in Rome as focussing point of an early cultural tourism has been mentioned) for the emigrants of the pre-World War II period becomes an existential necessity.

> 'In exile, the coffee house becomes house and home, church and parliament, desert and pilgrim's aim, a cradle of illusions and a cemetery. Exile makes you lonely and kills. In exile the coffee house is the only continuous locality. I have been sitting in cafés in a dozen exile countries and it was like I always sat in the same café, at the seaside, between mountains, in London, in Paris, next to Amsterdam's canals, between the monasteries of Bruges. I sat in the coffee house named exile and wrote.'[95]

The third café of the mythical trio in Paris' Saint-Germain is the 'Café de Flore'. Here we find Raymond Queneau (1903–1976) author of *Zazie dans le Metro*, made into a film by Louis Malle (1932–1995) in 1960, or Georges Bataille (1897–1962), Albert Camus (1913–1960), Alberto (1901–1966) and brother Diego (1902–1982) Giacometti, Jean Louis Barrault (1910–1994), whose later appearance in *Les enfants du paradis* made this film cult. Amongst 'Flor's' aficionados also counted actors such as Simone Signoret (1921–1985), Gérard Philippe (1922–1959), Brigitte Bardot (b.1934) and film directors like Roman Polanski (b.1933), Jean Rouch (1917-2004) or Joseph Losey (1909–1984).[96] Jacques Lacan (1901–1981) turned up every day as well as Roland Barthes (1915–1980) every morning. Pablo Picasso every night sat opposite the door amongst Spanish friends, in a sort of continuation of his stays in the Barcelona café 'Els Quatre Gats', where he had exhibited his first paintings as a sixteen-year-old.[97]

The intellectual, stimulating atmosphere of coffee houses certainly had the effect to facilitate the production of sketches and notes for writers and artists, but this did not mean that every café automatically became an orderly room. With 'Café de Flore' however, this was nearly the case. Jean-Paul Sartre, who lived next door to the 'Flore' in the Rue du Seine in the hotel La Louisiane, made use of the café as his working place. 'As a teacher with little lebte ich in einem Hotel ... und wie alle Leute, die in Hotels wohnten, verbrachte ich den größten Teil des Tages im Café."[98] (Abb. 27) „Simone de Beauvoir und ich haben uns im Flore mehr oder weniger häuslich niedergelassen."[99] Auf den Marmortischen standen statt Getränken Tintenfässer. „Wir arbeiteten", schreibt Simone de Beauvoir (1908–1986), „von neun Uhr morgens bis Mittag, wenn wir zum Essen gingen. Um zwei Uhr kamen wir zurück und unterhielten uns mit Bekannten bis vier, worauf wir wieder bis acht Uhr arbeiteten. Nach dem Abendessen verabredeten wir uns dort mit allerlei Leuten."[100] Wenn Norbert Elias (1897–1990) von einer Verhäuslichung menschlicher Aktivitäten spricht,[101] so findet im Kaffeehaus das Gegenteil statt. Im Kaffeehaus wird der privatisierte Bereich des Wohnens um einen zusätzlichen Lebensraum erweitert. „Ist mein Café kein hübsches Schreibzimmer eines Poeten?"[102]„Schon damals ging ich hauptsächlich ins Café, um zu schreiben",[103] so Hermann Kesten. Und der Blick aus den Kaffeehausfenstern ist wie der Blick aus den Fenstern einer Wohnung auf das Treiben der großen Stadt.[104]

„Ich sehe in einer Stunde ein Dutzend Komödien und höre ein Echo von Tragödien, die keiner schreibt"[105] notiert Kesten, der sich während seines Exils die Kaffeehäuser als pied-à-terre ausgesucht hatte. Dem neugierig-sensiblen Beobachter war das Kaffeehaus beides, Kammertheater im Inneren und Breitwandbühne auf der Straße. Bereits 1787 berichtet Carlo Goldoni (1707–1793) über das Café de Foy, in dem ja Desmoulins seinen historischen Auftritt hatte.

> „Ein unendliches Menschengewimmel, eine erstaunliche Menge von Wagen, kleine Händler mit allerhand Ware, die sich zwischen Pferde und Räder werfen, Stühle auf dem Bürgersteig für solche, die sehen, und solche, die gesehen werden wollen, Cafés mit einem Orchester und italienischen und französischen Sängern, Pastetenbäcker, Köche, Gastwirte, Marionetten, Luftspringer und Ausrufer, welche Riesen, Zwerge, wilde Tiere, Meerungeheuer, Wachsfiguren, Maschinenmenschen und Bauchredner ankündigen ..."[106]

Goldoni ist auch einer der ersten, der das Kaffeehaus zum Thema einer Prosakomödie macht.[107] „Retrospektiv erklärt Goldoni, dass im Mittelpunkt von *La Bottega del Caffè*[108] weder eine Geschichte noch eine Leidenschaft oder ein Charakter, sondern ein Kaffeehaus stehe. Das

27

28

27

The coffee house becomes a locality for holding court—for example, Jean Paul Sartre and Simone de Beauvoir in 'Café Flore' ● It also turns into a writing location for literati: a portrait of Fernando Pessoa from around 1964 (oil painting by José de Almada-Negreiros)

Das Kaffeehaus dient dem Schrifsteller zur Hofhaltung, wie Jean Paul Sartre und Simone de Beauvoir das Café Flore. ● Das Kaffeehaus wird auch zur Schreibstube: Porträt von Fernando Pessoa um 1964 (Gemälde von José de Almada-Negreiros).

28

Leipzig's 'Richtersches Caffee Haus' could hold up to 700 people at any one time. Friedrich Schiller, in all probability the man with the hat in the background in this copperplate engraving, commended the fruitful mental atmosphere

Bis zu 700 Personen konnten das Richtersche Caffee Haus in Leipzig gleichzeitig besuchen. Friedrich Schiller, auf diesem Kupferstich von 1794 im Hintergrund mit Hut zu vermuten, lobte die geistig lebendige Atmosphäre.

money I lived in a hotel … and like everybody that lives in a hotel, I spent most of the day in the café.'[98] 'Simone de Beauvoir (1908–1986) and I more or less settled down in the café.'[99] (fig. 27) On the marble table one could find inkwells instead of beverages. 'We worked', Simone de Beauvoir writes 'from nine in the morning till noon, when we went to eat. At two we came back and had conversations with acquaintances till four, whereupon we worked again till eight. After dinner we made appointments there with all sorts of people.'[100] If Norbert Elias (1897–1990) speaks of a 'housing in of human activities'[101], in a coffee house the exact opposite takes place. In it the privatized domain of dwelling is being enlarged by additional living space. 'My coffee house, is it not a handsome writing room for a poet?'[102] And: 'Already then I frequented the café mainly to do my writing', Hermann Kesten notes.[103] The glimpse out of coffee house windows resembles the gaze out of the windows of a flat upon the goings-on of a great city.[104]

'Within one hour I watch a dozen comedies und listen to the echoes of tragedies nobody will ever write down',[105] Kesten notes during his exile. To the curious and sensitive looker-on the coffee house was both: intimate theatre inside combined with wide-screen stage outside. In 1787 Carlo Goldoni (1707–1793) reports on the 'Café de Foy', where revolutionary Desmoulins had had his historical moment.

> 'A never ending milling of the crowd, an amazing number of cars, small scale retailers peddling manifold wares who throw themselves between the horses and wheels, seats on the pavement for those who want to watch and those who want to be watched, cafés with orchestras and Italian and French singers, pastry cooks, cooks, landlords, marionettes, acrobats and hawkers who advertise giants, dwarfs, wild beasts, sea monsters, wax figures, mechanical men and ventriloquists…'[106]

Goldoni is also one of the first to make the coffee house the centre of a prose comedy.[107] In retrospective the playwright declares that in the centre of *La Bottega del Caffè*[108] neither a story, nor a passion or a character is to be found, but the coffee house itself. 'The never changing stage in his comedy brings about that the acting personnel always meets in a public space and communicates there.'[109] This exactly mirrors the role that the coffee house for a long time occupied.

unverändert bleibende Bühnenbild in seiner Komödie bedingt, dass die handelnden Personen sich immer in einem öffentlichen Raum begegnen und dort miteinander kommunizieren."[109] Und das ist ja gerade die Rolle, die das Kaffeehaus spielt.

Die Gelegenheiten, zu denen Literaten und Künstler Kaffee und Kaffeehaus in ihren Arbeiten thematisieren, sind unzählig. Ein Werk jedoch darf nicht unerwähnt bleiben: die „Kaffeekantate" von Johann Sebastian Bach (1685–1750). Leipzig hatte als Messestadt eine Vielzahl berühmter Kaffeehäuser (Abb. 28).[110] In „Zimmermanns Caffe-Hauß" fanden jeden Freitagabend die Veranstaltungen des Collegium musicum statt. Dies blieb auch so, als Bach die Leitung des Collegiums zwischen 1729 bis 1740 übernahm. Hier wird wohl dann auch 1734 die „über den Kaffee Cantata" (Text: Christian Friedrich Henrici) uraufgeführt worden sein.[111] In der Musik finden wir jedoch auch die Kaffeeverdammung thematisiert, wie zum Beispiel im Kanon „Sei doch kein Muselmann - C-A-F-F-E-E".[112]

Musik, Theater, Literatur – prominente Vertreter dieser Kunstgattungen haben sich des Themas angenommen; aber auch unter der Vielzahl der Architekten und Dekorateure, die den Kaffeehäusern ihr Aussehen verliehen haben, findet sich die Prominenz der Architekturgeschichte: Piranesi wurde bereits erwähnt, in England Robert Adam (1728–1792) – die Brüder Adam waren übrigens enge Vertraute von Piranesi, ihnen dediziert er seine *Antichità Romane* – in Frankreich Claude-Nicolas Ledoux (1736–1806) 1762 mit dem Café des Officiers[113], in Deutschland Karl Friedrich Schinkel (1781–1841) 1825 mit dem Kaffeehaus Fuchs, Unter den Linden.[114] Auch im 20. Jahrhundert beugen sich berühmte Architekten über die Entwurfsaufgabe Kaffeehaus. Adolf Loos (1870–1933), der auch für die American Bar in Wien zeichnet, gestaltet das Café Museum[115] bereits 1899 äußerst nüchtern, was Spötter dann veranlasst, diesem Kaffeehaus am Karlsplatz den Beinamen „Café Nihilismus" zu verleihen. Leider nicht realisiert wird das Projekt für ein „Café Pittoresque" im vorrevolutionären Moskau. An dem Entwurf sind unter anderem Wladimir Tatlin (1885–1953) und Alexander Rodtschenko beteiligt. Das Café sollte „die ästhetischen Probleme der modernen Stadt aufwerfen und sowohl in der Malerei als auch in den anderen Zweigen der Kunst die Grundlagen [eines] neuen Stils schaffen."[116] Dem theoretischen Anspruch der Synthese von Kunst, Literatur und Theater zu entspre-

Examples in which literates and artists make coffee houses their theme are manifold. One musical work however must not be omitted here: Johann Sebastian Bach's (1685–1750) 'Kaffeekantate—Coffee Cantata'. Leipzig as prominent place for trade fairs possessed a wealth of famous coffee houses.[110] Each Friday night in 'Zimmermanns Caffe-Hauß' the 'Collegium Musicum' met. This remained so too after Bach took over as leader of the Collegium between 1729 and 1740. It was here in all probability that in 1734 the première of Bach's *Coffee Cantata* took place (words by Christian Friedrich Henrici, called Picander, 1700–1764).[111] There are on the other hand works of art too, that condemn the use of coffee, like for example Carl Gottlieb Hering's (1766–1853) canon 'C-A-F-F-E-E'.[112]

In the realm of music, theatre and literature many prominent members of these arts have treated the topic of the coffee house, but also within the ranks of the many architects and decorators, who gave coffee houses their shape, we find well-known exponents of architectural history: Piranesi has been mentioned before, in England one may name Robert Adam (1728–1792)—the brothers Adam by the way were intimate confidents of Piranesi, it is to them he dedicates his *Antichità Romane*. In France there is Claude-Nicholas Ledoux (1736–1806) and his 'Café des Officiers'[113], in Germany we find Karl Friedrich Schinkel (1781–1841) and his Berlin coffee house 'Fuchs' Unter den Linden.[114] In the twentieth century too, the design of coffee houses is an important task for famous architects. Adolf Loos (1870–1933), who also is responsible for Vienna's 'American Bar', designs the highly austere 'Café Museum'[115] in the same city. Its very character made scoffers name this Karlsplatz café 'Café Nihilism'. Alas never carried out was a project by Wladimir Tatlin (1885–1953) and Alexander Rodtschenko (1891–1956) for a 'Café Pittoresque' in pre-revolutionary (pre-1917) Moscow. This café was to 'treat basic aesthetic questions of the modern city and create the fundament for a new style in painting as well as in the other branches of art.'[116] To be in theoretical accordance with the demands of a synthesis of art, literature and theatre was also the ambition of a coffee house in Strasbourg. In 1926/1927 Hans Arp (1887–1966) gets the commission for 'Café Aubette'. Together with his wife Sophie Täuber-Arp (1889–1943) and Dutch De Stijl protagonist Theo van Doesburg (1883–1931), he works for two years redecorating the place, which is opened on 17. February 1928.[117] Café-

chen, ist ebenfalls Anliegen eines Cafés in Straßburg. 1926/27 erhält Hans Arp (1887–1966) den Auftrag für das Café Aubette. Mit seiner Frau Sophie Taeuber-Arp und dem holländischen De-Stijl-Protagonisten Theo van Doesburg arbeitet er zwei Jahre an der Umgestaltung (Eröffnung am 17. Februar 1928).[117] Café-Brasserie, Café-Restaurant, Teesalon, Aubette-Bar, Kabarettkeller, Bar Américain und Billardsaal sind als Zimelien der Architektur der 1920er Jahre nach der Restaurierung in ihren Originalzustand zurückversetzt worden (Abb. 29).[118]

Nach diesem Exkurs zur Gestaltung von Kaffeehäusern soll von ihnen noch einmal die Rede sein als Verweilorte für Künstler und Literaten. Eine exzellente Quelle sind hier Literaturführer und literarische Städteporträts (Anthologien). Im Buch *Literarisches Zürich*[119] ist zu erfahren, dass Tristan Tzara im Umfeld des Züricher Café Voltaire das Wort DADA[120] 1916 erfunden hat,[121] der Dadaismus somit dortselbst geboren wurde. Schlägt die Geburtsstunde des Existenzialismus im Pariser Café de Flore, in dem wir Sartre und de Beauvoir finden, so treffen sich die künftigen Autoren der „Beat Generation" Jack Kerouac und Allan Ginsberg im West End Café am Broadway in New York.[122] Ebenfalls in New York, im Caffè Torino, wurde Edward Albee zu seinem berühmtesten Theaterstück inspiriert. Über der Bar im Souterrain hing ein Spiegel, vollgekritzelt mit Graffiti unter anderem dem späteren Titel des Stücks: *Who's Afraid of Virginia Woolf?*[123] Dies alles ist nachzulesen in *Spaziergänge durch das literarische New York*. Hier ist auch zu erfahren, welche Rolle Bar und Café-Restaurant des Hotels Algonquin (44th Street) für die Literatur und die Gründung des Magazins *The New Yorker*[124] gespielt haben. Erwähnung findet als Zentrum der jungen New Yorker Literaturszene der 1990er Jahre das Nuyorican Poets Café in der East 3rd Street. Hier wurden zuerst Open-Mike-Abende veranstaltet, offene Lese- oder Musikveranstaltungen, bei denen dem Publikum die Bühne gehört.[125] Wenn man an die historische Bühne Kaffeehaus denkt, kann wohl kaum die Rede von einer Erfindung, eher von einer Reinkarnation sein.

Zu den aufschlussreichsten Publikationen gehören zwei *Théories des Cafés*[126] betitelte, in Frankreich erschienene Bände. Die ausgewählten Quellen illustrieren unter anderem für Italien die Rolle, die die Kaffeehäuser für die futuristische Bewegung[127] gespielt haben. Filippo Tommaso Marinetti, der „Papst" der italienischen Futuristen, berichtet über die gewaltigen Schlachten, die sich

29

30

29
From the end of the eighteenth century, the coffee house became a challenge for architects. Famous examples from the Modern period are Viennas 'Café Museum' by Adolf Loos ● And 'Aubette' in Straßburg by Hans Arp, Sophie Taeuber-Arp, and Theo van Doesburg

Seit dem Ende des 18. Jahrhunderts avanciert das Kaffeehaus zu einer architektonischen Entwurfsaufgabe. Berühmte Beispiele der Moderne sind das Wiener Café Museum von Adolf Loos. ● Und das Straßburger Aubette von Hans Arp und Sophie Taeuber-Arp sowie Theo van Doesburg.

30
Adolf Loos and Peter Altenberg (photograph, ca. 1900)—the architect with a grudge against ornamentation and the Bohemian poet—met in 'Café Central' and 'Griensteidl'

Adolf Loos und Peter Altenberg. Der Bohèmedichter und der Ornamente verdammende Architekt (Fotografie um 1900) trafen vor allem im Café Central und im Griensteidl aufeinander.

brasserie, café-restaurant, tea room, Aubette-Bar, basement cabaret, Bar Americain as well as the billiard room have been put back into their original state as is well due to this cimelium of the architectural history of the 1920s (fig. 29).[118]

After this detour touching on the design of coffee houses, we once more will turn to them as refuges for artists and literates. An excellent source for this are literary guidebooks and literary portraits of cities with an anthological character. From the guide *Literary Zurich*[119] we learn that Tristan Tzara (1896–1963) in 1916 invented the term 'DADA'[120] as habitué of 'Café Odeon',[121] Dadaism consequently has been born in this city. If the birth hour of existentialism was announced in Paris' 'Café de Flore', where we find Sartre and de Beauvoir, the future authors of the 'Beat Generation', Jack Kerouac (1922–1969) and Allen Ginsberg (1926–1997) meet in New York's 'West End Café'[122] on Broadway. Also in New York, in the 'Caffè Torino' Edward Albee (b.1928) had been inspired to his famous drama *Who's afraid of Virginia Woolf*: Behind the bar there was a mirror covered with graffiti, amongst which he found the question that he was to use as the title of his play.[123]

In *Walks through literary New York* one can also read about the role that the bar and café-restaurant of the hotel 'Algonquin' on 44th Street played in the history of literature generally and especially for the founding of the *New Yorker*[124] magazine. Reference is made also to the centre of the young 1990s New York literary scene East 3rd Street's 'Nuyorican Poet's Café'. Here, the famous 'Open Mike nights' were invented, free reading or music events, where the public occupies the stage.[125] Thinking of the historical character of the coffee house as a stage, one can hardly speak of an invention here, it is more of a reincarnation

Another informative publication are the two volumes of *Théories des Cafés*, published in France.[126] Selected sources here illustrate the role of the coffee houses in the development of the Futuristic Movement in Italy[127]. Filippo Tommaso Marinetti (1876–1944) gives an account of the 'gigantic battles' poets, painters and sculptors waged amidst gallons of coffee and choice Florentine ice cream treats in the 'Caffè delle Giubbe Rosse' in Florence.[128] The true arena and place of invention of the 'Futuristic Manifesto' however was 'Caffè Centro' in Milan. In the 1930ies, the bar 'Craja'—'Example'—takes over as meeting point of Milan's intellectuals and heart of the cultural life of the city. 'It was in February of 1909,

Dichter, Maler und Bildhauer im Angesicht von Kaffee und köstlichsten Florentiner Eisspezialitäten im Caffè delle Giubbe Rosse in Florenz lieferten.[128] Eigentlicher Entstehungsort des „Futuristischen Manifests" ist das Caffè Centro in Mailand. In den 1930er Jahren übernimmt die Bar Craja als intellektueller Treffpunkt die Hauptrolle im kulturellen Leben der Stadt.

> „Es war im Februar 1909, als Boccioni, Russolo und ich Marinetti, der in der via Senato wohnte, trafen", schreibt Carlo Carrà.[129] „Eine Generation wie die meine hat das Kaffeehaus als Zweigniederlassung des Ateliers interpretiert … In einem mit persischen Teppichen luxuriös dekorierten Salon entschieden wir, uns in einem Manifest an junge italienische Künstler zu wenden, um sie einzuladen, sich aus der jegliche Ambition unterdrückenden Lethargie zu lösen."[130]

In den darauffolgenden Tagen wurde das „Futuristische Manifest" zur Druckreife gebracht.

„Ich glaube, es war der irische Schriftsteller George Moore – oder war es Stendhal? –, der auf die Frage, wie die Kunst am besten zu fördern sei, die verblüffende Antwort gab: ‚Gründet Cafés!'"[131] Welche Rolle Kaffeehäuser für Literaten gespielt haben, macht der von Karl Kraus (1874–1936) beklagte Verlust eines solchen deutlich. In einem 1897 erschienenen Pamphlet, „Die demolierte Literatur" betitelt, schreibt er:

> „Wien wird jetzt zur Großstadt demoliert. [Hier nimmt Kraus eine ähnliche Haltung ein wie Victor Hugo im Angesicht der Haussmannschen Interventionen in Paris] … bald wird ein respektloser Spaten auch das ehrwürdige Griensteidl dem Boden gleichgemacht haben. Unsere Literatur sieht einer Periode der Obdachlosigkeit entgegen, der Faden der dichterischen Produktion wird grausam abgeschnitten … Mehr als ein Vorzug hat dem alten Locale seinen Ehrenplatz in der Literaturgeschichte gesichert. Wer gedenkt nicht der schier erdrückenden Fülle von Zeitungen und Zeitschriften, die den Besuch unseres Kaffeehauses gerade für diejenigen Schriftsteller, welche nach keinem Kaffee verlangten, zu einem wahren Bedürfnis gemacht hatte? Braucht es den Hinweis auf sämtliche Bände von Meyers Conversationslexikon, die, an leicht zugänglicher Stelle angebracht, es jedem Literaten ermöglichten, sich Bildung anzueignen? Auf das reiche Schreibmaterial, das für unvorhergesehene Einfälle stets zur Hand

31

when Boccioni (1882–1916), Russolo (1883–1947) and I', Carlo Carrà (1881–1966)[129] wrote,

> 'met Marinetti who lived in Via Senato…a generation like mine interpreted the café as an extension of the atelier…in a salon lavishly decorated with Persian carpets we decided to address young Italian artists in a manifesto to invite them to free themselves from a lethargy that suppressed every ambition.'[130]

In the following days the 'Futuristic Manifesto' was given its final shape.

'I think it was the Irish writer George Moore [1852–1933], or was it Stendhal [1783–1842], who answered the question how art was to be furthered best with: 'Open cafés!"[131] Of how much importance coffee houses were for literates, Karl Kraus (1874–1936)—quasi ex negativo—

31

'Café Griensteidl', founded in 1847 (watercolour by A. Völkel, 1880), was demolished in connection with urban planning around the Michaelerplatz in Vienna. An essay by Karl Kraus speaks of 'demolished literature'

Das 1847 gegründete Café Griensteidl (Aquarell von A. Völkel, 1880) wurde 1897 im Zusammenhang mit Neuplanungen am Wiener Michaelerplatz abgerissen. Karl Kraus spricht in einem Pamphlet von der „demolierten Literatur".

32

In the 1960s and 1970s 'Hawelka' sheltered intellectuals, artists, and students. It was able to keep its patina and its character ● With 'Café Central', renovated in the 1980s, the effect is more that of a tourist-flooded stage backdrop

In den 1960er und 1970er Jahren ist das Hawelka der Aufenthaltsort der Intellektuellen, Künstler und Studenten von Wien. Es hat seine Patina und seinen Charakter behalten, ● wohingegen die Wiederbelebung des Café Central in den 1980er Jahren eher eine von Touristen besuchte Kulisse bleibt.

33

'Café Schwarzenberg' in Vienna (photograph from the 1990s) is one of the establishments that still draw their inspiring atmosphere from the physical proximity of visitors, sounds, smells, delights, and distinguished service

Das Café Schwarzenberg (Fotografie aus den 1990er Jahren) in Wien ist eines der Häuser, die ihre inspirierende Kraft noch aus dem physischen Neben- und Miteinander der Besucher, den Geräuschen, Gerüchen und Genüssen sowie dem distinguierten Service ziehen.

32

33

makes clear. In a pamphlet of 1897 'Literature Demolished' he writes

> 'Vienna now will be demolished into a metropolis [here Kraus takes a similar position to that of Victor Hugo (1802–1885) facing Haussmann's destructive interventions in the Paris cityscape] ... soon a disrespectful spade will level the venerable Griensteidl [coffeehouse]. Our literature is facing a period of homelessness, the thread of poetical production will be cruelly broken...more than one advantage has secured this venerable locality a place of honour in literary history. Who does not commemorate the truly overwhelming number of newspapers and magazines, that have made visiting our coffee house a real necessity for those writers, who did not ask for coffee? Is it necessary to refer to the complete volumes of Meyer's Universal Dictionary that—easy of access—enabled every literary person to obtain an education? Or to the lavish range of writing utensils that always were there for sudden inspirations? Namely the younger poets will miss that intimate, old-Vienna-like interior that compensated by the right mood that what may have been lacking in comfort.'[132]

Around 1900, in an atmosphere of 'dream and reality'[133], Austrian literature reaches—also thanks to the coffee house culture in this country—a peak with writers such as Robert Musil (1880–1942), Arthur Schnitzler (1862–1931), Karl Kraus, Hermann Bahr (1863–1934), Alfred Polgar (1873–1955), Peter Altenberg (1859–1919) or Felix Salten (1869–1945) (fig. 30).[134] The history of the Vienna literary coffee house reaches back to the eighteenth century. Here the literary scene exchanges the 'Kramersche Etablissement', which soon after its inauguration in 1771 is called 'the erudite coffee house' by Michael Hertl, for 'Kaffeehaus Neuner', that in 1820 because of the solid quality of its furnishings was called 'the silver coffee house' by its owner, Ignaz Neuner. Nikolaus Lenau (1802–1850) who has been called the Austrian-Hungarian pendant to Lord Byron, whom he admired, lived under the same address and for more than 22 years was to be seen at 'Neuner's' several times a day, busy with 'the fragrant Arabic beverage, a pipe in his mouth and always a fresh concept in his head'.[135] Amongst the many other illustrious guests were Franz Grillparzer (1791–1872) and Ludwig van Beethoven (1770–1827), who in the same way as later on father and son Johann Strauss (1804–1845; 1825–1899) performed in coffee houses and their

> war? Namentlich die jüngeren Dichter werden das intime, altwienerische Interieur schmerzlich entbehren, welches, was ihm an Bequemlichkeit gefehlt, jederzeit durch Stimmung zu ersetzen vermocht hat."[132]

Um 1900 in einer Atmosphäre von „Traum und Wirklichkeit"[133] erreicht die österreichische Literatur – auch dank der Kaffeehäuser – mit Robert Musil, Arthur Schnitzler, Karl Kraus, Hermann Bahr, Alfred Polgar, Peter Altenberg, Felix Salten[134] einen Höhepunkt (Abb. 30). Die Wiener Literatenkaffeehausgeschichte geht auf das 18. Jahrhundert zurück. In Wien wechselte die Literaturszene vom Kramerschen Etablissement, das schon bald nach seiner Eröffnung durch Michael Hertl 1771 als „gelehrtes Kaffeehaus" bezeichnet wird, zu dem 1820 von Ignaz Neuner wegen seiner gediegenen Ausstattung – sogar die Türdrücker und Kleiderhaken waren aus reinem Silber – auch „silbernes Kaffeehaus" genannten Kaffeehaus Neuner über. Nikolaus Lenau (1802–1850), der als österreichisch-ungarisches Pendant zu dem von ihm bewunderten Lord Byron galt und der im selben Haus wohnte, war 22 Jahre lang mehrmals am Tage bei Neuner anzutreffen, beschäftigt mit „dem duftenden arabischen Trank, einer Pfeife im Munde und immer einer neuen Idee im Kopfe."[135] Zu den vielen anderen illustren Gästen zählten unter anderem Franz Grillparzer und Ludwig van Beethoven, der – wie später auch Vater und Sohn Johann Strauss – in Kaffeehäusern und deren Sommerdependancen im Prater musizierte.[136] 1847 dann vertauscht Heinrich Griensteidl den Beruf des Apothekers mit dem des Cafetiers. Bis zu seiner von Kraus beschriebenen Auslöschung ist das im Palais Dietrichstein ansässige Café der Künstlertreff schlechthin. (Abb. 31) Neben den Literaten verkehren hier auch die Komponisten Hugo Wolf und Arnold Schönberg. Der neue Parnass wird ab 1876 das Café Central, das sich neben dem Café Herrenhof (ab 1918) und dem Café Landtmann (ab 1873) die Rolle des *primus inter pares* erobert hatte, hauptsächlich dank der Person von Peter Altenberg, der das Etablissement sozusagen zu seinem Wohnsitz erkoren hatte und um den sich Adolf Loos, Egon Friedell, Alfred Polgar und andere scharten. Auch der aus dem Griensteidl exilierte Karl Kraus hatte hier seinen Stammtisch.

Wien gibt dann die Rolle an Berlin ab. In den 1920er Jahren machen sich nach einer Phase von Luxusetablissements wie dem Café Bauer im deutschsprachi-

summer branches in the Prater gardens.[136] In 1847 Heinrich Griensteidl exchanges his professional role of apothecary with that of cafétier. Until its extinction lamented by Karl Kraus, the 'Griensteidl' that was situated in the Palais Dietrichstein, is the meeting point par excellence of artists (fig. 31), where besides the literary crowd composers like Hugo Wolf (1860–1903) and Arnold Schönberg (1874–1951) are to be seen. The new Parnassus from 1876 on will be 'Café Central' that, next to 'Café Herrenhof' (from 1918 on) and 'Café Landtmann' (from 1873) conquered the rank of a *primus inter pares*. This happened mainly thanks to Peter Altenberg, who more or less made it his residence, and around whom Adolf Loos, Egon Friedell (1878–1938) and Alfred Polgar (1873–1955) grouped. Karl Kraus, exiled from the 'Griensteidl', took a regular table here as well.

Later Vienna relinquishes its role as the leading coffee house metropole to Berlin. In the 1920s Berlin coffee houses—after a phase dominated by big luxury establishments such as 'Café Bauer' for example—win a leading position in the German speaking world as cultural meeting points. Two coffee houses may be named here as proxies for many: The 'Café des Westens' (since 1893 'Kleines Café', renamed 1898) and the 'Romanisches Café' (from 1916). Siegfried Kracauer (1889–1966) gives an atmospheric description of coffee house life in his time. In Vienna, conditions comparable to the era of 'Griensteidl' and 'Central' arise only after World War II with 'Café Hawelka' (fig. 32).

> 'There was one, outwardly unostentatious, in Dorotheengasse. This I used to frequent [Hans Weigel (1908–1991) is speaking here] in the course of the afternoon. There I would write articles, work on books…this café was also one of the few keeping open after midnight, without music and the other bothersome attributes of the night café.'[137]

It is Weigel who takes colleagues with him from the 'Café Raimund', a meeting place of journalists, publishers and writers, to 'Hawelka'. Later the usual process of the birth of a cult locality commences: local intellectuals, amongst whom we find the great Praeceptor Austriae, Heimito von Doderer (1896–1966), are followed by international ones: Henry Miller (1891–1980), Günter Grass (1927-2015) etc.

In Vienna and Paris most historical coffee houses survived, in Berlin they fell victim to the bombings of

gen Raum die Berliner Cafés einen Namen als kulturelle Sammelpunkte. Zwei Kaffeehäuser seien hier stellvertretend genannt, das Café des Westens (ab 1893 Kleines Café, 1898 umbenannt) und das Romanische Café (ab 1916). Siegfried Kracauer liefert eine atmosphärische Beschreibung des Kaffeehauslebens dieser Zeit. In Wien kommt es zu einer mit dem Griensteidl und dem Central vergleichbaren Reputation erst wieder nach dem Zweiten Weltkrieg mit dem Café Hawelka. Hans Weigel berichtet:

> „Da war eines, äußerlich unauffällig, in der Dorotheengasse. Dieses suchte ich im Lauf des Nachmittags auf. Dort schrieb ich dann Artikel, arbeitete an Büchern (…). Dieses Café war auch eines der wenigen, die noch nach Mitternacht geöffnet waren, ohne Musik und andere störende Attribute des Nachtcafés."[137]

Es ist Weigel selbst, der aus seinem Stammcafé, dem Café Raimund, einen Tross von Journalisten, Verlegern und Schriftstellerkollegen mit ins „Hawelken" nimmt (Abb. 32). Danach beginnt der übliche Prozess des Werdens einer Kultstätte: den heimischen Intellektuellen – unter ihnen der große Praeceptor Austriae Heimito von Doderer – folgen die ausländischen: Henry Miller, Günter Grass et cetera.

In Wien und Paris überleben die historischen Kaffeehäuser, in Berlin fallen sie dem Zweiten Weltkrieg zum Opfer. In London lebt in den 1950er Jahren eine Espresso-Kultur auf, die übrigens auch in Budapest floriert.[138] In Paris mit der Neubelebung des Procope (1987) und in Wien in den 1980er und 1990er Jahren mit der Rekonstruktion des Café Central und des Café Griensteidl versucht man die Kaffeehauskultur als Teil des metropolitanen Branding einzusetzen. Wer aber die Atmosphäre des Authentischen sucht, ist im Prückel, Zartl, im Sperl, Schwarzenberg oder Landtmann[139] besser aufgehoben (Abb. 33). Letzteres in der Nähe von Parlament, Rathaus, Universität und Burgtheater ist noch heute Brennpunkt von Politik, Wissenschaft und Kunst. Dies entspricht exakt der Situation in der Pariser Brasserie Lipp in Saint-Germain. Im Wiener Café Stein hatte Christian Ide Hintze nach dem Vorbild der „Jack Kerouac School" (West End Café, New York) eine „Schule für Dichtung" eingerichtet. Hier konnte man einmal wöchentlich persönlich oder über das Internet mit Hintze diskutieren.[140] In den Nach-1968er-Jahren wird in Berlin mit dem Café Einstein in der Kurfürstenstraße – inzwischen

World War II. In the London of the 1950s, an Espresso-culture flourishes, equally in Budapest.[138] With the rejuvenation of the 'Procope' in Paris (1987) and in the Vienna of the 1980s and 1990s with the reconstruction of 'Café Central' and 'Griensteidl' the coffee house culture revival is treated as part of metropolitan branding. Whoever though is looking for an atmosphere of authenticity better visits 'Prückel', 'Zartl', 'Sperl', 'Landtmann' or 'Schwarzenberg' (fig. 33).[139] The latter, situated near parliament, town hall, university and Burgtheater, even today is a focal point of politics, science and art. This is exactly the situation the Paris 'Lipp' in Saint-Germain finds itself in. In Vienna's 'Café Stein' Christian Ide Hintze (1953-2012) established a 'school of poetry' following Jack Kerouac's New York—'West End Café' example. Here once a week one could have discussions with Hintze either in person or via the internet.[140] In Berlin after 1968 'Café Einstein' in Kurfürstenstrasse revives the old coffee house culture, nowadays also at Savigny Platz and in the central part of Berlin Unter den Linden, where prominent politicians from nearby Reichstag are part of the clientele. In the old West, 'Café im Literaturhaus' in Fasanenstrasse represents a mixture of café, garden café, exhibition rooms and a book store. Selling books in cafés is a habit dating back to the eighteenth century, but in the Copenhagen of the 1960s quite a number of book-cafés came into being. One recent example of this type is 'Café Literaire' in Berne, Switzerland (2005).[141]

Besides all those famous metropolitan coffee houses as points of attraction for tourists there are the more anonymous historical coffee houses of Italy[142], of Vienna or Paris. Ambience and clientele here amalgamate and form a convincing whole. In times of an observable renaissance of the coffee house culture only those places—no matter whether electronically connected with the whole world or not—will flourish culturally, that further a certain social togetherness. 'Coffee houses are visited by people who want to be on their own and need company to do so',[143] Alfred Polgar wrote. The secret of the coffee house was and is to be the stage for the 'L'être et paraître'.

Conclusion

In its early phases as a place for public congregation the main difference between coffee house on the one hand and taverns, pubs, inns and restaurants on the other lay in the fact that here predominantly coffee was consumed as

auch unter anderem am Savigny Platz und mit einer Filiale Unter den Linden – die Kaffeehauskultur neu belebt. Im Café im Literaturhaus in Berlin in der Fasanenstraße findet sich eine Kombination aus Café, Gartencafé, Ausstellungs- und Veranstaltungsräumen und einer Buchhandlung. Der Verkauf von Büchern in Kaffeehäusern wurde seit dem 18. Jahrhundert praktiziert. In den 1970er Jahren gibt es in Kopenhagen eine ganze Reihe von Buchcafés. Eines der jüngsten Beispiele dieses Typus ist das Café Literáire in Bern (seit 2005).[141]

Neben den berühmten, zu touristischen Anziehungspunkten avancierten metropolitanen Kaffeehäusern gibt es die unbekannteren historischen Kultstätten in italienischen Städten[142], in Wien, in Paris et cetera. Ambiente und Clientèle fügen sich hier zu einer überzeugenden Einheit. In einer Zeit der Renaissance von Kaffeehäusern werden, gleich ob mit der Welt elektronisch verkabelt oder nicht, nur die Orte kulturell erfolgreich sein, die dem sozialen Mit- und Nebeneinander förderlich sind. „Ins Kaffeehaus geht, wer alleine sein will und dazu Gesellschaft braucht",[143] hatte Alfred Polgar geschrieben. Das Geheimnis und die Anziehungskraft des Kaffeehauses ist es, Bühne für das „L'être et paraître" zu sein.

Conclusio

Das Kaffeehaus unterscheidet sich in der Frühphase seiner Existenz als Ort öffentlicher Geselligkeit von Bistro, Pub, Kneipe und Restaurant vor allem durch den vorwiegenden Konsum des den Geist anregenden Genussmittels Kaffee. Heute sind die Grenzen der Konsumption fließender. Im Kaffeehaus bekommt man alkoholische Getränke und in jeder Kneipe und jedem Restaurant ist Kaffee zu bekommen.

Die weltweite Wanderung des Kaffees beginnt im 13. Jahrhundert in Äthiopien. Der Handel mit diesem Genussmittel, wie auch mit Tee, Kakao und Gewürzen, ist eng mit der aggressiven Kolonialpolitik der Europäer verbunden. Seit sich, zunächst im Osmanischen Reich und später in Europa und Nordamerika Orte für den Kaffeekonsum konstituierten, trugen diese zur gesellschaftlichen und politischen Emanzipierung bei. Die Geburtsstunde der freien Meinungsäußerung sowie die Liberalisierung des Handels ist – wie weiter oben bereits ausgeführt – eng mit der Existenz von Kaffeehäusern verknüpft. Aus diesem Grunde sahen die jeweiligen politischen Machthaber in ihnen eine Bedrohung ihrer

a beverage that enlivens the spirit in stead of dampening it like alcohol does. Today the borderlines are not drawn so distinctly anymore. In a coffeehouse all kinds of alcohol is served and it is no problem to get coffee in pubs or restaurants.

The global migration of coffee starts in Ethiopia in the thirteenth and fourteenth century. Trade of this luxury good as well as the one with tea, cocoa or spices is intimately interwoven with an aggressive colonial policy of the European powers involved in it. Since the point in time at which specific places for the consumption of coffee started to open, first within the Osman Empire and later in Europe and North America, they contributed to the social and political emancipation of its customers. The birth of the right to free speech as well as the liberalization of trade is, as has been shown, closely linked to the existence of the coffee house. For this reason the respective political powers saw a grave threat here to their monopolistic claims und thus coffee houses became centers of intense spying activities, too.

Besides being strongholds of political and civic emancipation, coffee houses at the same time served as Parnassus for many literary people and artists. The specific and extraordinary atmosphere of coffee houses is equally characterized by a dialectic between restriction and independence as well as by the contradiction between leisure and activity.

In the biotope-like sphere of the coffee house specific patterns of social interaction between owners, staff and client develop, from which all sides draw a profit. To make this phenomenon flourish, a certain permanency of dwelling in such a place is pre-conditional, which opens the possibility to sink down ones roots according to the deepest psychological disposition of the human being. The aura of familiarity and the possibility for a creative productivity is impossible to achieve, when there is a permanent fluctuation of staff or a too limited span of time one spends in a café—both circumstances common today.

In this context it is interesting to observe, that in cities such as Paris or Vienna, where there still and again a certain metropolitan culture of the coffee house is alive, the type of quick-consumption-coffee place seems to have little chance of being successful. Here classic as well as creatively stimulating new coffee houses fulfill a civic demand for public gregariousness. Remake-type or over-renovated coffee houses like the 'Procop' in Paris

Machtansprüche und so werden Kaffeehäuser gleichzeitig Zentren politischer Bespitzelung.

Waren sie Horte politischer und bürgerlicher Emanzipation, so waren sie gleichzeitig auch ein Parnass für viele Literaten und Künstler. Die spezifische und außergewöhnliche Atmosphäre der Kaffeehäuser ist durch eine Dialektik von Gebundenheit und Ungebundenheit einerseits und von Müßiggang und Betriebsamkeit andererseits geprägt.

In der biotopgleichen Sphäre des Kaffeehauses bilden sich charakteristische Muster sozialen Verhaltens heraus, von denen alle Seiten profitieren. Bedingung für diese Fruchtbarkeit ist eine gewisse Permanenz des Verweilens, die, der psychischen Konditioniertheit des Menschen entsprechend, eine Verwurzelung ermöglicht. Ein Fluidum der Vertrautheit und die Möglichkeit zu schöpferischer Produktivität lässt sich bei einer ständigen Fluktuation des Personals und bei kurzen Verweilzeiten nicht herstellen.

In diesem Zusammenhang ist interessant, dass in Paris und vor allem in Wien, wo noch eine gewisse metropolitane Kaffeehauskultur fortbesteht, das Quick-Consumption-Kaffeehaus kaum Chancen zur Ansiedlung erhielt. Hier erfüllen klassische wie auch neugegründete, schöpferisch stimulierende Verweilorte das gesellschaftliche Bedürfnis nach öffentlicher Geselligkeit. Die Remakes oder überrenovierten historischen Kaffees wie das Procope in Paris, das Central oder das Griensteidl in Wien wirken im Vergleich zum Sperl oder Spröckl eher anämisch. Fazit ist, dass ein wahrhaft qualitätvolles Kaffeehaus seine Reputation aus einem Zusammenspiel von festem Personal, Kunden, Konsum- und Lektüreangebot, Inneneinrichtung sowie Lage in der Stadt bezieht, sowie auch davon, dass an solchen Orten Chronos seine Schwingen nicht allzu heftig bewegt. Denn die Muße und die Verlangsamung erst machen das Kaffeehaus zu einem geschützten Beobachtungsposten der hektischen metropolitanen Bühne. Sie ermöglichen den Ausblick und gleichermaßen den Rückzug. „Die meisten Leute gehen ins Café wie auf Urlaub vom täglichen Leben", schreibt Hermann Kesten.[144]

Wie ist es nun um die kulturpolitische Relevanz der Kaffeehäuser heute bestellt?

Spiegelt sich im Revival der Cafés seit den 1980er Jahren ein gesellschaftliches Bedürfnis wider oder handelt es sich hier nur um die Kapitalisierung einer modischen Marktlücke? Für das Kaffeehaus gilt, was für

and 'Central' or 'Griensteidl' in Vienna appear anemic in comparison with places like 'Sperl' or 'Spröckl'.

To sum it up, to be of real quality and justified reputation, a coffee house has to maintain a delicate balance between permanent staff, clientele, a wide range of things to eat, drink and read, as well as a suitable location within the city and above all a slowed down movement of God Chronos' wings. Only an atmosphere of leisure, a gentle slowing down make the coffee house a suitable observation post, from which to observe the hectic metropolitan stage. It embodies the possibility of an outlook and at the same time of retreat. 'Most people go to a café as if they go on holiday, leaving behind day-to-day life',[144] Hermann Kesten writes as the voice of somebody representing the interbellum and early post-World War II point of view.

But what about the possible cultural and political relevance of coffee houses today?

Does the revival movement of coffee houses since the 1980s mirror a true social need or does it merely represent the attempt to capitalize on a fashionable market niche? Here one has to say that it is true for the coffee house what is true for all such commercial chains and brands: these standardized pre-fab offers completely lack any *anima*.

Without being nostalgic, it can be said that they are still there, these coffee houses 'with a soul'. But what role do those repositories of age-old bourgeois emancipation movements play today? It seems that even nowadays many of them, at least in the metropoles, are centers of informal meeting possibilities for the most divers representatives of culture and the political sphere. But are rearguard actions fought here or do coffee houses become bastions of a counter-culture and thus win back their original historic functions? May longer lasting stays in a coffee house, in a consciously chosen atmosphere of leisure, be seen as evidence for a critical stance vis-à-vis a so-called 'efficient' use of time? Can coffee houses, or more precisely the sojourn in them, help reflect on essential values? Could they help retarding the impoverishment of our psyche's fundaments?

alle Kommerzketten und Marken gilt: Retortenangeboten fehlt die *anima*.

Ohne nostalgisch zu sein, lässt sich behaupten: Es gibt sie noch, die Kaffeehäuser mit „Seele". Aber welche Rolle spielen diese Aufbewahrungsorte bürgerlicher Emanzipationsbewegungen heute? Immer noch sind in den Metropolen viele von ihnen Zentren des informellen Zusammentreffens unterschiedlicher Vertreter aus Kultur und Politik. Aber finden in ihnen Rückzugsgefechte statt oder entwickeln sie sich zu Bastionen einer Gegenkultur und rücken sie somit wieder in ihre historischen Funktionen ein? Ist das längerdauernde Verweilen in einem Kaffeehaus, die bewusst gewählte Muße, als Indiz für eine kritische Haltung gegenüber dem sogenannten „effizienten" Zeitverbrauch zu werten? Können Kaffeehäuser oder besser der Aufenthalt in ihnen in heutiger Zeit zur Besinnung auf das Wesentliche beitragen? Können sie die Verarmung psychischer Fundamente aufhalten?

Notes

1 *Meyers Großes Konversations-Lexikon*, 6th ed., Leipzig and Wien 1905, vol.10, p. 421

2 William H. Ukers analyzed 1380 books over seventeen years for his 1922 New York book *All about Coffee*. My sources draw—next to primary sources—mainly on:
Clayton, Antony: *London's Coffee Houses. A stimulating story*, London 2003
Christophe, Delphine and Georgina Letourny (Eds.): *Paris et ses cafés*, Paris 2004
Hattox, Ralph S.: *Coffee and Coffeehouses. The origins of a Social Beverage in the Medieval Near East*, Seattle and London 1985
Jardin, Edélstan: *Le cafetier et le café*, Paris 1895
Jünger, Wolfgang: *Herr Ober, ein' Kaffee. Illustrierte Kulturgeschichte des Kaffeehauses*, München 1955
Heise, Ulla: *Kaffee und Kaffeehaus. Eine Kulturgeschichte*, Hildesheim, Zürich, New York 1987
Lemaire, Gérard-Georges: *Théories des cafés*, 2 vols., Paris 1987
Lepage, Auguste: *Les cafés politiques et litteraires de Paris*, Paris 1885
Robinson, Edward: *The Early History of Coffee Houses in England*, London 1893
Söhn, Gerhart: *Von Mokka bis Espresso*, Hamburg 1957
Weigel, Hans, Christian Brandstätter und Werner J. Schweiger (Eds.): *Das Wiener Kaffeehaus*, Wien, München, Zürich 1978

3 Schultz, Howard: in 'Business Review', *The Independent*, 24 May 2000

4 Melville, Herman: *Moby Dick; or The Whale*, New York 1851

5 Amongst Viennese variants count: 'very light, medium light, dark, black coffee with or without 'Schlagobers (whipped cream)'; coffee prepared in the Espresso machine or in the Turkish way (the latter variant 'nature' or ' passed', which does not mean [zugestoßen] or [überquert] but sieved).
Amongst the generic names that regrettably are more and more diminished nowadays, are 'a cup of gold', 'nut-gold', 'nut-brown', 'Kapuziner (very dark)', 'Obers gespritzt (very light-coloured)'. 'Einspänner (black coffee in a glass, an ample amount of whipped cream on top)', 'Melange (not prepared in an Espresso machine), a 'stretched' or 'shortened' coffee—all these quotes from Weigel, Hans, op.cit., p. 12

6 Clayton, Anthony, op.cit. p. 173

7 Christophe, Delphine, op.cit., p. 33

8 Mercier, Louis-Sébastien: *Tableau de Paris*, 1781, quoted from Heise, Ulla , op.cit., p.102

9 Haine, W. Scott: *The World of the Paris Café Sociability among the French Working Class 1789–1914*, London 1996

10 Christophe, Delphine, op.cit., p. 165

11 Quoted after Söhn, Gerhart, op.cit., p. 96

12 Linné, Carl von: *Systema naturae, sive regna tria naturae systematice proposita*, 7 vols., Leiden 1735

13 In French: Cafe; in Spanish: Café; in Portuguese: Café; in Italian: Caffè; in Dutch: Koffie; in English: Coffee; in Danish: Kaffee; in Swedish: Kaffee; in Norwegian: Kaffee; in Czech: kava; in Polish: kawa; in Russian: kophe; in Hungarian: kávé; in Roumanian: cafea; in Greek: kaféo. From: Gerhart Söhn, op.cit., p. 72

14 Jünger, Wolfgang, op.cit., p 13. James Bruce since 1762 was—amongst other functions—British consul in Algiers

15 Hattox, Ralph S., op.cit., p. 72

16 Alpinus, Prosper: *De plantis Aegypti liber*, Venice 1592
Dufour, Sylvestre: *Traitez nouveaux & curieux du café, du thé et du chocolate*, La Haye 1685 (1st ed. 1671)
Carolus Clusius (Charles de l'Ecluse): Exoticorum libri decem, o.O. 1605
Niebuhr, Carsten: *Travels through Arabia and other Countries in the East*, Translated from German by Robert Heron, 2 volumes,

Anmerkungen

1 *Meyers Konversations-Lexikon*, 6. Aufl. Leipzig und Wien 1908, Bd. 10, S. 421

2 Nicht weniger als 1380 Titel hat William H. Ukers in 17 Jahren für sein 1922 in New York erschienenes Buch *All about Coffee* ausgewertet. Meine Quellen beschränken sich auf weitaus weniger. Die wichtigsten sind
Clayton, Antony: *London's Coffee Houses. A Stimulating Story*. London 2003
Christophe, Delphine und Georgina Letourny, (Hg.): *Paris et ses cafés*. Paris 2004
Hattox, Ralph S.: *Coffee and Coffeehouses. The Origins of a Social Beverage in the Medieval Near East*. Seattle and London 1985
Jardin, Edélstan: *Le cafetier et le café*. Paris 1895
Jünger, Wolfgang: *Herr Ober, ein' Kaffee. Illustrierte Kulturgeschichte des Kaffeehauses*. München 1955
Heise, Ulla: *Kaffee und Kaffeehaus. Eine Kulturgeschichte*. Hildesheim, Zürich, New York 1987
Lemaire, Gérard-Georges: *Théories des cafés*, 2 Bde., Paris 1987
Lepage, Auguste: *Les cafés politiques et literaires de Paris*. Paris 1885
Robinson, Edward: *The Early History of Coffee Houses in England*. London 1893
Söhn, Gerhart: *Von Mokka bis Espresso*. Hamburg 1957
Weigel, Hans Christian Brandstätter, Werner J. Schweiger (Hg.): *Das Wiener Kaffeehaus*. Wien, München, Zürich 1978

3 Schultz, Howard in „Business Review", *The Independent*, 24. Mai 2000

4 Melville, Herman: *Moby Dick; or, The Whale*. New York 1851

5 In Wien gehört zu den Varianten: ein „ganz heller, mittelheller, dunkler, schwarzer Kaffee; mit und ohne Schlagobers; mittels Espressomaschine oder konventionell oder auf türkische Manier zubereitet; letztere Variante „natur" oder „passiert" (Was nicht „zugestoßen" bedeutet und nicht „überquert", sondern: geseiht). Unbeschadet auch der vielen Gattungsnamen (die sich leider in letzter Zeit anschicken, allmählich aus unserem Vokabular zu verschwinden): Schale Gold, Schale Nussgold, nussbraun, Kapuziner (ganz dunkel), Obers gespritzt (sehr hell), Einspänner (Schwarzer im Glas, darüber reichlich Schlagobers), Melange (nicht in der Espressomaschine bereitet). Verlängerter, Kurzer." Weigel, Hans, op. cit., S. 12

6 Clayton, Antony, op. cit., S. 173

7 Christophe, Delphine, op. cit., S. 33

8 Mercier, Louis-Sébastien: *Tableau de Paris*, 1781, zitiert nach Heise, Ulla, op. cit., S. 102

9 Haine, W. Scott: *The World of the Paris Café. Sociability Among the French Working Class 1789–1914*. London 1996

10 Christophe, Delphine, op. cit., S. 165

11 Zitiert nach: Söhn, Gerhart, op. cit., S. 96

12 Linné, Carl von: *Systema naturae, sive regna tria naturae systematice proposita*, 7 Bde., Leiden 1735

13 Französisch: Café; Spanisch: Café; Portugiesisch: Café; Italienisch: Caffè; Holländisch: Koffie; Englisch: Coffee; Dänisch: Kaffe; Schwedisch: Kaffe; Norwegisch: Kaffe; Tschechisch: káva; Polnisch: kawa; Russisch: kophe; Ungarisch: kávé; Rumänisch: cafea; Griechisch: kaféo aus: Söhn, Gerhart, op. cit, S. 3

14 Jünger, Wolfgang, op. cit., S. 13. James Bruce war unter anderem ab 1762 britischer Konsul in Algier.

15 Hattox, Ralph S., op. cit., S. 72

16 Alpinus, Prosper: *De plantis Aegypti liber* Venedig 1592;
Dufour, Sylvestre: *Traitez nouveaux & curieux du café, du thé et du chocolate*. La Haye 1685 (1. Aufl. 1671);

Edinburgh 1792
Olearius, Adam: *Beschreibung der Neuen Orientalischen Reise*, Schleswig 1647
Rauwolf, Leonard: *Eigentliche Beschreibung der Raisz, so er vor dieser Zeit gegen Aufgang in die Morgenländer vollbracht*, Lauingen 1582
Rocque, Jean de la: *Voyage de l'Arabie heureuse*, Paris 1716
Tavernier, Jean-Baptiste: *Six voyages de Jean Baptiste Tavernier qu'il a fait en Turquie, en Perse et aux Indes, pendant l'espace de 40 ans*, Paris 1676
Thévenot, Jean de: *Relation d'un voyage fait au Levant*, Rouen 1665
Valle, Pietro della: *Reiszebeschreibung in unterschiedliche Theile der Welt. Nemlich in Türckey*, Geneva 1671

17 Hattox, Ralph S., op.cit., p. 13ff.
18 Arasaratnam, Sinnapah: *Dutch Power in Ceylon 1658–1687*, New Delhi 1988
19 Ibid., pp. 181–193
20 Heise, Ulla, op.cit., pp. 17–21
21 Ibid., p. 16
22 *Sehsucht. Das Panorama als Massenunterhaltung des 19. Jahrhunderts.* Exhibition Catalogue, Ausstellungs- und Kunsthalle der Bundesrepublik Deutschland, Bonn 1993
23 Charles-Louis de Secondat, Baron de Montesquieu: *Lettres Persanes*, published in Amsterdam in 1721 paint, twenty years before Louis-Sébastien Mercier's *Tableaux de Paris*, an acidly mocking but also scientifically exact canvas of the mores of Parisian society. The *Lettres Persanes* are the product of two fictional Persian noblemen.
24 Hattox, Ralph S., op.cit., p. 73
25 Habermas, Jürgen: *Strukturwandel der Öffentlichkeit*, Frankfurt am Main 1961
26 Söhn, Gerhart, op.cit., pp. 48–49
27 Grote, Ludwig: *Albrecht Dürer, Reisen nach Venedig*, Munich and New York 1998. Dürer visits Venice in 1494/95 and in 1505–1507
28 Reato, Danilo: *La bottega del caffè, i caffè veneziani tra '700 e '900*, Verona 1991, p. 13
29 Schivelbusch, Wolfgang: *Das Paradies, der Geschmack und die Vernunft*, Munich and Vienna 1980, pp. 30–31
30 Clayton, Anthony, op.cit., p. 10
31 Ibid., p. 10
32 Ibid., p. 43
33 Two drawings survive as part of a collection of fire place mantle pieces, some of them in the Egyptian style. They are plates 45 and 46 from 'Diverse maniere d'adornare i camini ed ogni altra parte degli edifizi desunte dall'architettura egizia, etrusca, greca e romana Toscana' Rome 1769
34 Weinlig, Christian Traugott: *Briefe über Rom …* (Letters on Rome), entry of the 26 December 1767, quoted from Heise, Ulla, op.cit., p. 205
35 One of the most visited convivial places at the time of the ancien règime was the 'Café du Caveau'. In front of its garden arcades there was a roomy, well-furnished tent, that offered seats for more than a hundred persons.
36 Jünger, Wolfgang, op.cit., p. 190
37 Ibid., p. 188
38 This is impressively demonstrated in the pastry maker museum of Coltura in Bergell in Engadine, Switzerland.
39 Stirner's only literary work was 'Der Einzige und sein Eigentum' ('Individual man and his property'). He was the founder of a company that provided fresh milk to Berliners.
40 Gysi, Klaus and Kurt Böttcher (Ed.): *Unsterblicher Volkswitz, Adolf Glasbrenners Werk in Auswahl* (Eternal Popular Witticism—Adolf Glasbrenner's Selected Works), 2 vols., Berlin 1954, vol.1, p.82, quoted from: Heise, Ulla, op.cit., p. 135
41 *Süsse muss der Coffee sein*, exhibition catalogue, Stadtgeschichtliches Museum Leipzig 1994, p. 17. Probably

Clusius, Carolus (Charles de l'Ecluse), 1574;
Niebuhr, Carsten: *Travels Through Arabia and Other Countries in the East.* Translated from German by Robert Heron, 2 Bde., Edinburgh 1792;
Olearius, Adam: *Beschreibung der Neuen Orientalischen Reise.* Schleswig 1647;
Rauwolf, Leonard: *Eigentliche Beschreibung der Raisz, so er vor dieser Zeit gegen Aufgang in die Morgenländer vollbracht.* Lauingen 1582;
de la Rocque, Jean: *Voyage de l'Arabie heureuse.* Paris 1716;
de Thévenot, Jean: *Relation d'un voyage fait au Levant.* Rouen 1665;
Valle, Pietro della: *Reiszebeschreibung in unterschiedliche Theile der Welt. Nemlich in Türckey.* Genf 1671

17 Hattox, Ralph S., op. cit., S. 13 ff.
18 Arasaratnam, Sinnapah: *Dutch Power in Ceylon, 1658–1687.* New Delhi 1988
19 Ibid., S. 181–193
20 Heise, Ulla, op. cit., S. 17–21
21 Ibid., S. 16
22 Kunst- und Ausstellungshalle der Bundesrepublik Deutschland (Hg.): *Sehsucht. Das Panorama als Massenunterhaltung des 19. Jahrhunderts* (Ausstellungskatalog). Frankfurt am Main 1993
23 Charles-Louis de Secondat, Baron de Montesquieu: *Lettres persanes.* Amsterdam 1721, malen 20 Jahre vor den *Tableaux de Paris* von Louis-Sébastien Mercier mit beißendem Spott, aber auch wissenschaftlichem Ernst ein Sittenbild der Pariser Gesellschaft – aus der Feder zweier fiktiver persischer Standesherren.
24 Hattox, Ralph S., op. cit., S. 73
25 Habermas, Jürgen: *Strukturwandel der Öffentlichkeit.* Frankfurt am Main 1961
26 Söhn, Gerhart, op. cit., S. 48–49
27 Grote, Ludwig: *Albrecht Dürer. Reisen nach Venedig.* München und New York 1998. Dürer besucht Venedig 1494/95 und 1505–1507
28 Reato, Danilo: *La bottega del caffè, i caffè veneziani tra '700 e '900.* Verona 1991, S. 13
29 Schivelbusch, Wolfgang: *Das Paradies, der Geschmack und die Vernunft.* München und Wien 1980, S. 30–31
30 Clayton, Antony, op. cit., S. 10
31 Ibid.
32 Ibid., S. 43
33 Zwei Zeichnungen sind erhalten als Teil einer Sammlung von Kaminummantelungen, darunter mehrere im ägyptischen Stil. Es sind die Tafeln 45 und 46 aus: Piranesi, Giovanni Battista: *Diverse maniere d' adornare i cammini ed ogni altra parte degli edifizi desunte dall'architettura Egizia, Etrusca, e Grecae romana Toscana.* Rom 1769
34 Weinling, Christian Traugott: *Briefe über Rom …*, Eintragung vom 26.12.1767, zitiert nach: Heise, Ulla, op. cit., S. 205
35 Zu einer der meistbesuchten Geselligkeitsstätten gehörte in der Zeit des Ancien Régime das Café du Caveau. Vor seinen Gartenarkaden befand sich ein geräumiges, gut eingerichtetes Zelt, das mehr als 100 Personen Sitzgelegenheit bot.
36 Jünger, Wolfgang, op. cit, S. 190
37 Ibid., S. 188
38 Das Zuckerbäckermuseum in Coltura im Graubündner Bergell dokumentiert dies auf eindrückliche Weise.
39 Der durch sein Werk *Der Einzige und sein Eigentum* nur einmal in die Literaturgeschichte eingegangene Stirner hatte auch eine Gesellschaft zur Belieferung der Berliner mit frischer Milch gegründet.
40 Gysi, Klaus/Böttcher, Kurt (Hg.): *Unsterblicher Volkswitz. Adolf Glassbrenners Werk in Auswahl* (2 Bde.). Berlin 1954, Bd. 1, S. 82, zitiert nach: Heise, Ulla, op. cit., S. 135

coffee was already known through the procurement of Dirich Zobel, a Bremen citizen and merchant's son, who was brought back from Constantinople in 1614, ibid., p. 19
42 Heise, Ulla, op.cit., p. 106
43 Söhn, Gerhart, op.cit., pp. 43–45
44 Heise, Ulla (Ed.): *Kaffeekultur. Bilder aus der Geschichte des Kaffees*, Ausstellungskatalog, Sammlung Eduscho, Bremen undated, p. 35
45 'This very quotation is used by the Oxford English Dictionary…with the meaning "a deceptive means of allurement: a person…held out as a lure", quoted from Hattox, Ralph, op.cit., p. 109
46 There is an engraving in the Paris museum of Carnavalet to prove this. Christophe, Delphine, op.cit., p. 39. The painter and engraver Giovanni Volpato (1735–1803) too, shows a boy serving dishes in his copperplate engraving after a painting by Magrotto 'Divertissement de Venice'. In: *Giovanni Volpato 1735–1803*, exhibition catalogue, Bassano 1980, pp. 70 and 75
47 *Paris. Die schönsten Restaurants*, Cologne 1994, pp. 116–117
48 Likewise the English pub was, as Christoph Grafe shows, at first an entirely male domain. Cf. Grafe, Christoph and Franziska Bollerey: *Cafés and Bars. The Architecture of Public Display*, Abingdon (2007) 2008
49 Said, Edward: *Orientalism*, New York 1979
50 Original in 1298/1299, rediscovered in Toledo in 1933. First title presumably 'Le livre de Marco Polo, Citoyen de Venise, dit Million, oú l'on conte les merveilles du monde'
51 It was closed in 1977. The last Lyons corner shop closed in 1981. This imperium as a veritable synonym of the British habit to consume tea really merits a renaissance.
52 Clayton, Anthony, op.cit., pp. 135–138
53 Lummel, Peter: 'Erlebnisgastronomie (event gastronomy) um 1900. Das 'Haus Vaterland in Berlin'', in: May, Herbert and Andrea Schilz: *Gasthäuser. Geschichte und Kultur*, Petersberg 2004, p. 196
54 Giedion, Sigfried: *Mechanization Takes Command. A contribution to anonymous history*, New York 1948
55 As early as 1687 the French developed a coffee machine mounted on an alcohol burner. In 1800 the Frenchman de Belloy invented a precursor of the percolator system. The real inventor of this principle is the American Count Rumford, alias Benjamin Thompson (1753–1814). Söhn, Gerhart, op.cit., pp. 160–169
56 According to *Meyers Großes Konversationslexikon*, Leipzig, Wien 1903, vol. 3, p. 241 there were exchanges in Bruges and Antwerp (1531), Lyon and Toulouse (1549), Hamburg (1558), London (1566, founded by Sir Thomas Gresham, banker to the court) and Amsterdam (1603)
57 'Il buon e il cattivo governo', from 1338, fresco in the Palazzo Pubblico, Siena
58 Here again I will deal with the origins of sherbet, already mentioned in connection with Procopio dei Coltelli: 'Sherbet (Arabian for drink, from which derives 'sorbetto' in Italian), in the Orient a cool drink or lemonade, in Persia part of the daily meal': *Meyers Großes Konversationslexikon*, Leipzig/Wien 1907, vol.17, p. 739
59 Clayton, Anthony, op.cit., p.64
60 Pepys, Samuel: *Memoirs of Samuel Pepys, Comprising his diary from 1659 to 1669*, London 1825
61 Clayton, Anthony, op.cit., p. 90
62 Ibid., p. 10
63 Heise, Ulla, op cit., pp. 131–134; also: Lentzsch, Franziska: *Füssli, The Wild Swiss*, exhibition catalogue, Kunsthaus Zürich 2005
64 It was common to buy the right of access and to a cup of coffee with a penny, in more exclusive houses with two pennies. Later tokens became common. Amongst others the municipal historical museum of Leipzig owns a considerable collection.

41 Heise, Ulla (Hg.): *Süße muß der Coffee sein! Drei Jahrhunderte europäische Kaffeekultur und die Kaffeesachsen* (Ausstellungskatalog Stadtgeschichtliches Museum). Leipzig 1994, S. 17. Wahrscheinlich aber war der Kaffee bereits kurz nach 1614 durch die Übermittlung des aus Konstantinopel zurückgeholten Kaufmannssohnes Dirich Zobel bekannt, ibid., S. 19
42 Heise, Ulla, op. cit., S. 106
43 Söhn, Gerhart, op. cit., S. 43–45
44 Heise, Ulla (Hg.): *Kaffeekultur. Bilder aus der Geschichte des Kaffees* (Ausstellungskatalog Sammlung Eduscho). Bremen o. J., S. 35
45 „This very quotation is used by the „Oxford English Dictionary … with the meaning, a deceptive means of allurement; a person … held out as a lure", quoted from: Hattox, Ralph, op. cit., S. 109
46 Ein im Pariser Musée Carnavalet aufbewahrter Stich illustriert dies. Christophe, Delphine, op. cit., S. 39. Auch der Stecher und Maler Giovanni Volpato (1735–1803) zeigt auf einem Kupferstich den servierenden Knaben, nach einem Gemälde von Magrotto *Divertissement de Venice*. In: Marini, Giorgio (Hg.): *Giovanni Volpato 1735–1803* (Ausstellungskatalog). Bassano 1988, S. 70 und 75
47 *Paris. Die schönsten Restaurants.* Köln 1994, S. 116–117
48 Auch der englische Pub war vorerst eine reine Männerdomäne, wie Christoph Grafe in seinem Beitrag zeigt: Cf. Grafe, Christoph and Franziska Bollerey: *Cafés and Bars. The Architecture of Public Display*, Abingdon (2007) 2008
49 Said, Edward: *Orientalism*. New York 1979
50 Urschrift 1298/99, die erst 1933 in Toledo wiederentdeckt wurde und deren Titel vermutlich *le livre de Marco Polo, Citoyen de Venise, dit Million, oú l'on contre les merveilles du monde* lautet.
51 Es wird 1977 geschlossen. Die letzte Lyons-Filiale schloß 1981. Das für den britischen Teekonsum nahezu zum Synonym gewordene Imperium verdiente eine Renaissance.
52 Clayton, Antony, op. cit., S. 135–138
53 Lummel, Peter: „Erlebnisgastronomie um 1900. Das ‚Haus Vaterland in Berlin'". In: May, Herbert, Andrea Schilz: *Gasthäuser. Geschichte und Kultur*. Petersberg 2004, S. 196
54 Giedion, Sigfried: *Mechanization Takes Command. A Contribution to Anonymous History*. New York 1948
55 Bereits 1687 hatten die Franzosen eine auf einen Spirituskocher montierte Kaffeemaschine konstruiert und 1800 hatte der Franzose de Belloy einen Vorläufer des Percolator-Systems entwickelt. Eigentlicher Erfinder ist Graf Rumford, alias Benjamin Thompson (1753–1814). Söhn, Gerhart, op. cit., S. 160–169
56 Laut *Meyers Konversationslexikon*, Leipzig und Wien 1908, Bd. 3, S. 241, gibt es 1531 in Brügge und Antwerpen, 1549 in Lyon und Toulouse, 1558 in Hamburg, 1566 in London (Gründung des Hofbankiers Sir Thomas Gresham), 1603 in Amsterdam Börsen.
57 *Il buon e il cattivo governo*, ab 1338, Fresko im Palazzo Pubblico in Siena
58 Hier sei noch einmal auf die Herkunft des bereits in Zusammenhang mit Procopio dei Coltelli erwähnten Sorbet eingegangen: „Scherbet (arab. Trank, davon ital. Sorbetto), im Orient kühlendes Getränk, Limonade, in Persien Bestandteil der täglichen Mahlzeit", *Meyers Konversationslexikon*, Leipzig und Wien 1909, Bd. 17, S. 738
59 Clayton, Antony, op. cit., S. 64
60 Pepys, Samuel: *Memoirs of Samuel Pepys, Comprising his Diary from 1659 to 1669*. London 1825
61 Clayton, Antony, op. cit., S. 90
62 Ibid., S. 10
63 Heise, Ulla, op. cit., S. 131–134
64 Es war üblich, sich mit einem Penny, in exklusiven Häusern

Heise, Ulla: *Süße muß der Coffee sein*, op.cit. p. 106
65 Clayton, Anthony, op.cit., p.79
66 Westerfrölke, Hermann: *Englische Kaffeehäuser als Sammelpunkte der literarischen Welt im Zeitalter von Dryden und Addison*, Jena 1924, p. 62
67 Ibid.
68 Zweig, Stefan: *Die Welt von gestern. Erinnerungen eines Europäers*, posthumous Stockholm 1942, quoted from Martinek, Thomas: *Kaffeehäuser in Wien. Ein Führer durch die Wiener Kaffeehäuser*, Wien 1996, p.19
69 Thomas Martinek, op.cit., p. 19
70 Hattox, Ralph S., op.cit., p.32
71 '... in theory at least, all aspects of human activity fall into the reign of the shari'a, the holy law. Nonetheless, it would be foolish to ignore the fact that concern for the strict adherence of the believers to holy law was not always the sole anxiety of the governing powers'; ibid., p. 42
72 Quoted from: Jünger, Wolfgang, op.cit., p. 26
73 Hobbes, Thomas: *Elementorum philosophiae section prima de corpore: sectio secunda de homine; section tertia de cive*, Paris 1642. First English Edition in 1651, 'Philosophical Rudiments concerning Government and Society'.
74 Clayton, Anthony, op.cit., p. 16
75 Ibid.
76 After: Markman, Ellis: *The Coffee House—Architectural History*, London 2004, p. 89
77 Jünger, Wolfgang, op.cit., pp. 84–85
78 Quoted from Jünger, Wolfgang, op.cit., p. 89
79 Necker had succeeded in doubling the number of representatives of the 'Third Estate' in the States General. He also is said to be the originator of the cockade. His followers wore a rosette folded from plant leaves in the coffee houses and gardens of the Palais Royal that later was to become—in the national colours—the emblem of the French Revolution.
80 Roth, Joseph: *Zipper und sein Vater*, München 1928, pp. 137–138
81 Morrow, W.C.: *Bohemian Paris of To-Day*, London 1899, pp. 213–214
82 Jünger, Wolfgang, op.cit., p. 73
83 Morrow, W.C., op.cit., p. 219
84 Christophe, Delphine, op.cit., p. 18
85 In the times of Procopio dei Coltelli the licensing costs for a licence for a cafetier or limonadier were considerably above those of the manager of a restaurant. More refinement was expected from the first. This division was given up in 1791.
86 Fargue, Léon-Paul: *Le piéton de Paris*, Paris 1998 (1. ed. 1939), pp. 140–141
87 Nesbit, Molly and Françoise Reynaud: *Eugène Atget, interieurs parisiens: Un album du Musée Carnavalet*, Paris 1992, p. 25
88 In 1920 Marcelin Cazes takes over the brasserie 'Des Bords du Rhin', founded by Léonard Lippman in 1877 and rechristens it in commemoration of its first owner.
89 Léon-Paul Fargue, op.cit., p 154
90 Hemingway, Ernest: *Paris. A Moveable Feast*, New York 1964
91 'Magot'—dog-ape or grotesque Chinese porcelain figure
92 Stupanitsch, Gianni: 'Jeux d'ombre et de lumières au Caffè Garibaldi', in: Gérard-Georges Lemaire, op.cit., pp. 113–117
93 Concerning Joyce, Svevo and Saba, the city of Trieste has edited City guides in the series 'Itinerari Triestini—Triestine Itineraries'.
94 Christophe, Delphine, op.cit., p. 107
95 Kesten, Hermann: *Dichter im Café*, München, Wien, Basel 1959, pp. 12–13
96 The same kind of people, mixed with Italian colleagues, are to be found in the cafés of Rome's Via Veneto in the 1950ies.
97 Besides Barcelona, the most important meeting places for Spanish writers and artist were in Madrid. In the 'Café del Pombo' all international 'isms' receive their Spanish colouring.

auch mit zwei Pennys den Zutritt und das Recht auf einen Kaffee zu erkaufen. Später werden auch Zahlmarken gebräuchlich. Unter anderem im stadtgeschichtlichen Museum der Kaffeestadt Leipzig befindet sich eine anschauliche Sammlung. Heise, Ulla: *Süße muß der Coffee sein,* op. cit., S. 106
65 Clayton, Antony, op. cit., S. 79
66 Westerfrölke, Hermann: *Englische Kaffeehäuser als Sammelpunkte der literarischen Welt im Zeitalter von Dryden und Addison.* Jena 1924, S. 62
67 Ibid.
68 Zweig, Stefan: *Die Welt von gestern. Erinnerungen eines Europäers* (posthum veröffentlicht). Stockholm 1942, zitiert nach: Martinek, Thomas: *Kaffeehäuser in Wien. Ein Führer durch die Wiener Kaffeehäuser.* Wien 1996, S. 19
69 Martinek, Thomas, op. cit., S. 19
70 Hattox, Ralph. S., op. cit., S. 32
71 „in theory at least, all aspects of human activity fall into the realm of the shari'a, the holy law. Nonetheless, it would be foolish to ignore the fact that concern for the strict adherence of the believers to holy law was not always the sole anxiety of the governing powers", ibid., S. 42
72 Zitiert nach: Jünger, Wolfgang, op. cit., S. 26
73 Hobbes, Thomas: *Elementorum philosphiae sectio prima de corpore; sectio secunda de homine; sectio tertia de cive.* Paris 1642. Die erste englische Ausgabe erschien 1651 als *Philosophical Rudiments concerning Government and Society.*
74 Clayton, Antony, op. cit., S. 16
75 Ibid.
76 Nach: Markman, Ellis: *The Coffee House—Architectural History*, London 2004, S. 89
77 Jünger, Wolfgang op. cit., S. 84–85
78 Zitiert nach Jünger, Wolfgang, op. cit., S. 89
79 Necker hatte 1788 eine Verdopplung des Dritten Standes in den Generalständen durchgesetzt. Er gilt auch als Urheber der Kokarde. Seine Anhänger trugen in den Kaffeehäusern und -gärten des Palais Royal eine aus Blättern gefaltete Rosette, die später aus Stoff in den Nationalfarben das Emblem der Revolution wird.
80 Roth, Joseph: *Zipper und sein Vater.* München 1928, S. 137–138
81 Morrow, W. C.: *Bohemian Paris of To-Day.* London 1899, S. 213–214
82 Jünger, Wolfgang, op. cit., S. 73
83 Morrow, W.C., op. cit., p. 219
84 Christophe, Delphine, op. cit., S. 18
85 Zu Zeiten von Procopio dei Coltelli war die Lizenz für einen Cafetier und Limonadier weit über der eines Restaurantbetreibers angesiedelt. Von ihm erwartete man mehr Rafinesse. Diese Trennung wird 1791 aufgehoben.
86 Fargue, Léon-Paul: *Le piéton de Paris.* Paris 1998 (1. Ausg. 1939), S. 140–141
87 Nesbit, Molly und Françoise Reynaud: *Eugène Atget, interieurs parisiens: Un album du Musée Carnavalet.* Paris 1992, S. 25
88 1920 übernimmt Marcelin Cazes die 1877 von Léonard Lippman eröffnete Brasserie „Des Bords du Rhin" und tauft sie in Erinnerung an den ersten Besitzer um.
89 Fargue, Léon-Paul, op. cit., S. 154
90 Hemingway, Ernest: *Paris. A Moveable Feast.* New York 1964. Dt. Ausgabe: *Paris – ein Fest fürs Leben.* Reinbek 1965.
91 Im Fremdwörterduden steht Magot für Handaffe oder groteske chinesische Porzellanfigur.
92 Stuparitsch, Gianni: „Jeux d'ombre et de lumières au Caffè Garibaldi" In: Lemaire, Gérard-Georges, op. cit., S. 113–117
93 Zu Joyce, Svevo und Saba hat die Stadt Triest in ihrer Reihe *Itinerari Triestini* Stadtführer herausgegeben.
94 Christophe, Delphine, op. cit., S. 107

Here, Ramón Gómez de la Serna invents a literary formula of paradoxical character: 'Greguerias' that hence influences all Spanish poetry. In the 1920s and 30s 'Café de Gijón', opened in 1916, becomes a transhipment place of Spanish culture. Ortega y Gasset(1883–1955) sits here habitually as well as Federico Garcia Lorca (1898–1936), who in turn is portrayed in 1924 by another coffee house customer of 'Café Oriente', Salvador Dali (1904–1989). In Portugal it is Lisbon's 'Café A Brasilieira', erected in 1904 in the style of Portuguese Modernismo, that literates like Fernando Pessoa (1888–1935) *(fig. 27)* make their domicile. Cf. Ulla Heise, op.cit., pp. 200–201

98 Fitch, Noël Riley: *Die literarischen Cafés von Paris*, Hamburg 1993, p. 12

99 Ibid., p. 29

100 Hoffmann, Raoul: 'Die Cafés von Paris—Bilder aus einer Tradition', in: *Ausland* 1981, pp. 439-440

101 Elias, Norbert: *Über den Prozeß der Zivilisation. Soziogenetische und psychogenetische Untersuchungen*. 2 Bde., Frankfurt am Main 1978 (1939)

102 Kesten, Hermann, Dichter im Café, op.cit., p. 14

103 Ibid., p. 10

104 Cf. Bollerey, Franziska: *Mythos Metropolis. Die Stadt als Sujet für Schriftsteller, Maler und Regisseure*, Berlin (2001) 2006, pp. 40–49

105 Kesten, Hermann, op. cit., p. 7

106 Goldoni, Carlo: *Memorie del Goldoni per servire all'istoria della sua vita e quella del suo teatro: traduzione dal francese*, Firenze 1787–1789, German: Mein Theater—mein Leben, Berlin 1949, p.467, quoted from: Heise, Ulla, op.cit., p. 153

107 Jens, Walter (ed.): *Kindlers Literaturlexikon*, München 1992, vol. 6, pp. 577–578

108 Première in Mantova, 2.5.1750

109 Jens, Walter, op.cit., p. 578

110 Friedrich Schiller writes in 1785: 'My most agreeable recreation so far has been to visit Richter's coffee house, where I always find Leipsic's half tout monde gathered and can widen my acquaintance amongst locals and friends.' (cf. *fig. 28*) Quoted from Jünger, Wolfgang, op.cit., p 167. Leipzig's first coffee house was 'Zum arabischen Coffeebaum—At the Arabic Coffee Tree', later also called 'Lehmannisches Coffee-Haus'. It had been founded by the court's chocolatier Johann Lehmann.

111 Heise, Ulla, op cit., p. 152

112 'C-A-F-F-E-E, do not drink so much coffee, not for children this Turkish drink is suited, weakens the nerves and makes you pale and ill.' 'Do not be a musulman that cannot help drinking coffee', round by Carl Gottlieb Hering (1766-1853)

113 Reconstructed including its original wainscoting

114 In 1825, Fuchs, former private cook at the court of Friedrich Wilhelm III opened here one of the most elegant places. One of the rooms was furnished as 'Schweizerhaus' (Swiss cottage)—a cultural transfer from the Engadine. Schinkel was commissioned with the design of the mirrorhall. Cf. Jünger, Wolfgang, op. cit., p. 197–199

115 Rukschcio, Burkhardt and Roland Schachel: *Adolf Loos*, Wien 1982, pp. 66–69, pp. 418–420

116 Heise, Ulla, op cit., p. 206

117 Van Straaten, Evert: *Theo van Doesburg. Painter and Architect*, 1988, pp. 196–219

118 It was reopened on 8 June 2006. The colour scheme, which is of the utmost importance for the character of this place, was scientifically reconstructed by the Dutch Mariël Polman

119 Kosch, Arlette: *Literarisches Zürich. Der Dichter und Denker Stadtplan*, Jena 2002

120 *DADA*, exhibition catalogue, Centre Pompidou, Paris 2005, 2006, pp. 986–1014

121 Ibid., pp. 35–36

122 Arndt, Gudrun: *Spaziergänge durch das literarische New York*, Zürich/Hamburg 1997, pp. 166–167

95 Kesten, Hermann: *Dichter im Café*. München, Wien, Basel 1959, S. 12–13

96 Die gleichen Personen, durchmischt mit ihren italienischen Kollegen, finden sich in den 1950er Jahren in den Cafés der Via Veneto in Rom.

97 Außer in Barcelona befanden sich die wichtigsten Künstler und Literaturtreffpunkte in Madrid: Das Café del Pombo, von dem aus alle internationalen Ismen ihre spanische Prägung erhalten. Hier wird von Ramón Gómez de la Serna die literarische Paradoxformel, Greguerias, erfunden, die darauf die spanische Lyrik prägt. In den 1920er und 1930er Jahren wird das 1916 eröffnete Café de Gijón Umschlagplatz spanischer Kultur. Ortega y Gasset (1883–1955) sitzt hier als Stammgast ebenso wie Federico Garcia Lorca (1898–1936), den ein anderer Kaffeehausgänger im Café Oriente, Salvador Dalí, 1924 porträtiert. In Portugal ist es in Lissabon das 1904 im Stil des portugiesischen Modernismo erbaute Café A Brasileira, das die Literaten, unter ihnen Fernando Pessoa, zu ihrem Domizil machen. Siehe Heise, Ulla, op. cit., S. 200–201

98 Fitch, Noël Riley: *Die literarischen Cafés von Paris*. Hamburg 1993, S. 12

99 Ibid., S. 29

100 Hoffmann, Raoul: „Die Cafés von Paris – Bilder aus einer Tradition". In: *Ausland*, 1981, S. 439–440

101 Elias, Norbert: *Über den Prozeß der Zivilisation. Soziogenetische und psychogenetische Untersuchungen*. 2 Bde., Frankfurt am Main 1978 (1. Ausg. 1939)

102 Kesten, Hermann, op. cit., S. 14

103 Ibid., S. 10

104 Siehe Bollerey, Franziska: *Mythos Metropolis. Die Stadt als Sujet für Schriftsteller, Maler und Regisseure*. Berlin (2001) 2006, S. 40–49

105 Kesten, Hermann, op. cit., S. 7

106 Goldoni, Carlo: *Memorie del Goldoni per servire all'istoria della sua vita e a quella del suo teatro: traduzione dal francese*. Florenz 1787–89. Deutsch: *Mein Theater – mein Leben*. Berlin 1949, S. 467, zitiert nach: Heise, Ulla, op. cit., S. 153

107 Jens, Walter (Hg.): Kindlers Literaturlexikon. München 1952, Bd. 6, S. 577–578

108 Uraufführung in Mantua am 2. Mai 1750

109 Jens, Walter, op. cit., S. 578

110 Friedrich Schiller schreibt 1785: „Meine angenehmste Erholung ist bisher gewesen Richters Kaffeehaus zu besuchen, wo ich immer die halbe Welt Leipzigs zusammenfinde und meine Bekanntschaft mit Einheimischen und Freunden erweitere." Zitiert nach: Jünger, Wolfgang, op. cit., S. 164. Leipzigs erstes Kaffeehaus war das von Hofchocolatier Johann Lehmann unter dem Namen Zum arabischen Coffeebaum – später auch Lehmannisches Coffee-Haus eingerichtete Etablissement.

111 Heise, Ulla, op. cit., S. 152

112 „C-A-F-F-E-E, trink nicht so viel Kaffee.
Nicht für Kinder ist der Türkentrank,
schwächt die Nerven macht dich blaß und krank.
Sei doch kein Muselmann, der ihn nicht lassen kann". Kanon „C-A-F-F-E-E" von Carl Gottlieb Hering (1766–1853)

113 Mit der originalen Täfelung heute im Musée Carnavalet in Paris rekonstruiert

114 1825 hatte Fuchs, der ehemalige Mundkoch am Hofe Friedrich Wilhelms III., eines der elegantesten Häuser eröffnet. Einer der Räume war als Schweizerhaus ausgestattet (Kulturtransfer der Engadiner), den Entwurf des Spiegelsaals vertraute er Schinkel an. Siehe: Jünger, Wolfgang, op. cit., S. 197–199

115 Rukschcio, Burkhardt und Roland Schachel: *Adolf Loos*. Wien 1982, S. 66–69, S. 418–420

116 Heise, Ulla, op. cit., S. 206

123 Ibid., pp. 35-36
124 A literary magazine founded by Harald Ross and Jane Grant. First edition: 21. February 1921. The *New Yorker* is famous for its many short stories which it published since the mid-twentieth century, as well as for its reports, reviews, essays and cartoons.
125 Arndt, Gudrun, op.cit., pp. 84-85
126 Lemaire, Gérard-Georges, op.cit. Both volumes are accompanying a 1996 exhibition in the Musée des Beaux Arts in Caen: one catalogue volume and one anthology
127 Hulten, Pontus (Ed.): *Futurismo & Futurismi*, exhibition catalogue, Palazzo Grassi, Venice 1986
128 Marinetti, Filippo Tommaso and Albert Viviani: 'Gigantesque bataille de poets, peintres et sculpteurs', in: Lemaire, Gérard-Georges, op.cit., pp. 85–87
129 Carrà, Carlo: 'Invention de la peinture futuriste au Caffè Centro', in: Lemaire, Gérard-Georges, op.cit., pp. 102–103
130 Ibid.
131 Prévot, Réné: *Bohéme*, München 1922, p. 91
132 Kraus, Karl: *Demolierte Literatur*, Wien 1897, quoted from: Weigel, Hans, op.cit., p.62
133 Thus the name of an exhibition held in Vienna in 1985: 'Traum und Wirklichkeit. Vienna 1870–1930', Exhibition, Historisches Museum der Stadt Wien im Künstlerhaus, Vienna 1985
134 Felix Salten is the author of the story (made into a film by Walt Disney): *Bambi. Eine Lebensgeschichte aus dem Walde*, Berlin 1923, as very probably also of the pornographic novel: Josephine Mutzenbacher: *Die Geschichte einer Wienerischen Dirne, von ihr selbst erzählt*, Wien 1906
135 Jünger, Wolfgang, op.cit., p. 145
136 The inventor of coffee house concerts, that until well into the twentieth century were very popular, is said to be Martin Wiegand, who near Vienna's 'Kärntner Tor' organized a first one in the year of the French Revolution, 1789
137 Weigel, Hans, op.cit., p.15
138 Bodor, Ferenc: *Die Pressos der Stadt*, Budapest 1992
139 The most prominent guests of 'Café Landtmann' were Oskar Kokoschka (1886–1980), Max Reinhardt (1873–1943), Marlene Dietrich (1901–1992), Gary Cooper (1901–1961) or Oskar Werner (1922–1984)
140 Rössner, Michael: 'Aperçus de la vie de café', in: Lemaire, Gérard-Georges, op.cit., p. 57
141 Schweitzer, Claus: '68 Prose Cafés, Stadtcafés zum Wohlfühlen', in: *Swiss Magazine* 11/2005, pp. 68–71
142 Cf. Guagnini, Enrico: *Locali storici d'Italia—Historical Places of Italy, Cafés, Restaurants, Hotels*, Milan 2000
143 Polgar, Alfred in: Weigel, Hans, op.cit., p. 69
144 Kesten, Hermann, op.cit.,p. 8

117 van Straaten, Evert: *Theo van Doesburg. Painter and Architect.* Den Haag 1988, S. 196–219
118 Die Wiedereröffnung fand am 8. Juni 2006 statt. Die für den Charakter dieses Ortes äußerst wichtige Farbgestaltung wurde von der Niederländerin Mariël Polman wissenschaftlich rekonstruiert.
119 Kosch, Arlette: *Literarisches Zürich. Der Dichter und Denker Stadtplan*. Jena 2002
120 *DADA* (Ausstellungskatalog, Centre Pompidou). Paris 2005/2006, S. 986–1014
121 Ibid, S. 197–198
122 Arndt, Gudrun: *Spaziergänge durch das literarische New York*. Zürich und Hamburg 1997, S. 166–167
123 Ibid., S. 35–36
124 Ein von Harald Ross und Jane Grant gegründetes Literaturmagazin. Die erste Ausgabe erschien am 21. Februar 1921. *The New Yorker* ist bekannt für die zahlreichen Kurzgeschichten, die es in der Mitte des 20. Jahrhunderts veröffentlichte, sowie für seine Reportagen, Kritiken, Essays und Cartoons.
125 Arndt, Gudrun, op. cit., S. 84–85
126 Lemaire, Gérard-Georges, op. cit. Beide Bände, ein Katalogband und eine Anthologie, sind Begleitpublikationen einer 1996 im Musée des Beaux-Arts in Caen gezeigten Ausstellung.
127 Hulten, Pontus (Hg.): *Futurismo & Futurismi* (Ausstellungskatalog Palazzo Grassi). Venedig 1986
128 Marinetti, Filippo Tommaso und Alberto Viviani: „Gigantesque bataille de poètes, peintres et sculpteurs“. In: Lemaire, Gérard-Georges, op. cit., S. 85–87
129 Carrà, Carlo: „Invention de la peinture futuriste au Caffè Centro“. In: Lemaire, Gérard-Georges, op. cit., S. 102–103
130 Ibid.
131 Prévot, Réné: *Bohème*. München 1922, S. 91
132 Kraus, Karl: *Demolierte Literatur*. Wien 1897, zitiert nach Weigel, Hans, op. cit., S. 62
133 So der Titel einer Wiener Ausstellung aus dem Jahre 1985: „Traum und Wirklichkeit. Wien 1870–1930“, Ausstellung, Historisches Museum der Stadt Wien im Künstlerhaus. Wien 1985
134 Felix Salten ist sowohl Autor der von Walt Disney verfilmten „Bambigeschichte“ (*Bambi. Eine Lebensgeschichte aus dem Walde*. Berlin 1923), wie auch des pornografischen Romans: Josephine Mutzenbacher: *Die Geschichte einer Wienerischen Dirne, von ihr selbst erzählt*, Wien 1906
135 Jünger, Wolfgang, op. cit., S. 145
136 Als Erfinder der Kaffeehauskonzerte, die bis in das 20. Jahrhundert hinein zu den Attraktionen gehörten, gilt Martin Wiegand, der nahe dem Kärtner Tor 1789, im Jahr der Stürmung der Pariser Bastille, ein solches zum ersten Mal veranstaltete.
137 Weigel, Hans, op. cit., S. 15
138 Bodor, Ferenc, *Die Pressos der Stadt*. Budapest 1992
139 Zu den prominentesten Gästen des Landtmann gehörten Oskar Kokoschka, Max Reinhardt, Marlene Dietrich, Gary Cooper und Oskar Werner.
140 Rössner, Michael: „Aperçus de la vie de café“. In: Lemaire, Gérard-Georges, op. cit., S. 57
141 Schweitzer, Claus: „68 Prose Cafés. Stadtcafés zum Wohlfühlen“. In: *Swiss magazine* 11/2005, S. 68–71
142 Siehe hierzu: Guagnini, Enrico: *Locali Storici d'Italia/Historical Places of Italy. Cafés, Restaurants, Hotels*. Mailand 2000
143 Polgar, Alfred, in: Weigel, Hans, op. cit., S. 69
144 Kesten, Hermann, op. cit., S. 8

The Cosmos of the Hotel

Der Kosmos des Hotels

Here we give a short history of accommodation and its typological analysis to sketch the evolvement of the building type of the hotel, especially of the 'Grand Hotel': 'From Inn to Luxury Hotel'. Furthermore the phenomenon of social segregation is illustrated by the hotel as a mirror of the urban macrocosm: 'On and Behind the Stage'. In addition we want to show what role the hotel played as a motor of urbanization in the context of a growing tourism: 'From Purpose-Oriented Travel to Tourism: The Urbanization of the Countryside'. Finally, the chapter 'Surface Culture' treats the exploitation of the names of famous guests as well as the use of handsome historical buildings.

From Inn[1] to Luxury Hotel

'Hospitality is the custom of accommodating strangers in need of shelter, food and protection.'[2] This either took the form of hospitableness—as already mentioned in Homer's *Odyssey* or was practised professionally (commercialisation of hospitality). To be a host was only possible if one had appropriate rooms at one's disposition. The guest's answer to hospitality commonly was a gift or donation. In the context of temple visits or the Olympic Games professional accommodation evolved in ancient Greece. Mainly in Athens and Sparta the job was done by means of simple hostels called *leschen* (*lechos* = pallet). Later on in all big cities, *pandokeen* developed for the use of discerning travellers, if those lacked personal relations in the respective cities. Along the country roads with their increasing traffic, *katagonias* served as accommodation for strangers (without service of food).[3] Amongst many other Roman emperors Nero (37–68 A.D.) and Hadrian (76–138 A.D.) decreed the building of *tabernae* and *praetoriae* along country and military roads as well as on the coast of the Red Sea. Juridically, long before this time a categorisation for the *hospitium* (later hospice) as a house of accommodation was defined. One discerned between *caupo* and *stabularius*. A *caupo* was someone 'qui patitur viatores in caupona manere'—who accommodated travellers commercially. A *stabularius* was a person 'qui permittit, iumenta apud eum stabulari', i.e. who combined stables with his inn.[4] Moreover, Romans made a difference between *tabernarius*, the eating house and *popinarius* the taproom. For people not travelling on foot mule, horse and horse-and-cart were the customary means of transport. Guesthouses, inns, *auberges* or *albergi* till the

Hier soll zunächst anhand einer kurzen Geschichte der Beherbergung und einer typologischen Analyse die Herausbildung der Baugattung Hotel, insbesondere des Grand Hotels geschildert werden: „Von der Herberge zum Luxushotel". Des weiteren wird die im Hotel als Widerspiegelung des urbanen Makrokosmos anzutreffende soziale Segregation beleuchtet: „Vor und hinter den Kulissen". Darüber hinaus soll aufgezeigt werden, welche Rolle infolge des wachsenden Tourismus dem Hotel als einem Motor der Urbanisierung zukommt: „Von der Zweckreise zum Tourismus. Die Verstädterung der Landschaft". Abschließend behandelt das Kapitel „Der Schrei nach dem schönen Schein" die Instrumentalisierung des Namens berühmter Gäste wie auch die Nutzung attraktiver historischer Bauten.

Von der Herberge[1] zum Luxushotel

„Hospitality is the custom of accommodating strangers in need of shelter, food, and protection."[2] Dies geschah aus Gastfreundschaft – schon in der *Odyssee* ist davon die Rede – oder gewerbsmäßig (Kommerzialisierung der Gastfreundschaft). Gastgeber konnte nur sein, wer über entsprechende Räumlichkeiten verfügte. Der Gast revanchierte sich mit Geschenken. Die gewerbsmäßige Unterbringung in Griechenland bildete sich im Zusammenhang mit Tempelbesuchen und den Olympischen Spielen heraus. Vor allem in Athen und Sparta waren dies einfachere Herbergen, die *Leschen* (*leschos* = Lagerbett). Später entstanden in allen größeren Städten *Pandokeen* für anspruchsvollere Reisende, wenn diesen die Gastfreundschaftsbeziehungen am Ort fehlten. An den Landstraßen dienten mit zunehmendem Reiseverkehr *Katagonien* der Unterbringung (ohne Bewirtung) von Fremden.[3] Zur Zeit des römischen Imperiums haben neben vielen anderen römischen Kaisern Nero (37–68 n. Chr.) und Hadrian (76–138 n. Chr.) über die Anlage von *Tabernen* und *Praetoria* an Heer- und Landstraßen in Thrakien und entlang des Roten Meeres verfügt. Juristisch existierte schon lange davor eine Kategorisierung für das *Hospitium* (später Hospiz), das Haus zum Übernachten. Man unterschied zwischen *Caupo* und *Stabularius*. Ein „Caupo war, 'qui patitur viatores in caupona manere', wer also Fremde gewerbsmäßig beherbergte. Stabularius, 'qui permittit, iumenta apud eum stabulari', d. h., wer Viehunterstände mit seinem Gasthause verband."[4] Darüber hinaus unterschieden die Römer noch das *Tabernarius*,

introduction of modern means of transportation usually offered stabling, too.

Since Roman times, guest houses and inns bear names.[5] The habit of naming inns after a coat of arms goes back to the custom of travelling sovereigns to fix their coat of arms to the door or window of an inn. Frequently travelling noblemen also left their escutcheons as an acknowledgement of services rendered. Therefore it served as a recommendation for an inn to possess as many of those escutcheons as possible. Here we have the beginnings of a tendency and a marketing mechanism that was to play an important role up to the days of the Grand Hotel and even today. If a hotel can count prominent clients among its guests, the kudos and with it the degree of booking can be boosted.

A specific reason to establish professional inns was offered by pilgrimages and crusades. Since the council of Carthage in 398 a bishop was obliged to 'erect a hostel near the church'.[6] Wherever monasteries were not able to offer sufficient shelter themselves, monastic orders installed hospices or taverns that also catered for commercial travellers. The most famous kind of accommodation for travelling salesmen were caravanserais. In the Orient, they served as accommodation along the caravan routes spaced for the distance of a day's journey.[7] In China, the inns were similar to the caravanserais.

As a rule, the travellers brought their own bedclothes along.[8] For centuries the roadhouses were—with few exceptions—not places of refinement. In his *colloquia* Erasmus of Rotterdam criticises that nobody cares for arrivals, that the water to wash hands was so dirty that one had to look for another source of water to remedy the result of the first ablution. In a single room frequently more than 80 or 90 guests were assembled:

> 'Wayfarers, horsemen, merchants, boatmen, wagoners, farmers, boys, women, healthy and sick persons. Here somebody combs his hair, there another gets rid of his sweat, still another one may clean shoes or boots, somebody belches with garlic, in short it is a tangle of languages and people like at the construction of the tower of Babylon.'[9]

Like the present, also the past knew differences in quality of houses of hospitality. Michel de Montaigne in his diaries also reports positive things about them. There is talk of a pumping station in an Augsburg inn, which

das Speisehaus, und das *Popinarius*, die Schankstube. Maulesel, Pferd und Pferdefuhrwerk waren für den, der nicht zu Fuß ging, die gebräuchlichen Transportmittel. Gasthof, *Inn*, *Auberge*, *Albergo* boten bis zur Einführung moderner Transportmittel neben der Beherbergung in den meisten Fällen Stallungen an.

Seit Römerzeiten tragen Wirtshäuser und Gasthöfe Namen.[5] Die Sitte, ein Wirtshaus nach einem Wappen zu benennen, geht auf die Gewohnheit reisender Fürsten und Herren zurück, die ihr Wappenschild am Tor oder Fenster eines Gasthauses befestigten. Oftmals ließen adlige Reisende als Anerkennung geleisteter Dienste ihre Wappenschilder zurück. So galt es als besondere Empfehlung, möglichst viele dieser Wappenschilder zu haben. Hier bahnt sich eine Tendenz, ein Vermarktungsmechanismus, an, der dann in der Hochzeit der Grand Hotels und bis heute eine Rolle spielt. Zählt ein Hotel berühmte Persönlichkeiten zu seinen Gästen, so steigen Renomée und damit Buchungszahlen.

Einen besonderen Antrieb zur Errichtung gewerbsmäßiger Herbergen und Herbergsstationen boten Wallfahrten und Kreuzzüge. Bereits seit dem Konzil von Karthago im Jahr 398 war ein Bischof verpflichtet, „in der Nähe der Kirche eine Herberge zu errichten."[6] Wo die Klöster nicht selbst oder nur unzureichende Unterkunft boten, errichteten Mönchsorden Hospize und Tabernen, die auch der Unterbringung von Handelsreisenden dienten. Die berühmteste Form der Unterbringung von Handlungsreisenden sind die Karawansereien. Im Orient dienten sie, jeweils im Abstand von Tagesreisen an den Karawanenstraßen angeordnet, den Handelskarawanen als Unterkunft.[7] Die Herbergen in China glichen diesen Karawansereien.

Auch brachte der Reisende sein eigenes Bettzeug mit.[8] Über Jahrhunderte ist – mit wenigen Ausnahmen – das Gasthaus keine Stätte der Zivilisation. In seinen *Familiarum Colloquiorum Formulae* bemängelt Erasmus von Rotterdam, dass sich kein Mensch um den Ankommenden kümmere, dass das Wasser zum Händewaschen so dreckig sei, dass man sich nach anderem umsehen müsse, um die eben vorgenommene Waschung abzuspülen. In einem Raum kamen häufig 80 bis 90 Gäste zusammen:

> „Reisende zu Fuß, Reiter, Kaufleute, Schiffer, Fuhrleute, Bauern, Knaben, Weiber, Gesunde und Kranke. Hier kämmt einer sich das Haupthaar, dort wäscht sich ein

1
Thomas Rowlandson's 1791 caricature 'Inn Yard on Fire' shows an inn typical of the time, with galleries and accommodation for horses and coaches

Mit Galerien, Unterstellmöglichkeiten für Pferde und Wagen zeigt diese Karikatur „Feuer in einem Gasthofe" von Thomas Rowlandson, 1791, eine zeittypische Herberge

according to need was able to supply kitchens and every other place with fresh water—in the sixteenth century a truly rare domestic installation of a technological character. The following makes one think of the extravaganzas of the Grand Hotels of the Belle Époque:

> 'We stayed at the Krone, a decent inn. Into the wainscoting of the dining hall a kind of cage was inserted, in which a greater number of birds found room. Poised gangways, hung from brass wires crossed the room and enabled the birds to promenade.'[10]
>
> 'Mr. Montaigne there also made the attempt to cover himself in bed by a duvet which is in use there and was very content with it; he saw that it was an equally warm and lightweight cover.'[11]

anderer den Schweiß ab, noch ein anderer reinigt sich die Schuhe oder Reitstiefel, jenem stößt der Knoblauch auf, kurz, es ist ein Wirrwarr der Sprachen und Personen wie beim Turmbau zu Babel."[9]

Wie die heutige, so kannte auch die damalige Zeit Qualitätsunterschiede bei den Beherbergungshäusern. Michel de Montaigne weiß in seinen Reisetagebüchern Positiveres zu berichten. So ist die Rede von einem Pumpwerk in einem Gasthaus in Augsburg, das nach Bedarf die Küche und jeden anderen Ort mit Wasser versorgen konnte – im 16. Jahrhundert wahrlich eine außergewöhnliche haustechnische Installation. An die Extravaganzen der Grand Hotels der Belle Époque lässt die folgende Schilderung Montaignes denken:

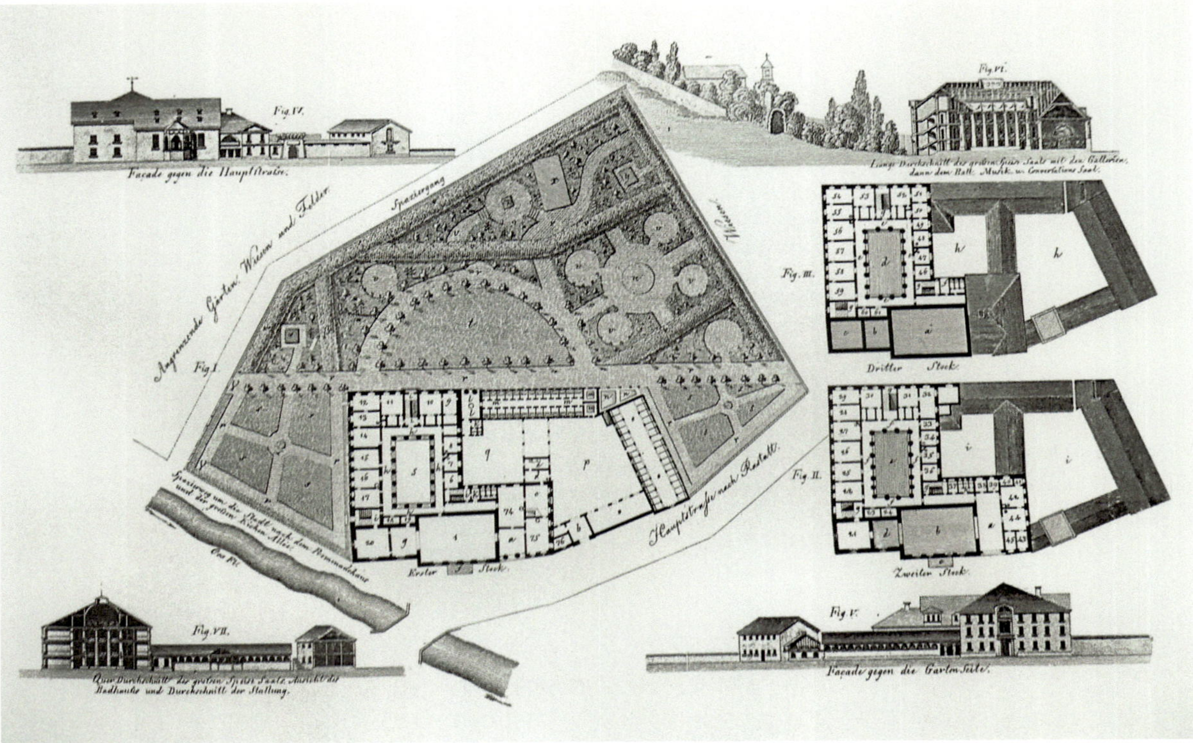

2

Hotel 'Badischer Hof', 1807–1809, Baden-Baden, by Friedrich Weinbrenner

Hotel Badischer Hof, 1807–1809, von Friedrich Weinbrenner, in Baden-Baden

3

'Tremont House', Boston, 1829, by Isaiah Rogers ● 'Astor Hotel', New York, 1794-1796, by Benjamin H. Latrobe

Hotel Tremont House, 1829, von Isaiah Rogers, in Boston ● Astor Hotel, 1794-1796, von Benjamin H. Latrobe, in New York

Much more typical however for the accommodation at the time were situations like those described by Johann Wolfgang von Goethe:

> 'In the first place the doors do not have locks … secondly the windows are covered by oiled paper instead of glass, thirdly a most necessary facility is lacking… When I asked the servant for a certain facility, he pointed down into the courtyard 'Qui abasso può server si!' I asked: 'Dove?'—'Da per tutto, dove vuol' (1786, from Italy).[12] (fig. 1)

And Prosper Mérimée reports:

> 'We arrived at the tavern ... one big room served as kitchen and equally as dining hall and dormitory. On a slab of stone in the middle of the room an open fire was burning. Along the wall one could see five or six greasy mule blankets spread out; those were the beds for the night lodgers.'[13]

Where there were bedsteads, one protected oneself by calf-, goat- or deerskins against the vermin that existed in abundance. In cities as well as in swanky holiday destinations[14] the conditions of accommodation looked better. Reference reading here is William Makepeace Thackeray who in his novel *Vanity Fair* describes hotels on the Rhine, in Brussels and London in Napoleon's time.[15]

The Baden-Baden hotel 'Badischer Hof' (fig. 2), built from 1807–1809, is regarded as an early prototype of the European luxury hotel. Its American pendant may be seen in Boston's 'Tremont House' from 1829 (fig. 3). Its 170 rooms by far outclassed the considerably smaller number of rooms of its contemporaries. The Tremont had one and two-bed rooms and 'service included such novelties as an individual lock on the door, a bowl and a pitcher and free soap for every guest room.'[16] '[T]he claim was made for or of being the 'pioneer first-class hotel in America.'[17] Charles Dickens during his first stay in America called it 'a very excellent one'.[18] 'Badischer Hof' with its 70 rooms was indeed considerably smaller than the American 'Tremont House'. But in Baden-Baden we have—in an epoch of a scarcely developed art of running a hotel and a table d'hôte—the first evidences of the type of a real luxury hotel. The two developers of 'Badischer Hof', the Baden privy councillor Johann Ludwig Klüber and renowned publisher Johann Friedrich Cotta ('Cotta, the Napoleon amongst the booksellers'[19]),

> „Wir wohnten in der Krone, einem hübschen Gasthaus. In das Tafelwerk des Speisesaals war eine Art Käfig eingebrochen, in dem eine große Anzahl Vögel Platz fanden. Schwebegänge, die mit Messingdrähten aufgehängt waren und von einem Ende des Zimmers bis zum anderen gingen, dienten den Vögeln zum Spazierengehen."[10]
> „Der Herr Montaigne machte dort auch einen Versuch, sich im Bett mit einer Federdecke zu bedecken, wie es dort Gebrauch ist und war sehr damit zufrieden; er sah, daß es eine zugleich warme und leichte Bedeckung war."[11]

Typisch für die Beherbergung aber waren Situationen, wie sie Johann Wolfgang von Goethe im Folgenden beschreibt:

> „erstlich haben die Türen keine Schlösser … zweitens sind die Fenster mit Ölpapier statt mit Glasscheiben geschlossen, drittens fehlt eine höchst nötige Bequemlichkeit … Als ich den Hausknecht nach einer gewissen Gelegenheit fragte, deutete er in den Hof hinunter ‚Qui abasso può servir si!' Ich fragte: 'Dove?' – 'Da per tutto, dove vuol.'" (1786, aus Italien).[12] (Abb. 1)

Und auch Prosper Mérimée berichtet:

> „Wir langten bei der Schenke an. … Ein großer Raum diente als Küche, Eß- und Schlafzimmer zugleich. Auf einem flachen Stein mitten im Zimmer brannte ein offenes Feuer .. Die Wand entlang sah man auf dem bloßen Boden fünf oder sechs schmierige Maultierdecken ausgebreitet; das waren die Betten für die Schlafgänger."[13]

Dort, wo Bettgestelle vorhanden waren, schützte man sich durch Kalbs-, Ziegen- oder Hirschhäute gegen das reichlich vorhandene Ungeziefer. In den Städten sowie in mondänen Feriendestinationen[14] sahen die Beherbergungskonditionen besser aus. Nachzulesen ist das unter anderem bei William Makepeace Thackeray, der in seinem Roman *Vanity Fair* in napoleonischer Zeit Hotels am Rhein, in Brüssel und London beschreibt.[15]

Als ein früher Prototyp des luxuriösen Hotels in Europa gilt der Badische Hof (Abb. 2) in Baden-Baden (1807–1809). Als sein amerikanisches Pendant ist das Tremont House in Boston (1829) anzusehen (Abb. 3). Mit 170 Zimmern übertraf es bei weitem die bislang üblicherweise nicht mehr als 30 Zimmer zählenden Beherbergungsstätten. Das Tremont hatte Ein- und

4

The dining hall of the 'Badischer Hof', ca. 1810, by J. St. Schaffroth ● Hotel 'Beau-Rivage et d'Angleterre', Geneva, 1865, by Antoine Krafft ● 'Hotel Verenahof', Baden-Baden, 1845, by Kaspar Joseph Jeuch

Speisesaal Badischer Hof um 1810, von J. St. Schaffroth ● Hotel Beau-Rivage et d'Angleterre, 1865, von Antoine Krafft, in Genf ● Hotel Verenahof, 1845, von Kaspar Joseph Jeuch, in Baden-Baden

'wanted the perfect hotel palace that offered its guests in the different price brackets a good kitchen, luxurious possibilities to take a bath (12 rooms had bathing installations) a garden, a theatre with casino, rooms for balls and billiard, a library, even a bookshop. Taken together with the fact that a good deal of foodstuffs came from the hotel's chicken run and vegetable garden, the hotel resembled a kind of city within the city.'[20]

As architect one could enroll Friedrich Weinbrenner[21], one of the most prominent architects of the neo-classicism period. For the 'Badischer Hof', Weinbrenner probably was lured by the task of converting a monastery into a modern hotel furnished with all imaginable comfort. The requirements included to 'convert the monastery's central space into a hall that takes its light from a cupola and around which on all three levels a gallery will run in front of the sitting rooms, from which one can look down on the hall.'[22] This model survives to the present day as the type of 'atrium' hotel that is exemplified amongst others by the Barcelona hotel 'Rey Juan Carlos . In 14 storeys, behind the glass parapets of the balconies the doors to the individual rooms become visible.[23] As someone who rediscovered the galleries under a glass-domed inner yard such as in 'Badischer Hof' John Calvin Portman is regarded. Here, the atriums of Jean Baptiste André Godin's Familistère[24] (1859), inspired by François Marie Charles Fourier come to mind. In the 1967 Atlanta as well as in the San Francisco 'Hyatt Regency' the atrium serves as a three-dimensional stage 'where interactivity is possible again that since the period of the palace hotels was not possible any more.'[25] (fig. 4) But let us get back to the hotel 'Badischer Hof' that Weinbrenner would have liked to have called 'Karlsbad' so as to profit from the reputation of the celebrated Bohemian spa of that name. In Baden Baden the name remained 'Badischer Hof'. Beside the disposition of the rooms it was to anticipate still another feature of the future Grand Hotels. Into the pattern of rooms, Weinbrenner integrates the model of the culture of leisure of the royal and noble palaces and that of the bourgeois ballrooms. To this purpose the church of the unutilised Capuchin monastery was to be reused as conversation-, gambling-, concert- or ballrooms as well as 'for a small convertible theatre'[26] for the use of longer-staying guests.

Much more pragmatic and exclusively aimed at the accommodation of short-stay-guests Jean Nicolas Louis

Zweibettzimmer, „service included such novelties as an individual lock on the door, a bowl and a pitcher and free soap for every guest room."[16] „[T]he claim was made for or of being the ‚pioneer first class-hotel in America'."[17] Charles Dickens bezeichnet es während seines ersten Amerikaaufenthaltes als „a very excellent one."[18] Der Badische Hof war mit circa 70 Zimmern zwar kleiner als das amerikanische Tremont House. Aber hier in Baden-Baden sind – in einer Zeit, zu der die Kunst der Hotellerie und Gastronomie noch wenig entwickelt war – erste Ansätze hin zum Luxushotel zu erkennen. Die beiden Bauherren, der badische Staatsrat Johann Ludwig Klüber und der renommierte Verleger Johann Friedrich Cotta, „Cotta, der Napoleon unter den Buchhändlern"[19],

„wollten den perfekten Hotelpalast, der seinen Gästen in verschiedenen Preisklassen eine gute Küche, luxuriöse Bademöglichkeiten (zwölf Zimmer mit eigener Badeeinrichtung), eine Gartenanlage, ein Theater mit Spielcasino, Säle für Bälle und Billard, eine Bibliothek, ja eine eigene Buchhandlung anbieten sollte. Nimmt man hinzu, dass ein Großteil der Viktualien aus dem Hühnerhof und Gemüsegarten des Hotels stammte, so stellte es eine Art Stadt in der Stadt vor."[20]

Als Architekten konnten sie mit Friedrich Weinbrenner[21] einen der renommiertesten Architekten des Klassizismus gewinnen. Weinbrenner wird am Badischen Hof vor allem die Umwandlung eines Klosters in ein modernes, mit allem erdenklichen Komfort ausgestattetes Hotel gereizt haben. Vorgaben waren: „Den Mittelraum im Kloster in einen Saal zu verwandeln, der sein Licht durch eine Kuppel erhält, und um welchen in allen drei Etagen die Gallerie vor den Wohnzimmern herumläuft, so dass man von solcher in den Saal herabsieht."[22] Ein Prinzip, das bis heute in Atrium-Hotels fortlebt, wie unter anderem im Barceloneser Hotel Rey Juan Carlos. In 14 Obergeschossen werden hinter gläsernen Balkonbrüstungen die Türen zu den Hotelzimmern sichtbar.[23] Als Wiederentdecker der im Badischen Hof um einen glasüberdeckten Innenhof angelegten Galerien (zu denken ist hier auch an die von François Marie Charles Fouriers Phalanstère inspirierten Innenhöfe des Familistère[24] von Jean Baptiste André Godin, ab 1859) gilt John Calvin Portman. Im Hyatt Regency Atlanta, 1967, wie auch im Hyatt Regency in San Francisco dient das Atrium als dreidimensionale Bühne, „wo wieder

5
'Caravanserai de Cachan' and 'Caravanserai près de Sultanie, en Perse' (from C.N.L. Durand: Recueil, 1800)

„Carawanserai de Cachan" und „Caravanserai près de Sultanie, en Perse" (von C.N.L. Durand: *Recueil*, 1800)

Durand's design for the 'Hotellerie et Poste' comes along. After Johann Bernhard Fischer von Erlach[27], Durand is the first to establish in 1800, 1801–05 and 1821 building typologies.[28] As teacher at the École Polytechnique in Paris he analyses the procedural development of building typologies. Concerning the hotel, for him it is the derivation from the caravanserai that seems exemplary.[29] In 1800 he publishes samples in his *Recueil et parallèles des édifices....* In his *Précis des leçons d'architecture...*, 1801–05, the caravanserai serves as a model for his design for a hotel.[30] (fig. 5)

As one can see from the example of Durand's considerations and the 'Badischer Hof', different categories of hotels can be discerned. Diversification increases with growing tourism and the growing number of hotels in its wake. Parameters that signify these differences are:

Duration of stay (a few nights up to semipermanent or permanent residence in 'boarding houses' and 'apartment hotels'[31] or 'pensions'). Location of the hotel in the city centre as middle class or Grand Hotel; special type of railway[32] or (today) airport hotel; in the countryside as spa, wellness or resort hotel. Categories or class of a hotel chiefly are determined by the requirements and financial potential of the clientele. 'The first class hotel or *grand*

Interaktion möglich ist wie in Hotels seit den Zeiten der Palasthotels nicht mehr."[25] (Abb. 4) Aber kehren wir zurück zum Badischen Hof, den Weinbrenner gern „Karlsbad" benannt hätte, um von der Reputation des berühmten böhmischen Kurbades zu profitieren. Es blieb bei Badischer Hof. Und dieser nimmt neben der räumlichen Disposition der Zimmer noch ein anderes Phänomen der späteren Grand Hotels vorweg. Er integriert in sein Raumangebot die Freizeitkultur der königlichen und adligen Paläste und der bürgerlichen Redouten. So sollte für die länger verweilenden Gäste die Kirche des ungenutzten Kapuzinerklosters zu Konversations-, Spiel-, Konzert- und Ballsälen „nebst einem kleinen wandelbaren Theater"[26] umgenutzt werden.

Weitaus pragmatischer und ausschließlich auf die Beherbergungs- und Bewirtungsanforderungen eines Kurzaufenthaltes beschränkt, sieht der Entwurf von Jean-Nicolas-Louis Durands „Hotellerie et Poste" aus. Nach Johann Bernhard Fischer von Erlach[27] ist Durand in der Neuzeit der erste, der 1800, 1801–1805 und 1821 Bautypologien aufstellt.[28] Als Lehrer an der École Polytechnique in Paris analysiert er die prozessmäßige Entwicklung von Gebäudetypologien. In Bezug auf das Hotel ist das bei ihm die Herleitung von der Karawan-

6
Georges Auguste Escoffier, 1846–1935 ● César Ritz, 1850–1918
Georges Auguste Escoffier, 1846–1935 ● César Ritz, 1850–1918

hotel by and by has obtained a cosmopolitan character, thanks to the proliferation of wealth and the compensating influence of international communication. One can therefore abstain from designating the national characteristics of modern hotels in the capitals of Europe', Eduard Guyer writes as early as 1874.[33]

After the Second World War one can hardly speak of a national, respectively individual-typological character of most of the hotels any more. With Conrad Hilton[34] at the latest the suggestion is to identify a hotel as part of a chain of hotels and not as part of a specific location. Man the nomad[35] changes countries and continents but is to find an identical ambience to help with his orientation. Of course, symptoms of fatigue occur because of this uniformity. Design-, Art- or Boutique-hotels are the answer today. Even if Guyer denies the Grand Hotels a national identity, they at least each had their individual flair. In terms of style, they followed contemporary pluralisms such as Historicism, Art Nouveau or Art Deco. What gave them an individual note however, was the specific management of a hotel. One of the elements was the celebration of the guest's sojourn.

Primus inter pares amongst these stage directors of hotel life no doubt was César Ritz. 'In theatrical terms,

serei, die ihm als vorbildlich erscheint.[29] 1800 publiziert er in seinen *Recueil et parallèles des édifices* … Beispiele. In den *Précis des leçons d'architecture* … 1801–1805 dann dient ihm die Karawanserei als Basis für seinen Hotelentwurf.[30] (Abb. 5)

Wie am Beispiel des Vorschlags von Durand und am Badischen Hof zu sehen ist, sind bereits früh Hotelgattungen zu unterscheiden. Die Diversifizierung nimmt mit dem wachsenden Tourismus und den in seiner Folge entstehenden Hotels zu. Faktoren, die diese Unterschiedlichkeit kennzeichnen sind: die Verweildauer (wenige Nächte bis hin zu semi- bis permanentem Verbleib in Boarding Houses und Apartmenthotels[31] oder Pensionen); die Lage des Hotels (in der Stadt als Mittelklasse- oder Grand Hotel oder als Sondertypus eines Bahnhofs-[32] oder heute Flughafenhotels oder in der Landschaft als Bade-, Kur- oder Naturszenenhotel (Resort- Hotel)). Auch wird die Gattung und Klasse eines Hotels von den Ansprüchen und finanziellen Möglichkeiten der Clientèle bestimmt. „Das Hotel ersten Ranges, das *grand hotel*, hat allmählich einen kosmopolitischen Charakter angenommen dank der Verbreitung des Wohlstandes und dem ausgleichenden Einfluss des internationalen Verkehrs. Es kann daher von einer Kennzeichnung der

7

The lavish extravagance of a stage production in the Grand Hotel: Madame Ritz, wearing a Louis-XVI-fancy dress ● Horse dancing the waltz, 'Hotel Taj Mahal', Bombay, 1952 ● Serge Lifar's 'Ballets Russes' in the 'Hotel des Bains', Venice, 1920s ● Banquet (George Kessler) in the flooded courtyard of 'Hotel Savoy', London, 1906

Extravagante Inszenierungen im Grand Hotel: Madame Ritz im Louis-XVI.-Kostüm, 1880er Jahre ● Walzer tanzendes Pferd, 1952, im Hotel Taj Mahal in Bombay ● Serge Lifar: „Ballets Russes" im Hotel des Bains in Venedig, 1920er Jahre ● Festessen (George Kessler) im gefluteten Innenhof des Hotel Savoy in London, 1906

Ritz was a showman, a brilliant director and producer, who set the stage for the star performances by the clientele.'[36] Reception as well as sojourn, everything was painstakingly matched to the respective guest and stage-managed just for him. It was a matter of course to import green figs and mangoes for Aga Khan's breakfast: 'Ritz shrewedly noted the needs and tastes of both the 'old' and the 'new' groups, whether it was ice-water for the Americans or Egyptian cigarettes for Albert Edward, Prince of Wales'.[37] Already during the Vienna World Exhibition of 1873 serving as a temporary waiter in the 'Imperial Pavilion', Ritz never failed to commit to memory the requests and habits of his renowned guests such as the Prince of Wales. The Vienna restaurant served him as a trial stage for his own qualification and promotion in the same way as should be the case for Thomas Mann's Felix Krull much later. After many stages in the hotel and restaurant business in 1880 in the Grand Hotel in Monte Carlo, Ritz joined forces with Auguste Escoffier. Under the device 'Comfort, Cuisine and Service'[38] the two further on worked in tandem (fig. 6). When the 1888 London Savoy, initiated by the London theatre impresario Richard D'Oyly Carte neared its finishing stages, he asked Ritz to take over the management.

> 'He wants the clientele I can give him … the people who come here, who go to Baden, who were my patrons at Lucerne and Monte-Carlo … he wants the Vanderbilts and Morgans, he wants the Rothschilds. He wants to make his hotel the hotel de luxe of London and of the world',[39]

Ritz notes down. The Savoy ascends to the metropolitan luxury hotel par excellence, a visit of its restaurant, the 'Dining at the Savoy' became an obligation of fashion.

> 'Whatever one may think about music as an accompaniment of the best food, it is certain that if there is to be music it must be the best music. It was Ritz who started that fashion in London, and he started it with no less a musician than Johann Strauss.'[40] (fig. 7)

Little wonder that the Prince of Wales, the later King Edward VII was moved to the following dictum: 'Where Ritz goes, I go'.[41] So he transferred his residence in Paris from the hotel 'Bristol'[42] to the 'Ritz', erected by Ritz in

nationalen Eigenthümlichkeiten moderner Hotels in den Hauptstädten Europas abgesehen werden," schreibt Eduard Guyer bereits 1874.[33]

Nach dem Zweiten Weltkrieg kann dann wohl überhaupt nicht mehr von nationalen bzw. individualtypischen Eigenschaften eines Hotels gesprochen werden. Spätestens mit Conrad Hilton[34] sollen Kettenhotels als zur Kette und nicht zum Ort gehörig identifiziert werden. Der nomadisierende moderne Mensch[35] wechselt die Länder und die Kontinente, soll aber als Orientierungshilfe stets ein identisches Ambiente vorfinden. Hier tritt ein Ermüdungseffekt ein, auf den Design-, Art- und Boutiquehotels heute eine Antwort zu geben versuchen. Auch wenn Guyer den Grand Hotels nationale Identität abspricht, so hatten sie doch ihr individuelles Flair. Stilistisch folgten sie dem Stilpluralismus des Historismus, dem Jugendstil, dem Art déco. Was ihnen aber eine persönliche Note gab, war das Management eines Hotels. Hierzu gehörte die Zelebrierung des Hotelaufenthaltes. Primus inter pares dieser Regisseure des Hotellebens war César Ritz. „In theatrical terms, Ritz was a showman, a brilliant director and producer, who set the stage for the star performances by the clientèle."[36] Empfang und Aufenthalt, alles war aufs Sorgfältigste und auf den jeweiligen Gast abgestimmt, inszeniert. Die grünen Feigen und Mangos für die Frühstücke von Aga Khan zu importieren war eine Selbstverständlichkeit. „Ritz shrewdly noted the needs and tastes of both the ‚old' and the ‚new' groups, whether it was ice-water for the Americans or Egyptian cigarettes for Albert Edward, Prince of Wales."[37] Nach vielen Stationen im Hotel- und Restaurantgewerbe tat sich Ritz 1880 im Grand Hotel in Monte Carlo mit Georges Auguste Escoffier zusammen. Unter dem Motto „Comfort, Cuisine and Service"[38] arbeiteten diese beiden Genies im Tandem (Abb. 6). Als sich die Fertigstellung des vom Londoner Theaterimpresario Richard D'Oyly Carte initiierten Hotelbaus, des Savoy, 1888 dem Ende näherte, bat er Ritz, die Leitung zu übernehmen.

> „He wants the clientèle I can give him … the people who come here, who go to Baden, who were my patrons at Lucerne and Monte-Carlo … he wants the Vanderbilts and Morgans; he wants the Rothschilds. He wants to make his hotel the Hotel de luxe of London and of the world",[39] notiert Ritz.

8

9

10

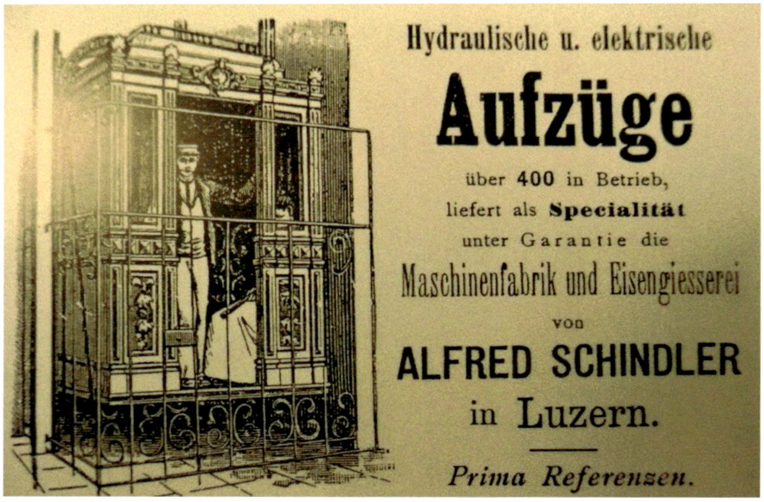

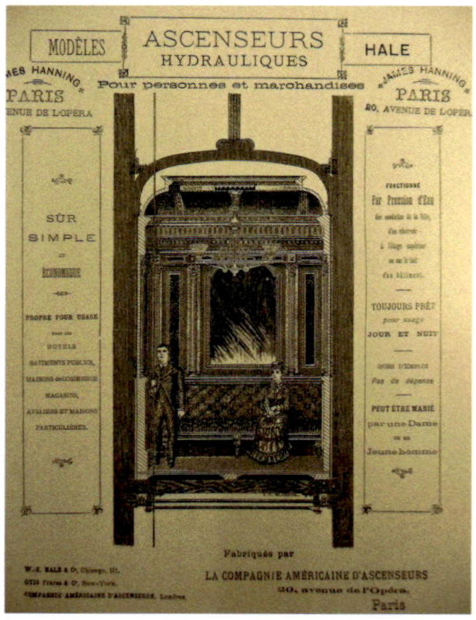

8

Bathroom in the 'Hotel Savoy,' London, around 1900 ● Bathroom in the 'Hotel Majestic', Paris, ca. 1908

Badezimmer im Savoy Hotel in London, um 1900 ● Badezimmer im Hotel Majestic in Paris, um 1908

9

'The Electrical Hotel', booklet by 'Gelsenkirchener Elektrizitätswerke'

Das elektrische Hotel, Werbebroschüre der Gelsenkirchener Elektrizitätswerke

10

Advertising brochures by the 'Compagnie Américaine d'ascenseurs' and the elevator firm Alfred Schindler, 1902

Prospekt der Compagnie Américaine d'ascenseurs und Werbebroschüre der Aufzugsfirma Alfred Schindler, 1902

1898 in the Place Vendôme.[43] Marcel Proust was one of the first clients here.

> 'The big hotel became his second home, to make up for the palaces of Cabourg[44], Venice and Evian, that he was never to see again … In the Ritz he found again the emotions and mysteries of a miniature world, the comfort and safety of family life, the gratification of his lifelong longing for rendered services and appropriate gratitude. He did his writing in his cork-protected bedroom, but to experience life, he went to the Ritz.'[45]

Ernest Hemingway who makes the Ritz his steady Paris address after the first of his book successes exults:

> 'When I dream of a later life in heaven, all is taking place in the Ritz. I down a few Martinis at the bar. Then comes a magnificent dinner under a flowering chestnut tree in the so-called 'Petite Jardin'. After a couple of Brandies I go up to my room and sink into one of these gigantic Ritz beds that all have a brass bedstead.'[46]

These brass beds as well as the assignment of a bathroom to each room were innovations introduced by Ritz. Rightly his widow in her book *César Ritz: Host to the World* asserts 'that Ritz "was one of the greatest civilizing influences of his time as regards the point of hygiene and sanitation" a claim that is by no means fanciful' [47]. How unusual this sanitary equipment was in the Europe of the 1880s, is shown by an analysis of hotel ground plans found in architectural manuals.[48] The relation between the number of rooms and of bathrooms and toilets was incredibly poor. As late as 1889 Richard D'Oyly Carte was laughed at when he wished for a better ratio of numbers for his London 'Savoy' hotel.

> 'When D'Oyly stipulated that the Savoy should have seventy bathrooms the builder asked him if he were providing for amphibian guests: if he had stipulated then for a bathroom for every room (what Ritz later offered in Paris) he might have been asked if he were erecting an aquarium. Spain is notoriously conservative, but in December 1901 the leading hotel in Madrid had only one bathroom situated in a kind of vault for the use of which a charge of five pesetas was levied from the eccentric guest who wanted to use it, and in those days that was a quarter of the daily charge for board and lodging. Even in London

Das Savoy avanciert zum metropolitanen Luxushotel par excellence, der Besuch seines Restaurants, das „dining out at the Savoy" wird zur modischen Verpflichtung.

> „Whatever one may think about music as an accompaniment of the best food, it is certain that if there is to be music it must be the best music. It was Ritz who started that fashion in London, and he started it with no less a musician than Johann Strauss."[40] (Abb. 7)

Kein Wunder, dass der Prince of Wales, der spätere König Edward VII., zu folgendem Ausspruch gelangte: „Where Ritz goes, I go."[41] So verlegte er seinen Aufenthalt in Paris vom Hotel Bristol[42] in das von Ritz an der Place Vendôme 1898 errichtete Ritz.[43] Marcel Proust war dort einer der ersten Gäste.

> „Das große Hotel wurde zu seinem zweiten Heim, zum Ersatz für die Paläste von Cabourg[44], Venedig und Evian, die er nie wiedersehen sollte … Im Ritz fand er wieder die Regungen und Rätsel einer Miniatur-Welt, die Behaglichkeit und Sicherheit von Familienleben, die Befriedigung seiner lebenslangen Sehnsucht nach erwiesenem Dienst und entsprechendem Dank. Er schrieb in seinem korkgeschützten Schlafzimmer, aber um zu leben, ging er ins Ritz."[45]

Und Ernest Hemingway, der das Ritz nach seinen ersten Bucherfolgen zu seiner festen Pariser Adresse macht, jubelt:

> „Wenn ich von einem späteren Leben im Himmel träume, dann spielt sich alles immer im Ritz ab. Ich kippe in der Bar … ein paar Martinis. Dann kommt ein wunderbares Dîner unter einem blühenden Kastanienbaum im sogenannten ‚Petit Jardin'. Nach ein paar Brandys gehe ich dann hinauf in mein Zimmer und sinke in eines dieser riesigen Ritzbetten, die alle ein Messinggestell haben."[46]

Diese Messingbetten wie auch die Zuordnung eines Bades zu jedem Zimmer waren Neuerungen, die Ritz einführte. Zu Recht behauptet seine Witwe in ihrem Buch *César Ritz: Host to the World* „that Ritz ‚was one of the greatest civilizing influences of his time as regards this point of hygiene and sanitation' a claim that is by no means fanciful."[47] Wie ungewöhnlich diese Sanitärausstattung noch in den 1880er Jahren in Europa

11

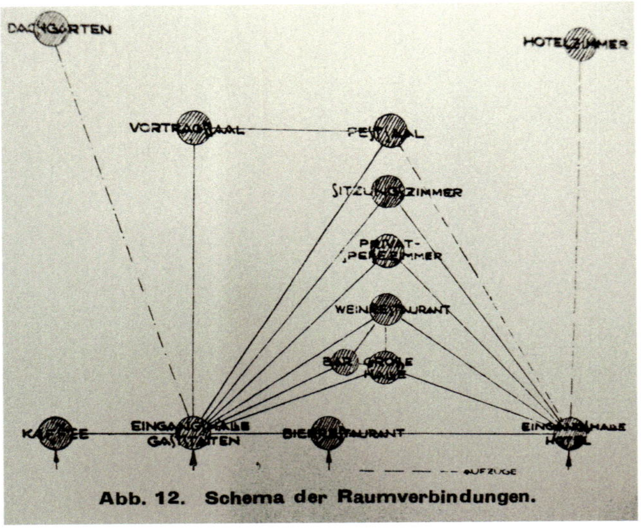

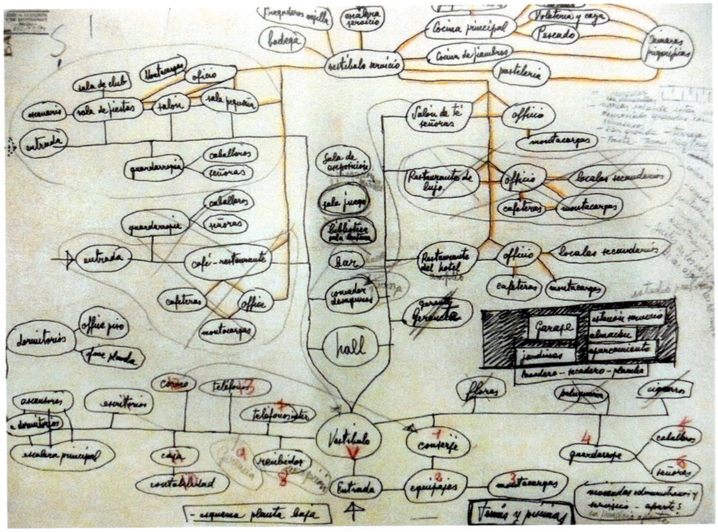

11
Diagram of the relations of rooms in a hotel ● Sketch of service and room relations, by J. A. Coderch de Sentmenat, 1962

Schema der Raumverbindungen in einem Hotel ● Skizze der Service- und Raumzuordnungen, von J. A. Coderch de Sentmenat, 1962

12
Hotel floorplans: hotel in North America by Hermann von der Hude and F. Baumann, Chicago, 1885 ● ‚Hotel Bellevue', Wildbad, 1842 ● ‚Hotel Austria', Vienna, by Fränkel

Hotelgrundrisse: Nordamerikanisches Hotel, 1885, von Hermann von der Hude und F. Baumann in Chicago ● Hotel Bellevue in Wildbad, 1842 ● Hotel Austria in Wien, 1870er Jahre, von Fränkel

the Hotel Victoria, opened two years before the Savoy at a cost of £ 520,000, had only four bathrooms for five hundred visitors, and no more had been added in 1897. In fact, the astonishing number of bathrooms at the Savoy, upon which D'Oyly Carte insisted, was indeed an innovation and set the standard for the future.'[49] (fig. 8)

'It were the devices that made the modern hotel modern'[50], Jefferson Williams writes in *The American Hotel*. 'Homes are becoming more hotel-like' the hotel men say, and they are thinking of the way in which hotels have pioneered in such things as bathtubs (even German emperor Wilhelm I. (1871–1888) has a bathtub brought to the chateau from the 'Hôtel de Rome'[51]), modern heating arrangements, and comfortable beds.'[52]

In Europe, Swiss hotels play a pioneering role. In 1847 the Geneva 'Hotel des Bergues' had the first flush lavatories, in 1866 the Samedan 'Hotel Bernina' had

war, zeigt eine Analyse der in einschlägigen Handbüchern zu findenden Hotelgrundrisse.[48] Das Verhältnis von Zimmerzahl und Anzahl der Bäder und WCs war unglaublich schlecht. Noch 1889 war Richard D'Oyly Carte verlacht worden, als er für sein Londoner Savoy-Hotel ein besseres Zahlenverhältnis wünschte.

„When D'Oyly stipulated that the Savoy should have seventy bathrooms the builder asked him if he were providing for amphibian guests: if he had stipulated then for a bathroom for every room [was Ritz dann in Paris anbot] he might have been asked if he were erecting an aquarium. Spain is notoriously conservative, but in December 1901 the leading hotel in Madrid had only one bathroom situated in a kind of vault for the use of which a charge of five pesetas was levied on the eccentric guest who wanted to use it, and in those days that was a quarter of the daily charge for board and lodging. Even in London

12

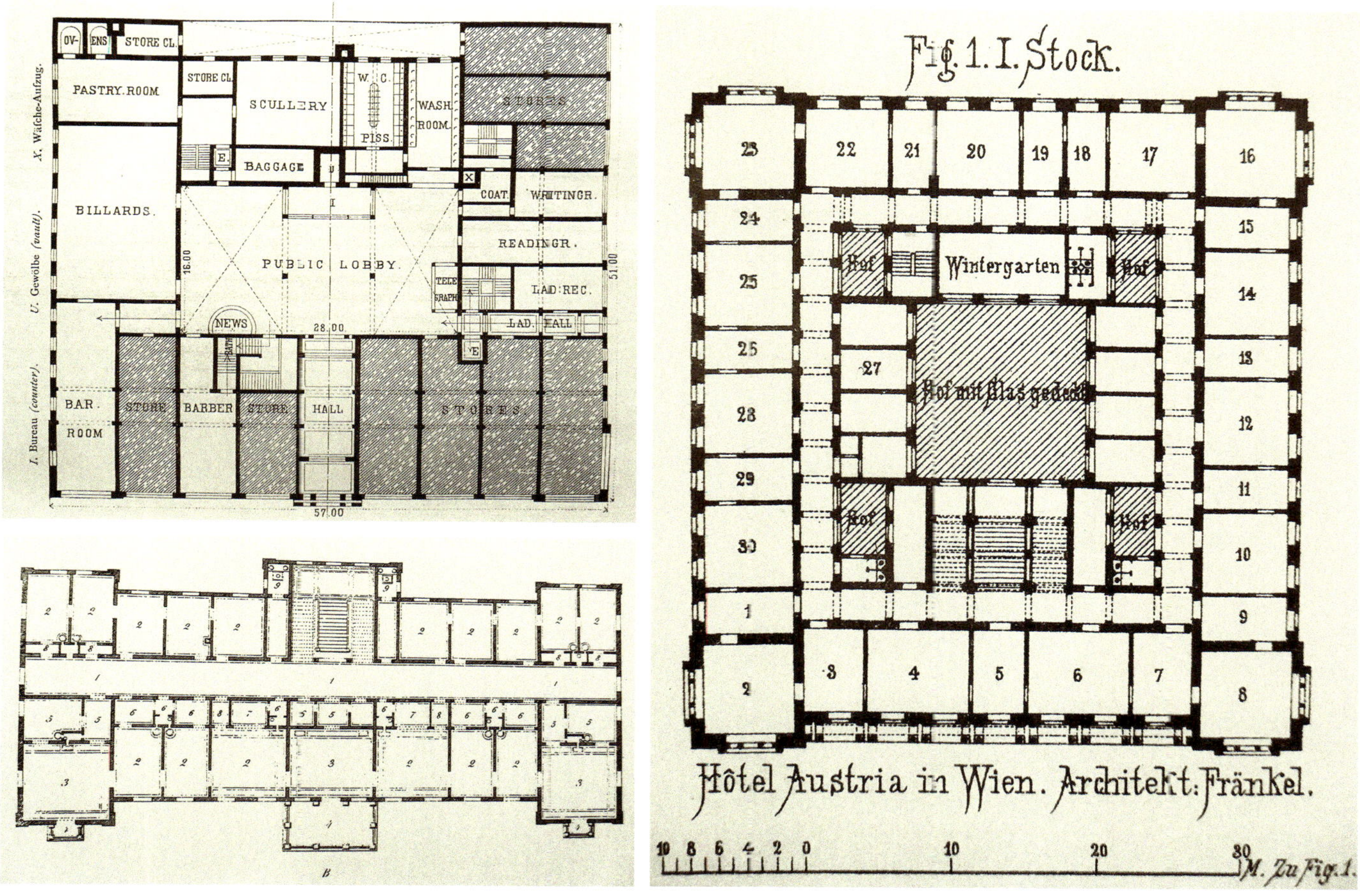

bathrooms. In the 1860s, gas lighting and in 1879 in St. Moritz in the 'Hotel Engadiner Kulm' electric illumination (fig. 9) is introduced.[53]

Another essential innovation was the lift, also called 'vertical train' (fig. 10). Besides other constructive preconditions this was the actual prerequisite for the building of multi-storey high rises. 'There were (in 1889) six lifts at the Savoy which the American Elevation Company claimed were the largest and most efficient in Europe. There are now thirty-two lifts in the Savoy, twenty-three of which are needed for service',[54] we hear in 1953. The number of the service lifts points to the complicated internal operations of a hotel. The most extravagant requests of the guests were to be fulfilled by day and night. To guarantee this, a refined logistical system is necessary that intermeshes the storage of goods and foodstuffs, their preparation and distribution as well as all other services (fig. 11). A diversified choice is only possible when there are

the Hotel Victoria, opened two years before the Savoy at a cost of £ 520,000, had only four bathrooms for five hundred visitors, and no more had been added in 1897. In fact, the astonishing number of bathrooms at the Savoy, upon which D'Oyly Carte insisted, was indeed an innovation and set the standard for the future."[49] (Abb. 8)

"It were the devices that made the modern hotel modern",[50] schreibt Jefferson Williams in *The American Hotel*. „,Homes are becoming more hotel-like', the hotel men say, and they are thinking of the way in which hotels have pioneered in such things as bathtubs [der deutsche Kaiser Wilhelm I. lässt sich in Berlin aus dem Hôtel de Rome noch jeweils eine Badewanne ins Schloss bringen][51], modern heating arrangements and comfortable beds."[52]

In Europa nehmen die Schweizer Hotels eine Vorreiterrolle ein. 1847 hatte in Genf das Hotel des Bergues die ersten Toiletten mit Wasserspülung, 1866 das Hotel

sufficient numbers of guests. This was already known to François Marie Charles Fourier, who envisioned a widely diversified spectrum of activities for his social palace, the 'Phalanstère' (a mix of work and leisure around 1800).[55]

To combine recreation and entertainment, repose and distraction as well as boarding, a specific architectural disposition was needed. Here, we have to discern different ground plan designs: the square or rectangular composition with projecting middle and side parts, a building with wings in the classical disposition—now and then with a *cour d'honneur*—or with angled wings or special shapes like triangular or v-shaped ground plan (fig. 12, 13, 14). Hermann von der Hude discerns in his typology of elements the criteria still valid today:[56]

a) characteristics and general disposition
b) Elements and facilities
- guest rooms
- lounges
- rooms for administration
- operational rooms
c) rooms for public concourse

In a fourth chapter Hude describes examples starting with the characteristic features of American hotels:

> 'On the ground floor the public lobby forms the centre of the entire complex and resembles in its disposition and size the main courts of our European hotels of recent origin. The lobby is lighted from above. It is a frequently visited space. Always guests linger there, sitting down, standing, walking and conversing. Particularly in the evenings the lobby is tersely filled. One is looking for friends and acquaintances, one debates the state of the stock exchange. The counter, a telegraph, an outlet for newspapers and the porter's lodge are also to be found in the lobby[57].' (fig. 15)

In the pattern of rooms the lobby is the pivotal point of the social rooms and lounges. Similar to Frank Lloyd Wright's disposition of rooms where the fireplace takes central stage, from the lobby 'arms' reach at other spatial functions. In most cases, it is grouped axially behind an entryway and a vestibule (provided there is one) and combined with entrance hall and leads to a winter garden, great dining hall or lounge.

'The big hall in a way serves as the market place of the hotel, its decoration mainly is dictated by fashion:

Bernina in Samedan Badezimmer. In den 1860er Jahren wird die Gasbeleuchtung und 1879 werden in St. Moritz im Hotel Engadiner Kulm elektrische Lampen (Abb. 9) eingeführt.[53]

Eine andere wesentliche Neuerung war der auch „vertical train" genannte Lift (Abb. 10). Er ist neben baukonstruktiven Vorgaben die eigentliche Voraussetzung für den vielgeschossigen Hochhausbau. „There were [in 1889] six lifts at the Savoy which the American Elevation Company claimed were the largest and most efficient in Europe. There are now thirty-two lifts in the Savoy, twenty-three of which are needed for service",[54] heißt es 1953. Die Anzahl der Service-Lifte verweist auf die komplizierten internen Abläufe in einem Hotel. Die extravagantesten Wünsche der Gäste sollen 24 Stunden hindurch erfüllt werden. Um dies zu garantieren, ist ein raffiniertes logistisches System nötig, das Vorratshaltung von Gütern und Lebensmitteln, die Zubereitung und Verteilung derselben sowie alle anderen Dienstleistungen miteinander vernetzt (Abb. 11). Ein diversifiziertes Angebot ist erst bei einer entsprechenden Anzahl von Gästen möglich. Das wusste schon François Marie Charles Fourier, der ein weit gefächertes Spektrum von Aktivitäten (eine Mischform aus Arbeit und Freizeit) in seinem „Sozialpalast" Phalanstère vorsah.[55] Um Erholung und Unterhaltung, Ruhe und Ablenkung sowie die Beköstigung zu kombinieren, bedurfte es einer spezifischen architektonischen Disposition. Hier sind verschiedene Grundrissformen zu unterscheiden: die quadratische und rechteckige Anlage mit hervorspringenden Mittel- und Seitenteilen, der Flügelbau in seiner klassischen Form – mitunter mit einem Cours d'honneur – oder mit angewinkelten Flügeln sowie Sonderformen von Dreiecks- und V-Grundrissen (Abb. 12, 13, 14). In seiner Typologisierung unterscheidet Hermann von der Hude die heute noch gültigen Kriterien[56]:

a) Charakteristik und Gesamtlage
b) Bestandteile und Einrichtung Fremdenzimmer
- Gesellschaftsräume
- Verwaltungsräume
- Wirtschaftsräume
- Verkehrsräume
c) Konstruktion, Ausstattung und Baukosten

In einem weiteren Kapitel werden Beispiele beschrieben, beginnend mit den Charakteristika eines nordamerikanischen Hotels:

13

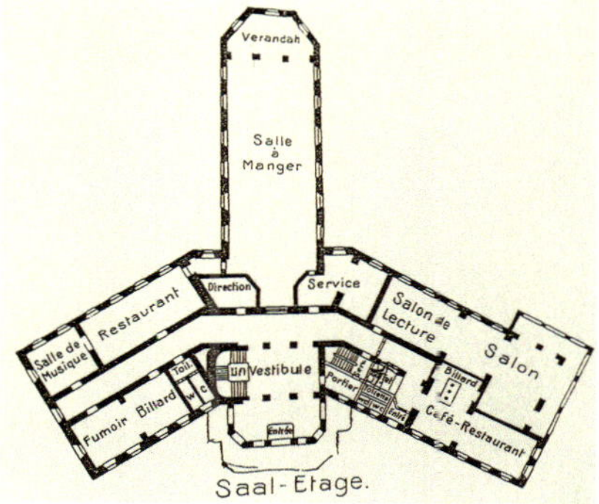

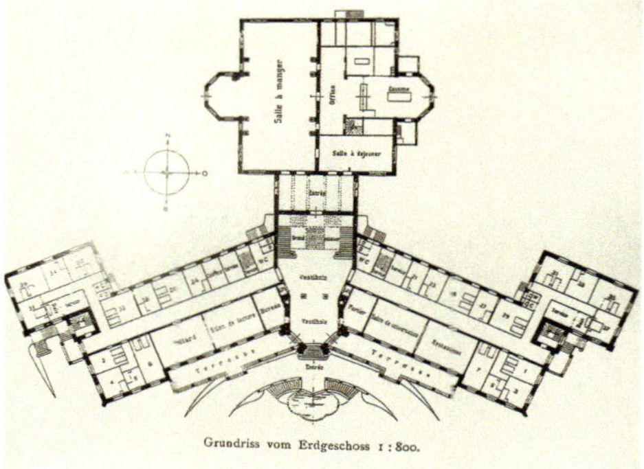

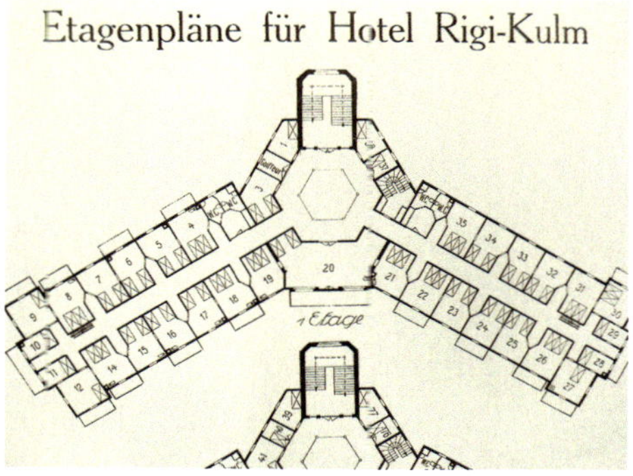

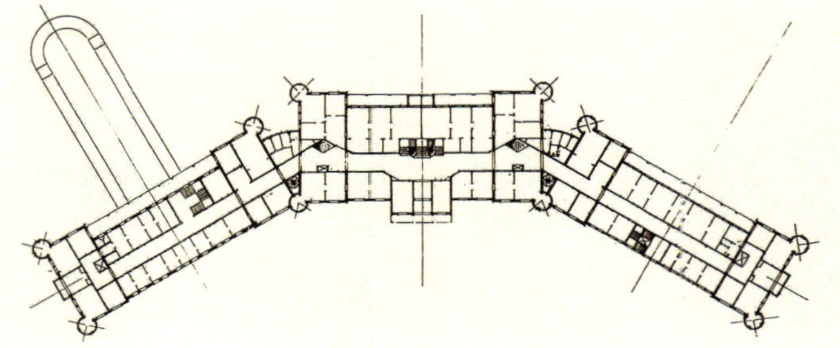

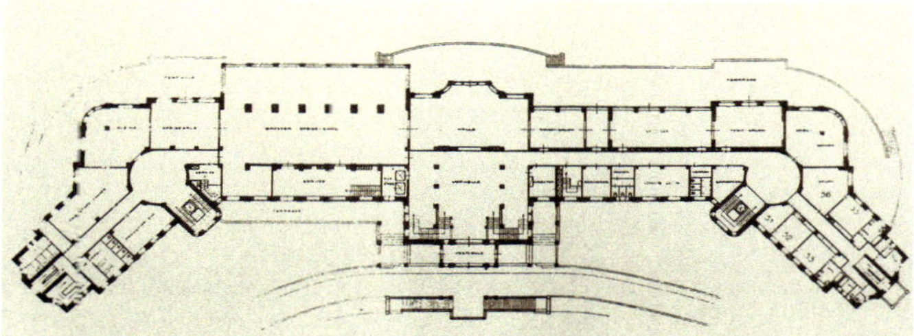

Abb. 106 KARLSBAD, Hotel Imperial, Erdgeschoß-Grundriß.

14

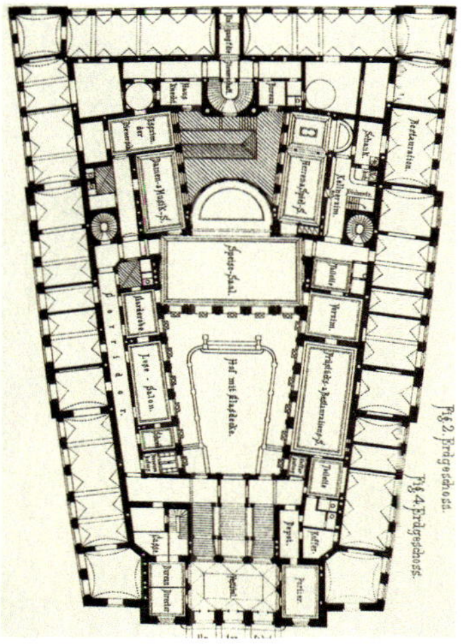

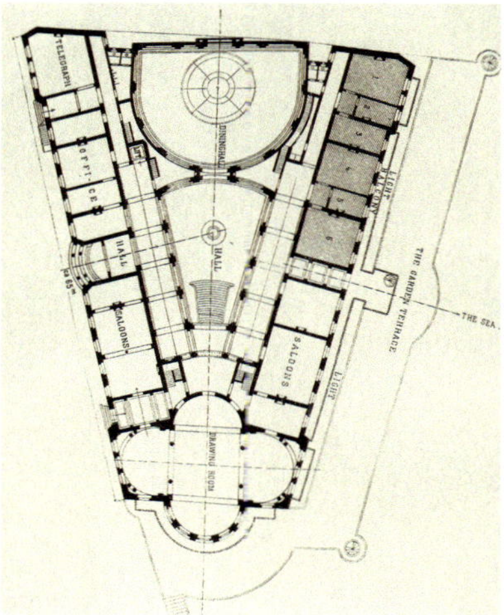

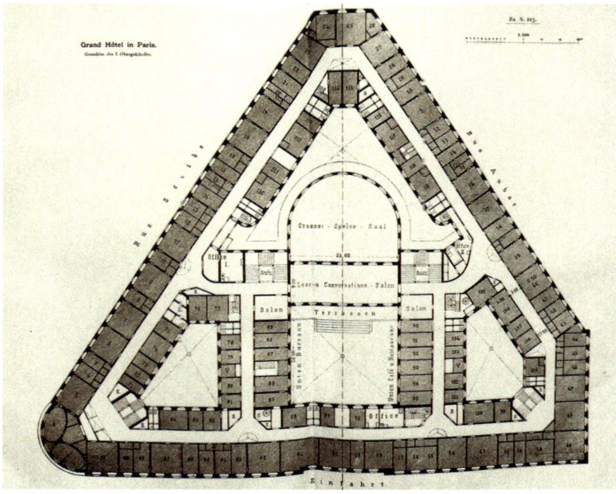

13

'Hotel Bernina', Samedan, 1866 ● 'Grand Hotel Dolder', by Jacques Gros, Zurich, 1898/99 ● 'Hotel Rigi Kulm', by Horace Edouard Davinet, 1875 ● 'Hotel Waldhaus', by Nicclaus Hartmann sen., Vulpera, 1896/97 ● 'Hotel Imperial', by E. Hébrard (J. Kronfuß), Karlsbad, 1912

Hotelgrundrisse: Hotel Bernina, 1866, in Samedan ● Grand Hotel Dolder, 1898/99, von Jacques Gros in Zürich ● Hotel Rigi Kulm, 1875, von Horace Edouard Davinet ● Hotel Waldhaus, 1896/97, von Nicolaus Hartmann sen. in Vulpera ● Hotel Imperial, 1912, von E. Hébrard (J. Kronfuß) in Karlsbad

14

'Hotel Métropole', by C. Schumann and L. Tischler, Vienna, 1871–73 ● 'Grand Hotel', by Cuthbert Brodrick, Scarborough, 1863–67 ● 'Grand Hotel' (10,000 square metres floorspace) by Alfred Armand, Paris, 1861–62

Hotel Métropole, 1871–73, von C. Schumann und L. Tischler in Wien ● Grand Hotel, 1863–67, von Cuthbert Brodrick in Scarborough ● Grand Hotel (10.000 m² Grundfläche), 1861–62, von Alfred Armand in Paris

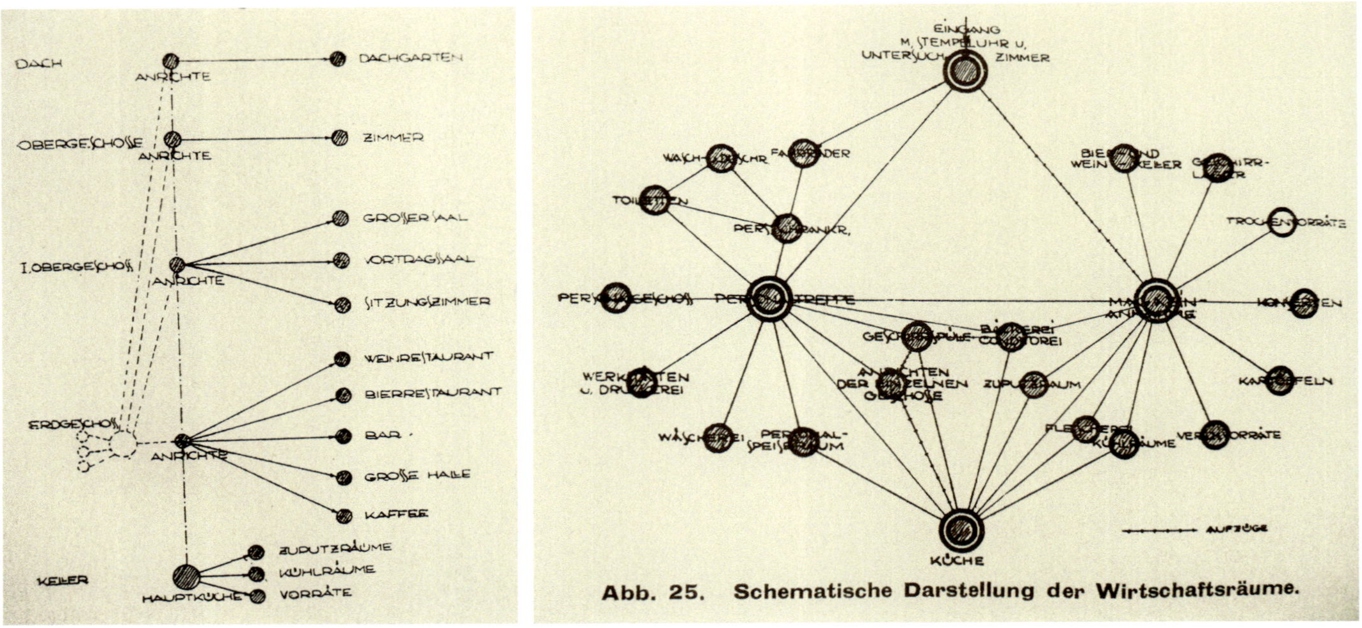

15
Diagrams of the utility and public rooms of a hotel, Karl Wilhelm Just, 1933

Schematische Darstellungen der Wirtschafts- und Gesellschaftsräume, Karl Wilhelm Just, 1933

for its aesthetic language as well as for its application to society's needs', Wilhelm Just annotates.[58] Hude counts the lobby, along with the interior yards, the entrance halls, staircases for guests and personnel, corridors, lifts for persons, baggage and food amongst the concourse zones. The dining halls are part of the spaces made accessible by the lobby: a big dining hall for the 'table d'hôte', smaller ones for cafés and restaurants where dining à la carte is customary. Attached to these spaces there are pantry rooms or offices that serve as intermediary zones between the working room of the kitchen and the areas serving restauration purposes. Public rooms are also reading and conversation rooms, writing rooms, in American hotels a bar, a 'barbershop', music rooms, porches, various halls (according to the reputation of the hotel ballrooms, theatre and conference halls. Saloons and other public rooms sometimes are also on the first floor, in the different storeys one has smaller saloons, serving in a way as social buffer zones between the private space of the hotel room and the public nature of the big society rooms. The great number of operational rooms mirrors most distinctively the labyrinthine but nevertheless impeccably functioning cosmos of the Grand Hotel. Next to the pantry already

> „Im Erdgeschoss bildet die *public lobby* den Mittelpunkt der ganzen Anlage und entspricht hierin sowohl, als auch in den Dimensionen den Haupthöfen unserer europäischen neueren Hotels. Sie ist durch Deckenlicht erhellt. Die *public lobby* ist ein sehr besuchter Raum; stets verweilen Gäste dort, sitzend, stehend, gehend und plaudernd. Insbesondere ist sie des Abends fast gedrängt voll. Man sucht dort Freunde und Bekannte auf; man verhandelt dort den Stand der Börse. Das Bureau (*counter*), ein Telegraphen-Bureau, eine Verkaufsstelle für Zeitungen, die Loge des Portier (*clerc*) befinden sich in der *lobby*."[57] (Abb. 15)

Raumkompositorisch ist sie der Dreh- und Angelpunkt der Verkehrs- und Gesellschaftsräume. Ähnlich wie in Frank Lloyd Wrights Grundrissdispositionen der Kamin eine zentrale Rolle einnimmt, so greifen von der Lobby aus „Arme" in andere Funktionseinrichtungen aus. Sie ist meist axial hinter der Vorfahrt, einem Vestibül – so vorhanden –, oft kombiniert mit einer Vorhalle, angelegt und leitet in der Achse in einen Wintergarten, großen Speisesaal oder einen Ball- oder Konversationssaal über. „Die große Halle ist gewissermaßen der Marktplatz des Hotels. Ihre Ausgestaltung ist zum größten Teil der Mode

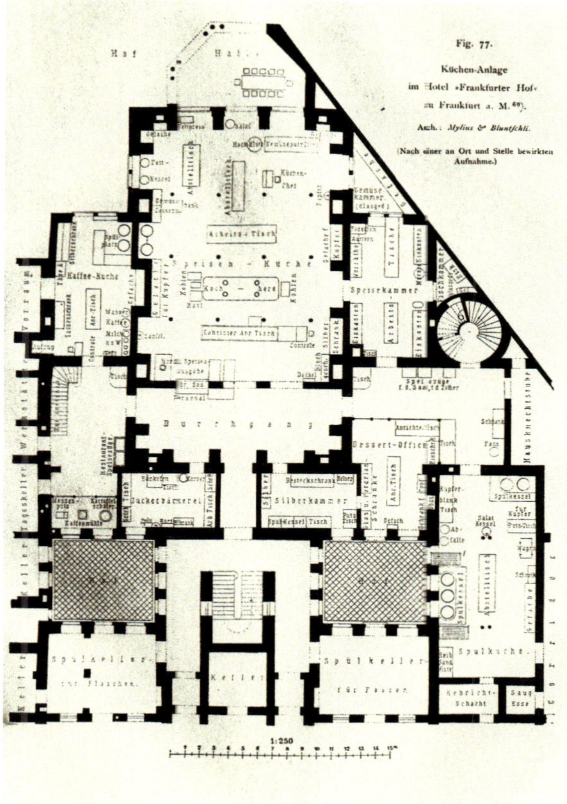

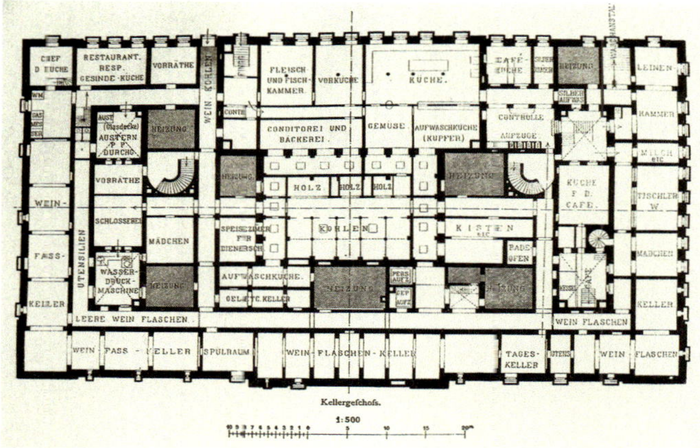

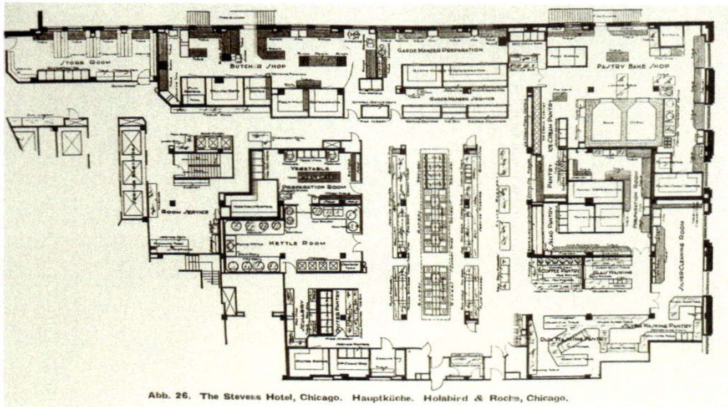

16

Kitchen of the hotel 'Frankfurter Hof', by Mylius & Bluntschli, Frankfurt am Main, 1875/76 ● Kitchen of the 'Hotel Kaiserhof', by Hermann von der Hude & Julius Hennicke, Berlin, 1878–80 ● Kitchen of hotel the 'The Stevens' (3,000 rooms), by Holabird & Roche, Chicago 1926/27

Küche des Hotel Frankfurter Hof, 1875/76 von Mylius & Bluntschli in Frankfurt am Main ● Küche des Hotel Kaiserhof, 1878–80 von Hermann von der Hude und Julius Hennicke in Berlin ● Küche des The Stevens (3000 Zimmer), 1926/27, von Holabird & Roche in Chicago

17

The kitchen of the 'Adelphi Hotel,' by Frank Atkinson, respectively Liverpool, 1914, photograph taken 1920 ● Kitchen of 'Hotel Suvretta House,' by Karl Koller, St. Moritz Bad, 1911/12, photograph taken 1920

Küche im Adelphi Hotel, 1914, von Frank Atkinson in Liverpool, Aufnahme 1914 ● Küche im Hotel Suvretta House, 1911/12 von Karl Koller in St. Moritz Bad, Aufnahme 1920

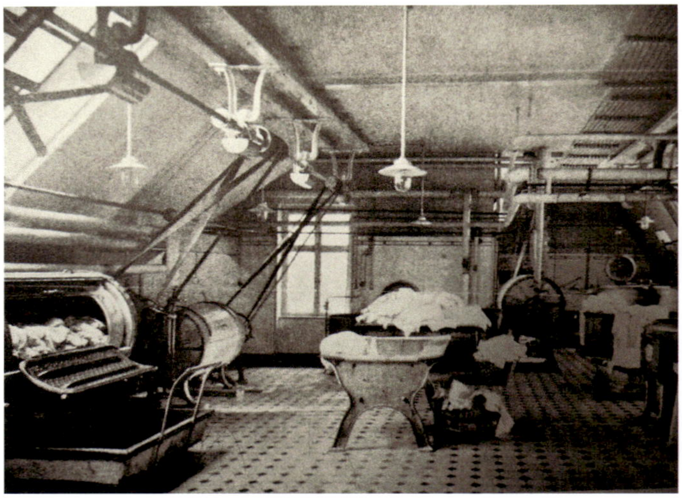

18

Grand Hotels resembled ocean liners with storage rooms, wine cellars, taprooms (here in the Ciga hotel chain, Venice) and laundries ('Hotel Adlon,' Berlin), private electrical generating stations, central heating rooms ('Grand Hotel,' Paris)

Mit Vorratshaltung, Weinkellern, Abfüllräumen (hier Ciga-Hotelkette in Venedig) und Wäschereien (Hotel Adlon, Berlin) wie eigenen Kraftzentralen, Heizräumen (Grand Hotel, Paris) et cetera waren die Grand Hotels so autark wie transatlantische Passagierschiffe.

mentioned, there are main kitchen ('a practical kitchen disposition is much more important and influences much more deeply the running of a hotel than is usually assumed'[59]), preparatory kitchen, washing up rooms for table and copperware, coffee kitchen with washing up room, adjoined by storages for tea, coffee, sugar, etc. (fig. 16, 17) There are also milk cellar for the storage of butter and milk, rooms for cleaning vegetables, silver vault, bakery, dessert room, kitchen and eating room for the servants, more storage room for preserves, smoked food, cans and other durable goods. 'The meat chamber … must be situated in a cool place and needs fresh air. One must provide ice containers and basins with running water for living fishes.'[60] In the day-cellar, adjoining the wine cellar, the beverages for day-to-day use are stored. An ice house was necessary before electrical cooling was possible and where there was no supply by the municipal ice-works. Furthermore one needs laundry facilities and workshops for fitters, carpenters, plumbers and paper hangers as well as a heating room for the steam operated central heating (fig. 18) and the preparation of warm water for the bathrooms and finally a basement for fuels. One also needs sleeping rooms for employees and other personnel—the latter usually slept on the attic floor[61]—and eating rooms for servants brought along by guests. The director's flat—should he be housed in the hotel—as well as his office Hude subsumes under administrative rooms. The 'bureau', or offices, the porter's lodge, a room for the house-servant, luggage, toilets and cloakrooms were all to be situated near the entrance, main hall or porch. Either on the ground floor in central position or decentralised on the different floors chambers for linen, bedclothes and tablecloths were situated.

In 1885 Hude assumes that for 500 guests you needed 130 employees and servants. Next to the chef de reception, accountant and teller, to hall and kitchen supervisors, cellarmaster, office clerk, matrons and housekeepers Hude reckons with ca. 25 waiters, 30 maids, 25 house servants and 6 grooms in a hotel. Towards the turn of the century the number of pages and bell hops is increasing. Furthermore 4–5 boilermen and workmen, 3–4 coopers, 7 sub-cooks and 3–5 backup porters and night watchmen are employed. In 1895 the entire personnel of the Paris 'Grand Hotel' consisted of 600 persons.[62]

Shortly before World War One in Swiss hotels with a capacity of 70.000 beds nearly 100,000 people worked 'behind the backdrops of the fairy magic'.[63]

unterworfen: sowohl in der künstlerischen Formensprache als auch in der Verwendung für gesellschaftliche Zwecke", notiert Wilhelm Just.[58] Hude rechnet sie wie die Innenhöfe, die Eingänge und Eintrittshallen, Treppen für Gäste und Personal, Korridore, Personen-, Gepäck- und Speiseaufzüge zu den Verkehrsräumen. Zu den von der Lobby erschlossenen Gesellschaftsräumen gehören die Speisesäle: ein großer Speisesaal für die „table d'hôte", kleinere für die Cafés und Restaurants, wo das Speisen nach der Karte gebräuchlich ist. Diesen Räumlichkeiten zugeordnet ist ein Anrichteraum oder *office*, der als Übergangszone zwischen dem Wirtschaftsraum Küche und den der Restauration dienenden Räumen zu sehen ist. Des weiteren zählen zu den Gesellschaftsräumen: Lese- und Konversationssalon, Schreibzimmer, in amerikanischen Hotels eine Bar, ein *barbershop*, Musikzimmer, Veranden, diverse Säle (je nach Größe und Reputation des Hotels Ball-, Theater- und später Konferenzsäle). Salons und Gesellschaftsräume befinden sich teilweise auch im ersten Geschoss, auch sind auf den Etagen kleinere Salons untergebracht, gewissermaßen als sozialer Puffer zwischen dem Privaten des Zimmers und der Öffentlichkeit der großen Gesellschaftsräume. Die Vielzahl der Wirtschaftsräume spiegelt am deutlichsten den labyrinthischen und dennoch reibungslos funktionierenden Kosmos eines Grand Hotels. Neben dem bereits erwähnten Anrichteraum zählen zu diesem: Hauptküche („Eine praktische Kücheneinteilung ist viel wichtiger und greift viel tiefer in den Betrieb eines Hotels ein, als gewöhnlich angenommen wird"[59]), Vorbereitungsküche, Aufwaschraum für das Tafel- und Kupfergeschirr, Kaffeeküche mit Aufwaschraum, an den sich der Vorratsraum für Tee, Kaffee, Zucker et cetera anschließt (Abb. 16, 17), Milchkeller für die Lagerung von Butter und Milch, Gemüseputzraum, Silberkammer, Backstube, Dessert-Raum, Gesindeküche und -speisezimmer, weitere Vorratskammern für Eingemachtes, geräucherte Waren, Konserven und sonstige haltbare Waren. „Die Fleischkammer … muß kühl gelegen sein und gut gelüftet sein. Eisbehälter sowie Bassins mit stetig fließendem Wasser für lebende Fische sind vorzusehen."[60] Im Tageskeller, der an den Flaschenkeller anschließt, werden die Getränke für den Tagesbedarf gelagert. Ein Eiskeller war vor der Erfindung von Kühlräumen und dort, wo das Eis nicht aus den städtischen Eiswerken bezogen wurde, nötig. Ferner müssen Waschanstalten und Werkstätten für Schlosser, Tischler, Klempner und Tapezierer sowie ein Heizraum für die Zentraldampfheizung und die Aufbereitung warmen Wassers für die Bäder samt einem Keller für

The fortunes of a hotel porter is the central motif of Friedrich Wilhelm Murnau's film *Der letzte Mann*, 1924. The social position of this protagonist and the social calamities of the hotel personnel in contrast to the luxurious hotel life of the guests is the theme of the following chapter.

On and Behind the Stage

'For some are in the dark
and others in the light
you can see those in the light
those in the dark you do not see'[64]

The hotel is the one place that concentrates the urban macrocosm of social segregation upon the narrowest space. Exposed to sight and helped by a generous offer of ample room, the well to do together with society's climbers move as on a stage. Behind-the-scenes work, badly paid and badly acommodated, the real guarantors of the frictionless operation of a hotel (fig. 19).

In his film *Der letzte Mann*, Friedrich Wilhelm Murnau portrays, both on the macro level of the city and the micro level of the hotel, this segregation.[65] He contrasts pulsating big city life with the world of the poor's tenement houses. On the one hand we see the prestigious façade of the hotel Atlantic in its affluent surroundings—on the other hand the backyard (fig. 20). Here the to and fro of people in the hotel lobby—there worker's wives on the backstairs. And bluntly emphasizing this contrast[66] he contrasts hotel guests luxuriously slurping oysters with the doorman-protagonist's wife bringing him lunch in a canteen. This doorman however appears here as more than a mere representative of the working class. Daily he transgresses the borders between two worlds. He is some kind of mediator in the way prescribed by his function in the hotel. Here, he is the interfering figure between the external world of the street and the interior sphere of the hotel. He supervises the arrival as well as the departure of the guests, organizes approach and farewell and also the transport of the luggage via a side door. He is the first and last ambassador of the hotel. He reigns over the revolving door[67] that sucks the guests inside and conveys them—depending on their rank in society accompanied by the hotel manager—outside. The transgression mentioned above of the borders between the segregated levels of proletariat and 'affluent society', i.e.

Brennmaterialien vorhanden sein (Abb. 18). Schlafräume für Beamte und übriges Personal (letztere wurden meist im Dachgeschoss[61] untergebracht) sowie Speisezimmer für von den Gästen mitgebrachte Dienerschaft sollten ebenfalls vorhanden sein. Die Wohnung des Direktors – so dieser im Hotel untergebracht ist – sowie dessen Büro subsumiert Hude unter den Verwaltungsräumen. Das „Bureau" oder die Büroräume, wie die Portiersloge, ein Raum für Hausdiener und Gepäck sowie die Toiletten und die Garderobe sollten alle an der Eingangs-, Haupthalle (Lobby) oder der Vorhalle liegen. Im Erdgeschoss zentriert oder dezentral auf den Etagen liegen die Leinwand, Bett- und Tischwäschekammern.

1885 geht Hude davon aus, dass 500 Gästen 130 Beamte und sonstige Bedienstete zur Verfügung stehen sollten. Neben dem *chef de reception*, dem Buchhalter, Kassierer, den Saal- und Küchenvorständen, dem Kellermeister, den Bürobeamten, Hausdamen und Haushälterinnen rechnet er mit circa 25 Kellnern, circa 30 Mädchen, 25 Hausdienern sowie circa sechs Jungen (*grooms*) im Hotel. Zur Jahrhundertwende hin nimmt die Zahl der Pagen oder auch *bell-hops* dann noch zu. Darüberhinaus sind vier bis fünf Heizer und Handwerker, drei bis vier Küfer, etwa sieben Unterköche sowie drei bis fünf Hilfsportiers und Nachtwächter angestellt. 1895 betrug die Gesamtzahl des im „Grand Hotel" in Paris arbeitenden Personals 600 Personen.[62]

Kurz vor dem Ersten Weltkrieg waren in Schweizer Hotels bei einer Bettenzahl von 70.000 nahezu 100.000 Menschen im Hotelgewerbe „hinter den Kulissen des ‚Märchenzaubers'"[63] tätig.

Das Schicksal eines Portiers ist das zentrale Thema von Friedrich Wilhelm Murnaus Film *Der letzte Mann* aus dem Jahr 1924. Dessen gesellschaftliche Stellung wie die soziale Degradierung des Hotelpersonals als Antipode zum luxuriösen Hotelleben sind Thema des folgenden Kapitels.

Vor und hinter den Kulissen

„Denn die einen sind im Dunkeln
Und die anderen sind im Licht.
Und man siehet die im Lichte
Die im Dunkeln sieht man nicht."[64]

Das Hotel ist der Ort, an dem der urbane Makrokosmos sozialer Segregation auf engstem Raum konzentriert

19

Bootblack in the 'Hotel Claridge', Paris ● Jeanne Moreau in the 'Hotel Meurice', Paris, 1964

„The boot-black": Schuhputzer im Hotel Claridge in Paris ● Jeanne Moreau im Hotel Meurice in Paris, 1964

20
Film stills from 'The Last Laugh', 1924, directed by Friedrich Wilhelm Murnau

Standbilder aus *Der letzte Mann*, 1924, Regie: Friedrich Wilhelm Murnau

21

Receptionist, page boy and coachman of the 'Élysée Palace Hotel', Paris ● Footman and page boy of the 'Hotel Savoy', London ● Film still from *Hotel Adlon*, directed by Joseph von Baky

Empfangschef, Page und Chauffeur im Élysée Palace Hotel in Paris ● Diener und Page im Hotel Savoy in London ● Standbild aus *Hotel Adlon*, 1955, Regie: Joseph von Baky

in this specific case the contact with the latter, is made possible by his position and the corresponding uniform. The uniform as a status symbol guarantees him access to and abidance in the hotel and in the lobby. In his private environment this position serves him and his family as an element of social upgrading. He becomes the ambassador of a world that he represents by means of his richly adorned frock coat-cum-epaulettes which is inaccessible to the proletariat. The hotel—more precisely its specific dress code in its highly diversified hierarchy—serves here as a synonym for the Upper Class. Murnau's film however insists on still another strand of a plot: the reversal of the social status—the hotel as a stage on which the actors change their roles. In fiction as in reality the hotel with its willingness to compromise vis-à-vis solvent customers[68] is the perfect setting to demonstrate such a status-switch. In front of habitué guests arrogantly amusing themselves and of the grimacing waiters, the doorman, having become rich through an unexpected inheritance but not used to the environment of a luxury restaurant as a paying guest, has to be served nevertheless. For him is not applicable anymore what Thomas Mann in *Felix Krull*[69] characterizes as follows: '[T]o the rich Poverty is a flaw … therefore very detestable … and so to society it seems wisest to turn a blind eye towards such a faulty product within their order.'[70] Nowhere poverty and wealth are so near each other as in a hotel. They meet in the lobby, in the lift, in the dining room, on the corridors. For the rich, according to a careful management, the working and living conditions of the hotel personnel remain invisible. Footboys, commis, valets, liftboys, suitcase carriers, porters and chamber maids are liveried and gloved for their appearance and contact with the hotel guests (fig. 21)—and what is more—by their sheer number and dress code they are meant to suggest courtly etiquette.[71]

> 'It is also nothing but a dazzlement of the eyes and mainly caused by this great coat à la Saint James and Albany with its velvet applications and gold buttons, which is nothing but the adornment of my position, without which I look like nothing'[72]

Thomas Mann makes Felix Krull remark. And in another part of his novel with a critical glance at the nouveau riche's world, that more and more count amongst the clientele of the Grand Hotels we read:

ist. Die Wohlhabenden wie auch die „society climbers" bewegen sich durch ein großartiges Raumangebot wie auf einer Bühne. Hinter den Kulissen arbeiten schlecht bezahlt und schlecht untergebracht die eigentlichen Garanten des reibungslosen Ablaufs eines Hotelbetriebs (Abb. 19).

Seinen Film *Der letzte Mann* (1924)[65] siedelt Friedrich Wilhelm Murnau sowohl auf der Makroebene der Stadt als auch auf der Mikroebene des Hotels an. Er kontrastiert das pulsierende Großstadtleben mit der Welt der Mietskaserne: hier die repräsentative Fassade des Hotel Atlantic und seiner affluenten Umgebung – dort der Hinterhof (Abb. 20). Hier das Wogen der Menschen in der Lobby – dort die Arbeiterfrauen im Treppenhaus. Und als zugespitzte Thematisierung dieses Gegensatzes:[66] Hier die genüsslich Austern schlürfenden Gäste – dort die Frau des Hauptprotagonisten, des Portiers, dem sie in einem Kochgeschirr das Mittagessen bringt – eine bis in die erste Hälfte des 20. Jahrhunderts hinein übliche Versorgung auch der Fabrikarbeiter. Der Portier jedoch ist mehr als nur ein Vertreter der arbeitenden Klasse. Er überschreitet täglich die Grenzen zweier Welten. Er ist eine Art Mediator, wie ihm dies auch seine Funktion im Hotel vorschreibt. Dort ist er die vermittelnde Figur zwischen der Außenwelt der Straße und der Binnenwelt des Hotels. Er überwacht die Ankünfte und Départs, organisiert die Vor- und Abfahrten sowie den Gepäcktransport. Er ist der erste und letzte Repräsentant des Hotels. Er herrscht über die Drehtür[67], die die Hotelgäste einsaugt oder, entsprechend ihrer gesellschaftlichen Stellung vom Hotelmanager begleitet, hinausbefördert. Die oben angesprochene Grenzüberschreitung zwischen den segregierten Schichten des Proletariats und der „affluent society", das heißt im konkreten Fall den Kontakt zu letzterer, ermöglicht ihm seine Position und die dazugehörige Uniformierung. Die Uniform als Statussymbol ist Garant für seinen Zugang zum und seinen Aufenthalt im Hotel und in der Lobby. In seinem Lebensumfeld gerät sie ihm und seiner Familie zur Aufwertung im sozialen Milieu. Mit seinem üppig goldbetressten und epaulettierten Gehrock wird er zum Botschafter einer dem Proletariat unzugänglichen Welt. Das Hotel – im konkreten Fall die ihm eigene Kleiderordnung in ihrer weitgefächerten Hierarchisierung – steht hier als Symbol der gesamten Gesellschaft. Murnaus Film aber behält sich noch einen weiteren Handlungsstrang vor: die Umkehrung des sozialen Status. Das Hotel als

> 'It was the motif of exchangeability: after changing their dress, their styling, the servants could as well have been the gentlefolk, and many of those sprawling in the deep wicker chairs, a cigarette in the side of their mouths, could have been the waiters. It was pure coincidence that things were the other way around—the accident of wealth; for the aristocracy of money is an interchangeable aristocracy by happenstance.'[73]

Until today, the invasion of the nouveau riches into society's temple, the hotel with its conserving exclusive cohesiveness has to be counterbalanced.

Felix Krull, in his Paris hotel 'Saint James and Albany'[74], not only constitutes a change in status from liftboy to headwaiter, but also exemplifies a role change that is possible within the frame of hotel ambience. 'Away from home', free from day-to-day social control and 'social gossip', hotel guests are less inhibited—without ever busting out of the circle of the purely formal and conventional completely, as Thomas Mann illustrates by the example of Eleanor Twentyman, Lord Necton Kilmarnock and last not least Madame Houpflé. Felix Krull himself, like an actor changing his role, mutates into the 'Marquis de Venosta'. A careful analysis of the hotel-stage with its up-and-downs of appearance and real substance, where physical proximity goes along with social distance, provides him with the tools for his performance as man-of-the-world. Norman S. Hayner[75], the author already mentioned, from the academic environment of the Chicago School of Sociology centered around Robert E. Park[76], speaks of a habitus characteristic for a hotel guest who protects himself against manifold external influences by inner dissociation. We have here a mechanism of adaptation and coming to terms that Georg Simmel generally ascribes to the big city dweller. If we substitute big city with hotel and the city dweller with hotel guest, the latter has to react to external conditions.

> 'Restlessness, i.e. the difficulty or inability to adjust to the anonymous, impersonal atmosphere of a hotel; individuation, i.e. the unimpeded movement of impulses free of constraints; a blasé attitude as defensive reaction against these irritations and agitations that are part of hotel life, and finally a cultivated or 'man-of-the-world attitude', a kind of immunisation against the influences of the hotel milieu.'[77]

Bühne, auf der die Schauspieler ihre Rollen wechseln. Auch hier ist in der Literatur und der Realität das Hotel mit seiner Kompromissbereitschaft gegenüber zahlungskräftigen Gästen[68] der geeignete Ort, um einen solchen Statuswandel zu demonstrieren. Im Angesicht der sich arrogant amüsierenden Stammgäste und der verächtlich dreinblickenden Bedienung wird der über eine Erbschaft zu Reichtum gelangte, mit dem Angebot des Luxusrestaurants jedoch nicht vertraute Portier dennoch bedient. Auf ihn trifft nicht mehr zu, was Thomas Mann in *Felix Krull*[69] wie folgt charakterisiert: „Armut ist den Besitzenden ein Makel .. also sehr widerwärtig … und somit scheint es der Gesellschaft am weisesten über ein solches Fehlprodukt ihrer Ordnung wie blind hinwegzusehen."[70] Dennoch: Nirgendwo sind Armut und Reichtum einander so nah wie im Hotel. In der Lobby, im Lift, im Speisesaal, auf den Gängen begegnen sie sich. Für die Reichen sind wohlweislich die unwürdigen Arbeits- und Lebensbedingungen des Hotelpersonals nicht zu erkennen. Pagen, Commis, Kammerdiener, Liftführer, Kofferträger, Pförtner und Zimmermädchen sind für ihre Auftritte und Kontakte mit den Gästen (Abb. 21) livriert und behandschuht, ja mehr noch, sie sollen in ihrer Vielzahl und Kleiderordnung höfische Etikette vorgaukeln.[71]

> "Es ist auch nur Augenverblendung und kommt größtenteils von diesem Frack à la Saint James and Albany mit dem Samtbesatz und den Goldknöpfen, der nichts als Putz meiner niederen Stellung ist, ohne den ich nach gar nichts aussehe"[72],

lässt Thomas Mann Felix Krull bemerken. An anderer Stelle mit einem kritischen Blick auf die Welt der Neureichen, die mehr und mehr zur Clientèle der Grand Hotels zählen, heißt es:

> „Es war der Gedanke der Austauschbarkeit: Den Anzug die Aufmachung gewechselt, hätten sehr vielfach die Bedienenden ebenso gut Herrschaft sein und hätte so mancher von denen, welche, die Zigarette im Mundwinkel, in den tiefen Korbstühlen sich rekelten – den Kellner abgeben können. Es war der reine Zufall, daß es sich umgekehrt verhielt – der Zufall des Reichtums; denn eine Aristokratie des Geldes ist eine vertauschbare Zufallsaristokratie."[73]

22
Roof garden of the 'Hotel Montclair', New York ● Chamber maids at the call-board in a German Grand Hotel, 1930

Dachgarten im Hotel Montclair in New York ● Zimmermädchen an der Anzeigetafel in einem deutschen Grand Hotel, 1930

Felix Krull in his role as Marquis de Venosta convincingly had mastered this man-of-the-world attitude.

A much unhappier course the plot of Thomas Mann's story *Tod in Venedig (Death in Venice)* takes, settling the events in the 'Hotel des Bains' in Venice.[78] There, the great number of lounges, passages and restaurant rooms gives the protagonist Aschenbach ample opportunity to more or less blatantly observe young Tadzio, the object of his adoration daily anew. A direct approach he forbids himself (social distance in spite of physical nearness). What is applicable to the macrocosm of the big city is true also for the microcosm of the hotel. Robert E. Park calls it 'meeting but not knowing one another' and Georg Simmel analyses it as early as the beginning of the twentieth century in *Soziologie des Raumes (Sociology of Space)*.[79] Different from his novelette *Death in Venice*[80] in *Felix Krull*, Thomas Mann describes hotel architecture: 'A magnificent crown hall with porphyry columns and a gallery running round it on the level of the entresol … where plenty humankind moves to and fro.'[81] He also throws light on the 'backstage':

> 'Dormitory no. Four … eight beds with grey coarse blankets and thin pillows, visibly not washed for a longer time, were arranged in berths, one on top of each other along the side walls … else wise the room whose window point-

Das Eindringen der Neureichen in den Gesellschaftstempel Hotel mit seiner bewahrenden exklusiven Geschlossenheit gilt es bis heute auszubalancieren.

Felix Krull ist im Pariser Hotel Saint James and Albany[74] nicht nur ein Beispiel für den Statuswechsel vom Liftboy zum Oberkellner, sondern exemplifiziert auch einen Rollenwechsel, wie er sich vor allem im Ambiente des Hotels anbahnen kann. *Away from home*, der alltäglichen sozialen Kontrolle und dem *social gossip* entronnen, sind die Gäste enthemmter – ohne den Rahmen des rein Formellen und Konventionellen zu sprengen, wie Thomas Mann das an Eleanor Twentyman, Lord Necton Kilmarnock und last but not least Madame Houpflé vorführt. Felix Krull selbst mutiert gleich einem Schauspieler, der seine Rolle wechselt, zum Marquis de Venosta. Die sorgfältige Analyse der Hotelbühne mit ihrem Auf und Ab von Schein und Sein, in der körperliche Nähe mit sozialer Distanz einhergeht, liefert ihm das Rüstzeug für seinen Auftritt als Weltmann. Der der Chicago School of Sociology um Robert E. Park[75] nahestehende Autor Norman Hayner[76] spricht von einem dem Hotelgast eigenen Habitus, der sich aufgrund einer Vielzahl von Eindrücken durch innere Distanzierung schützt – ein Adaptions- und Bewältigungsmechanismus, wie ihn Georg Simmel ganz allgemein dem Großstädter zuschreibt. Setzt man Großstadt mit Hotel und Groß-

23
Hotel Room, painting by Edward Hopper, 1931
Hotelzimmer, von Edward Hopper, 1931

ed towards a ventilation shaft, offered no kind of convenience.'[82]

In 1933 George Orwell who worked as *plongeur*—dishwasher[83]—in Paris restaurants and a hotel[84], describes his impressions: 'I came across the strangest accounts in the hotel. There was talk of drug addicts and old debauchees that visited the hotel to look for pretty liftboys, of theft and fraud'.[85]

> 'It was funny, if you looked around the dirty little scullery and thought that it was merely separated from the dining hall by a double door. There they all sat, the guests in their splendour—spotless tablecloths, flower bowls, gilded mouldings and painted cherubim; and us, just a few meters away, in our foul dirt. It really was nauseating dirt. Until evening, there was no time to wipe the floor and we were skidding in a mixture of soapy brine, salad leaves, torn paper and scrunched food.'[86]

> 'Our cafeteria showed perennial dirt in all its dark corners and the bread container was flooded by cockroaches.'[87]

Equally extreme are Maria Leitner's descriptions in her novel *Hotel Amerika*[88]. In an admittedly propagandistic black-and-white portrayal she contrasts the conditions

städter mit Hotelgast gleich, so hat letzterer auf äußere Konditionen zu reagieren:

> „Ruhelosigkeit, d. h. die Schwierigkeit oder Unfähigkeit, sich an die anonyme, unpersönliche Atmosphäre im Hotel zu gewöhnen; Individuation, d. h. das freie Spiel der von Zwängen entlasteten Impulse; Blasiertheit als Abwehrreaktion gegenüber den Reizungen und Erregungen, die mit dem Leben im Hotel verbunden sind, und schließlich Kultiviertheit oder ‚weltmännische Art', eine Art Immunisierung gegenüber den Einflüssen des Hotel-Milieus."[77]

Felix Krull in seiner Rolle als Marquis de Venosta hat sich überzeugend diese weltmännische Art zu eigen gemacht.

Einen weit unglücklicheren Verlauf nimmt Thomas Manns Geschichte aus dem Hotel des Bains[78] in Venedig. Die reichlich vorhandenen Gesellschafts- und Restaurationsräume bieten dem Protagonisten Aschenbach die Möglichkeit, mehr oder minder verhohlen den jungen Tadzio, das Objekt seiner Adoration, täglich aufs Neue zu beobachten. Eine direkte Annäherung verbietet er sich (sozialer Abstand verbietet körperliche Nähe). Es gilt für den Mikrokosmos Hotel, was für den Makrokosmos Großstadt gilt und was Robert E. Park als „meeting but not knowing one another" charakterisiert und was

of the residence of the staff with that of the hotel guests. In his review of the book, Siegfried Kracauer speaks of 'a luxury hotel seen from below'.[89] The authoress researches the 'conditions of life of the countless hotel employees … light is thrown on that which usually recedes into darkness: that province of an enormous empire in which chambermaids, scrubbing women, waitresses and waiters, porters, night watchmen, pages and kitchen helps dwell.'

> 'The personnel on the lowest level receive bedclothes that no longer can be repaired. The lacerated mattress shows its filling of seaweed through torn sheets … cockroaches and bugs wander unhurriedly around in spite of the brightness (The rooms of the guests are visited daily by pest-control personnel). But here it can be dirty, here it can remain dirty.'[90]

The 'Down and Out'—socially as well as spatially—have to content themselves in the third underground level with water soup and potatoes in their jacket. The social climbers sip champagne on the roof terrace at the afternoon dances (fig. 22). Thus the depictions of exclusive extravagances are part of the same self-contained hotel cosmos. A ballroom in *Hotel Amerika* is furnished for a wedding: 'From the West Indies and Surinam, flowers and shrubs and trees together with their roots … have been transported to New York … exotic butterfly and moth larvae also have been delivered … all are to hatch on wedding day.' It was an abundant luxuriance of forms and colours:

> 'Butterflies with blue bodies and translucent, gold coloured wings surround roses from the Caribbean islands with their rich … petals in the colour of yellowed ivory … also butterflies whose one wing is of a poisonous green whereas the other shows red, blue and yellow lines on tobacco coloured background flutter around them'.[91]

But it is not only the lounges that are stages for excessive life. In the extravagant hotel imagined by Leitner, we hear of the room of a proprietress of a coffee plantation, who has 'transformed it into a miniature forest: with two palm trees, a monkey … a parrot and a white cockatoo.'[92] Sarah Bernhardt however only brought, when she stayed in the 1884 luxury apartment house that later became the Chelsea Hotel, with her only the coffin that she carried around on all her journeys and in which she slept.[93]

Georg Simmel bereits Anfang des 20. Jahrhunderts als die Soziologie des Raumes analysiert.[79]

Anders als in seinem Roman *Der Tod in Venedig*[80] liefert Thomas Mann in *Felix Krull* neben der Beschreibung der Bühne („Ein prachtvoller Kronensaal mit Porphyrsäulen und einer in der Höhe des Entresols umlaufenden Galerie … wo viel Menschheit hin und wider wogte“[81]) auch eine Ansicht der Hinterbühne:

> „Dortoir Nummer Vier … Acht Betten mit grauen Friesdecken und flachen, sichtlich längere Zeit nicht gewaschenen Kopfkissen waren kojenartig je zwei und zwei übereinander an den Seitenwänden angeordnet … Somit bot das Zimmer, dessen einziges Fenster auf einen Luftschacht zu gehen schien, keinerlei Behaglichkeit.“[82]

Georg Orwell, der als *plongeur*, Tellerwäscher[83] in Pariser Restaurants und Hotels gearbeitet hat, beschreibt 1933 seine Eindrücke:[84]

> „Ich hörte die seltsamsten Geschichten in dem Hotel. Da war die Rede von Rauschgiftsüchtigen, von alten Lüstlingen, die in die Hotels gingen, um nach hübschen Pagen Ausschau zu halten, von Diebstahl und Betrug.“[85]

> „Es war komisch, wenn man sich in der verdreckten kleinen Spülküche umsah und daran dachte, daß man nur durch eine Doppeltür vom Speiseraum getrennt war. Da saßen sie alle, die Gäste in all ihrer Pracht – makellosen Tischtüchern, Blumenschalen, vergoldeten Gesimsen und bemalten Cherubim; und wir hier, nur wenige Meter entfernt, in unserem widerlichen Schmutz. Es war tatsächlich ekelerregender Schmutz.“[86]

> „Unsere Cafeteria hatte jahrealten Dreck in allen dunklen Ecken, und der Brotbehälter war überschwemmt mit Kakerlaken.“[87]

Noch extremer sind die Schilderungen in Maria Leitners Roman *Hotel Amerika*.[88] In einem zugegebenermaßen propagandistischen Schwarzweiß-Gemälde kontrastiert sie die Aufenthaltsbedingungen des Personals mit denen der Gäste. Von einem „Luxushotel von unten gesehen“[89] spricht Siegfried Kracauer in seiner Rezension des Buches. Die Autorin erforscht die „Daseinsbedingungen der zahllosen Hotelangestellten … Belichtet ist, was sonst ins Dunkel zurücktritt: jene Provinz des gewal-

24
Department store 'Galeries Lafayette', Paris, 1895 ● 'Hotel Hermitage', Monte Carlo, 1906

Warenhaus Galeries Lafayette, 1895, in Paris ● Hotel Hermitage, 1906, in Monte Carlo

But also those rooms behind the stage of a public appearance offer a descent into anonymity and into the uncontrolled, individual self-fulfilment. The fascination with palace hotels has as much to do with the figures who gave the establishments their distinctive style as with their architecture and technical background'.[94] Hayner speaks of a 'free play of impulses when released from restraint'. [95] If the concierge is informed, he keeps silent. This is part of the codex of a hotel. Of course, three musicians in the Paris Ritz cannot come in or go out without being noticed, when they provide an American playboy with a musical background for his tête-à-tête as can be watched in Billy Wilder's *Love in the Afternoon*.[96] Surely the universe of the hotel—in literature and film[97], even in painting, if we keep Edward Hopper's scenes of isolation in mind—never has been

tigen Reichs, in der die Stubenmädchen, Scheuerfrauen, Kellnerinnen und Kellner, Gepäckträger, Nachtwächter, Pagen und Küchenbediensteten hausen."

> „Das Personal auf der letzten Stufe bekommt Bettzeug, das nicht mehr ausgebessert werden kann. Die aufgerissene Matratze zeigt die Seegrasfüllung durch zerrissene Laken … Schaben und Wanzen wandern trotz der Helligkeit gemächlich umher (Die Hotelzimmer der Gäste werden täglich von einem Kammerjäger besucht). Hier kann es schmutzig sein, hier kann es dreckig bleiben."[90]

Die Abgesunkenen – sozial wie räumlich – müssen sich im dunklen Untergeschoss mit einer Wassersuppe und Pellkartoffeln begnügen. Die Aufgestiegenen nippen auf der Dachterrasse beim Tanztee am Champagner

25

Hôtel Bellevue et le Wetterhorn.
5865. Wengernalpbahn. Station Scheidegg.

26

27

Aug Vautier Dufour

28

anything else as the reflection of all our fears[98], wishes and dreams (fig. 23).

From Purpose-Oriented Travel to Tourism: The Urbanization of the Countryside

Within the cities Grand Hotels from the last quarter of the nineteenth century act—similar to the big railway stations and department stores—as promoters of urban densification.[99] Moreover they resemble each other stylistically, even their interior disposition points to consistencies with features like glazed cupolas, lobbies, entrance halls and prestigious staircases (fig. 24). They all possess a multifunctional character that in various ways combines possibilities to consume, for leisure activities, refreshment and work. The epitome of such a multifunctional amalgam is the 'Palais Royal'[100], where in an ingenious way in a sort of 'unité multifonctionelle' galleries, theatres, shops and luxurious apartments are combined by arcades.

Such a combination of functions furthering the leisure needs of demanding hotel clients the Grand Hotels were to offer that sprang into existence at the shores of Atlantic or Mediterranean Sea, the Baltic or North Sea and later of the Pacific, as well as in the mountains and at lakesides, in spas or in attractive landscapes. Implanted solitary or massed together into the countryside (fig. 25, 26), they are—concerning architecture, interior decoration and technological innovation—representative of urban culture. They were built for a clientele that—temporarily fleeing the cities—nevertheless was not willing to renounce their right to habitual comfort.

25
'Hotel Bellevue', Kleine Scheidegg, ca. 1895 ● 'Hotel Waldhaus', Vulpera, ca. 1900

Hotel Bellevue, Kleine Scheidegg, ca. 1895 ● Hotel Waldhaus, Vulpera, ca. 1900

26
Engelberg, ca. 1910 ● Davos, 1923

Engelberg, ca. 1910 ● Davos, 1923

27
'Promenade des Anglais', Nice, 1880

Promenade des Anglais, Nizza, 1880

28
The 800-metre-promenade of the 'Palace Hotel', Caux, 1950

800 Meter lange Promenierterrasse des Palace Hotel in Caux, 1950

(Abb. 22). So sind die Schilderungen exklusiver Extravaganzen Teil des gleichen geschlossenen Hotelkosmos. Ein Ballsaal in *Hotel Amerika* wird für eine Hochzeit ausgestattet: „Aus Westindien und Surinam waren Blumen und Sträucher und Bäume samt Wurzeln … nach New York transportiert … Exotische Schmetterlings- und Falterpuppen . . wurden gleichfalls mitgeliefert … Alle sollten sich am Hochzeitsstag entpuppen." Es war eine üppige Formen- und Farbenpracht:

> „Falter mit blauen Leibern und durchsichtigen, goldfarbenen Flügeln umgeben die Rosen von den karibischen Inseln mit ihren reichen … Blütenblättern in den Farben von vergoldetem Elfenbein … Auch Schmetterlinge, deren einer Flügel giftgrün ist, während der andere auf tabakfarbenem Grund rote, blaue und gelbe Linien aufweist, umschwirren sie."[91]

Was für eine Wonne für einen Lepterologen!

Doch nicht nur die Gesellschaftsräume sind Schauplätze exzessiven Lebens. Im von Leitner imaginierten extravaganten Hotel ist von dem Zimmer einer Kaffeeplantagenbesitzerin die Rede, die dieses in „einen Miniaturурwald verwandelt hat: mit zwei Palmen, einem Affen, … einem Papagei und einem weißen Kakadu."[92] Sarah Bernhardt brachte (nur!) wenn sie in New York im 1884 als Luxusapartmenthaus gebauten späteren Chelsea Hotel übernachtete, ihren Sarg, den sie auf allen Reisen mit sich führte und in dem sie schlief, mit.[93]

Aber auch die Zimmer hinter der Kulisse des öffentlichen Hotelauftritts bieten ein Abtauchen in die Anonymität und in verstärktem Maße in die unkontrollierte individuelle Entfaltung. „Die Attraktivität von Palasthotels basiert nicht nur auf der Architektur und dem technischen Komfort, sondern auch auf dem individuellen Stil eines Hauses, für das herausragendes Personal die Verantwortung trägt."[94] Hayner spricht in diesem Zusammenhang im Bezug auf die Gäste vom „freien Spiel der Impulse, frei von jeglichen Zwängen."[95] Ist der Concierge informiert, so bewahrt er Schweigen. Das gehört zum Verhaltenskanon eines Hotels. Denn selbstverständlich können nicht unbemerkt drei Musiker in einem Hotel wie dem Pariser Ritz ein- und ausgehen, wo sie einem amerikanischen Playboy die musikalische Untermalung für sein Tête-à-Tête geben – so zu sehen in Billy Wilders *Love in the Afternoon*.[96] Das Universum des Hotels ist in Literatur und Film[97] – aber auch in der

One example for a scenery urbanized by hotels and places of leisure may be seen in the French Riviera. The railway in the second half of the nineteenth century offers to a multitude of travellers the opportunity to rapidly reach faraway destinations. At an early date the railway networks are extended to attractive holiday landscapes. In 1864 the *Chemins de fer du Sud* from Paris reach via Lyon the Côte d'Azur. A hotel boom starts and around 1900 reaches its climax. 'Au début du XXme siècle, toute la promenade des Anglais (à Nice) n'est pas qu'une suite des palaces, entre lesquels villas réussissent encore à s'intercaler'.[101] (fig. 27)

One more phenomenon of urbanization of the nineteenth century can be seen in the construction of holiday villas in resorts. Mild winter climate and—as an additional attraction—the casinos make for a steady flow of guests. '[U]ne monde de viveurs et de joueurs surtout où le "rastaquouérisme" et l'élement mondain prédominent de plus en plus. Pour ceux-là, Nice n'est que l'etape d'hiver au soleil dans la vie brûlée de la fête perpétuelle'[102] we hear in 1897.

The process of 'hotelization' starts in a modest way as early as the eighteenth century. In 1763 it is the enthusiastic reporting of British physician Tobias George Smollet[103] about the beneficial climate of the Riviera that set in motion the flood of Englishmen towards the French coast. After the fall of Napoleon they together with other representatives of the European aristocracy and the early moneyed bourgeoisie form the bulk of the hotel guests. To please them, already in 1822 in the shape of *Chemin des Anglais*—later called *Promenade des Anglais*—an urban boulevard is created by the Englishman Lewis Way.[104]

Many hotel names are also pointing to an English clientele: 'West End', 'Westminster', 'Hôtel des Anglais' or 'Victoria on the Riviera', 'Beau-Rivage et d'Angleterre' in Geneva and Lausanne, or 'Inghilterra' in Rome. Italy was teeming with hotels called 'Isole Britanniche' and names such as 'Londra', 'Villa di Londra' etc.

This 'English Flood' paired with a push for urbanization Leo N. Tolstoi in 1857 makes the theme of his short novel 'Lucerne'.

> 'Now one has, owing to the tremendous onrush of Englishmen and in consideration of their needs, their taste and their money pulled down the old bridge and in its place constructed a dead straight base dam and erected on this dam several straight-lined five-storey houses planted

Malerei – man denke an die Szenen der Vereinsamung bei Edward Hopper – nie etwas anderes als die Widerspiegelung unserer Ängste[98], Wünsche und Träume (Abb. 23).

Von der Zweckreise zum Tourismus – die Verstädterung der Landschaft

In den Städten sind die Grandhotels ab dem letzten Viertel des 19. Jahrhunderts ähnlich wie die großen Bahnhöfe und Warenhäuser Beschleuniger der urbanen Verdichtung.[99] Darüber hinaus gleichen sie einander stilistisch, selbst die innenarchitektonische Anordnung weist mit Glaskuppeln, Vor- und Eingangshallen sowie repräsentativen Treppenanlagen auf Übereinstimmungen hin (Abb. 24). Allen gemeinsam ist dabei eine Multifunktionalität, die in verschiedenen Variationen Konsummöglichkeiten, Freizeitangebote, Restauration und Arbeit kombiniert. Das *pars pro toto* dieses Amalgams ist das Pariser Palais Royal, in dem auf ingeniöse Weise und von François Marie Charles Fourier bewundert[100] in einer „unité multifonctionelle" Galerien, Theater, Läden und Luxuswohnungen durch Arkadengänge miteinander verbunden sind.

Diese Bündelung von Funktionen zum Wohle der Freizeitbedürfnisse anspruchsvoller Hotelgäste sollten auch die an den Küsten des Atlantiks und des Mittelmeers, der Ost- und Nordsee und später des Pazifiks, in den Bergen und an den Seen in Kurorten oder landschaftlich attraktiven Gegenden entstehenden Grandhotels aufweisen (Abb. 25, 26). Als Solitäre oder auch massiert in die Landschaft implantiert sind sie, was Architektur, Interieur und technische Innovation angeht, die Repräsentanten urbaner Kultur. Gebaut sind sie für eine Clientèle, die, der Stadt auf Zeit entflohen, dennoch nicht auf den gewohnten Komfort verzichten will.

Als ein Beispiel einer durch Hotels und Vergnügungsorte verstädterten Landschaft kann die französische Riviera gelten. Die Eisenbahn bietet in der zweiten Hälfte des 19. Jahrhunderts einer Vielzahl von Reisenden die rasche Möglichkeit, entfernte Ziele zu erreichen. Schon früh werden dabei die Netze auf attraktive Ferienlandschaften ausgedehnt. 1864 erreichen die „Chemins de fer du Sud" von Paris über Lyon die Côte d'Azur. Der Hotel-Bauboom nimmt damit seinen Anfang und erreicht um 1900 seinen Höhepunkt. „Au début du XXiéme siècle, toute la promenade des Anglais à Nice n'est qu'une suite de palaces, entre lesquels villas réussissent encore à s'intercaler"[101] (Abb. 27).

29
Bath at Leuk, Valais, around 1600 and around 1850
Bad zu Leuk im Wallis um 1600 und um 1850

two rows of lime trees in front of the houses and supported them by poles. Between the lime trees one has according to custom distributed green-painted benches. This is the promenade; here English ladies in Swiss straw hats are strolling as well as Englishmen in their practical and comfortable suits and they are enjoying their creation. It may be possible that the quays and the houses, lime trees and Englishmen somewhere else might look pretty, but in any case not here in the midst of this strangely majestic and at the same time indescribably harmonic and gentle landscape.'[105]

Promenade and boulevard are urbanistic elements serving the 'Corso'.[106] To See and Be Seen was a social requirement the tourists brought with them. Inside the hotel, social and public spaces served this desire. Switched between landscape and architecture, patios, arcades or colonnades offered the adequate outer frame. The 800-metre-promenade-terrace of the hotel 'Palace' in Caux (fig. 28) defines the culmination of what Tolstoi calls an insensitive intrusion into a harmonic landscape.

Appropriately Prosper Mérimée finally characterizes the purpose of travelling as a status symbol, as a hunt for new sensations with which one could make an impression after coming back from a journey. Here, we come across a modern phenomenon of the consumer society: Travelling and reporting of it become a question of prestige. 'Initially, Miss Lydia was flattered by the thought to see

Der im 19. Jahrhundert in Ferienorten einsetzende Bau von Ferienvillen ist ein weiteres Verstädterungsphänomen. Das milde Klima im Winter und – als zusätzliche Attraktion – das Spielcasino sorgen für einen ständigen Strom von Gästen. „[U]ne monde de viveurs et de joueurs surtout où le ‚rastaquouérisme' et l'élément mondain prédominent de plus en plus. Pour ceux-là, Nice n'est que létape d'hiver au soleil dans la vie brûlée de la fête perpétuelle",[102] heißt es 1897.

In einem bescheidenen Maße hatte die Hotelisierung bereits im 18. Jahrhundert begonnen. Es sind 1763 die enthusiastischen Berichte des schottischen Arztes und Schriftstellers Tobias George Smollett[103] über das wohltätige Klima der Riviera, die den Strom der Engländer an die französische Küste in Gang setzen. Nach dem Sturz Napoleons bilden sie neben anderen Vertretern der europäischen Aristokratie und des frühen Geldbürgertums den Hauptanteil der Gäste. Ihnen zu Gefallen wird schon 1822 von dem Engländer Lewis Way mit dem Chemin des Anglais – später Promenade des Anglais genannt – ein städtischer Boulevard angelegt.[104]

Ebenfalls auf eine englische Clientèle verweisen viele Hotelnamen wie West End, Westminster, Hôtel des Anglais, Victoria an der Riviera, Beau-Rivage et d'Angleterre in Genf und Lausanne oder Inghilterra in Rom. Italien war übersät mit Hotels namens Isole Britanniche, Londra, Villa di Londra et cetera.

30
The Lauteraar Glacier, 1775, Caspar Wolf
Lauteraargletscher, 1775, von Caspar Wolf

things beyond the Alps that nobody before her had seen and about which she would be able to converse with really cultured persons.'[107] Again Mérimée: Soon the continued admiration of the pleasure travellers had reversed into its opposite: 'the erupting Vesuvius (they found) hardly more meaningful than the chimneys of the factories in Birmingham'. But 'never before an Englishwoman had been to Corsica, so she had to go there'[108] Here we meet as early as 1840 the onrush of sensations that Georg Simmel attributed to modern big city life, but also the restless hunt for novelty, a phenomenon that was to constantly culminate well into the 21st century: 'Consuming, not Digesting'.

Urbanization of the countryside therefore is the inevitable consequence of a development from purpose-oriented travel to travelling as an end in itself. People trav-

Diese „Engländerschwemme", gepaart mit einem Urbanisierungsschub macht Leo N. Tolstoi 1857 in seiner Novelle „Luzern" zum Thema.

> „Nun hat man dank dem ungeheuren Andrang von Engländern und aus Rücksicht auf ihre Bedürfnisse, ihren Geschmack und ihr Geld die alte Brücke abgebrochen und an ihre Stelle einen schnurgeraden Sockeldamm angelegt, auf dem Damm mehrere geradlinige, fünfstöckige Häuser erbaut, vor den Häusern noch zwei Reihen Linden gepflanzt und sie mit Pfählen gestützt. Zwischen den Linden hat man, wie es überall üblich ist, grün angestrichene Bänke verteilt. Das ist die Promenade; hier ergehen sich die Engländerinnen mit schweizerischen Strohhüten und die Engländer in ihren praktischen und bequemen

elling to the markets, salesmen, pilgrims and messengers undertook purpose-oriented journeys. From late mediaeval times on there was a certain spa tourism (fig. 29). In the 16th century there followed the tour for nature studies or geographic and geological purposes.[109] Approximately from the middle of the eighteenth century the purpose of travelling changes. One travels to regions unknown 'out of pleasure and to widen one's horizon. Travelling as educational task was herewith institutionalized.'[110] Educational journeys, frequently in the company of an architect, were as 'Grand Tour'[111] part of fashionable social customs. Destinations of these travels at first were the places of ancient cultures in Italy, Greece, and the Middle East. By and by the Alpine world becomes a travel destination, as part of an experience of nature inspired by its idealization by Jean-Jacques Rousseau, whose writings were part of the literary canon of the educated nobility and supported also by Albrecht Haller's poem 'The Alps'.[112] Thus still in the eighteenth century, travelling in Switzerland becomes an integral part of the 'Grand Tour', from which the term 'tourism' and 'tourist' derives, as Hans Magnus Enzensberger demonstrates.[113] 1798, in the year of the French Revolution, William Coxe publishes his travel guide *Travels in Switzerland*.[114] In 1804/1805 one can read in Johann Gottfried Ebel's travel instructions:

> 'All the Great, Sublime, Extraordinary and Astonishing, everything horrible and dreadful, defiant, gaunt and melancholic, everything romantic, gentle, amiable, serene, quiet, sweetly refreshing, idyllic and mellow of the whole ample nature seems to have united in a small space to make this land the garden of Europe.'[115] (fig. 30)

Such propaganda did not lack in efficiency: from 1844 Carl Baedeker's travel guide is a companion to the German tourist, like already from 1836 John Murray's *Handbook for Travellers on the Continent* for English speaking voyagers. Both contain information concerning lodgings. It was Murray who first introduced a categorical classification of tourist sights which is still current today. No less a person than Mark Twain in the last third of the nineteenth century travels according to the instructions of current travel guides: 'Thinking over my plans, as mapped out, I perceived that they did not take the Furka Pass, the Rhone Glacier, the Finsteraarhorn, the Wetterhorn etc. I immediately examined the guide-book to see if these were important, and found they were.'[116] Twain laments the

> Anzügen, und sie freuen sich alle ihrer Schöpfung. Es ist ja möglich, dass die Kais und die Häuser, Linden und Engländer sich irgendwo ganz hübsch machen würden, jedenfalls aber nicht hier, inmitten dieser seltsam majestätischen und zugleich unbeschreiblich harmonischen und weichen Landschaft."[105]

Promenade und Boulevard sind städtebauliche Elemente, die dem „Corso"[106] dienen. Sehen und gesehen werden, das war ein soziales Bedürfnis, welches die Touristen mitbrachten. Im Hotel dienten Gesellschafts- und Verkehrsräume diesem Verlangen. Zwischen Landschaft und Architektur geschaltet, boten Terrassen, Wandelgänge und Arkaden einen entsprechenden Rahmen. Was Tolstoi als unsensibles Eindringen in eine harmonische Landschaft bezeichnet, erfährt mit der 800 Meter langen Promenadenterrasse des Palace Hotel in Caux einen Höhepunkt (Abb. 28).

Zutreffend charakterisiert Prosper Mérimée dann schließlich den Zweck des Reisens als Statussymbol, als eine Jagd nach neuen Reizen, mit denen man dann nach Rückkehr von der Reise Eindruck machen konnte. Hier begegnen wir einem modernen Phänomen der Konsumgesellschaft: Die Reise und die Berichterstattung von derselben werden zu einer Prestigefrage. „Anfangs hatte Miss Lydia der Gedanke geschmeichelt, jenseits der Alpen Dinge zu sehen, die niemand vor ihr gesehen hätte und über die sie mit ‚feingebildeten Leuten' … sprechen könne."[107] Bald jedoch hatte sich die fortgesetzte Bewunderung der Vergnügungsreisenden in ihr Gegenteil verkehrt: „den ausbrechenden Vesuv [fanden] sie kaum bedeutender als die Schornsteine der Fabriken in Birmingham. Es galt aber auch: ‚noch nie war eine Engländerin auf Korsika gewesen, also mußte sie hin."[108] Hier begegnet man bereits 1840 der von Georg Simmel dem modernen Großstadtleben zugeschriebenen Reizüberflutung, aber auch der rastlosen Jagd nach Neuem, einem Phänomen, das unter dem Motto *consuming, not digesting* seine Zuspitzung bis in das 21. Jahrhundert hinein erfahren sollte.

Die Urbanisierung der Landschaft ist dann die unausweichliche Folge der Entwicklung von Zweckreisen hin zur Reise als Selbstzweck. Marktfahrer, Händler, Pilger und Kuriere hatten zweckbedingte Reisen unternommen. Ab dem späten Mittelalter gab es dann einen gewissen Bädertourismus (Abb. 29). Im 16. Jahrhundert folgt die der naturkundlichen, geografischen und geologi-

implantation of municipal hotel architecture emerging in a first building phase from 1860 on and in a second boom from the 1880s in Inner, Western and Eastern Switzerland as well as in the Ticino:

> 'One does not find out what a hold the chalet has taken upon him until he presently comes upon a new house—a house which is aping the town fashions of Germany and France, a prim, hideous, straight-up-and-down thing, plastered all over on the outside to look like stone, and altogether so stiff, and formal, and ugly, and forbidding, and so out of tune with the gracious landscape, and so deaf and dump and dead to the poetry of its surroundings, that it suggests an undertaker at a picnic, a corpse at a wedding, a puritan in paradise.'[117]

Twain sets this in opposition to the quality of the ancestral regional chalet: 'Set such a house against the fresh green of the hillside, and it looks ever so cosy and inviting and picturesque, and is a decidedly graceful addition to the landscape.'[118] The same phenomenon is described equally in the 1880s by Alphonse Daudet:

> 'Switzerland nowadays is nothing but an enormous Kursaal, opened from June till September, a casino with a panorama, in which people from all continents amuse themselves. This business is run by a society owning hundreds of millions and billions with company seats in Geneva and London. Just imagine how much money had to be spent to furnish this entire landscape of lakes and forests, mountains and waterfalls, to polish it to a glossy finish, maintain an entire army of extras and employees and to build luxury hotels with gas, telegraph and telephone on the highest peaks. Just look about the country. You will find no corner not furnished with mechanical devices and tricks like an opera stage: lighted waterfalls, turnstiles at the entrance to glaciers and a great number of trains of all varieties to climb up the mountains.'[119] (fig. 31)

The urbanification of the countryside as described by Mark Twain and Alphonse Daudet, on the one hand takes place by amplifying existing houses (fig. 32), on the other hand after demolishing old buildings and thirdly as building of solitary houses in the open country. The same demolishing-constructing procedure we find in metropolitan building types such as the railway stations already mentioned.[120] Here, the early stations of the first

schen Neugierde gewidmete Reise.[109] Etwa seit der Mitte des 18. Jahrhunderts ändert sich dann der Reisezweck. Man reist in unbekannte Gegenden „aus Vergnügen und zur Erweiterung des eigenen Horizonts. Das Reisen als Bildungsaufgabe war damit institutionalisiert."[110] Bildungsreisen des englischen Adels, oft in Begleitung von Architekten, gehörten als Grand Tour[111] zu den angesagten gesellschaftlichen Gepflogenheiten. Ziel dieser Reisen waren zunächst die Stätten antiker Kultur in Italien, Griechenland und Vorderasien. Im 18. Jahrhundert wird, auch infolge der Idealisierung der Natur durch Jean-Jacques Rousseau, dessen Schriften zum Lesekanon des gebildeten Adels gehörten, das Naturerlebnis und dann speziell, besonders durch Albrecht von Hallers Gedicht „Die Alpen"[112] angeregt, die Alpenwelt zum Reiseziel. So wird noch im 18. Jahrhundert die Bereisung der Schweiz integrativer Bestandteil der Grand Tour – von deren Bezeichnung, sich die Begriffe Tourismus und Tourist herleiten, wie Hans Magnus Enzensberger nachweist.[113] 1789, im Jahr der französischen Revolution, schreibt William Coxe den Reiseführer *Travels in Switzerland*.[114] 1804/1805 liest man in einer Reiseanleitung für die Schweiz bei Johann Gottfried Ebel:

> „Alles Grosse, Erhabene, Ausserordentliche und Erstaunenswürdige, alles Schreckliche und Schauderhafte, alles Trotzige, Finstere und Melancholische, alles Romantische, Sanfte, Reitzende, Heitre, Ruhige, Süsserquickende und Idyllenliebliche der ganzen weiten Natur scheint sich hier in einem kleinen Raume vereinigt zu haben, um dieses Land zu dem Garten von Europa zu bilden."[115] (Abb. 30)

Eine derartige Propaganda blieb nicht ohne Wirkung. Ab 1844 begleitet die deutschsprachigen Touristen der Reiseführer von Carl Baedeker, wie bereits ab 1836 John Murrays *Handbook for Travellers on the Continent* die englischsprachigen Schweizreisenden. Beide enthalten auch Hinweise auf Unterkünfte. Es ist Murray, der als Erster eine Kategorisierung der Sehenswürdigkeiten, wie sie bis heute üblich ist, vornimmt. Kein Geringerer als Mark Twain bewegt sich im letzten Drittel des 19. Jahrhunderts gemäß der Anweisungen gängiger Reiseführer. „Thinking over my plans, as mapped out, I perceived that they did not take the Furka Pass, the Rhone Glacier, the Finsteraarhorn, the Wetterhorn etc. I immediately examined the guide-book to see if these were important, and found they were."[116] Und bereits Mark Twain beklagt

31

Vitznau-Rigi railway, 1874 ● 'The Railway at its Destination. Three Victims of Progress', humorous postcard from around 1900. From left to right: the Jungfrau, Mönch, and Eiger as suffering mountains ● Hammetschwand lift at Bürgenstock, 1905, Franz-Josef Bucher-Durrer ● Giessbach railway above Lake Brienz, 1879

Die Vitznau-Rigibahn, 1874 ● „Die Bahn am Ziel. Drei Opfer des Fortschritts", humoristische Postkarte um 1900. Von links nach rechts: die bedrohten Berge Jungfrau, Mönch und Eiger ● Hammetschwand-Aufzug am Bürgenstock, 1905, von Franz-Josef Bucher-Durrer ● Die Giessbachbahn über dem Brienzer See, 1879

32

KULM

33

EXETER CHANGE
ROYAL MENAGERIE
BILLIARD ROOM
SIMPSON
ANDREWS

half of the nineteenth century after 1850 are replaced by monumental buildings in the historicist manner. Likewise, department stores like the Paris 'Au Bon Marché', 'Printemps' or 'Samaritaine'[121] grow from small retail shops or small scale department stores into complexes occupying whole city blocks. The same process of crowding out historic substance or swallowing it up one can also observe with big city or metropolitan hotel construction. London's Savoy hotel and theatre for example thus replaces the 'Beaufort Buildings' from 1695 'which was a combination of residential street and workshops'.[122] (fig. 33) In New York, Henry Willard the railway king's listed building from 1883 was ingested by the new 51-storey hotel 'Helmsley Palace'.[123]

There are many examples for the process of integrating or transforming historical building matter besides the already mentioned hotel 'Badischer Hof'. In Venice, the 14th century palace Palazzo Dandolo becomes hotel 'Danieli' in 1822. In Paris, the 'Bristol' (1878) goes back to a palace of 1718 and 'Crillon' to another from 1765. César Ritz in 1898 respected the façade from 1704 at the Place Vendôme. For the Alexandria 'Beau Rivage' (1922) two villas from 1897 are combined. In Cairo the 1869 'Gezira Palace' that housed Empress Eugènie during the opening of the Suez Canal becomes the hotel 'Ismail Palace' and in 1982 is augmented by two 20 storey towers. In Kandy, Sri Lanka, the governor's palace from 1825 turns into the hotel 'Mount Lavinia' in 1877. Although we will not be concerned with the so-called 'Oriental Hotels' here, since their concept differs from that of the Grand Hotel, two may be mentioned because they represent the paradigm of 'demolition/replacement': In Singapore, the 'Raffles', opened only in 1887, is replaced by a new hotel building

32
First 'Rigi-Kulm' hotel, 1847/48 ● second 'Kulm-Hotel,' 1857 ● 'Rigi-Kulm Grand Hotel,' by Schreiber 1875

Rigi-Kulm, erstes Hotel, 1847/48 ● zweites Kulm-Hotel 1857 ● Rigi-Kulm Grand Hotel von Schreiber, 1875

33
'The Strand', 1829 ● and 1889 after construction of 'Savoy Hotel', London

The Strand, 1829 ● und 1889 nach dem Neubau des Savoy Hotel in London

die Implantate städtischer Hotelarchitektur, die in einer ersten Bauphase ab den 1860er und in einem zweiten Bauboom ab den 1880er Jahren in der Inner-, West- und Ostschweiz sowie im Tessin entstehen:

> „One does not find out what a hold the chalet has taken upon him until he presently comes upon a new house – a house which is aping the town fashions of Germany and France, a prim, hideous, straight-up-and-down thing, plastered all over on the outside to look like stone, and altogether so stiff, and formal, and ugly, and forbidding, and so out of tune with the gracious landscape, and so deaf and dumb and dead to the poetry of its surroundings, that it suggests an undertaker at a picnic, a corpse at a wedding, a puritan in Paradise".[117]

Er konfrontiert damit die Qualitäten des angestammten regionalen Chalets: „Set such a house against the fresh green of the hillside, and it looks ever so cosy and inviting and picturesque, and is a decidedly graceful addition to the landscape".[118] Das gleiche Phänomen beschreibt ebenfalls in den 1880er Jahren Alphonse Daudet.

> „Die Schweiz … ist heutzutage nur noch ein riesiger Kursaal, geöffnet von Juni bis September, ein Kasino mit Panorama, in dem sich Leute aus allen Erdteilen vergnügen. Betrieben wird dieses Unternehmen von einer Hunderte von Millionen und Milliarden reichen Gesellschaft mit Sitz in Genf und London. Stellen Sie sich nur vor, wie viel Geld es gebraucht hat, um diese ganze Landschaft mitsamt ihren Seen und Wäldern, Bergen und Wasserfällen einzurichten und auf Hochglanz zu polieren, ein ganzes Heer von Statisten und Angestellten zu unterhalten und auf den höchsten Gipfeln Luxushotels mit Gas, Telegraf und Telefon zu erbauen … Schauen Sie sich nur um im Lande. Sie werden keinen Winkel finden, der nicht mit mechanischen Einrichtungen und Tricks wie in der Opernbühne ausgestattet ist: beleuchtete Wasserfälle, Drehkreuze am Eingang zu Gletschern und zur Erklimmung der Berge eine Vielzahl von Bahnen aller Art."[119] (Abb. 31)

Die Verstädterung der Landschaft, wie sie von Alphonse Daudet und Mark Twain beschrieben wird, findet einmal als Erweiterung bestehender Häuser, zum anderen nach Abbruch von Altbausubstanz und zum

34

35

34

City map of Montreux, in 1830, 1870, and 1914, and photographs of 1894 and 1906

Stadtplan von Montreux 1830, 1870, 1914 und Aufnahmen von 1894 und 1906

35

'Hotel Montreux Palace', postcard, ca. 1906

Hotel Montreux Palace, Postkarte, ca. 1906

in 1899. In Tokyo, the hotel 'Imperial'[124] from the late 1890s has to give way to Frank Lloyd Wright's building from 1915–1922 that itself was to be demolished in 1967.

But to return to Switzerland: The necessity to spend the night somewhere in this country is mainly caused by having to cross the Alps, be it in combination with military actions—the most famous being Hannibal's crossing in antiquity[125]—or be it for economic purposes or during pilgrimages. The hospice on Great St. Bernard in an altitude of 8,110 feet (2,472 meter), goes back to the year 962 A.D.[126] More than 900 years had to pass, before in the nineteenth and early tweentieth century in Switzerland pensions became resort hotels and villages hotel cities of an international standing. In his most competent publication *Hotel Palaces. Between Dream and Reality*[127], Roland Flückiger-Seiler compares the settlement structure of Montreux in the years 1830, 1870 and 1914 and correctly speaks of a 'hotel city'.[128] (fig. 34) Here, high above Lac Léman Switzerland's presumably most imposing hotel-chateau is situated, 'Montreux Palace'.[129] (fig. 35) Here too, as with the urban Grand Hotels, an urbanization as well as a process of growth into large-scale dimensions happened. In 1904, the boarding house 'Pilivet' was demolished, situated directly next to the 'Hotel de Cygne' from 1834. In its place in 1905/06 an annex is built for the 'Montreux Palace' that includes a theatre and an ostentatious ballroom as well as a vestibule, several halls, staircases, dining halls, parlours, patios and verandas. 'Life in a hotel was to be as varied as for example a trip on an ocean liner'.[130] The background for this development was the speculation upon the Simplon railway line, completed in 1906, on which swanky guests now were able to reach Montreux hassle free by first class club cars. Amongst the many prominent guests in the course of time was the writer Vladimir Nabokov who between 1961 and 1977 had his permanent residence here.

The motor of urbanization in the shape of an explosively growing hotel sector in St. Moritz was provided again by the railway that in 1904 reaches the Engadine spa (fig. 36). The upswing in St. Moritz Bad as well as in St. Moritz Dorf can be exemplary measured by the hotel 'Engadiner Kulm'—the number of overnight stays grew from 80 in the year 1850 to 6,000 in the year 1920.[131] In 1840, Johannes Caspar Badrutt establishes the boarding house 'Faller' in an existing farm building that he enlarges in 1856 and renames 'Hotel Kulm'. Step by step nearly all adjoining farm buildings are incorporated as hotel

dritten als Solitärbau auf freiem Gelände statt (Abb. 32). Demselben Abbruch-Neubau-Prozedere begegnet man auch bei großstädtischen Bautypen wie den eingangs erwähnten Warenhäusern und Bahnhöfen[120], bei welch letzteren die frühen Stationsgebäude der ersten Hälfte des 19. Jahrhunderts nach der Jahrhundertmitte durch Monumentalbauten ersetzt werden, die dem Historismus verpflichtet sind. Warenhäuser wie das Pariser Au Bon Marché, Printemps oder Samaritaine[121] werden vom Einzelhandelsgeschäft oder Kleinkaufhaus zu ganze Baublöcke einnehmenden Volumen ausgebaut. Dasselbe Phänomen der Verdrängung historischer Bausubstanz oder ihrer Integration ist auch beim großstädtischen und metropolitanen Hotelbau festzustellen. So tritt unter anderem Londons Savoy Hotel und Theater an die Stelle der „Beaufort Buildings" aus dem Jahr 1695 „which was a combination of residential street and workshops."[122] (Abb. 33) In New York wird das aus dem Jahr 1883 stammende Haus des Eisenbahnkönigs Henry Willard als denkmalgeschütztes Objekt in den 51-geschossigen Hotelneubau des Helmsley Palace integriert.[123] Die Umwandlung oder Integration historischer Bausubstanz kennt neben dem bereits genannten Hotel Badischer Hof viele Beispiele. In Venedig wird der Palazzo Dandolo aus dem 14. Jahrhundert 1822 in das Hotel Danieli umgewandelt. In Paris gehen das Bristol (1878) auf einen Palast von 1718 und das Crillon (1909) auf einen Palast von 1765 zurück. Ritz seinerseits hat an der Place Vendôme eine Fassade von 1704 respektiert. In Alexandria entsteht das Beau Rivage (1922) aus der Zusammenlegung zweier Villen aus dem Jahr 1897. In Kairo wird der 1865 erbaute Gezira-Palast in das Hotel „Ismail Palace" umgewandelt und 1982 durch zwei Türme ergänzt. In Kandy, Sri Lanka entsteht aus dem 1825 errichteten Gouverneurspalast 1877 das Hotel Mount Lavinia. Obwohl die sogenannten Oriental Hotels hier nicht behandelt werden, da ihr Konzept dem der Grand Hotels nicht entspricht, seien zwei hier dennoch erwähnt, da sie Beispiele für das Vorgehen von Abbruch und anschließendem Neubau abgeben: In Singapur wird das 1887 eröffnete Raffles bereits 1899 durch einen Neubau ersetzt. Und in Tokio muss das Imperial[124] aus den späten 1890er Jahren dem Neubau von Frank Lloyd Wright (1915–1922) weichen, der dann seinerseits 1967 zerstört werden wird.

Doch kehren wir zurück in die Schweiz. Die Notwendigkeit von Übernachtungen bestand hier vor allem bei Alpenüberquerungen, sei es im Zusammenhang militä-

annexes. In 1886–87 Nicolaus Hartmann sen. enlarges the complex further. In 1911—meanwhile the winter season too is a period of travel—Nicolaus Hartmann jun. amplifies the complex to a several-hundred-room-hotel.[132] (fig. 37) Most Grand Hotels that intensify the moment of urbanization explosively, are built after the railway reaches the respective places.[133] St. Moritz, like the Riviera, Montreux or Cabourg constitutes an example of procedural hotelization, i.e. an urbanization of the countryside. After the Second World War in the Alps and on the coasts holiday resorts like 'La Grande Motte', 'Flaine' or 'Les Menuires'[134] are mushrooming in very short periods of time.

In Spain, this taking over of a landscape is aptly called *urbanización*. Along with the construction of hotels the erection of thousands of holiday residences had devastating consequences for the Spanish coastal regions. As a side effect of newly erected hotels the construction of private villas—based on speculative expectations—in the immediate vicinity of the hotels goes also back to the nineteenth century. The building contractors of 'Hotel Kursaal de la Maloja' next to the hotel built numerous villas in the 'Swiss wood style' for rent or purchase as element of an additional urbanization of the mountainside. The solitaire building of the 'Hotel Kursaal de la Maloja' however is an example of megalomaniac volumina (fig. 38). As an oversized foreign object it is rammed into the sublime landscape of the elevated plain between St. Moritz and Bergell, painted by artists like Giovanni Segantini and Giovanni Giacometti (fig. 39). For its initiator, Belgian nobleman Count Camille de Renesse, the hotel was to become the 'Monte Carlo of the Alps'.[135] In 1882 building activities and in 1884 hotel operations began in the 200-metre long edifice that after the Zurich Polytechnic was the second largest building in Switzerland. The architectural shape followed Neo-Renaissance forms, the big ballroom-cum-stage, the flat roof of which served customers as sun deck, was held in Neo-Rococo. Up to the epoch of Art Nouveau, architectural styles à la Louis XIV, XV, and XVI were leading. The naming of hotel halls and lounges as 'Pompadour', 'Versailles' or 'Trianon' additionally pointed to High Baroque and Rococo. The guests were to associate the court culture of the French kings or generally a noble chateau and palace culture. Accordingly, certain accretions to the word 'hotel' are further indices. Thus part of the hotel's program is a culture of festivities that offers balls, opera or theatre performances. In the ballroom of the 'Kursaal

rischer Handlungen – berühmt wurde Hannibals Überquerung in der Antike[125] –, Handel treibend oder auf Pilgerfahrt. Das auf dem Großen St. Bernhard in einer Höhe von 8110 Fuß (circa 2600 Meter) errichtete Hospiz geht auf das Jahr 862 zurück.[126] Mehr als 900 Jahre sollte es dauern, bis in der Schweiz im 19./20. Jahrhundert aus Pensionen Resorthotels und aus Dörfern Hotelstädte internationalen Ranges wurden. Roland Flückiger-Seiler vergleicht in seiner äußerst kompetenten Publikation *Hotelpaläste zwischen Traum und Wirklichkeit*[127] die Siedlungsstruktur von Montreux in den Jahren 1830, 1870 und 1914 und spricht mit Recht von einer Hotelstadt.[128] (Abb. 34) Hier liegt hoch über dem Genfer See das wohl imposanteste Hotelschloss der Schweiz, das Montreux Palace.[129] (Abb. 35) Auch hier findet sich also wie bei städtischen Grand Hotels die Verstädterung, die Großmaßstäblichkeit. 1904 wurde die neben dem seit 1834 bestehenden Hotel de Cygne gelegene Pension Pilivet abgebrochen. An ihrer Stelle entstand für das Montreux Palace 1905/06 ein Anbau mit Theater und einem prunkvollen Festsaal, Vestibül, diversen Hallen, Treppenhäusern, Esssälen, Salons, Rauchzimmern, Terrassen und Veranden. „Das Leben in einem Hotel sollte so abwechslungsreich sein wie zum Beispiel die Fahrt auf einem Ozeandampfer".[130] Diesem Kalkül folgte auch die 1906 fertiggestellte Simplonlinie der Eisenbahn, mit der die Gäste in mondänen Salonwagen Erster Klasse Montreux erreichen konnten. Zu den vielen prominenten Gästen Montreuxs gehörte unter anderem der Schriftsteller Vladimir Nabokov, der von 1961 bis 1977 seinen ständigen Wohnsitz im Hotel Montreux Palace hatte.

Motor der Verstädterung, das heißt des explosiven Wachstums der Hotellerie, ist auch in St. Moritz die Bahn, die den Engadiner Kurort 1904 erreicht. (Abb. 36) Der Aufschwung von sowohl St. Moritz Bad als auch Dorf – ein Anstieg der Übernachtungszahlen von 80 im Jahr 1850 auf 6000 im Jahr 1920[131] – lässt sich beispielhaft am Hotel Engadiner Kulm aufzeigen. 1840 richtet Johannes Caspar Badrutt in einem bestehenden Bauernhaus die Pension Faller ein, die er 1856 erweitert und in Hotel Kulm umbenennt. Sukzessive werden nahezu alle angrenzenden Bauernhäuser als Dépendancen einbezogen. Der Komplex wird 1886/87 von Nikolaus Hartmann sen. erweitert. 1911, inzwischen zählen auch die Wintermonate zur Reisesaison, findet durch Nikolaus Hartmann jun. eine erneute Erweiterung zum Mehrere-Hundert-Betten-Hotel statt.[132] (Abb. 37) Die meisten

36

St. Moritz Dorf, 1848, 1880, and 1934

St. Moritz Dorf 1848, 1880 und 1934

37

'Hotel Engadiner Kulm', picture postcard from around 1900 ● Floorplan of the ground floor with Faller boarding house integrated into the northwest corner

Hotel Engadiner Kulm, Ansichtskarte um 1900 ● Grundriss des Erdgeschosses mit der im Nordwesten integrierten Pension Faller

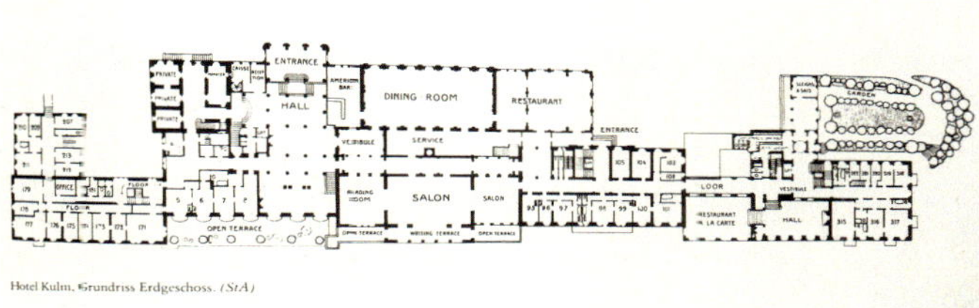

Maloja' one could admire stars of the Metropolitan Opera of New York or the Paris 'Comédie Française' as well as film presentations since the turn of the century.

In the hotel's heydays, twice daily concerts with musicians of the Milan 'Scala' took place.[136] The dining room to the right of the lobby housed 300 diners at the 'table d'hôte'. In the upper storeys 300 rooms for 450 guests were situated. The technical furnishings—with the notable exception of the sanitary arrangements—

Grand Hotels, die die Urbanisierung schlagartig vorantreiben, entstehen nach dem Anschluss an die Bahn.[133] St. Moritz ist wie die Riviera, Montreux, Cabourg et cetera ein Beispiel für die prozessuale Hotellisierung, das heißt die Verstädterung der Landschaft. Nach dem Zweiten Weltkrieg werden in den Alpen und an den Küsten Ferienstädte wie zum Beispiel La Grande Motte, Flaine oder Les Menuires[134] in einem Guß aus Beton aus dem Boden gestampft.

Dieses Phänomen der Landschaftsübernahme wird durch die in Spanien gebräuchliche Bezeichnung *urbanización* treffend charakterisiert. Zusammen mit dem Hotelbau hatte der Bau von Tausenden von Ferienresidenzen verheerende Folgen für unter anderem die spanischen Küsten. Als Begleiterscheinung neu errichteter Hotels geht – basierend auf spekulativen Erwartungen – die Errichtung von Privatvillen in unmittelbarer Umgebung

38
'Hotel Kursaal de la Maloja', photograph around 1900
Hotel Kursaal de la Maloja, Aufnahme um 1900

39

The Hay's Harvest 1889–1898, Giovanni Segantini ● Dining hall of the 'Hotel Kursaal de la Maloja', 1885

Heuernte, 1889–1898, von Giovanni Segantini ● Speisesaal des Hotel Kursaal de la Maloja, um 1885

were extremely modern. Parts of the advanced building equipment were lifts, central heating and electric illumination. The lighting of the interior and the big forecourt by carbon filament light bulbs produced by Siemens was made possible by the hotel's own electrical power station. Unparalleled in Switzerland was the air conditioning system (fig. 40). Part of the attractions was an elaborate park, situated towards the 'Silver Lake'. Most Grand Hotels offered parks. Assuming the shape of urban parks or villa gardens, they were alien elements in the respective countrysides like the hotel buildings themselves. Tennis courts, a 9-hole golf course, a skating rink, carriage service, an Anglican and a catholic church rounded off the choices.

Already in the summer of 1885 high nobility and pecunious bourgeoisie flocked into 'Kursaal Maloja'. In the visitors' book besides many other celebrities we find

des Hotelneubaus auf das 19. Jahrhundert zurück. Die Baugesellschaft des Hotel Kursaal de la Maloja erstellt neben dem Hotel als Element einer zusätzlichen Urbanisierung der Gebirgswelt zahlreiche Villen im „Schweizer Holzstil", die zum Verkauf oder zur Vermietung angeboten wurden. Das Hotel Kursaal de la Maloja ist jedoch als Solitärbau ein Beispiel megalomaner Volumina (Abb. 38). Als überproportionierter Fremdkörper ist es auf dem Hochplateau zwischen St. Moritz und dem Bergell in die erhabene Landschaft, wie sie Giovanni Segantini oder Giovanni Giacometti in Bilder gebannt haben, hineingestampft (Abb. 39). Für den Initiator, den belgischen Adligen Graf Camille de Renesse, sollte das Hotel „Monte Carlo der Alpen" werden.[135] 1882 begann der Bau und 1884 der Hotelbetrieb des mit 200 Metern Fassadenlänge nach dem Polytechnikum in Zürich zweitgrößten Gebäudes der Schweiz. Das architektonische Erschei-

40
Air conditioning system of the 'Hotel Kursaal de la Maloja', 1885
Klimaanlage im Hotel Kursaal de la Maloja, 1885

Edmund Baron Rothschild, Count Zeppelin, Sir Arthur Conan Doyle and the Impératrice Eugénie. The latter set the standard for luxuriant otiosity in her palais in Biarritz during the Second Empire that Grand Hotels took as a guideline. In 1887 Friedrich Nietzsche writes to his mother:

> 'In the hotel Maloja … the season runs very well this time (ca. 300 persons) … To give an idea of the frequency: On the 9th of August at the Maloja, at the hotel ca. 900 carriages operated, 500 of which were coaches or equipages. Very Nizza-like, whereas our Sils sticks to its idyllic character'.[137]

nungsbild folgte der Neorenaissance, der große Festsaal mit Bühne, dessen Flachdach den Gästen als Liegeterrasse diente, war in Neorokoko gestaltet. Bis zum Jugendstil war die Formensprache à la Louis XIV., Louis XV. und Louis XVI. tonangebend. Auch die Benennung der Hotelsäle und -salons verwies mit „Pompadour", „Versailles", „Trianon" auf Hochbarock und Rokoko. Der Gast sollte die Hofkultur der französischen Könige, ja ganz allgemein die Schloss- und Palastkultur assoziieren. So gehört auch zum Programm der Hotels eine Festkultur, die Bälle, Opern- und Theaterveranstaltungen anbietet. Zu bewundern waren im Kursaal Maloja Stars der Metropolitan Opera New York und der Pariser Comédie Française wie auch seit der Jahrhundertwende Filmvorführungen.

In der Blütezeit des Hotels fanden zweimal täglich Konzerte mit Musikern der Mailänder Scala statt.[136] Der zur Rechten des Vestibüls (Lobby) gelegene Speisesaal hatte Platz für 300 Personen an der „table d'hôte". In den Obergeschossen befanden sich 300 Zimmer für 450 Gäste. Die technische Ausstattung war – mit der bemerkenswerten Ausnahme der Sanitäranlagen – sehr fortschrittlich. Zur avancierten Haustechnik gehörten Lifte, Heizung und elektrische Beleuchtung. Die Beleuchtung der Innenräume und des großen Vorplatzes mittels Kohlefaden-Glühlampen der Firma Siemens war durch ein hoteleigenes Kraftwerk gesichert. Einmalig in der Schweiz war die Klimaanlage. Zum Angebot gehörte auch ein zum Silsersee hin gelegener, aufwändiger Park. Parkanlagen waren Teil der meisten Grand Hotels: gestaltet wie Stadtparks oder Villengärten waren sie ebenso wie die Hotelarchitekturen Fremdkörper im Landschaftsbild. Tennisplätze, ein Neun-Loch-Golfplatz, im Winter eine Eisbahn, ein Kutschendienst, eine anglikanische und eine katholische Kirche komplettierten das Angebot.

Bereits im Sommer 1885 strömten der Hochadel und die Geldbourgeoisie ins Kursaal Maloja. Im Gästebuch finden sich neben vielen anderen Zelebritäten Baron Edmund Rothschild, Graf Zeppelin, Lord Arthur Conan Doyle und die Impératrice Eugénie. Letztere setzte als Gemahlin von Napoleon III. in ihrem Palais in Biarritz während des Zweiten Kaiserreiches Maßstäbe für luxuriösen Müßiggang, an dem sich auch die Grandhotels orientierten. 1887 schreibt Friedrich Nietzsche an seine Mutter:

> „Im Hotel Maloja … ist die Saison dieses Mal sehr gut (ca. 300 Personen) … Um einen Begriff von der Frequenz

41

Maloja, 1899/1900, by Giovanni Segantini ● Transport of luggage to the 'Hotel Kursaal de la Maloja', around 1900

Maloja, 1899/1900, von Giovanni Segantini ● Gepäcktransport zum Hotel Kursaal de la Maloja, um 1900

'Nizza-like' Nietzsche calls that element of spatial and social alienation that adheres to the Grand Hotel implanted into the open countryside.

Out of proportion with the scale of regional architecture, the hotel 'Kursaal Maloja' constitutes a metropolitan citation. The cultural program with protagonists from New York, Paris, and Milan imports urban attractions. The staff mainly consists of non-residents thus creating a cultural mix typical for urban environments. Furthermore the locals are confronted with a civilization alien to them, with apparel and habits of an urban population that they on the one hand disapprove of and on the other hand imitate. The hotel guests in turn regard the locals as an exoticum (fig. 41). To watch them becomes part of consumption like watching the landscape or the imported music from Milan. The specific folkloristic flavour develops into the marketing strategy of the Grand Hotels. The experience of the landscape more and more degenerates into a stage production.[138] On a world scale, autochthon populations of the most diverse races are presented to the tourists as attractions. The most recent trend is slum sightseeing.[139] Living in luxury hotels one lets reality pass by like a film, today in the same way as yesterday (fig. 42).

Surface Culture

As insignia of an urbanizing world hotels were positioned in the midst of so far untouched landscapes—as shown at the Swiss example. At an early date Swiss hotel owners and after them foreign investors realized the marketing potential of the scenery. The Alps constituted an attraction: one simply had to see the sunrise on the Rigi, had to experience the awe of the grandiose world of the mountains. Here we can discern a first tendency for the marketing of attractions. Next to World Exhibitions and Olympic Games—as we see already in the Sparta of antiquity—they are an essential prerequisite for the building of hotels as well as winning an economic profit from them. Where there was no authenticity of place (Riviera, the Alps or Paris, London, Venice, etc.) artificial attractions had to be created, as was to be the case with Las Vegas. Again in its role as promoter of an early mass tourism, the railway here in 1903 reaches the Nevada desert. It is gambling halls and casinos, theatrical shows of every kind that up to today drive a mass public into the hotels of Las Vegas. Trendsetters too—if on another level—were the Grand Hotels, as we have shown using the example of the 'Ritz',

zu geben: Am 9ten August verkehrten in Maloja, bei dem Hotel, ca. 900 Wagen, davon ca. 500 Kutschen und Equipagen. Sehr nizza-mäßig, dagegen hält unser Sils seinen idyllischen Charakter fest".[137]

Mit „nizza-mäßig" charakterisiert Nietzsche jenes Element der räumlichen und gesellschaftlichen Entfremdung, das dem in die Landschaft implantierten Grandhotel anhaftet.

Mit seinen Dimensionen die Maßstäbe der regionalen Architektur sprengend, ist das Hotel Kursaal de la Maloja ein großstädtisches Zitat. Das kulturelle Angebot mit Protagonisten aus New York, Paris und Mailand importiert urbane Attraktionen. Das Hotelpersonal setzt sich zu großen Teilen aus Ortsfremden zusammen, somit findet eine ebenfalls als städtisches Phänomen zu interpretierende Durchmischung statt. Darüber hinaus wird die einheimische Bevölkerung mit einer ihr fremden Zivilisation, Kleidung und den Gewohnheiten des urbanen Menschen konfrontiert, denen sie ablehnend oder auch adaptierend gegenübersteht. Der Hotelgast wiederum betrachtet den Einheimischen als ein Exotikum (Abb. 41). Seine Betrachtung wird konsumiert wie die Landschaft oder die aus Mailand importierte Musik. Das spezifische Lokalkolorit wird Teil der Vermarktungsstrategie der Grandhotels. Das Landschaftserlebnis gerät immer mehr zu einer Bühneninszenierung.[138] Weltweit wird die autochthone Bevölkerung der unterschiedlichsten Ethnien dem Touristen vorgeführt. Neuester Trend ist die Besichtigung von Slums.[139] Man lebt abgeschirmt im Luxushotel und lässt die Realität als Film an sich vorbeiziehen, heute wie gestern (Abb. 42).

Kultur der Oberflächen – der Schrei nach dem schönen Schein

Wie Insignien einer sich verstädternden Welt wurden die Hotels – wie am Beispiel der Schweiz dargestellt – in die Landschaft gesetzt. Schon früh erkannten die Schweizer Hoteliers und in ihrer Folge ausländische Investoren, dass sich die Landschaft vermarkten ließ. Die Alpen waren eine Attraktion: Den Sonnenaufgang auf der Rigi musste man gesehen, den Schauder vor der grandiosen Bergwelt erfahren haben. Neben Weltausstellungen und Olympischen Spielen – das galt schon in Sparta – wurde die Landschaft als Attraktion eine wesentliche Voraus-

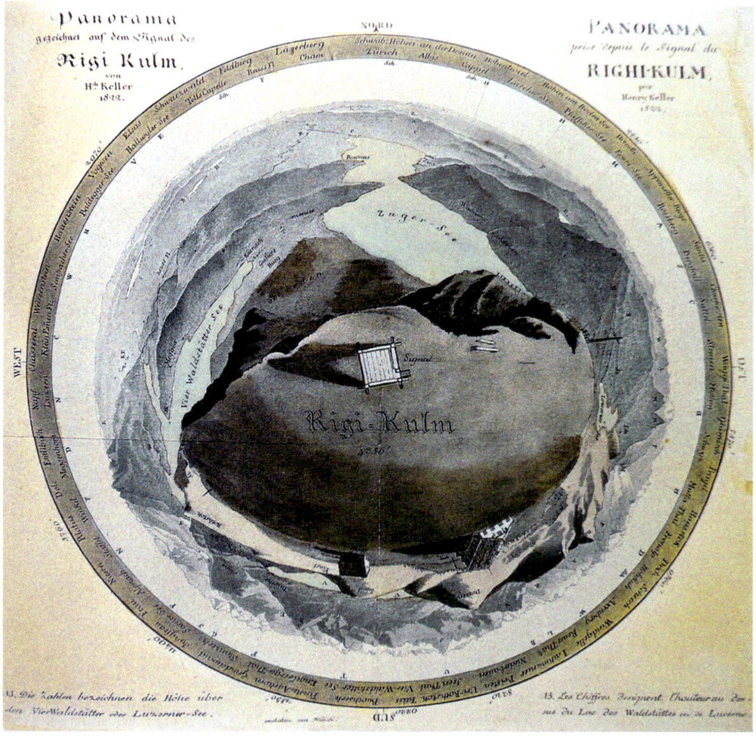

the 'Hotel Kursaal de la Maloja', the Côte d'Azur casinos or those in Monte Carlo (from 1863).

As an object of investment and rates of return the hotel depends on marketing. Again, this trend was initiated a long time ago. From around 1830, travel guides override

42
The experience of nature and a metropolitan quality of service: Rigi-Kulm panorama, Erich Keller, 1822 ● 'Order-clock' in the 'Élysée Palace Hotel', Paris

Naturerlebnis und großstädtische Servicequalität: Rigi-Kulm Panorama, 1822 von Heinrich Keller ● Bestelluhr im Élysée Palace Hôtel in Paris

setzung für den Hotelbau und den aus ihm zu schöpfenden ökonomischen Gewinn. Dort wo die Authentizität des Ortes (Riviera, Alpen oder auch Paris, London, Venedig et cetera) nicht gegeben war, mussten künstliche Attraktionen geschaffen werden. Las Vegas ist hierfür ein Beispiel. 1903 erreicht die Eisenbahn – auch hier wieder Beförderer des frühen Massentourismus – die Wüste von Nevada. Spielsalons und Casinos sowie schaustellerische Angebote jeglicher Art sind die Attraktionen, die bis heute ein Massenpublikum in die Hotels von Las Vegas bringen. Trendsetter – wenn auch auf einem anderen Niveau – waren die Grand Hotels, wie am Beispiel Ritz, dem Hotel Kursaal de la Maloja, den Casinos an der Côte d'Azur oder in Monte Carlo (ab 1863) aufgezeigt.

Als Objekt von Investition und Rendite ist das Hotel abhängig von der Vermarktung. Auch hier wurden die Weichen bereits in der Geschichte gestellt. Die Jahrhunderte lange mündlich oder in Reiseberichten erfolgte Übermittlung der Reputation einer Herberge oder eines

the century-old role of conveying the reputation of an inn or a hotel by word-of-mouth or travel reports. Part of a marketing strategy is, besides the actual qualities of 'comfort, service, cuisine' the purposeful decision of the hotel owner concerning the establishment's name. Why does one call a Japanese (Fukuoka) hotel 'Il Palazzo', why hotels were called 'Palace Hotels' or 'Castle Hotels'? The answer is clear. The unequivocal intention was to suggest to the client that he was completely being lifted out of his daily experience. The recourse on historic styles and the celebration of a quasi-courtly culture (balls, formal dinners) were the means.

Famous guests also contributed to the fame of a hotel or a café or restaurant[140] because their stay in these establishments could be exploited in a promotionally successful way. 'The name means something to us ... each hotel depends on the reputation of its guests. A famous actress like you ... brings attention for the hotel and ... guests' we already read in Theodore Dreiser's novel Sister Carrie.[141] Hotel leaflets as well as signs at room doors point to outstanding personalities like Mark Twain, Tennessee Williams, James Joyce, Thomas Mann, Agatha Christie, Marcel Proust, Charlie Chaplin, Marilyn Monroe and others. Of course also today, in terms of marketability, the visit of 'celebrities' augments the fame of a hotel and draws a 'society-climber' clientele. Thus hotel management is compelled like in the epoch of the Grand Hotels to coordinate the demands of a cultivated elite with that of the nouveau riches.

Since quite a while now, luxury hotels are in the hands of international corporate groups. The 'Kempinski' hotels for example are by majority stake owned by the Thai 'Crown Property Bureau'. Concerning the market entry of Asian investors into the Paris hotel market, the American news magazine *Time* titles: 'Paris Hotel Wars. Asian chains take on the city's grandes dames by offering a modern spin on luxury'.[142] For more than a century, Paris Grand Hotels like the 'Ritz', 'Crillon', 'George V', 'Meurice' 'Plaza Athenée' or 'Bristol' saw themselves as guardians of an outstanding hotel service. 'Their iconic status kept their rooms filled through most of the recession...'[143] The guests mainly come from the ranks of the international money oligarchy of the twenty-first century[144] and it is they that are targeted by the Asian investors. The Singapore 'Raffles Group' invested into the reopening of the Paris 'Le Royal Monceau' dating back to 1928, the firm 'Shangri-La' from Hong Kong convert-

Hotels übernehmen ab circa 1830 die Reiseführer. Zur Vermarktungsstrategie gehört neben den tatsächlichen Qualitäten von „comfort, service, cuisine" als zielgerichtete Entscheidung des Hoteliers die Namensgebung. Warum wohl wird in Japan (Fukuoka) ein Hotel Il Palazzo, warum wurden die Hotels Palast- oder Schlosshotel benannt? Die Antwort ist eindeutig. Die Intention war, dem Gast die Illusion zu vermitteln, im Hotel der Alltagskultur vollständig enthoben zu sein. Der Rückgriff auf historische Stile und die Zelebrierung einer quasi-höfischen Kultur (Bälle, Diners) taten das ihrige.

Zum Ruhm eines Hotels – wie auch zu dem von Cafés und Restaurants[140] – trugen auch berühmte Gäste bei, deren Aufenthalt sich dann wiederum werbewirksam nutzen ließ. „Der Name ist uns etwas wert ... Jedes Hotel hängt von dem Ruf seiner Gäste ab. Eine bekannte Schauspielerin wie Sie ... verschafft dem Hotel Beachtung und ... Gäste", heißt es schon in Theodore Dreisers Roman *Sister Carrie*.[141] Hotelprospekte, Schilder an Zimmern oder Suiten verweisen auf Mark Twain, Tennessee Williams, James Joyce, Thomas Mann, Agatha Christie, Marcel Proust, Charlie Chaplin, Marilyn Monroe und so weiter und so fort. Selbstverständlich hebt auch heute – vermarktungstechnisch gesehen – der Besuch von *celebrities* den Ruf eines Hotels und zieht die *society-climber*-Clientèle an. Somit wird das Hotelmanagement – wie in den Zeiten der Grand Hotels – gezwungen, die Ansprüche einer kultivierten Elite mit denen der neuen Reichen zu koordinieren.

Schon längst befinden sich Luxushotels in den Händen internationaler Konzerne. Die Kempinski-Hotels zum Beispiel sind mehrheitlich im Besitz des thailändischen Crown Property Bureau. Den Einstieg asiatischer Investoren in Paris beschreibt das amerikanische Nachrichtenmagazin *Time* unter dem Titel: „Paris Hotel Wars. Asian chains take on the city's grandes dames by offering a modern spin on luxury".[142] Etwa 100 Jahre lang haben Pariser Grand Hotels wie das Ritz, das Crillon, das George V., das Meurice, das Plaza Athénée und das Bristol sich als Wächter hoch stehenden Hotelservices gesehen. „Their iconic status kept their rooms filled through most of the recession ..."[143] Kunden sind vor allem die Geldoligarchen des 21. Jahrhunderts.[144] Asiatische Investoren zielen auf diese Gäste ab. Die in Singapur ansässige Raffles Group investierte in Paris in die Wiedereröffnung des Le Royal Monceau aus dem Jahr 1928, die Firma Shangri-La aus Hongkong hat den Stadtpalast von

ed the town palace of Napoleon's grand nephew into a hotel with price levels between 1000 and 1300 dollars per night. In the immediate neighbourhood of the Louvre in 2011 the 'Mandarin Oriental' opened. The name-giving clearly points to the expected clientele. The investment per room was 1.6 million dollar. 'The newly rich of China and India (and one has to add Russia) are becoming active tourists filling hotel rooms and dining out.'[145] 'Dining out at the Savoy' at the beginning of the twentieth century was a novelty introduced by César Ritz.

The general manager of the 'Royal Monceau' swears to the intermix of international guests with Parisians. He hopes that 'the hotel's public spaces will seduce locals giving guests the clichéd sense of place they seek.'[146] To underpin this cliché, Philippe Starck furnished the grand foyer with typical French finds from flea markets and even strategically placed tomes of Marcel Proust in carefully chosen positions. 'Surface culture' Walter Benjamin called this phenomenon. An in-depth-attitude is not in fashion any more, neither with the perception of the surroundings nor with that of people. 'Nobody bothers about anyone else. Everyone is alone with himself. The events that happen do not constitute entire human destinies complete and rounded off. They are fragments merely, scraps, pieces … A glance that travels up does not reach the eyes. It stops at one's clothes.'[147]

The hotel provides the background for this non-committal attitude. For the ambiance of these encounters that do not oblige one to anything, one increasingly looks at the historical Grand Hotels. On a worldwide scale they—like palaces[148]—are brought to new life: the 'Cathay' (1929) with its Art Deco glass cupola in Shanghai[149], the hotel 'Metropole' (1885) today 'Corinthian' in London and, also in the British metropole, the 'Savoy'[150] and the 'St. Pancras Renaissance'. 'Despite modern touches here like an underground swimming pool and spa, Old world elegance reigns. The sweeping lobby—made by enclosing an old taxi rank—melds glass ceiling with red brick walls and elaborate (historic) ironwork.'[151]

'Russian and Chinese consumers like old looking buildings, but if the shower or the wi-fi doesn't work properly it turns them off completely', thus the 'Oriental Mandarin's'[152] manager. 'It were devices that made modern hotels modern',[153] Norman S. Hayner stated in the 1930s and remarks simultaneously 'The rage for mechanical devices may be the ruin of a once good hotel; for the basis of righteousness in a hotel is not mechanical

Napoleons Großneffen hotellisiert. Preisniveau: zwischen 1000 und 1300 Dollar pro Nacht. Im Juni 2011 eröffnete in unmittelbarer Nähe des Louvre das Mandarin Oriental. Die Namensgebung verweist auf die intendierte Clientèle. Die Investition beträgt 1,6 Millionen Dollar pro Zimmer. „The newly rich of China and India [man muss Russland hinzufügen] … are becoming active tourists filling hotel rooms and dining out."[145] *Dining out at the Savoy* war Anfang des 20. Jahrhunderts eine von César Ritz eingeführte Novität.

Der Geschäftsführer des Le Royal Monceau beschwört die Durchmischung der internationalen Gäste mit Parisern: die Vermarktung des Lokalkolorits. Er hofft, dass „the hotel's public spaces will seduce locals giving guests the clichéd sense of place they seek."[146] Um diesem Klischee ein Fundament zu geben, hat Philippe Starck das große Foyer mit „typisch französischen" Fundstücken von Trödelmärkten ausgestattet und an sorgfältig ausgewählten Stellen Proustbände platziert! „Oberflächenkultur" benennt Walter Benjamin dieses Phänomen. Tiefgang ist nicht gefragt, weder bei der Wahrnehmung der Umgebung, noch bei der Wahrnehmung der Menschen. „Niemand kümmert sich um den Anderen. Jeder ist allein mit sich selbst. Die Veranstaltungen die sich zutragen, repräsentieren in keiner Weise vollständige und abgerundete menschliche Schicksale. Sie sind eher Fragmente, Fetzen, Stückwerk … Ein aufwärts wandernder Blick erreicht die Augen nicht. Er bleibt an der Kleidung hängen".[147]

Das Hotel liefert den perfekten Rahmen für diese Unverbindlichkeit. Das Ambiente für die zu nichts verpflichtenden Begegnungen wird zunehmend in historischen Grand Hotels gesucht. Weltweit werden sie, wie auch Paläste[148], zu neuem Leben erweckt: das Cathay (1929) mit seiner Art-Déco-Glaskuppel in Shanghai[149], das Hôtel Métropole (1885) – heute Corinthian – in London und ebenfalls in der britischen Metropole das Savoy[150] und das St. Pancras Renaissance. „Despite modern touches like an underground swimming pool and spa, old world elegance reigns. The sweeping lobby – made by enclosing an old taxi rank – melds glass ceiling with red brick walls and elaborate (historic) ironwork."[151]

„Russian and Chinese consumers like old looking buildings, but if the shower or the Wi-fi doesn't work properly it turns them off completely", so der Manager des Mandarin Oriental.[152]

devices but personal human contacts.'[154] In the Paris hotel war French hotel owners counterattack:

> 'You can come from China and build outstanding bathrooms … But our guests are looking for soul. That isn't in the marble or the gilt. Luxury today needs to have a story, so the Crilllon emphasizes that Marie Antoinette took piano lessons in the drawing rooms and the Ritz honors Coco Chanel's 30-year residency there.'[155]

The history written by Grand Hotels is exploited here. History and stories as merchandise, as marketing label. In this, hotels act in conformity to the capitalist economy. They represent the culture of the surface, a way once paved by the Grand Hotels. 'The detachment, freedom, loneliness and release from restraints that mark the hotel population are only to a lesser degree characteristic of modern life as a whole'[156] Norman S. Hayner wrote in 1936 and thus defines a deficit beyond the anxious unfolding of contemporary glamour.

„It were devices that made modern hotels modern",[153] konstatierte Norman S. Hayner in den 1930er Jahren und erkennt gleichzeitig: „The rage for mechanical devices may be the ruin of a once good hotel; for the basis of righteousness in a hotel is not mechanical devices but personal human contacts."[154] Im Pariser Hotelkrieg kontern die französischen Hotelbetreiber:

> „You can come from China and build outstanding bathrooms … But our guests are looking for soul. That isn't in the marble or the gilt. Luxury today needs to have a story, so the Crillon emphasizes that Marie Antoinette took piano lessons in the drawing rooms and the Ritz honors Coco Chanel's 30-year residency there."[155]

Die Geschichte, die die Grand Hotels geschrieben haben, wird hier instrumentalisiert. Geschichte und Geschichten als Ware, als Label für die Vermarktung. Hiermit verhalten sich Hotels konform zur kapitalistischen Wirtschaft. Sie sind Repräsentanten einer Oberflächenkultur, der einstmals die Grand Hotels den Weg ebneten. „Die Alltagsferne, die Freiheit, Einsamkeit und das Fehlen von Einschränkungen die die Hotelklientel kennzeichnen, sind nur noch in geringem Masse charakteristisch für das moderne Leben als Ganzes",[156] schrieb Norman S. Hayner und benennt damit ein Defizit jenseits der bemühten Entfaltung zeitgenössischen Glamours.

Notes

1 Concerning the history of accomodation, cf. Ludy, Robert: *Historic Hotels of the World*, Philadelphia (1927) 2009; Hayner, Norman S.: *Hotel Life*, Chapel Hill 1936, p. 1–27; von der Hude, Hermann: 'Hotels', in: *Handbuch der Architektur*, 4th part, 4th halfbinding: *Entwerfen, Anlage und Einrichtung der Gebäude. Gebäude für Erholungs-, Beherbergungs- und Vereinszwecke*, Darmstadt 1885, p. 174–75; Firebaugh, W. C.: *The Inns of Greece and Rome. And a History of Hospitality from the Dawn of Time to the Middle Ages*, New York (1928) 1972; Glücksmann, Robert: *Das Gaststättenwesen*, Stuttgart 1927, p. 1–56

2 Hayner, Norman S., op.cit., p. 11

3 Cf. *Meyers Großes Konversationslexikon*, 6th edition, Leipzig and Vienna 1908, vol. 7, p. 379–380

4 Glücksmann, Robert, op.cit., p. 27ff.

5 Very often the hanging out of signs was controlled by guilds. 'For France, Fournier names the year 1313 as demonstrably earliest date, for Germany Grohne names 1410' Glücksmann, Robert, op.cit., p. 27ff.

6 Ibid., p. 6–7

7 'Caravanserais are those kinds of public buildings within the city or along the trading routes, in which these travelling companies with their horses and camels find accommodation. In the cities they normally take the shape of square buildings of one or two storeys executed with splendour with rooms in the upper storeys that open towards galleries around a yard. In these rooms the merchants and their wares are accommodated, whereas the ground level and basement is occupied by the animals. In the centre of such an inn usually a water basin is found to water the animals and serve as washing basins before prayer. The caravanserais, usually called chane (today han) in Turkey, mostly are pious endowments by rich merchants, highly positioned dignitaries and baronial persons'. (*Meyers Großes Konversationslexikon*, op.cit., vol. 10, p. 616)

8 'The traveller carries his own bedding, which is spread out upon a few boards stretched over two trestles' (Williams, Edward T.: *China. Yesterday and Today*, New York 1923, p. 125). As late as the end of the eighteenth century the Englishwoman Mariana Starke (Letters from Italy between 1792 and 1798) recommends to pack the following items: a bedstead that can be converted into a divan, two sheepskin bags, a pair of pillows, a pair of woollen blankets, a pair of bedside carpets, bed sheets, two bed covers, a mosquito net made of fine veil-like cloth, a padlock (theses padlocks one can already find in London and fix it to doors in less than five minutes); towels, tablecloths, napkins (not fine ones, but ones durably to use); pistols, knives, a pocket knife for meals, silver spoons, table and tea spoons, salt spoons, a silver or doublé teapot, a tin kettle for making tea; a box with fire steel and tinder or a simple pocket lighter, a tea box and one more for sugar, a soldier's confort … tea, Cayenne pepper, ginger, nutmegs, oatmeal…'. Cited after: Imorde, Joseph: 'Schmutzige Laken. Die Kehrseite der Grand Tour', in: *Daidalos, Architektur. Kunst. Kultur*, issue 62, 1996, p. 56–57. A lot of these things are objects that in the Grand Hotels of 1900 as well as nowadays fall pray to souvenir hunters.

9 Desiderius Erasmus von Rotterdam (1466 or 1469-1536): *Familiarium Colloquiorum Formulae, auch Colloquia Familiaria*, Basel 1518, 1527. Cited after: Glücksmann, Robert, op.cit., p.13

10 Montaigne, Michel de (1533–1592): *Reisetagebuch,* translated and introduced by Otto Flake, Leipzig 1903, vol. 7 of the Collected Works. Cited after: Glücksmann, Robert, op.cit., p. 15

11 Ibid., p.15–16

12 Goethe's Works, ed. By Gerhard Fricke, Tübingen, n.y., vol. 7, p. 26. Cited after: Imorde, Joseph, op.cit., p. 64

13 Mérimée, Prosper: 'Carmen', Paris 1845, in: Mérimée, Prosper:

Anmerkungen

1 Zur Geschichte der Beherbergung vgl. Ludy, Robert: *Historic Hotels of the World*. Philadelphia (1927) 2009; Hayner, Norman S.: *Hotel Life*. Chapel Hill 1936, S. 1–27; Hude, Hermann von der: „Hotels". In: *Handbuch der Architektur*. 4. Teil, 4. Halbband: *Entwerfen, Anlage und Einrichtung der Gebäude. Gebäude für Erholungs-, Beherbergungs- und Vereinszwecke*. Darmstadt 1885, S. 174/175; Firebaugh, W. C.: *The Inns of Greece and Rome. And a History of Hospitality from the Dawn of Time to the Middle Ages*. New York (1928) 1972; Glücksmann, Robert: *Das Gaststättenwesen*. Stuttgart 1927, S. 1–56

2 Hayner, Norman S., op. cit., S. 11

3 Vgl. *Meyers Großes Konversationslexikon*, Leipzig und Wien 1908, Bd. 7, S. 379/380

4 Glücksmann, Robert, op. cit., S. 2

5 Das Aufhängen von Schildern stand oft unter Kontrolle einer Zunft. „Für Frankreich gibt Fournier das Jahr 1313 als nachweisbar frühesten Zeitpunkt [hierfür] an, für Deutschland Grohne das Jahr 1240." (Glücksmann, Robert, op. cit., S. 27 ff.)

6 Ibid., S. 6/7

7 „Karawansereien sind die öffentlichen Gebäude in den Städten und an der Handelsstraße, in denen jene Reisegesellschaften mit ihren Pferden und Kamelen Unterkunft finden. In Städten bestehen sie zumeist aus viereckigen, oft mit Pracht ausgeführten, ein oder zwei Stock hohen Gebäuden, deren Zimmer in den obern Stockwerken auf rund um einen Hof laufende Galerien sich öffnen. In diesen Zimmern wohnen die Kaufleute mit ihrer Ware, während das Erdgeschoß und die Kellerräume von den Tieren eingenommen werden. In der Mitte einer derartigen Herberge befindet sich meist ein Wasserbassin zum Tränken der Tiere und zu den Waschungen vor dem Gebet. Die Karawansereien, in der Türkei gewöhnlich Chane (heute Han) genannt, sind zumeist fromme Stiftungen reicher Kaufleute, hoher Würdenträger und fürstlicher Personen." (*Meyers Großes Konversationslexikon*, op. cit., Bd. 10, S. 616)

8 "The traveller carries his own bedding, which is spread out upon a few boards stretched over two trestles" (Williams, Edward T.: *China: Yesterday and Today*. New York 1923, S. 125). Noch Ende des 18. Jahrhunderts empfiehlt die Engländerin Mariana Starke (*Letters from Italy between 1792 and 1798*) folgendes mit einzupacken: „Eine Liegestatt, die in einen Diwan umgewandelt werden kann; zwei Säcke aus Schaffell, ein Paar Kissen, ein Paar Wolldecken, ein Paar Bettvorleger, Bettücher, zwei Bezüge, ein Moskitonetz aus feinem Schleierstoff, ein Vorhängeschloß (diese Schlösser kann man schon in London finden und in weniger als fünf Minuten bequem an jede Tür anbringen); Handtücher, Tischtücher, Mundtücher (Nicht schöne, sondern dauerhafte in Gebrauch); Pistolen, Messer, ein Taschenmesser für die Mahlzeiten, silberne Esslöffel, Suppen- und Teelöffel, Salzlöffel, eine Teekanne aus Silber oder auch Doublé, eine Blechkanne zum Kochen des Teewassers: eine Schachtel mit dem Feuerstahl und dem phosphorigen Zunder oder ein einfaches Taschenfeuerzeug, eine Teedose und eine weitere für Zucker, ein soldier's confort … Tee, Cayennepfeffer, Ingwer, Muskatnuß, Hafermehl …". Zitiert nach Imorde, Joseph: „Schmutzige Laken. Die Kehrseite der Grand Tour". In: *Daidalos. Architektur. Kunst. Kultur*. Heft 62, 1996, S. 56/57. Eine Menge der aufgezählten Dinge gehören zu den Objekten, die heute Souvenirjägern zum Opfer fallen.

9 Desiderius Erasmus von Rotterdam (1466 oder 1469–1526): *Familiarum Colloquiorum Formulae*, auch *Colloquia Familiaria*. Basel (1518). 1527 (dt.: Vertraute Gespräche). Zitiert nach Glücksmann, Robert, op. cit., S. 13

10 Montaigne, Michel de (1533–1592): *Reisetagebuch*. Übersetzt und eingeleitet von Otto Flake. Leipzig 1908, 7. Bd. der gesammelten Schriften. Zitiert nach: Glücksmann, Robert, op. cit., S. 15

Collected Short Novels, München 1982, p. 522

14 Cf. the chapter 'From Purpose-Oriented Travel to Tourism: The Urbanisation of the Countryside'

15 Thackeray, William Makepeace: *Vanity Fair*, or: *A Novel without a Hero*, London 1847/48

16 Hayner, Norman S., op.cit., p. 22. 'Tremont House', built by Isaiah Rogers replaced the burnt down 'Exchange Coffee House' of 1806-09 (architect Asher Benjamin), a seven-storey house with 200 rooms seating 300 persons for dinner. The earliest American hotel was New York's 'City Hotel', erected from 1794–96 by Benjamin Henry Latrobe (1764–1820). William H. Eliot's 'A Description of Tremont House, with Architectural Illustrations', 1830, for half a century served as compendium of hotel architecture (Watkin, David, op. cit., p. 13-15). Another milestone of hotel architecture in America was the 'Astor Hotel' in New York, for which from 1830 several designs by Alexander Jackson Davis existed.

17 Ludy, Robert B., op.cit., p. 210

18 'The hotel (a very excellent one) is called Tremont House. It has more galleries, colonnades, piazzas and passages than I can remember, or the reader would believe' Dickens writes in 1842. Ibid., p. 211

19 Characterization by the Berlin publicist Friedrich Buchholz. Cited after: Fischer, Bernhard: 'Der Badische Hof. 1807–1830. Cottas Hotel in Baden-Baden', in: *Marbacher Magazin*, 79/1997, Marbach am Neckar 1997, p. 2. Cotta edited Schiller, Alexander von Humboldt, Schelling and Herder, but also political magazines and cultural journals. After Schiller's death, with whom Cotta had an intimate friendship, he befriended Goethe. Both frequented spas. Cotta travelled to the South-West of Germany, in the Allgäu and to Switzerland, Goethe to Pyrmont or mostly Bohemia, for example Karlsbad. One incitement for the erection of the hotel was that both then could have the opportunity to meet more frequently in Baden-Baden.

20 Fischer, Bernhard, op.cit., p. 5

21 Weinbrenner, Friedrich (1766–1826) from 1800 acted as senior director of construction in the grand duchy of Baden. Part of his responsibility were public buildings, amongst others the urban planning of Karlsruhe

22 Fischer, Bernhard: op.cit., p. 17

23 Architects: Carlos Ferrater and José Maria Cartañá, 1995

24 Cf. Bollerey, Franziska: *Architekturkonzeptionen der utopischen Sozialisten. Alternative Planung und Architektur für den gesellschaftlichen Prozeß*, Berlin (1977) 1991, p. 150–167

25 Keck, Herbert: 'Profitable Raumverschwendung. Das Atriumhotel', in: *Daidalos*: op.cit., p. 42-51. Cf. Downey, Claire: 'Das Portman Hotel. Die Evolution einer Design Philosophie', in: *Archithese. Zeitschrift und Schriftenreihe für Architektur*, issue 2, 1988, p. 19–25

26 Fischer, Bernhard, op.cit., p. 17

27 Fischer von Erlach, Johann Bernhard: *Entwurff einer historischen Architectur*, Wien 1721, 2nd ed. 1725

28 Durand, Jean-Nicolas-Louis (1760–1834), *Recueil et parallèles des édifices de tous genres, anciens et modernes, remarquables par leur beauté, par leur grandeur ou par leur singularité, et dessinés sur une même échelle.* Paris 1801; ibid.,: *Précis des leçons d'architecture: données à l'École Polytechnique.* Paris, 1802–1805; ibid.: *Partie graphique des cours d'architecture faits à l'École Royale Polytechnique depuis sa réorganisation; précédée d'un sommaire relatif à ce nouveau travail.* Paris, 1821

29 Durand, Jean-Nicolas-Louis: *Recueil et parallèles...*, op.cit., table 30 (Hospices, Lazarets, Caravanserails, Cimitières)

30 'Les hôtelleries, destinées à recevoir des voyageurs ne sont dans la plus grande partie de l'Europe que des édifices particuliers qui n'offrent pas, pour la plupart, plus d'ordre, de commodité, de propreté que la majeure partie de nos fermes. En Orient, au contraire, ces mêmes lieux, nommés caravansérails, sont des édifices publics bâtis et entretenus avec le plus grand soin

11 Ibid., S. 15/16

12 *Goethes Werke.* Hg. von Gerhard Fricke. Tübingen o. J., Bd. 7, S. 26. Zitiert in: Imorde, Joseph, op. cit., S. 64

13 Mérimée, Prosper: „Carmen". Paris 1845. In: ders.: *Sämtliche Novellen.* München 1982, S. 522

14 Siehe auch das Unterkapitel „Von der Zweckreise zum Tourismus: Die Verstädterung der Landschaft"

15 Thackeray, William Makepeace: *Vanity Fair, or, A Novel without a Hero.* London 1847/48

16 Hayner, Norman S., op. cit., S. 22. Das von Isaiah Rogers erbaute Tremont House trat an die Stelle des abgebrannten Exchange Coffee House von 1806–09 (Architekt Asher Benjamin), ein Gebäude mit sieben Geschossen, 200 Räumen und Speisemöglichkeiten für 300 Gäste. Das früheste amerikanische Hotel war das von Benjamin Henry Latrobe (1764–1820) 1794–1796 errichtete City Hotel in New York. William H. Eliots *A Description of Tremont House, with Architectural Illustrations*, 1830, diente ein halbes Jahrhundert als Handbuch der Hotelarchitektur (Watkin, David, op. cit., S. 13–15). Ein weiterer Meilenstein im amerikanischen Hotelbau war das Astor Hotel in New York, ab 1830 diverse Entwürfe von Alexander Jackson Davis (1803–1892)

17 Ludy, Robert B., op. cit., S. 210

18 „The hotel (a very excellent one) is called Tremont House. It has more galleries, colonnades, piazzas and passages than I can remember, or the reader would believe", schreibt Charles Dickens 1842. Ibid., S. 211

19 Charakterisierung des Berliner Publizisten Friedrich Buchholz. Zitiert in: Fischer, Bernhard: „Der Badische Hof. 1807–1830. Cottas Hotel in Baden-Baden". In: *Marbacher Magazin*, 79/1997, Marbach am Neckar 1997, S. 2. Cotta verlegte Goethe, Schiller, Alexander von Humboldt, Schelling und Herder, aber auch politische Zeitungen und Kulturzeitschriften. Nach dem Tod Schillers, mit dem er eng befreundet war, freundete er sich mit Goethe an. Beide waren Bädertouristen. Cotta im Südwestdeutschen, im Allgäu und in der Schweiz, Goethe in Pyrmont oder meist in Böhmen, zum Beispiel in Karlsbad. Ein Motiv für den Hotelneubau war auch, dass beide sich dann öfter in Baden-Baden hätten treffen können.

20 Fischer, Bernhard, op. cit., S. 5

21 Friedrich Weinbrenner (1766–1826) war ab 1800 Oberbaudirektor im Großherzogtum Baden. In seine Verantwortlichkeit fielen alle öffentlichen Bauten, unter anderem die Stadtplanung von Karlsruhe.

22 Fischer, Bernhard, op. cit., S. 17

23 Architekten: Carlos Ferrater und José Maria Cartañá, 1995

24 Vgl. Bollerey, Franziska: *Architekturkonzeptionen der utopischen Sozialisten. Alternative Planung und Architektur für den gesellschaftlichen Prozeß*, Berlin (1977) 1991, S. 150–167

25 Keck, Herbert: „Profitable Raumverschwendung. Das Atriumhotel". In: *Daidalos*, op. cit., S. 42–51. Vgl. Downey, Claire: „Das Portman Hotel. Die Evolution einer Designphilosophie". In: *Archithese. Zeitschrift und Schriftenreihe für Architektur*, Heft 2, 1988, S. 19–25

26 Fischer, Bernhard, op. cit., S. 17

27 Fischer von Erlach, Johann Bernhard: *Entwurff einer historischen Architectur.* Wien 1721, 2. Ausgabe 1725

28 Durand, Jean-Nicolas-Louis (1760–1834): *Recueil et parallèle des édifices de tout genre, anciens et modernes, remarquables par leur beauté, par leur grandeur ou par leur singularité, et dessinés sur une même échelle.* Paris 1801; ders.: *Précis des leçons d'architecture: données à l'École Polytechnique.* Paris 1802–1805; ders.: *Partie graphique des cours d'architecture faits à l'École Royale Polytechnique depuis sa réorganisation; précédée d'un sommaire relatif à ce nouveau travail.* Paris 1821

29 Durand, Jean-Nicolas-Louis, *Recueil et parallèles…*, op. cit., Tafel 30 („Hospices, Lazarets, Caravanserails, Cimitières")

30 „Les hôtelleries, destinées à recevoir des voyageurs ne sont dans

par le Gouvernement. Ces édifices disposés de la manière la plus simple, offrent au regard de tous les voyageures le plus bel aspect. On sait combien celui de nos hôtelleries en général est ignoble et repoussant. Il ne faudrait pour cela que donner a leur disposition la convenance et la simplicité qu' elles exigent...'. In: Durand, Claude Nicolas Louis: *Précis des leçons...*, op.cit., 2nd vol., p. 19, table 32. Hermann von der Hude rightly points out that at the latest since the Renaissance, a type of guest house existed very similar to the caravanserai. Through a vaulted thoroughfare, one reached a yard surrounded by open wood or stone galleries. A staircase led to the upper-storey-galleries with the guest rooms. A second staircase linked the stables that were also situated in the courtyard to the galleries.
From the thoroughfare, the tavern and inn could be reached, behind them kitchen and storages. In the front building, a kind of entrance hall or large hallway was situated (sort of a prototype to the later lobbys). Von der Hude, Hermann, op.cit., p. 175

31 Norman S. Hayner speaks of 50% of permanent or similarly high-grade use of 'residential hotels' in the 1930s in the USA. But also in Grand Hotels apartments or suites are rented permanently. Thus the Aga Khan occupied a suite in the Paris Ritz for 40 years. Vladimir Nabokov from 1961–1977 resided in the 'Montreux Palace', just to name two of a great number of permanent hotel guests.

32 Probably the most famous of the European railway hotels is the 'Midland Grand Hotel' of the 'Midland Railway', erected by George Gilbert Scott from 1868-1873 in front of the St. Pancras railway station in London that today serves as the terminal of the 'Eurostar' train from the continent. Hotel activities have been restarted in a modern annex. The old 'Midland Grand' has been converted to apartments. Cf.: Bradley, Simon: *St. Pancras Station* London 2006; Frost, Barbara: *Memories of the Midland (the one in Manchester at the other end of the line)*, Manchester 1993; North British Railway Company's Station Hotels (Edinburgh and Glasgow), Guide book, n.y.) Another famous hotel is 'Gare d'Orsay', erected in 1898-99 for the Paris World Exhibition of 1900 with 370 rooms. After interior conversion by Italian architect Gae Aulenti the station itself was opened in 1986 as museum of the nineteenth century. Cf.: Bradley, Simon: *St. Pancras Station*. London 2007; Mathieu, Caroline: *Orsay. From Station to a Museum*, Paris 1999; Frost, Barbara: *Memories of the Midland*. Manchester 1993; *North British Railway Company's Station Hotels*. Guide Book, n.y.

33 Guyer, Eduard: *Das Hotelwesen der Gegenwart*, Zürich 1874 (2nd amplified ed. 1885), p. 12–14 and 232–236. Cited after von der Hude, Hermann, op.cit., p.175

34 The Dallas Hilton in 1925 was the first hotel built by Conrad Hilton (1888–1979), more followed in the USA. The 'Hilton Hotels Corporation' empire, founded in 1946, during the 1950s and 60s became the first international hotel chain with 188 hotels in the USA and 54 in other countries. Hilton put his experiences into writing in two books: *Be my Guest*. Autobiography of Conrad Hilton in 1959 and *Inspirations of an Innkeeper* in 1963. In the first book he describes a visit at 'The Stevens Hotel' 1926/27 in Chicago that left an impression by its sheer dimensions: 3,000 rooms, 6,000 people (guests and employees), social and public spaces of more than 12,000 square meters, a daily consumption of 3,000 litres of coffee, ten heads of cattle, etc. Also a private hospital ward complete with an operation theatre, 26 storeys, three basement levels

35 'The hotel population is essentially an aggregation of displaced people' Norman S. Hayner writes, op.cit., p. 181

36 D'Ormesson, Jean and Watkin, David a.o.: *Grand Hotel. The Golden Age of Palace Hotels. An Architectural and Social History*, New York 1984, p. 149

37 Montgomery-Massingberd, Hugh: 'A Homage to César Ritz', in: D'Ormesson, Jean, op.cit., p. 147

la plus grande partie de l'Europe que des édifices particuliers qui n'offrent pas, pour la plupart, plus d'ordre, de commodité, de propreté que la majeure partie de nos fermes. En Orient, au contraire, ces mêmes lieux, nommés caravansérails, sont des édifices publics bâtis et entretenus avec le plus grand soin par le Gouvernement. Ces édifices disposés de la manière la plus simple, offrent au regard de tous les voyageurs les plus bel aspect. On sait combien celui de nos hôtelleries en général est ignoble et repoussant. Il ne faudrait pour cela que donner á leur disposition la convenance et la simplicité qu'elles exigent …" In: Durand, Jean-Nicolas-Louis, *Précis des leçons …*, op. cit., 2. Bd., S. 19, Tafel 32. Hermann von der Hude weist mit Recht darauf hin, dass spätestens seit der Renaissance ein der Karawanserei ähnlicher Typus von Gasthaus bestand. Über eine Torhalle gelangte man in einen mit offenen Stein- oder Holzgalerien umbauten Hof. Eine Treppe führte in die Hofgalerien der oberen Geschosse mit den Gastzimmern. Eine zweite Treppe verband die im Hof gelegenen Stallungen ebenfalls mit den Galerien. Von der Torhalle aus sind Schenke und Wirtsstube zu erreichen, hinter ihnen Küche und Vorratsräume. Im Vorderhaus befand sich eine Art Vorsaal oder große Diele (Frühform einer Lobby). (Hude, Hermann von der, op. cit., S. 175)

31 Norman S. Hayner spricht von 50 Prozent permanenter sowie gleichprozentiger Nutzung der Residential Hotels in den 1930er Jahren in den Vereinigten Staaten. Aber auch in Grand Hotels werden Appartements oder Suiten permanent angemietet. Der Aga Khan hatte 40 Jahre lang im Pariser Ritz eine Suite. Vladimir Nabokov wohnte von 1961 bis 1977 im Montreux Palace, um nur zwei Beispiele aus der Vielzahl permanenter Hotelgäste zu nennen.

32 Die wohl berühmtesten europäischen Bahnhofshotels sind das von George Gilbert Scott 1868–1873 errichtete Midland Grand Hotel der Midland Railway im Bahnhof St. Pancras in London, heute Endstation des „Eurostar" (das alte Midland Grand wurde teilweise in Appartements umgewandelt, der Hotelbetrieb dort und in einem Anbau wieder aufgenommen) und das 1898/99 für die Pariser Weltausstellung 1900 erbaute, 370 Zimmer zählende Hotel des Gare d'Orsay, der bis 1986 durch Gae Aulenti zu einem Museum umgebaut wurde. Vgl. hierzu für London: Bradley, Simon: *St. Pancras Station*. London 2007; für Paris: Mathieu, Caroline: *Orsay. From Station to a Museum*. Paris 1999; für Manchester: Frost, Barbara: *Memories of the Midland*. Manchester 1993; für Edinburgh und Glasgow: *North British Railway Company's Station Hotels*. Guide Book, o. J.

33 Guyer, Eduard: *Das Hotelwesen der Gegenwart*. Zürich 1874 (zweite erweiterte Auflage 1885), S. 12–14 und 232–236. Zitiert bei: Hude, Hermann von der, op. cit., S. 175

34 Das Dallas Hilton, 1925, war das erste der von Conrad Hilton (1888–1979) gebauten Hotels, dem weitere in den Vereinigten Staaten folgten. Das als „Hilton Hotels Corporation" 1946 gegründete Imperium wurde mit 188 Hotels in Amerika und 54 außerhalb in den 1950er und 1960er Jahren die erste internationale Hotelkette. Seine Erfahrungen hat Hilton in zwei Büchern niedergelegt: *Be my Guest. Autobiography of Conrad Hilton* (1958) und *Inspirations of an Innkeeper* (1963). In letzterem schildert er auch einen Besuch im The Stevens Hotel, 1926/27 in Chicago, das durch seine schieren Quantitäten beeindruckte: 3000 Zimmer, 6000 Personen (Gäste und Angestellte), Gesellschafts- und Verkehrsräume von mehr als 12.000 Quadratmetern, ein täglicher Konsum von 3000 Litern Kaffee, zehn Rindern et cetera, einer eigenen Krankenstation mit Operationssaal, 26 Obergeschosse, drei Untergeschosse.

35 „The hotel population is essentially an aggregation of displaced people", schreibt Norman S. Hayner, op. cit., S. 181

36 D'Ormesson, Jean und David Watkin u.a.: *Grand Hotel. The Golden Age of Palace Hotels. An Architectural and Social History*. New York 1984, S. 149

38 Ibid., p. 178
39 Ibid.
40 MacKenzie, Compton: *The Savoy of London*, London, Toronto, Wellington, Sidney 1953, p. 57. Extravaganzas in the Savoy went on: 'Krupp gave a party in May 1906 when the majolica fountain in the old courtyard gushed champagne, and in that same year the old courtyard was flooded for dinner to be served in a gondola to the guests of George Kessler, the champagne magnate.' (MacKenzie, Compton, op.cit., p. 73)
41 D'Ormesson, Jean, op.cit., p. 148
42 Today, the Bristol still is one of the first addresses with a restaurant dating back to the year 1929, at the same time however with the most ample and modern bathrooms of the city. Woody Allen's latest film 'Midnight in Paris' shown in Cannes in May 2011, will further contribute to the hotel's glory (*Time Magazine*, 2 May 2011)
43 Architect was the Alsatian architect Charles F. Mewès (1858–1914) who, together with the Englishman Arthur J. Davis (1878–1951) was also responsible for the London Ritz. (Both were pupils of the Ècole des Beaux-Arts in Paris) Ritz originally intended to put up a more modern building. Mewès however convinced him to preserve the Place Vendome façade of Jules Hardouin Mansart (1690/1704), a speculation object under Louis XIV and his minister of finances, Colbert. The interior was designed following Paris contemporary taste employing neo-styles between Louis XIV and Empire. The hotel was financed by the wine merchant Alexandre Marnier-Lapostolle. A liqueur created for the Savoy, Ritz baptised 'Le Grand Marnier'.
44 The 'Grand Hotel Cabourg' that the asthmatic Proust visited every summer from 1907 till the outbreak of the First World War, was situated in the centre of an agglomeration created at the end of the nineteenth century out of a void in the department of Calvados not far from the mouth of the river Seine. It developed into a gentrified seaside resort for Parisians. The establishment served as the model for the hotel 'Balbec' in Proust's *À la recherche du temps perdu*, but also impressions of other luxury hotels such as the Venice 'Danieli' went into the account of his memoirs.
45 Painter, George D., cited in: Künzli, Lis (Ed.): *Hotels. Ein literarischer Führer*, Frankfurt/Main 1996, p. 111
46 Hemingway, Ernest, cited after: Künzli, Lis, op.cit., p. 112
47 (Becker) Ritz, Marie Louise: *César Ritz. Host to the World*, Philadelphia 1938, cited after: D'Ormesson, Jean, op.cit, p. 148
48 The earliest typological analysis is Eduard Guyer's *Das Hotelwesen der Gegenwart* from 1874. It is followed by: Klasen, Ludwig: *Grundrissvorbilder von Gebäuden aller Art, Abth. II, Grundrissvorbilder von Gasthäusern, Hôtels und Restaurants*, Leipzig 1884. After that: von der Hude, Hermann: 'Hotels', in: *Handbuch der Architektur*, 4th part, 4th halfbinding: *Entwerfen, Anlage und Einrichtung der Gebäude. Gebäude für Erholungs-, Beherbergungs- und Vereinszwecke*, Darmstadt 1885 and as modern amendment: Just, Karl Wilhelm: 'Hotels, Restaurants', in: *Handbuch der Architektur*, 4th part, 4th halfbinding, issue 1, Leipzig 1933
49 MacKenzie, Compton, op.cit., p. 42
50 Williams, Jefferson: *The American Hotel: An anecdotal History*, New York 1930, p. 77
51 Bollerey, Franziska: 'Palasthotels', in: *Boulevard Spezial zum Thema Hotel*, broadcast by Deutschlandfunk, 20.9.1997
52 Hayner, Norman S., op.cit., p. 179–180
53 Cf. Flückiger-Seiler, Roland: *Hotelpaläste zwischen Traum und Wirklichkeit. Schweizer Tourismus und Hotelbau 1830–1920*, Zürich (2003) 2005, p. 102–103, 110
54 MacKenzie, Compton, op.cit., p. 43
55 Bollerey, Franziska: *Architekturkonzeptionen der utopischen Sozialisten. Alternative Planung für den gesellschaftlichen Prozeß*, Berlin (1977) 1991, p. 118–123, 142–145

37 Montgomery-Massingberd, Hugh: „A Homage to Cesar Ritz". In: D'Ormesson, Jean, op. cit., S. 147
38 Ibid., S. 178
39 Ibid.
40 Mackenzie, Compton: *The Savoy of London*. London 1953, S. 57. Die Extravaganzen im Savoy wurden fortgesetzt. „Krupp gave a party in May 1906 when the majolica fountain in the old courtyard gushed champagne, and in that same year the old courtyard was flooded for dinner to be served in a gondola to the guests of George Kessler, the champagne magnate." (Mackenzie, Compton, op. cit., S. 73)
41 D'Ormesson, Jean, op. cit., S. 148
42 Heute ist das Bristol immer noch eine der ersten Hoteladressen mit einem Restaurant, das auf das Jahr 1929 zurückgeht, aber bereits die größten und modernsten Badezimmer der Stadt aufwies. Woody Allens 42ter Film *Midnight in Paris*, der im Mai 2011 in Cannes uraufgeführt wurde, trug zum weiteren Ruhm bei (*Time Magazine*, 2. Mai 2011)
43 Architekt war der Elsässer Charles F. Mewès (1858–1914), der zusammen mit dem Engländer Arthur J. Davis (1878–1951) – beide Schüler der École des Beaux-Arts in Paris – auch für das Londoner Ritz verantwortlich zeichnet. Ritz schwebte ursprünglich ein moderner Bau vor. Mewès überzeugte ihn, die Fassade (1690–1704) von Jules Hardouin Mansart an der Place Vendôme, einem urbanistischen Spekulationsobjekt unter Ludwig XIV. und seinem Finanzminister Colbert, zu erhalten und das Interieur dem Pariser Zeitgeschmack entsprechend in Neostilen zwischen Louis XIV. und Empire zu gestalten. Die Finanzierung des Hotelbaus übernahm der Weinhändler Marnier Lapostolle. Einen von ihm bereits für das Savoy kreierten Likör tauft Ritz „Le Grand Marnier".
44 Das Grand Hotel Cabourg, das Proust als Asthmatiker schon 1907 bis zum Ausbruch des Ersten Weltkriegs jeden Sommer besuchte, lag im Zentrum einer Ende des 19. Jahrhunderts aus dem Boden gestampften Agglomeration im Department Calvados unweit der Seine-Mündung und entwickelte sich rasch zu einem mondänen Badeort für die Pariser. Das Etablissement war Vorbild für das Hotel Balbec in Prousts Roman *Auf der Suche nach der verlorenen Zeit*. Aber auch Eindrücke anderer Nobelherbergen wie zum Beispiel des Danieli in Venedig sind in die Erinnerungsaufzeichnungen eingeflossen.
45 George D. Painter, zitiert in: Künzli, Lis (Hg.): *Hotels: ein literarischer Führer*. Frankfurt am Main 1996, S. 111
46 Ernest Hemingway zitiert in: Künzli, Lis, op. cit., S. 112
47 (Becker) Ritz, Marie-Louise: *César Ritz: Host to the World*. Philadelphia 1938. Zitiert in: D'Ormesson, Jean, op. cit., S. 148
48 Die früheste bautypologische Analyse ist Eduard Guyers *Das Hotelwesen der Gegenwart*, 1874. Ihm folgen Klasen, Ludwig: *Grundrissvorbilder von Gebäuden aller Art, Abth. II, Grundrissvorbilder von Gasthäusern, Hôtels und Restaurants*. Leipzig 1884. Dann: Hude, Hermann von der: „Hotels". In: Wagner, Heinrich/Schmitt, Eduard u. a.: *Handbuch der Architektur*. Vierter Teil, 4. Halbband: *Entwerfen, Anlage und Einrichtung der Gebäude. Gebäude für Erholungs-, Beherbergungs- und Vereinszwecke*. Darmstadt 1885 und als moderne Ergänzung: Just, Karl Wilhelm: „Hotels, Restaurants". In: *Handbuch der Architektur*. IV. Teil, 4. Halbband, Heft 1, Leipzig 1933
49 Mackenzie, Compton, op. cit., S. 42
50 Williams, Jefferson: *The American Hotel: An Anecdotal History*. New York 1930, S. 77
51 Bollerey, Franziska: „Palasthotels". In: *Boulevard Spezial* zum Thema Hotel. Deutschlandfunk, 20.09.1997
52 Hayner, Norman S., op. cit., S. 179/180
53 Vgl. hierzu: Flückiger-Seiler, Roland: *Hotelpaläste.Zwischen Traum und Wirklichkeit. Schweizer Tourismus und Hotelbau. 1830–1920*. Zürich (2003) 2005, S. 102/103/110
54 Mackenzie, Compton, op. cit. S. 43

56 Von der Hude, Hermann, op.cit., p. 174–220. Together with Hennicke he built the hotel 'Kaiserhof' in Berlin 1873–1875. The four upper storeys had 60–70 rooms with 75–85 beds. Nearly every room had a balcony but there were only two bathrooms per storey. There was a generous number of lounges and saloons arranged around the central glass-canopied courtyard

57 Ibid., p. 197

58 Just, Wilhelm, op.cit., p. 19

59 Guyer, Eduard, cited after: Flückiger-Seiler: *Hotelträume*, op.cit., p. 60

60 Von der Hude, Hermann, op.cit., p. 191

61 Cf. Chapter: 'On and Behind the Stage'

62 In the epoch of Haussmann's urban improvements the Grand Hotel was Europe's largest hotel. D'Ormesson, Jean, op.cit. p. 54

63 Flückiger-Seiler: *Hotelträume*, op.cit., p. 44

64 Brecht, Bertold: *Gesammelte Werke*, vol. 2, Frankfurt/Main 1967, p. 497

65 *Der letzte Mann* (English title: *The Last Laugh*), Germany 1924. Director: Friedrich Wilhelm Murnau, producer: Erich Pommer, script: Carl Meyer, camera: Karl Freund

66 The topic of 'Hunger and Voracity' also appears as a convincing collage of contrast in Walter Ruttmann's film *Berlin. Die Sinfonie der Großstadt* (English title: *Berlin. Symphony of a Great City*), 1927. Cf. Bollerey, Franziska: *City Symphonies – Film Manifestos of Urban Experiences*, Eselsohren. Journal of History of Art, Architecture and Urbanism, Vol. II, 2014, No. 1, 2.

67 'In 'The Last Laugh', this revolving door becomes an obsession. The film opens with a magnificent tracking shot that shows guests moving through the never stopping revolving door—a camera focus that returns over the whole duration of the film and that represents a cross between a carousel and a roulette wheel'. Kracauer, Siegfried: *Von Caligari bis Hitler*, (Princeton 1947) Frankfurt/Main 1979, p.112. Cf. also Seger, Cordula: *Grand Hotel. Schauplatz der Literatur*, Köln, Weimar, Wien 2005, p. 286–303

68 As early as 1936 Hayer, Norman S. in his book: *Hotel Life*, Chapel Hill, (The University of North Carolina Press 1936. Appeared 1928 under the title of 'Hotel Life and Personality', his dissertation), in the chapter 'Problems of Human Nature' reports a compensatory dispensation for a Princeton student. 'The son of a rich man held a party' in a hotel. 'Every breakable thing was smashed. Even the tiles and the plumbing fixtures in the bathroom were torn out.', p. 170

69 Mann, Thomas: *Bekenntnisse des Hochstaplers Felix Krull. Der Memoiren erster Teil*, Frankfurt/Main 1954, paper back edition Frankfurt 1990

70 Ibid., p. 391

71 'The washerwomen wear blue, the errand girls from the laundry rose, the scrubbing women striped, the parlour maids white, the waitresses in the soda fountain ochre, those in the tearoom lilac working clothes' (Leitner, Maria: *Hotel Amerika* {1930} Dresden 1950, p. 13)

72 Mann, Thomas, op.cit., p. 479

73 Ibid., p. 491-492

74 The hotel exists till our days: 202, Rue de Rivoli

75 Hayner, Norman S., op.cit., Hayner's book appeared in 1928 under the title *Of Hotel Life and Personality* as his dissertation.

76 The Chicago School of Sociology was an institutionalized research movement that was founded in the 1920s at the University of Chicago. It oriented itself on the basic principles of the pragmatistic theory of action of George Herbert Mead and John Dewey and had a shared interest in a common research subject, the city of Chicago. With the help of process-analytical and reconstructive methods, one explored the social microcosm to describe the interdependency between economic and political developments.

77 Lindner, Rolf *Die Entdeckung der Stadtkultur. Soziologie aus*

55 Bollerey, Franziska: *Architekturkonzeptionen der utopischen Sozialisten. Alternative Planung und Architektur für den gesellschaftlichen Prozeß.* Berlin (1977) 1991, S. 118-123, 142-145

56 Hude, Hermann von der, op. cit., S. 174–220. Zusammen mit Hennicke ist er Erbauer des Hotels Kaiserhof (1873–1875) in Berlin. Die vier Obergeschosse hatten 60–70 Zimmer mit 75–85 Betten. Fast jedes Zimmer hatte einen Balkon, aber pro Etage gab es nur zwei Badezimmer. Das Angebot der um den glasüberdachten Lichthof arrangierten Gesellschaftsräume war großzügig.

57 Ibid., S. 197

58 Just, Wilhelm, op. cit., S. 19

59 Eduard Guyer zitiert in: Flückiger-Seiler, Roland: *Hotelträume. Zwischen Gletschern und Palmen. Schweizer Tourismus und Hotelbau 1830–1920.* Baden (2001) 2005, S. 60

60 Hude, Hermann von der, op. cit., S. 191

61 Vgl. Unterkapitel „Vor und hinter den Kulissen"

62 Zur Zeit von Haussmanns Umstrukturierungen in Paris war das „Grand Hotel" das größte Hotel Europas. D'Ormesson, Jean, op. cit., S. 54

63 Flückiger-Seiler, Roland Hotelträume, op. cit., S. 44

64 Vgl. Brecht, Bertolt: *Gesammelte Werke*, Bd. 2. Frankfurt am Main 1967, S. 497

65 *Der letzte Mann*, Deutschland 1924. Regie: Friedrich Wilhelm Murnau, Produzent: Erich Pommer, Drehbuch Carl Meyer, Kamera: Karl Freund

66 Das Thema taucht als überzeugende Kontrastcollage auch in Walter Ruttmanns Film *Berlin. Die Sinfonie der Großstadt* von 1927 auf. Vgl. Bollerey, Franziska: *City Symphonies – Film Manifestos of Urban Experiences*, Eselsohren, II, 2017, Nr. 1, 2.

67 Vgl.: Seger, Cordula: *Grand Hotel. Schauplatz der Literatur.* Köln, Weimar und Wien 2005, S. 286–303. In dem Film *Der letzte Mann* wird die Drehtür zu einer Obsession. „Den Film eröffnet eine Kamerafahrt, die zeigt, wie die Gäste durch die nie stillstehende Tür strömen, eine Einstellung, die bis zum Schluß erschöpfend wiederholt wird und ein Mittelding zwischen Karussell und Rouletterad darstellt." Kracauer, Siegfried: *Von Caligari bis Hitler.* (Princeton 1947) Frankfurt am Main 1979, S. 112

68 Bereits 1936 berichtet Norman S. Hayner in seinem Buch *Hotel Life* im Kapitel „Problems of Human Nature" von einem Wiedergutmachungsdispens für einen Princeton-Studenten: „The son of a rich man, held a party" in einem Hotel. "Every breakable thing was smashed. Even the tiles and the plumbing fixtures in the bathroom were torn out", S. 170

69 Mann, Thomas: *Bekenntnisse des Hochstaplers Felix Krull. Der Memoiren erster Teil.* Frankfurt am Main 1954, Taschenbuchausgabe Frankfurt am Main 1990

70 Ibid., S. 391

71 „Die Wäscherinnen tragen blaue, die Laufmädchen aus der Wäscherei rosa, die Scheuerfrauen gestreifte, die Stubenmädchen weiße, die Kellnerinnen in der Sodaquelle ockergelbe, die in dem Teeraum fliederfarbene Arbeitskleider." (Leitner, Maria: *Hotel Amerika.* Dresden (1930) 1950, S. 13)

72 Ibid., S. 479

73 Ibid., S. 491-492

74 Das Hotel besteht heute noch. 202, Rue de Rivoli, Paris

75 Die Chicago School of Sociology war eine institutionalisierte Forschungsbewegung, die in den 1920er Jahren an der University of Chicago begründet wurde. Neben Robert E. Park und Ernest W. Burgess waren unter anderem Louis Wirth, Frederic Thrasher, Clifford R. Shaw, Roderick McKenzie und Henry D. McKay bedeutende Forscher innerhalb dieser Schule. Sie orientierten sich an den Grundbegriffen der pragmatistischen Handlungstheorie von George Herbert Mead und John Dewey und teilten das Interesse an einem gemeinsamen Forschungsgegenstand, der Stadt Chicago. Mit Hilfe von prozessanalytischen und rekonstruktiven

der Erfahrung der Reportage, Frankfurt am Main and New York 2007, p. 92–93

78 The 'Hotel des Bains' was erected as a luxury hotel in 1900 on Lido di Venezia. Just, Karl Wilhelm: *Hotels, Restaurants. Handbuch der Architektur*, op.cit., p. 41, names as architects: Ing. Fromesco Marsich & Comm. and Ing. Giovanni Sicher, Venice. Amongst other reasons, the hotel became famous because of Thomas Mann's stay in 1911, that inspired him to write his short novel *Der Tod in Venedig - Death in Venice*

79 Simmel, Georg: 'Soziologie des Raumes', in: Georg Simmel, *Aufsätze und Abhandlungen 1901–1908*, vol. 1 of the seven-volume complete edition, Frankfurt am Main 1995, p. 132–183

80 Mann, Thomas: *Der Tod in Venedig*, Berlin 1912

81 Mann, Thomas: *Bekenntnisse des Hochstaplers Felix Krull*, op.cit., p. 393

82 Ibid., p. 397–398

83 'A typical slave of modern times' Orwell calls the 'plongeur'. Orwell, George: *Down and Out in Paris and London*, Paris and London 1933, cited after: Orwell, George: *Erledigt in Paris und London*, Zürich 1987, p. 156

84 It was the hotel Lotti in Rue Castiglione near the Place Vendôme. Cf. Künzli, Lis: *Hotels, ein literarischer Führer*, Frankfurt/Main 1996, p. 103-104

85 Orwell, George: *Erledigt in Paris und London*, op.cit., p. 113

86 Ibid., p. 92–93

87 Ibid., p. 108

88 Leitner, Maria: *Hotel Amerika*, op.cit. Cf. also: 'Electric Stimulations', in: Ward, Janet: *Weimar Surfaces. Urban Visual Culture in 1920s Germany*, (first edition 1930) Berkeley, Los Angeles, London 2001, p. 135

89 Kracauer, Siegfried: 'Luxushotel von unten gesehen', in: *Frankfurter Zeitung*, 28.12.1930, 2. morning edition

90 Leitner, Maria, op.cit., p. 8

91 Ibid., p. 212–213

92 Ibid., p. 50

93 Schulte, Michael: 'Weder Staubsauger noch Vorschriften. Geschichten aus dem Chelsea', in: *Daidalos. Architektur, Kunst Kultur*, vol. 62, December 1996, p. 83–89

94 Montgomery-Massingberd, op.cit., p. 150

95 Hayner, Norman S., op.cit., p. 176

96 *Love in the Afternoon*, USA 1956. Director Billy Wilder, script: Billy Wilder

97 Arns, Alfons: *Hotel als Fim*. In: Daidalos, op.cit., p. 32–41

98 Hayner, Norman S., op.cit., p. 4 speaks of a 'tragic climax of demoralizing lonesomeness that often accompanies mobility and detachment.'

99 Bollerey, Franziska: *Palasthotels*. In: *Boulevard Spezial* concerning hotels, broadcast by Deutschlandfunk, 20.9.1997

100 For the Palais Royal cf. Dupezard, Emile: *Le Palais Royal, Architecture et Décoration de Louis XV à nos jours*, Paris 1911; N.N.: *Palais Royal, Domaine de la Couronne. Histoire du Palais Royal*, Paris 1934; D'Espelel, Pierre: *Le Palais Royal*, Paris 1936; Champier, Victor and Sandoz, G.-Roger: *Le Palais Royal d'après des documents inédits* (1629–1900), 2 tomes, Paris 1900. Cf. Bollerey, Franziska : *Architekturkonzeptionen der Utopischen Sozialisten : Alternative Planung und Architektur für den gesellschaftlichen Prozeß*, Berlin (1977) 1991, p. 128–130

101 Saudan, Michel and Yolande Blanc a.o.: *De l'hotel-palais en Riviera*, Geneva 1985, p. 98

102 Joanne, Paul: *Les Stations d'hiver de la Méditerranée, Collections des guides-Joanne*, Paris 1897

103 Ibid.

104 An initiative of Englishman 'Révérend Père Lewis Way' who financed it himself. Cf. Saudan, Michel, op.cit., p. 95

105 Tolstoi, Leo N.: *Aus den Aufzeichnungen des Fürsten D. Nechljudow* (From the chronicle of Prince D. Nechljudow), Luzern 8 July 1857, in: Tolstoi, Leo N.: *Frühe Erzählungen*, München 1961, p. 476

Methoden untersuchten sie dessen sozialen Mikrokosmos, um die Wechselwirkung zwischen ökonomischen und politischen Entwicklungen (Industrialisierung, Urbanisierung und Einwanderung) zu verstehen und den Wandel sozialer und kultureller Ordnungen zu beschreiben.

76 Hayner, Norman S., op. cit., 1928 war unter dem Titel *Hotel Life and Personality* Hayners Doktorarbeit erschienen.

77 Lindner, Rolf: *Die Entdeckung der Stadtkultur. Soziologie aus der Erfahrung der Reportage*. Frankfurt am Main und New York 2007, S. 92–93

78 Das Hotel des Bains wurde im Jahr 1900 auf dem Lido di Venezia als Luxushotel erbaut. Bekannt wurde das Hotel unter anderem durch Thomas Manns Aufenthalt im Jahr 1911, der ihn zu der Novelle *Der Tod in Venedig* inspirierte. Ebenso wurde Luchino Viscontis gleichnamiger Film dort 1971 gedreht. Heute ist das Hotel in Appartements umgewandelt.

79 Simmel, Georg: „Soziologie des Raumes", In: Simmel, Georg, *Aufsätze und Abhandlungen 1901–1908*, Frankfurt am Main 1995, S. 132–183

80 Mann, Thomas: *Der Tod in Venedig*. Berlin 1912

81 Mann, Thomas: *Bekenntnisse des Hochstaplers Felix Krull*, op. cit., S. 393

82 Ibid., S. 397–398

83 „A typical slave of modern times", nennt Orwell den „plongeur". Orwell, George: *Down and Out in Paris and London*. Paris and London 1933. Deutsche Ausgabe: *Erledigt in Paris und London*, Zürich 1987, S. 156

84 Es ist das Hotel Lotti in der Rue Castiglione nahe der Place Vendôme. Siehe: Künzli, Lis: *Hotels, ein literarischer Führer*. Frankfurt am Main 1996, S. 103–104

85 Orwell, George, op. cit., S. 113

86 Ibid., S. 92–93

87 Ibid., S. 108

88 Leitner, Maria: *Hotel Amerika*. Dresden (1930) 1950. Siehe auch: „Electric Stimulations". In: Ward, Janet: *Weimar Surfaces. Urban Visual Culture in 1920s Germany*. Berkeley, Los Angeles und London 2001, S. 135

89 Kracauer, Siegfried: „Luxushotel von unten gesehen". In: *Frankfurter Zeitung*, 28.12.1930, 2. Morgenblatt

90 Leitner, Maria, op. cit., S. 8

91 Ibid., S. 212–213

92 Ibid., S. 50

93 Schulte, Michael: „Weder Staubsauger noch Vorschriften. Geschichten aus dem Chelsea". In: *Daidalos. Architektur, Kunst, Kultur*, Heft 62, Dezember 1996, S. 83–89

94 Montgomery-Massingberd, op. cit., S. 150

95 Hayner, Norman, op. cit., S. 176

96 *Love in the Afternoon*, USA 1956. Regie und Drehbuch: Billy Wilder

97 Arns, Alfons: „Hotel als Film". In: *Daidalos*, op. cit., S. 32–41

98 Hayner, Norman S., op. cit., S. 4 spricht vom „tragic climax of demoralizing lonesomeness that often accompanies mobility and detachment."

99 Bollerey, Franziska: „Palasthotels". In: *Boulevard Spezial* zum Thema Hotel. Deutschlandfunk, 20.09.1997

100 Zum Palais Royal siehe: Dupezard, Emile: *Le Palais Royal, Architecture et Décoration de Louis XV à nos jours*, Paris 1911; N.N.: *Palais Royal, Domaine de la Couronne. Histoire du Palais Royal*, Paris 1934; D'Espelel, Pierre: *Le Palais Royal*, Paris 1936; Champier, Victor und G.-Roger Sandoz: *Le Palais Royal d' aprés des documents inédits (1629–1900)*, 2 Bde., Paris 1900. Siehe auch: Bollerey, Franziska: *Architekturkonzeptionen der Utopischen Sozialisten: Alternative Planung und Architektur für den gesellschaftlichen Prozeß*. Berlin (1977) 1991, S. 128–130

101 Saudan, Michel und Yolande Blanc u.a.: *De l'hotel-palais en Riviera*. Genf 1985, S. 98

102 Joanne, Paul: *Les Stations d'hiver de la Méditerranée* (Collections des Guides Joanne). Paris 1897

106 'Corso'—to show oneself strolling in public, to observe, to pause for a conversation—all this is a component part of the Italian culture. '...and this stroll becomes dearer and dearer the more often one visits it (the corso) conjointly with the inhabitants of this city that all come together here...for one of the most entertaining promenades..., because one observes the whole living Rome moving up and down ... As soon as the day's heat has retired, everybody is crowding together to enjoy the cool evening air '....' 'Carriages and pedestrians move between Porta del Popolo up to the Ponte Molle'. The most lively area of the corso is near the church of St. Carlo, where the street Condotti crosses the Corso.' 'Karl Philipp Moritz', In: Günther, Horst (Ed.): *Karl Philipp Moritz Werke*, vol. 2, Frankfurt am Main 1993, p. 359

107 Mérimée, Prosper: *Colomba* (Paris 1840), in: *Sämtliche Novellen*, München 1982, p. 309

108 Ibid., p. 312

109 Flückiger-Seiler, Roland: *Hotelträume zwischen Gletschern und Palmen. Schweizer Tourismus und Hotelbau 1830-1920*, Zürich (2003), 2005 p 15. Here travellers are mentioned such as: Thomas Platter (1499–1582), Johannes Stumpf (1500–1566), Aegidius Tschudi, a disciple of Zwingli (1505–1572) and Conrad Gessner (1516–1563)

110 Ibid., p. 17

111 For Grand Tour, cf.: Attilio, Brilli: *Als Reisen eine Kunst war – Vom Beginn des modernen Tourismus: Die „Grand Tour"*, Berlin 2001; Freller, Thomas: *Adelige auf Tour*, Ostfildern 2006; Henning, Christoph: *Reiselust – Touristen, Tourismus und Urlaubskultur*, Frankfurt am Main 1999; Kroll, Gabriele M.: *Kulturgeschichte des Reisens. Von der Pilgerfahrt zum Badeurlaub*, Darmstadt 2006; Krempien, Petra: *Geschichte des Reisens und des Tourismus. Ein Überblick von den Anfängen bis zur Gegenwart*, Limburgerhof 2000

112 Ibid., p. 18, footnote 15. Haller first publishes this poem in 1732 in his collection *Versuch Schweizerischer Gedichte*

113 Enzensberger, Hans Magnus: 'Eine Theorie des Tourismus', in: Enzensberger, Hans Magnus: *Einzelheiten I*, München 1962, p. 147–168

114 Coxe, William: *Travels in Switzerland*, 3 vols., London 1789

115 Ebel, Johann Gottfried: *Anleitung auf die nützlichste und genußvollste Art in der Schweiz zu reisen*, Zürich 1793, 2nd ed. 1804/1805, vol. 1, p. 10. Cited after: Flückiger-Seiler, Roland: *Hotelträume*, op.cit., p. 19

116 Twain, Mark (i.e. Samuel Langhorne Clemens), *A Tramp Abroad*, 1880, edition Chatto&Windus, London 1880, p. 163

117 Ibid., p. 171

118 Ibid.

119 Daudet, Alphonse: *Tartarin sur les Alpes*, Paris 1886. Cited after: Flückiger-Seiler, Roland: *Hotelträume*, op.cit., p. 39

120 Cf. Meeks, Caroll L.V.: *The Railroad Station. An Architectural History*, New Haven 1956; Krings, Ulrich: *Deutsche Großstadtbahnhöfe des Historismus*, München 1985; Berger, Manfred: *Historische Bahnhofsbauten Sachsens, Preußens, Mecklenburgs u. Thüringens*, 4 vols., Berlin and Stuttgart 1980–1996

121 Cf. Marrey, Bernhard: *Les grands magazines des origines à 1939*, Paris 1979

122 Construction of this project initiated by Richard D'Oyly Carte started in 1884. The name 'Savoy' goes back to a palace that Peter, count of Savoy 'who started a tradition of entertainment and hospitality which has endured centuries' had built around 1248 under Henry III 'in vico vocato le Straunde' as 'fairest manor in Europe'. (MacKenzie, Compton: *The Savoy of London*, *London*, Toronto, Wellington, Sydney 1953, p. 9–10)

123 *The Helmsley Palace*, with a foreword by Henry-Russell Hitchcock, New York 1980

124 Ludy, Robert: *Historic Hotels of the World. Past and Present*, Philadelphia 1927 (reprint 2009), p. 16

103 Ibid.

104 Eine Iniative des „Révérend Père Lewis Way". Vgl. Saudan, Michel, op. cit., S. 95

105 Tolstoi, Leo N.: „Aus den Aufzeichnungen des Fürsten D. Nechljudow", Luzern 8. Juli 1857, in: Tolstoi, Leo N.: *Frühe Erzählungen*, München 1961, S. 476

106 Der „Corso", das öffentliche Flanieren und Sich-Zeigen, Beobachten, für ein Gespräch Innehalten, ist Bestandteil der italienischen Kultur. „und dieser Gang wird einem immer lieber, je öfter man ihn [den Corso] gemeinschaftlich mit den Einwohnern dieser Stadt besucht, die alle hier zusammen strömen ... zu einem der unterhaltsamsten Spaziergänge ..., weil man das ganze lebende Rom sich hier auf und nieder bewegen siehet ... So wie die Hitze des Tages sich gelegt hat, drängt sich alles zusammen, um die kühle Abendluft zu genießen." Equipagen und Fußgänger bewegen sich zwischen der „Porta del Popolo bis nach der Ponte Molle". „Die lebhafteste Gegend auf dem Korso ist bei der Kirche St. Carlo, da wo die Straße Condotti den Korso durchkreuzt." (Moritz, Karl Philipp: *Reisen eines Deutschen in Italien 1786–88*. In: ders.: *Werke*. Hg. von Horst Günther. Frankfurt am Main 1993, Bd. 2, S. 359

107 Mérimée, Prosper: „Colomba" (Paris 1840), in: ders.: *Sämtliche Novellen*. München 1982, S. 309

108 Ibid., S. 312

109 Flückiger-Seiler, Roland: *Hotelträume zwischen Gletschern und Palmen. Schweizer Tourismus und Hotelbau. 1830–1920*. Zürich (2003) 2005, S. 15 erwähnt hier: Thomas Platter (1499–1582), Johannes Stumpf (1500–1566), Aegidius Tschudi (1505–1572), einen Schüler Zwinglis und Conrad Gessner (1516–1563).

110 Ibid., S. 17

111 Zur Grand Tour siehe auch: Brilli, Attilio: *Als Reisen eine Kunst war – Vom Beginn des modernen Tourismus: Die „Grand Tour"*. Berlin 2001; Freller, Thomas: *Adelige auf Tour*. Ostfildern 2006; Henning, Christoph: *Reiselust – Touristen, Tourismus und Urlaubskultur*. Frankfurt am Main 1999; Knoll, Gabriele M.: *Kulturgeschichte des Reisens. Von der Pilgerfahrt zum Badeurlaub*, Darmstadt 2006 und Krempien, Petra: *Geschichte des Reisens und des Tourismus. Ein Überblick von den Anfängen bis zur Gegenwart*, Limburgerhof 2000

112 Ibid., S. 18, Fußnote 15: Haller veröffentlichte dieses Gedicht erstmals 1732 in seiner Sammlung *Versuch Schweizerischer Gedichte*.

113 Enzensberger, Hans Magnus: „Eine Theorie des Tourismus". In: Enzensberger, Hans Magnus: *Einzelheiten I*. München 1962, S. 147–168

114 Coxe, William: *Travels in Switzerland*. 3 Bde., London 1789

115 Ebel, Johann Gottfried: *Anleitung auf die nützlichste und genussvollste Art in der Schweiz zu reisen*. Zürich 1793, 2. Ausgabe 1804/1805, Bd. I, S. 10. Zitiert bei Flückiger-Seiler, Roland, *Hotelträume*, op. cit., S. 19

116 Mark Twain (d. i. Samuel Langhorne Clemens): *A Tramp Abroad* (1880). Ausgabe Chatto & Windus, London 1880, S. 163

117 Ibid., S. 71

118 Ibid.

119 Daudet, Alphonse: *Tartarin sur les Alpes*. Paris 1886. Zitiert bei: Flückiger-Seiler, Roland, *Hotelträume*, op. cit., S. 39

120 Vgl. hierzu: Meeks, Caroll L. V.: *The Railroad Station. An Architectural History*. New Haven 1956; Krings, Ulrich: *Deutsche Großstadtbahnhöfe des 19. Jahrhunderts*. München 1985; Berger, Manfred: *Historische Bahnhofsbauten Sachsens, Preußens, Mecklenburgs und Thüringens*. Berlin 1980

121 Vgl. hierzu: Marrey, Bernhard: *Les grands magazins des origines à 1939*. Paris 1979

122 Der Bau des von Richard D'Oyly Carte initiierten Projektes begann 1884. Der Name Savoy geht zurück auf einen Palast, den Peter, Count of Sayoy, „who started a tradition of entertainment and hospitality which has endured centuries" um

125 It was re-established by the Savoyard nobleman St. Bernard de Menthon. Most Alpine hospices were run by Augustinians. Ludy, Robert, op.cit., p. 18–19
126 Ludy, Robert, op.cit., p. 17–18
127 Flückiger-Seiler, Roland: *Hotelpaläste. Zwischen Traum und Wirklichkeit. Schweizer Tourismus und Hotelbau 1830-1920*, Baden (2003) 2005; the same: *Hotelträume*, op.cit.
128 Flückiger-Seiler, Roland: *Hotelpaläste*, op.cit., p. 18–19
129 In 1903 Alexander Emrey bought 'Hotel de Cygne' and gave the architect Eugène Jost the commission to enlarge it. Jost became generally known as architect of a number of palace hotels as well as of Montreux' railway station and the Lausanne post office. Remarkable is the façade opening up wide to the lake.
130 R.F.: 'Montreux Palace', in: *Schweiz.Suisse.Svizzera Switzerland. Monatszeitschrift der Schweizerischen Bundesbahn*, 3/1981, p. 44
131 1900: 3,700; 1910: 5,350; (Rätisches Museum (Ed.): *Bündner Hotellerie um 1900 in Bildern*, Chur 1992, p. 13)
132 Rucki, Isabelle: *Das Hotel in den Alpen. Die Geschichte der Oberengadiner Hotelarchitektur von 1860–1914*, Zürich 1989, p. 192–193; Nicolaus Hartmann sen. (1838–1903), Nicolaus Hartmann jun. (1880–1956) cf. Hartmann, Kristiana: *Baumeister und Architekten für Graubünden*, Chur 2016
133 Parkhotel Kurhaus 1905; Grand Hotel 1910; Chantarella and Suvretta House 1912; Carlton 1913
134 La Grande Motte was created as a tourist destination in the 1960s with the intention to 'redirect' tourist flow away from the Spanish beaches. Hallmarks of the place are its terraced high-rises. Flaine in Haute Savoye is a typical example for covering a formerly untouched landscape with housing. The ensemble from the early 1960s, conceived by the former Bauhaus teacher Marcel Breuer, counts nowadays as a listed monument. Les Menuires in the Savoy Alps also came into existence in the 1960s in an altitude of 1,850 meters as one of the first retort cities for winter sport mass tourism
135 Flückiger-Seiler, Roland: *Hotelpaläste*, op.cit., p. 209
136 Cited after: Böckli, Peter: *Bis zum Tode der Gräfin. Das Drama um den Hotelpalast des Grafen Renesse in Maloja*, Zürich 1998, in: Flückiger-Seiler, Roland, p. 211
137 Nietzsche, Friedrich, cited after: Peter Böckli, op.cit., p. 98 f.
138 Cf. Schmid, Daniel and Peter Christian Bener: *Die Erfindung vom Paradies*, Glattbrug 1983. Swiss film director Daniel Schmid, grown up in the Flims hotel 'Schweizerhof' himself, very arrestingly depicted hotel life in his film *Hors saison* of 1992 from the viewpoint of the hotelier
139 Today, in Asia, Latin America and Africa guided visits to slums are offered as part of tourist programs. As early as 1911/12, in *King's View of New York* we find an advertisement for 'slumming', i.e. an organized tour through New York's slums. Cf. Bollerey, Franziska: *The Good and the Evil City*, in: *Ezelsoren*, vol. II, no. 3, p. 22–23
140 Grafe, Christoph and Franziska Bollerey (Ed.): *Cafés and Bars. The Culture of Public Display*, Abingdon (2007) 2008
141 Dreiser, Theodore: *Sister Carrie,* New York 1900, cited after the German translation, Berlin and Weimar 1980, p. 412
142 Adams, William Lee: 'Paris Hotel wars. Asian chains take on the city's grandes dames by offering a modern spin on luxury.' *Time Magazine*, vol. 177, April 2011, p. 39–40
143 Ibid.
144 Ibid. 'The target clientele is a growing market elite. The number of millionaire households rose 14% worldwide in 2009 to include 11,2 million people, according to the Boston Consulting Group and China alone saw a spike of 31%'
145 Ibid., p. 40: 'According to the U.N. World Tourism Organization, the number of Chinese travelling outside the country rose to 4.7 million in 2009, 54% more than in 2005'
146 Ibid.
147 Baum, Vicky: *Grand Hotel*, New York 1931, (German edition Berlin 1929), p. 237, 299

1248 unter Henry III. „ín vico vocato le Straunde" als „fairest manor in Europe" erbauen ließ. (Mackenzie, Compton: *The Savoy of London*. London, Toronto, Wellington und Sidney 1953, S. 9–10)
123 *The Helmsley Palace*, mit einem Vorwort von Henry-Russell Hitchcock, New York 1980
124 Ludy, Robert B.: *Historic Hotels of the World. Past and Present.* Philadelphia 1927 (Reprint 2009) S. 16
125 Es war eine Gründung des savoyardischen Adligen St. Bernhard de Menthon. Die meisten alpinen Hospize wurden von Augustinern geführt. Ludy, Robert B., op. cit., S. 18–19
126 Ludy, Robert B., op. cit., S. 17–18
127 Flückiger-Seiler, Roland: *Hotelpaläste. Zwischen Traum und Wirklichkeit. Schweizer Tourismus und Hotelbau 1830-1920*, Baden 2003/2005 und ders.: *Hotelträume*, op. cit.
128 Flückiger-Seiler, Roland, *Hotelpaläste*, op. cit., S. 18–19
129 1903 hatte Alexander Emrey das Hotel de Cygne gekauft und dem Architekten Eugène Jost den Auftrag für die Erweiterung gegeben. Jost war als Architekt verschiedener Palasthotels sowie des Bahnhofs in Montreux und der Post von Lausanne bekannt geworden. Bemerkenswert ist die völlige Auflösung der zum See hin orientierten Fassade.
130 R.F.: „Montreux Palace". In: *Schweiz.Suisse.Svizzera. Switzerland. Monatszeitschrift der Schweizerischen Bundesbahn* 3/1981, S. 44
131 1900: 3700; 1910: 5350 Übernachtungen (O.V.: *Bündner Hotellerie um 1900 in Bildern*. Hg. vom Rätischen Museum, Chur 1992, S. 13)
132 Rucki, Isabelle: *Das Hotel in den Alpen. Die Geschichte der Oberengadiner Hotelarchitektur von 1860 –1914*. Zürich 1989, S. 192–193; vgl. auch: Hartmann, Kristiana: *Baumeister und Architekten für Graubünden*, Chur 2016
133 Parkhotel Kurhaus 1905, Grand Hotel 1910, Chantarella und Suvretta House 1912, Carlton 1913
134 La Grand Motte wurde als Touristenort ab den 1960er Jahren mit dem Ziel geschaffen, die Touristenströme aus den spanischen Badeorten hierher „umzuleiten". Kennzeichnend für den Ort sind terrassenförmig angelegte Hochhäuser. Flaine in Hochsavoyen ist ein typisches Beispiel für die Verbauung einer ehemals unberührten Landschaft. Das Ensemble aus den frühen 1960er Jahren, das vom ehemaligen Bauhauslehrer Marcel Breuer konzipiert wurde, ist mittlerweile als Denkmal anerkannt. Les Menuires in den Savoyer Alpen entstand ebenfalls in den 1960er Jahren auf 1850 Meter Höhe als einer der ersten Retortenorte für den Ski-Massentourismus weltweit.
135 Flückiger-Seiler, Roland, *Hotelpaläste*, op. cit., S. 209
136 Zitiert nach Böckli, Peter: *Bis zum Tode der Gräfin. Das Drama um den Hotelpalast des Grafen Renesse in Maloja*. Zürich 1998, in: Seiler-Flückiger, Roland, *Hotelpaläste*, op. cit., S. 211
137 Nietzsche, Friedrich zitiert in: Böckli, Peter, op. cit., S. 98 f.
138 Dazu Schmid, Daniel und Peter Christian Bener: *Die Erfindung vom Paradies*. Glattbrugg 1983. Der Schweizer Regisseur Daniel Schmid, selber im Hotel Schweizerhof in Flims aufgewachsen, hat auf eindrucksvolle Weise mit seinem Film *Hors saison*, 1992, das Hotelleben aus der Sicht des Hoteliers geschildert.
139 Heute werden in Asien, Lateinamerika und Afrika Besuche in Elendsvierteln als Teil touristischer Programme angeboten. Bereits 1911/12 ist in New York in *King's Views of New York* eine Anzeige zum „Slumming", das heißt eine organisierte Tour durch die New Yorker Slums zu finden. Vgl. auch: Bollerey, Franziska: „The Good and the Evil City". In: *Ezelsoren* vol. II, no.3, S. 22–23
140 Grafe, Christoph und Franziska Bollerey: *Cafés and Bars. The Culture of Public Display*. Abingdon (2007) 2008
141 Dreiser, Theodore: *Sister Carrie*. New York 1900. Deutsch zuerst Wien 1929; hier Berlin und Weimar 1980, S. 412
142 Adams, William Lee: „Paris Hotel wars. Asian chains take on

148 Spence, Rachel, in: *Time Magazine*, vol. 175, April 20, 2009, p. 31. In 2008 the 'Palazzo della Gherardesca (15th century) in Florence together with an adjacent monastery from the 16th century was converted to a five-star-hotel. The Çirağan palace (1855–57) in Istanbul since 1992 serves as another 5-star-hotel of the Kempinski group, to name but two from a multitude of examples
149 Bergmann, Justin: 'Peace in Our Time', in: *Time Magazine*, vol. 176, November 1, 2010, p. 41
150 Wu, Daven: 'Spoiled for Choice. Add another London hotel to the list', in: *Time Magazine*, vol. 177, 8 April 2011, p. 53
151 Adams, William Lee: 'Back on Track. A London railway icon lives on', in: *Time Magazine*, vol. 177, 14 March 2011, p. 49
152 cf. note 142, p. 40
153 Hayner, Norman S., op.cit., p. 24
154 Ibid., p. 178
155 cf. note 142, p. 40
156 Hayner, Norman S., op.cit., p. 182

the city's grandes dames by offering a modern spin on luxury." In: *Time Magazine,* vol. 177, 4. April 2011, S. 39–40
143 Ibid.
144 Ibid. „The target clientele is a growing emerging market elite. The number of millionaire households rose 14% worldwide in 2009 to include 11.2 million people, according to the Boston Consulting Group and China alone saw a spike of 31%." (Ibid.)
145 Ibid., S. 40. „According to the U.N. World Tourism Organization, the number of Chinese travelling outside the country rose to 47.7 million in 2009, 54% more than in 2005."
146 Ibid.
147 Baum, Vicki: *Menschen im Hotel*. Berlin 1929, S. 237 und S. 299
148 Spence, Rachel, in: *Time Magazine*, vol. 175, 20. April 2009, S. 31. In Florenz wurde 2008 der Palazzo de la Gherardesca (15. Jh.) mit einem angrenzenden Kloster aus dem 16. Jahrhundert in ein Fünf-Sterne-Hotel umgewandelt. Der Çırağan-Palast in Istanbul (1855–57) ist seit 1992 ein Luxushotel der Kempinski-Gruppe, um nur zwei aus der Vielzahl der Beispiele zu nennen.
149 Bergmann, Justin: „Peace in Our Time". In: *Time Magazine,* vol. 176, 1. November 2010, S. 41
150 Wu, Daven: „Spoiled for Choice. Add another London hotel to the list." In: *Time Magazine,* vol. 177, 8. April 2011, S. 53
151 Adams, William Lee: „Back on Track. A London railway icon lives on." In: *Time Magazine,* vol. 177, 14. März 2011, S. 49
152 Wie Anm. 142, S. 40
153 Hayner, Norman S., op. cit., S. 24
154 Ibid., S. 178
155 Wie Anm. 142, S. 40
156 Hayner, Norman S., op. cit., S. 182

The Birth of the Restaurant and the Rise of 'Haute Cuisine'

Die Geburt des Restaurants und der Aufstieg der „Haute Cuisine"

1
‚To live, you must eat; one lives to eat‘, caricature from around 1820

Man muß essen, um zu leben, man lebt, um zu essen,
Karikatur um 1820

A thin man gesturing to his plate says, *'Il faut manger pour vivre'* ('You must eat to live') to a fat man, who, with hand raised to mouth, hair fashionably coiffed, replies *'Il faut vivre pour manger'* ('You must live to eat'). In culinary literature, this caricature[1] is usually illustrated by a modest rectangular-shaped table covered with a slightly-too-small tablecloth and placed opposite a much grander table, piled high with opulent delicacies and graced with elegantly draped linen. Each detail is contrasted to the maximum: a water jug versus champagne and wine bottles, a modest soup and bean stew versus fowl and a generous assortment of vegetables and desserts. Simple and basic tableware on one side, ornate on the other. Here a glass, there a champagne flute. These two diners are the personification of

„Il faut manger pour vivre", „um zu leben, muss man essen", spricht ein Magerer, mit dem Finger auf seinen Teller zeigend, zu einem Fetten, der, die Hand zum Mund erhoben, die Haare modisch aufgetürmt, erwidert: „Il faut vivre pour manger", „man lebt, um zu essen". Ein bescheiden mit knappem Tischtuch gedeckter, rechteckiger Tisch wird in dieser in der gastronomischen Literatur immer wieder abgebildeten Karikatur[1] antipodisch einem überbordenden, mit wallendem Tischtuch bedeckten Tisch gegenübergestellt. Bis in die Details werden die Gegensätze ausgereizt: Wasserkaraffe gegen Champagner- und Weinflasche, Suppe und Bohnengericht gegen Geflügel, diverse Gemüse und Dessert. Hier einfaches, dort Dekorgeschirr, hier ein Glas, dort eine Champag-

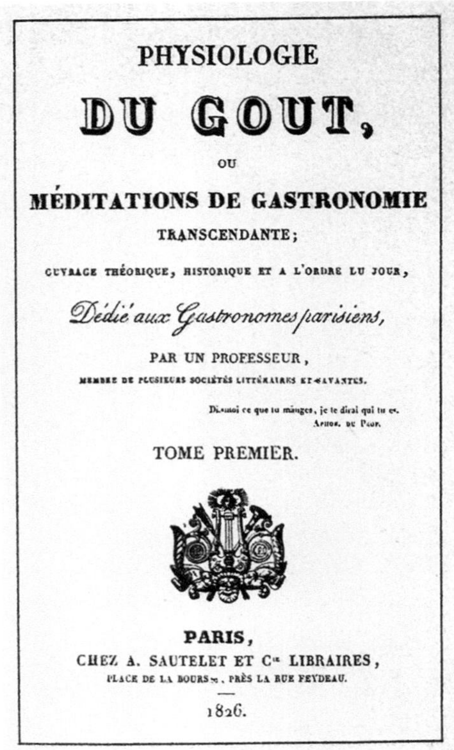

PHYSIOLOGIE

DU GOUT,

OU

MÉDITATIONS DE GASTRONOMIE

TRANSCENDANTE;

OUVRAGE THÉORIQUE, HISTORIQUE ET A L'ORDRE DU JOUR,

Dédié aux Gastronomes parisiens,

PAR UN PROFESSEUR,

MEMBRE DE PLUSIEURS SOCIÉTÉS LITTÉRAIRES ET SAVANTES.

Dis-moi ce que tu manges, je te dirai qui tu es.
APHOR. DU PROF.

TOME PREMIER.

PARIS,

CHEZ A. SAUTELET ET Cie LIBRAIRES,

PLACE DE LA BOURSE, PRÈS LA RUE FEYDEAU.

1826.

2
Portrait of Jean Anthelme Brillat-Savarin ● Titlepage of *Physiologie du goût*, 1826

Porträt von Jean Anthelme Brillat-Savarin ● Titel *Physiologie du goût*, 1826

nutrition versus *gourmandise*. One man is sitting under a shop sign promoting a seed, vegetable, and feed business offering green beans from Soissons while the other reposes beneath a lantern bearing the inscription *'magazine comestibles'*; in other words, a delicatessen. This might not actually be a true restaurant scene that pits luxury and fine dining against a simple inn, but it nonetheless addresses the subject of gastronomy (fig. 1).

Even if the term 'restaurant' is defined as a place of culinary pleasure in a sophisticated atmosphere with extravagant personal service and an assortment of elaborate dishes, it should not be limited to this definition—its initial function is the preparation and presentation of food. Social and economic conditions determine what is considered edible, and how it is to be prepared, as well as the rules involved in its consumption, amount, exorbitance, necessity, and luxury. The following will mainly address 'western' society and its culinary culture.

nerflöte. Die beiden Esser können als Personifizierung von Ernährung und *gourmandise* gesehen werden. Der eine sitzt unter dem Ladenschild eines Samen-, Gemüse- und Futterhandels. Grüne Bohnen aus Soissons werden angeboten. Der andere thront unter einer Laterne mit der Aufschrift „Magazin comestibles", ein Feinkostgeschäft. Auch wenn es sich hier nicht um eine Restaurantszene handelt, die ein einfaches Gasthaus einem Luxusrestaurant gegenüberstellt, trifft sie doch das Thema der Gastronomie (Abb. 1).

Selbst wenn man das Restaurant als einen Ort kulinarischer Genüsse in gepflegtem Ambiente und mit gehobenem, individuellem Service und einer Vielzahl von elaborierten Speisen definiert, so sollte nicht allein dem Raum als solchem Aufmerksamkeit geschenkt werden, sondern seiner primären Daseinsberechtigung, nämlich dem Essen, seiner Inszenierung und Zubereitung. Was als essbar gilt, welche Normen der Zubereitung, welche

3
Chapter title vignettes for *Physiologie du goût*

Kapitel-Titelvignetten der *Physiologie du goût*

This first chapter, 'Inventing, Consuming, and Describing Food, and Displaying Food and Those Who Eat It' discusses the development of the art of cooking, those at its forefront, and the modern renowned culinary philosophers and critics such as Jean Anthelme Brillat-Savarin and Alexandre Grimod de la Reynière. 'The Birth of the Restaurant or a Name and its Consequences' deals with the origins of the restaurant as an expression of modern standards of living. The section 'Fast Meals' is dedicated to 'fast food restaurants' and street food as a phenomenon of 'street selling'. And finally, 'Nothing New Under the Sun—Or Is There?' attempts to assess new trends in gastronomy with regard to their traditional circumstances.

Inventing, Consuming, and Describing Food, and Displaying Food and Those Who Eat It

Apologists for the Physiology of Taste

'The discovery of a new dish does more for the happiness of mankind than the discovery of a new star,'[2] according to Brillat-Savarin.[3] He sums up the personification of food and *gourmandise* described at the beginning of this chapter in his *The Physiology of Taste*[4] as *besoin* and *désir*.[5] *The Physiology* was published in 1826, long before the bourgeoisie began to associate social guilt with their debaucheries. Hence, Brillat-Savarin (fig. 2) was able to almost cynically counterpoise *appétit naturelle*, which is the pure need to feed oneself, with *appétit de luxe*. 'As to the physical effects… eyes grow brighter… as to the moral effects: wits are sharpened' and the *gourmandise* comes to its merits. His book of aphorisms is dedicated to 'the passionate, defensible, and customary preference for things that please the sense of taste'. It is the first comprehensive written work on the philosophy of eating and the psychology of gourmets[6] and it is still being published today. In a book of thirty essays entitled *Meditation*, (fig. 3), Brillat-Savarin examines food, gastronomy, nutrition (including obesity and thinness) the kitchen, dinner hosts, appetite, thirst, and digestion. The book is fundamentally a reflection on the senses, as is typical of almost every piece of literature dealing with gastronomy and the culinary arts. 'The senses (are) the organs by the use of which man communicates with his surroundings.'[7] And they are all activated in a restaurant: sight, hearing, smell, taste, touch. Brillat-Savarin writes that

Regeln beim Verzehr, Maß und Maßlosigkeit, Notwendigkeit und Luxus, ist von gesellschaftlichen und kulturellen Rahmenbedingungen abhängig. Im Folgenden wird im Wesentlichen von den sogenannten westlichen Gesellschaften und ihrer Gastrokultur die Rede sein.

Mit der Entwicklung der Kochkunst, ihren Protagonisten und ihren in der Neuzeit berühmten französischen Gastrosophen und Gastronomiekritikern wie Jean Anthelme Brillat-Savarin und Alexandre Grimod de la Reynière beschäftigt sich das Kapitel „Essen erfinden, verzehren, beschreiben, das Essen und den Essenden zur Schau stellen". „Die Geburt des Restaurants oder ein Name und seine Folgen" behandelt dann die Genese des Restaurants als Ausdruck moderner Lebensformen. Ein weiteres, „Schnelle Mahlzeiten" betiteltes Kapitel widmet sich den Fast-Food-Restaurants sowie dem Straßenverkauf und -verzehr. Abschließend versucht das Kapitel „Nichts Neues unter der Sonne – oder?" neuere Tendenzen der Gastronomie an ihren historischen Gegebenheiten zu messen.

Essen erfinden, verzehren, beschreiben, das Essen und den Essenden zur Schau stellen

Apologeten der Physiologie des Geschmacks

„Die Entdeckung eines neuen Gerichts ist für das Glück der Menschheit wichtiger als die Entdeckung eines neuen Gestirns",[2] sagt Brillat-Savarin.[3] Die eingangs beschriebenen Personifizierungen von Ernährung und *gourmandise* subsummiert er in seiner *Physiologie des Geschmacks*[4] als *besoin* und *désir*.[5] In einer Zeit, in der die Vertreter der Bourgeoisie sich bei ihren Ausschweifungen keinerlei sozialer Schuld bewusst sind – die *Physiologie* erscheint 1826 – kann Brillat-Savarin (Abb. 2) nahezu zynisch dem *appétit naturelle*, dem Bedürfnis, sich zu ernähren den *appétit de luxe* gegenüberstellen. „In physischer Hinsicht erheitert sich das Antlitz … in moralischer … schärft sich der Geist" und die *gourmandise* kommt auf ihre Kosten. „Der leidenschaftlichen, begründeten und gewohnheitsmäßigen Vorliebe für Dinge, die dem Geschmackssinn schmeicheln" ist sein in Aphorismen gehaltenes Buch gewidmet. Es ist die erste umfassende Abhandlung über die Philosophie des Essens und die Psychologie der Feinschmecker[6], sie wird bis heute immer wieder neu aufgelegt. In 30 „Meditation" (Abb. 3) benannten Essays untersucht er unter anderem Nahrungsmittel, behandelt

4

5

4
'The Five Senses'. From *Groupes Physionomiques, connus sous le nom de Grimaces par Boilly* Louis-Léopold Boilly, beginning of the nineteenth century

Die fünf Sinne. Aus: *Groupes Physionomiques, connus sous le nom de Grimaces par Boilly*, Louis-Léopold Boilly, Anfang 19. Jahrhundert

5
'Taste'. Jan P. Saenredam after H. Goltzius: *The Five Senses*, 1595/96 ● 'Gourmandise or Taste', Jeremias Falck, 1644/45

Das Schmecken. Jan P. Saenredam nach H. Goltzius: Die fünf Sinne, 1595/96 ● *Die Gourmandise oder der Geschmack*, Jeremias Falck, 1644/45

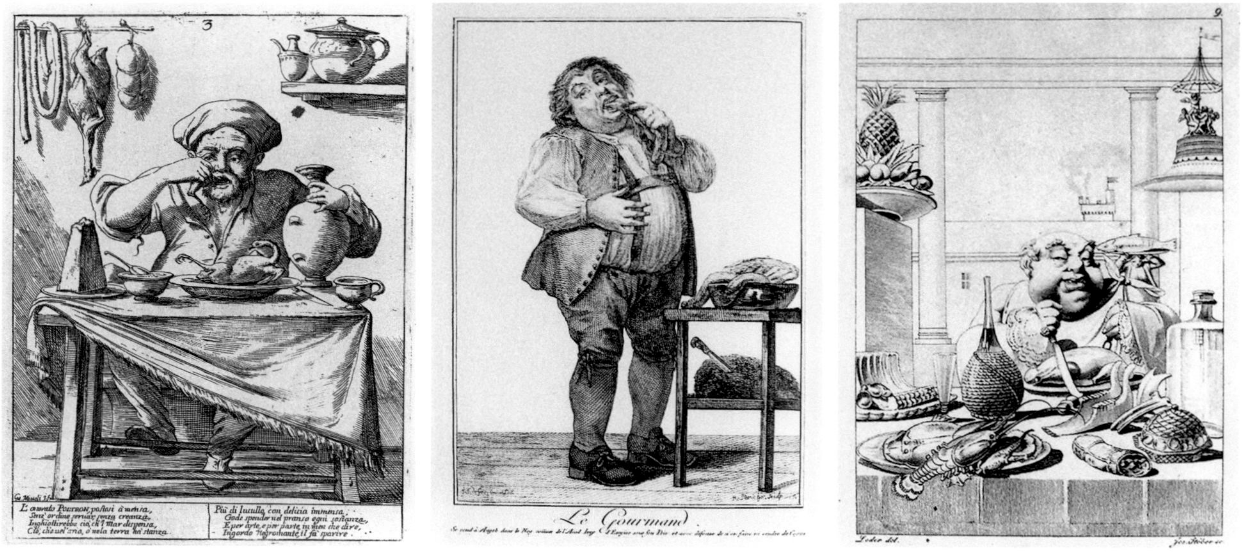

6

‚Poltrone as glutton', Guiseppe Maria Mitelli, 1683 ● *Le Gourmand, (the Glutton)*, Joseph Baron von Goez, 1784 ● *The Insatiable*, Joseph Stöber, 1818

Poltrone als Fresser, Guiseppe Maria Mitelli, 1683 ● *Le Gourmand, der Vielfraß*, Joseph Freiherr von Goez, 1784 ● *Der Nimmersatt*, Joseph Stöber, 1818

'sight, which embraces space, and, through the medium of light, reveals the existence and colour of bodies which surround us; hearing, which through the medium of air receives vibrations set up by sonorous bodies; smell, which enables us to discern the odours which certain bodies exhale; taste, by means of which we approve the sapidity and esculence of things; touch, which determines the consistency and surface of bodies …'[8] (fig. 4)

Restaurant guests absorb the interior design of a dining establishment, the arrangement of furniture, the laid tables, and the dishes served. Amidst the general sound of human voices, they can make out individual words spoken by someone at a neighbouring table. The scent of the dishes stimulates their appetite. Taste enables them to discern between the different meals they consume. The sense of touch is perhaps the sense least used in this context, unless of course, one hand caresses another—but the feel of tablecloths, napkins, glasses, flatware, and porcelain is also a sensory experience. The sense of taste experiences a particular elevation in 'gourmandism'. The *gourmandise* is usually depicted as either a

die Gastronomie, die Ernährung – einschließlich Fettleibigkeit und Magerkeit – die Küche, die Speisewirte, den Appetit, den Durst sowie die Verdauung. Aufmacher ist eine Betrachtung der Sinne, wie sie fast in jeder Publikation zur Gastronomie und Kulinarik zu finden ist.

„Die Sinne [sind] diejenigen Organe, durch welche der Mensch sich mit der Außenwelt in Beziehung setzt."[7] Im Restaurant werden sie alle mobilisiert: das Sehen, das Hören, das Riechen, das Schmecken, das Fühlen. „Das Gesicht, welches den Raum umfaßt und uns mittelst des Lichtes die Existenz und die Farben der Körper erkennen läßt, die uns umgeben; das Gehör, welches mittelst der Luft die Schwingungen der schallenden oder tönenden Körper aufnimmt; der Geruch, mittelst dessen wir die Gerüche der riechenden Körper wahrnehmen; der Geschmack, mittelst dessen wir alle eßbaren oder schmackhaften Körper beurteilen; das Gefühl, das die Oberfläche und Dichte der Körper zum Gegenstande hat …"[8],

schreibt Brillat-Savarin (Abb. 4). Der Restaurantgast nimmt also die Inneneinrichtung, die Anordnung

voluptuous woman (fig. 5) or an overindulgent man (fig. 6). Philosophical and physiological musings about them are an intrinsic element of all gastronomic literature. Brillat-Savarin, with his own philological flair, introduces not only new gastronomic terms, but also distinguishes between voracity, gluttony and gourmandism. French utopian socialist François Marie Charles Fourier ascribes a new social order to both gourmandism and taste in his psycho-hedonistic draft:

> 'Il faut généraliser la vertu gourmandise et élever le genre humain au raffinement gastronomique, même sur le mets le plus commun.'[9]

In Fourier's sensualistic worldview, the *gourmandise* plays a pivotal role in the welfare of all, not just that of a small minority.

> 'Le bon goût est relégné en civilisation chez quelques adeptes seulement, et ne s'étend jamais à la multitude.'[10]

The second of the famous French culinary authors, Alexandre Balthazar Laurent Grimod de la Reynière, dedicates his work to these selected few[11] in his *Almanach des gourmands* published between 1803 and 1812 (fig. 7). The volumes were published annually and each began with engravings by the Parisian painter François Marie Neveu,[12] one of which appears to depict the editor (fig. 8). '*Le plus lettré des gourmands, le plus gourmand des lettrés*', wrote Charles Monselet, the editor of the weekly publications, *Le Gourmet* and *Le Gourmand* (fig. 9, top), in 1857 about Grimod de la Reynière.[13] In his *Manuel des Amphytrions*[14] from 1808, Grimod de la Reynière refers to the hospitable Greek king,[15] a frequently recurring subject of literature. The *Manuel* was planned as a lexical work, but was never implemented as such. It was not until many years later in 1873 under Napoleon III, at the height of the era of the bourgeoisie, that Alexandre Dumas the Elder, author of *Le comte de Monte-Cristo*, took up the idea again with his *Grand Dictionnaire de cuisine*[16] (fig. 9, bottom). Grimod de La Reynière first caught the attention of Parisians as early as 1783 with a banquet held at his palace on the Champs-Élysées. It was designed as a Roman *Coena*, which reflected that period's predilection for antiquity.

> 'Twenty-two people gathered together, including two women in men's clothing. We first crossed through a

der Möbel, die gedeckten Tische und die ihm servierten Speisen wahr. Vor der Kulisse des allgemeinen Stimmengewirrs lauscht er den Worten des Tischnachbarn. Die Gerüche der Speisen stimulieren seinen Appetit. Der Geschmackssinn ermöglicht ihm die Beurteilung der verzehrten Speisen. Der Tastsinn kommt vielleicht am wenigsten zu seinem Recht, es sei denn, eine Hand streichelt die andere, aber auch das Berühren von Tischdecken, Servietten, Gläsern, Besteck und Porzellan ist eine sinnliche Erfahrung. Der Geschmackssinn erfährt in der Feinschmeckerei eine besondere Überhöhung. Die *gourmandise* wird grafisch als wollüstiges Weib (Abb. 5) und männlicher Vielfresser dargestellt (Abb. 6). Die philosophischen und physiologischen Auslassungen über sie fehlen in keinem Werk zur Gastronomie. Mit dem ihm eigenen philologischen Spürsinn führt Brillat-Savarin nicht nur neue gastronomische Termini ein, sondern räumt auch mit der Verwechslung der Begriffe Gefräßigkeit, Völlerei und Feinschmeckerei auf. Letzterer wie auch dem Geschmack schenkt der französische utopische Sozialist François Marie Charles Fourier in seinem psycho-hedonistischen Entwurf einer neuen Gesellschaftsordnung seine Aufmerksamkeit.

> „Il faut généraliser la vertu gourmandise et élever le genre humain au raffinement gastronomique, même sur le mets le plus commun."[9]

In seinem sensualistischen Weltbild spielt die *gourmandise* eine zentrale Rolle für das Wohlbefinden aller, nicht nur einer kleinen Minderheit.

> „Le bon goût est relégné en civilisation chez quelques adeptes seulement, et ne s'étend jamais à la multitude."[10]

An diese wenigen Eingeweihten wendet sich auch der zweite der berühmten französischen Gastro-Autoren, Alexandre Balthazar Laurent Grimod de la Reynière[11] (Abb. 7) mit seinem zwischen 1803 und 1812 herausgegebenen *Almanach des gourmands*. Die jährlich erscheinenden Bände werden jeweils mit Kupferstichen des Pariser Malers François Marie Neveu[12], auf denen man den Herausgeber zu erkennen vermeint, aufgemacht (Abb. 8). „Le plus lettré des gourmands, le plus gourmand des lettrés", schreibt Charles Monselet, selbst Herausgeber der Wochenzeitschriften *Le gourmet* und *Le gourmand* (Abb. 9, oben), 1857 über Grimod de la Reynière.[13] Mit seinem

7

A.B.L. Grimod de la Reyniere, né à Paris, le 20 9.bre 1758.

8

Bibliothèque d'un Gourmand
du XIX.e Siècle.
Les audiences d'un Gourmand.
Séance d'un Jury de Gourmands dégustateurs.
Les méditations d'un Gourmand.
Le premier devoir d'un Amphitrion.
Les Rêves d'un Gourmand.
Le lever d'un gourmand
Le plus mortel ennemi du diner.

darkened hall, and then a theatre curtain suddenly lifted revealing the ballroom. In the middle of the table there was an elevated catafalque. There was a gallery surrounding the festival hall, which was intended for an audience to enjoy the view of the festivities. M. de la Reynière had invited approximately 300 guests to the gallery, and at the appointed hour gave the order for them to enter, but no one could linger very long because they soon had to vacate their places to make room for new guests.'[17]

Nicolas Edme Restif de La Bretonne describes a similar scene in *Les Nuits de Paris ou le spectateur nocturne*[18] (fig. 10). The entire event was staged by the actor and master of ceremonies, Joseph-Jean-Baptiste Albouy Dazincourt,[19] who was also employed by Marie Antoinette and later Napoleon I. Here, Grimod de la Reynière takes up this tradition of the dinner as a showpiece event. At the same time, because it makes courtly gourmandism accessible to entirely new social strata, it clears the way for restaurants to come. The '*Diners philosophiques*' he later arranged for selected members of these social strata combined stimulating conversation with the enjoyment of eating. De La Reynère also introduced a type of product information. After each course, the dining guests, persevering until the wee hours, were informed about the sources of the various dishes and ingredients in an enlightening and promotional performance. Grimod de la Reynière went personally to the halls and markets to shop—something completely unheard of at that time for someone of his class and standing. In 1785, he put his point of view, which was critical of the monarchy, in writing in his successful book, *Lorgnette philosophique*. But, as previously mentioned, his *Almanach des gourmands* nevertheless had the nobility, bourgeoisie, and restaurant owners in mind. In response, one of the editors of the almanac, François Guillaume Ducray-Duminil,[20] published the *Almanach des pauvres diables. Annales de l'Inanition pour servir de pendant à l'Almanach des gourmands*[21] in 1808, as

7
Portrait of Alexandre Balthazar Laurent Grimod de la Reynière

Porträt von Alexandre Balthazar, Laurent Grimod de La Reynière

8
Title copper plates of the 'Almanach des Gourmands', 1804–1812, François Marie Neveu

Titelkupfer des *Almanach des Gourmands*, 1804–1812, François Marie Neveu

Manuel des Amphytrions[14] von 1808 bezieht sich Grimod de la Reynière auf den auch in der Literatur immer wieder behandelten gastfreien griechischen König.[15] Das *Manuel* war als lexikalisches Werk geplant, wurde aber als solches nicht realisiert. Erst Jahre später greift unter Napoleon III. im Jahre 1873, in der Hochzeit der Bourgeoisie, der Verfasser des *Le conte de Monte-Christo*, Alexandre Dumas d. Ä., mit seinem *Grand dictionnaire de cuisine*[16] das Projekt wieder auf (Abb. 9, unten).

Bereits 1783 macht Grimod de la Reynière mit einem Gastmahl in seinem Palais an den Champs-Élysées auf sich aufmerksam. Es war gemäß der damaligen Vorliebe für die Antike einer römischen *coena* nachempfunden.

> „Es hatten sich 22 Personen eingefunden, darunter zwei Frauen in Männerkleidern. Zuerst durchquerten wir ein verdunkeltes Vorzimmer, dann hob sich plötzlich ein Theatervorhang und gab den Blick auf den Festsaal frei. In der Mitte des Tisches ... erhob sich ein Katafalk ... Rings um den Festsaal lief eine Galerie, die für die Zuschauer bestimmt war, welche sich am Anblick der Festivität erfreuen wollten. M. de la Reynière hatte ungefähr 300 Einladungen für die Galerie verteilt, und zur angegebenen Stunde gab er den Befehl, die Leute einzulassen, aber keiner durfte lange bleiben, jeder mußte bald seinen Platz für die Nachrückenden räumen."[17]

Ähnliches beschreibt auch Nicolas Edme Restif de La Bretonne in *Les nuits de Paris ou le spectateur nocturne*[18] (Abb. 10). Das Ganze wurde von dem Schauspieler und Zeremonienmeister sowohl Marie Antoinettes als auch später Napoleons I., Joseph-Jean-Baptiste Albouy Dazincourt[19] in Szene gesetzt. Grimod de la Reynière greift hier die Tradition der Schauessen auf. Gleichzeitig ebnet er den Weg zu den späteren Restaurants, indem er höfische Feinschmeckerei neuen gesellschaftlichen Schichten zugänglich macht. Seine hernach arrangierten „Diners philosophiques" kombinieren dann für ausgewählte Vertreter dieser Schichten das angeregte Gespräch mit dem Genuss am Essen. De La Reynère führt auch eine Art Produktinformation ein. Nach den einzelnen Gängen wurden den Speisenden, die bis in den Morgen ausharrten, in einer aufklärenden und werbenden Aktion die Quellen der verarbeiteten Produkte mitgeteilt. Grimod de la Reynière ging selber in den Hallen und auf den Märkten einkaufen – ein absolut unkonventioneller Vertreter seiner Klasse. Seine monarchiekriti-

Première année — N° 21. 20 CENTIMES Dimanche 1er Août 1858.

LE GOURMET

Parait tous les Dimanches

LE GOURMET

JOURNAL DES INTÉRÊTS GASTRONOMIQUES

RÉDACTEUR EN CHEF : M. CHARLES MONSELET.

PRINCIPAUX ARTICLES

PUBLIÉS PAR LE GOURMET

LE POIVRE ET LE PIMENT

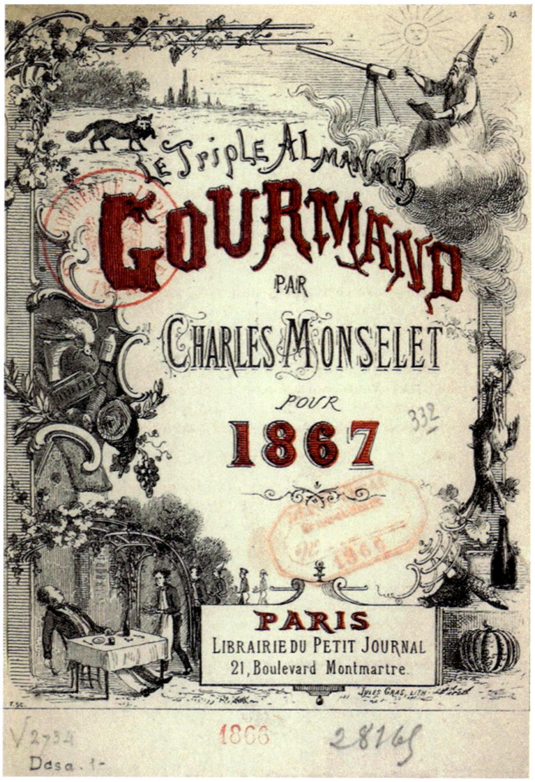

LE TRIPLE ALMANACH

GOURMAND

PAR

CHARLES MONSELET

POUR

1867

PARIS

LIBRAIRIE DU PETIT JOURNAL

21, Boulevard Montmartre.

GRAND DICTIONNAIRE

DE

CUISINE

PAR

ALEXANDRE DUMAS

PARIS

ALPHONSE LEMERRE, ÉDITEUR

27–29, PASSAGE CHOISEUL, 27–29

M DCCC LXXIII

9

Title of *Le Gourmet*, 1858, edited by M. Charles Monselet ● Title of *Le Triple Almanach Gourmand*, 1867, edited by M. Charles Monselet ● Title of *Grande dictionnaire de cuisine*, 1873, edited by Alexandre Dumas the Elder

Titel des von M. Charles Monselet herausgegebenen *Le Gourmet*, 1858 ● Titel des von M. Charles Monselet herausgegebenen *Le triple Almanach Gourmand*, 1867 ● Titel des von Alexandre Dumas d.Ä. herausgegebenen *Grande dictionnaire de cuisine*, 1873

an anti-Grimod publication. Except for a very few exceptions, the starving population in the countryside and cities was not a subject of gastronomic discourse. Apart from Fourier, who is mentioned above, the only others occupied with this question at this time were Charles-Louis Cadet de Gassicourt,[22] who was thinking about developing a nutritional powder for soldiers during the time of the Napoleonic Wars, and Benjamin Thompson, Count of Rumford,[23] who invented a nourishing soup for the poor made from a variety of low-cost ingredients. There was also Queen Victoria's head chef, Charles Elme Francatelli,[24] who wrote *A Plain Cookery Book for the Working Classes* in 1852, and Alexis Soyer with *A Shilling Cookery Book for the People* (1855).[25] The critical *Dictionary of National Biography* calls Francatelli a cost-efficient gourmand. Yet his findings include a fact still highly relevant today: thousands of families could easily be fed by the food that is thrown away in London on a daily basis. The topic of 'hunger and voracity,' including the waste and destruction of food, would be a very appropriate subject here, but it would go far beyond the scope of this essay.

To return once again to the eight volumes of the *Almanach des gourmands*: there is also something enduring and fundamental to be discovered among the many writings on gourmandism, food, and dining culture. They contain a system of values comparable in significance to the arts and sciences. Grimod de la Reynière would regularly meet with selected tasters in the *Jury dégustateurs* he established. They convened in academic-like conferences that had the aura of a freemasons' secret rendezvous. Over a total of 465 meetings, a canon of judgments formed that eventually developed into a qualification system for the Parisian restaurants, and even into a forerunner of today's system of awarding stars. He also anticipated the restaurant review stickers that are today mounted on or next to restaurant doors or in menus. The certificate (also issued by his jury) for caterers—the most famous among them being *Corcellet* and *Chevet*[26]—had to be purchased and could subsequently be used for promotional purposes. Grimod de la Reynière is a pioneer of the modern restaurant. The way in which his meals were staged and presented, as well as the varying and numerous courses, were geared towards courtly culture. He was an admirer of Louis XIV. And perhaps this is where Grimod de La Reynière found the idea for audience participation at his famous *catafalque-banquet*; adopted from the king, who in fact did put himself on display eating in Versailles. It

sche Haltung hat er 1785 in seinem erfolgreichen Buch *Lorgnette philosophique* niedergelegt. Aber wie bereits erwähnt, standen ihm mit dem *Almanach des gourmands* der Adel, die Bourgeoisie und die Gastronomen vor Augen. Als Reaktion hierauf veröffentlicht 1808 einer der Redakteure des Almanach, François Guillaume Ducray-Duminil,[20] als Anti-Grimod-Publikation den *Almanach des pauvres diables. Annales de l'Inanition pour servir de pendant à l'Almanach des gourmands*[21]. Bis auf wenige Ausnahmen ist die hungerleidende Bevölkerung auf dem Land und in den Städten nicht Gegenstand gastronomischer Diskurse. Außer dem erwähnten Fourier haben sich nur noch Charles-Louis Cadet de Gassicourt[22], der zur Zeit der napoleonischen Kriege an ein Ernährungspulver für Soldaten denkt oder Benjamin Thompson Graf von Rumford[23], der eine aus allerlei preisgünstigen Bestandteilen komponierte nahrhafte Suppe für die Armen erfand, dieser Frage gewidmet. Weiter gab es den Küchenchef Königin Victorias, Charles Elmé Francatelli[24] mit seinem *A Plain Cookery Book for the Working Classes* aus dem Jahr 1852 sowie Alexis Soyer mit *A Shilling Cookery Book for the People* von 1855.[25] Das kritische *Dictionary of National Biography* nennt Francatelli einen ökonomischen Kulinariker. Zu seinen Feststellungen gehört die noch heute hochaktuelle Erkenntnis, dass Tausende von Familien von dem ernährt werden könnten, was in London täglich an Lebensmitteln weggeworfen wird. „Hunger und Völlerei", eingeschlossen die Verschwendung und Vernichtung von Lebensmitteln wäre ein hochrelevantes Thema, würde aber den Rahmen dieses Beitrages sprengen.

Hier sei noch einmal auf die acht Bände des *Almanach des gourmands* zurückgekommen. In den substanziellen Beiträgen zu Feinschmeckerei, zu Lebensmitteln und zur Tafelkultur lässt sich etwas Dauerhaftes und Grundlegendes entdecken: Es handelte sich hier um ein System von Werten, dem man die gleiche Bedeutung beimaß wie den Künsten und Wissenschaften. Wie bei den Akademiesitzungen und nahezu von einer Aura von Freimaurerei umgeben trifft sich Grimod de la Reynière mit ausgewählten Verkostern in der von ihm begründeten „Jury dégustateurs". In insgesamt 465 Sitzungen entwickelt sich ein Kanon der Beurteilungen, der sich als Qualifizierung der Pariser Restaurants, ja sogar als Vorläufer der heutigen Sternevergabe herauskristallisiert. Auch die heute auf oder neben den Restauranttüren oder neben den Speisekarten angebrachten Bewertungsauf-

10

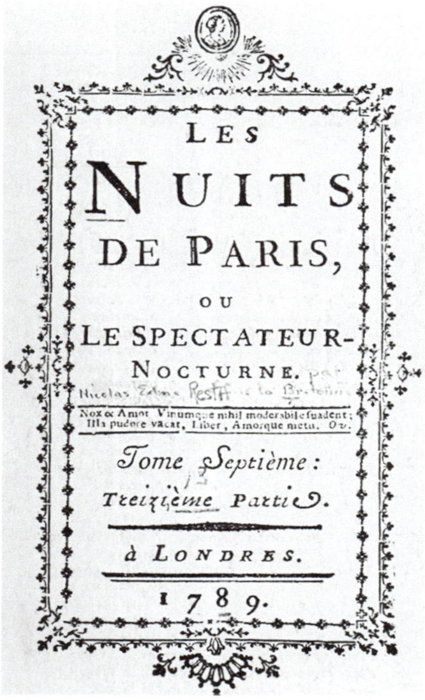
LES
NUITS
DE PARIS,
OU
LE SPECTATEUR-
NOCTURNE.
Nox & Amor Vinumque nihil moderabile suadent;
Illa pudore vacat, Liber, Amorque metu. Ov.
Tome Septième:
Treizième Partie.
à LONDRES.
1789.

11

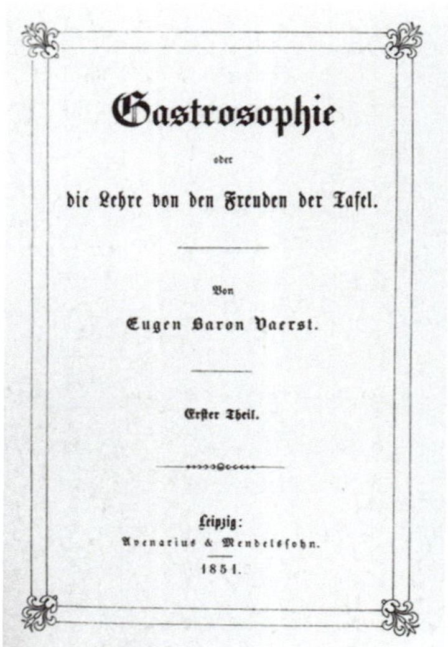
Gastrosophie
oder
die Lehre von den Freuden der Tafel.
Von
Eugen Baron Vaerst.
Erster Theil.
Leipzig:
Avenarius & Mendelssohn.
1851.

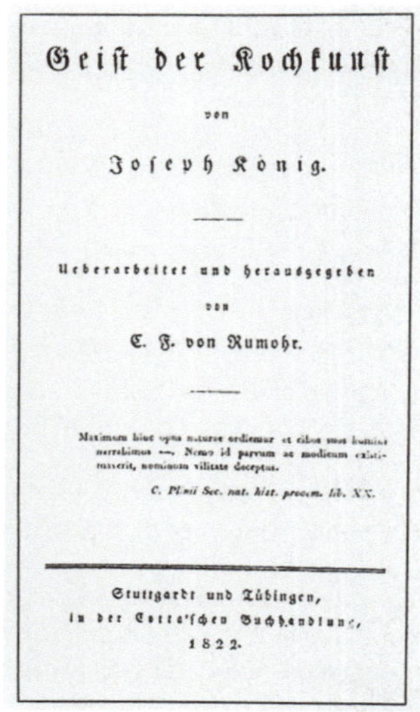
Geist der Kochkunst
von
Joseph König.
Ueberarbeitet und herausgegeben
von
C. F. von Rumohr.
C. Plinii Sec. nat. hist. procem. lib. XX.
Stuttgart und Tübingen,
in der Cotta'schen Buchhandlung,
1822.

10
Title of the seventh volume of *Les nuits de Paris ou le spectateur nocturne* by Nicolas Edme Restif de La Bretonne, 1789 ● Banquet at Grimod de la Reynière, from 'La Bretonne'

Titel des 7. Bandes der *Les nuits de Paris ou le spectateur nocturne* von Nicolas Edme Restif de La Bretonne ● *Gastmahl bei Grimod de la Reynière*, aus *La Bretonne*

11
Title of 'Gastrosophie or The Lesson of the Pleasures of the Table' by Eugen Baron von Vaerst, 1851 ● Design for the title of 'Spirit of the Art of Cooking', around 1822 ● Title of 'The Spirit of the Art of Cooking', around 1822

Gastrosophie oder die Lehre von den Freuden der Tafel, Eugen Baron von Vaerst, 1851 ● Idee für das Titelblatt zu *Geist der Kochkunst*, um 1822 ● Titel *Geist der Kochkunst*, um 1822

is, however, more likely that this well-educated man was familiar with the historical significance of the showcase banquet, which will be discussed later.

The annual volumes of the almanac not only set future trends and standards, but were also received internationally. In London in 1815, the anonymously published *The Epicure's Almanack, or Calendar of Good Living in London* was equivalent to the Parisian model. As in Paris, it also became the first restaurant guide to London—which its subtitle implies: *First Directory to London's Inns, Taverns, Coffee-Houses, Eating Houses and Other Places of Elementary Resort.* Abraham Heyward and William Blanchard Jerrold also pay tribute to both Grimod de la Reynière and Brillat-Savarin in *The Art of Dining: or Gastronomy and Gastronomers*[27] and *The Epicure's Yearbook and Table Companion.*[28] The two French gastronomers were lawyers, and were therefore interested in laws as well as interpretations. This may well be the root of their great success in the age of transition from a feudal to a bourgeois society. Louis-Eustache Ude, a naturalised British citizen, made direct reference to French cuisine with *The French Cook* in 1813.[29] Grimod de la Reynière's first *Almanac* was a bestseller, as was Louis-Sébastien Mercier's *Tableau de Paris.*[30] In several editions it reached a circulation of 20,000 copies, which was considerable at the time. In Germany, a pirated edition entitled *Almanach der Leckermäuler* appeared (fig. 11, left).[31] Friedrich Christian Eugen von Vaerst would have been aware of this German translation and would have had it in mind while writing his *Gastrosophie oder die Lehre von den Freuden der Tafel.*[32] Von Vaerst is one of the triumvirate of German *Feinschmecker* (literally 'fine taster'), which also includes Carl Friedrich Baron von Rumohr with *Der Geist der Kochkunst von Joseph König* (fig. 11, centre, and right)[33] from 1822, and Gustav Blumröder with *Vorlesungen über Eßkunst*[34] from 1838. Rumohr was an opponent of gluttony: 'I understand gluttony as a certain wasteful hedonism or a hedonistic waste.'[35] With his virtuous doctrine of temperance, he preferred to campaign against the excesses of Epicureans.[36] Von Vaerst, on the other hand, was more positive about epicurean hedonism. As the title suggests, his 'gastrosophy' is specifically dedicated to the pleasures of the table. He refers to Brillat-Savarin's stated differentiation between *gourmandism* and gluttony in order to clarify the difference between gourmand, gourmet, and 'gastrosopher'. 'The gourmand is eager for anything that tastes good without regard for health, the gourmet is merely lustful,

kleber nimmt er vorweg. Das ebenfalls von seiner Jury für Traiteure – die berühmtesten unter ihnen waren „Corcellet" und „Chevet"[26] – ausgegebene Zertifikat musste gekauft und konnte dann zu Werbezwecken genutzt werden.

Grimod de la Reynière ist ein Wegbereiter des modernen Restaurantwesens. Die Inszenierung seiner Mahlzeiten sowie die variierenden und zahlreichen Gänge orientierten sich an der höfischen Kultur. Vielleicht hatte Grimod de la Reynière als Bewunderer von Louis XIV. die zuschauende Teilhabe an seinem berühmten Katafalkgastmahl auch von ihm, dem sich essend in Versailles zur Schau stellenden Potentaten übernommen. Wahrscheinlicher aber ist, dass der Literat mit den historischen Schauessen, von denen noch die Rede sein wird, vertraut war.

Die Jahresbände des Almanachs setzen nicht nur zukunftsweisende Maßstäbe, sondern werden auch international rezipiert. In London sollte das 1815 anonym erschienene *The Epicure's Almanack, or Calendar of Good Living in London* dem Pariser Vorbild entsprechen. Wie in Paris dient es – der Untertitel *First Directory to London's Inns, Taverns, Coffee-Houses, Eating Houses and Other Places of Elementary Resort* besagt es – als erster Restaurantführer für London. Abraham Heyward und William Blanchard Jerrold würdigen mit *The Art of Dining: or Gastronomy and Gastronomers*[27] und *The Epicure's Yearbook and Table Companion*[28] sowohl Grimod de la Reynière als auch Brillat-Savarin. Beide französischen Gastrosophen waren Juristen und somit Gesetzmäßigkeiten wie auch Auslegungen auf der Spur. Hierin liegt wohl die Ursache ihres großen Erfolges im Zeitalter des Aufbruchs von einer feudalen in eine bürgerliche Gesellschaft. Direkten Bezug auf die französische Kochkunst nimmt der in England naturalisierte Louis-Eustache Ude mit *The French Cook* 1813.[29] Grimod de la Reynières erster *Almanach* war wie Louis-Sébastien Merciers *Tableau de Paris*[30] ein Bestseller. In mehreren Editionen erreichte er die für die damalige Zeit beträchtliche Auflagenhöhe von 20.000 Exemplaren. In Deutschland erschien ein *Almanach der Leckermäuler* betitelter Raubdruck.[31] (Abb. 11, links) So wird wohl auch Friedrich Christian Eugen von Vaerst diese deutsche Übersetzung gekannt und sie in seiner 1851 erschienenen *Gastrosophie oder die Lehre von den Freuden der Tafel*[32] berücksichtigt haben. Von Vaerst gehört zu dem Dreigestirn deutschsprachiger Gastrosophen, neben Carl Friedrich Baron von Rumohr mit *Der*

12

13

Ein new Kochbuch/

Das ist Ein grundtliche beschreibung

wie man recht vnd wol/ nicht allein von vierfüssigen/ heymischen vnd wilden Thieren/ sondern auch von mancherley Vögel vnd Federwildpret/ darzu von allem grünen vnd dürren Fischwerck/ allerley Speiß/ als gesotten/ gebraten/ gebacken/ Presolen/ Carbonaden/ mancherley Pasteten vnd Füllwerck/ Gallrat/ etc. auff Teutsche/ Vngerische/ Hispanische/ Italianische vnnd Frantzösische weiß/ kochen vnd zubereiten solle: Auch wie allerley Gemüß/ Obß/ Salsen/ Senff/ Confect vnd Latwergen/ zuzurichten seye.

Auch ist darinnen zu vernemmen/ wie man herrliche grosse Pancketen/ sampt gemeinen Gastereyen/ ordentlich anrichten vnd bestellen soll.

Allen Menschen/ hohes vnd nidriges Standts/ Weibs vnd Manns Personen/ zu nutz jetzundt zum ersten in Druck gegeben/ dergleichen vor nie ist außgegangen/

Durch

M. Marxen Rumpolt/ Churf. Meintzischen Mundtkoch.

Mit Röm. Keyserlicher Maiestat special Priuilegio.

15 81.

Sampt einem gründtlichen Bericht/ wie man alle Wein vor allen zufällen bewaren/ die bresthafften widerbringen/ Kräuter vnd andere Wein/ Bier/ Essig/ vnd alle andere Geträncke/ machen vnd bereiten soll/ daß sie natürlich/ vnd allen Menschen vnschädlich/ zu trincken seindt.

Gedruckt zu Franckfort am Mayn/ In verlegung M. Marx Rumpolts/ Churf. Meintz. Mundtkochs/ vnd Sigmundt Feyerabendts.

Kochbuch M. Marx Rumpolts/

Nun folgen vier Bancket der Königen in Vngern vnd Böhem/ darinn vermeldet/ was für Speiß vnd Trachten/ nicht allein auff die Fleisch/ sondern auch auff die Fasttage/ zuzurichten seyen.

Der erste Gang zum Frümahl/ am Fleischtag.

EIn groß stück Rindfleisch/ vnnd geräuchert Fleisch darbey/ von allerley geräuchert Fleisch. 1

Zwen Kapaunen in einer Suppen/ vnd von allerley Gebratens darauff/ wie hernach folgt/ nemlich/ Ein Hirschen Ruckbraten/ auch ein Kälbern Hachsen Braten/ vnnd an eim Heßlen Spiß gebraten/ ein theil mit Knobloch gestrichen/ Ein Kälbern Bratwurst/ Ein Schweine Bratwurst/ vnnd kleine Vögel gebraten/ alles zu den Kapaunen auff die Suppen gelegt/ Das heißt man ein Vngerische gesattelte Suppen. 2

Der ander Gang.

Dreyssig Junge Hüner gelb auff Vngerisch gekocht/ darvon dem Hofmeister zwey/ dem Kuchenmeister zwey/ vnnd zwey dem ders kocht/ die andern vier vnd zwentzig in silber angericht. 3

Sechtzig

14

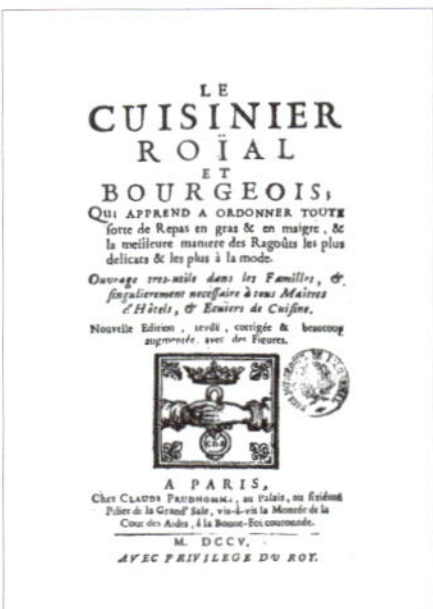

LE CUISINIER ROÏAL ET BOURGEOIS,

Qui apprend a ordonner toute sorte de Repas en gras & en maigre, & la meilleure maniere des Ragoûts les plus delicats & les plus à la mode.

Ouvrage tres-utile dans les Familles, & singulierement necessaire à tous Maîtres d'Hôtels, & Ecuiers de Cuisine.

Nouvelle Edition, revûë, corrigée & beaucoup augmentée, avec des Figures.

A PARIS,

Chez Claude Prudhomme, au Palais, au sixiéme Pilier de la Grand' Sale, vis-à-vis la Montée de la Cour des Aides, à la Bonne-Foi couronnée.

M. DCCV.

AVEC PRIVILEGE DU ROY.

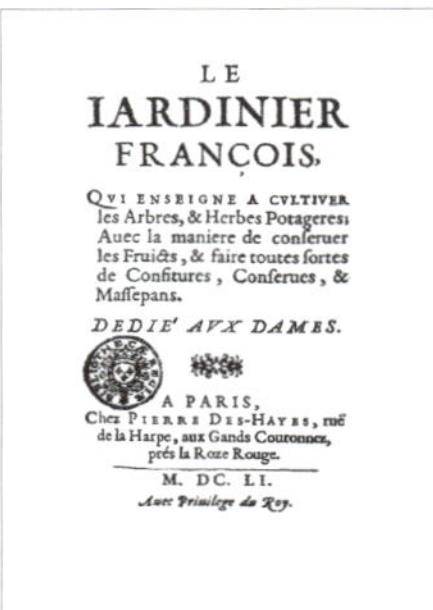

LE IARDINIER FRANÇOIS,

QVI ENSEIGNE A CVLTIVER les Arbres, & Herbes Potageres; Auec la maniere de conseruer les Fruicts, & faire toutes sortes de Confitures, Conserues, & Massepans.

DEDIE' AVX DAMES.

A PARIS,

Chez Pierre Des-Hayes, ruë de la Harpe, aux Gands Couronnez, prés la Roze Rouge.

M. DC. LI.

Auec Priuilege du Roy.

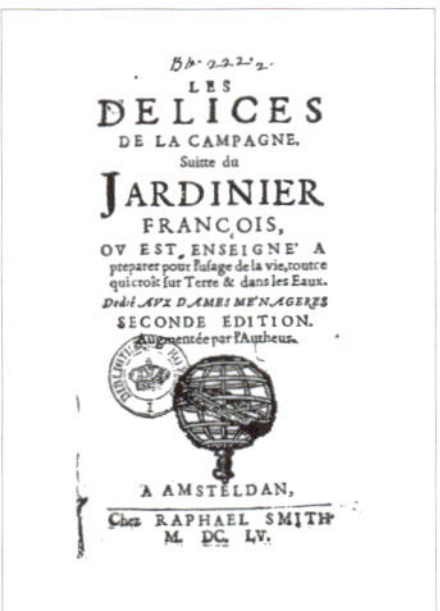

Bb. 2222.

LES DELICES DE LA CAMPAGNE.

Suitte du

JARDINIER FRANÇOIS,

OV EST ENSEIGNE' A preparer pour l'usage de la vie, tout ce qui croît sur Terre & dans les Eaux.

Dedié AVX DAMES ME'NAGERES

SECONDE EDITION.

Augmentée par l'Autheur.

A AMSTELDAN,

Chez RAPHAEL SMITH

M. DC. LV.

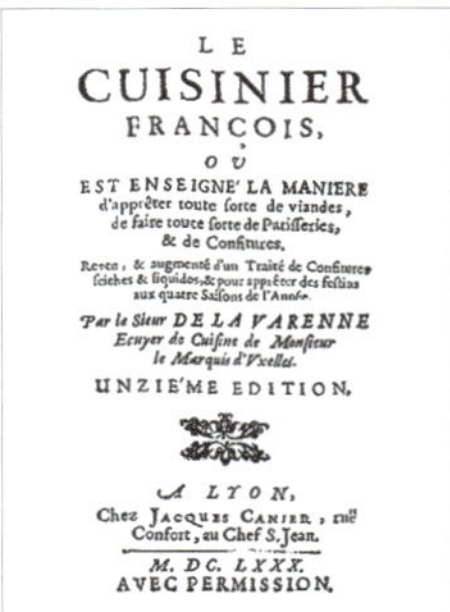

LE CUISINIER FRANÇOIS,

OV

EST ENSEIGNE' LA MANIERE d'apprêter toute sorte de viandes, de faire toute sorte de Patisseries, & de Confitures.

Reveu, & augmenté d'un Traité de Confitures seiches & liquides, & pour apprêter des festins aux quatre Saisons de l'Année.

Par le Sieur DE LA VARENNE Ecuyer de Cuisine de Monsieur le Marquis d'Vxelles.

UNZIE'ME EDITION.

A LYON,

Chez Jacques Canier, ruë Confort, au Chef S. Jean.

M. DC. LXXX.

AVEC PERMISSION.

but only for that, which attracts the eye and tongue. By contrast, the gastrosopher selects the best from the good, in its most beautiful form, with scrupulous regard for health and propriety'.[37] Von Vaerst's distinction between gourmand and gourmet brings to mind films such as *La Grande Bouffe*[38] and *Babette's Feast*.[39]

The Wisdom of Cooks

Almost all culinary-gastrosophical and restaurant-related writings can be traced back to antiquity. In the first century BC, physicians had already begun exploring the effects of food and writers were singing the praises of feasts such as those held by Lucius Licinius Lucullus. The single most important source of information is *De re coquinaria* by Marcus Caelius Apicius, which was based on Greek cuisine and published until the eighteenth century (fig. 12). The book analysed and described food and philosophised about its preparation and consumption.

Throughout history, chefs in particular have imparted their knowledge of plant and animal substances, their preparation, and the physiological effects of food. Today's high quality and standard of the culinary arts owe much to the knowledge that these early chefs recorded in manuscripts and books. Culinarily-demanding preparation was as important here as the sequence of dishes. A thoughtful combination of dishes can be found in Bartholomew de Sacchi's *De honesta voluptate et valitudine*,[40] written as early as 1474, and mentioning 'the honourable, pleasurable, and even admissible lust of the abdomen'.

12
De re coquinaria by Apicius, edition 1709

De re coquinaria von Apicius, Ausgabe 1709

13
Title of *Ein new Kochbuch* (A New Cookbook) by Marx Rumpolt, 1581 • Banquet of the kings of Hungary and Bohemia, by Marx Rumpolt

Titel *Ein new Kochbuch* von Marx Rumpolt, 1581 • Bankett der Könige von Ungarn und Böhmen, von Marx Rumpolt

14
Title of *Le cuisinier royal et bourgeois* by François Massialot, 1691 • Portrait of Johann Coler, author of the *Oeconomia ruralis et domestica*, 1593 • Title of *Le Jardinier François* by Nicolas de Bonnefons, 1651 • Title of *Délices de la campagne* by Nicolas de Bonnefons, 1654 • Title of *Le Cuisinier François* by François Pierre de la Varenne, 1653

Titel *Le cuisinier royal et bourgeois* von François Massialot, 1691 • Porträt von Johann Coler, Autor der *oeconomia ruralis et domestica*, 1593 • Titel *Le jardinier françois* von Nicolas de Bonnefons, 1651 • Titel *Délices de la campagne* von Nicolas de Bonnefons, 1654 • Titel *Le cuisinier françois* von François Pierre de la Varenne, 1653

Geist der Kochkunst von Joseph König (Abb. 11, mittig und rechts)[33] von 1822 und Gustav Blumröder mit *Vorlesungen über Eßkunst*[34] von 1838. Rumohr kämpft gegen die Schlemmerei: „Unter Schlemmerei verstehe ich eine gewisse vergeudende Gefräßigkeit oder gefräßige Vergeudung".[35] Mit seiner Tugendlehre der Mäßigkeit zieht er gegen die Exzesse der Epikuräer zu Felde.[36] Von Vaerst hingegen war ein Anhänger eben dieses epikuräischen Hedonismus. Seine Gastrosophie ist, wie aus dem Titel hervorgeht, den Freuden der Tafel gewidmet. Die von Brillat-Savarin vorgegebene Differenzierung zwischen *gourmandise* und Völlerei greift er nochmals auf, um den Gourmand, den Gourmet und den Gastrosophen voneinander zu scheiden. „Der Gourmand ist begierig auf alles, was gut schmeckt ohne Rücksicht auf die Gesundheit … der Gourmet ist bloß lüstern, doch nur nach alledem, was Zunge und Auge anlockt. Aber der Gastrosoph wählt aus dem Guten das Beste, in schönster Form, mit gewissenhafter Rücksicht auf Gesundheit und Schicklichkeit."[37] Bei von Vaersts Unterscheidung von Gourmand und Gourmet drängt sich die Assoziation zu den Filmen *Das große Fressen*[38] und *Babettes Fest*[39] auf.

Die Weisheit der Köche

Fast alle kulinarisch-gastrosophischen und damit das Restaurant tangierenden Schriften gehen auf die Antike zurück. Mediziner erforschten damals bereits die Wirkung der Nahrungsmittel, Schriftsteller besangen Gastmähler wie zum Beispiel die des Lucius Licinius Lucullus im 1. Jahrhundert v. Chr. Die mit Abstand wichtigste Informationsquelle ist *De re coquinaria* des Marcus Caelius Apicius, die – auf der griechischen Küche fußend – bis in das 18. Jahrhundert aufgelegt wurde (Abb. 12). Speisen werden hier analysiert und beschrieben, über ihre Zubereitung und ihren Verzehr wird philosophiert.

Im Verlauf der Geschichte vermitteln vor allem die Köche ihre Kenntnis von pflanzlichen und tierischen Substanzen, von ihrer Zubereitung und der physiologischen Wirkung der Speisen. Ihnen und ihrem in Manuskripten und Büchern niedergelegten Wissen verdankt die Kochkunst ihr hohes Niveau. Kulinarisch anspruchsvolle Zubereitung ist hier ebenso wichtig wie die Speisenfolge. Eine überlegte Zusammenstellung der Gerichte findet sich bereits in Bartholomäus de Sacchis *De honesta voluptate et valitudine*[40] von 1474, wenn er „von der eerlichen zinnlichen auch erlaubten wolust des leibs" spricht.

'The first course should consist of vegetables and fruit, which open the body, while apples, pears, radishes and hard cheese will help to digest the consumed food, will close the stomach and keep evil vapours from rising into the head and brain.'[41]

Even today, cheese is served in restaurants as the finale of a meal. In 1500, Thomas Pynson published *A Boke of Cokery* in England. *Ein new Kochbuch* by Marx Rumpolt in 1581 is considered the first German cookbook.[42] Before Rumpolt became the personal chef to the Elector of Mainz, he worked in the service of other European nobles, including at the Viennese court of Ferdinand II.

Rumpolt's knowledge of diverse regional cuisines is included in his cookbook, which, according to custom at that time, was intended purely for royal kitchens (fig. 13). It was not until 110 years later, in 1691, that the inventor of the 'crème brulée', François Massialot, divulged this recipe in *Le cuisinier royal et bourgois* (fig. 14, top left)[43] to the non-aristocratic, affluent society that would eventually become the supporter and guarantor of restaurant culture in the nineteenth century. A large percentage of literature on gastronomic knowledge was devoted to the cultivation of crops. John Evelyn's *Acetaria. A Discourse of Sallets* from 1699[44] is one of the lesser-known sources. One hundred years earlier, between 1593-1603, the *Oeconomia ruralis et domestica* was published by Johann Coler (fig. 14, top right).[45] Nicolas De Bonnefon's *Le Jardinier François* appeared in 1651, and in 1654 his *Délices de la campagne* (fig. 14, left).[46] Bonnefons was a chamber footman at the court of Louis XIV. In *Délices de la campagne* ('The joys of country life') he reflects the aristocracy's rural exodus, which began in the 1640s. The book focuses, however, on cooking instructions for the middle nobility and bourgeoisie. The first part is dedicated to the 'Women of Paris', who were responsible for kitchen supervision. The second part, 'From the Roots,' deals with the cultivation and preparation of vegetables as a full source of food, and not merely a supplementary one. 'People should grow roots in France and like to eat them.' The entire work is dedicated to the Capuchin monastic order, which lends the German name, *Kapuzinerkresse*, to the flowering plant and herb watercress. 'They are devoted to horticulture with far more curiosity than any other monastic order.'[47] The third part focuses on the chamberlain, the true director of courtly eating. The books *Le Cuisinier François* from 1651 and *Le Patissier François* from 1653, written by

„Der erste gang soll aus gemüse und obst bestehen, die den leib offen behelt, während äpfel, birnen, rettich und hartkäse die genomene speyß sehr helfe verdwenen, ja den magen beschlüsse und verhinder, daß die böse dempfe nicht ubersich in das haubt und hirn steigen".[41]

Noch heute wird Käse in Restaurants als Abschluss eines Essens serviert. Im Jahr 1500 veröffentlicht Thomas Pynson in England *A Boke of Cokery*. *Ein new Kochbuch* von Marx Rumpolt gilt 1581 als erste deutsche Publikation der Kochkunst.[42] Bevor Rumpolt Mundkoch des Mainzer Kurfürsten wurde, ist er in Diensten anderer europäischer Adliger, unter anderem am Wiener Hof von Ferdinand II.

Seine Kenntnisse der unterschiedlichsten regionalen Küchen fließen in sein Kochbuch ein, das, wie in jener Zeit üblich, nur für die höfische Küche bestimmt war (Abb. 13). Erst 110 Jahre später, 1691, wendet sich der Erfinder der „crème brulée", François Massialot, in *Le cuisinier royal et bourgois* (Abb. 14, oben links)[43] auch an nicht-adlige, affluente Gesellschaftsschichten, die dann im 19. Jahrhundert Träger und Garanten der Restaurantkultur werden. Ein Großteil der gastronomische Kenntnisse verbreitenden Literatur widmet sich *in extenso* dem Anbau von Nutzpflanzen. Zu den unbekannteren Quellen zählt John Evelyns *Acetaria. A Discourse of Sallets* von 1699.[44] Bereits 100 Jahre zuvor, von 1593 bis 1603, war die *Oeconomia ruralis et domestica* von Johann Coler erschienen (Abb. 14, oben rechts).[45] 1651 erschien Nicolas De Bonnefons' *Le jardinier françois* und 1654 *Délices de la campagne* (Abb. 14, links).[46] Bonnefons war ein Kammerlakai am Hofe Louis' XIV. Sein Werk über die „Freuden des Landlebens" spiegelt die Landflucht des Adels seit den 1640er Jahren. Doch nicht diese, sondern Anweisungen zum Kochen für den mittleren Adel und das Bürgertum sind der Inhalt. Der erste Teil ist den „Damen von Paris" gewidmet, denen die Küchenaufsicht oblag. Der zweite Teil „Von den Wurzeln" behandelt den Anbau und die Zubereitung von Gemüse als vollwertigem Nahrungsmittel und nicht nur als Beikost. „Man soll in Frankreich Wurzeln züchten und gern essen." Das Gesamtwerk ist den Kapuzinern gewidmet (Kapuzinerkresse). „Sie widmen sich mit viel mehr Neugier dem Gartenbau als irgendein anderer Mönchsorden." Der dritte Teil wendet sich an die Haushofmeister, die eigentlichen Intendanten höfischen Essens.[47] Direkt an diesen Berufsstand gerichtet sind auch die Bücher François

François Pierre de Varenne,[48] were specifically addressed to this profession (fig. 14, right). De Varenne is considered the inventor of genuine French cuisine, which set itself apart from the Italian influences introduced to the French court by Catherine and Maria de Medici. Although he recommends the administration of vegetables again and again, his numerous recipes also provide for carnivores. Abstaining from meat (animals bred for meat, poultry, and game) was out of the question. One recommendation, made much later by Viennese writer Peter Altenberg while pondering the 'taste buds', would certainly have made people in the decadent, baroque society sneer:

> 'From now on, he prefers the taste of bean puree, lentil puree, pea puree, foamy raw eggs, or curd and unripened cheeses to the expensive and superfluous delicacies previously surveyed by stupid palates!'[49]

But the conditions of an absolutist, affluent society cannot be compared with the Vienna of 1918. It should be noted here that it was the food problem that ignited the French Revolution in the first place, especially concerning the general public's participation.[50] Jules Michelet wrote: 'As long as the story of hunger remains unwritten, the terror of the Revolution will never be understood.'

Table Manners

On one side bounty, on the other, starvation. The enveloping ornamental elements were of great significance in the production of extravagantly laid tables. As items of representation, they were as important as the ornately fashioned variety of dishes made from local and exotic goods and wares. The staging of festive banquets first became popular in the Middle Ages and remained so until the nineteenth century. Towards the end of the Middle Ages, decorative cups and trophies, sideboards, serving boards, and elaborate salt and spice containers appeared—made of tin and silver, demonstrating the wealth of the host. The use of patterned tablecloths (fig. 15) and drinking fountains[51] also remained popular. During the Renaissance, these table scenes became even more lavish, reaching their decorative highpoint in the seventeenth and eighteenth centuries (fig. 16, top). Beautifully presented, pastry-wrapped meat dishes were ornate showpieces fashioned from game and poultry (including swans) to look as naturalistic as possible. Landscapes, architectural and mythological scenes, even garden parterres *à la Le Nôtre*

Pierre de La Varennes[48] *Le cuisinier françois* von 1651 und *Le pâtissier françois* von 1653 (Abb. 14, rechts). Ihm wird die Erfindung der genuin französischen Küche zugeschrieben, die sich von den von Katharina und Maria von Medici am französischen Hof eingeführten italienischen Einflüssen absetzt. Obwohl die Verabreichung von Gemüse immer wieder empfehlend, wenden sich seine zahlreichen Rezepte auch an „carnivore" Menschen. An einen Fleischverzicht (Zuchttiere, Geflügel, Wild) war nicht zu denken. Eine Empfehlung, wie sie der Wiener Schriftsteller Peter Altenberg, über die „Geschmacksnerven" sinnierend, formuliert, hätte in der barocken Verschwendergesellschaft Hohnlachen hervorgerufen:

> „Von nun an schmeckten ihm Bohnen-Püree, Linsen-Püree, Erbsen-Püree, gesprudelte rohe Eier, Topfen, junger Käse besser als die bisher vom blöden Gaumen begutachteten teuren und überflüssigen Leckerbissen!"[49]

Doch die Lebensbedingungen der absolutistischen Überflussgesellschaft lassen sich nicht mit denjenigen im Wien von 1918 vergleichen. Hier sei dennoch angemerkt, dass sich die Französische Revolution, vor allem, was die Beteiligung der Massen angeht, am Ernährungsproblem entzündete.[50] Jules Michelet schreibt: „Solange die Geschichte des Hungers nicht geschrieben ist, wird niemand den Terror der Revolution verstehen."

Tafelsitten

Hier „Hülle und Fülle", dort extremer Hunger. Die Hülle war als Inszenierung der Tafelextravaganzen von hoher Relevanz, als Bestandteil der Repräsentation ebenso wichtig wie die Vielzahl der Gänge aus heimischen und exotischen Produkten. Das In-Szene-Setzen festlicher Gastmähler hatte im Mittelalter einen ersten Höhepunkt und war bis in das 19. Jahrhundert üblich. Gegen Ende des Mittelalters zierten Becher und Pokale, Kredenzen, Essbrettchen, geschmückte Salz- und Gewürzfässer – dem Wohlstand des Gastgebers entsprechend in Zinn oder Silber gehalten – die Tafel. Auch die Verwendung gemusterter Tafeltücher (Abb. 15) und von Trinkbrunnen[51] ist überliefert. In der Renaissance werden die gedeckten Tafeln üppiger und erreichen im Barock ihren dekorativen Höhepunkt (Abb. 16, oben). Die aufgetragenen, ummantelten Fleischgerichte waren Schaustücke von Wild und Geflügel – Schwäne eingeschlossen – und wurden so der Natur nachgebildet. Landschaften, archi-

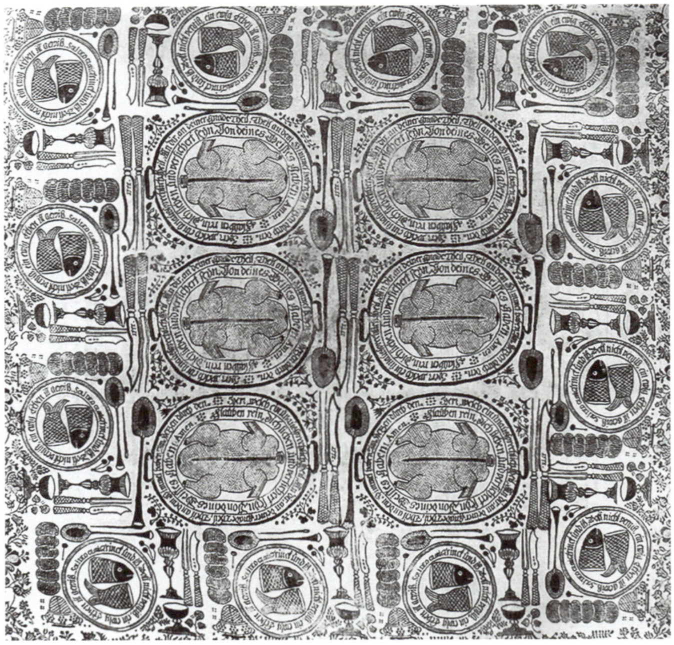

15

Tabletop, Bavaria, 1743 ● Tablecloth, Saxony, 1772

Tischplatte, Bayern, 1743 ● Tischdecke, Sachsen, 1772

16

Buffet in a grotto-like surrounding, Marcantonio Chiarini, Bologna, 1693 ● Table arrangement for fifty plates, Paris, around 1770

Grottenbuffet, Marcantonio Chiarini, Bologna, 1693 ● Tafelarrangement für 50 Gedecke, Paris, um 1770

(fig. 16, bottom) adorned the table while intricately crafted fruit and vegetable sculptures were intended to stimulate the eye. Entire brigades of staff, divided into different hierarchies, worked inside and outside the kitchen. The tradition of serving staff, *Vorschneider* or meat carver (also called *Trincierer*), cupbearer, and—to prevent poisoning—a taster can be traced back to the Middle Ages (fig. 17). The sumptuous and physiological qualities of food and its preparation were recorded in books, along with instructions for presentation, food design, and the arrangement of the tables—a central axis or a U-shaped table (fig. 18)—and the seating arrangements of the hosts and their guests. Nowadays, the ceremonial and personal manner in which guests were once directed to their seats has been usurped by the place card. Again and again, we see how table manners as rudiments of courtly culture were passed on via the intermediate stage of the restaurant into the households of the bourgeoisie and petty bourgeoisie.

The wealth of imagination given to the lavish and time-consuming folded napkin art pieces, as they were known from the sixteenth century onward (fig. 19), has completely disappeared from restaurants, where you now perhaps, at best, might hope for a napkin folded into a simple cone-like form. Even at the end of the nineteenth century, this art of folding produced objects such as lotus flowers, cardinal hats, ram horns, lighthouses, and belvederes—even the Eiffel Tower. The first publication of patterns and folding instructions is *Li Tre Trattati* from 1639 by Matthias Jäger, who, under the name Mattia Giegher, taught the art of folding at the University of Padua (fig. 20, top left).[52] Georg Philipp Harsdörffer published a German translation in 1652 entitled *Trincir-Buch*, (fig. 20, bottom left).[53] However, in 1549, one hundred years earlier, Christoforo di Messisbugo, a Fleming at an Italian court, wrote about the arrangement of banquets, and Bartolomeo Scappi, the head chef of the Popes (including Pius V) recorded in 1570 that for a meeting between the Pope and Emperor Charles V 'the table had to be laid with four perfumed tablecloths, folded in a special way, twelve napkins and five credence service sets' (fig. 20, right).[54] Giacomo Procacchi's *Trincier oder Vorlegebuch*,[55] published in 1620 and translated into German in 1624, shows a *Vorschneider* on one of the cover pages, who holds a large piece of meat skewered on a fork in the Italian style (fig. 21, left). The ritual demanded that it be divided up without ever placing it on the table

tektonische und mythologische Szenen, auch Gartenparterres à la Le Nôtre (Abb. 16, unten) schmückten die Tafel. Aufwendig gestaltete Gemüse- und Obstskulpturen zielten auf optische Stimulanz. Ganze Brigaden von Personal, in unterschiedlichste Hierarchien gegliedert, waren innerhalb und außerhalb der Küche tätig. Die Tradition der Vorleger, Vorschneider, auch Trincierer genannt, sowie Mundschenke und – um Giftmorde zu vermeiden – auch Vorkoster geht bis auf das Mittelalter zurück (Abb. 17). Wie in Büchern die lukullischen und physiologischen Qualitäten des Essens und seiner Zubereitung festgehalten wurden, so gab es auch Anweisungen zur Darreichung und optischen Aufbereitung, zur Anordnung der Tische – mittelachsig oder in U-Form (Abb. 18) – zur Platzierung des Gastgebers und seiner Gäste. Heute ist die zeremonielle, persönliche Platzanweisung durch Platzkarten ersetzt. Immer wieder sind Tischsitten als Rudimente der höfischen Kultur, tradiert über das Zwischenstadium Restaurant, im bürgerlichen und kleinbürgerlichen Haushalt zu finden.

Die fantasievollen, zeitaufwendigen Serviettenkunststücke, wie sie seit dem 16. Jahrhundert gebräuchlich waren (Abb. 19), sind heute aus den Restaurants vollkommen verschwunden. Allenfalls bemüht man sich noch um die Faltung eines simplen Kegels. Noch Ende des 19. Jahrhunderts waren unter anderem Lotusblüten, Kardinalshüte, Widderhörner, Leucht- und Aussichtstürme, ja sogar der Eiffelturm Objekte der Faltkunst. Erste Muster und Anweisungen finden sich im 1639 erschienenen *Li Tre Trattati* von Matthias Jäger, der als „Mattia Giegher" (Abb. 20, links oben)[52] die Faltkunst an der Universität Padua lehrte. Unter dem Titel *Trincir-Buch* veröffentlicht Georg Philipp Harsdörffer 1652 eine deutsche Übersetzung dieses Buches (Abb. 20, links unten).[53] Bereits rund 100 Jahre zuvor, 1549, hatte Christoforo di Messisbugo, ein Flame an einem italienischen Hof, über die Komposition von Banketten geschrieben und Bartolomeo Scappi, der päpstliche Chefkoch (unter anderem in den Diensten Pius' V.), hält 1570 fest, dass für ein Treffen des Papstes mit Kaiser Karl V. „der Tisch mit vier parfümierten, auf besondere Weise gefalteten Tischdecken, zwölf Servietten und fünf Kredenz-Servicen" gedeckt werden musste (Abb. 20, rechts).[54] In Giacomo Procacchis 1620 erschienenem, 1624 ins Deutsche übertragenen *Trincier oder Vorlegebuch*[55] ist auf dem Titelblatt ein Vorschneider zu sehen, der im italienischen Stil ein großes Stück Fleisch – aufgespießt auf einer Gabel – hält

17

18

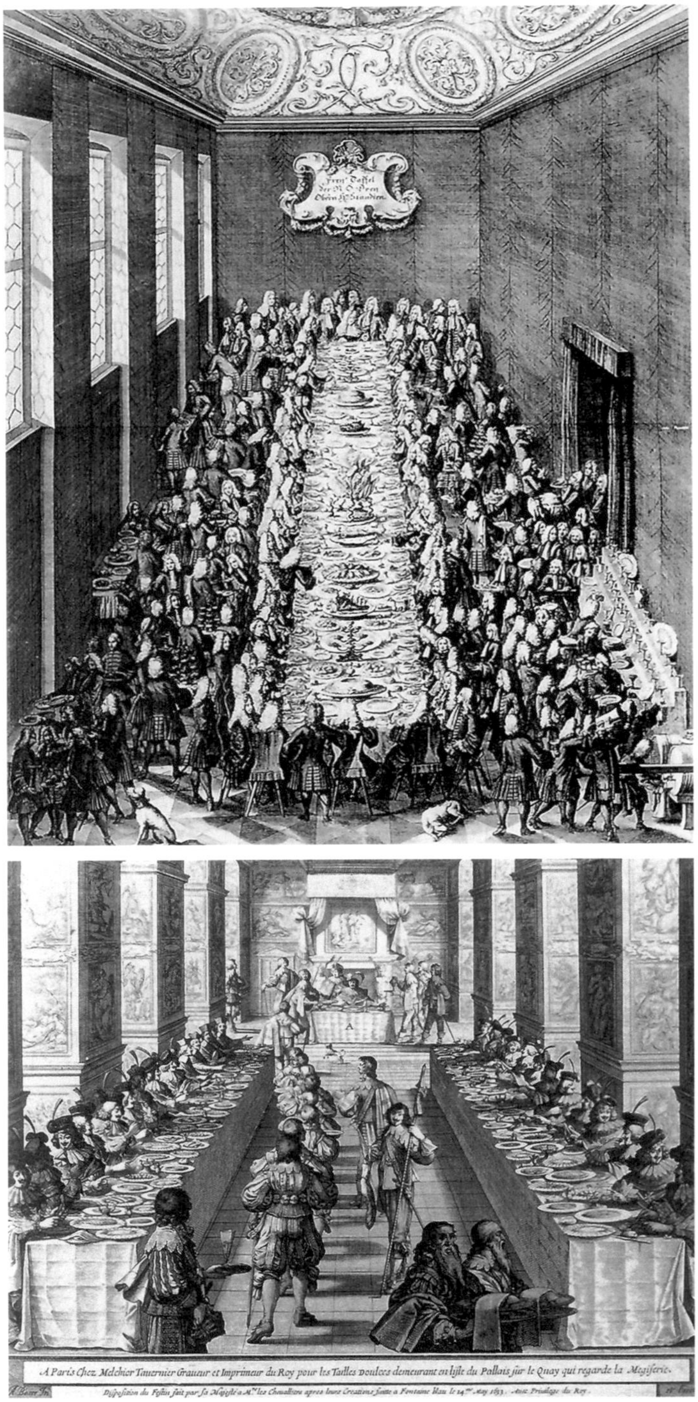

17

Salomon's banquet, Michael Wohlgemut, 1491

Das Festmahl des Salomon, Michael Wohlgemut, 1491

18

Knight's Table of the Order of the Holy Spirit at Fontainebleau, Abraham Bosse, Paris, 1633 ● *Public banquet of the fourth Rank, at the occasion of the hereditary tribute for Maria Theresia*, Vienna, 1740

Rittertafel des Heilig-Geist-Ordens in Fontainebleau, Abraham Bosse, Paris, 1633 ● *Öffentliche Tafel des vierten Standes anläßlich der Erbhuldigung für Maria Theresia*, Wien, 1740

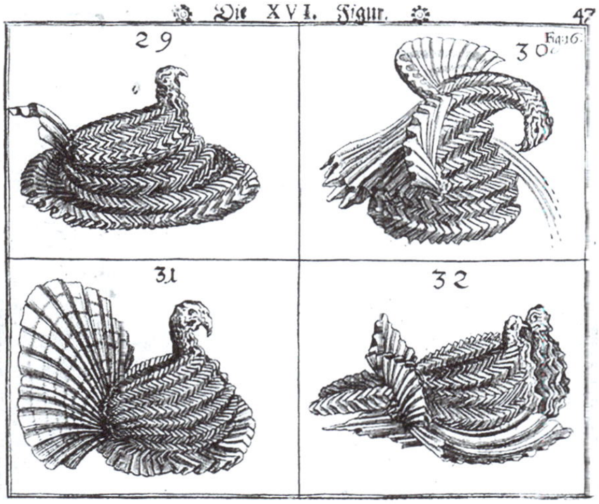

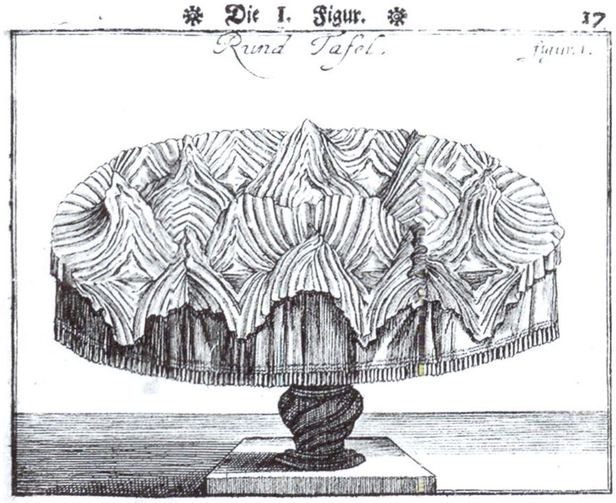

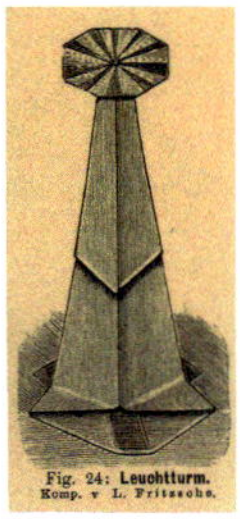

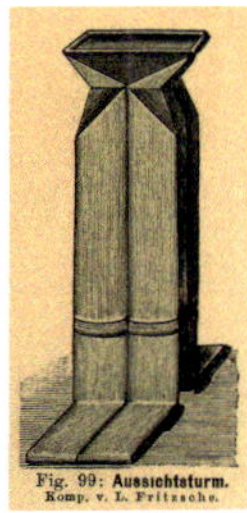

19

Suggestions for the folding of napkins from Georg Philipp Harsdörffer, 1652 ● The folding of napkins, end of the nineteenth century: lighthouse, Eiffel tower, observation tower

Vorschläge zur Serviettenfaltung aus Georg Philipp Harsdörffer ● Serviettenfaltungen Ende des 19. Jahrhunderts: Leucht-, Eiffel- und Aussichtsturm

(fig. 21, centre and right). Observations report a virtuoso carving performance on swirling forks. Now, similar spectacles are occasionally exhibited by dough-juggling pizza bakers. Corresponding codes for servers did not appear in France until the Baroque age, such as *L'école des officiers de bouche parfaite* in 1662 or *L'art de bien Traiter* in 1674 by Massialot, mentioned earlier.

It was hard to outperform the opulence and theatrical staging of the laid tables and buffets typical of the feasts and banquets held by Louis XIV. One of the many extraordinary dramaturgical events of Versailles' stage was a nocturnal buffet held in an inner courtyard. A column supported by volutes and surrounded by candles rose from

(Abb. 21, links). Das Ritual verlangte, dass es zerteilt wurde, ohne es auf dem Tisch abzulegen (Abb. 21, mittig und rechts). Kommentare berichten von virtuos die Gabel wirbelnden Tranchierern. Ähnliche Schauspiele lassen sich heute noch hin und wieder bei teigjonglierenden Pizzabäckern beobachten. Entsprechende Serviercodes erschienen in Frankreich erst in der Barockzeit, wie zum Beispiel *L'école parfaite des officiers de bouche* von 1662 oder *L'art de bien traitér* des bereits erwähnten Massialot aus dem Jahr 1674.

An Opulenz und theatralischer Inszenierung waren die Gastereien Louis' XIV. in Form von gedeckten Tafeln und Büffets kaum zu überbieten. Eine der vielen außer-

20

21

TRINCIER
Oder
Vorlege Buch/
Darinnen berichtet wird/
Wie man allerhand gebratene und gesottene Speisen/ so auff Fürstliche und andere Taffeln getragen werden mögen/ Nach Italianischer/ und vornemlich Romanischer Art/ anschneiden/ und auff der Gabel zierlich zerlegen sol.
Vor dessen von
GIACOMO PROCACCHI
In Italianischer Sprach beschrieben/ und von jhm zum andern mal mit dem Obst trinciren, vielen Capitteln/ und unterschiedenen arten vermehret/ So an jetzo auffs new widerumb ubersehen/ in da[illegible]deutsche trewlich versetzet/ und mit den signirten Kupfferstichen auffs best und fleissigste[illegible]zieret worden.
Leipzig/
In Verlegung Henning Grossen des Jüngern S. nachgelassenen Erben.
Im Jahr
M. DC. XXIV.

IL
MASTRO
DI CASA
DEL SIG. CESARE
PANDINI,
MASTRO DI CASA DELL'ILLVSTRISS.
& Reuerendiss. Sig. Cardinal Farnese.
Ragionamento fatto tra il Caualier Reale Fusorito
da Narni Trinciante, & esso Mastro di Casa.
CON PRIVILEGIO.
IN VENETIA, M. DC. X.
Appresso Alessandro de' Vecchi.

22

an octagonal table arrangement, which was supposed to refer to the Roman models of Hadrian and Aurelian (fig. 22). Most dining ceremonies during the seventeenth and eighteenth centuries at European courts were held inside, though. Typical for these banquet events was the *service à la française*. Here, a wide selection of artfully designed dishes was arranged on plates, in terrines, and in bowls, in a double-axis symmetry around which the guest's dinner plates were arranged (fig. 23). Since the arrangement of plates and tureens was pre-established, and the serving bowls and plates for each subsequent course had to each be placed on the same spot, it was necessary to consis-

20
Self-portait of serving cutter Mattia Giegher, Padua, 1639 ● Portrait of Georg Philipp Harsdörffer, ca. 1652 ● Portrait of M. Bartolomeo Scappi, ca. 1579

Selbstbildnis des Vorschneiders Mattia Giegher, Padua, 1639 ● Porträt von Georg Philipp Harsdörffer, ca. 1652 ● Porträt von M. Bartolomeo Scappi, ca. 1579

21
Title of the German edition of *Trincier oder Vorlegebuch* (Book of cutting and serving), 1624 by Giacomo Procacchi ● Titlepage of *Il mastro di casa* by Cesare Pandini, 1610 ● Detail from 'Il mastro di casa'

Titel der deutschen Ausgabe von Giacomo Procacchis *Trincier oder Vorlegebuch*, 1624 ● Titel *Il mastro di casa* von Cesare Pandini, 1610 ● Detail aus *Il mastro di casa*

22
Celebratory table in the inner courtyard of Versailles: arrangement by Jean Le Pautre, 1674

Festtafel im Innenhof von Versailles, Arrangement: Jean Le Pautre, 1674

gewöhnlichen dramaturgischen Ereignisse der Versailler Bühne war ein in einem Innenhof angerichtetes nächtliches Büffet. Über einem oktogonalen Tischarrangement erhob sich, gestützt durch Voluten, eine kerzenumringte Säule, die an die römischen Vorbilder Hadrians und Aurelians erinnerte (Abb. 22). Die meisten Tafelzeremonien an den europäischen Höfen des 17. und 18. Jahrhunderts aber vollzogen sich in den Innenräumen. Hier herrschte beim Esszeremoniell das „Service à la française". Zahlreiche kunstvoll gestaltete Gerichte wurden auf Platten, in Terrinen und Schüsseln in doppelter Achsensymmetrie arrangiert. Rund um dieses geometrische Ensemble verteilten sich die Speiseteller (Abb. 23). Da die Anordnung der Platten und Terrinen festgelegt war und an jeweils denselben Standorten die Behältnisse eines jeden neuen Ganges niedergesetzt wurden, war eine gleiche Grundzahl der einzelnen Gänge beizubehalten. Bestand der erste Gang zum Beispiel aus sechs „hors d'oeuvres, entrées", Suppen und „relevés", so hatten alle nachfolgenden Gänge die gleiche Anzahl zu haben. Die grafische Gestaltung einer Menükarte aus dem Jahre 1757 für ein Souper von Louis XV. (Abb. 24) zeigt anschaulich den geometrisch-logistischen Charakter des „Service à la française". Im Zentrum der Tafel standen dekorative Elemente, ein *dormant* oder ein *surtout* sowie Tafelschiffe, kunstvolle Gebilde, aus Gold, Silber, Bronze, Porzellan oder Fayence gefertigt. Formenreich waren auch die Behältnisse für Pfeffer, Salz, Öl, Essig, Soßen, Senf,

tently have the same number of basic individual courses. The first course, for example, would typically consist of six hors d'oeuvres, *entrées*, soups, and *relevés*, meaning that all subsequent courses would have to be of the same number. The design of a menu card from 1757 for a supper given by Louis XV (fig. 24) shows the geometrical logistical character of a *service à la française*. Decorative elements are placed at the centre of the table: a *dormant* or *surtout*, as well as *Tafelschiffe*, elaborate structures made of gold, silver, bronze, porcelain, or earthenware. The receptacles for individual seasoning, such as pepper, salt, oil, vinegar, sauces, mustard, sugar, and lemons were equally ornate.[56] They survive in restaurant culture as small or large cruet stands. In addition to the table setting décor, cutlery and crockery were also highly distinguished up to its peak in the Baroque and designed for specific uses. 'Eating with your fingers' transformed into the mandatory use of highly specified cutlery, each with a shape corresponding to that of the serving cutlery placed near a specific dish. Before forks were later introduced in luxury restaurants for specific dishes such as fish, lobster, or dessert, the fork and its use first had to be mastered at court. The original function of the two-pronged fork was to spear sticky confection, yet as it eventually transformed in the sixteenth and seventeenth centuries into a five-pronged device it became customary to use for dishes of all kinds. An early lampoon describes how difficult it was for some diners to get used to the new cutlery.

> 'They took the meat with forks to their mouths, then stretched their neck and their entire bodies out to the plate … because it is forbidden in this country to touch the meat with their hands, how difficult whatsoever that may be, they would prefer that this little pronged instrument touched their lips, and not their hands. Then artichokes, asparagus, peas, and beans were served, and it was amusing to watch them eat these with forks. Because those diners, who were not as well practised, allowed most of the food on the way to their mouths to fall back onto the bowls and plates.'[57]

In addition to the *service à la française*, there was the *à l'anglaise* and *à la russe*. It was reported in England at the beginning of the twentieth century that 'food was not served by servants, but requested from those diners seated before the desired dish'.[58] 'Rinsing bowls' were also mentioned. These were bowls made of crystal glass, which

Zucker und Zitronen zum individuellen Nachwürzen.[56] Als kleine oder große Menagen haben sie in den Restaurants überlebt. Parallel zum Tafeldekor differenzierte sich auch das Besteck und Geschirr bis zu seinem Höhepunkt im Barock. Aus dem Essen mit den Fingern wurde der zwingende Gebrauch von individuell zu nutzenden Besteckteilen, deren Form ähnlich wie die der Vorlegeteile den unterschiedlichen Speisen entsprach. Bevor die später in Luxusrestaurants gebräuchliche Diversifizierung von Menü-, Fisch-, Hummer- und Dessertgabel eingeführt wurde, musste die Gabel und ihr Gebrauch erst hoffähig werden. Während der ursprüngliche Zweck zweizinkiger Gabeln das Aufspießen klebrigen Konfektes war, wurde ihr Gebrauch – und hier wandelte sie sich zwischen dem 16. und 18. Jahrhundert zu einem fünfzinkigen Gerät – für alle Arten von Speisen üblich.

Eine frühe Spottschrift schildert, wie gewöhnungsbedürftig für die Speisenden die Ingebrauchnahme von neuen Besteckteilen war.

> „Sie führten das Fleisch mit Gabeln zum Munde, streckten dabei ihren Hals und ihren ganzen Körper zum Teller hinaus, … denn in diesem Land ist es verboten, das Fleisch mit den Händen zu berühren, wie schwierig auch immer das ist, sie wollen lieber, daß dieses kleine gezinkte Instrument ihre Lippe berührt als ihre Hände … Danach gab es Artischocken, Spargel, Erbsen, Bohnen, und es war ein Vergnügen zu sehen, wie sie das mit den Gabeln aßen. Denn die es nicht ganz so gut konnten, ließen das meiste in die Schüsseln fallen, auf die Teller oder unterwegs auf dem Weg zum Mund."[57]

Neben dem „Service à la française" unterscheidet man das „à l'anglaise" und das „à la russe". Aus England wird Anfang des 19. Jahrhunderts berichtet: „Es werden die Speisen nicht durch die Dienerschaft gereicht, sondern von den Gästen bei demjenigen erbeten, vor dessen Platz die gewünschte Speise aufgestellt ist."[58] Weiter ist die Rede von „rinsing bowls", Schalen aus Kristallglas, die man nutzte, um bei Tisch den Mund auszuspülen, die sich auch am Wiener Hof großer Beliebtheit erfreuten.

> „… daß die Sache, wie sie da betrieben wurde, mir nicht ganz appetitlich vorkam, denn obgleich das Wasser in schönen großen Kristalltassen mit extrafeinen Servietten jedem einzelnen Gast gereicht wurde, klang doch

23

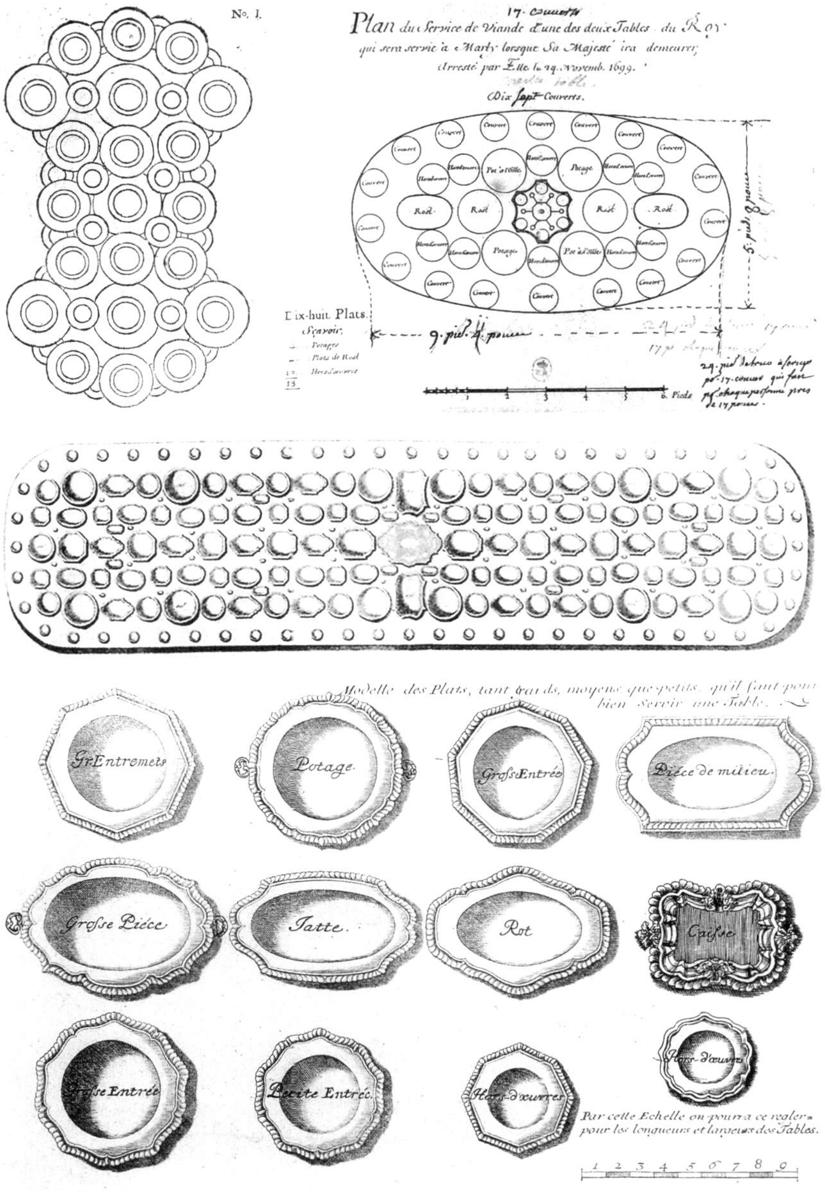

24

23

Table set 'à la française', from *Traiteur à la mode* by Hans Schupp, 1698 ● Plan for a table for a dinner hosted by Louis XIV in Marly, 1699 ● Table with sixty covers, from *Le cuisinier moderne* by Vincent La Chapelle, 1742 ● Parts of a service, from *Le cuisinier moderne*, 1742

„À la française" gedeckte Tafel, aus: *Traiteur à la mode* von Hans Schupp, 1698 ● Tafelplan für ein Abendessen gegeben von Louis XIV. in Marly, 1699 ● Tafel mit 60 Gedecken, aus: *Le cuisinier moderne* von Vincent La Chapelle, 1742 ● Serviceteile, aus: *Le cuisinier moderne*, 1742

24

Menu for Louis XV, in the chateau of Choissy ● Round menu, representing the geometrical character of the 'Service à la française', 1757

Menukarte für Louis XV. im Schloß Choissy ● Runde Menukarte, die plakativ den geometrischen Charakter des „Service à la française" widergibt, 1757

were used to rinse out the mouth at the table. This was also very popular at the Viennese court:

> 'The manner in which this act was performed was not very appetizing to me, because although water was served to every single guest in beautiful, large crystal cups with extra fine napkins, the general sound of gurgling lent something almost eerie to the scene—like the murmuring of underground wells',[59]

reports Gustav Blumröder. Johanna Schopenhauer writes that,

> 'the entire society busy in this manner often reminded us of a circle of Tritons, as they are seen spouting water around fountains.'[60] (fig. 25)

This spitting-ritual is still common amongst sommeliers, while bowls can be found today in most restaurants as finger bowls when eating shellfish and crustacea.

The Russian method now was one revolutionising the former traditions of eating, whether English or French, and even anticipated what was to come in the way of dining in restaurants. In the *service à la russe*, there were no prepared or garnished plates and bowls on the table at all. The dishes of the different courses were placed on plates in the kitchen and brought by servants to the seats in the dining hall. This necessitated a completely different organisation of kitchen logistics; it required that even large restaurant kitchens comply with the *à la minute* method of preparing food. Economically, it meant less food wastage, since the portions were easier to calculate, and because you could better gauge the amount of ingredients needed on the basis of menu cards and the number of guests. Diners were also given menu cards—another anticipation of restaurant culture, which, since the dishes were no longer on display, enabled them to have an overview of the expected food.

> 'One might well accuse the Russian serving method of lowering the standard of elegance that the French method offered; but I strongly disagree, since a table can be more beautifully decorated … with decorative and ornate elements … than with food and dishes, even if they are skilfully arranged and prepared',

> das allgemeine Gegurgel fast etwas schauerlich, wie das Murmeln unterirdischer Quellen,"[59]

berichtet der bereits erwähnte Gustav Blumröder. Johanna Schopenhauer schreibt:

> „Die ganze so beschäftigte Gesellschaft erinnerte uns oft an einen Kreis Tritonen, wie man sie wasserspeiend um Fontänen sieht."[60] (Abb. 25)

Es ist dies ein Spuckritual, wie es heute noch bei Sommeliers geläufig ist. Bowls findet man heutzutage in Restaurants allenfalls noch als Fingerschalen beim Verzehr von Schalen- und Krustentieren.

Eine die bisherigen Essgewohnheiten – seien sie englisch oder französisch – umwerfende, ja revolutionierende und das Bedienen in Restaurants vorwegnehmende Art und Weise war die russische Methode. Beim „Service à la russe" standen keine angerichteten und garnierten Platten und Schalen auf der Tafel. Die Gerichte der unterschiedlichen Gänge wurden in der Küche auf die Teller aufgetragen und von Dienern an die Plätze im Esssaal gebracht. Dies erforderte eine vollkommen andere Logistik in der Küche, der größere Restaurantküchen unter dem Zwang des „à la minute"-Zubereitens noch heute unterworfen sind. Ökonomisch bedeutete dies, da die Portionen kalkulierbarer waren, auch eine geringere Verschwendung von Lebensmitteln, weil man die Zutaten auf der Basis von Menükarten und der Anzahl der Gäste besser berechnen konnte. Menükarten erhielten auch die Speisenden – dies ebenfalls als eine Vorwegnahme der Restaurantkultur – die sich, da die Gerichte nicht mehr aufgedeckt waren, einen Überblick über die zu erwartenden Speisen verschaffen konnten.

> „Man könnte nun noch der russischen Methode des Servierens vorwerfen, daß dieselbe eine geringere Eleganz der Tafel als die französische nach sich zieht; ich muß diesem aber entschieden widersprechen, da eine Tafel sich durch geschmackvolle Aufsätze … sehr viel schöner ausschmücken läßt, als durch Gerichte und Speisen, mögen dieselben auch noch so kunstfertig angerichtet und gearbeitet sein",

schreibt Ernst von Malortie 1842.[61] Hervorzuheben ist, dass das System des Tellerservice mehr Platz für dekorative Elemente bot und die Dessertdekoration, die von

25

'La Dégustation', from *Groupes physionomiques, connu sous le nom de grimaces par Boilly*, Louis-Léopold Boilly, beginning of the nineteenth century

La Dégustation, aus: *Groupes physionomiques, connu sous le nom de grimaces par Boilly*, Louis-Léopold Boilly, Anfang des 19. Jahrhunderts

26

DIEU DU GOUT.
LE
PATISSIER
Pittoresque.
OUVRAGE
Contenant cent vingt cinq Sujets,
Composés et Dessinés
Par M. A. Carême.
Paris.
chez l'Auteur, Rue Neuve S.t Roch, N.o 41.

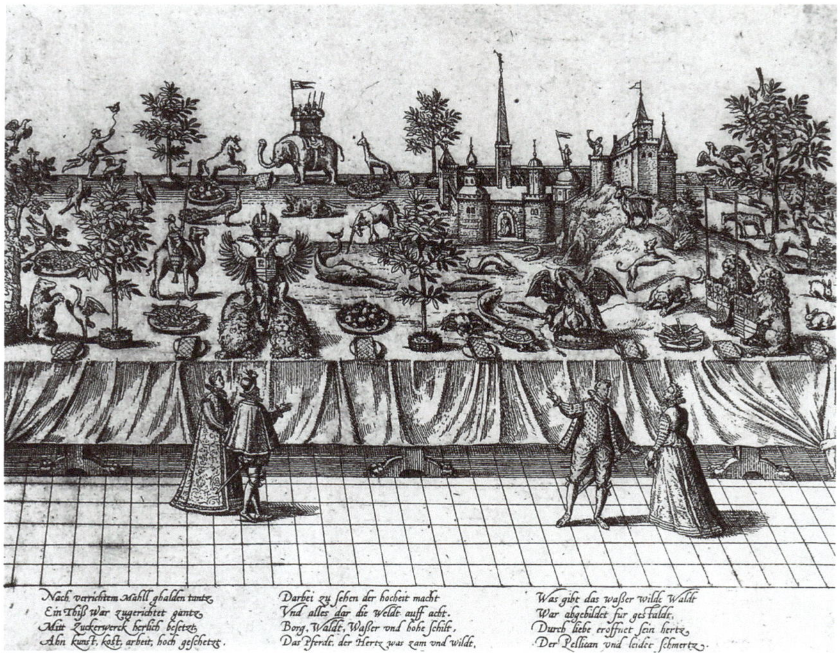
Nach verrichtem Mahll ghalden tantz
Ein Thiß war zugerichtet gantz
Mitt Zuckerwerck herlich besetzt,
Ahn kunst, kost, arbeit, hoch geschetzt.
Darbei zu sehen der hocheit macht
Vnd alles dar die Weldt auff acht.
Borg, Waldt, Waßer vnd hohe schilt,
Das Pferdt, der Hertz was zam vnd wildt,
Was gibt das waßer wilde Waldt
War abgebildet fur gestaldt,
Durch liebe eroffnet sein hertz
Der Pellican vnd leidet schmertz.

L'Art
de La Cuisine
FRANÇAISE
AU XIX.e SIECLE
PAR Antonin CARÊME DE PARIS.
Deuxieme Edition.
A PARIS
CHEZ L'AUTEUR, RUE NEUVE ST ROCH, N.o 41.
Robert
Boucher
Daniel
Lasne
Legagneur
Riquette
Normandie
Périgord
Provence
Champagne
Bourgogne
Bordeaux

27

FÊTE & REPAS DONNÉS AU PEUPLE PAR S. M. L'EMPEREUR.

VUE D'UNE DES 240 TABLES DRESSÉES POUR LE PEUPLE
sur la place de Devitchié-polé.

wrote Ernst von Malortie in 1842.[61] But what is of significance here is that this method of service allowed for more decorative elements, and the dessert arrangement—which graced the table from the very beginning of the meal—presented an admirably attractive table decoration. The 'confectioner',[62] which had been a traditional profession since the Middle Ages, experienced a climax with Marie-Antoine Carême,[63] the 'architect' of confectioners. His *pièces montées* were unsurpassed. His patisserie sculptures, based on historic architecture, were extraordinary, as illustrated in a selection on the cover of his book *Le patisseur*,[64] published in 1828: his repertoire included Chinese pagodas, ancient temples, and Russian hermitages, as well as artwork reflecting the architectural projects of Étienne Louis Boullée, Claude-Nicolas Ledoux, and Jean-Jaques Lequeu. Carême requested that his artwork be given equal status to that of other fine arts,

> 'of which there are five … namely painting, sculpture, poetry, music, and architecture, whose main branch is confectionery art',

as he explains rather immodestly.[65] He researched his ideas in libraries and calculated the dimensions and material needs for his sweet 'architecture in miniature' with the meticulousness of an architect (fig. 26). Throughout his career, which also took him to the British and Russian courts as a cook, he introduced a new system of structure to the still-uncoordinated wealth of up to 322 specific dishes for as many as one hundred people. His motto was 'order and flavour'. He separated beef, poultry, and fish,

26

Title of *Le patissier pittoresque* by Marie Antoine Carême, 1828 ● Title of *Le cuisinier parisien ou l'art de la cuisine française au XIXe siècle*, 1843-1844 ● Midnight banquet of sweets at a celebratory wedding meal in Düsseldorf, Franz Hogenberg, 1585

Titel *Le patissier pittoresque* von Marie Antoine Carême, 1828 ● Titel *Le cuisinier parisien ou l'art de la cuisine française au XIXe siècle*, 1843-1844 ● Mitternächtliche Konfekttafel eines festlichen Hochzeitsessens in Düsseldorf, Franz Hogenberg, 1585

27

Celebratory meal for 11 000 people at Moscow's Field of Virgins, a the occasion of the crowning of Tzar Nicholas I, 1826

Festessen für das Volk 11.000 Personen) auf dem Jungfrauenfeld in Moskau anlässlich der Krönung von Zar Nikolaus I., 1826

Anfang an die Tafel zierte, einen vortrefflichen Schmuck darstellte. Die seit dem Mittelalter tradierte Zuckerbäckerei[62] erfährt mit Marie Antoine Carême,[63] dem „Architekten" unter den Zuckerbäckern, einen Höhepunkt. Seine *pièces montées* waren unübertroffen. Von besonderer Ausdruckskraft waren die architekturhistorischen Patisserieskulpturen, wie er sie in einer Auswahl auch auf dem Titel seines 1828 erschienenen Buches *Le patisseur*[64] abbildete: chinesische Pagoden, antike Tempel, russische Eremitagen sowie die Architektur Étienne-Louis Boullées, Claude-Nicolas Ledoux' und Jean-Jacques Lequeu zitierende Kunstwerke gehörten zu seinem Repertoire. Carême plädiert für eine Gleichrangigkeit seiner Kunst mit anderen schönen Künsten,

> „von denen es fünf gibt … nämlich die Malerei, die Skulptur, Dichtkunst, Musik und Architektur, deren Hauptzweig die Konditorkunst ist",

wie er nicht gerade bescheiden notiert.[65] Seine Vorbilder holte er sich aus Bibliotheken und bestimmte mit der Akribie eines Architekten Maße und Material seiner süßen „architecture en miniature" (Abb. 26). Im Laufe seiner Karriere, die ihn als Koch auch an den englischen und russischen Hof führte, brachte er in die dort noch unkoordinierte Fülle der bis zu 322 für manchmal bis zu 100 Personen bestimmten Speisen eine neue Struktur. Sein Motto war „Ordnung und Geschmack". Carême separierte Rind, Geflügel und Fisch, die bis dahin oft auf einer einzigen Platte aufgetragen wurden, um so die individuellen Geschmacksnuancen besser zur Geltung zu bringen. Er war der Spitzenkoch seiner Zeit. Im Dienst von Charles Maurice de Talleyrand war er mit zum Wiener Kongress gereist und ihm wird nachgesagt, dass seine Kochkunst wesentlich dazu beitrug, Frankreichs Verhandlungsposition zu verbessern. Als Gourmand war Talleyrand dafür bekannt, seine exquisiten Gastmähler manipulativ für diplomatische Ziele einzusetzen. Essenseinladungen – und das gilt bis in die heutige Restaurantzeit hinein – dienten oft neben dem reinen Genuss am Essen bestimmten Intentionen. Talleyrands nie mehr als zehn bis zwölf Personen zählende Tafelzeremonien würde man heutzutage wohl unter den Begriff „Business-Lunch" subsumieren.

Hatten Schauessen des Adels oder auch städtischer Obrigkeiten noch die Absicht zu repräsentieren, so haben für das Volk veranstaltete Bankette deutlich propagan-

28

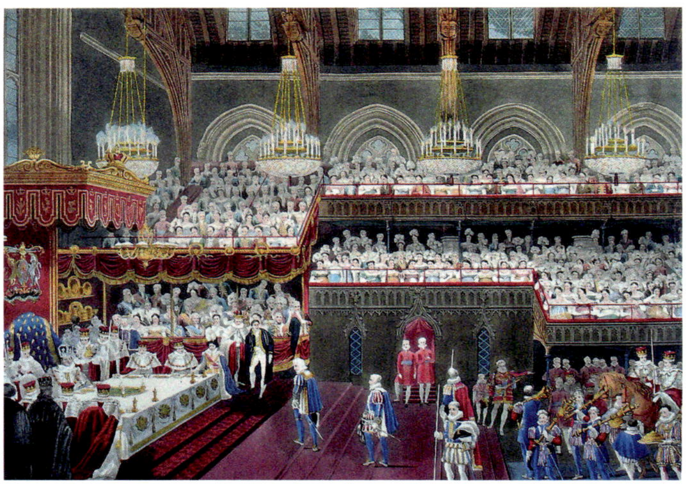

29

28

Knight's table at the declaration of knights of the Bath Order, London, 1725 ● Coronation banquet of George IV of England, 1820 ● Coronation banquet of Ferdinand I at the Prague castle, 1836

Rittertafel anlässlich der Ernennung der Ritter des Bath-Ordens, London, 1725 ● Krönungsbankett von Georg IV. von England, 1820 ● Krönungsbankett von Ferdinand I. in der Prager Burg, 1836

29

The 'Grand Couvert' of Louis XIV in a waxworks cabinet, around 1780

Das *grand couvert* von Louis XIV. im Wachsfigurenkabinett, circa 1780

which until then had often been placed on a single plate, in order to allow the individual flavours a better advantage. He was the star chef of his times. He travelled to the Congress of Vienna in the service of Charles Maurice de Talleyrand, and it is said that his culinary talents significantly helped to improve France's negotiating position. As a gourmand, Talleyrand was known to use his exquisite banquets as a manipulative tool for diplomatic objectives. Dinner invitations—and we still see this in today's restaurant culture—often have underlying intentions in addition to the pure enjoyment of eating. Talleyrand's table ceremonies of never more than ten or twelve people would nowadays probably be considered a 'business lunch'. If such showcase banquets by the nobility or urban authorities were intended to represent social status, then banquets hosted specifically for the populace had the obvious objective of propaganda. One example of this is the banquet organised in 1826 for the coronation of Nicholas I on the Frauenfeld in Moscow. In the tradition of the Roman culture of *panem et circenses*, two hundred and forty tables were set, each with forty-six seats. Tens of thousands of onlookers waited behind barricades for the Tsar's orders allowing them to descend upon the tables (fig. 27).[66] This is one case where curiosity was converted into actual participation, but in fact most showcase banquets merely served to flaunt the privileged diners. They satisfied the curiosity and stimulated the desire of the audience restricted to the stands (fig. 28). For those with the available financial means, this denial of participation in courtly banquets translated into an imitation thereof at one's own palace, including the aforementioned banquet staged by Grimod de la Reynière in 1783. The *non-plus-ultra* of satisfying gastronomic curiosity in the *ancien régime* was, at least for those who could not travel to Versailles, where Louis XIV displayed himself dining live, was a lifelike wax replica of the *grand couvert*—the King and his family *à table* (fig. 29).[67] Towards the end of the eighteenth century the society that could afford such grand displays multiplied. This was the case in all major European metropolises. In Paris, however, *Feinschmeckerei* played a central role for the burgeoning restaurant culture. This grew from the courtly cuisine and was made popular by gastrosophers such as Grimod de la Reynière and Brillat-Savarin, thus supplying a new clientele. On the eve of the French Revolution there were fifty restaurants in Paris; at the end of the Napoleonic era twenty-five years later, there were more than 3,000.

distische Ziele. In der Tradition der römischen „panem-et-circenses"-Kultur werden zum Beispiel 1826 zur Krönung von Nikolaus I. auf dem Frauenfeld in Moskau 240 Tische mit je 46 Plätzen gedeckt. Zehntausende von Schaulustigen, hinter Absperrungen wartend, durften sich dann, der Aufforderung des Zaren folgend, auf diese Tische stürzen (Abb. 27).[66] Hier konnte die Schaulust in Teilhabe umgewandelt werden. Im Gegensatz dazu dienten die meisten Schauessen ausschließlich der Zurschaustellung privilegierter Essender. Sie befriedigten die Neugierde und stimulierten die Begierde der auf Tribünen platzierten Zuschauer (Abb. 28). Dort, wo die finanziellen Mittel vorhanden waren, wurde die verweigerte Teilhabe an höfischen Gastmählern in eine Imitation im eigenen Palais umgewandelt. Hierzu gehörte das bereits erwähnte, von Grimod de la Reynière 1783 inszenierte Gastmahl. Das Nonplusultra zur Befriedigung gastronomischer Schaulust im Ancien Régime war für diejenigen, die nicht nach Versailles kommen konnten, wo Louis XIV. sich tatsächlich essend zur Schau stellte, eine naturgetreue Wachsnachbildung des *grand couvert* – des gedeckten Tischs des Königs und seiner Familie (Abb. 29).[67] Gegen Ende des 18. Jahrhunderts hatte sich die Schicht, die sich solche repräsentativen Essen leisten konnte, exponentiell vergrößert. Dies gilt für alle europäischen Metropolen. In Paris aber spielt für die aufblühende Restaurantkultur, die auf der höfischen Küche basierende Feinschmeckerei, von Gastrosophen wie Grimod de la Reynière und Brillat-Savarin popularisiert und einer neuen Klientel zugeführt, eine wichtige Rolle. Am Vorabend der Revolution gab es in Paris 50, am Ende der napoleonischen Ära 25 Jahre später über 3000 Restaurants.

Die Geburt des Restaurants oder ein Name und seine Folgen

Der Begriff „Restaurant", der sich in seiner endgültigen Form erst in den 1820er Jahren in Paris durchsetzt, wird bereits seit dem 17. Jahrhundert für eine deftige Fleischbrühe[68], die der Kräftigung des Essers dient, benutzt. Rebecca L. Spang berichtet in *The Invention of the Restaurant* von Jacques Minet, der 1767 in Paris einen der ersten „salles du restaurateur" eröffnet.[69] Der Traiteur Jean François Vacossin unterstreicht die wiederherstellende Wirkung seiner „soupe de santé" auf seinem Ladenschild: „Accurite ad me omnes qui stomacho laboratis et

Tables d'hôte

Tables d'hôte are abominable for strangers, although they depend upon them. One dines there in the midst of a dozen strangers, and one who is polite or shy does not get his money's worth. Near the midst of the table where the platters with the main dishes are positioned, the regulars make themselves at home … if the thing is to provide the stomach with the biggest and tastiest morsels. With the gluttony of antique creatures they attack the dishes and clear whole tables in a matter of minutes… Woe to the one that chews his mouthfuls slowly! Wedged in the midst of these greedy guts and swift cormorants he sees himself condemned to fasting in the midst of the meal. The same uncivilized vultures, however that only a minute ago crammed the tremendous cavities of their bowels at the expense of their neighbours, turn, barely sated, into merciless chatterboxes. The echo of their smutty yelping then fills the smoke-filled vaults of the dining halls. Besides, it would equal a miracle, if one succeeded in quitting the joint without somebody's crude and clumsy hands leaving some smudges on one's clothes. Furthermore, there are some cookshops, also called Noah's Arches, where it is possible to get food for no more than twenty-two *sous*. These are the regular haunts of the less prosperous, who, after the meal, pride themselves on the promenade or in the theatre of having dined outwards, just as if it were a disgrace to eat cheaply, if one is not capable to do otherwise.

Louis-Sébastien Mercier: Tableau de Paris, Hamburg/Neuchâtel 1781, p. 129–131

FIG. I

'The Birth of the Restaurant, or A Name and Its Consequences'

With the term 'restaurant', we are actually dealing with the invention of a name. The final name, which was not established until the 1820s in Paris, had already been in use in the seventeenth century to denote a hearty broth,[68] which served to strengthen those who ate it. Rebecca L. Spang writes in *The Invention of the Restaurant* about Jacques Minet, who opened one of the *first salles du restaurateur* in 1767 in Paris.[69] The *traiteur* Jean François Vacossin emphasised the restorative effect of his 'soupe de santé' on his shop sign: 'Accurite ad me omnes qui stomacho laboratis et ego vos restaurabo.'[70] Another supplier of this healthy bouillon praised it with the following words: 'Boulanger offers divine restaurants.'[71] The name of this particular broth eventually became the name for guesthouses that offered food and would often list this restorative soup at the top of their menu cards. In 1770, *Réstif de La Bretonne* criticised such a restaurant:

ego vos restaurabo".[70] Ein anderer Anbieter der Gesundheits-Bouillon preist sich mit folgenden Worten an: „Bei Boulanger gibt es göttliche Restaurants".[71] Der Name dieser besonderen Brühe wurde der Name für Speisegaststätten, die dann noch oft die restaurierende Suppe an erster Stelle auf ihren Speisekarten führten. Der bereits erwähnte *Réstif de La Bretonne* beschreibt 1770 kritisch eine solche Gaststätte:

> „Ich bat sie, mich zu stärken [je demandai à me restaurer]. Man bot mir eine Reissuppe, ein paar frische Eier, ein Stück Huhn oder ein Stück Kalbsbraten an. Ich sah hier nichts Stärkenderes als anderswo. Ich bestellte die Suppe und einen Hühnerflügel. Ich wurde in mürrischer Weise von einem Jungen bedient. Es war kein Leben an diesem Ort. Jeder restauré aß stumm an einem kleinen runden Tisch ohne Tischtuch."[72]

Von der *table d'hôte* zum Restaurant

Seit jeher waren Reisende zur Verköstigung und Übernachtung auf Gasthöfe angewiesen. In den Städten gab

'I asked them to restore me [*je demandai à me restaurer*]. I was offered a rice soup, some fresh eggs, a piece of chicken, or a piece of roast veal. I saw nothing here any more restorative than I had seen elsewhere. I took the soup and a chicken wing. I was served grumpily by a boy. There was no life to the place. Each *restauré* supped silently at a little round table without a tablecloth.'[72]

From *Table d'hôte* to Restaurant

For centuries, travellers needed inns where they could eat and sleep. The cities had public houses and taverns. The following is said of Samuel Pepys, in London in the 1630s:

> 'Having bought a lobster in Fish Street and bumping into some friends carrying a sturgeon, whereupon the group repaired to Sun Tavern in order to get their fish cooked and enjoy it together. The sociability of taverns made them natural places to do business, and Pepys often entertained colleagues there, and was frequently schmoozed himself. Taverns ruled supreme in London's social and business life for several centuries.'[73]

One decisive factor for a restaurant was that it should be a place for socialising and communication. Another factor was that various dishes were prepared so they could be selected individually. These were either listed on a blackboard, or on a bill of fare, or on menu cards—dating back to the *service à la russe*—both methods of announcement still in use today. With just a few exceptions, the restaurants[74] provided food only at specified times, and the quality of these meals was very poor, as noted by scholar Joachim Nemeitz at the beginning of the eighteenth century:

> 'Forced to eat at an innkeeper's or traiteur's ... table d'hôte, the simple visitor to Paris would quickly discover that he "does not fare well at all, either because the meat is not properly cooked, or because they serve the same thing every day and rarely offer any variety".'[75]

However, the dishes and meal times were specified at a *table d'hôte*—customary in Grand Hotels until long after 1900.[76] (FIG. I) In Paris, there was a famous exception to these restricted eating times: the *Marmite Perpétuelle*, or 'Ever-simmering Pot', a guesthouse serving food that was acclaimed by Grimod de la Reynière in 1810, and which is said to have served 300,000 capons since

es Schenken und Tavernen. Von Samuel Pepys heißt es 1630 in London:

> „Having bought a lobster in Fish Street and bumping into some friends carrying a sturgeon, whereupon the group repaired to Sun Tavern in order to get their fish cooked and enjoy it together. The sociability of taverns made them natural places to do business, and Pepys often entertained colleagues there, and was frequently schmoozed himself. Taverns ruled supreme in London's social and business life for several centuries".[73]

Ort der Geselligkeit und Kommunikation zu sein, gehört zu den Charakteristika eines Restaurants. Ein weiteres Kriterium sind die über den ganzen Tag angebotenen, individuell auszuwählenden Speisen. Diese sind bis heute entweder auf einer Tafel oder auf Speise- oder – zurückgehend auf das „service à la russe" – auf Menükarten notiert. Mit wenigen Ausnahmen waren die Gaststätten[74] bis zum Ende des 18. Jahrhunderts nur Anbieter von Essen zu festgelegten Zeiten und ihre Qualität äußerst mangelhaft, wie der Gelehrte Joachim Nemeitz im frühen 18. Jahrhundert feststellt:

> „Hergegen aber speiset man in denen Gast-Höfen eben nicht so gar sonderlich, theils, weil das Essen insgemein nicht wohl zugerichtet, theils, weil man alle Tage einerley isset, und gar selten eine Veränderung hat."[75]

An einer *table d'hôte* – noch lange nach 1900 in Grand Hotels gebräuchlich[76] – waren die Gerichte und die Essenszeiten vorgegeben (FIG. I). In Paris gab es eine berühmte Ausnahme für zeitungebundenes Essen, den Marmite perpétuelle, den „immerbrodelnden Kessel", eine 1810 von Grimod de la Reynière gelobte Speisegaststätte, die seit ihrer Eröffnung 1724 300.000 Kapaune serviert haben soll. Ebenfalls von der Uhrzeit unabhängig war das Angebot der Traiteure und Feinkostladenbesitzer. Am Anfang dieses Kapitels wurde der unter einem „Comestible"-Schild sitzende Genießer beschrieben. Traiteure waren in einer Gilde zusammengeschlossen und beargwöhnten und bekämpften die neue Gruppe der Restaurateure und Gastronomen. Traiteure boten nicht nur Delikatessen, Wein und Champagner, Pasteten oder Ragouts von hoher Qualität an – Honoré de Balzac spricht von der „riche et savoureuse bibliothèque [des Traiteurs] Chevet ... et les jouissances promises par un

its opening in 1724. The *traiteur* and delicatessen owner's wares were also available at flexible times. At the beginning of this essay a connoisseur was described sitting under a sign advertising a *comestible. Traiteurs* were united in a guild and were wary of, and opposed to, the new group of restaurant owners and gastronomes. They offered not only delicacies, wine and champagne, pies and stews, and more of high quality—Honoré de Balzac speaks of the 'riche et savoureuse bibliothéque (des traiteurs) Chevet … et les jouissances promises par un pâté foie gras de Strasbourg'[77]—but also served diners at all desired hours of the day and night. If required, dishes, glasses, cutlery, table linen, and even servants would also be included. Gourmand and author of *La Comédie humaine* Balzac was not only a customer of Chevet, but treated him in his novels[78] with the same high regard as he did noble restaurants such as 'Rocher de Cancale', 'Véry', and 'Chez Véfour'. Balzac was considered completely unreliable when it came to paying his bills. He assumed, because he promoted the catering establishments by contributing to their publicity and reputation, that he owed them nothing at all.

Caterers had their heyday at the end of the *ancien régime*:

> 'As successful and comfortable merchants and entrepreneurs, they shared in the intellectual and cultural life of Paris; their customers included dukes and actresses, clergymen and philosophers; they numbered minor officeholders, lawyers and fellow merchants. They worked within and between established systems, not hampered by them but manipulating them to their own advantage.'[79]

This was an area that, as a result, restaurateurs successfully conquered. As early as 1782, Antoine Beauvilliers left the court of the later Louis XVIII to open a restaurant in the arcades of the Palais Royal. In 1786, the restaurant 'Les trois frères Provençeaux' followed. Beauvilliers was the first to recognise the needs of an emerging new society. He satisfied these by bringing the culinary privileges of the aristocracy to the public sphere. It is up for debate, as Eric Hobsbawm suggests, as to whether this might be an early indication of societal democratisation. Danton 'eats venison from silver plates',[80] shouts Robespierre to the crowd; the Revolutionary tribunal convenes *ad infinitum.* Victims were sought even among diners in restaurants. It was announced in 1793 in Jacobin circles that,

pâté foie gras de Strasbourg"[77] – sondern richteten zu allen gewünschten Tages- und Nachtzeiten auch Diners aus. Wenn nötig, gehörten auch Geschirr, Gläser, Bestecke, Tischwäsche wie auch Diener zum abrufbaren Angebot. Der Gourmand Balzac, Autor von *La comédie humaine*, ist nicht nur Kunde bei Chevet, sondern behandelt ihn wie auch andere Nobelrestaurants, zum Beispiel Rocher de Cancale, Véry oder Chez Véfour auch in seinen Romanen.[78] Balzac galt als vollkommen unzuverlässiger Bezahler von Rechnungen und ging eigentlich davon aus, dass er, zu Publizität und Renommée der Gastronomiebetriebe beitragend, diesen keine Begleichung schuldig war.

Die Hochzeit der Traiteure beginnt am Ende des Ancien Régime.

> „As successful and comfortable merchants and entrepreneurs, they shared in the intellectual and cultural life of Paris; their customers included dukes and actresses, clergymen and philosophers; they numbered minor officeholders, lawyers and fellow merchants. They worked within and between established systems, not hampered by them but manipulating them to their own advantage."[79]

Ein Terrain, welches sich in der Folge auch die Betreiber der Restaurants erfolgreich eroberten. Bereits 1782 verlässt Antoine Beauvilliers den Haushalt des späteren Louis XVIII., um in den Arkaden des Palais Royal ein Restaurant zu eröffnen. 1786 folgt dort das Restaurant Les trois frères Provençeaux. Beauvilliers erkennt als erster die Bedürfnisse aufstrebender neuer Gesellschaftsschichten. Er befriedigt sie, indem er kulinarische aristokratische Privilegien in den öffentlichen Raum überträgt. Ob es sich, wie Eric Hobsbawm behauptet, schon um eine Art Demokratisierung handelt, sei dahingestellt. Danton „ißt das Wildbret von silbernen Tellern"[80], ruft Robespierre in die Menge. Das Revolutionstribunal tagt ununterbrochen. Opfer sucht man unter den Restaurantbesuchern.

> „Es wird notwendig, den Gastwirten, Restaurantbesitzern und Hoteliers Besuche abzustatten, um festzustellen, wer bei ihnen für 100 Livres gegessen hat. Wer solche Mahlzeiten eingenommen hat, ist genauso suspekt wie die, die sie serviert haben …"[81],

verlautet es 1793 aus Jakobinerkreisen. Restaurants und Cafés waren bis in das 20. Jahrhundert hinein immer auch Orte der Bespitzelung.[82]

'It becomes neccassary to visit the innkeepers, restaurateurs and hoteliers to see who has eaten there for a hundred livres. Anyone who has taken such a meal is just as suspect as those who have served it.'[81]

Well into the twentieth century, restaurants and cafés were always good places for spying.[82]

However, it would be too short-sighted to claim that restaurants emerged simply because the royal head chefs, *rôtisseurs*, pastry chefs, *sauciers*, and so on were made unemployed after the revolution of 1789. Unlike those working in the kitchens of the aristocracy, a restaurant owner had to secure his own premises and its equipment, create its design, and worry about attracting a clientele. Very early on, Beauvilliers recognised the importance of good relations with diplomats and foreign businessmen—and the meeting of these two specimens would form the foundation for what would later be called the 'business dinner'. Many restaurant tables became conference tables. A German traveller reported, 'The name Vérys and Beauvilliers soon became known to many … deputies to great prestige.'[83] Beauvilliers knew that excellent service and a personal touch were guarantors of success. Who does not enjoy being greeted personally by name by the owner? Reputation, therefore, was not only a product of gastronomic-sensual pleasure. A restaurant also had to be advertised. This was achieved not only by means of a store window display—Grimod de la Reynière and Balzac called them 'bibliothèques'—but also by relying on the age-old tradition of inn signs.[84] Heinrich von Kleist has provided us with an apt description of this competitive effort.

'When you're walking through the streets of Paris observing the traffic, the merchants, craftsmen, innkeepers, and so on: a character begins to emerge … that … is very different to the nature of our simple-minded German intercourse. Above all, it is important to know that the merchant does not merely display a sample of his wares for all to see, which is common in our culture: the product itself, which is the best and most precious thing that he possesses, is spread out in the most pleasing … and proud manner. Store signs that protrude from both sides into the street give importunate and flattering information in long rates about the priceworthiness … of the goods … the *Cafetier*, for example, who lives at the top of the street, would perhaps write with white letters on a simple small

Das Aufkommen der Restaurants ausschließlich auf die nach der Revolution von 1789 arbeitslosen höfischen Chefköche, Rôtisseurs, Pâtissiers, Sauciers zurückzuführen, wäre zu kurz gegriffen. Anders als in den Küchen des Adels musste sich ein Restaurantbesitzer um eigene Räumlichkeiten, ihr Aussehen, ihre Ausstattung – und vor allem um Gäste kümmern. Früh hatte Beauvilliers erkannt, wie wichtig gute Beziehungen auch zu Diplomaten und ausländischen Geschäftsleuten waren, die mit ihren Zusammenkünften den Grundstein für die später sogenannten Geschäftsessen legten. Mancher Restauranttisch wurde zum Konferenztisch. Ein deutscher Reisender berichtet: „Die Namen Vérys und Beauvilliers gelangten bald auch bei vielen … Deputierten zu großem Ansehen."[83] Beauvilliers wusste, dass eine persönliche Note – wer wird nicht heute noch gerne vom Restaurantbesitzer namentlich begrüßt – und ein hervorragender Service Garanten des Erfolgs waren. Die Reputation war demnach nicht nur vom gastronomisch-sensuellen Genuss abhängig. Werbung für ein Restaurant war notwendig. Diese fand nicht nur durch Schaufensterauslagen – von Grimod de la Reynière und Balzac werden sie als „bibliothèque" bezeichnet – statt, sondern auch durch die auf eine lange Tradition zurückgehenden Wirtshausschilder.[84] Eine treffende Schilderung dieses Konkurrenzkampfes liefert uns Heinrich von Kleist.

„Wenn man in den Straßen von Paris, den Verkehr, den Kaufleute, Handwerker, Schenkwirte, usw. treiben, beobachtet: so zeigt sich ein Charakter … der … absticht gegen den Charakter unseres einfältigen deutschen Verkehrs. Zuförderst muß man wissen, daß der Kaufmann nicht wie bei uns eine Probe seiner Ware zur Schau stellt: die Ware selbst das Kostbarste und Beste, was er besitzt, wird … auf die wohlgefälligste und ruhmredigste Weise, ausgebreitet. Aushängeschilder, die von beiden Seiten in die Straße hineinragen, geben, in langen Tarifen, zudringliche und schmeichlerische Auskunft über die Wohlfeilheit … der Waren … der Cafetier zum Beispiel, der am Eingang einer Straße wohnt, affichiert vielleicht, auf einem bloßen schwarzen Brett, mit weißen Lettern: Café; einige Artikel führt er, auf einfache Weise, mit ihren Preisen an; er hat den Vorteil, er ist der erste. Der zweite, um ihm den Rang abzulaufen, fügt schon überall bei der Enumeration seiner Leckereien hinzu: du plus exquis; de la meilleure qualité; und: le tout au plus modique prix; sein

blackboard: *café*; he would list in an unpretentious fashion some items he has on offer, as well as their prices; he has the advantage, he is the first one on the street. The second, to outdo him, augments the enumeration of his treats: *du plus exquis; la meilleure qualité*; and: *le tout au plus modique prix*; his board is now brightly coloured, be it yellow, red, or blue, and, in order to catch more attention, he extends it even further into the street. The third writes: 'Café des Connoisseurs', or 'Café des Turcs'; he helps himself by extending his sign one or two feet even further into the street; and his letters, on a black or white background, are, in a strange and bizarre way, also brightly coloured themselves. The fourth situation seems desperate; nevertheless made humorous by the despair, it outdoes all of his predecessors. He writes: 'Café au non plus ultra', in man-sized letters, such that it is impossible to read up close, and his sign, which uses all of the colours in the rainbow, protrudes up into the very middle of the street. But what to make of the fifth? It is hopeless to accomplish anything by charlatanism, self-praise, and exaggeration, he resorts to the absolute simplicity of the first patriarch. 'Café', he writes, with ordinary letters, and includes: 'Entrez et puis jugez.'[85]

The Emergence of Restaurants in Metropolitan Cities

The beginning of the nineteenth century also saw the birth of the restaurant guide, at first still a supplement in Grimod de la Renière's *Almanach*—the latter, similarly to Balzac, incidentally also speculated on service free of charge. From 1800, restaurants and delicatessens began to fundamentally change the physiognomy of the Parisian city centre. In 1805, in the Palais Royal alone, there were fifteen restaurants and cafés, and eighteen gaming tables.[86] In London, taverns, inns, and chophouses would prevail for sometime to come. Similar to the French *traiteurs, confectionists* also began to offer food, starting in the eighteenth century. *Haute cuisine* emerged on the London scene through the clubs and their head chefs.[87] *The Epicure's Almanack*,[88] mimetic of Grimod de la Reynière's *Almanach*, mentions three eating establishments with French names near Leicester Square. It was not until the mid-nineteenth century that the term 'restaurant' gradually established itself in London. They were

Brett ist bunt gefärbt, es sei nun gelb, rot oder blau, und er schiebt es, um die Aufmerksamkeit damit zu fangen, noch tiefer in die Straße hinein. Der dritte schreibt: Café des Connoisseurs, oder Café des Turcs; er hilft sich noch, indem er sein Schild, um noch einen oder zwei Fuß tiefer in die Straße reckt; und seine Lettern, auf schwarzem oder weißem Grunde, sind, auf sonderbare und bizarre Weise, bunt gefärbt in sich. Des vierten Lage scheint verzweifelt; gleichwohl durch die Verzweiflung selbst witzig gemacht, überbietet er noch alle seine Vorgänger. Café au non plus ultra, schreibt er: seine Lettern sind von Mannsgröße, dergestalt, daß sie in der Nähe gar nicht gelesen werden können, und sein Schild, das den ganzen Regenbogen spielt, ragt bis auf die Mitte der Straße hinaus. Aber was soll der fünfte machen? Hoffnungslos, durch Scharlatanerie, Selbstlob und Übertreibung etwas auszurichten, fällt er in die Ureinfalt der ersten Patriarchen zurück. Café, schreibt er, mit ganz gewöhnlichen Lettern, und darunter: entrez et puis jugez".[85]

Das Aufkommen der Restaurants in den Metropolen

Das beginnende 19. Jahrhundert ist auch die Geburtsstunde der Restaurantführer, vorerst noch verpackt in Grimod de la Renières *Almanach* – letzterer spekulierte übrigens ähnlich wie Balzac auf kostenlose Bewirtung. Ab 1800 veränderten Restaurants und Delikatessenläden die Physiognomie des Pariser Zentrums grundlegend. 1805 gab es allein im Palais Royal 15 Restaurants, 20 Cafés und 18 Spieltische.[86] In London herrschten noch lange die *taverns, inns* und *chop houses* vor. Ähnlich den französischen Traiteurs boten seit dem 18. Jahrhundert *confectionists* Speisen an. Die *haute cuisine* hält über die Clubs und ihre bereits erwähnten Chefköche ihren Einzug in London.[87] The *Epicure's Almanack*[88], Grimod de la Reynières *Almanach* nachahmend, erwähnt in der Nähe des Leicester Square drei Speisegaststätten mit französischem Namen. Erst gegen die Mitte des 19. Jahrhunderts setzte sich in London die Bezeichnung „Restaurant" allmählich durch.

„To distance themselves from the traditional dining rooms, which were associated with business and trade, and to reposition themselves in the most fashionable sector of the market."[89] (Abb. 30, links)

30

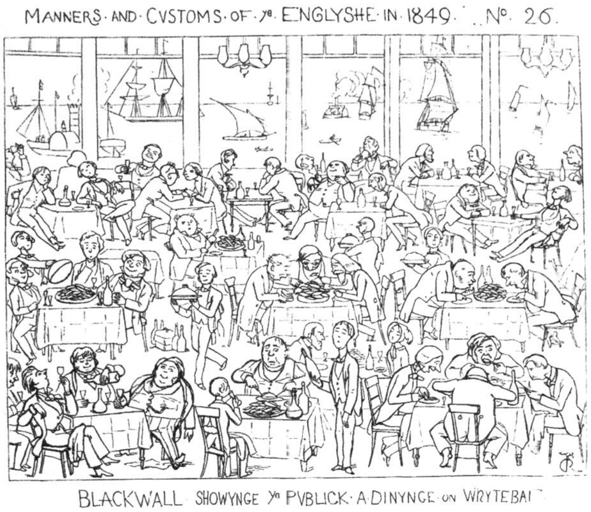

30

A 'Whitebaitdinner' in the 'Lovegrave Tavern' in Blackwell, London, Richard Doyle, 1845 ● Carvers in the old 'Simpson's'. Waiters, who frequently served the restaurant for more than a quarter of a century, guaranteed tradition

Ein „whitebaitdinner" in der Lovegrave Tavern in Blackwell, London, Richard Doyle, 1845 ● Tranchierer im alten Restaurant Simpson's. Für die Tradition sorgten Kellner, die oft mehr als ein Vierteljahrhundert im Restaurant Dienst taten

31

31

Interior view of the wine restaurant 'F.W. Borchardt', Berlin, photo from around 1900

Innenansicht des Weinrestaurants F.W. Borchardt, Berlin, Foto um 1900

'to distance themselves from the traditional dining rooms, which were associated with business and trade, and to reposition themselves in the most fashionable sector of the market.'[89] (fig. 30, left)

Elaborate interiors as well as good service were also an important criterion of the new restaurant culture in London. 'Simpson's Grand Restaurant' on the Strand in 1848 played a pioneering role here. A unique feature of restaurants specialising in English cuisine was the 'carving' of roasted meat, which was brought to the table on silver service trolleys (fig. 30, right).[90] As described earlier, carving was a service skill that became ever more highly refined throughout the centuries. In London, however, restaurants that maintained French cuisine were praised, such as the renowned theatre restaurant 'Criterion', designed in 1874 by Thomas Verity. The Café-Restaurant 'Royal', opened in 1865 by the Frenchman Daniel Nicolas Thévenon, also offered its guests dishes 'absolument comme à Paris'. This is where the bohemian society would gather around 1900, among its ranks James McNeill Whistler, Aubrey Beardsley, and Oscar Wilde.[91]

In Berlin, restaurant culture did not emerge until 1870–1871, and it experienced a second heyday in the 1920s. In this youngest of all European metropolitan cities, though, we find the oldest inn: 'Zum Nussbaum', which dates back to 1507. Another historic inn in Berlin on the River Spree, dating back to 1699, was what would later become the hotel 'King of Portugal', with its gourmet restaurant frequented by the likes of Franz Grillparzer, Gotthold Ephraim Lessing, and E.T.A. Hoffmann.[92] The table d'hôte in 'Hôtel de Brandenbourg' was also well known. Theodor Fontane mentions it in his novel *Der Stechlin*.[93]

Typical for Berlin were its wine bars. Simon Habel, the sommelier of Frederick the Great, opened the first such establishment in 1779. The wine bar of Gebrüder Habel Unter den Linden became famous because of its illustrious guests from various fields, such as politics, the military, and the arts.[94] But the most notable of all wine bars was 'Lutter & Wegner'. It was the hangout of E.T.A. Hoffmann, whose drawings adorned the walls. Heinrich Heine, Ludwig Devrient, Theodor Körner, and many others were also counted among its guests. Christoph Lutter and August Friedrich Wegner opened it in 1806 in a building designed by Carl Gontard. There was a restaurant on the mezzanine floor, and beginning in 1835,

Aufwendige Inneneinrichtung sowie der Service bildeten auch in London ein wichtiges Kriterium der neuen Restaurantkultur. Simpson's Grand Restaurant von 1848 am Strand spielt hier eine Vorreiterrolle. Eine Besonderheit des auf die britische Küche spezialisierten Restaurants war das *carving* des auf silbernen Servierwagen an die Tische gefahrenen Bratens (Abb. 30, rechts).[90] Wie bereits beschrieben, war das Tranchieren eine seit Jahrhunderten hochentwickelte Servierkunst. Grundsätzlich aber rühmten sich in London Restaurants, die auf sich hielten, französische Küche anzubieten, so das renommierte Theaterrestaurant Criterion, 1874 von Thomas Verity entworfen. Auch das 1865 von dem Franzosen Daniel Nicolas Thévenon eröffnete Café-Restaurant Royal bot seinen Gästen Gerichte „absolument comme à Paris" an. Um 1900 versammelte sich hier die Bohéme, unter ihnen James McNeill Whistler, Aubrey Beardsley und Oscar Wilde.[91]

In Berlin setzt ein Restaurantboom erst nach 1870/71 ein und erlebt in den 1920er Jahren einen zweiten Höhepunkt. In dieser jüngsten aller europäischen Metropolen wird das älteste Gasthaus Zum Nußbaum 1507 nachgewiesen. Ebenfalls ein historisches Gasthaus an der Spree aus dem Jahre 1699 war das spätere Hotel König von Portugal mit seinem Speiserestaurant, in dem sich Franz Grillparzer, Gotthold Ephraim Lessing und E. T. A. Hoffmann einfanden.[92] Berühmt waren die *table d'hôte* im Hôtel de Brandenbourg. Theodor Fontane erwähnt es in seinem Roman *Der Stechlin*.[93]

Typisch für Berlin waren seine Weinrestaurants. Das erste eröffnete 1779 Simon Habel, der Kellermeister Friedrichs des Großen. Die Weinstube der Gebrüder Habel Unter den Linden wurde durch illustre Gäste aus Politik, Militär und Kunst berühmt.[94] Das namhafteste aller Weinlokale aber war Lutter & Wegner. Es war das Stammlokal von E. T. A. Hoffmann, dessen Handzeichnungen die Wände zierten. Hier verkehrten Heinrich Heine, Ludwig Devrient, Theodor Körner und viele andere. 1811 hatten es Christoph Lutter und August Friedrich Wegner in einem 1806 von Carl von Gontard entworfenen Haus eröffnet. Es gab ein Restaurant im Hochparterre und ab 1835 den berühmten historischen Weinkeller.[95] Verglichen mit den gastronomischen Verlockungen in Paris war Berlin allerdings eine Provinzstadt. Erst 1853 eröffnet August F. W. Borchardt in der Französischen Straße ein Restaurant, das dem Pariser Niveau entspricht (Abb. 31).

the famous historic wine cellar.[95] Berlin was, however, provincial compared to the gastronomic temptations in Paris. It was not until 1853 that August F.W. Borchardt opened a restaurant in Französische Strasse that could compare with Parisian standards (fig. 31).

> 'A relatively small restaurant, very discreet and with elegant furnishings, and highly valued by gourmets who had every meal prepared for them according to a recipe developed after long and thorough special consultation. Small side rooms, in which the crown prince sometimes supped with his entourage after the theatre, or the Imperial Guard celebrated an evening among comrades.'[96]

In combination with a delicatessen shop and wine store, the establishment worked along the lines of French caterers and even as delivery kitchen that supplied the Emperor. A second branch was opened in 1895 on Gendarmenmarkt.[97] The above-mentioned reputation was essentially due to the fame of its guests. An establishment would become popular—be it a restaurant, café,[98] or hotel—if it possessed a certain magnetism, if there was a tendency to want to be part of it socially. To see and be seen in a restaurant, at the opera or the theatre—to display oneself in public—was an integral part of the ritualised life of the bourgeoisie, the playboys, and the social climbers. This was true up until the twentieth century and it still applies to the twenty-first. In Chicago in 1900, Theodore Dreiser wrote that

> 'Rector's, with its polished marble walls and floor, its profusion of lights, its show of china and silverware, and, above all, its reputation as a resort for actors and professional men, seemed to him the proper place for a successful man to go … He loved fine clothes, good eating, and particularly the company and acquaintanceship of successful men. At Rector's he could always obtain this satisfaction, for there one could encounter politicians, brokers, actors, some rich young "rounders" of the town, all eating and drinking amid a buzz of popular commonplace conversation.' [99]

'Diner à deux'

There was, however, another social code practised in restaurants: that of gallantry, or the conquest of a woman. This *diner à deux* had a rather long tradition (fig. 32, top), but in newly opened restaurants, it was held mostly on

> „Ein verhältnismäßig kleines Lokal, sehr diskret und vornehm eingerichtet und hochgeschätzt von den Gourmets, die sich jedes Gericht nach besonderem, lange und gründlich beratenem Rezept anfertigen lassen. … Kleine Nebensäle, in denen der Kronprinz manchmal mit seiner Umgebung nach dem Theater soupiert und die Garde-Kavallerie kameradschaftliche Abende feiert."[96]

In Kombination mit einem Delikatessengeschäft und einer Weinhandlung arbeitete das Etablissement nach dem Vorbild französischer Traiteure auch als Versandküche und belieferte sogar den Kaiser. Eine zweite Filiale eröffnete man 1895 am Gendarmenmarkt.[97] Die bereits angesprochene Reputation nährt sich im Wesentlichen vom Bekanntheitsgrad der Gäste. Öffentliche Orte aufzusuchen – seien es Restaurants, Cafés[98] oder Hotels – unterlag einem gewissen Magnetismus, einer sozialen Tendenz, dazugehören zu wollen, deren Attraktivität bis heute nicht verblichen ist. Das Sehen und Gesehenwerden, gleich ob im Restaurant, in der Oper oder im Theater, das Sich-Zeigen in der Öffentlichkeit war fester Bestandteil des ritualisierten Lebens der Bourgeoisie, der Lebemänner und Emporkömmlinge. Dies galt bis ins 20., ja gilt auch noch im 21. Jahrhundert. Zu Chicago um 1900 heißt es bei Theodore Dreiser:

> „Rector's Restaurant mit seinen glatten Marmorwänden und -böden, dem Überfluß an Licht, dem Prunk von Porzellan und Silber und vor allem seinem Ruf als Stelldichein für Schauspieler und Künstler dünkte ihn der Ort, den ein erfolgreicher Mann aufsuchen mußte … Bei Rector war es ihm immer möglich, sich diese Genugtuung zu verschaffen, denn hier konnte man Politiker, Börsenmakler, Schauspieler, reiche junge Lebemänner aus der Stadt treffen, die alle inmitten des Summens alltäglicher Gespräche aßen und tranken."[99]

Diner à deux

Im Restaurant wurde und wird noch ein anderer, der Galanterie oder der Eroberung einer Frau geschuldeter gesellschaftlicher Code mit langer Tradition praktiziert: das *diner à deux* (Abb. 32). In den neueröffneten Restaurants wurden hierfür meist im oberen Geschoss die sogenannten *chambres séparées* vorgehalten. Man kann sie als Orte der Liberalisierung sexueller Anbahnung bezeichnen. Eine Einladung in ein Restaurant war und ist Teil von Annäherungsstrategien zwischen den Geschlechtern.

32

A Merry Mealtime around 1760 ● *An oyster meal for two*, Jean Baptiste Bernard Coclers, 1780 ● *Dinner in the Ambassadeur*, Paris, Jean Béraud, around 1890 ● *The Diwan*, Pablo Picasso, 1899

Die fröhliche Tischzeit, um 1760 ● *Ein Austernessen zu zweit*, Jean Baptiste Bernard Coclers, 1780 ● *Diner im Ambassadeur*, Paris, Jean Béraud, um 1890 ● *Der Divan*, Pablo Picasso, 1899

the upper floor in what was known as *chambres séparées*. These can be described as places for the liberalisation of sexual courting. An invitation to a restaurant was and still is an important rapprochement strategy between the sexes. 'When eating, one can hint at a dissolving of propriety and decorum or even completely surrender them in favour of physical enjoyment',[100] writes Hans Ottomeyer. In *Sister Carrie*, Theodore Dreiser delivers a concise account of the rise of a working girl to her becoming a prima donna. Restaurants play a central role in this ascent—first in Chicago in a middle-class restaurant, then in New York in an establishment of fine dining.

> 'Drouet selected a table close by the window, where the busy route of the street could be seen. He loved the changing panorama of the street—to see and be seen as he dined... Carrie looked over the large bill of fare... She was very hungry, and the things she saw there awakened her desires, but the high prices held her attention... She had dimly heard of these things, but it seemed strange to be urged to order from the list... That little soldier of fortune took her good turn in an easy way.' [101]

Later, in New York:

> 'Young Ames held Carrie's elbow as he helped her up the steps... Here was the place where the matter of expense limited the patrons to the moneyed or pleasure-loving class... Here was the splendid dining chamber, all decorated and aglow, where the wealthy ate... Once seated, there began that exhibition of showy, wasteful, and unwholesome gastronomy as practiced by wealthy Americans... Ames was looking away rather abstractedly at the crowd and showed an attractive profile to Carrie. She felt as if she would like to be agreeable to this young man.'[102]

French authors such as Guy de Maupassant, Gustave Flaubert, Balzac, and Emile Zola wrote about seduction by means of restaurant dining:

> 'The next course was tender, dainty lamb cutlets, lying on a thick layer of tiny asparagus tips... They ate them slowly, relishing the delicate meat and the rich creamy vegetable. "When I love a woman," continued Duroy, "everything else vanishes apart from her." He spoke with conviction, inspired by the pleasures of the table in which he was indulging',[103]

„Beim Essen kann eine Auflösung von Sitte und Anstand zugunsten physischen Genusses angedeutet oder ganz ausgespielt werden"[100], schreibt Hans Ottomeyer. Es ist wiederum Theodore Dreiser, der in *Sister Carrie* eine prägnante Schilderung des Aufstiegs einer Arbeiterin zur Primadonna liefert. Restaurants spielen dabei eine zentrale Rolle, vorerst ein Mittelklasse-Restaurant in Chicago, dann in New York ein Speiselokal der gehobenen Art.

> „Drouet wählte einen Tisch nahe am Fenster, von wo sie das geschäftige Straßentreiben überblicken konnten. Er liebte das wechselnde Schauspiel der Straße, liebte es, beim Speisen zu sehen und gesehen zu werden ... Carrie blickte auf die lange Speisekarte ... sie war sehr hungrig, und die angeführten Speisen erregten ihr Verlangen, aber die hohen Preise schreckten sie ... von solchen Dingen hatte sie wohl gehört, aber es dünkte sie seltsam, daß sie sie nun bestellen sollte ... die kleine Glücksritterin nahm die gute Wendung leichten Herzens an."[101]

Später in New York:

> „Der junge Ames hielt Carrie am Ellbogen, als er sie die Treppe hinaufführte ... hier war die Stätte, wo die Höhe der Preise den Kreis der Gäste auf die wohlhabende oder vergnügungssüchtige Klasse beschränkte ... hier war nun der herrliche Speisesaal, reich verziert und strahlend von Licht, wo die Reichen dinierten ... Als sie glücklich saßen, begann jene Schaustellung prunkender, verschwenderischer und ungesunder Gastronomie, wie sie wohlhabende Amerikaner üben ... Ames blickte etwas zerstreut auf die Menge und zeigte Carrie sein anziehendes Profil, [sie] fühlte, daß sie dem jungen Manne gefallen wollte."[102]

Es sind vor allem die französischen Autoren wie Guy de Maupassant, Gustave Flaubert, Balzac und Emile Zola, die das Thema der Verführung durch Speisen am Verführungsort Restaurant immer wieder aufgreifen.

> „Man brachte zarte, leichte Lammkoteletts auf einem zierlichen, dichten Bett von Spargelspitzen ... Sie aßen bedächtig, genossen das feine Fleisch und das ölig weiche Gemüse wie Creme. ‚Wenn ich eine Frau liebe', fuhr Duroy fort, ‚so versinkt alles neben ihr.' Er sagte das überzeugt und fühlte sich bei den köstlichen Tafelfreuden beschwingt von dem Gedanken an so genießerische Liebe."[103]

writes Maupassant. Flaubert portrays another seduction scene:

> 'As he was married (he would have been afraid of compromising himself in his own house), I was taken to a private room in a restaurant, and told that I would be happy, that I would get a lovely present. The only seat in the room was a sofa close beside the table... The table was covered with a heap of things I had never seen before. Nothing seemed nice to me... Pushing aside one of the pillows ... I found under my hand a kind of album or notebook; they were obscene pictures...'[104] (Fig. 32, bottom)

The French demimondaines' demand for exquisite dining at restaurants in a *chambre séparée*, or for a staged feast arranged especially for them, is well depicted in *The Splendours and Miseries of Courtesans* by Balzac, *Sentimental Education* by Flaubert, and *Nana* by Zola. In 1928, Ilya Ehrenburg wrote of 'Café Schottenhaml' in Berlin, 'Sometimes they are in a *café séparée*, which look like stable boxes. Whipped cream costs twenty *Pfennig* more there.'[105]

The restaurant—as a place of seduction, a meeting point for gourmets, a stage for the upper classes, the home of artists and writers—is a product of a modern society in the process of disengaging from traditional economic and social systems. On the one hand, it owes its existence to the passing-on of culinary skills, which had been developed and constantly refined over centuries and whose enjoyment was now no longer limited to the privileged few. On the other hand, it is also rooted in the ancient tradition of hosting travellers on highways and in cities.

The Genesis of the Dining and Service Establishment

The words 'auberge' (French), 'albergo' (Italian) and 'Gasthof' and 'Gasthaus' (both German) all allude to the economic and cultural amalgamation of the lodging and catering systems. This is also implied in the English word 'inn', while 'tavern' is derived etymologically from the Latin word *taberna*. In addition to the Roman *tabernae*, a distinction was made between *caupona*, *fornix*, *popina*, and *termopolium*, which refer to the different products and services on offer. They were in the city centre, along the main roads, especially near theatres, spas, and gladiator barracks. There were absolutely none located in the

so Maupassant. Flaubert schildert eine weitere Verführungsszene:

> „Er [Frederic] war verheiratet und hätte fürchten müssen, in seinem eigenen Hause erwischt zu werden, und so führte man mich in einem Restaurant ins Chambre séparée. Man hatte mir gesagt, ich werde glücklich sein und obendrein ein schönes Geschenk bekommen ... Die einzige Sitzgelegenheit war ein Diwan vor dem Tisch ... Der Tisch war mit einer Menge Sachen vollgestellt, die ich nicht kannte. Nichts schmeckte mir ... Als ich eines von den Kissen wegschob ... geriet mir eine Art Album, ein Heft in die Hand. Es waren unzüchtige Bilder ...“[104] (Abb. 32, unten)

In *Glanz und Elend der Kurtisanen* schildert Balzac, in *Lehrjahre des Herzens* Flaubert und in *Nana* Zola den Anspruch der französischen Lebedamen auf exquisites Essen im Restaurant, im Chambre séparée wie auch auf eigens für sie inszenierten Festgelagen. „Manchmal gibt es in einem Café séparées, die aussehen wie Boxen im Pferdestall. Dort ist die Schlagsahne zwanzig Pfennig teurer“,[105] schreibt noch 1928 Ilja Ehrenburg über das Café Schottenhaml in Berlin.

Das Restaurant ist als Ort der Verführung, als Treffpunkt der Gourmets, als Bühne gehobener gesellschaftlicher Schichten, als Domizil von Künstlern und Literaten ein Produkt einer sich aus überkommenen wirtschaftlichen und sozialen Systemen lösenden modernen Gesellschaft. Seine Existenz verdankt es einerseits der Übertragung einer in Jahrhunderten entwickelten und stets verfeinerten Kochkunst, deren Genuss nicht mehr zu den Privilegien Weniger zählt. Andererseits basiert es auch auf althergebrachten Traditionen der Bewirtung von Reisenden auf Landstraßen und in Städten.

Die Genese des Bewirtungsortes

In den Wörtern *auberge*, *albergo*, Gasthof oder Gasthaus zeichnet sich die wirtschaftliche und kulturelle Verquickung des Beherbergungs- und Verpflegungswesens ab, wohingegen das englische Wort *inn* dies nicht andeutet und *tavern* etymologisch direkt auf die antike *taberna* verweist. Neben den *tabernae* des Römischen Reiches unterschied man *caupona*, *fornix*, *popina* und *termopolium*, die auf unterschiedliche Gattungen des Angebots verweisen. Sie befanden sich im Stadtzentrum, an den Hauptstraßen, vornehmlich in der Nähe von Theatern,

wealthy districts, where the population frowned upon going to taverns.

> 'The taverns consisted of one or more rooms that were open to the street and could be closed at closing time with wooden shutters. Facilities included a mostly rectangular bar counter, covered by colourful or white marble slabs. There were hollow areas on the top for wine and food. Its sides were equipped with brick, stair-like elements on which drinking vessels could be stacked. The guest rooms, depending on the standard, were equipped with shelves, tables, chairs, klinai, or encircling benches (fig. 33, left). In smaller guesthouses, the cooking, serving, and carousing would all take place in the same room. In larger inns there were private kitchen facilities and private latrines. The walls were mostly decorated by paintings whose content revolved around food, drink, and hospitality.'[106]

From the Middle Ages (fig. 33, centre) to the early nineteenth century, simple inns became increasingly similar and were comparable to a Swiss guesthouse described by Johann Wolfgang von Goethe in 1779:

> 'It differed in nothing from usual buildings of the same kind, except that the great room in the centre was at once the kitchen, the anteroom, and general gathering-place… On the one side was the fire, which was burning on the ground on some stone slabs; while a chimney built durably and neatly of planks, received and carried off the smoke in front of a wide chimney… The doors of the oven were located in the corner. All the rest of the floor was made of wood, with the exception of a small piece near the window around the sink, which was paved. Moreover, all around and overhead, on the beams, a multitude of domestic articles and utensils were arranged in beautiful order, and all kept nice and clean.'[107] (Fig. 33, right.)

The recesses in the bar counters of Roman taverns were now replaced by tin and wooden plates at the guesthouses. Guests brought their own wooden spoons, and later, metal knives and forks. Wealthy travellers had fine cutlery cases. There usually was not a great selection of what to eat. The meals were pre-set, as we see later in the *table d'hôte* culture. There were primitive and upmarket guesthouses and taverns, depending on the ambitions of their owners. But the real pioneering step into a cultured ambience came in the form of the restaurant in the nine-

Thermen und Gladiatorenkasernen. In den Quartieren der wohlhabenden Bevölkerung fehlten sie vollständig; in dieser Schicht war es verpönt, eine Taverne aufzusuchen.

> „Zur Straße hin waren die aus einem oder mehreren Räumen bestehenden Lokale offen und konnten nach Feierabend mit hölzernen Läden verschlossen werden. Zur Ausstattung zählte ein meist rechtwinkliger Schanktisch, der mit bunten oder weißen Marmorplatten verkleidet war. Oben waren Ausnehmungen für Wein bzw. Speisen eingelassen. Zu seinen Seiten fanden sich oft gemauerte, treppenartige Aufsätze, die dem Stapeln der Trinkgefäße dienten. Im Gastraum befanden sich je nach Standard Regale, Tische, Stühle, Klinen oder aber umlaufende Sitzbänke (Abb. 33, links). In kleineren Betrieben wurde im selben Raum gekocht, ausgeschenkt und gezecht. In größeren Gasthäusern gab es eigene Küchenräume und auch Latrinen. Die Wände waren meist mit Malereien versehen, deren Inhalt sich um Essen, Trinken und Gastlichkeit drehte.“ [106]

Vom Mittelalter (Abb. 33, mittig) bis ins frühe 19. Jahrhundert hinein glichen sich dann die einfachen Gasthöfe und entsprachen einem von Johann Wolfgang von Goethe 1779 beschriebenen Schweizer Gasthaus:

> „Es unterschied sich … von gewöhnlichen Gebäuden in nichts, als daß der große Raum mitteninne zugleich Küche, Versammlungsplatz, Vorsaal ist … Auf der einen Seite war an dem Boden auf steinernen Platten das Feuer angezündet, davor ein weiter Schornstein … In der Ecke waren die Türen zu den Backöfen, der ganze Fußboden übrigens gedielet … ringsherum, auch in der Höhe über den Balken, eine Menge Hausrat und Gerätschaften.“[107] (Abb. 33, rechts)

An die Stelle der in Rom üblichen Vertiefungen in den Schanktischen der Tavernen traten in den Gasthöfen Zinn- und Holzteller. Holzlöffel und später metallene Messer und Gabeln brachten die Gäste selbst mit. Wohlsituierte Reisende hatten kostbare Besteckketuis. Auswahlmöglichkeiten von Speisen gab es kaum. Ähnlich wie bei der späteren *table d'hôte* waren die Gerichte vorgegeben. Entsprechend der Ambitionen der Wirte gab es primitive und gehobene Gast- und Wirtshäuser. Den bahnbrechenden Schritt in ein kultivierteres Ambiente stellen

33

Thermopolium in Pompeii. Before being destroyed in 79 AD, the city of 20,000 inhabitants boasted more than 20 pubs and 120 wine inns ● *The landlord Jörg Starz*, from: *House Book of the Mendel's Twelve Brothers Foundation*, around 1450 ● *Italian eating establishment*, Johann Heinrich Meyer, around 1780

Thermopolium in Pompeji. Vor ihrer Zerstörung 79 n.Chr. verfügte die 20.000-Einwohner-Stadt über 20 Gasthäuser und 120 Weinlokale ● *Der Wirt Jörg Starz*, aus: *Hausbuch der Mendelschen Zwölfbrüderstiftung*, um 1450 ● *Italienisches Speisehaus*, Johann Heinrich Meyer, 1780er Jahre

teenth century. These eating establishments differed from their predecessors in that menu cards were provided, from which a variety of selected dishes could be enjoyed throughout the day with elegant service in beautifully decorated premises. The interior design and furnishings of the first gastronomic establishments at that time followed the prevailing predilection for classical models–Herculaneum and Pompeii were excavated in 1738 and 1748. Based on advice from art historians, philosophers, and encyclopaedias, the adaptation of antiquity became the fashion of the *Empire*. In German-speaking countries this gave birth to the *Biedermeier* style, and in England to the Regency stlye. From now on, the design of restaurants[108] would always be subject to respective style dictates: the style re-editions of Historicism, Jugendstil, Functionalism, and, in the 1950s, the Scandinavian formal canon (fig. 34). Even Futurism makes its appearance: in New York, Fortunato Depero designed the 'Zucca Ristorante'; in Barcelona, Catalan Modernismo can be seen in 'Els Quatre Gats', and in Vienna the secession (fig. 35).

Cult Cuisine

In the last quarter of the nineteenth century, not only did the number of restaurants increase, but they also took on different spatial dimensions to accommodate the increas-

dann erst Anfang des 19. Jahrhunderts die Restaurants dar. Sie unterschieden sich von den bisherigen Speisenanbietern durch eine auf Menükarten präsentierte Vielzahl ausgewählter Speisen, die man zu beliebigen Zeiten mit gepflegtem Service in aufwendig ausgestatteten Räumlichkeiten einnahm. Raumgestaltung und Möblierung der ersten gastronomischen Etablissements folgten dem damaligen Zeitgeschmack entsprechend klassizistischen Vorbildern – 1738 und 1748 waren Herculaneum und Pompeij ausgegraben worden. Vermittelt über Kunstwissenschaftler, Philosophen und die Enzyklopädie entwickelte sich die Adaptation der Antike zur Mode des Empire, im deutschsprachigen Raum zu der des Biedermeier und in England der des Regency.

Von nun an war die Ausgestaltung der Restaurants[108] stets den jeweiligen Stildiktaten unterworfen, den Stil-Re-Editionen des Historismus, dem Jugendstil, dem Funktionalismus und in den Fünfzigerjahren dem weitgehend von skandinavischen Gestaltern vorgegebenen Formenkanon (Abb. 34). Selbst der Futurismus verschafft sich Gehör: in New York gestaltet Fortunato Depero das Ristorante Zucca. In Barcelona meldet sich in Els Quatre Gats der katalanische Modernismo zu Wort, so wie in Wien die Sezession (Abb. 35).

ing number of guests. The types of rooms also diversified into main and auxiliary dining rooms, lounges, festivity rooms, and so on. Accordingly, the kitchens also grew in size, as did the pantry and storage rooms, the number of dishes, glasses, cutlery, and table linen. The kitchen is the 'cult site of prescribed laws, (where) the raw becomes civilised and nutritional goods (become) proper food',[109] writes Elias Canetti (fig. 36). Larger kitchens in particular—as they were to be found in the Grand Hotels—had to submit to a very precise system of logistics. Similar to the courtly and military traditions—Massialot spoke of the 'officiers de bouche'—the service and kitchen staff had to adhere to a strict dress code according to rank.

> 'Immediately in front of us, a group of black-clad waiters are standing at the pass (the long steel counter where orders are dispatched), gazing at the white-hatted chefs beyond, who worked with concentrated precision, apparently oblivious to the waiter's eyes trained on them. The "chef de cuisine" is also at the pass, barking out orders to his "brigade," who shout back without once looking up from their work. The military terminology is not misplaced. A professional kitchen at full throttle resembles nothing so much as an army unit under siege. Flames burst forth like mortar shells, faces are grim and determined, and tasks are carried out with soldier-like focus and urgency. Teamwork and discipline are vital in a kitchen such as this, since it is split into different sections ("parties"), each of which performs a different culinary function—hors d'oeuvres, sauces, roasting, grilling and so on—so that a miracle of co-ordination is required to assemble each dish at precisely the right moment.'[110]

Diversification in Typology

Restaurants, which in their early days had to satisfy a select clientele, now saw themselves confronted by a public rapidly growing in numbers. More and more international guests joined the local customers, because travel conditions (railway and steamship) had improved greatly. The restaurant as a building type is subject to the same laws as hotels and railway stations, which were increasingly oriented towards mass transit. If it was not upgraded, it was to be demolished. Pompous new buildings were replacing the architecture of the past. French haute cuisine restaurants also were no longer individual establishments, but were now often connected with hotels or railway stations. Before dining cars were established

Kultort Küche

Im letzten Viertel des 19. Jahrhunderts erhöhte sich nicht nur die Zahl der Restaurants, sondern diese erreichten mit dem Ansteigen der Gästezahl auch andere räumliche Dimensionen. Zudem diversifizierte sich das Raumangebot in Haupt- und Nebenspeisesäle, Salons, Festzimmer et cetera. Dementsprechend wuchsen auch die Küchen, die Räume für Vorratshaltung, Geschirr, Gläser, Bestecke und Tischwäsche. Die Küche ist der „Kultort mit festgeschriebenen Gesetzen, [wo] das Rohe zum Zivilisierten und der Nährstoffträger zum richtigen Essen [wird]"[109], schreibt Elias Canetti (Abb. 36). Vor allem größere Küchen, wie sie in Grand Hotels zu finden waren, mussten sich einer präzisen Logistik unterwerfen. Nach dem Vorbild höfischer und militärischer Gepflogenheiten – Massialot sprach von den „officiers de bouche" – war das Service- wie auch das Küchenpersonal gemäß seiner Rangordnung einer strengen Kleiderordnung unterworfen.

> „Immediately in front of us, a group of black-clad waiters are standing at the pass (the long steel counter where orders are dispatched), gazing at the white-hatted chefs beyond, who worked with concentrated precision, apparently oblivious to the waiter's eyes trained on them. The chef de cuisine is also at the pass, barking out orders to his ‚brigade' who shout back without once looking up from their work. The military terminology is not misplaced. A professional kitchen at full throttle resembles nothing so much as an army unit under siege. Flames burst forth like mortar shells, faces are grim and determined, and tasks are carried out with soldier-like focus and urgency. Teamwork and discipline are vital in a kitchen such as this, since it is split into different sections (parties), each of which performs a different culinary function – hors d'oeuvres, sauces, roasting, grilling and so on – so that a miracle of co-ordination is required to assemble each dish at precisely the right moment."[110]

34

ENGELHARDT
BAMBERGER-HOFBRAU
PILSNER
RESTAURANT LEUCHTTURM
ENGELHARDT-BRAU

35

36

34
The 'Turkish Tent' was one of Berlin's most popular restaurants in Charlottenburg during the nineteenth century ● Rosensaal-wine rooms in the 'Trarbach' restaurant. Architect: Richard Riemerschmid, photo from around 1905 ● Restaurant of the Engelhardt-Brewery, also called 'Lighthouse', near the S-Bahn station of Friedrichstrasse, Berlin. Architect: Rudolf Fränkel, 1930/31 ● Restaurant 'Giraffe' in Berlin-Tiergarten (Interbau 1957). Architects: Klaus Müller-Rehm and Gerhard Siegmann

Das Türkische Zelt war im 19. Jahrhundert eines der beliebtesten Ausflugsrestaurants in Charlottenburg bei Berlin ● Die Rosensaal-Weinstuben im Restaurant Trarbach, Architekt: Richard Riemerschmid, Foto um 1905 ● Das Restaurant Engelhardt-Bräu, auch Leuchtturm genannt, am S-Bahnhof Friedrichstraße, Berlin, Architekt: Rudolf Fränkel, 1930/31 ● Restaurant Giraffe im Berliner Tiergarten (Interbau 1957), Architekten: Klaus Müller-Rehm und Gerhard Siegmann

35
Restaurant 'Els Quatre Gats', Barcelona. Architect: Josep Puig i Cadafalch, 1895–1904 ● Great dining hall of the hotel 'Bristol' in Warsaw. Architect: Koloman Moser, 1901 ● Restaurant 'Zucca', New York. Architect: Fortunato Depero, 1930

Restaurant Els Quatre Gats, Barcelona, Architekt: Josep Puig i Cadafalch, 1895–1904 ● Großer Esssaal des Hotels Bristol in Warschau, Architekt: Koloman Moser, 1901 ● Restaurant Zucca, New York, Architekt: Fortunato Depero, 1930

36
Title of the German translation from 1542 of Bartholomaeus de Sacchi's *De honesta voluptate et valitudine*, 1474 ● Working areas of a kitchen, from: Florinus, *Oeconomus prudens et legalis*, around 1702 ● Kitchen of the hotel 'Suvretta House', St. Moritz Bad. Architect: Karl Koller, 1911/1912, photo from 1920

Titel der deutschen Übersetzung von 1542 von Bartholomäus de Sacchi *De honesta voluptate et valitudine*, 1474 ● Die Arbeitsbereiche der Küche, aus: *Florinus Oeconomus prudens et legalis*, um 1702 ● Küche des Hotels Suvretta House, St. Moritz Bad, Architekt: Karl Koller, 1911/1912, Foto 1920

Diversifizierung des Typus

Die Restaurants, die in ihrer Frühzeit eine ausgewählte Klientel zu befriedigen hatten, sahen sich einem stets wachsenden Publikum gegenüber. Zu den lokalen Gästen gesellte sich dank der durch Eisenbahn und Dampfschiff verbesserten Reisebedingungen eine Vielzahl auswärtiger Gäste. Als Bautypus unterliegt das Restaurant hier denselben Gesetzen wie die auf den zunehmenden Massenverkehr ausgerichteten Hotels und Bahnhöfe. Dort, wo nicht erweitert werden konnte, wurde abgerissen. An die Stelle von Vorgängerarchitekturen treten pompöse Neubauten. Auch tritt das Restaurant der französischen *haute cuisine* nicht mehr als Solitär auf, sondern nun häufig in Verbindung mit Hotels und Bahnhöfen. Bevor 1868 in den USA, später in Europa und ab 1880 in Deutschland Speisewagen eingesetzt wurden, war der Reisende auf die Restaurationsbetriebe in den Bahnhöfen angewiesen. In den Metropolen erobern diese sich auch nicht-bahnreisende Gäste: in Paris das Le train bleu im Gare de Lyon, das wie der Bahnhof selbst für die Weltausstellung des Jahres 1900 gebaut wurde; die von der Offizin Rafael Guastavino 1911–1913 entworfene Oyster Bar in New Yorks Grand Central Station oder das von

in trains in 1868 in the US—later in Europe and from 1880 in Germany—travellers had to rely on eating establishments in train stations. In large cities, these were besieged even by non-rail-travelling guests: in Paris at 'Le Train Bleu' at the Gare de Lyon, which was built for the Universal Exhibition of 1900, as was the train station itself; at the 'Oyster Bar' in New York's Grand Central Station, designed between 1911 and 1913 by Rafael Guastavino, or at the restaurant in Kazan Train Station, Moscow, designed by Aleksei Shchusev between 1913–1926 (fig. 37).

Combining a restaurant and a second cultural institution, such as a theatre or opera house, started very early on. The 'Königsstädtische Theater' built in Berlin between 1823 and 1824 was described as follows:

> 'On the ground floor, the patisserie and restaurant were located on both sides of the vestibule, the round room, and the foyer, and were easily accessible from inside and outside the theatre.'[111]

The three dining rooms in the original South Kensington Museum, known today as the Victoria and Albert Museum, were one early example of a restaurant integrated in a museum. 'The Green Dining Room' was designed by William Morris between 1865 and 1867 and was also one of the first important contracts for the company Morris, Marshall, Faulkner & Co. (fig. 38, left).[112] Expensive restaurants in museums, as well as snack food stands, are once again in vogue at, for instance, the MoMA in New York, the Musée d'Orsay in Paris, the Kunsthistorisches Museum in Vienna, or in the Rijksmuseum in Amsterdam. Moreover, the restaurant that opened in the latter in October 2014 is a theme restaurant that creates dishes to resemble Dutch and Flemish still lives of the seventeenth century (fig. 38, right).

The boundaries of the restaurant as a thing in itself began to blur as it fused with other institutions, but also as other genres started emerging, such as the café-restaurant, the brasserie, the bistro, and so on. Yet the public houses of the workers, the 'corner bars', remained unique to themselves: in England, the pubs, in France, *L'Assommoir*—also the title of the novel by Émile Zola[113]—and the distilleries in Germany, a favourite subject matter of the Berlin painter Heinrich Zille. The term 'restaurant' was more and more watered down and attached to other words like garden, terrace, view, journey, highway, airport, and so on.

37

Alexej Schtschussew 1913–26 im Kasaner Bahnhof in Moskau gestaltete Restaurant (Abb. 37).

Eine Kombination von Restaurants und anderen kulturellen Einrichtungen wie dem Theater oder der Oper setzt schon früh ein. So heißt es vom 1823/24 in Berlin erbauten Königsstädtischen Theater:

> „Im Erdgeschoß waren Konditorei und das Restaurant beidseitig von Vestibül, Rundraum und Foyer untergebracht und waren von innen wie außen hervorragend zugänglich."[111]

Eines der frühen Beispiele der Integration eines Restaurants in ein Museum sind die drei Speisesäle im ursprünglichen South Kensington Museum (heute Victoria and Albert Museum), wobei der „Green Dining Room" 1865 bis 1867 von William Morris entworfen wurde und einer der ersten wichtigen Aufträge für die Firma Morris, Marshall, Faulkner & Co. war[112] (Abb. 38, links). Hochpreisige Restaurants in Museen sind neben dem Snackverzehr heute wieder en vogue, sei es im MoMA in New York, im Musée d'Orsay in Paris, im Kunsthistorischen Museum in Wien oder im Rijksmuseum in Amsterdam. Dessen Ende Oktober 2014 eröffnetes Restaurant ist sogar ein Themenrestaurant, das seine Gerichte optisch an den flämischen Stillleben des 17. Jahrhunderts orientiert (Abb. 38, rechts).

Einerseits verwischen sich die Grenzen des Restaurants als einem im eigenen Recht bestehenden Ort durch

38

39

37

Restaurant of the Kasan railway station in Moscow, architect: Aleksei Shchusev, 1913–1916

Restaurant im Kasaner Bahnhof in Moskau, Architekt: Alexej Schtschussew, 1913–1916

38

'The Green Dining Room', Victoria and Albert Museum, London. Architect: William Morris, 1865–1867 ● The restaurant of the Amsterdam 'Rijksmuseum' uses Flemish still life motifs as a reference

The Green Dining Room im Victoria und Albert Museum London. Architekt: William Morris, 1865–1867 ● Das Restaurant im Amsterdamer Rijksmuseum orientiert sich mit seinen Gerichten an den flämischen Stillleben

39

Restaurant of the 'Minerva' hotel, Florence. Architect: Carlo Scarpa, 1958–1964 ● Restaurant and beer hall in Sapporo. Architect: Aldo Rossi, 1989

Restaurant im Hotel Minerva, Florenz, Architekt: Carlo Scarpa, 1958–1964 ● Restaurant und Bierhalle in Sapporo, Architekt: Aldo Rossi, 1989

40

41

"AL · PASSO · DI · S. GIACOM. PESCATORE
CONFORTO · SARÀ · IL · WAGRISTORATORE"

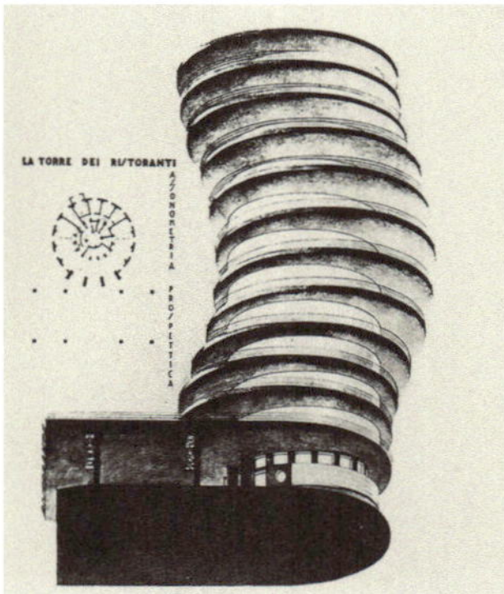
LA TORRE DEI RISTORANTI
ASSONOMETRIA

It stopped representing a specific character and began to pave the way for a certain arbitrary usage of the word.

Extravagant Designs

The flair—apart from a few exceptions—is lost. If the first surge of democratisation was from the royal court to the bourgeoisie, then after World War II the second was a surge towards mass culture, which also affected other leisure activities such as travelling. We have already discussed how restaurant design reflects style periods throughout the years. In addition to lesser-known designers, many famous architects also took on the task of designing restaurants: for instance, Carlo Scarpa in Modena in 1973, or Aldo Rossi in Sapporo in 1989 (fig. 39). Like all architectural genres, the restaurant can also result in extravagant fantastical designs that have been either fully or partially realised. Restaurants with a view are the most spectacular—the first of which, still in the style of the Belle Époque, opened on the Eiffel Tower in 1889. The revolving restaurant, which can be seen today on many television towers, we first see in 1932 in a design by the Danish architect Arne Jacobsen for a 'Bellevuetårn' (fig. 40, bottom left).[114] Panorama restaurants can be found near lakes and rivers and on mountain ranges like the Alps—for instance, the 'Glacier Paradise' of the Zermatt mountain railways at 3883 metres on the Kleines Matterhorn (fig. 40, top).[115]

A unique form of restaurant is one that extends out over a cliff to allow for a double-sided view, such as the complex that was designed by Maurice Braillard in

40

Restaurant 'Glacier Paradise' of the Zermatt mountain railway on Little Matterhorn at 3,883 meters. Architects: Peak 2009 ● Katarina elevator, Stockholm late 1930s. Architect: Olof Thunström ● Observation tower plus restaurant in Copenhagen's Bellavista quarter. Architect: Arne Jacobsen, 1932 ● Top terminal, hotel and cable railway 'Salève'. Architect: Maurice Braillart, 1931/32 ● Mooring and restaurant 'Vkhutemas'. Design by Nikolai Alexandrowitsch Ladowski, 1922

Das Restaurant Glacier Paradise der Zermatt Bergbahnen auf dem kleinen Matterhorn auf 3.883 Meter, Architekten: Peak, 2009 ● Katarina Aufzug, Stockholm, späte 1930er. Architekt: Olof Thunström ● Aussichtsturm mit Restaurant im Kopenhagener Bellavista, Architekt: Arne Jacobsen, 1932 ● Bergstation, Hotel und Restaurant der Luftseilbahn Salève, Architekt: Maurice Braillard, 1931/32 ● Anlegestelle und Restaurant Vchutemas, Entwurf von Nikolai Alexandrowitsch Ladowski, 1922

41

'Wagristoratore' at Swiss San Giacomo Pass at 2,300 metres. Architect: Piero Portaluppi, 1929 ● Lake restaurant. Architect: Walter Loos, 1945 ● Restaurant tower. Architect: M. Ridolfi, 1928

Wagristoratore am San Giacomo Pass auf 2.300 Meter, Architekt: Piero Portaluppi, 1929 ● Restaurant am See, Architekt: Walter Loos, 1945 ● Der Turm des Restaurants, Architekt: M. Ridolfi, 1928

die Verschmelzung mit anderen Institutionen, andererseits entstehen das Café-Restaurant, die Brasserie, das Bistro und andere Mischformen. Deutlich abgrenzen lassen sich die Schankgaststätten der Arbeiter, die sogenannten Eckkneipen: in England die Pubs, in Frankreich das *L'Assommoir* – so auch der Titel eines Romans von Émile Zola[113] – und in Deutschland die Destillen, ein Lieblingsmotiv des Berliner Malers Heinrich Zille. Die Bezeichnung „Restaurant" wird immer weiter verwässert und an Worte wie Garten, Terrasse, Aussicht, Ausflug, Autobahn, Flughafen et cetera angehängt. Er steht nicht mehr für einen bestimmten Ort mit spezifischem Charakter, sein Gebrauch unterliegt einer gewissen Beliebigkeit.

Extravagante Entwürfe

Das Flair ist – bis auf wenige Ausnahmen – verloren. Fand der erste sogenannte Demokratisierungsschub vom Hof zur Bourgeoisie statt, so ereignet sich der zweite nach dem Zweiten Weltkrieg als Bewegung hin zu einer Massenkultur, die auch andere Freizeitaktivitäten wie zum Beispiel das Reisen betrifft. Dass die Gestaltung des Restaurants die jeweiligen Stilepochen widerspiegelt, wurde bereits gesagt. Neben weniger bekannten Entwerfern nehmen sich auch berühmte Architekten wie zum Beispiel Carlo Scarpa 1973 in Modena oder Aldo Rossi 1989 in Sapporo dieser Bauaufgabe an (Abb. 39). Wie alle Baugattungen kennt auch das Restaurant extravagante, teilweise verwirklichte oder auch nicht realisierte, fantastische Entwürfe. Spektakulär sind vor allem Aussichtsrestaurants, dessen erstes – noch ganz im Stil der Belle Époque – sich seit 1889 auf dem Eiffelturm befindet. Dem sich drehenden Restaurant, das heute auf vielen Fernsehtürmen anzutreffen ist, begegnet man bereits 1932 in einem Entwurf des dänischen Architekten Arne Jacobsen für einen „Bellevuetårn" (Abb. 40, unten links).[114] Panoramarestaurants finden sich an Seen und Flüssen und in Berglandschaften wie den Alpen, wie beispielsweise das Glacier Paradise der Zermatt-Bergbahnen auf 3883 Metern am Kleinen Matterhorn (Abb. 40 oben).[115]

Eine Sonderform stellen über den Abgrund auskragende, beidseitige Aussichten ermöglichende Restaurants dar, wie der von Maurice Braillard 1931/1932 entworfene Komplex in Salève (Abb. 40, unten mittig).[116] Er gleicht auffällig dem 1935 in Stockholm eröffneten Restaurant Gondolen (Abb. 40, oben rechts).[117] Bei beiden assozi-

1931/1932 in Salève (fig. 40, bottom center).[116] It is strikingly similar to the restaurant 'Gondolen' (fig. 40, top right) that opened in Stockholm in 1935.[117] Both recall a Vkhutemas restaurant design from 1922 (fig. 40, bottom right),[118] and of course, Eleazar Markovich Lissitzky's 'Wolkenbügel.' The 'Wagristoratore,' built in 1929 at the Swiss San Giacomo Pass, also offered double-sided views. The name is indicative: railway wagons sat on top of concrete foundations (fig. 41, left).[119] Noteworthy is also the design by Walter Loos for Argentina of a restaurant as a bridge arch with its foundations in water (fig. 41, top right).[120] Mario Ridolfo designed a restaurant tower in 1928 that was developed from a circular shape (fig 41, bottom right)[121] and spirals upward over twelve stories in a jutting upward motion. All these restaurant types appeal above all to two senses: sight and taste, or to the enjoyment of eating. Restaurants with a view are about a more contemplative vision (fig. 42, left), but this changes when the view is directed at sporting events and the consumption of food becomes almost incidental. One example here is the restaurant at Wembley Stadium:

> 'The restaurant is located under the roof of an existing grandstand. It is about fifty-five metres long and consolidates the top nine rows of seats in the stands into three broader ranks, where tables are set each for four persons. This allows each guest to have an unobstructed view.'[122] (Fig. 42, right.)

The Berlin project for a restaurant on a mound of earth above a blown-up bunker can be traced back to a competition entitled 'Around the Zoo' from 1948. Sergius Ruegenberg and Günther Kühne presented their designs in 1954.

> 'The gently sloping hill would be accessible from the zoo area by means of the marina of the Landwehrkanal and a wide bridge. Via winding paths and stairways, a person on foot would be able to first reach a wide, partially covered observation deck and above that, the terraced restaurant on the top of the hill' (fig. 43, top).[123]

An 'archaeological site' as a park, designed by Jasper Halfmann and Clod Zillich, was supposed to be built in 1978 on the highest 'mountain' in Berlin, a post-war landfill in the western half of the city between Lübars and the residential satellite city 'Märkisches Viertel'. The 'garbage-

iert man einen Wchutemas-Restaurantentwurf von 1922 (Abb. 40, unten rechts)[118] und selbstverständlich Eleazar Markowitsch Lissitzkys Wolkenbügel. Den doppelseitigen Blick ermöglichte auch das 1929 am Schweizer San Giacomo Pass errichtete „Wagristoratore“. Der Name deutet es an: es handelte sich um auf Betonfundamente aufgeständerte Bahnwaggons (Abb. 41, links).[118] Beachtenswert ist auch der Entwurf eines für Argentinien als Brückenbogen im Wasser fundamentierten Restaurants von Walter Loos (Abb. 41, oben rechts).[120] Aus der Kreisform entwickelt ist der sich in zwölf Geschossen in einer abknickenden Spirale nach oben schraubende Restauranttturm von Mario Ridolfo von 1928 (Abb. 41, unten rechts).[121] Bei all diesen Restauranttypen kommen vor allen Dingen zwei Sinne zu ihrem Recht: das Sehen und der Essensgenuss. Ist es beim Aussichtsrestaurant ein beschauliches Sehen (Abb. 42, links), so verändert sich dies an Orten, wo der Blick auf sportliche Ereignisse gerichtet ist und die Nahrungsaufnahme nahezu zweitrangig wird. Ein Beispiel dafür ist das Restaurant im Wembley-Stadium.

> „Das Restaurant liegt unter dem Dach einer vorhandenen Zuschauertribüne. Es ist etwa 55 Meter lang und fasst die oberen neun Sitzreihen der Tribüne zu drei breiteren Rängen zusammen, auf denen Tische für je vier Personen stehen. Jeder Gast hat so eine ungehinderte Aussicht.“[122] (Abb. 42, rechts)

Das Berliner Projekt für ein Restaurant auf einem Schutthügel über einem gesprengten Bunker geht auf einen 1948 ausgelobten Wettbewerb „Rund um den Zoo“ zurück. 1954 stellt Sergius Ruegenberg zusammen mit Günther Kühne seine Entwürfe vor.

> „Über Bootsanlegestellen (am Landwehrkanal) und eine breite Brücke wäre der sanft ansteigende Hügel vom Zoobereich erreichbar gewesen. Die Fußgänger hätten über Serpentinen und Treppenanlagen zunächst eine breite, zum Teil überdachte Aussichtsplattform und darüber, auf dem Gipfel des Hügels, das terrassenförmig angelegte Restaurant erreichen können.“[123] (Abb. 43, oben)

Auf dem höchsten „Berg“ Berlins, einer Nachkriegs-Mülldeponie im Westen der Stadt zwischen Lübars und dem Wohnstadttrabanten Märkisches Viertel, sollte nach den Plänen von Jasper Halfmann und Clod Zillich

42

The Berlin transmission tower restaurant. Architect: Heinrich Straumer, 1926 ● Restaurant of Wembley stadium, London. Architect: Sir Owen Williams, 1922/23

Das Restaurant auf dem Berliner Funkturm, Architekt: Heinrich Straumer, 1926 ● Restaurant des Wembley Stadions bei London, Architekt: Sir Owen Williams, 1922/23

43

Restaurant on a rubble mountain in the Berlin Zoo grounds. Architect: Sergius Ruegenberg, 1954 ● 'Rubble-Casino/Schinkel Café'. Top of a Berlin garbage dump. Architects: Jasper Halfmann and Clod Zillich, 1978

Restaurant auf dem Bunkerberg auf dem Zoogelände in Berlin, Architekt: Sergius Ruegenberg, 1954 ● Müll-Casino/Schinkel-Café, Bekrönung einer Mülldeponie in Berlin. Architekten: Jasper Halfmann und Clod Zillich, 1978

Casino / Schinkel-Café' rises upward from the landfill like the capital of a Doric column. The notes mention a lift in a glass shaft which allows the guest to see the individual pieces of debris and thus have 'a real or illusionistic insight into the history of the reconstruction'(fig. 43, bottom).[124]

Quick Meals

Ultimately, the subject matter was always the restaurant, regardless of whether the discussion was of the *physiologie du gout*, the theories and practices of food preparation, the opulent display of feasts, or the place of upscale public food consumption. However, public consumption of food, even without protection from the elements, has a long tradition and is still common today.

Lunchtime in downtown Manhattan: small pushcarts rush out from streets all around to take position on plazas that are still half-deserted (fig. 44), and in no time at all, long lines form behind them. The spectrum of the food they have transported here is diverse: Chinese cuisine, fruits and juices, chili con carne, hot dogs, ice cream, beverages, vegetarian, and so on. Outside of peak hours you will find these carts on every street, mostly on the corners. They are a part of New York, in the same way that pineapple, mango, and fruit salads are sold on the streets of Bogotá, or how in autumn and winter in Paris you can buy the Maghrebins' roasted chestnuts and corn on the cob from converted shopping carts. Outside the metro stations in Moscow you can find small stalls offering baked potatoes with different sauces; in Copenhagen *pølser*; in London, fish and chips; in Berlin, *currywurst*; in Amsterdam, herring with onions.

Fast consumption of food on the road is an urban phenomenon that does not demand a commitment, such as the ceremony of being shown to a seat when visiting a restaurant, from the person eating. The mobile small traders and small kitchens, in a way the forerunners of the 'diner', are a global phenomenon and can be found on all five continents. An exhibition in 2012, 'Ma cantine en ville. Voyages au coeur de la cuisine de rue', on display in the former railway viaducts of the Paris 'Promenade plantée', which was used as a leisure and green space long before the new redevelopment of New York's 'High Line', gave an impression of the variety, functionality, and imagination of the micro-food vendors.[125]

Georg Friedrich Lichtenberg wrote in his 1775 *English letters* of the 'howling of those vendors at the corners

1978 als Ausflugspark eine „archäologische Grabungsstätte" entstehen. Als Kapitell einer dorischen Säule ragt das „Müll-Casino/Schinkel-Café" aus dem Müllberg. Die Erläuterungen erwähnen einen Fahrstuhl in einem gläsernen Schacht, der die Sicht auf die einzelnen Müllablagerungen freigeben sollte und somit „einen realen oder illusionistischen Einblick" in die Geschichte des Wiederaufbaus gegeben hätte (Abb. 43, unten).[124]

Schnelle Mahlzeiten

Von der *physiologie du gôut*, den Theorien und Praktiken der Essenszubereitung, der Zurschaustellung von Gastmählern und dem Ort der gehobenen öffentlichen Nahrungsaufnahme, kurz: vom Restaurant war die Rede. Aber auch die Nahrungsaufnahme in der Öffentlichkeit, und dies ohne eine vor dem Wetter schützende Räumlichkeit, hat eine lange Tradition und ist noch heute gebräuchlich.

Mittagszeit in Downtown Manhattan: Aus allen Straßen schießen kleine Karren auf die eben noch fast menschenleeren Plazas (Abb. 44). Schnell bilden sich an ihnen Schlangen. Das Spektrum ihres mitgeführten Speiseangebots ist vielfältig: Chinesisches, Früchte und Säfte, Chili con Carne, Frankfurter, Eis und Getränke, Vegetarisches .... Außerhalb der Stoßzeiten findet man die Karren auf allen Straßen, bevorzugt an Straßenecken. Sie gehören zum Straßenbild New Yorks wie die Ananas, Mango und Fruchtsalate verkaufenden Händler in den Straßen Bogotás. In Paris bieten im Herbst und Winter auf umgerüsteten Supermarktwagen Magrebins geröstete Maroni und Maiskolben an. In Moskau stößt man beim Verlassen der Metro auf Buden, die Pellkartoffeln mit unterschiedlichsten Soßen anbieten, in Kopenhagen werden Pølser, in London Fish and Chips, in Berlin Currywürste, in Amsterdam Hering mit Zwiebeln angeboten.

Der schnelle Verzehr auf der Straße ist ein städtisches Phänomen, das dem Essenden keine Verbindlichkeiten, wie zum Beispiel die Zeremonie des Platzanweisens beim Besuch eines Restaurants, abverlangt. Die mobilen Kleinsthändler und Kleinstküchen, quasi Vorläufer des „Diner", sind ein weltweites Phänomen und auf allen fünf Kontinenten anzutreffen. Eine 2012 in den Viadukten der Pariser „Promenade plantée", einer ausgedehnten ehemaligen Eisenbahntrasse, die lange vor der Umnutzung der New Yorker „High Line" als Freizeit- und

44
Street selling in Downtown Manhattan, Financial District, around 2000
Straßenverkauf in Downtown Manhattan, Financial District, circa 2000

of the alley in the hot and cold open air.'[126] Normally a customer looks for a restaurant, but street vendors needed to look for customers. Their favourite locations were bustling streets and squares, especially on market days and holidays, and this is where they loudly praised their merchandise. As suppliers of food and beverages before the introduction of stores, they were part of a variety of scenes involving mobile merchants, artisans, and showmen.[127] They have been depicted as *Kaufruf* (German for: market cry) illustrations that date back to the 1480s.[128] First summarised together on a sheet of paper, the *Kaufrufe* were made more individual in 1600 (fig. 45). As such, they provide insight into both national and historic eating habits (fig. 46). Mobile food was offered in Europe and North America well into the industrial age, and continues to be to this day also on other continents.

The Diner

'Into ... dull-streeted communities came the lunch wagon, its cheery light shining like a hospitable deed in a chilly world ... here met all sorts and conditions of men on democratic footing ... here gathered night workers with an hour to spend in eating and chatting, the night

Grünfläche neu genutzt wurde, gezeigte Ausstellung „Ma cantine en ville. Voyages au coeur de la cuisine de rue" vermittelte einen Eindruck von der Vielfalt, der Funktionalität und Phantasie der Mikro-Essensanbieter.[125]

Georg Friedrich Lichtenberg schreibt 1775 in seinen „Briefen aus England" von dem „Heulen derer, die an den Ecken der Gasse unter freiem Himmel Kaltes und Warmes feilhalten".[126] Ein Kunde sucht ein Restaurant auf, Straßenverkäufer aber mussten ihrerseits die Kunden aufsuchen. Belebte Straßen und Plätze, besonders an Markt- und Festtagen, waren ihre bevorzugten Standorte. Hier priesen sie lauthals ihre Ware an. Als Anbieter von Speisen und Getränken waren sie vor der Einführung von Ladengeschäften Teil einer Vielzahl ambulanter Händler-, Handwerker und Schaustellerszenen.[127] Ihre bildliche Darstellung gehört in den Bereich der sogenannten „Kaufruf"-Grafik, die bis auf die 1480er Jahre zurückgeht.[128] Die vorerst noch auf einem Blatt zusammengefassten Kaufrufe werden dann um 1600 individualisiert (Abb. 45). Als solche vermitteln sie einen Einblick sowohl in nationale wie auch historische Essgewohnheiten (Abb. 46). Noch weit in das Industriezeitalter hinein wird Essen in Europa und Nordamerika

45

'Oyster seller', Jean Le Clerc, ca. 1600 ● 'Vendor of sorbet', sixteenth century ● 'Vendor of baked apples and pears', Bologna, 1660 ● 'Egg-cream vendor', Paris, ca. 1737 ● 'Vendor of licorice water', Paris, 1774 ● 'Vendor of rice jelly', Constantinople, 1799

Austern-Verkäufer, Jean Le Clerc, ca. 1600 ● *Sorbet-Verkäufer*, 16. Jahrhundert ● *Bratäpfel- und Birnenverkäufer*, Bologna 1660 ● *Eiercreme-Verkäuferin*, Paris, ca. 1737 ● *Lakritzwasser-Verkäufer*, Paris 1774 ● *Reissülze-Verkäufer*, Konstantinopel 1799

46

'Oyster seller', Naples, 1825 ● 'Dumpling vendor', Vienna, 1844 ● 'Coffee stand', Charles Hunt, London, 1881 ● 'Vendor of hot gingerbread', London, 1804 ● 'Caviar vendor', St. Petersburgh, 1809 ● 'Vendor of hot rolls', Russia, 1830s ● 'Woman roasting chestnuts', Lisbon, 1819 ● 'Roast chestnut vendor', Paris, Henri de Toulouse-Lautrec, 1897 ● 'Roast chestnut vendor', Paris, 2013

Austern-Verkäufer, Neapel 1825 ● *Knödel-Verkäuferin*, Wien 1844 ● *Ein Kaffeestand*, Charles Hunt, London 1881 ● *Verkäufer heißer Pfefferkuchen*, London 1804 ● *Kaviar-Verkäufer*, St. Petersburg 1809 ● *Verkäufer von heißen Brötchen*, Russland 1830er Jahre ● *Maronirösterin*, Lissabon 1819 ● *Maroni-Verkäufer*, Paris, Henri de Toulouse-Lautrec, 1897 ● *Maroni-Verkäufer*, Paris 2013

owl who sought sustenance before turning in and he who had no place into which he might turn. Often were found in the company dingy men … who could spout Homer in his own tongue; could discuss philosophies … in the lunch wagon atmosphere one might hear the views of the men on the street on the vital questions—anything and everything … here gathered the satirist, the humourist, raconteur, and over a post-prandial cup of coffee offered leisurely contribution to the discussion.'[129]

This apt characterisation of a diner was published on the occasion of the death of Samuel Messer Jones in 1926, under the title 'A Gallery of Night Owls' in the *New York Times Magazine*. Samuel Messer Jones was the person who, in 1884, first introduced the walk-in dining car on a street in Worcester (Massachusetts). 'Seven people could perch on stools in relative comfort, for others there was standing room.'[130] Since 1872, food had only been served from the wagon but eaten outside. In the same year, Walter Scott travelled the streets of Providence (Rhode Island), for the first time with his horse-drawn lunch cart, equipped with windows and a roof that offered goods mainly at night. Until this time, street food had been sold from handcarts. The system of 'passing over the counter' was born, as would become typical of fast food chain restaurants. In contrast to the mass production of these chain restaurants, Scott's food was 'homemade'—which could also be clearly read on the sign on his cart. 'For my chicken sandwich … I bought the best of native birds and cooked them under the best conditions.'[131] Nevertheless, his merchandise was affordable: for a nickel you could get a ham and butter sandwich with a boiled egg or a piece of fruit cake. Scott, who died in 1917 at the age of seventy-six, rightly claimed, 'I guess I've done my share in putting the night lunch on the map.'[132]

In the meantime, these vehicles, which at that point still looked like the wagons of the great American trek westward, were constantly being improved. The discarded railway carriages, which people had been already converting for reuse for some time, were followed by the professional and specific production of 'walk-in lunch wagons'. Conversely, in 1891 in Worcester, Charles H. Palmer announced his patent for the 'Night Lunch Wagons': 'The Owl' and the 'Fancy Night Café' (fig. 47, top left). The three units were each separated according to function into kitchen, counter, and dining room, and were arranged to make optimal use of space (fig. 47, top centre).

– und bis heute noch auf anderen Kontinenten – ambulant angeboten.

Der Diner

„Into … dull-streeted communities came the lunch wagon, its cheery light shining like a hospitable deed in a chilly world … here met all sorts and conditions of men on democratic footing … here gathered night workers with an hour to spend in eating and chatting, the night owl who sought sustenance before turning in and he who had no place into which he might turn. Often were found in the company dingy men … who could spout Homer in his own tongue; could discuss philosophies … in the lunch wagon atmosphere one might hear the views of the men on the street on the vital questions – anything and everything … here gathered the satirist, the humourist, raconteur, and over a post-prandial cup of coffee offered leisurely contribution to the discussion.“[129]

Diese treffende Charakterisierung eines Diners findet sich anlässlich des Todes von Samuel Messer Jones 1926 unter dem Titel „A Gallery of Night Owls“ im *New York Times Magazine*. Samuel Messer Jones war derjenige, der 1884 den ersten begehbaren Speisewagen auf einer Straße in Worcesterr (Massachusetts) einführte. „Seven people could perch on stools in relative comfort, for others there was standing room.“[130] Seit 1872 wurde aus dem Lunchwagen lediglich serviert, gegessen aber wurde im Freien. In diesem Jahr war Walter Scott zum ersten Mal auf den Straßen von Providence (Rhode Island) mit seinem pferdegezogenen, mit Fenstern versehenen und überdachten „Lunch Cart“ unterwegs, der vor allem des Nachts seine Ware anbot. Bislang waren für den Straßenverkauf von Esswaren Handkarren benutzt worden. Das System des „Durchreichens“, wie es dann typisch für Fast-Food-Kettenrestaurants werden sollte, war geboren. Im Unterschied zu den Massenprodukten dieser Kettenrestaurants jedoch war Scotts Devise – wie auf seinen Wagen zu lesen war – „home made“. „For my chicken sandwich … I bought the best of native birds and cooked them under the best conditions.“[131] Dennoch war seine Ware preisgünstig: für einen Nickel – fünf Cent – konnte man ein Schinken-, ein Butterbrot mit einem gekochten Ei oder ein Stück Obstkuchen bekommen. Scott, der 1917 76-jährig starb, konnte mit Recht von sich sagen „I guess I've done my share in putting the night lunch on the map.“[132]

Despite the limited in cooking facilities, the menus were extended to include greater variety. Moreover, several vendors now assembled entire fleets of these 'wagons'. The most successful was Tom H. Buckley, who, between 1893 and 1898 on the basis of an early franchising process, had 'lunch wagons' located in more than 275 cities. As a former wagon builder himself, he began producing snack wagons in 1892 while developing a catering system. These elements would evolve to become the fast-food chain.

Compared with the simple, functional design of early snack wagons, Buckley had his 'White House' series lavishly decorated. There were colourful hunting scenes, marine pictures, and historical motifs on an opal white background, framed by blue and gold cartouches. This made the outside of the 'wagons' look rather like circus wagons and less like eating establishments (fig. 47, top right). But the insides looked more like quirky art historical cabinets—most likely in an attempt to imitate the restaurants of the Parisian *Belle Époque*—with coloured glazing, bevelled mirrors, tiles, and bronze and silver sculptures and cash registers rather imitating art cabinets (fig. 47, bottom centre and right). Probably precisely because of this ornate variety of decorative detail, they also enjoyed the popularity that Buckley had hoped for. They advertised themselves, but they also served other propaganda purposes as well. For instance, the Buckley wagons were also used for the purpose of conversion. The Temperance Movement in New York offered cheap meals in eight of these dining cars in conjunction with educational activities.[133] Twenty-five people could be served meals at the same time either in front of factory gates or at mass events.

The mobile snack carts may have been able to travel to their customers, but ultimately they could not compete with stationary restaurants and were ultimately forced to settle at fixed locations. In order to attract customers, they advertised their round-the-clock opening times: 'Always open', 'We Never Close', 'Open Day and Night'. Patrick Tierney coined the term 'diner' as a replacement for 'lunch wagon' in New York State. His intention was to copy a railway dining car (fig. 48, top) and bring back the classic atmosphere of the Pullman railway car 'with lengthy counters with stools along one wall and booths along the other, enlarged kitchen, storage spaces and toilet facilities'.[134] Water, gas, and sewage systems made this possible. In the 1930s, these 'deluxe diners' also appear on the highways where they were like a beacon of light against the darkness of night for travellers (fig. 48, top right). Today

In der Zwischenzeit waren die anfangs noch an die Wagen der großen amerikanischen Trecks nach Westen erinnernden Gefährte stets verbessert worden. Der ebenfalls seit geraumer Zeit praktizierten Umnutzung ausrangierter Eisenbahnwaggons folgte die professionelle und spezifische Herstellung von „Walk-In-Lunch-Wagons".

Wiederum in Worcester meldet 1891 Charles H. Palmer seine Patente für „Night Lunch Wagons" – „The Owl" und „Fancy Night Cafés" (Abb. 47, oben links) an. Die drei voneinander separierten Funktionseinheiten Küche, Tresen und Essraum waren aufs raumökonomischste angeordnet (Abb. 47, oben mittig).

Trotz dieser kochtechnischen Einschränkungen wird das Angebot erweitert. Mehrere Anbieter bauen nun ganze Flotten solcher „Wagons" auf. Am erfolgreichsten ist Tom H. Buckley, der zwischen 1893 und 1898 auf der Basis eines frühen Franchising-Verfahrens in mehr als 275 Städten seine „Lunch Wagons" zu stehen hat. Als ehemaliger Wagenbauer hatte er seit 1892 mit der Produktion von Imbisswagen begonnen und parallel dazu ein Cateringsystem entwickelt. Hier sind bereits die Elemente der späteren Fast-Food-Ketten vorweggenommen.

Im Vergleich zum einfachen, funktionalen Design der frühen Imbisswagen ließ Buckley speziell seine „White-House"-Serie üppig dekorieren. Auf opalweißem Grund fanden sich, von blau-goldenen Kartuschen gerahmt, farbige Jagdszenen, Marinebilder und historische Motive. So glichen die „Wagons" von außen eher Zirkuswagen (Abb. 47, oben rechts) als solchen, in denen gegessen werden sollte. Innen erinnerten sie – wohl die Restaurants der Pariser Belle Époque imitierend – mit Farbverglasungen, facettierten Spiegeln, Kacheln und bronzenen wie versilberten Skulpturen und Kassen eher an skurrile kunsthistorische Kabinette (Abb. 47). Wohl gerade wegen dieser Schmuck- und Dekorationsvielfalt erfreuten sie sich dann auch der von Buckley angestrebten Beliebtheit. Sie dienten als Werbeträger in eigener Sache, kamen darüber hinaus aber auch anderen Propagandazwecken zugute. So wurden die Buckley-Wagen auch zum Zwecke der Bekehrung eingesetzt. In acht solcher Speisewagen bot in New York die Temperance-Bewegung in Verbindung mit Aufklärungsaktivitäten billige Mahlzeiten an.[133] 25 Personen konnten zum Beispiel vor Fabriktoren oder bei Massenveranstaltungen gleichzeitig bedient werden.

47

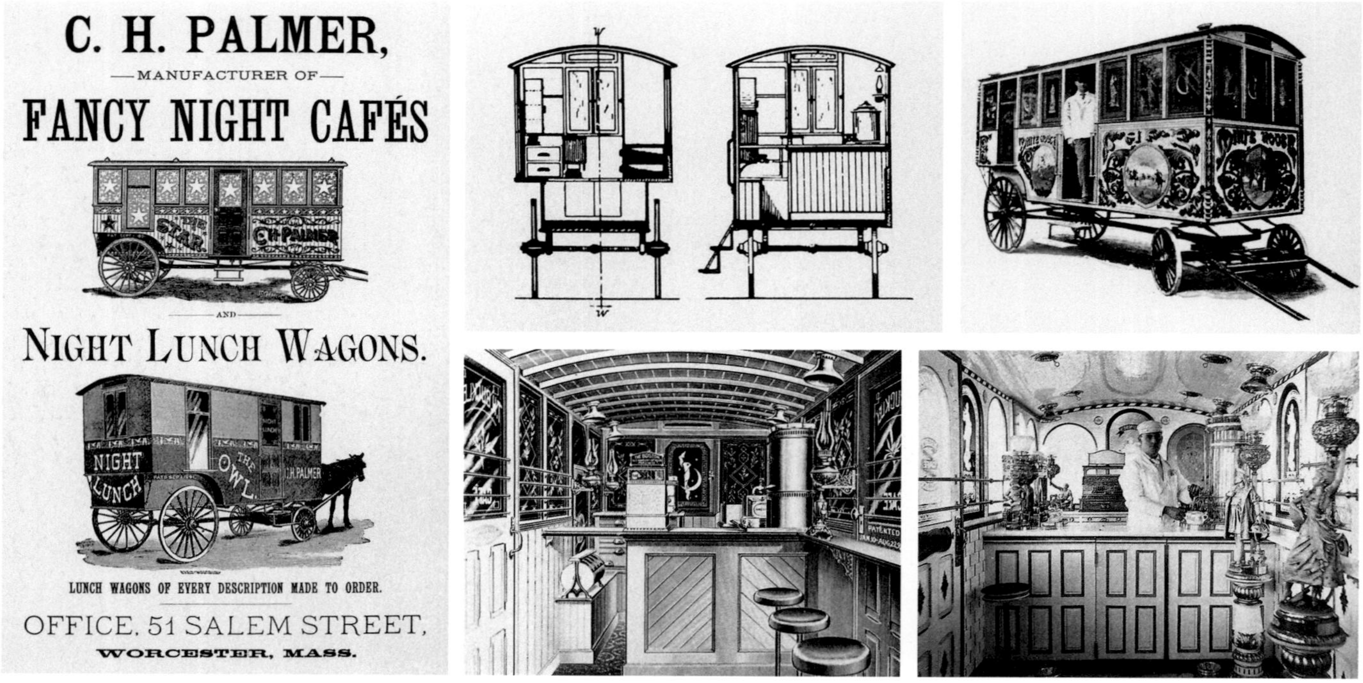

a dining car from the Orient Express serves as a dining room for the restaurant 'Wagon Bleu' in Paris.[135]

The initially real mobility of the original 'lunch wagons' now became the illusion of speed. The high-speed train served as a metaphor for motion and the guarantee of fast service, and suggested that the visitor could eat here in a hurry—which is why locomotives were chosen as design motifs. The owner of the 'Sterling Streamliner' in Philadelphia brought this to a climax when he installed the kitchen in an actual tunnel, from which the train—aka diner—was to shoot out (fig. 48, bottom right).

Diners—especially Buckley's—also alluded to the luxury of the Pullman dining car. Both presented an interior architectural challenge posed by the need for spatial economy. The idea of constant coming and going in their design reflects the fact that food consumption for Americans had become more of a necessity than a pleasure. The Art Deco style of Raymond Loewy's streamline shaped diner of the late 1920s and early 1930s became a metaphor for American culture up until the mid-1950s (fig. 49, top left).

Die mobilen Imbisswagen mit ihrer Möglichkeit, sich zum Kunden zu bewegen, konnten aber dem Druck der ortsfesten Restaurants nicht standhalten und wurden gezwungen, sich an festen Standorten niederzulassen. Um weiterhin attraktiv zu bleiben, warben sie mit ihren durchgehenden Öffnungszeiten: „Always open", „We never close", „Open day and night". Die Bezeichnung „Diner" wurde als Ersatz für „Lunch Wagon" von Patrick Tierney im Staat New York geprägt. Seine Intention war es, einen Eisenbahn-Speisewagen zu kopieren (Abb. 48, oben links) (*railroad dining car*) und die klassische Atmosphäre des Pullman-Eisenbahnwagens wiederaufzunehmen: „with lengthy counters with stools along one wall and booths along the other, enlarged kitchen, storage spaces and toilet facilities".[134] Wasser-, Gas- und Kanalisationsanschluss ermöglichten dies. In den 1930er Jahren erscheinen diese „Deluxe Diners" auch an den Überlandstraßen, wo sie in der Nacht dem Autofahrer entgegenleuchteten (Abb. 48, oben rechts). Heute dient in Paris ein Speisewagen des „Orient Express" dem Restaurant „Wagon bleu" als Räumlichkeit.[135]

48

'The diner came to symbolise a kind of commonplace theatre. Author Joseph Manzo described breakfast at the typical diner as follows: "A cacophony of sounds, smells and sights would start the customer's day. The rattling of cups and the rustling of newspapers mixed with the chatter of customers, snappy talking waitresses and a manager greeting people provided the backdrop for the diner's food."[136] The cook juggled orders at the grill, performing a kind of ballet. Waitresses scurried to refill coffee cups

47

'Night Lunch Wagons' from the firm of C.H. Palmer, Worcester, 1889 ● The economic disposition of a 'Night Lunch Wagon' ● A 'Buckley Lunch Wagon', 1890s ● Interiors of 'Buckley Lunch Wagons'

„Night Lunch Wagons" der Firma C.H. Palmer, Worcester 1889 ● Die ökonomische Einrichtung eines „Night Lunch Wagon" ● Ein „Buckley Lunch Wagon", 1890er Jahre ● Interieurs von „Buckley Lunch Wagons"

48

'Diners' in a stationary position ● A 'Streamline Diner' with eating space in the wagon and kitchen in the simulated tunnel mouth

Diners, stationär aufgestellt ● Ein „Streamline Diner" mit Essbereich im Wagenteil und der Küche im simulierten Tunnelmund

Die ursprünglich ja tatsächlich gegebene Mobilität der „Lunch Wagons" wird zu einer Illusion von Geschwindigkeit ausgebaut. Der Hochgeschwindigkeitszug dient als Metapher für Schnelligkeit und soll rapiden Service garantieren sowie eine kurze Verweildauer suggerieren. Bevorzugt werden deshalb Lokomotiven als Gestaltungsmotive gewählt. Auf einen Höhepunkt bringt es der Besitzer eines „Sterling Streamliner" in Philadelphia. Die Küche installiert er in einem Tunnel, aus dem der Zug – alias Diner – hervorschießen sollte (Abb. 48, unten rechts).

Angespielt wird bei den Diners – speziell denen von Buckley – auch auf den Luxus der Pullman-Speisewagen, beider Raumökonomie stellte eine innenarchitektonische Herausforderung dar. Mit dem Motiv des ständigen Kommens und Gehens spiegeln sie die Tatsache, dass Essen für die Amerikaner eher eine notwendige Nahrungsaufnahme denn ein Genuss ist.

Speziell die im Sinne des Art-déco-Stils eines Raymond Loewy stromlinienförmig gestalteten Diner der späten 1920er und frühen 1930er Jahre werden bis in

49

50

EAT
DINER
EMPIRE
DINER

51

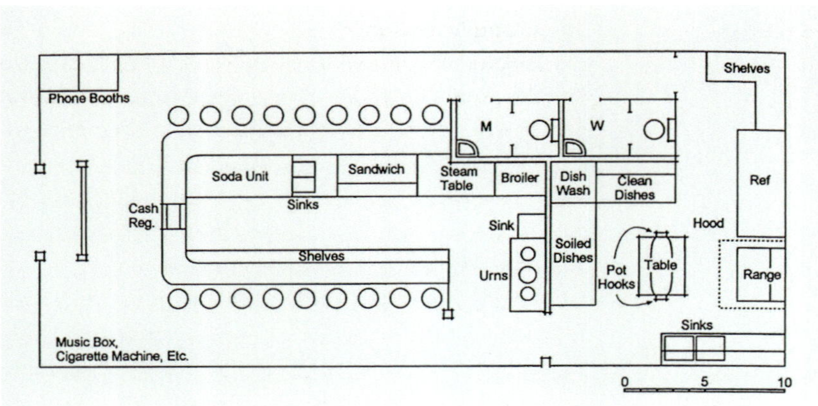
Phone Booths
Shelves
M
W
Soda Unit
Sinks
Sandwich
Steam Table
Broiler
Dish Wash
Clean Dishes
Ref
Cash Reg.
Sink
Hood
Shelves
Soiled Dishes
Urns
Pot Hooks
Table
Range
Sinks
Music Box, Cigarette Machine, Etc.
0
5
10

when not delivering plates or cleaning away dishes. The smell of coffee and frying bacon permeated the air. At the counter sat business proprietors, construction workers, clerks and truck drivers—a cross-section of America, the nation's democratic ideals apparently validated.'[137]

'Most diners placed employees and customers in almost intimate proximity.'[138] Like all types of restaurants, diners reflect the social contexts in which they are embedded. As places of everyday processes of socialisation, political activists have seen them as platforms for action. 'When African-Americans set about to confront segregation laws, they organised sit-ins at lunch counters.[139] As a typical phenomenon of the 'American Way of Life,' and having been spawned from it, diners appear in a variety of American motion pictures—for example, Barry Levinsons 1982 film 'Diner.' The New York 'Empire Diner' (fig. 50)[140] in West Chelsea has been used as a set location in several films including Woody Allen's 'Manhattan' (1979) and Barry Sonnenfeld's 'Men in Black' (1997). It has been operating under the name 'Highliner' since 2011.

'Soda Fountains'

Another precursor of the quick-service establishment is the 'soda fountain'. In France and Italy the *limonadier* and *limonadières* were first heard of as early as the seventeenth century, and their stores were often the starting points for coffee houses.[141] In the United States in 1837, Eugene Roussel, a perfumer in Philadelphia, mixed carbonated water with syrups of different flavours, and with that invented the soda fountain. A specialty of soda fountains was the development of new beverage variations such as 'birch beer', 'pepsin', 'ginger ale', 'sarsaparilla', and so on. Robert Green's combination of ice cream and soda water from 1874 can most likely be traced back to what the Italians called *sorbetto*, which was a translation from the Arab

49
Art Deco design in diners
Art déco Design im Diner

50
The 'Empire Diner', today the ,High Liner', in New York
Der Empire Diner, heute der Highliner in New York

51
Ground plan of a 'Luncheonette' with its typical U-shaped eating counter
Grundriss einer Luncheonette mit der typischen U-förmigen Esstheke

die Mitte der 1950er zu Aushängeschildern amerikanischer Kultur (Abb. 49, links oben).

> „The diner came to symbolize a kind of commonplace theatre. Author Joseph Manzo described breakfast at the typical diner as follows: 'A cacophony of sounds, smells and sights would start the customer's day. The rattling of cups and the rustling of newspapers mixed with the chatter of customers, snappy talking waitresses and a manager greeting people provided the backdrop for the diner's food.'" [136] „The cook juggled orders at the grill, performing a kind of ballet. Waitresses scurried to refill coffee cups when not delivering plates or cleaning away dishes. The smell of coffee and frying bacon permeated the air. At the counter sat business proprietors, construction workers, clerks and truck drivers – a cross-section of America, the nation's democratic ideals apparently validated."[137] „Most diners placed employees and customers in almost intimate proximity."[138]

Wie alle Typen von Restaurants spiegeln Diners die sozialen Zusammenhänge, in die sie eingebettet sind. Als Orte des alltäglichen Sozialisierungsprozesses haben politische Aktivisten sie als Handlungsräume gesehen. „When African-Americans set about to confront segregation laws, they organized sit-ins at lunch counters."[139] Als typisches Phänomen des „American way of life" und aus ihm erwachsen, tauchen die Diners in einer Vielzahl amerikanischer Spielfilme auf, so in Barry Levinsons *Diner* von 1982. Spezifisch der New Yorker „Empire Diner"[140] (Abb 50) in West Chelsea ist in vielen Filmen Schauplatz, so unter anderem in Woody Allens *Manhattan* (1979) oder Barry Sonnenfelds *Men in Black* (1997). Seit 2011 firmiert er als „Highliner".

„Soda Fountains"

Ein anderer Vorläufer der Quick-Service-Etablissements sind die „Soda Fountains". In Frankreich und Italien sind die „Limonadier" und „Limonadières" seit dem 17. Jahrhundert bekannt, oft wurden ihre Ladengeschäfte zum Ausgangspunkt von Kaffeehäusern.[141] In den Vereinigten Staaten mischt 1837 der Parfümhändler Eugene Roussel in Philadelphia kohlensäurehaltiges Wasser mit Sirup unterschiedlicher Geschmacksrichtungen und kreiert damit die „Soda Fountains". Eine Spezialität der „Soda Fountains" war die Entwicklung von neuen Getränkevariationen wie „Birch Beer", „Pepsin", „Ginger Ale",

sherbet. As early as the 1660s, the *limonadier* Francesco Procopio dei Coltelli served sorbets; in 1686 he founded the famous Parisian café 'Procope'. John S. Pemberton, a chemist in Atlanta, Georgia, invented a unique American beverage creation. He flavoured sugar syrup with cola leaves and cola nut extract. Diluted with soda water, it was sold to the public as 'Coca-Cola'.[142] Backed by aggressive advertising, it developed throughout the decades into a worldwide synonym for an American beverage 'culture'. By 1908, there were no less than 75,000 'soda fountains' located in drugstores and candy stores or in shops of their own. In the early 1880s they began offering light dishes, mainly sandwiches, and equipped their stores with counters at which customers could sit. This was the birth of the 'Luncheonette' (fig. 51). 'Lunch grabbed on the fly', is what they called fast food that was always available.

> 'It's time for lunch. The streets are filling up again. In New York nobody goes home for lunch: One eats locally, either in the office, at work (as mentioned above, on the street) or in clubs or cafeterias. In the popular restaurants thousands of people eat, hat on head, in a row, as in a stall, otherwise fresh and appetising looking food at a much lower price than ours. They pounce on platefuls of meatball, while others are already waiting to take their place'

reported the Frenchman Paul Morand in 1930.[143] The mealtime no longer seems to exist for its own sake. It is not defined and certainly not ritualised, and more than everything else, food seems to be consumed in much haste. In other words, criticism of the hasty meal that consisted of coffee, soft drinks, and sandwiches was increasing in the 1920s. 'Good meals … are rapidly supplanted by sugary concoctions of the soda jerker's ingenuity.' Such was the opinion of the doctor Paul Morand, continuing:

> 'This indiscreet eating with almost a total lack of exercise, now features the life of the average businessman. Up at eight in the morning; a hasty breakfast, ride downtown in an automobile; a ten minute lunch, of miscellaneous sugary drinks in the quick lunch or drug store, back to the office, home in an automobile—they call that a day. The consequences are indigestion, bad nerves, decaying teeth, restless nights and cutting down the span of life.'[144]

The 75,000 soda fountains listed statistically in 1908 also promoted themselves in their own magazines.[145] In

„Sarsaparilla" und Ähnlichem. Robert Greens Kombination aus Eiscreme und Sodawasser aus dem Jahre 1874 geht wohl auf das von den Italienern „Sorbetto" genannte arabische „Scherbet" zurück. Bereits in den 1660er Jahren servierte der Limonadier Francesco Procopio dei Coltelli Sorbets, er wurde 1686 zum Begründer des berühmten Pariser Cafés Procope. Eine eigenständig amerikanische Getränkeschöpfung gelang dann dem Drogisten John S. Pemberton aus Atlanta. Er aromatisierte Zuckersirup mittels Kolablättern und Kolanussextrakt. Mit Sodawasser verdünnt war damit die „Coca-Cola" auf den Markt gebracht.[142] Unterstützt durch aggressive Werbung, wurde sie im Laufe der Jahrzehnte weltweit zu einem Synonym amerikanischer Getränke-Kultur. Bereits 1908 gab es, in eigenen Ladengeschäften oder in Drugstores und Süßwarengeschäften untergebracht, nicht weniger als 75.000 „Soda Fountains". Seit dem Beginn der 1880er Jahre boten sie leichte Gerichte, vor allem Sandwiches, an und statteten ihre Lokalitäten mit Tresen aus, an denen man sitzen konnte. Dies war die Geburtsstunde der „Luncheonette" (Abb. 51). „Lunch grabbed on a fly", so wird das jederzeit schnell verfügbare Essen charakterisiert.

> „Es ist Zeit für das Mittagessen. Die Straßen füllen sich wieder. In New York geht niemand mittags nach Hause: Man ißt vor Ort, entweder in den Büros, bei der Arbeit (wie bereits erwähnt, auf der Straße) oder in den Clubs oder Cafeterias … In den populären Restaurants verschlingen tausende Menschen, den Hut auf dem Kopf, in einer Reihe aufgestellt, wie in einem Stall, ansonsten frisch und appetitlich aussehende Speisen zu einem viel geringeren Preis als bei uns. Sie stürzen sich auf Teller voll mit Fleischbällchen, während hinter ihnen bereits andere auf ihren Platz warten",

berichtet 1930 der Franzose Paul Morand.[143] Die Essenszeit scheint nicht mehr für sich selbst zu bestehen. Sie ist nicht abgegrenzt und schon gar nicht ritualisiert und vor allem scheint die Essensaufnahme unter Zeitdruck zu stehen. So mehrten sich bereits in den 1920er Jahren die Kritiken an dem hastigen aus Kaffee, „softdrinks" und Sandwiches bestehenden Essen. „Good meals … are rapidly supplanted by sugary concoctions of the soda jerker's ingenuity." Der eben zitierte Mediziner Morand fährt dann fort:

how far the name is meant to be a subliminal reference to drinking spring water at spas remains unclear. In any case, the word 'fountain' is derived etymologically from the Latin *fontana*[146] and the French *fontaine*. Such spa treatments had been known since antiquity and, in Paris, were very fashionable in the 1830s. Passy and Auteuil possessed numerous artesian wells, whose water was also sold in bottles in pharmacies.[147] The alchemists of beverage production experimented further: to this day, the trend of marketing stylish drinks continues unabated. 'Ice tea' also became one of these drinks. The World Fair in St. Louis in 1904 contributed to this drink's fame when an East Indian tea merchant distributed tea cooled with ice during the unusual heat wave. Before the Unilever-owned Lipton tea company manufactured instant 'iced tea' in powdered form in 1972, another multinational food company, Nestlé, had already offered the powdered 'Nestea' as early as 1948.

Main Street Restaurants, Cafeterias, and Automated Restaurants

In fact, 'Main Street restaurants' do not necessarily belong in the category of quick-service culture. But they are worth mentioning in this context because of their quick service and limited menu.[148] Much like *Kneipen* in Germany, French bistros (the latter being, as a rule, expensive), pubs and inns in Britain, bars in Italy, or *bodegas* in Spain, they are all places of social contact and thus comparable to the 'diner'.

> 'Dad was in his element in a place like this. He liked to "josh" the waitress; he knew all kinds of comic things to say, funny names for things to eat. He would order his eggs "sunny side up" or "with their eyes open", please…'[149]

wrote Upton Sinclair in his novel *Oil!* This is a totally different atmosphere to the night mood that Edward Hopper portrays in his famous painting *Nighthawks*.

Cafeterias, however, do not have any service personnel, which introduced the principle of self-service.[150] 'Emulating the factory assembly line, customers pushed trays along elongated counters as they moved along.'[151] After taking a tray and cutlery, hungry guests would be tempted by desserts, salads, entrees, and drinks before they loaded their tray with other dishes. Sliding a tray along a counter located beneath the food on display is still characteristic of canteens and cafeterias, as well as muse-

> „This indiscreet eating with almost a total lack of exercise, now features the life of the average businessman. Up at 8 in the morning; a hasty breakfast, ride downtown in an automobile; a ten minute lunch, of miscellaneous sugary drinks in the quick lunch or drug store, back to the office, home in an automobile – they call that a day … The consequences are indigestion, bad nerves, decaying teeth, restless nights and cutting down the span of life."[144]

Die 1908 in der Statistik aufgeführten, bereits erwähnten 75.000 „Soda Fountains" aber propagierten ihre Existenz in eigenen Zeitschriften.[145] Inwieweit die Namensgebung unterschwellig und werbewirksam hier auf das Trinken von Brunnenwasser in Kurorten verweisen soll, bleibt eine Vermutung. Etymologisch leitet sich *fountain* ohnehin vom lateinischen *fontana*[146] und der französischen Benennung ab. Das Kuren war seit der Antike bekannt und in Paris ab den 1830er Jahren große Mode. Passy und Auteuil verfügten über eine Vielzahl artesischer Brunnen, deren Wasser abgefüllt auch in Apotheken verkauft wurde.[147] Die Alchimisten der Getränkeherstellung experimentierten weiter: bis zum heutigen Tag ist die Tendenz, Trendgetränke auf den Markt zu bringen, ungebrochen. Zu einem solchen Getränk avancierte auch der Eistee. Zu seiner Bekanntheit trug die Weltausstellung in St. Louis von 1904 bei, wo ein ostindischer Teehändler bei ungewöhnlicher Hitze mit Eis heruntergekühlten Tee ausschenkte. Bevor der zum Unilever-Konzern gehörende Teehändler Lipton 1972 „iced tea" in pulverisierter Form trinkfertig anbot, hatte der andere multinationale Lebensmittelkonzern, Nestlé, 1948 bereits den Pulvertee „Nestea" auf den Markt gebracht.

Main Street Restaurants – Cafeterias – Automatenrestaurants

Eigentlich gehören die Main Street Restaurants nicht unbedingt in die Kategorie der Quick-Service-Kultur. Ausschließlich ihr schnell zu servierendes und auf einer wenig umfangreichen Speisekarte beruhendes Essensangebot gestattet eine Erwähnung in diesem Zusammenhang.[148] Ähnlich wie Kneipen in Deutschland, Bistros in Frankreich – dort neuerdings im Hochpreis-Niveau –, Pubs und Inns in Großbritannien, Bars in Italien oder Bodegas in Spanien sind sie Orte sozialer Kontaktaufnahme und gleichen somit dem amerikanischen Diner.

52

53
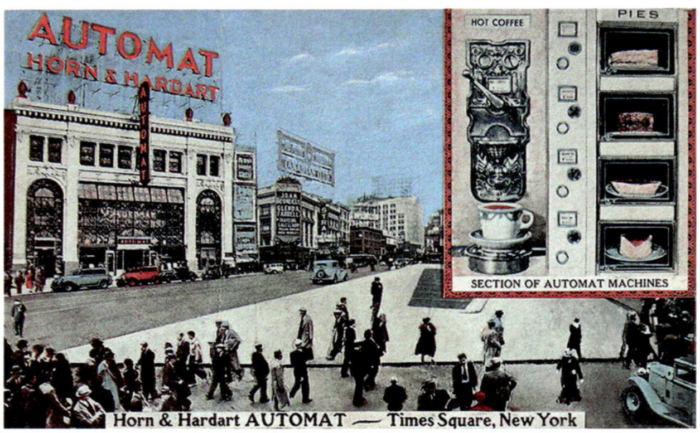

52
One of the first electrified automated restaurants in Berlin, end of the nineteenth century ● The new branch. Architect: Bruno Schmitz, 1905

Eines der ersten elektrischen Automatenrestaurants in Berlin, Ende des 19. Jahrhunderts ● Die neue Filiale, Architekt: Bruno Schmitz, 1905

53
The automated restaurant 'Horn and Hardart's' in New York's Times Square, 1939

Das Automatenrestaurant Horn and Hardart's am Times Square in New York, 1939

um snack restaurants. This makes the category of cafeteria, as self-service restaurant, far less personal than that of the diner, luncheonette, or the 'Main Street restaurant'. Yet the absolute least personal of all is the now almost obsolete automated restaurant.

As early as 1900/01, there was a restaurant on Leipziger Strasse in Berlin called 'Automat'. It was operated by the Berlin entrepreneur Silaff, who ran similar restaurants in other cities and exported the idea to New York in 1902. The first Berlin branch was located behind a neo-Gothic façade (fig. 52, top left). The second location on Friedrichstrasse was designed by Bruno Schmitz in 1904/05 in ornate *Jugendstil* (fig. 52, top right). Auto-

> „Dad was in his element in a place like this. He liked to ‚josh' the waitress; he knew all kinds of comic things to say, funny names for things to eat. He would order his eggs ‚sunnyside up' or ‚with their eyes open', please",[149]

schreibt Upton Sinclair in seinem Roman *Oil!*. Dies ist eine gänzlich andere Atmosphäre als die nächtliche, die Edward Hopper in seinem berühmten Gemälde *Nighthawks* einfängt.

Ohne Servierpersonal kommen dagegen die Cafeterias aus, mit denen das Prinzip der Selbstbedienung ins Spiel kam.[150] „Emulating the factory assembly line, customers pushed trays along elongated counters as they

mated restaurants and department stores both tried to evoke a new type of consumer attitude. The automated restaurant opened in 1902 by 'Horn & Hardart's' in Philadelphia is hence—as often wrongly assumed—not really a genuine American invention. Even a Swedish model has been cited. 'Borrowed was an idea previously perfected in Sweden for dispensing food through banks of small windows.'[152] Sandwiches, salads, desserts, and so on were placed behind glass windows that would open when a coin was inserted. Depending on the size of the automated restaurant, there would be between thirty[153] and over one hundred such glass dispensers arranged along the walls. Diners ate mostly at round bistro tables. Many American celebrities commented on 'Horn & Hardart's', located on New York's Times Square. Gregory Peck said, 'I have always thought that the Automat in New York has the best scrambled eggs in the world,' and Woody Allen: 'I went to the Automat all the time. I grew up going to the Automat. And its food was wonderful'.[154] (fig. 53)

In the 1920s and 1930s, the bar-, automated-, buffet- and vending machine restaurants experienced a heyday. The Parisian restaurant which Leo Faust commissioned De Stijl artist and architect Piet Zwart to design was given the name 'machine à manger'. Zwart was to design the architecture, interior design, and menu card as a corporate design.[155] Everything was to look very practical and stark: the 'crank mechanism of a mirrored window borrowed from a car, service as fast as in the dining car of a train', said Zwart. 'Chez Leo Faust' was not just a place for the Dutch in Paris. The renowned photographer André Kertész took portrait photos of the guests at the opening, among whom were Piet Mondriaan, Michel Seuphor, the above-mentioned Curnonsky and Rouff, food critic and novelist, Adolf Loos, Willi Baumeister, the Italian Futurist Enrico Prampolini, and Piet Zwart himself.[156]

The effect of a *machine à manger* was then driven to a cruel climax in Charlie Chaplin's film 'Modern Times' from 1936, in which a worker is almost force-fed by a machine.

Chain Restaurants

'You get the same clean, appetizing food at Childs as at any cafeteria or automated restaurant ... Childs is a byword for inexpensive food in America ... Anywhere in New York you can say: let's eat at Childs, and they will never be more than a ten-minute walk away',

moved along".[151] Nach der Entgegennahme von Tablett und Besteck wurde der hungrige Gast durch Desserts, Salate, Entrées und Getränke in Versuchung gebracht, bevor er sein Tablett mit anderen Gerichten belud. Das Tablettschieben auf einem unterhalb der zur Schau gestellten Esswaren durchlaufenden Bord charakterisiert noch heute Kantinen und Mensen, aber auch Museums-Snackrestaurants. Der Typus Cafeteria als Selbstbedienungsrestaurant ist somit weit unpersönlicher als Diner, Luncheonette oder das Main Street Restaurant. Am unpersönlichsten aber waren die heute weitestgehend verschwundenen Automatenrestaurants.

Bereits 1900/01 gibt es in Berlin in der Leipziger Straße ein Restaurant namens Automat. Eigentümer ist der Berliner Unternehmer Silaff, der gleichartige Restaurants auch in anderen Städten betrieb und die Idee 1902 nach New York exportierte. Die erste Berliner Filiale verbirgt sich hinter einer neogotischen Fassade (Abb. 52, oben links). Der zweite Standort in der Friedrichstraße ist, entworfen von Bruno Schmitz 1904/05, in materialaufwendigem Jugendstil gehalten (Abb. 52, oben rechts). Automatenrestaurants versuchen wie die Kaufhäuser ein neues Konsumentenverhalten zu evozieren. Das 1902 von Horn & Hardart's in Philadelphia eröffnete Automatenrestaurant ist somit – wie oft unterstellt – keine genuine amerikanische Erfindung. Auch ein schwedisches Vorbild wird angeführt. „Borrowed was an idea previously perfected in Sweden for dispensing food through banks of small windows".[152] Hinter aufklappbaren Glasscheiben waren belegte Brötchen, Salate, Desserts et cetera platziert, deren Freigabe durch den Einwurf einer Münze geschah. Je nach Größe eines Automatenrestaurants waren entlang der Wände etwa 30 bis über 100 Fächer[153] angeordnet. Gegessen wurde meist an runden Stehtischen. Das am New Yorker Times Square gelegene Horn & Hardart's vereinigt auf sich die Kommentare vieler amerikanischer Berühmtheiten. So schreibt Gregory Peck „I have always thought that the Automat in New York has the best scrambled eggs in the world", und Woody Allen: „I went to the Automat all the time. I grew up going to the Automat. And its food was wonderful."[154] (Abb. 53)

In den 1920er und 1930er Jahren erleben die Bar-, Automaten- und Büffetrestaurants eine Blütezeit. Eine „machine à manger" wird das von Leo Faust beim De-Stijl-Künstler und -Architekten Piet Zwart 1926 in Auftrag gegebene Pariser Restaurant genannt. Zwart soll-

reported Ilya Ilf and Yevgeni Petrov to Moscow in 1935.[157] The uniformity of these restaurants, with their over one hundred branches in the 1920s, often situated at busy locations in the immediate vicinity of a subway station, were designed specifically for a high level of recall factor by their uniform shop fronts. There were separate entrances for the bar and restaurant. The customer was either served by 'waitresses in white dresses', or they got their food themselves. William and Samuel Childs had opened their first restaurant on the ground floor of the Merchant's Hotel in New York in 1899, before founding, in 1908, the 'tray-line' that was typical of the above-mentioned cafeterias.[158] All the steps needed for the end product of a meal were centralised. Suppliers, processors, and staff were all components in a rationally structured system. The unique aspect of the Childs' restaurant chain was the employment of predominant architects. The Childs, of course, had their trademark show window, but their architect of over thirty years, John Corley Westerveld, was responsible for the elongated restaurants, always situated at a right angle to the street. Also involved were William van Alen, the architect of the Chrysler Building, and the École des Beaux Arts-influenced bigshots McKim, Mead & White, who designed many New York buildings including the Municipal Building, the Metropolitan Museum, Pennsylvania Station, and the Columbia University campus.

Aschinger

In Berlin, the brothers August and Karl Aschinger—one originally a cook, the other a waiter—also understood the valuable role architecture played in the recall factor of their restaurants. Every additional restaurant built during their early expansion phase was an exact replica of their first eating establishment, founded in 1892.[159] In the Prussian metropolis, their trademark of Bavarian cosy hospitality was blue-white rhombuses (fig. 54, top). By 1901 they had as many as thirty locations in Berlin.

> 'Long before their immense expansion during the Weimar era, the giant of the German gastronomy sector demonstrated that making a commercial venture out of dining away from home and aligning this with market principles was not only viable, but could find a wide resonance among the urban population.'[160]

To entice customers, food was arrayed appetizingly behind shop windows so that it could be seen from the

te Architektur, Inneneinrichtung und Speisekarten als Corporate Design entwerfen.[155] Alles sollte äußerst praktisch und sachlich sein, dem „Kurbelmechanismus eines Autos entlehnte Spiegelfenster, eine schnelle Bedienung wie im Speisewagen", so Zwart. Chez Leo Faust war nicht nur ein Ort für Niederländer in Paris. Der renommierte Fotograf André Kertész hat die zur Eröffnung geladenen Gäste porträtiert, unter denen sich Piet Mondriaan, Michel Seuphor, Curnonsky und Rouff, Gastrokritiker und Romanschriftsteller, Adolf Loos, Willi Baumeister, der italienische Futurist Enrico Prampolini und Piet Zwart selbst befanden.[156]

Auf einen grausamen Höhepunkt wird die Idee einer „machine à manger" dann in Charlie Chaplins Film *Modern Times* von 1936 getrieben, wo ein Arbeiter per Maschine quasi zwangsernährt wird.

Kettenrestaurants

> „Bei Childs erhält man das gleiche saubere, appetitliche Essen wie in der Cafeteria oder aus dem Automaten … Childs ist in Amerika ein Inbegriff für preiswertes Essen … An jedem beliebigen Ort in New York kann man sagen: lass uns bei Childs essen, und man wird nicht länger als zehn Minuten zu laufen haben,"

berichten Ilja Ilf und Jevgeni Petrow 1935 nach Moskau.[157] Die in den 1920er Jahren über 100 Filialen, an publikumsreichen Standorten, oft in unmittelbarer Nähe von U-Bahnstationen gelegen, sollten sich durch einheitliche Geschäftsfronten einprägen. Bar und Restaurant hatten getrennte Zugänge. Weißgekleidete Kellnerinnen bedienten oder man holte sich sein Essen selbst. 1908 begründeten William und Samuel Childs, die 1899 im Erdgeschoss des Merchant's Hotel in New York ihr erstes Restaurant eröffnet hatten, die für die erwähnten Cafeterias typische „tray-line".[158] Alle für das Endprodukt einer Mahlzeit notwendigen Schritte waren zentralisiert. Zulieferer, Verarbeiter und Personal waren Teile eines rationell durchstrukturierten Systems.

Außergewöhnlich bei Childs war die Heranziehung tonangebender Architekten. Zwar hatten die Childs ihre immer gleichen markenzeichenartigen Schaufenster, aber ihr Kontaktarchitekt über 30 Jahre, John Corley Westerveld, engagierte für die langgestreckten, stets im rechten Winkel zur Straße gelegenen Gaststätten unter anderem William van Alen, den Architekten des Chrysler Building, und die an der École des Beaux-Arts orien-

street. This turned the dishes into a displayed commodity. 'Aschinger' restaurants had large shop windows, and, similar to the shop windows of department stores and retail outlets, they were specifically intended to animate customers to consume (in this case, to eat) their products. In addition to beverages, the first restaurants of this chain marketed exclusively cold dishes, with the Berlin *Schrippe* with *Hackepeter* being its most popular dish.[161] Later, the offer was extended to include other varieties of filled bread rolls. Eventually hot items were added, such as 'baby peas with bacon, roast goose with applesauce, or beer sausages with salad'.[162] They were mind-reading exactly what Berliners wanted to eat.

> 'Everything at 'Aschinger' "tasted like Mama made it"; they counted on the Berlin palate, and when the corporate group began selling oysters, it was also a success.'[163]

The restaurant's 'all you can eat' Berliner *Schrippe*, free of charge, became the 'Aschinger' legend and trademark. Incidentally, as early as the 1830s, Honoré de Balzac mentions free bread *à discretion* at the legendary Parisian student restaurant 'Flicoteaux'.[164]

The combination of reliable, consistent dishes together with an affordable price was the major key to success. In order to save money on tipping, customers could even get their own food and drinks themselves from a counter. Pricing and standardisation were in line with industrial large-scale operations. At 'Aschinger', certain goods for consumption were produced in their own industrial-sized kitchens (fig. 54, bottom). They had their own meat and sausage production as well as a soda water factory with a daily production of 20,000 bottles. In 1900 they built a large bread factory that was expanded in 1912[165]—which was the year 'Aschinger' also went on the stock exchange. Rolls, pretzels, and cheese sticks were delivered not only to the restaurant outlets, but also to baked goods stores operated by 'Aschinger'.

> 'Aschinger' has a large cafe and restaurant. If you don't have a paunch you can get one there, and if you do, it can be enlarged as desired. Nature does not cheat! Those who think they can use artificial additives to improve bread and baked goods made from devalued white flour are fooling themselves and their customers. Nature has its natural laws and avenges every abuse. Our failing health has its origins in the consuming of devalued and artificially

tierte Groß-Offizin McKim, Mead & White, zu deren zahlreichen New Yorker Bauten das Municipal Building, das Metropolitan Museum (Seitenflügel), die Pennsylvania Station sowie der Campus der Columbia University gehörten.

Aschinger

In Berlin setzten die Brüder August und Karl Aschinger – der eine ursprünglich Koch, der andere Kellner – ebenfalls auf den Wiedererkennungseffekt ihrer Restaurantarchitektur. Alle Restaurants der frühen Expansionsphase waren eine Nachbildung der ersten Speisewirtschaft von 1892.[159] Ihr Markenzeichen bayerischer Gemütlichkeit in der preußischen Metropole waren die blau-weißen Rauten (Abb. 54, oben). Bereits 1901 hatten sie in Berlin 30 Lokale.

> „Lange vor seiner gewaltigen Expansion zu Weimarer Zeiten stellte der Gigant des deutschen Gastronomiegewerbes unter Beweis, daß die Speisung außer Haus kommerziell betrieben und nach marktwirtschaftlichen Prinzipien ausgerichtet, nicht nur lebensfähig war, sondern breiteste Resonanz bei der großstädtischen Bevölkerung finden konnte."[160]

Die von der Straße aus zu sehenden, appetitlich hinter Schaufenstern aufgereihten Speisen stellten den verlockenden Anreiz dar. Die Speisen wurden somit zu einer zur Schau gestellten Ware. Aschingers großflächig durchfensterte Geschäftsfronten sollten ähnlich wie die Schaufenster der Warenhäuser und Einzelhandelsgeschäfte zum Konsum – hier zum Verzehr – animieren. Die ersten Restaurants der Kette vermarkteten neben Getränken ausschließlich Speisen der kalten Küche, in deren Zentrum die Berliner „Schrippe mit Hackepeter" stand.[161] Später wurde das Angebot um weitere Sorten belegter Brötchen erweitert. Dann kamen auch warme Speisen hinzu wie zum Beispiel „Löffelerbsen mit Speck, Gänsebraten mit Apfelmus oder Bierwürste mit Salat".[162] Sie lasen den Berlinern ihre Gaumenwünsche quasi von den Lippen ab.

> „Alles bei den ‚Aschingern' schmeckte ‚wie bei Muttern', sie verließen sich auf die Berliner Zunge und als der Konzern dazu überging, auch noch Austern zu verkaufen, wurde es ebenfalls ein Erfolg".[163]

54
A branch of the Berlin 'Aschinger' chain in Leipziger Strasse, around 1936 ● Female workers in an 'Aschinger' central kitchen

Ein Restaurant der Berliner Kette Aschinger in der Leipziger Straße, ca. 1936 ● Arbeiterinnen in einer Aschinger Großküche

> refined foods. Fine sausages, also to take away, cheap liver sausage, and black pudding…'[166]

writes Alfred Döblin. Today's mass production of mainly inferior bread products, whether by 'Paul' in France, 'Kamps' in Germany, or any of many other chains, is among the many negative consequences of the industrialisation of the food industry. Sigfried Giedion was one of the first to question the consequences of the industrialisation of food production (FIG. II).

> 'In the 1930s, Aschinger was Europe's largest restaurant and hotel group, a company that owned more than one hundred cafes, hotels, bars, restaurants, and pastry shops and employed several thousand people.'[167]

Das freie Brötchen, die Berliner Schrippe als unbegrenzt und gratis zu verzehrendes Angebot der Restaurants wurde zu einer Legende und zum Markenzeichen für Aschinger. Bereits in den 1830er Jahren erwähnt übrigens Honoré de Balzac das kostenfreie Brot „à discretion" in dem legendären Pariser Studentenrestaurant Flicoteaux.[164]

Ein Schlüssel zum Erfolg waren diese verlässlichen, gleichbleibenden Gerichte sowie deren Preisgünstigkeit. Um das Trinkgeld zu sparen, konnte man sich das Essen und die Getränke auch selbst von der Theke holen. Preiskalkulation und Standardisierung fußten auf dem Prinzip industrieller Großbetriebe. Bei Aschinger stellte man die zum Verzehr bestimmten Waren in Großküchen selber her (Abb. 54, unten), übernahm Fleisch- und Wurstfabriken in eigene Regie und betrieb eine Selterwasserfabrik mit einer täglichen Abfüllung von 20.000 Flaschen. 1900 baute man eine bereits 1912 erweiterte gigantische Brotfabrik.[165] In diesem Jahr ging Aschinger auch an die Börse. Brötchen, Brezeln und Käsestangen wurden nicht nur an die Restaurantfilialen, sondern auch in von Aschinger betriebene Ladengeschäfte für Backwaren geliefert.

> „Aschinger hat ein großes Café und Restaurant. Wer keinen Bauch hat, kann einen kriegen, wer einen hat, kann ihn beliebig vergrößern. Die Natur läßt sich nicht betrügen! Wer glaubt, aus entwertetem Weißmehl hergestellte Brote und Backwaren durch künstliche Zusätze verbessern zu können, der täuscht sich und die Verbraucher. Die Natur hat ihre Lebensgesetze und rächt jeden Mißbrauch. Der erschütterte Gesundheitszustand hat seine Ursache im Genuß entwerteter und künstlich verfeinerter Nahrung. Feine Wurstwaren, auch außer dem Haus, Leberwurst und Blutwurst billig",

schreibt Alfred Döblin.[166] Die heutige Massenproduktion von meist minderwertigen Brotwaren, sei es durch „Paul" in Frankreich oder „Kamps" in Deutschland oder andere Ketten, gehört zu den vielen negativen Folgen der Industrialisierung der Lebensmittelindustrie. Als einer der Ersten hat Sigfried Giedion die Folgen der Industrialisierung der Nahrungsmittelproduktion hinterfragt (FIG. II).

> „In den 1930er Jahren war Aschinger Europas größter Restaurant- und Hotelkonzern, ein Unternehmen,

By 1905, 'Aschinger' had opened fifty branches in Berlin. Because the first 'Mitropa' dining cars did not appear in Germany until 1916, 'Aschinger' also had branches at Berlin's railway stations. Today, it is customary to see national and international fast-food chains located on the concourses and on station platforms.

'Aschinger' restaurants were initially located in the city centre, but branches were later opened in the working-class districts of the northern and eastern parts of the city. In the establishments in the centre different types of customers mingled, creating an equalisation of societal levels that took place as employees, public servants, office staff, male and female workers, businesspeople, and students came together to eat and drink in the same place (fig. 55). After World War II, in 1947, all of the 'Aschinger' branches in Berlin's Soviet sector were nationalised. In West Berlin only a handful of branches survived in, for instance, Neukölln, or 'Aschinger' at Zoologischer Garten. Even at the beginning of the 1970s, when the first 'McDonald's' outlets appeared on the gastronomy scene in Berlin, 'Aschinger' was still offering Berlin cuisine along with their famous free bread roll.[168] A French version of a low cost restaurant was 'Bouillon', which appeared in Paris at the second half of the nineteenth century (FIG. III).

The Franchising System in Catering

In the 1950s, licensing or 'franchising' became the basis for the emergence of the first American, and then global, fast food chains. Organised centrally, as was the case in the early stages with Buckley, licenses were awarded that granted the licensee the right to sell and market products or product lines in exchange for a license fee based on sales volume. The first licensor in America for the preparation and sale of prepared foods was 'A&W' root beer stands in 1924, followed by Howard Johnson in 1935 with the licensing of ice cream and other food products. The first franchise restaurant in the 'Dairy Queen' chain was opened in 1944. This chain of ice cream parlours was aimed at nationwide branches and by 1948 had opened a total of 2,500.[169] In the late 1930s, the 'Boy Hamburger' chain appeared. 'Burger King' followed in 1954, renamed from the original ineffective name of 'Justaburger', along with 'Kentucky Fried Chicken'. Today, the fast-food chains 'Burger King' and 'McDonald's' are criticised because of the trans-fatty acids contained in their burgers. The weight component of fat-absorbing batter is especially high in chicken nuggets. This is not even a piece

dem über hundert Cafés, Hotels, Bars, Restaurants und Konditoreien mit mehreren Tausend Beschäftigten angehörten.[167]

1905 bereits gab es in Berlin 50 Aschinger-Dependancen. Da es in Deutschland erst ab 1916 Mitropa-Speisewagen gab, unterhielt Aschinger auch auf den Berliner Bahnhöfen Filialen. Heute gehören Schnellrestaurants nationaler und internationaler Ketten in Bahnhofshallen und auf Bahnsteigen zur Normalität.

Aschingers Restaurants waren zunächst in der Innenstadt zu finden, erst später dehnte sich die Kette in die Arbeiterbezirke des Nordens und Ostens aus. In den Etablissements des Zentrums mischten sich die Kunden, die Klassengesellschaft mischte sich, wenn Angestellte, Beamte, Büropersonal, Arbeiter und Arbeiterinnen, Geschäftsleute und Studenten sich zum Essen und Trinken hier einfanden (Abb. 55). Nach dem Zweiten Weltkrieg wurden 1947 alle Aschinger-Betriebe in Berlins sowjetischem Sektor verstaatlicht. In West-Berlin überlebten nur wenige Filialen wie zum Beispiel in Neukölln oder Aschinger am Zoologischen Garten. Noch zu Beginn der 1970er Jahre, als in Berlin die ersten McDonald's-Filialen auf der Gastronomiebühne erschienen, bot Aschinger die Berliner Küche inklusive der berühmten kostenlosen Brötchen an.[168] Eine französische Variante eines preisgünstigen Restauranttyps waren ab der zweiten Hälfte des 19. Jahrhunderts die Pariser „Bouillons“ (FIG. III).

Das Franchising-System in der Massengastronomie

In den 1950er Jahren wird die Lizenzvergabe, das „Franchising“, zur Basis für das Entstehen erster amerikanischer und dann auch weltweit agierender Fast-Food-Ketten. Zentral organisiert, wie das bereits in einer frühen Phase bei Buckley der Fall war, wurden Lizenzen vergeben, die dem Lizenznehmer das Recht einräumten, Produkte oder Produktreihen gegen eine am Umsatz orientierte Lizenzgebühr zu übernehmen. Die ersten Lizenzgeber für die Zubereitung und den Verkauf fertiger Speisen in Amerika waren 1924 die „A&W“-Kräuterbierstände. 1935 folgte Howard Johnson mit der Lizenzvergabe für Speiseeis und andere Lebensmittel. Das erste Franchise-Restaurant der Kette Dairy Queen wurde im Jahr 1944 eröffnet. Diese Kette von Eissalons versuchte, auf landesweiter Ebene Fuß zu fassen und eröffnete bis zum Jahr 1948 insge-

Production of Bread

'Before mechanization, the fragrance of bread was of utmost importance … to increase production, carbon dioxide was then added to the dough instead of slow-working yeast.' 'Since the mid-nineteenth century, when chemicals such as gypsum, alum and sulphate of copper were used to make bread weightier or whiter and to compensate for bad quality of flour'.

The development of breadmaking from handicraft to fully mechanized assembly belt production is clear-sightedly analyzed by Sigfried Giedion in *Baking for Profit*. Perceptively, he describes the loss of quality from the individual product to uniform mass production. 'Contrary to the hand-kneaded bread, the fully mechanized product has reached the elasticity of a rubber sponge: when deformed, it inevitably returns to its original shape.' 'It seems like the consumer's need adapts more and more to that brand of bread (or every kind of food specimen) that accommodates most perfectly mass production and most rapid turnover.'

Sigfried Giedion: *Mechanization Takes Command. A Contribution to Anonymous History*, Oxford 1948, p. 169–208

FIG. II

Bouillon, a French Variety

As early as 1867 Baptiste-Adolphe Duval and his wife Ernestine, who in 1854 established their first Bouillon-restaurant in the centre of Paris, introduced wholesale buying for their French chain restaurants 'Bouillon Duval'. The 'Compagnie anonyme des Établissements Duval' had organized their direct buying in La Vilette, 'les Halles' and the wine cellars of Bercy, shortcutting any intermediate trade. Later, a proper Bordeaux wine production, a central slaughterhouse, as well as a central dairy was added. Part of the whole system was also mineral water production as well as the roasting of coffee. In the morning and at noon one baked bread under one's own direction. A steam laundry washed table linen and the personnel's clothing. A company-owned copper works produced pots and pans. A fleet of vehicles cared for supply for the fifteen subsidiaries in 1881 with their 1200 employees. This centrally organized operating as well as supply system [similar to the way, 'Aschinger' in Berlin worked] offered economic repasts. Another typical trait of 'Bouillon Duval' was the system of cashing up. When entering the restaurant, every customer was handed a menu card with price quotations. The dishes ordered were marked upon this card. Payment was effected through showing the marked card when leaving the restaurant at the central register.

Duval's success encouraged copies of the system. At the end of the nineteenth century, the family of Cartier possessed a similar chain with more than twenty subsidiaries. Three of them have been preserved in their original Art Nouveau style: the 'Restaurant Vagenande', the 'Bouillon Racine' and the 'Montparnasse 1900'. A fourth sub-branch from 1896 in Rue du Faubourg Montmartre has not only not changed its appearance, but also operates in the very tradition of the 'Bouillon' and is up to its reputation to offer Parisiens as well as guests from the provinces and from abroad a good meal at a reasonable price.

Excerpt from Paul Smith: *Paris, cafés et restaurants protégés au titre des monuments historiques*, manuscript, Paris 2009, p. 18–20

FIG. III

of fried chicken, but rather a product of food chemistry that includes more than two dozen ingredients, of which meat is just one. Robert Baker, the creator of nuggets, is also called the 'Edison of the chicken industry'.[170] The shift to chicken came right on cue for McDonald's. After the establishment of factory farming, chicken cost half as much as beef and pork.

> 'The Chicken McNugget turned a bird that once had to be carved at a table into something that could easily be eaten behind the wheel of a car. It turned a bulk agricultural commodity into a manufactured, value-added product. And it encouraged a system of production that has turned many chicken farmers into little more than serfs,'

Eric Schlosser writes in his book *Fast Food Nation*.[171] The founding of the 'McDonald's' empire by Ray Croc in the mid-1950s finds its roots in a 'drive-in' restaurant near Pasadena, opened in 1937 by Mac and Dick McDonald. A larger restaurant was opened in the 1940s in San Bernardino. After restructuring in 1948, a decision was made to concentrate on hamburgers and serve them fast and cheap. Crockery and cutlery were replaced by cardboard and paper bag packaging, and customers ate by hand (FIG. IV).[172] The basic elements of the concept, which still form the basis of the 'McDonald's' economic structure, were speed, sales volume, and cheapness. Both customer and staff were unconditionally subject to a smooth systematic procedure that was calculated well in advance. The individual operations of the staff were tracked by stopwatch. German investigative journalist Günter Wallraff got himself employed incognito in the 1980s at McDonald's and described the inhumane working conditions in his 1985 best-selling book *Ganz unten* ('Lowest of the Low').[173] George Ritzer analysed in his book entitled *The McDonaldisation of Society* how much society is marked by command and control, whereby much of that control over humans is exerted by 'nonhuman technologies'.[174]

Production line-comparable techniques of preparation and serving, as introduced by the early chain restaurants, replaced traditional cooking methods and personal service. The Macdonald brothers divided work into individual steps, similar to the assembly line techniques of the manufacturing industry, seen for example in the factories of Henry Ford—and presented by Charlie Chaplin with sarcastic accuracy in his film 'Modern Times'—or even

samt 2500 Lokale.[169] Ende der 1930er Jahre entstand die Kette Boy Hamburger. 1954 folgten Burger King, eine Umbenennung vom ursprünglichen, weniger werbewirksamen Justaburger, sowie Kentucky Fried Chicken. Heute werden die Fast-Food-Ketten Burger King oder McDonald's wegen der Transfettsäuren in ihren Brätlingen kritisiert. Der Gewichtsanteil fettsaugender Panaden fällt vor allem bei den „Chicken Nuggets" ins Gewicht. Hierbei handelt es sich nicht um ein Stück frittiertes Hühnerfleisch, sondern um ein Produkt der Lebensmittelchemie aus über zwei Dutzend Zutaten, wovon Fleisch nur eine ist. Schöpfer der „Nuggets" ist der auch als „Edison der Hühnerindustrie" bezeichnete Robert Baker.[170] Die Hinwendung zum Hühnerfleisch kam für McDonald's wie gerufen. Dessen Preis hatte sich auf der Basis der Massentierhaltung gegenüber Rinder- und Schweinefleisch mehr als halbiert.

> „Das Chicken McNugget machte aus einem Vogel, der einmal auf dem Tisch hatte zerlegt werden müssen, etwas, was man leicht hinter dem Steuerrad eines Autos essen konnte. Es machte aus einem Massenrohstoff der Agrikultur ein Fabrikprodukt mit Mehrwert. Und es förderte ein Produktionssystem, das viele Hühnerzüchter in wenig mehr als kleine Sklaven verwandelt",

schreibt Eric Schlosser in seinem Buch *Fast Food Nation*.[171] Die Gründung des McDonald's-Imperiums durch Ray Croc Mitte der 1950er Jahre geht auf ein 1937 von Mac und Dick McDonald in der Nähe von Pasadena eröffnetes Drive-In-Restaurant zurück. In den 1940er Jahren folgte ein größeres Restaurant in San Bernadino. Nach einer erneuten Umstrukturierung 1948 und einer Konzentration auf den Hamburger setzte man auf niedrigste Preise und größte Schnelligkeit. Geschirr und Besteck wurden durch Karton- und Tütenverpackungen ersetzt, zum Essen nahm man die Hand.[172] (FIG. IV) Die Grundelemente des Konzepts, wie sie noch heute die Wirtschaftsstruktur von McDonald's bestimmen, waren Geschwindigkeit, die Menge des Absatzes und Billigkeit. Sowohl die Kunden als auch das Personal waren bedingungslos dem reibungslosen Ablauf dieses Systems totaler Vorauskalkulation unterworfen. Die einzelnen Arbeitsgänge der Bediensteten wurden mit der Stoppuhr nachgehalten. Der deutsche Enthüllungsjournalist Günter Wallraff erfuhr die menschenunwürdigen Arbeitsbedingungen als inkognito bei McDonald's Beschäftigter und

55

Bei Aschinger—(At Aschinger's), Jeanne Mammen, ca. 1926 ● Ladies' circle at 'Aschinger' around 1910

Bei Aschinger, Jeanne Mammen, ca. 1926 ● Damenrunde bei Aschinger, um 1910

56
'McDonald's' fast food, offered during fashion weeks as 'McFancy' ● A 'McFancy' consumption room

Fast Food von McDonald's während Modewochen als McFancy angeboten ● Ein McFancy Verzehrraum

Hold the Relish: A lab-grown burger excites hopes but not taste buds

'True beef or not true beef? That is the question two volunteers masticating a burger in front of an invited audience in a London theatre attempted to answer [on August, 5, 2013]. Schmeat—or 'cultured beef'—is the culinary product of stem cells harvested from a cow's shoulder and lab-nurtured into strips of muscle. In Britain, beefeaters have experienced some of the downsides of industrialized farming and food production: an epidemic of bovine spongiform encephalopathy that spiked in the early 1990s, a foot-and-mouth epidemic a decade later and, this year, the revelation that the 'beef' in certain prepared foods was actually horse meat. Schmeat production, if scaled up enough to bring prices down, could help feed the world and reduce some of the pressures on the planet. One macerates the muscle cells in a broth that includes fetal calf serum, obtained by slaughtering pregnant cows. 'Our goal is to promote foods that don't use animals at all' says Ingrid Newkirk, president of People for the Ethical Treatment of Animals (PETA), an animal-rights organization.

Catherine Mayer, in: *Time Magazine*, August 19, 2013, p. 51

FIG. IV

older workflow systems in Chicago slaughterhouses. As on a production line, special units called *fillers*, *shakers*, *fryers*, and *decorators* created, step-by-step, the end product of this early fast food factory. Such a level of rationalisation was only possible if a very limited range of products were manufactured. With more than 30,000 branches, the corporation had now extended its range of classic American standard goods to include ethnic variations, such as salmon in Norway and *McUevo*, and *McQueso* in Uruguay. In Russia, where the fast-food empire competes with the *Russkoye Bistro* chain, you can order pierogies and blinis. In Thailand there is the *Samurai Burger*, a sandwich of pork marinated in teriyaki sauce; in Japan, a sandwich of fried chicken seasoned with soy sauce and ginger served with herb and mustard mayonnaise. In the Philippines, McDonald's offers a 'highlight of culinary experience' in the form of *McSpaghetti*, a noodle dish served with a sauce made from either tomatoes or Frankfurter sausage pieces.[175]

'The global food industry and the foodstuffs wholesale trade introduced a kind of general culinary syncretism, which functions according to the system that French soci-

beschrieb die Zustände in seinem 1985 veröffentlichten Bestseller *Ganz unten*.[173] George Ritzer analysiert in seinem Buch *Die McDonaldisierung der Gesellschaft* das Ausmaß gesellschaftlicher Steuerung und Kontrolle, „wobei ein Gutteil dieser Kontrolle auf nicht-humane Technologien zurückgeht".[174]

Fließbandähnliche Techniken der Zubereitung und des Servierens, wie die frühen Kettenrestaurants sie vorexerziert hatten, lösten die traditionellen Kochmethoden und den persönlichen Service ab. Nach dem Vorbild der Montagetechniken der Industrie, zum Beispiel in den Fabriken Henry Fords, von Charlie Chaplin mit sarkastischer Genauigkeit in seinem Film *Modern Times* karikiert, oder der noch älteren Abläufe in Chicagoer Schlachthöfen wurde bei den McDonald's-Brüdern die Arbeit in Einzelschritte zerlegt. Wie am Fließband sorgten in Spezialeinheiten „Füller", „Schüttler", „Brater" und „Dekorierer" für die Herstellung der Endprodukte dieser frühen Fast-Food-Fabriken. Eine derartige Durchrationalisierung war nur auf der Basis eines schmalen, standardisierten Angebotes möglich. Mit mehr als 30.000 Filialen hat der Konzern heute die Palette seiner klassischen amerikanischen Standardware um ethnische Varianten angereichert wie zum Beispiel Lachs in

ologist Edgar Morin, with the culture industry in mind, described in *Esprit du temps*.'[176]

The international agro-business, as well as the fast-food chains, do not only destroy local culinary specialties: they destroy and integrate at the same time, producing a kind of universal syncretic mosaic or, pursuant to the formula applied by Edgar Morin to the culture of the masses, effect a real analytical cracking, that transforms natural products into homogenised cultural products for mass consumption.[177]

> 'The food industry and the fast food chains thus remove local differences and peculiarities, but at the same time dispatch altered or standardised regional and exotic specialties to all five continents.'[178]

In order to entice even more customers, 'McDonald's' began offering special attractions on a worldwide scale as an incentive for food intake, as well as incentives that were specifically directed at children. It has been scientifically proven that children are particularly inspired by the gimmicks that go along with the *Happy Meal*. After all, as aptly described in Emile Zola's *Au bonheur des dames*[179] a Parisian department store in the 1860s had already used free balloons to entice customers. In 2012, 'McDonald's', in order to improve their dubious reputation and based on the statistic that one in three children in Britain did not own a single book, devised a strategy to grant a free book with each 'Happy Meal'. Critics of this literacy campaign called this a particularly perfidious trick to lure children and young people to the brand 'and to dress up poor nutrition[180] in good education ethics'.[181] In an attempt to entice customers at the other, more sophisticated end of the social scale, especially during fashion weeks, the label 'McFancy' was introduced:

> 'Part art installation and part gathering spot, the temporary eatery gives event attendants a stylish nod with a traditional McDonald's menu served in playful yet elegant packaging design.'[182]

The fast food French fries were donned with the label of either 'Hermes' or 'Gucci', the hamburger referred to as a 'Burberry Burger'. The plastic cutlery was embossed with a neo-baroque pattern (fig. 56).

Norwegen, McUevo und McQueso in Uruguay. In Russland, wo dem Fast-Food-Imperium die Kette „Russkoje Bistro" Konkurrenz macht, sind Pirogen und Blinis zu bekommen. In Thailand wird der „Samurai Burger", mit Teriyaki-Soße mariniertes Schweinefleisch, und in Japan das mit Sojasoße und Ingwer gewürzte Brathähnchen mit Kraut und Senfmayonaise als Sandwich angeboten. Auf den Philippinen schließlich werden bei McDonald's als „Höhepunkt der Esskultur" McSpaghetti mit einer Tomaten- oder einer aus Frankfurter-Wurststücken bestehenden Soße angeboten.[175]

> „Die weltumspannende Lebensmittelindustrie und der Lebensmittelgroßhandel führten eine Art allgemeinen kulinarischen Synkretismus ein, der nach dem System funktioniert, das der französische Soziologe Edgar Morin in *L'esprit du temps* im Hinblick auf die Kulturindustrie beschrieben hat."[176]

Das internationale Agro-Business wie auch die Fast-Food-Ketten zerstören nicht einfach die lokalen kulinarischen Besonderheiten: Sie zerstören und integrieren gleichzeitig, produzieren eine Art universelles synkretistisches Mosaik oder bewirken gemäß der Formel, die Edgar Morin auf die Kultur der Masse anwandte, „ein echtes analytisches Cracking, [das] die natürlichen Produkte in homogenisierte kulturelle Produkte für den Massenkonsum verwandelt."[177]

> „Die Lebensmittelindustrie und die Fast-Food-Ketten entfernen demzufolge die lokalen Unterschiede und Besonderheiten, entsenden aber gleichzeitig die veränderten oder standardisierten regionalen und exotischen Spezialitäten in alle fünf Kontinente."[178]

Auf Kundenfang offeriert McDonald's weltweit als Anreiz zur Nahrungsmittelaufnahme spezielle Attraktionen sowie vor allem Anreize für Kinder. Wissenschaftlich ist nachgewiesen, dass die Kleinen sich vor allem wegen der der Mahlzeit hinzugegebenen Gimmicks für das sogenannte „Happy Meal" begeistern. Schließlich ging, wie in Emile Zolas *Au bonheur des dames*[179] treffend beschrieben, schon in den 1860er Jahren ein Pariser Warenhaus mit Gratisluftballons auf Kinder- und damit Kundenfang. Um seinen zweifelhaften Ruf aufzubessern und basierend auf der Tatsache, dass jedes dritte Kind in Großbritannien kein einziges Buch besitzt, wurde 2012

Advertising is one element of the trinity of speed, packaging, and cheapness. Yet speed is not only important in terms of standardisation on the food product assembly line. It also plays an essential role in the turnover of customers. The work process is divided into sequences, but so is the duration of the guests' stay—and, of course, in the case of drive-in restaurants, this is reduced to practically zero. Twenty minutes is the maximum amount of time that a customer should stay at the restaurant. This no longer has anything to do with quality food experience. Canadian historian Harvey Levenstein speaks of 'smash-and-grab places.'[183] In *Labor and Monopoly Capital*, Harry Bravermann comes to the conclusion that fast-food restaurants, if they can even be called restaurants, are the total source of degradation of employees, customers, as well as food.[184] But if the aim is to increase profit maximisation, you of course need to produce reliable eaters. 'If people could exist on food in its natural state, they would never suffer from the evils caused by concentrated foods,' Sigfried Giedion cites Sylvester Graham.[185] The uniformity of such food and convenience meals, continues Giedion, can only prevail in a society that lives by forgetting, by forgetting their own fundamental basis of life. A countermovement to the disinterest, mass merchandising, and acceleration in the catering industry is the Slow Food movement and its related initiatives. In response to the opening of a 'McDonald's' restaurant on the Roman Piazza Navona, Carlo Petrini—not to be confused with the dégustateur Andrea Petrini—together with the editors of *Il Manifesto* organised a public food protest with traditional Italian dishes on the Spanish Steps. In 1986, Carlo Petrini and the 'Friends of Barolo' founded the association *Arcigola* in Bra in Piedmont. In 1989 at an international meeting in the Paris Comic Opera, this was renamed *Slow Food*. The restaurants of the Slow Food movement, which can be found in an annually published *Osteria Guide*, guarantee regional products, regional cuisine, and small guest rooms. And as in the case of Massimo Bottura with his 28-seat 'Osteria Francescana' in Modena, they have cooked up quite a few stars.[186]

Nothing New Under The Sun—Or Is There?

A restaurant earns its reputation due to a famous chef or because it has historical or architectural significance. It also gains appeal if its clientele includes public figures or celebrities. Restaurants that meet all three criteria are very

zum „Happy Meal“ ein Buch gratis gereicht. Kritiker dieser Alphabetisierungskampagne nennen dies einen besonders perfiden Trick, um Kinder und Jugendliche an die Marke zu binden „und schlechte Ernährung[180] mit einem guten Bildungsgewissen zu bemänteln“.[181] Vor allem anlässlich von Modewochen ist McDonald's mit dem Label „McFancy“ aber auch am anderen Ende der gesellschaftlichen Skala auf Kundenfang:

> „Part art installation and part gathering spot, the temporary eatery gives event attendants a stylish nod with a traditional McDonald's menu served in playful yet elegant packaging design.“[182]

Die Pommes Frites kommen mit der Etikettierung „Hermes“ oder „Gucci“, der Hamburger als „Burberry Burger“ daher. Das Plastikbesteck ist neobarock geprägt (Abb. 56).

Die Werbung gehört zur Trias Geschwindigkeit, Umschlag und Billigkeit. Geschwindigkeit herrscht nicht nur bei der Fließbandproduktion der standardisierten Esswaren. Sie spielt im Zusammenhang mit der Fluktuation der Kunden ebenfalls eine Rolle. So wie der Arbeitsprozess in Frequenzen zerlegt ist, so soll auch der Aufenthalt der Gäste getaktet sein. Bei den Drive-Ins reduziert sich die Verweilzeit ohnehin auf nahezu Null. In den Lokalen soll die Verweilzeit möglichst 20 Minuten nicht überschreiten. Von einer Qualität des Essenserlebnisses kann hier keine Rede mehr sein. Der kanadische Historiker Harvey Levenstein spricht von „smash-and-grab places“.[183] In *Labor and Monopoly Capital* kommt Harry Bravermann zu dem Schluss, dass das Fast-Food-Restaurant, wenn man hier überhaupt noch von einem Restaurant sprechen kann, eine einzige Quelle der Herabwürdigung sowohl der Beschäftigten als auch der Kunden und sogar der Nahrung darstellt.[184] Hier geht es im Sinne der Profitmaximierung vorrangig um die Fabrikation des zuverlässigen Essers. „Wenn der Mensch ausschließlich von Nahrung in ihrem natürlichen Zustand existieren müßte, würde er niemals an den Übeln leiden, die konzentrierte Nahrungsmittel verursachen“, zitiert Sigfried Giedion Sylvester Graham.[185] Die Uniformität der Nahrungsmittel bis hin zu den Fertiggerichten – so Giedion weiter – kann sich nur in einer Gesellschaft durchsetzen, die vom Vergessen lebt, vom Vergessen der eigenen Existenzgrundlagen. Eine Gegenbewegung zu Desinteressiertheit, Massenware und Akzeleration in der

57

Glass paper	**Aerial Meal** **(Recipe of futuristic „aerial“ painter Fillia)**
Red Silk	One serves to the right side of the eater a plate with black olives, fennel hearts and Chinese cabbage. To the left side of the eater one serves a rectangle, composed of glass paper, silk and velvet. The food must be directed by the right hand immediately to the mouth, whereas the left lightly and repeatedly strokes the touching-rectangle. Meanwhile the waiters spray the guest's necks with a sym-fragrance of carnations, while there comes a fierce sym-sound of the motor of an aeroplane and simultaneously a dis-music by Bach.
Black Velvet	

53

57

A recipe from Filippo Tommaso Marinetti's *Cucina futurista*, 1932

Rezept aus Filippo Tommaso Marinetti *Cucina futurista*, 1932

58

Vignette of the 'Spoerri' Restaurant in Düsseldorf, 1970 ● *L'ultima cena*, Daniel Spoerri, 1970

Vignette des Restaurants Spoerri in Düsseldorf, 1970 ● *L'ultima cena*, Daniel Spoerri, 1970

privileged. The opinion of a food critic in the qualitative assessment of a restaurant's kitchen still plays as important a role as it did during Grimod de la Reynières lifetime. His *jury de dégustateurs*, after many intermediate stages, was followed by Curnonsky and Marcel Rouff's[187] 1927 *Académie des gastronomes*. Today, Andrea Petrini[188] is considered a 'star-maker'. His statement concerning restaurant chefs, 'that everyone should follow their own personal endeavour',[189] can only be underscored. Yet cooking events such as *Paris des chefs* or *Gelinaz* seem to be primarily about showmanship. The latter was a twenty-three-course meal, for which Petrini had invited twenty-three of the world's best chefs to the Flemish city of Ghent to cook and to perform. It was designed 'not as a dinner, but as a performance'.[190] The price tag of 725 Euros per setting made this an elitist event. 'It was wasteful and, in its gluttony, markedly unhealthy',[191] wrote one critic. However, the synergistic effects, the amalgamation of cuisine, art, and music as a performative event, was more than likely not an attempt to refer to historic dining spectacles or the creativity of Carème. On the other hand, the imagination of the futurists, led by Filippo Tommaso Marinetti's *cucina futurista*,[192] (fig. 57) Daniel Spoerri with, for example, the *ultima cena*,[193] or Joseph Beuys' *Beethoven's Kitchen*[194] seems to hold more credible creative power. The Düsseldorf-based bar-restaurant *Spoerri*, managed by Carlo Schröter, for many years not only was a cult, but also a place of fertile and stimulating exchange (fig. 58). Petrini's desire for synergy between art and food developed at *Spoerri's* naturally and was not forced.

Paris is still the unrestricted capital of restaurants. A restaurant guide with more than 400-pages[195] presents 'the most beautiful' of 12,000 cafes and restaurants in all twenty *arrondissements*. Competition is tough under what Curnonsky referred to as the gastro-nomads. The black boards described by Kleist are back on the sidewalk in front of simple establishments. Radiant gas heaters, which could be seen as early as the 1920s on Berlin's Kurfürstendamm, are once again in vogue (fig. 59). Yet the more sophisticated restaurants display their special aura only inside, especially in the styles of Historicism, Art Nouveau, or Art Deco.[196] Additional attractions were also added to interior design features, as at 'Lasserre' in Paris, the restaurant visited on an almost daily basis by Salvador Dalí and André Malraux.

Gastronomie stellen die „Slow Food"-Bewegung und ihr verwandte Initiativen dar. Als Reaktion auf die Eröffnung einer McDonald's-Filiale auf der römischen Piazza Navona hat Carlo Petrini – nicht zu verwechseln mit dem Degustateur Andrea Petrini – zusammen mit Redakteuren von *Il Manifesto* ein öffentliches Protestessen mit traditionellen italienischen Gerichten an der Spanischen Treppe veranstaltet. 1986 hatten Carlo Petrini und die „Freunde des Barolo" in Bra im Piemont die Vereinigung „Arcigola" gegründet. 1989 erfolgt bei einem internationalen Treffen in der Pariser Komischen Oper die Umbenennung in „Slow Food". Die Restaurants der „Slow Food"-Bewegung, die in einem jährlich herausgegebenen „Osterienführer" zu finden sind, garantieren regionale Produkte und regionale Küche sowie kleine Gasträume. Als solche haben sie sich, wie im Fall von Massimo Bottura mit seiner 28 Gäste fassenden Osteria Francescana in Modena, auch Sterne erkocht.[186]

Nichts Neues unter der Sonne – oder?

Restaurants erwerben ihr Renommee dank eines berühmten Kochs oder als historische oder architektonische Attraktion. Sie gewinnen an Anziehungskraft, wenn zu ihrer Kundschaft Persönlichkeiten des öffentlichen Lebens zählen. Privilegiert sind solche, auf die alle drei Kriterien zutreffen. Wie zu Zeiten Grimod de la Reynières spielt das Urteil des Gastrokritikers eine wichtige Rolle bei der qualitativen Einstufung einer Restaurantküche. Auf die „Jury de dégustateurs" dieses Autors sollte nach vielen Zwischenstadien 1927 Curnonskys und Marcel Rouffs[187] „Académie des gastronomes" folgen. Heute positioniert sich Andrea Petrini[188] als „Starmaker". Wenn er von den Restaurantköchen sagt, „ everyone should follow their own personal endeavour"[189], kann man dies nur unterstreichen. Kochveranstaltungen wie „Paris des chefs" oder „Gelinaz" aber scheinen vor allem auf Publikumswirksamkeit ausgerichtet zu sein. Letzteres war ein 23-Gänge-Menü, zu dem Petrini 23 der weltbesten Köche nach Gent eingeladen hatte, um zu kochen und zu inszenieren. Es war „not as a dinner, but as a performance"[190] gedacht. Für 770 Dollar pro Gedeck war es eine elitistische Veranstaltung. „It was wasteful and in its gluttony markedly unhealthy",[191] schreibt eine Kritikerin. Ob jedoch die synergetischen Effekte des Amalgamierens von Kochkunst, Kunst und Musik als performativer Veranstaltung an die historischen Schauessen

'When you enter the Lasserre, you first pass the pigeon-aviary. With the help of a lift in the form of a litter you can ascend to the candy-dish decorated dining room … on the second floor.'[197]

A sliding ceiling ventilates and illuminates the hall, and offers guests an open view of the sky. At gala events, it was customary for famous guests to set pigeons free through the open ceiling. Whether restaurant owner Pierre Lasserre was aware of it or not, there is an obvious association with the Renaissance or Baroque gastro-experience culture. Castles and palaces as table decorations were common. In the sixteenth century a castle was reported:

'Its walls inside were filled with white rabbits decorated with coral, and its towers with hidden birds of different species. As the guests entered the dining hall accompanied by drums and trumpets and perfumed fireworks, the doors in the walls and towers were opened, freeing all of the rabbits and allowing the birds to fly away.'[198]

The staging and production here is part of the feast culture and bound to a fixed location. Today, 'pop-up-dinners' search out alternate locations in exotic places, such as the cab of a construction crane, or a Ferris wheel, an abandoned church, an unused quarry, and so on.

'Temporary restaurants are a model with staying power. The concept has been especially popular with up-and-coming chefs who want to test-drive a menu concept without investing a fortune in a permanent space.'[199]

It is a concept that is completely unprecedented in history. Catering and rented cooks, however, are a different situation. Caterers from Paris who moved to other major European cities were offering these services as early as the late eighteenth century. By 1792, there were already fourteen *traiteurs* in Vienna.'[200] Following the *traiteur* model, Stephen Leguillon founded 'La belle assiette' in 2013 in France. Five hundred and forty-five top chefs are now employed by 'La belle assiette' in France, as well as in Belgium, Switzerland, Luxembourg, Britain, and Germany. They guarantee a high standard of French cuisine. 'La belle assiette' accepts less than a quarter of all applicants for the position of cook. Customers may book up to twenty-four hours in advance of a dinner invitation. 'For as little $39

oder die Kreativität eines Carème heranreichen, bleibt zu bezweifeln. Da scheint die Fantasie der Futuristen, allen voran Filippo Tommaso Marinettis *La cucina futurista*[192] (Abb. 57) oder die eines Daniel Spoerri mit zum Beispiel *L'ultima cena*[193] oder Josef Beuys' *Beethovens Küche*[194] ein deutlicheres Zeichen schöpferischer Kraft zu sein. Das Düsseldorfer Bar-Restaurant Spoerri, geführt von Carlo Schröter, war nicht nur ein Kultort, sondern ein Platz fruchtbaren und stimulierenden Austausches (Abb. 58). Die von Petrini intendierte Synergie zwischen Kunst und Essen entwickelte sich hier prozessual und war nicht aufgezwungene Intention.

Paris ist noch immer die uneingeschränkte Hauptstadt der Restaurants. Ein über 400-seitiger Restaurantführer[195] stellt „die schönsten" der 12.000 Cafés und Restaurants in allen 20 Arrondissements vor. Der Konkurrenzkampf um die Gastro-Nomaden, wie sie Curnonsky bezeichnet, ist groß. Die von Kleist beschriebenen schwarzen Bretter werden vor einfacheren Etablissements wieder auf den Bürgersteig gestellt. Wärmestrahler, die in den 1920er Jahren bereits auf den Restaurantterrassen des Berliner Kurfürstendamms standen, sind wieder en vogue (Abb. 59). Restaurants der gehobenen Klasse entfalten ihre Aura nur innen, vor allem im Stil des Historismus, des Art nouveau oder Art déco.[196] Zur innenarchitektonischen Ausstattung kamen, wie zum Beispiel im Lasserre in Paris, dem fast täglich von Salvador Dalí und André Malraux besuchten Restaurant, zusätzliche Attraktionen hinzu.

„Wenn man das Lassere betritt, kommt man zuerst an der Tauben-Voliere vorbei … Mit Hilfe eines Aufzuges in Form einer Sänfte gelangt man in den wie eine Bonbonniere dekorierten Speisesaal"[197]

in der ersten Etage. Ein verschiebbarer Plafond dient der Belüftung und Beleuchtung des Saales und bietet den Gästen den Blick in den Himmel. Bei Galaveranstaltungen ist es Brauch, dass berühmte Gäste bei geöffnetem Plafond Tauben in die Freiheit entlassen. Ob dem Gastronomen Pierre Lasserre bekannt oder nicht, die Assoziation zur Gastro-Erlebniskultur der Renaissance oder des Barock liegt auf der Hand. Schlösser und Burgen als Tischdekoration waren gebräuchlich. Im 16. Jahrhundert wird von einem Schloss berichtet,

per person, the chef (cook) buys the ingredients, prepares and serves a meal, and even does the dishes afterwards.'[201]

In an age of the multiple and accelerated increase of information, food and cooking has also become a subject of interest in the media, but the focus is more often on the cooks, the ingredients, the preparation, and tasting, and rarely the restaurant itself. We previously discussed how the word 'restaurant' is used as a functional additive in relation to places where it is located. Other additions refer to national cuisines. This raises the question as to whether the many Chinese restaurants, pizzerias, and fast-food chains actually do more than merely restore physical strength. However, if 'restaurant' is defined in the classical sense as a place of culinary delights in a refined atmosphere with superior personalised service, where the gourmet lingers in pleasant company, then attention is again directed back to the art and the artists of cooking—and the cuisine. An American news magazine in 2013 appears under the headline *The Gods of Food*.[202] Pictured are David Chang from the USA, René Redzepi from Denmark, and Alex Atala from Brazil. In 2010, the 'kitchen gods' David Chang from the USA, Jamie Oliver from Great Britain, and Ferran Adrià from Catalonia were featured in the same magazine.[203] They, and many of their celebrated contemporaries, are part of a centuries-old tradition of gastronomic creativity. This is emphasised by one of its most experimental representatives: Ferran Adrià from Catalonia, with his molecular gastronomy. His restaurant, 'el Bulli', most likely in the twenty-first century the most famous restaurant in the world, closed its doors in July 2011. In Barcelona, 'el Bulli 1846' is planned to re-open with a 2500 square metre roof garden in the future, but for only one month a year. The number forty-six refers to the forty-six different courses available as well as the year French chef Auguste Escoffier was born, whose gastronomic imagination was unsurpassed even in times of privation.

In the famine period, during the siege of Paris in the Franco-German War of 1870-71, when even rats, mice, cats, and dogs were eaten, the latter prepared a *diner Parisien* using instead of calf and valuable poultry amongst the *rots* ('roasteds') mule, donkey, horse, *Gigot d'antelope, filet d'Elephant*, and, for the entremets, *bombes glacés à la Krupp* (fig. 60).[204]

The direct reference between Adrià and Escoffier points to the true objective of 'el Bulli 1846': 'Bulli DNA', a gastronomic laboratory, which aims to create a *Bulli-*

> „dessen ‚Mauern' innen voll von weißen, mit Korallen geschmückten Kaninchen und dessen Türme mit verborgenen Vögeln verschiedener Arten gefüllt waren. Als die Gäste mit Begleitung von Trommel- und Posaunenmusik bzw. von parfümiertem Feuerwerk in das Eßzimmer kamen, wurden die Türen in den Mauern und Türmen geöffnet, damit sich alle Kaninchen befreien und alle Vögel davonfliegen konnten."[198]

Die Inszenierung ist hier Teil der Gastmahlkultur und an einen festen Platz gebunden. Wechselnde Standorte suchen heute die sogenannten Pop-Up-Dinners an exotischen Plätzen wie zum Beispiel in der Kanzel eines Baukrans, der Kabine eines Riesenrades, in einer leerstehenden Kirche, einem ungenutzten Steinbruch et cetera.

> „Temporary restaurants are a model with staying power … The concept has been especially popular with up-and-coming chefs who want to test-drive a menu concept without investing a fortune in a permanent space."[199]

Diese Idee kennt keine Vorbilder in der Geschichte. Anders verhält es sich mit dem Catering und den Leihköchen. Seit dem Ende des 18. Jahrhunderts sind das die Dienstleistungen der Traiteure, die sich von Paris aus in den europäischen Großstädten ansiedelten. Bereits „1792 gab es in Wien vierzehn ‚Traiteure'".[200] Dem Traiteur-Vorbild folgend, hat Stephen Leguillon 2013 in Frankreich „La belle assiette" gegründet. Heute arbeiten 545 Chefköche, auch in Belgien, der Schweiz, Luxemburg, Großbritannien und Deutschland für „La belle assiette". Garantiert sind hohe Standards der französischen Küche. Weniger als ein Viertel aller Bewerber für „La belle assiette" werden angenommen. Die Buchung durch den Klienten ist bis 24 Stunden vor einer Essenseinladung möglich. „For as little as $ 39 per head, the chef (cook) buys the ingredients, prepares and serves a meal, and even does the dishes afterward."[201]

Im Zeitalter der multiplen und akzelerierenden Vervielfältigung von Informationen ist auch das Essen und Kochen ein Topos in den Medien geworden, wobei die Köche, die Ingredienzien und die Zubereitung, ja oft auch die Verkostung im Mittelpunkt stehen, seltener aber das Restaurant. Es wurde bereits gesagt, dass das Wort „Restaurant" als funktionales Additiv im Zusammenhang mit Örtlichkeiten, an denen es sich befindet, genutzt wird. Weitere Hinzufügungen verweisen auf

59

60

pedia 'decoding Western culinary history. The challenge at *el Bulli* was to create plates. Now it's to create those who create plates.'[205] Which actually means 'evaluate,' rather than 'create'. From Apicius, de Sacchi, Rumpolt, Bonnefons, de La Varenne, Evelyn, Massialot, Rumohr, von Vaerst, and so on, right up to Grimod de la Reynière and Brillat-Savarin, their footprints have also been left in the history of culture in this essay.

> 'Bullipedia's aim is to provide an online resource for anyone interested in gastronomy: its history, development, the emotional and cognitive factors involved in food, the elaboration of recipes and techniques—in simple terms, the hidden story behind everything we eat.'[206]

59
Outdoor radiation heaters in Berlin's Café Reimann, 1920s

Wärmestrahler im Café Reimann in Berlin, 1920er Jahre

60
Auguste Escoffier: menu of a dinner held during the occupation of Paris, 1870/71

Menu eines Diners während der Belagerung von Paris, Auguste Escoffier, 1870/71

nationale Küchen. Hier stellt sich die Frage, ob die Vielzahl von China-Restaurants, Pizzerien und Fast-Food-Ketten zu mehr als der baren Restaurierung körperlicher Kräfte dienen. Definiert man das Restaurant im klassischen Sinne jedoch als einen Ort kulinarischer Genüsse in einem gepflegten Ambiente mit gehobenem individuellem Service, in dem der Gourmet in angenehmer Gesellschaft verweilt, dann zentriert sich die Aufmerksamkeit wieder auf die Kochkunst und die Küche. Ein amerikanisches Nachrichtenmagazin titelt 2013 „The Gods of Food".[202] Abgebildet sind David Chang, USA, René Redzepi, Dänemark und Alex Atala, Brasilien. 2010 standen im selben Magazin die „kitchen gods" David Chang, USA, Jamie Oliver, Großbritannien und Ferran Adrià, Katalonien im Mittelpunkt.[203] Sie und viele ihrer berühmten Zeitgenossen sind Teil einer jahrhundertealten Tradition gastronomischer Kreativität. Dies unterstreicht einer ihrer experimentierfreudigsten Vertreter, der Katalane Ferran Adrià mit seiner Molekularküche. Das wohl international berühmteste Restaurant des 21. Jahrhunderts, Adriàs el Bulli schloss im Juli 2011 seine Türen. In Barcelona soll „el Bulli 1846" mit einem Dachgarten von 2500 qm künftig für jeweils nur einen Monat

The laboratory 'El Taller'—the workshop—and 'el Bulli DNA'

> 'will host experts in gastronomy as well as specialists in other fields from architecture to philosophy, botany, and anthropology. There will also be an exhibition tracing the evolution of the restaurant—"like walking through a movie" as Adrià describes it.'[207]

Adrià will not cease to experimentally investigating dissonance and harmony, anarchy and methodological systems, analysis versus creativity, in order to crown them with culinary creations. Of the different disciplines investigated for 'el Bulli DNA', psychology is to play an important role in the science of the senses. Innovative ideas for the restaurant emerged in fruitful discourse with architects in a Barcelona ideas forum, because the sensory experiences emphasised by Brillat-Savarin at the beginning of this essay should still be enjoyed in their complex and varied nature in restaurants today. The gastronomical and archaeological research of *Bullipedia* resulted in *nouvelle cuisine* with, for instance, Paul Bocuse and Alain Chapel. 'A compelling dish has symbolic character and is a colourful guide along the pilgrimage route of culture,' writes Chapel. *Nouvelle cuisine*,[208] after the birth of the French *haute cuisine*, once again put the gastronomic supremacy of this nation to the test and substantiated it with a ranking system of awarding stars. Following in the footsteps of Grimod de la Reynière and his introduction of the awarding of quality labels, the stars bestowed by Gault et Millau[209] and Michelin[210] are still decisive and highly influential. With the obligation to cook up three stars, Prince Rainier of Monaco in 1987 put his trust in Alain Ducasse to manage the restaurant located in the traditional 'Hôtel de Paris'. Within three years in the opulent Belle Epoque rooms, he succeeded. This was the starting point of his gourmet empire that included twenty-seven restaurants, earned nineteen stars, and sustained 1,400 employees. The commercialisation of the art of cooking and the building of a chain of 'haute cuisine' restaurants is an unprecedented phenomenon in the history of gastronomy. Top chefs market themselves, like fashion designers, as a 'label'. The restaurant as a place recedes behind the name of the cook. Guests eat at Ducasse's Adrià's, Alex Atala's, José Andrés', Chang's, Redzepi's, and so on, and drop these names like fashion labels. However, it is highly unlikely that all these gastro-tourists are discerning

im Jahr eröffnet werden. Die Zahl 46 bezieht sich auf die 46 wählbaren Gänge und auf das Geburtsjahr des französischen Chefkochs Auguste Escoffier, dessen gastronomische Phantasie selbst in Notzeiten unübertroffen war.

In der Hungerepoche der Belagerung von Paris während des deutsch-französischen Kriegs 1870/71, in der Ratten, Mäuse, Katzen und Hunde verzehrt wurden, führt er für ein „diner Parisien" anstelle von Kalb und wertvollem Geflügel unter den „Rots" (Geröstetem) Maultier, Esel, Pferd, „gigot d'Antilope", „filet d'Elephant" und bei den *entremets* „bombes glacés à la Krupp" auf (Abb. 60).[204]

Der direkte Bezug Adriàs zu Escoffier verweist auf den eigentlichen Zweck von „el Bulli 1846": „Bulli DNA", ein gastronomisches Laboratorium, dessen Ziel die Erstellung einer „Bullipedia" sein soll, sie „is decoding Western culinary history. The challenge at ‚el Bulli' was to create plates. Now it's to create those who create plates",[205] wobei bei letzterem wohl nicht „create" sondern „evaluate" gemeint ist. Von Apicius über de Sacchi, Rumpolt, Bonnefons, de La Varenne, Evelyn, Massialot, Rumohr, von Vaerst, bis hin zu Grimod de la Reynière und Brillat-Savarin wurde auch ihr Fußabdruck in der Kulturgeschichte in diesem Beitrag gestreift.

> „Bullipedia's aim is to provide an online resource for anyone interested in gastronomy: its history, development, the emotional and cognitive factors involved in food, the elaboration of recipes and techniques – in simple terms, the hidden story behind everything we eat."[206]

Das Laboratorium „El Taller"– die Werkstatt – und „el Bulli DNA" „will host experts in gastronomy as well as specialists in other fields from architecture to philosophy, botany and anthropology. There will also be an exhibition tracing the evolution of the restaurant – ‚like walking through a movie' as Adrià describes it."[207] Adrià wird nicht aufhören, im Experiment Dissonanzen und Harmonien, Anarchie und methodologische Systeme, Analyse versus Kreativität zu ergründen, um sie durch kulinarische Schöpfungen zu krönen. In der Aufzählung der für „el Bulli DNA" recherchierenden Disziplinen sollte die Psychologie als die die Sinne tangierende Wissenschaft eine Rolle spielen. In befruchtenden Diskursen mit Architekten könnten sich in Adriàs Denkforum innovative Lösungen für Restaurants herauskristallisieren, denn die eingangs von Brillat-Savarin hervorgehobe-

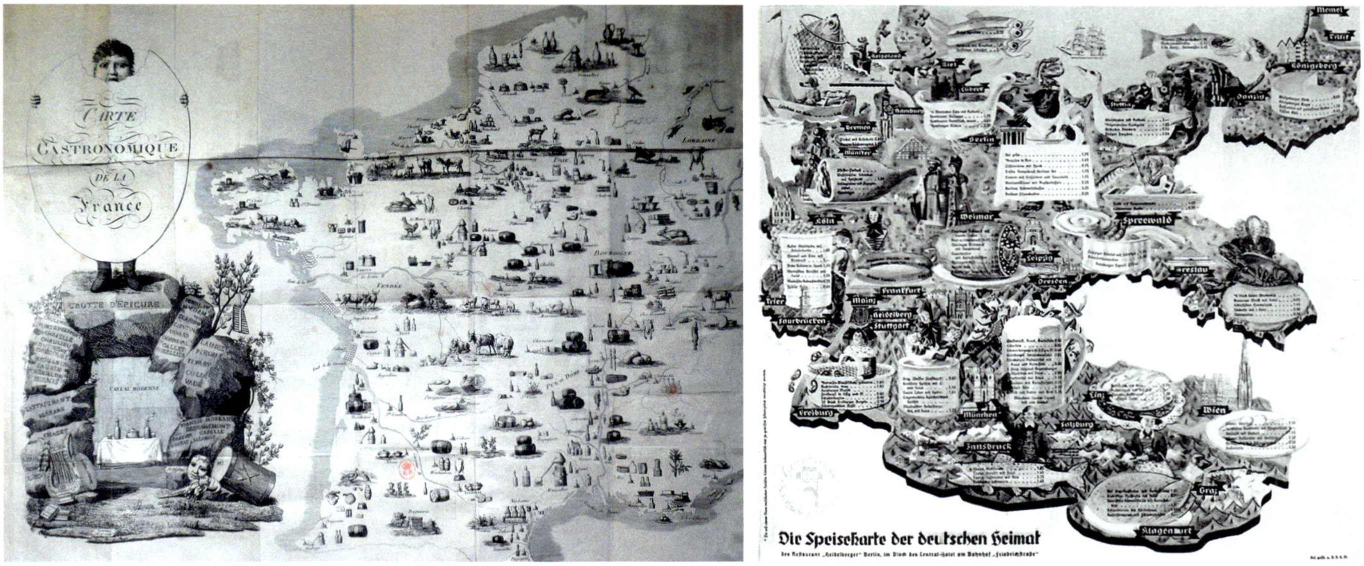

gourmets. The star chefs became quasi-idols and, due to their presence in the media, have significant widespread impact. After all, some of them do use their popularity to promote the importance of nutrition. New York-based star chef Chang—also an entrepreneur as the founder of the 'Momofuko' restaurant group—writes:

> 'The last U.N. report estimated that we throw away at least a third of all food (this brings us back to Francatelli) … and I think it is happening because we've lost the narrative that food takes time and life and energy … if we understood the process that went into getting our food, I don't think we would be as wasteful.'[211]

Other chef personalities, such as Jamie Oliver in London or Sarah Wiener in Berlin, are actively concerned with the healthy nutrition of schoolchildren. Michelle Obama was able to get 500 restaurant chefs involved in her initiative to fight child obesity.[212] Restaurant magnates in general want to raise awareness, also concerning the importance of seasonal and regional products (fig. 61),

61
Map with national products of France, Cadet de Gassicourt, 1809 ● Menu showing regional German dishes, restaurant 'Heidelberger', Berlin, 1938

Karte mit nationalen Produkten Frankreichs, Cadet de Gassicourt, 1809 ● Speisekarte mit regionalen deutschen Gerichten, Restaurant Heidelberger in Berlin, 1938

nen sinnlichen Erfahrungen sollten in ihrer Mehrschichtigkeit auch heute noch im Restaurant befriedigt werden. Die gastronomisch-archäologischen Recherchen der „Bullipedia" enden mit der „Nouvelle Cuisine" mit unter anderem Paul Bocuse und Alain Chapel. „Ein überzeugendes Gericht hat Zeichencharakter und ist ein farbiger Wegweiser auf der Pilgerstraße der Kultur",[208] schreibt Chapel. Die „Nouvelle Cuisine" hatte nach der Geburtsstunde der französischen „Haute Cuisine" ein weiteres Mal die gastronomische Vormachtstellung dieser Nation unter Beweis gestellt und diese mit dem Benotungssystem der Vergabe von Sternen untermauert. Nach der von Grimod de la Reynière eingeführten Verteilung von Qualitätssiegeln sind die von Gault et Millau[209] und Michelin[210] vergebenen Sterne noch immer maßstabgebend.

Mit der Auflage, drei Sterne zu erkochen, vertraute 1987 Fürst Rainier von Monaco Alain Ducasse das Restaurant im traditionsreichen Hôtel de Paris an. Innerhalb von drei Jahren gelang ihm das in den opulenten Belle-Epoque-Sälen. Von hier aus baute er ein Gourmetimperium mit 27 Restaurants, 19 Sternen und 1400 Mitarbeitern auf. Die Kommerzialisierung der Kochkunst sowie die Kettenbildung der „Haute Cuisine"-Restaurants ist ein in der Geschichte der Gastronomie noch nie dagewesenes Phänomen. Spitzenköche vermarkten sich ähnlich wie Modeschöpfer als „Label". Das Restaurant als Ort tritt hinter dem Namen des

62

Dinner menu for the 'gastronomes régionalistes', Paris 1927

Menu eines Diners der Gastronomes régionalistes, Paris 1927

which they use in their restaurants. Redzepi, as a regional food hunter, is setting the trend with his Copenhagen restaurant 'Noma'. 'Where many leading chefs seek to build empires, Redzepi wants only to dig deeper into his surroundings'.[213] Literature available on the history of gastronomy also provides a *déjà vu* effect here, for instance in the case of Evelyn in 1699, or even of Platina in 1474, which is also true in terms of the emphasis on regional cuisine, presented in the form of a dinner in Paris in 1927 for the general meeting of the *Association des gastronomes régionalistes* (fig. 62). An additional aspect of Regionalism—as demonstrated by Redzepi—is that many restaurant chefs not only acquire their products from surrounding areas, but also run their own farms. More recently, the *Locavore*[214] movement was established to counter 'eating contrary to geographical location and time' (meaning, bringing shellfish inland, or eating strawberries in winter). The restaurant gods are undoubtedly helping us to raise awareness of food cycles, because the consumption of

Kochs zurück. Man hat dann bei Ducasse, Adrià, Alex Atala, José Andrés, Chang, Redzepi et cetera gegessen und renommiert damit wie mit einer Modemarke. Es ist dabei zu bezweifeln, ob all die Gastro-Touristen urteilsfähige Gourmets sind. Die zu Idolen avancierten Sterneköche haben dank ihrer Medienauftritte erhebliche Breitenwirkung. Einige von ihnen nutzen ihre Popularität immerhin für ernährungsrelevante Botschaften. Der New Yorker Spitzenkoch Chang – auch er als Begründer der Momofuko-Restaurantgruppe ein Entrepreneur – schreibt:

> „The last U.N. report estimated that we throw away at least a third of all food [hier sei an Francatelli erinnert] ... and I think it is happening because we've lost the narrative that food takes time and life and energy ... if we understood the process that went into getting our food, I don't think we would be as wasteful."[211]

Andere Kochpersönlichkeiten wie unter anderem Jamie Oliver in London oder Sarah Wiener in Berlin haben die gesunde Ernährung von Schulkindern im Visier. Michelle Obama konnte 500 Restaurantköche für ihre Initiative gegen Fettleibigkeit bei Kindern gewinnen.[212] Ganz allgemein haben sich Restaurantmagnaten Aufklärung auf die Fahnen geschrieben. Ein zweites Plädoyer richtet sich auf die Verwendung jahreszeitlicher und regionaler Produkte (Abb. 61) in ihren Restaurants. Eine tonangebende Stelle nimmt hier in der Rolle eines regionalen *food hunter* Redzepi in seinem Kopenhagener Restaurant Noma ein. „Where many leading chefs seek to build empires, Redzepi wants only to dig deeper into his surroundings."[213] Ein Blick auf die historische Gastronomieliteratur ruft aber auch hier ein Déjà-vu hervor, zum Beispiel bei Evelyn 1699, ja sogar schon bei Platina 1474. Dies gilt auch in Bezug auf die Hervorhebung der regionalen Küche, die sich in Paris 1927 anlässlich der Generalversammlung der „Association des gastronomes régionalistes" (Abb. 62) mit einem Diner präsentierte. Zum Regionalismus gehört – wie am Beispiel Redzepis aufgezeigt – dass viele Restaurantköche nicht nur ihre Produkte aus dem Umland beziehen, sondern sogar eigene Agrikulturen betreiben. Das „gegen Raum und Zeit Essen" (zum Beispiel Krustentiere ins Landesinnere zu holen oder Erdbeeren im Winter zu verzehren) will neuerdings auch eine Bewegung wie die der „Locavoren"[214] bekämpfen. Ohne Zweifel tragen die Restaurantgötter dazu bei,

a meat or fish dish—whether at home or in the restaurant—is the result of the appropriating 'intention of one body over another'[215] (FIG. V). Already Johann Wolfgang von Goethe pondered on this point:

> 'The little worms eat fresh little seed leaves, the little lark fills its belly with little worms, and because I am also here to eat, I indulge in the little lark.'[216]

'It's what you eat, eats'[217] says Angel Léon, the chef of star restaurant 'Aponiente.' Now, high-price and high-quality restaurants, previously located almost exclusively in big cities, can be found outside urban centres, such as for instance the 'Aponiente' in Puerto de Santa Maria near Cadiz. Léon is interested in the sea. 'Léon will use almost anything from the ocean, so long as it is sustainable, including seaweed, bycatch and even plankton.'[218] Redzepi, who, like Adrià, was present only in print media, shares with many of his international counterparts an interest in forgotten products or products that have not yet been used in restaurants. Together they embark on search expeditions, in order to create dishes employing their own individual fantasies.

In the history of the restaurant, collaborative cooking according to uniform guidelines is a recent phenomenon. For example, Chang invited twelve top chefs to Italy for his event *Cook It Raw*. 'To see each guy's creativity, to watch his perfectionism was amazing',[219] says Chang. This event, to which fifty guests were invited, was designed to emphasise his concern with combining environmental awareness and creativity. Chang made a 'kimchi' from local radicchio. The regional product in this case is amalgamated with cooking techniques from other cultures. Marx Rumpolt, while cooking for the various courts of the Holy Roman Empire of the German Nation in the 16th century, appropriated the knowledge of 'German, Hungarian, Hispanic, Italian, and French' cuisines, but today, this range has become global.

The craft is learned in the restaurants of top chefs. Escoffier was the great teacher of the nineteenth century after Carème, under whom Francatelli served as apprentice. Bottura came from the school of Ducasse. Redzepi, who now has trainees in his restaurant himself, studied at 'el Bulli' under Adrià. The genealogy of the chefs is a family tree with globally reaching branches. Women are virtually non-existent. One exception is Fatéma Hal and her restaurant 'Mansouria' in Paris.[220] The French-naturalised

uns für die Nahrungskreisläufe zu sensibilisieren, denn der Verzehr eines Fleisch- oder Fischgerichtes – sei es zu Hause oder im Restaurant – ist das Resultat der aneignenden „Absicht des einen Körpers auf den anderen".[215] (FIG. V) Schon Johann Wolfgang von Goethe hat hierüber sinniert:

> „So frißt's Würmlein frisch Keimleinblatt / Das Würmlein macht das Lerchlein satt / Und weil ich auch bin zu essen hier / Mir das Lerchlein zu Gemüte führ." [216]

„Its what you eat, eats",[217] konstatiert Angel Léon, der Koch der Sternerestaurants Aponiente. So finden sich heute auch Hochpreis- und Qualitätsrestaurants, früher fast ausschließlich in den Großstädten angesiedelt, wie unter anderem das Aponiente in Puerto de Santa Maria in der Nähe von Cadiz, oft außerhalb urbaner Zentren. Léons Interesse gilt dem Meer. „Léon will use almost anything from the ocean, so long as it is sustainable, including seaweed, bycatch and even plankton."[218] Redzepi, der sich ebenso wie Adrià nur in Print-Medien zu Wort meldet, teilt seine Neugier auf vergessene oder noch nicht in Restaurants verarbeitete Produkte mit vielen seiner internationalen Kollegen. Gemeinsam begeben sie sich auf Suchexpeditionen, um sich dann mit dem Einsatz der je individuellen Phantasie an die Kreation von Gerichten zu machen.

In der Geschichte des Restaurantwesens neu ist auch das kooperative Kochen nach einheitlichen Vorgaben. So hatte Chang unter dem Motto „Cook it raw" zwölf Spitzenköche nach Italien eingeladen. „To see each guy's creativity, to watch his perfectionism was amazing",[219] sagt Chang. Diese Veranstaltung, zu der 50 Gäste geladen waren, sollte sein Anliegen unterstreichen, Umweltbewusstsein und Kreativität zu vereinen. Chang kochte ein „Kimchi aus heimischem Radicchio. Das regionale Produkt wird hier mit Kochtechniken anderer Kulturkreise amalgamiert. Hatte Marx Rumpolt sich im 16. Jahrhundert an den unterschiedlichsten Fürstenhöfen des Heiligen Römischen Reiches deutscher Nation kochend, die Kenntnisse der „teutsche[n], ungarische[n], hispanische[n], italienische[n] und französische[n]" Küche angeeignet, so hat sich das Spektrum heute globalisiert.

Das Handwerk wird im Restaurant eines Spitzenkochs erlernt. Nach Carème, bei dem Francatelli in die Lehre ging, war Escoffier der große Lehrmeister des

Circuits

I am eating cabbage and turnips, what the devil! Onions, carrots and radish, because we were compelled to get used to it and because we even have gotten to like it and also because nothing else is sprouting. But all this is by rights fodder for rabbits and goats, like grass and clover is fodder for horses and cows. When I gaze at a ripe corn field, for me there is no doubt at all that this grain in the ground has germinated for the beaks of sparrows and larks and not for my mouth. When I chew my bread, then I am stealing from the birds, same as becoming a thief of weasel and fox when I eat chicken. Are not quail, pigeon and partridge the natural prey of the sparrow hawk? Sheep, deer and ox not the big carnivores? More likely anyway than if we get them served up as roast, seasoned with truffles with the truffles having been dug out of the ground by especially drilled grunters.

Guy de Maupassant: *L'Inutile Beauté*, (Paris, 1890)

FIG. V

Moroccan once served Benjamin Netanyahu and Abbas Mahmoud among others at the same table.

> 'A dish exists to heal each one of our woes ... regardless of religious or political disputes, people can communicate when they share a meal.'[221]

> 'In a world in which what and how we eat has become fetishised, celebrity chefs are finding new ways to harness their star power—and not just make money.'[222]

The economic basis of the 'cooking gods,' in addition to the media marketing and brand marketing of their own products (food and related products) as well as the sale of consumer products (kitchen accessories), is also the restaurant itself. From here, they share their secrets, knowledge, and insights from the kitchens, which already boast a long tradition as laboratories of experimentation. What is new—and this applies to all information—is the dissemination of these findings in an electronically connected world. The grandiose spectacle banquets we know from history are now staged as culinary celebrations combined with cooking as a performance conveyed by the media. And as has been true for centuries, they are reserved primarily for the elite. Those who do not belong to this circle but still want to boast about their experi-

19. Jahrhunderts. Aus der Schule von Ducasse ist Bottura hervorgegangen. Redzepi, der heute in seinem Restaurant selbst Eleven hat, lernte im el Bulli bei Adrià. Die Genealogie der Köche zeigt sich in weltweit verzweigten Stammbäumen. Frauen sind dort kaum zu finden. Eine Ausnahme ist mit dem Restaurant Mansouria in Paris Fatéma Hal.[220] Die in Frankreich naturalisierte Marokkanerin bewirtete unter anderem an ein und demselben Tisch Benjamin Netanjahu und Mahmud Abbas.

> „A dish exists to heal each one of our woes ... regardless of religious or political disputes, people can communicate when they share a meal."[221]

> „In a world in which what and how we eat have become fetishized, celebrity chefs are finding new ways to harness their star power – and not just make money."[222]

Wirtschaftliche Grundlage der „Kochgötter" sind neben der Medienvermarktung und Markenwerbung für eigene Produkte (Nahrungs- und Genussmittel) sowie dem Verkauf von Konsumgütern (Küchenzubehör) die Restaurants selber. Von hier aus verbreiten sie Bekenntnisse, Kenntnisse und Erkenntnisse aus den Küchen, die schon von jeher Labore des Experimentierens waren. Neu ist – und dies gilt für alle Informationen – die Verbrei-

ence—*à propos* the fashion label comparison mentioned above—search out a top-notch restaurant. They do not only go to eat at the establishment of a star chef, but also in restaurants that have a reputation as a traditional location. 'Simpson's' in London, the 'Paris Bar' in Berlin, the 'Oyster Bar' in New York, but especially 'La Tour d'Argent' and 'Le Grand Véfour' in Paris, and so on. In other words, places that are, for the most part, tourist attractions.

From *taberna* to guesthouse, the hospitality business has a long history, and it is a reflection of the art of cooking. The styles of the times can be seen in the architecture and interior design of the restaurant itself. Encyclopaedists and physiocrats gave impetus to a social and economic liberalisation. As a result, the restaurant was born and, through its chefs and famous guests, has passed into glory. Speed and a supposed lack of time led to the invention of fast-food restaurants, mainly in the metropolises, around 1900, which developed into giant fast-food chains in the twentieth and twenty-first centuries. The *osterias* and *fondas* of the Slow Food movement emerged as an reaction to them and their 'industrialised' products, as did the denominations of cooking luminaries celebrated in the media.

tung dieser Erkenntnisse in einer elektronisch vernetzten Welt. Die aus der Geschichte bekannten grandiosen Schau-Essen finden heute, durch die Medien vermittelt, als kulinarische Zelebrationen in Kombination mit dem Schau-Kochen statt. Wie seit Jahrhunderten, sind erstere den Eliten vorbehalten. Wer nicht dazugehört und dennoch renommieren will – vom Vergleich mit dem Modelabel war bereits die Rede – sucht ein Spitzenrestaurant auf. Man geht aber nicht nur zu den Sterneköchen, sondern auch in Restaurants, die als traditionelle Standorte einen Namen haben. Simpson's in London, Paris Bar in Berlin, Oyster Bar in New York, aber vor allem in Paris La Tour d'Argent, Le Grand Véfour, um nur wenige zu nennen, Orte, die vor allem touristische Attraktionen sind.

Von der *taberna* über das Gasthaus hat die Bewirtung außer Haus eine lange Geschichte. In ihr spiegelt sich die Kultur des Kochens. An Architektur und Innenarchitektur der Restaurants selbst lassen sich die jeweils zeittypischen Stile ablesen. Enzyklopädisten und Physiokraten gaben den Anstoß zu einer gesellschaftlichen und wirtschaftlichen Liberalisierung. In ihrer Folge feiert das Restaurant seine Geburtsstunde und gelangt durch seine Köche und berühmte Gäste zu seinem Ruhm. Schnelligkeit und vermeintlicher Zeitmangel führen vor allem in den Metropolen um 1900 zur Gründung von Schnellrestaurants, die sich bis in das 21. Jahrhundert hinein zu gigantischen Fast-Food-Ketten auswachsen. Gegen sie und ihre „industrialisierten" Produkte richten sich die „Osterien" und „Fondas" der Slow-Food-Bewegung ebenso wie die Bekenntnisse der in den Medien gefeierten Koch-Koryphäen.

Notes

1 So for example in MacDonogh, Giles: *A palate in Revolution: Grimod de La Reynière and the almanach des gourmands* (London and New York 1987); Jean-Paul Aron, Der Klub der Bäuche (Stuttgart 1993). Original French title: *Le mangeur du XIXe siècle*, Paris 1973.

2 Jean Anthelme Brillat-Savarin: *Physiologie des Geschmacks oder physiologische Anleitung zum Studium der Tafelgenüsse. Dedicated by Brillat-Savarin to the gastronomes of Paris.* Translated into German with notes by Carl Vogt, Braunschweig 1865. French original title: *Physiologie du goût ou Méditation de gastronomie transcendente; ouvrage théorique historique et à l'ordre du jour dédiér aux gastronome Parisiens par un professeur, membre de plusieurs sociétés savantes*, published anonymously, Paris 1826, p. 23

3 Jean Anthelme Brillat-Savarin was born in 1755 in Belley at the foot of the Jura. After studying law, he worked as a civil judge and in 1791 as a department representative. In Paris he came into conflict with the revolutionary government. He settled in New York after short stays in Switzerland and Germany. In 1796 he returned to France. To compensate for the loss of all his property, the 'Board' awarded him a post as secretary of the General Staff of the French Armies in Germany, and then the post of Government Commissioner in Versailles. A position he retained until his death in 1826, the year his *Physiology* was published.

4 Brillat-Savarin, Jean Anthelme: op.cit. Because some recipes are included in this culinary work, it is often mistakenly referred to as a cookbook.

5 Ory, Pascal: *Le discours gastronomique français des origines à nos jours*, Paris 1998, p. 170

6 *Kindlers Literaturlexikon*: vol. 18, Munich 1974, p. 7500

7 Brillat-Savarin, Jean Anthelme, op.cit., p. 39

8 Ibid.

9 Ucciani, Louis: Book review: 'Simha, Suzanne: Du goût. De Montesquieu à Brillat-Savarin. De l'esthétique galante à l'esthétique gourmande', Paris 2012, quoted in: *Cahiers Charles Fourier. Le phalanstère représenté*, Dijon 2013, p. 141

10 'In civilisation, good taste is reserved for only a few insiders and never for the general public.' François Marie Charles Fourier, quoted in: Silberling, E.: *Dictionnaire de sociologie phalanstérienne. Guide des oeuvres complètes de Charles Fourier*, Paris 1911, Reprint New York 1966, p. 205. It continues: 'La gourmandise est un passion qui à aucun âge ne perd son empire' and 'La gourmandise est la plus puissante passion que la nature ait donnée à l'enfant,' p. 204–205

11 Alexandre Balthazar Laurent Grimod de la Reynière was born 1758 in Paris. He worked as a lawyer after first training as an attorney. After the death of his parents, he inherited a large fortune, which allowed him to devote himself to his passion for gourmandism. Beginning in 1782, he wrote the comedy 'Le flatteur,' and worked also as a theatre critic. He then began writing restaurant criticism. His *Almanac of the Gourmands* 1803–1812 and his *Manuel of Amphytrions* … in 1808, his banquets and restaurant reviews gained him celebrity status and his work is groundbreaking for modern gastronomy. He died in 1837 at his country home in Villiers-sur-Oger.

12 François Marie Neveu (1756–1808) worked as a figure, portrait, and landscape painter at the École Polytechnique. He was also a guest of the famous Grimod de la Reynière banquet on February 1, 1783, for which he made his first etching, a frontispiece entitled 'Bibliotheque d'un gourmand au XIXe siècle.' Subsequent frontispieces were published posthumously. It is said that Grimod de la Reynière is portrayed in all of the etchings.

13 Monselet, Charles: *Les oubliés et les dédaignés*, Alençon 1857 and *La cuisine poétique*, Leipzig 1859. Charles Monselet

Anmerkungen

1 So zum Beispiel in: MacDonogh, Giles: *A palate in revolution: Grimod de La Reynière and the almanach des gourmands.* London und New York 1987; Aron, Jean-Paul: *Der Klub der Bäuche.* Stuttgart 1993. Französischer Originaltitel: *Le mangeur du XIXe siècle.* Paris 1973

2 Nummer 9 der Aphorismen des Professors. In: Brillat-Savarin, Jean Anthelme: *Physiologie des Geschmacks oder physiologische Anleitung zum Studium der Tafelgenüsse. Den Pariser Gastronomen gewidmet von Brillat-Savarin. Übersetzt und mit Anmerkungen versehen von Carl Vogt.* Braunschweig 1865. Französischer Originaltitel: *Physiologie du goût ou Méditation de gastronomie transcendente; ouvrage théorique historique et à l'ordre du jour dédiér aux gastronome Parisiens par un professeur, membre de plusieurs sociétés savantes.* Paris 1826, anonym erschienen, S. 23

3 Jean Anthelme Brillat-Savarin wurde 1755 in Belley am Fuße des Jura geboren. Nach seinem Jurastudium arbeitete er als Zivilrichter, 1791 als Departementsvertreter. In Paris geriet er in Konflikte mit der Revolutionsregierung. In die Schweiz und nach Deutschland ausweichend, landet er schließlich in New York. 1796 kehrt er nach Frankreich zurück. Als Kompensation für den Verlust all seiner Güter entschädigte ihn das „Direktorium" mit einem Posten als Sekretär des Generalstabs der französischen Armeen in Deutschland und danach mit dem Posten eines Regierungskommissars in Versailles. Dieses Amt behielt er bis zu seinem Tode 1826, dem Jahr des Erscheinens seiner *Physiologie.*

4 Brillat-Savarin, Jean Anthelme, op. cit. Fälschlicherweise wird dieses gastrosophische Werk wegen der Aufnahme einiger Rezepte oft als Kochbuch bezeichnet.

5 Wobei das französische Wort „besoin" auch für Not und Mangel steht – und diese herrschten in den unteren Gesellschaftsschichten. Ory, Pascal: *Le discours gatronomique français des origines à nos jours.* Paris 1998, S. 170

6 *Kindlers Literaturlexikon*, Bd. 18. München 1974, S. 7500

7 Brillat-Savarin, Jean Anthelme, op. cit., S. 39

8 Ibid.

9 Ucciani, Louis: Buchbesprechung: Simha, Suzanne: *Du goût. De Montesquieu à Brillat-Savarin. De l'esthétique galante à l'estétique gourmande.* Paris 2012. In: *Cahiers Charles Fourier. Le phalanstère représenté.* Dijon 2013, S. 141

10 „Der gute Geschmack ist in der Zivilisation nur einigen wenigen Eingeweihten vorbehalten und nie der Allgemeinheit". François Marie Charles Fourier zitiert in: Silberling, E.: *Dictionnaire de sociologie phalanstérienne. Guide des oeuvres complèts de Charles Fourier.* Paris 1911, Reprint New York 1966, S. 205. Weiter heißt es: „La gourmandise est un passion qui à aucun âge ne perd son empire" und „La gourmandise est la plus puissante passion que la nature ait donnée à l'enfant", S. 204–205.

11 Alexandre Balthazar Laurent Grimod de la Reynière wurde 1758 in Paris geboren. Ausgebildet als Jurist, arbeitete er als Advokat. Nach dem Tod seiner Eltern fällt ihm ein großes Vermögen zu und er kann sich seiner Leidenschaft, der „Gourmandise", widmen. Seit 1782 ist er mit der Komödie *Le flatteur* als Literat und darüber hinaus als Theaterkritiker tätig. Er wechselt dann zur Gastronomiekritik. Mit seinem *Almanach des gourmands* 1803–12 und seinem *Manuel des Amphytrions* … 1808, seinen Gastmählern und Restaurantbeurteilungen erlangt er Berühmtheit und ist wegweisend für die moderne Gastronomie. 1837 stirbt er auf seinem Landsitz in Villiers-sur-Oger.

12 François Marie Neveu (1756–1808) war als Figuren-, Bildnis- und Landschaftsmaler an der École Polytechnique tätig und Gast des berühmten Grimod-de-la-Reynièreschen Gastmahls am 1. Februar 1783, für das er das erste Titelkupfer *Bibliotheque d'un gourmand au XIXe siécle* sticht. Die späteren Titelkupfer wurden posthum veröffentlicht. Man meint, auf allen Grimod de la Reynière selbst porträtiert zu sehen.

(1825–1888) was editor-in-chief of *Le gourmet. Journal des intérêts gastronomiques*, 1858 and *Le triple Almanach gourmand*, 1865–1869

14 Grimod de la Reynière, Alexandre Balthazar Laurent: *Manuel des Amphytrions contenant un traité de la discussion des viandes à table, la nomenclature des menus les plus nouveaux et des élements de politesse*, Paris 1808

15 Amongst others Titus Maccius Plautus, Molière 1668; John Dryden, 1690; Heinrich von Kleist 1807 and Jean Girodoux

16 Alexandre Dumas the Elder (1802–1870) wrote many novels, including in 1844/1845 *Le comte de Monte-Cristo*, 12 volumes; 1844 *Les trois mousquetaires*, 8 volumes. He was so prolific that he often worked on several different novels simultaneously. *Meyers Großes Konversationslexikon* coined the phrase 'a novel factory'. The *Grand dictionnaire de cuisine* was published posthumously in 1872/1873. Dumas' *Dictionnaire* in France was followed up by Joseph Favre, *Dictionnaire de cuisine et hygiène alimentaire*, Paris 1888

17 Bachaumont, Louis Petit de: *Mémoire secrets* 1783, London 1784, vol. 1, p. 242/243. Quoted in: Aron, Jean Paul, op.cit., p. 13/14

18 Restif de La Bretonne, Nicolas Edme: *Les nuits de Paris ou le spectateur nocturne*. 8 volumes. London 1788/89

19 Joseph-Jean Baptiste Albouy Dazincourt (1747–1809) was also a professor of rhetoric at the Paris Conservatoire. He also presided over the *Jury dégustateur*. After his death, Grimod de la Reynière dedicated the seventh edition of his almanac to him.

20 François Guillaume Ducray-Duminil (1761–1819) originally an *ingenieur-machiniste*, worked as a journalist and writer, first as an editor for the literature segment of the *Journal des annonces, affiches et avis divers* and from 1790 as editor-in-chief of the *Petites affiches de Paris*.

21 MacDonogh, Giles, op.cit., p. 70–71

22 Charles Louis Cadet de Gassicourt (1769–1821) writes in his *Cours gastronomiques ou les diners de Manant-Ville, seconde édition dediée à la societé épicurienne du caveau moderne*, Paris 1809. '… essayer de composer dans ces principes une poudre nourritive pour les soldats et les marins … une vingtaine de leurs repas dans une tabatiére', p. 182

23 Benjamin Thompson Count of Rumford (1753–1814) was awarded in 1776, as an American, a position at the English War Office. In 1784 he entered the State Council in the service of Bavaria. In 1799 he returned to England before settling in Paris in 1802. He founded schools for child soldiers, supported the interests of poor people in factories, invented 'Sparöfen', (economical ovens), promoted the cultivation of potatoes, and developed the famous Rumford's soup. His works include *Essays political and philosophical*, 3 volumes, London 1796–1803.

24 Charles Elmé Francatelli (1805–1876) was the son of an Italian immigrant. He learned his cooking craft in France from Antonin (Marie Antoine) Carême. He worked as a chef in England for different families of the Victorian upper class; after this he was employed at the *Crockford and St. James* clubs, then as *maître d'hôtel* and head chef of Queen Victoria. In 1845 he published *The Modern Cook* and in 1861 *The Cook's Guide and the Butler's Assistent*. His *Plain Cookery Book for the Working Class* of 1852 (reprint 2008) also contains recipes for the poor, such as *No. 240: How to prepare a large quantity of good soup for the poor* or *No. 241: Another method for making economic soups* or *No. 242: How to make fish soup in large quantities for distribution to the poor*.

25 Alexis Benoist Soyer (1810–1858) began a five-year apprenticeship in 1821 at the restaurant owned by George Rignon near Versailles. He then worked until 1830 in the Parisian restaurant of d'Ouix on Boulevard des Italiens. He then fled to England, where he cooked for the British aristocracy. In 1837 he was head chef at London's 'Reform Club', where he directed a breakfast for 2,000 people for the coronation of Queen Victoria. He designed a kitchen for the 'Reform Club' together with Charles Barry (1795–1860), to

13 Monselet, Charles: *Les oubliés et les dédaignés*. Alençon 1857 und ders.: *La cuisine poétique*. Leipzig 1859. Charles Monselet (1825–1828) ist Chefredakteur von *Le gourmet. Journal des intérêts gastronomiques*, 1858 und des *Le triple Almanach gourmand*, 1865–1869

14 Grimod de la Reynière, Alexandre Balthazar Laurent: *Manuel des Amphytrions contenant un traité de la discussion des viandes à table, la nomenclature des menus les plus nouveaux et des élements de politesse*. Paris 1808

15 Unter anderem von Titus Maccius Plautus, von Molière (1668), John Dryden (1690), Heinrich von Kleist (1807) und Jean Girodoux (1929).

16 Alexandre Dumas d. Ä. (1802–1870) verfasste eine Vielzahl von Romanen, darunter 1844/45 *Le comte de Monte-Cristo* (12 Bände), 1844 *Les trois mousquetaires* (8 Bände). Die Produktion war eine so rege, dass Dumas in der Regel an mehreren Romanen gleichzeitig arbeitete. *Meyers Großes Konversationslexikon* prägt den Begriff „Romanfabrik". Das *Grand dictionnaire de cuisine* erschien posthum 1872/73. Dumas' *Dictionnaire* findet in Frankreich seine Fortsetzung mit Joseph Favres *Dictionnaire de cuisine et hygiène alimentaire*, Paris 1888.

17 Bachaumont, Louis Petit de: *Mémoire secrets 1783*. London 1784, Band 1, S. 242–243. Zitiert in Aron, Jean Paul, op. cit., S. 13–14

18 Restif de La Bretonne, Nicolas Edme: *Les nuits de Paris ou le spectateur nocturne*. 8 Bde. London 1788/89

19 Joseph-Jean Baptiste Albouy Dazincourt (1747–1809) war auch Rhetorikprofessor am Pariser Konservatorium. Er saß der „Jury dégustateur" vor. Grimod de la Reynière widmete ihm nach dessen Tod den siebenten Jahrgang seines *Almanach*.

20 François Guillaume Ducray-Duminil (1761–1819), ursprünglich „ingenieur-machiniste", arbeitete als Journalist und Literat, erst als Redakteur für den Literaturteil des *Journal des annonces, affiches et avis divers* und ab 1790 als Chefredakteur der *Petites affiches de Paris*.

21 MacDonogh, Giles, op. cit., S. 70–71

22 Charles Louis Cadet de Gassicourt (1769–1821) schreibt in seinen *Cours gastronomiques ou les diners de Manant-Ville, seconde édition dediée à la societé épicurienne du caveau moderne …* (Paris 1809) : „essayer de composer dans ces principes une poudre nourritive pour les soldats et les marins … une vingtaine de leurs repas dans une tabatiére" (S. 182)

23 Benjamin Thompson Graf von Rumford (1753–1814) erhielt als Amerikaner 1776 eine Anstellung im englischen Kriegsministerium. 1784 trat er als Staatsrat in bayerische Dienste. 1799 kehrte er nach England zurück um sich dann 1802 in Paris niederzulassen. Er gründete Schulen für Soldatenkinder, legte im Interesse der Armen Manufakturen an, erfand Sparöfen, propagierte den Anbau von Kartoffeln und entwickelte die berühmte Rumfordsche Suppe. Zu seinen Werken gehört *Essays political and philosophical*, 3 Bände. London 1796–1803.

24 Charles Elmé Francatelli (1805–1876) war Kind italienischer Einwanderer, erlernte sein Kochhandwerk in Frankreich unter anderem bei Antonin (Marie Antoine) Carême. Als Küchenchef arbeitete er dann in England in verschiedenen Familien der viktorianischen *upper class*, dann in den Clubs Crockford und St. James, danach als Maître d'hôtel und Küchenchef Königin Victorias. 1845 veröffentlichte er *The Modern Cook*, 1861 *The Cook's Guide and the Butler's Assistant*. Das *Plain Cookery Book for the Working Class* von 1852 (Reprint 2008) enthält auch Rezepte für die Armenspeisung wie zum Beispiel „No. 240: how to prepare a large quantity of good soup for the poor. No. 241: another method for making economic soups. No. 242: how to make fishsoup in large quantities for distribution to the poor."

25 Alexis Benoist Soyer (1810–1858) begann 1821 eine fünfjährige Lehrzeit im Restaurant von George Rignon in der Nähe von Versailles, danach arbeitete er bis 1830 im Pariser Restaurant von d'Ouix am Boulevard des Italiens. Dann flieht er nach England, wo er für den britischen Adel kocht. 1837 wird er

whom, in collaboration with Augustus Pugin (1812–1852), London owes the construction of the Houses of Parliament. He introduced gas stoves with temperature control as well as a water cooling system. In 1847 he established a soup kitchen in Dublin to help feed the poor during the Irish famine. He also devoted much attention to the army's diet. He experimented with a mobile kitchen, and designed a field stove, the Soyer stove, which was part of the standard equipment of the British military up to the twentieth century. Moreover, he gave 'service institution' cooking courses to the army. In 1851 he initiated an unsuccessful 'gastronomic symposium' as a catering company at the World Exhibition in London. His publications include *A Shilling Cookery Book for the People*, 1855, *Gastronomic Regenerator*, 1846, *The Modern Housewife*, 1849, *History of Food in All Ages*, 1853

26 See the subchapter 'From *Table d'hôte* to Restaurant' in this book, p. 163

27 Hayward, Abraham: *The Art of Dining: Or Gastronomy and Gastronomers*, London 1852

28 Jerrold, Gerald and William Blanchard: *The Epicur's Yearbook and Table Companion*, London 1868, which dealt with the following subjects: 'Remarkable Dinners of 1867', 'London Dinners', 'Good Living in Paris', 'Cooks and the Art of Cookery' and 'The Epicure's Library'. Quoted in: Ehrmann, Edwina: 'Nineteenth Century'. In: *London Eats Out. 500 Years of Capital Dining*, exhibition catalogue, London 1999, p. 69

29 A detailed overview of English gastronomical literature can be found in: Tames, Richard: *Feeding London. A Taste of History*, London 2003, p. 200–203

30 Mercier, Louis-Sébastien: *Tableau de Paris*, Hamburg and Neuchâtel 1781

31 MacDonogh, Giles, op.cit., p. 65

32 Vaerst, Friedrich Christian Eugen von: *Gastrosophie oder die Lehre von den Freuden der Tafel.*, Leipzig 1851, Reprint Munich 1975. Unfortunately none of Axel Matthe's selected illustrations are assigned to their originators.

33 Carl Friedrich Baron von Rumohr (1785–1843), after his studies in Göttingen, occupied himself with painting and writing (fiction and art history). His *Geist der Kochkunst* was published in1822 and translated into English in 1832: *The Essence of Cookery* (Reprint London 1993). He was friends with Bettina von Arnim (who liked to see him sporting an apron at her manor in Wiepersdorf) as well as most of the representatives of German Romanticism. His influence on German literature is discussed in: Wierlacher, Alois: *Vom Essen in der deutschen Literatur. Mahlzeiten in der deutschen Erzählliteratur von Goethe bis Grass*, Stuttgart, Berlin, and Cologne 1987. Here, the chapter: 'Zur Wirkung Rumohrs auf Stifter, Keller und Fontane, Nietzsche und Thomas Mann.' See in comparison with Rumohr: Bastek, Alexander and Achatz von Müller: *Kunst, Küche und Kalkül. Carl Friedrich von Rumohr (1785-1843)* and *Entdeckung der Kulturgeschichte*, exhibition catalogue Lübeck 2010; and Kegel, Gerhard: 'The Essence of Cookery' in the life of Carl Friedrich Rumohr (1785-1843). In: *Cottas Kulinarischer Almanach*, 1995/96, pp 69–80. See also the edition by Wolfgang Koeppen published in Frankfurt am Main in 1978, for which he wrote the preface.

34 Antonius Anthus alias Gustav Blumröder (1802–1855) initially studied theology, then medicine, before specialising in psychiatry. He was involved in the National Assembly in 1848 and was jailed in Augsburg as one of its members. In his *Vorlesungen*, Anthus the gourmet calls for students to adhere to a level of cleanliness, which turns Rumohr's material purism into something of almost ethical essence.

35 Rumohr, Carl Friedrich von, op.cit., p. 29. Also see: Götze, Karl Heinz: 'Rechte Mitte. Carl Friedrich Rumohr als Gastrosoph' In: Bastek, Alexander and Achatz von Müller, op.cit.

36 As mentioned above, studying authors from antiquity, which

Küchenchef im Londoner Reform Club, wo er anlässlich der Krönung von Königin Victoria ein Frühstück für 2000 Personen ausrichtet. Zusammen mit Charles Barry (1795–1860), dem in Zusammenarbeit mit Augustus Welby Northmore Pugin (1812–52) London den Bau der Houses of Parliament verdankt, entwirft er im Reform Club eine Küche. Er führt Gasherde mit Temperaturregelung und ein Wasserkühlungssystem ein. 1847 wird zur Bekämpfung der irischen Hungersnot eine von ihm entwickelte Suppenküche in Dublin installiert. Große Aufmerksamkeit widmete er auch der Ernährung des Heeres. Er experimentierte mit einer mobilen Küche, entwarf einen Feldherd, den Soyer-Herd, der bis ins 20. Jahrhundert zur Standardausrüstung des britischen Militärs gehörte. Darüber hinaus gab er an der Service Institution Kochkurse für das Heer. 1851 initiierte er erfolglos ein *gastronomic symposium* als Cateringunternehmen der Londoner Weltausstellung. Zu seinen Veröffentlichungen zählen neben dem „Ein-Schilling-Kochbuch" (*A Shilling Cookery Book for the People*, 1855), *Gastronomic Regenerator*, 1846, *The Modern Housewife*, 1849, *History of Food in All Ages*, 1853

26 Siehe dazu das Unterkapitel „Von der *table d'hôte* zum Restaurant" in diesem Buch

27 Hayward, Abraham: *The Art of Dining: Or Gastronomy and Gastronomers*. London 1852

28 Jerrold, Gerald und William Blanchard: *The Epicur's Yearbook and Table Companion*. London 1868, welches folgende Themen behandelt: „Remarkable Dinners of 1867", „London Dinners", „Good Living in Paris", „Cooks and the Art of Cookery" und „The Epicure's Library". Zitiert in: Ehrmann, Edwina: „19th Century". In: *London Eats Out. 500 Years of Capital Dining* (Ausstellungskatalog). London 1999, S. 69

29 Eine ausführliche Übersicht englischer Gastro-Literatur findet sich in: Tames, Richard: *Feeding London. A Taste of History*. London 2003, S. 200–203

30 Mercier, Louis-Sébastien: *Tableau de Paris*. Hamburg und Neuchâtel 1781

31 MacDonogh, Giles, op. cit., S. 65

32 Vaerst, Friedrich Christian Eugen von: *Gastrosophie oder die Lehre von den Freuden der Tafel*. Leipzig 1851, Reprint München 1975. Leider sind die von Axel Matthes ausgewählten Bildbeigaben nicht ihren Urhebern zugeordnet.

33 Carl Friedrich Baron von Rumohr (1785–1843) war nach seinem Studium in Göttingen malend und schreibend (Belletristik und Kunstgeschichte) tätig. Sein 1822 erschienener *Geist der Kochkunst* wurde 1832 ins Englische übersetzt als *The Essence of Cookery* (Reprint London 1993). Zu seinen Freunden gehörten neben Bettina von Arnim, die ihn gerne mit der Küchenschürze auf Gut Wiepersdorf sah, die meisten Vertreter der deutschen Romantik. Seinen Einfluss auf die deutsche Literatur behandelt Wierlacher, Alois: *Vom Essen in der deutschen Literatur. Mahlzeiten in der deutschen Erzählliteratur von Goethe bis Grass*. Stuttgart, Berlin und Köln 1987. Hierin die Kapitel: „Zur Wirkung Rumohrs auf Stifter, Keller und Fontane, Nietzsche und Thomas Mann". Vgl. zu Rumohr: Bastek, Alexander und Achatz von Müller: *Kunst, Küche und Kalkül. Carl Friedrich von Rumohr (1785–1843) und die Entdeckung der Kulturgeschichte* (Ausstellungskatalog). Lübeck 2010 und Kegel, Gerhard: „„The Essence of Cookery' im Leben des Carl Friedrich Rumohr (1785–1843)". In: *Cottas Kulinarischer Almanach*, 1995/96, S. 69–80. Vgl. auch die von Wolfgang Koeppen 1978 mit einem Vorwort von ihm in Frankfurt am Main herausgegebene Ausgabe.

34 Antonius Anthus alias Gustav Blumröder (1802–1855) studierte anfänglich Theologie, dann Medizin und spezialisierte sich auf die Psychiatrie. Er engagierte sich 1848 in der Nationalversammlung und wurde als deren Mitglied in Augsburg inhaftiert. In seinen *Vorlesungen* hält der Esskünstler Anthus seine Schüler zu einer Sauberkeit an, die Rumohrs materiellen Purismus gleichsam ins Moralische wendet.

were mentioned at the beginning of this essay, is a prerequisite for all authors of culinary literature. 'Essentially there are five ancient authors whose works demonstrate a direct or indirect influence on Rumohr's basic alimentary philosophy: the Nicomachean Ethics of Aristotle, the gastronomic Satires of Horace, the Cena Trimalchionis by Petronius, Epicurus' Letter to Menoeceus, and the Epistolae Moralis ad Lucilium from the pen of Seneca.' In: Götze, Karlheinz, op.cit, p.107, footnote 32

37 Vaerst, Friedrich Christian Eugen, Baron von, op.cit., p. 10–11

38 *La Grande Bouffe*, Director: Marco Ferreri, a French-Italian production, 1973, duration 133 minutes

39 *Babettes Gaestebud*, Director: Gabriel Axel, a Danish production, 1987, duration 103 minutes

40 Bartolomeo Sacchi da Platina (1421–1481) or Platina Cremonensis published *De honesta voluptate et valitudine* in 1474. It was considered the first cookbook of the Renaissance. *De honesta…* is Platina's translation of the text *Liber de re coquinaria* by Maestro Martino from Como, who was in the service of the Bishop of Aquileia. The German translation from 1542 is by Stephanus Vigilius Paci Montanus. Including translations into English and French the book was reissued thirty times in a period of one hundred years.

41 Schmid, Emanuel and Ulrike Staudinger: "Die Kurfürstin ließ Katzen und Mäuse braten…" Tafelfreuden am Münchener Hof'. In: Zischka, Ulrike, Hans Ottomeyer and Susanne Bäumler: *Die anständige Lust: Von Eßkultur und Tafelsitten*, exhibition catalogue Munich 1993, p. 81

42 Rumpolt, Marx: *Ein new Kochbuch. Das ist ein grundliche Beschreibung, wie man recht und wol…allerlei Speiß gesotten, gebraten, gebacken…wie man herrliche große Pancketten samt gemeinsamen Gastereyen anrichten und bestellen soll…*, Mainz 1581

43 Massialot, François (1660–1733) : *L'art de bien traitér, divisé en trois parties*, 1693; idem: *Le cuisinier royale et bourgeois*, 1691; idem: *L' école parfaite des officiers de bouche*, 1710

44 John Evelyn (1620–1706) was one of the most extraordinary personalities in the England of Charles II In 1661, he denounced pollution in *Fumigium, or, The inconveniencie of the aer and smoak of London dissipated together with some remedies humbly proposed by J.E. esq. to His Sacred Majestie, and to the Parliament now assembled.* In 1666 he entered a plan in competion with Christopher Wren for the reconstruction of London after the great fire. *Acetaria. A Discourse of Sallets. Book of Directions for Gardening and Cooking*, his treatise on growing vegetables, salad, and fruit as well as cooking, was published in 1699.

45 Coler, Johann: *Oeconomia ruralis et domestica*, 1591/1593 until 1605, in six parts

46 Bonnefons, Nicolas de: *Les délices de la campagne*, second edition, Amsterdam 1654

47 Bonnefons, quoted in: Blond, Georges and Germaine: *Der Mensch war immer schon genüßlich*, Vienna and Hamburg 1965, pp. 286/287. Quoted in: Andressen, Michael B.: *Barocke Tafelfreuden. Tischkultur an europäischen Höfen*, Stuttgart and Zurich 1996

48 Varenne, François Pierre de La (1618–1678): *Le cusinier françois ou est enseigné la manière d'apprêter tout sorte de viande, de faire toutes sortes de patisseries…*1651

49 Erb, Elke (ed.), *Peter Altenberg: Die Lebensmechanerie. Feuilletons*, Leipzig (1980), 1988, p. 172

50 See: Manesse, Leon: *Les paysans et leur seigneur avant 1789*, Paris (not dated)

51 See: Wiewelhove, Hildegard: *Tischbrunnen. Forschungen zur europäischen Tafelkultur*, Berlin 2002; Ehlert, Trude: *Das Kochbuch des Mittelalters. Rezepte aus alter Zeit*, Düsseldorf 2000; Peschke, Peter von and Werner Feldmann: *Das Kochbuch der Renaissance*, Düsseldorf 2001; Ottomeyer, Hans and Michaela Völkel: *Die öffentliche Tafel. Tafelzeremoniell in Europa 1300–1900*, exhibition catalogue Berlin 2002; Andressen, Michael B.: op. cit.

35 Rumohr, Carl Friedrich von, op. cit., S. 29 Vgl. hierzu auch: Götze, Karl Heinz: „Rechte Mitte. Carl Friedrich Rumohr als Gastrosoph". In: Bastek, Alexander und Achatz von Müller: op. cit.

36 Wie eingangs erwähnt, ist das Studium antiker Autoren Voraussetzung für die Verfasser gastronomischer Literatur. „Im wesentlichen gibt es für Rumohr fünf antike Autoren, für deren Werke sich ein direkter oder indirekter Einfluß auf Rumohrs alimentäre Elementarlehre nachweisen läßt die Nikomachische Ethik des Aristoteles, die gastronomischen Sermones des Horaz, das cena trimalchionis des Petronius, der Menoikeus-Brief Epikurs und die Epistolae Moralis ad Lucilium aus der Feder Senecas". Götze, Karl Heinz, op. cit., S. 107

37 Vaerst, Friedrich Christian Eugen, Baron von, op. cit., S. 10–11

38 *La Grande Bouffe*, Regie: Marco Ferreri, Frankreich/Italien 1973, Laufzeit 133 Minuten

39 *Babettes Gaestebud*, Regie: Gabriel Axel, Dänemark 1987, Laufzeit 103 Minuten

40 Bartolomeo Sacchi da Platina (1421–1481) oder Platina Cremonensis veröffentlichte 1474 *De honesta voluptate et valitudine*. Es gilt als erstes Kochbuch der Renaissance. *De honesta* … ist Platinas Übersetzung des Textes *Liber de re coquinaria* des aus Como stammenden Maestro Martino, der in Diensten des Bischofs von Aquileia stand. Die deutsche Übersetzung von 1542 stammt von Stephanus Vigilius Paci Montanus. Mit den Übersetzungen ins Englische und Französische erzielte das Buch in 100 Jahren 30 Auflagen.

41 Schmid, Emanuel und Ulrike Staudinger: „Die Kurfürstin ließ Katzen und Mäuse braten …' Tafelfreuden am Münchener Hof". In: Zischka, Ulrike, Hans Ottomeyer und Susanne Bäumler: *Die anständige Lust: Von Eßkultur und Tafelsitten* (Ausstellungskatalog). München 1993, S. 81

42 Rumpolt, Marx: *Ein new Kochbuch. Das ist ein grundliche Beschreibung, wie man recht und wol … allerlei Speiß gesotten, gebraten, gebacken … wie man herrliche große Pancketten samt gemeinsamen Castereyen anrichten und bestellen soll….* Mainz 1581

43 Massialot, François (1660–1733): *L'art de bien traitér, divisé en trois parties*, 1693; ders.: *Le cuisinier royale et bourgeois*, 1691; ders.: *L'ecole parfaite des officiers de bouche*, 1710

44 John Evelyn (1620–1706) war eine der herausragendsten Persönlichkeiten im England von Charles II. 1661 prangert er in *Fumifugium, or, The inconveniencie of the aer and smoak of London dissipated together with some remedies humbly proposed by J.E. esq. to His Sacred Majestie, and to the Parliament now assembled* die Umweltverschmutzung an. 1666 liefert er in Konkurrenz zu Christopher Wren einen Wiederaufbauplan für das vom Brand zerstörte Londoner Zentrum. 1699 erscheint das den Gemüse-, Salat- und Obstanbau wie auch das Kochen behandelnde Traktat *Acetaria. A Discourse of Sallet. Book of Directions for Gardening and Cooking.*

45 Coler, Johann: *Oeconomia ruralis et domestica*. 1591/1593 bis 1605, sechs Teile

46 Bonnefons, Nicolas de: *Les delices de la campagne*. Zweite Auflage, Amsterdam 1654

47 Bonnefons, zitiert in: Blond, Georges und Germaine: *Der Mensch war immer schon genüßlich*. Wien und Hamburg 1965, S. 286/287. Zitiert in: Andressen, Michael B.: *Barocke Tafelfreuden. Tischkultur an europäischen Höfen*. Stuttgart und Zürich 1996

48 Varenne, François Pierre de La (1618–1678): *Le cusinier françois ou est enseigné la manière d'apprêter tout sorte de viande, de faire toutes sortes de patisseries* ….1651

49 Erb, Elke (Hg.): *Peter Altenberg. Die Lebensmechanerie. Feuilletons.* Leipzig (1980), 1988, S. 172

50 Vgl.: Manesse, Leon: *Les paysans et leur seigneur avant 1789.* Paris o. J.

51 Vgl. : Wiewelhove, Hildegard: *Tischbrunnen. Forschungen zur europäischen Tafelkultur.* Berlin 2002; Ehlert, Trude: *Das*

52 As suggested by the detailed title *Li Tre Trattati di Messer Mattia Giegher, Bavaro di Mosburg, Trinciante del' ill Ma. Natione Alemanna in Padova...* Giegher here appears as a *Vorschneider* who served at the table and not in the kitchen. 'Nel primo si mostra con facilità grande il modo di piegare...' the first chapter deals with folding textiles. See: Sallas, Joan: *Tischlein Deck Dich. Ursprung und Entwicklung des Serviettenbrechens* (exhibition catalogue), Freiburg im Breisgau and Salzburg 2008

53 Harsdörffer, Georg Philipp: *Vollständiges und von neuem vermehrtes Trincirbuch von Tafeldecken, Trinaeren, Zeitigung der Mundkoste, Schauessen und Schaugerichten, benebens XXIV Gast oder Tischfragen*, Nuremberg 1657, reprint Leipzig 1976

54 Scappi, Bartolomeo: *Opera di Bartolomeo Scappi. Cuoco secreto di papa Pio Quinto, Venezia MDXCVIII*, First Edition Venice 1570. 'Prima fu posa la tavola con quattro touaglie per fumate & laureate a diverse fogie, con dodici saluiette, con cinque seruiti di credenza'

55 Procacchi, Giacomo: *Trincier oder Vorlegebuch / darinnen berichtet wird, wie man allerhand gebratene und gesottene Speisen / so auff fürstliche und andere Taffeln getragen werden mögen / nach italienischer und vornehmlich romanischer Art...*, 1624. Quoted in: Ottomeyer, Hans and Michaela Völkel: *Die öffentliche Tafel*, op.cit., p. 216

56 The 'surtout' and 'dormant' are richly sculptured silver or gold elements, standing platters with openings in them for carafes and shakers, which were artistically integrated into the overall design of the table setting. Their names refer to their constant presence on the table.

57 Gouarier, Zeef et al: *Les Français et la table*. Exhibition catalogue Paris 1985, p. 26

58 Malortie, Ernst von: *Der Hofmarschall. Handbuch zur Einführung eines Hofhalts*, Hannover 1842. Quoted in: Andressen, Michael B., op.cit., p. 103

59 Quoted in: Andressen, Michael B., op.cit., p. 104

60 Ibid.

61 Malortie, Ernst von, op.cit., p. 111

62 Trude Ehlert describes in her book, op.cit., p. 225, the following arrangement: 'Castle (made from a four-coloured batter, with chicken and live birds). In order to make a castle, make four pancakes, one green, one red, one blue, and one yellow. A chicken and four live birds should be inside the castle.'

63 Marie Antoine Carême (1783–1833) was born the child of a poor stonemason in Paris. A curriculum can be found in Alexandre Dumas the Elder's *Grand Dictionnaire de Cuisine*. After an apprenticeship and a three-year stay with the most famous patisseur, Bailly, he first became a confectioner and head chef for Charles Maurice de Talleyerand (1754–1838), Minister of Foreign Affairs under the Directorate and under Napoleon I. As chef de cuisine he worked at the English and Russian courts, then in Paris in the service of Baron James de Rothschild where he was allowed the greatest possible freedom to experiment. He published his meticulous numerical notes on gastronomic art in books that justified the glory and fame of his achievements in the culinary arts.

64 Carême, Marie Antoine: *Le cusinier parisien ou l'art de la cuisine française au 19iéme siècle*, Paris 1843/1844. The same (under the nome de plume of 'Antonin Carême'): *Le maître d'hôtel français ou parallèl de la cuisine ancienne et moderne*, 2 volumes, Paris 1822; idem: *Le patissier pittoresque. Ouvrage contenant cent vingt cinque sujets. Composés et dessinés par M.A. Carême*, Paris 1828

65 Beusen, Paul, Sybille Ebert-Schifferer and Ekkehard Mai: *L'art gourmand. Stilleben für Auge, Kochkunst und Gourmets von Aertsen bis van Gogh*, exhibition catalogue, Darmstadt und Cologne 1996, p. 303

66 Klemp, Klaus and Karl Weber (Eds.): *Fragile—Die Tafel der Zaren und das Porzellan der Revolutionäre. Porzellan als Kunst und Instrument in Diplomatie, Wirtschaft und Gesellschaft. Die russische Tafelkultur des 18. bis 20. Jahrhunderts*, exhibition catalogue,

Kochbuch des Mittelalters. Rezepte aus alter Zeit. Düsseldorf 2000; Peschke, Peter von und Werner Feldmann: *Das Kochbuch der Renaissance.* Düsseldorf 2001; Ottomeyer, Hans und Michaela Völkel: *Die öffentliche Tafel. Tafelzeremoniell in Europa 1300-1900* (Ausstellungskatalog). Berlin 2002; Andressen, Michael B., op. cit.

52 Wie aus dem ausführlicheren Titel *Li Tre Trattati di Messer Mattia Giegher, Bavaro di Mosburg, Trinciante del' ill Ma. Natione Alemanna in Padova ...* hervorgeht, handelt es sich bei Giegher um einen Vorschneider, der an der Tafel und nicht in der Küche diente. „Nel primo si mostra con facilità grande il modo di piegare ...“ heißt es zum Falten der Textilien im ersten Traktat. Vgl.: Sallas, Joan: *Tischlein Deck Dich. Ursprung und Entwicklung des Serviettenbrechens* (Ausstellungskatalog). Freiburg im Breisgau, Salzburg 2008

53 Harsdörffer, Georg Philipp: *Vollständiges und von neuem vermehrtes Trincirbuch von Tafeldecken, Trinaeren, Zeitigung der Mundkoste, Schauessen und Schaugerichten, benebens XXIV Gast oder Tischfragen.* Nürnberg 1657, Reprint Leipzig 1976

54 Scappi, Bartolomeo: *Opera di Bartolomeo Scappi. Cuoco secreto di papa Pio Quinto, Venezia MDXCVIII.* Erstauflage Venedig 1570: „Prima fu posa la tavola con quattro touaglie pro fumate & laureate a diverse fogie, con dodici saluiette, con cinque seruiti di credenza.“

55 Procacchi, Giacomo: *Trincier oder Vorlegebuch / darinnen berichtet wird, wie man allerhand gebratene und gesottene Speisen / so auff fürstliche und andere Taffeln getragen werden mögen / nach italienischer und vornehmlich romanischer Art ...*, 1624. Zitiert in: Ottomeyer, Hans und Michaela Völkel, op. cit., S. 216

56 Das *surtout* wie auch das *dormant* sind reich skulptierte Silber- oder Goldaufsätze, Standplatten mit Einlassungen für Karaffen und Streuer, die aufs Kunstvollste in die Gesamtskulptur integriert sind. Beide Namen verweisen auf ihre stete Präsenz auf der Tafel.

57 Gouarier, Zeef und andere: *Les Français et la table* (Ausstellungskatalog). Paris 1985, S. 26

58 Malortie, Ernst von: *Der Hofmarschall. Handbuch zur Einführung eines Hofhalts.* Hannover 1842. Zitiert in: Andressen, Michael B., op. cit., S. 103

59 Zitiert in: Andressen, Michael B., op. cit., S. 104

60 Ibid.

61 Malortie, Ernst von, op. cit., S. 111

62 Trude Ehlert erwähnt in ihrem Buch, op. cit., S. 225, folgendes Arrangement: „Burg (aus vierfarbigem Teig, mit Huhn und lebendigen Vögeln). Willst Du eine Burg machen, so mach vier Pfannkuchen, einen grün, den anderen rot, den dritten blau, den vierten gelb. In die Burg soll ein Huhn und vier lebende Vögel.“

63 Marie Antoine Carême (1783–1833) wurde als Kind eines armen Steinmetzen in Paris geboren. Ein Lebenslauf findet sich in Alexandre Dumas d. Ä. *Grand dictionnaire de cuisine.* Nach einer Lehrzeit und einem dreijährigen Verbleib bei dem damals berühmtesten Patisseur, Bailly, wird er erst Confiseur und dann Chefkoch bei Charles Maurice de Talleyrand (1754–1838), dem Außenminister unter dem Direktorium und unter Napoleon I. Als Chef de cuisine arbeitete er am englischen und russischen Hof, um dann in Paris mit der größtmöglichen Freiheit in Diensten des Barons James de Rothschild experimentieren zu können. Seine akribischen numerischen Notizen zur gastronomischen Kunst publizierte er in Büchern, die ebenso wie seine Kocherfolge seinen Ruhm und Nachruhm begründeten.

64 Carême, Marie Antoine: *Le cusinier parisien ou l'art de la cuisine française au 19iéme siècle.* Paris 1843/44. Ders. (unter dem *nome de plume* „Antonin Carême“): *Le maître d'hôtel français ou parallèl de la cuisine ancienne et moderne*, 2 Bände. Paris 1822; ders.: *Le patissier pittoresque. Ouvrage contenant cent vingt cinque sujets. Composés et dessinés par M.A. Carême.* Paris 1828

65 Beusen, Paul, Sybille Ebert-Schifferer und Ekkehard Mai: *L'art gourmand. Stilleben für Auge, Kochkunst und Gourmets von Aertsen*

Schloß Bad Homburg 2008, p. 69ff., 190–191

67 Wax replicas were common up to the eighteenth century, especially in medicine, until a German named Curtius, actually Creutz, displayed his mythological figures, international potentates, criminals, writers, and so forth in his cabinets in Paris. Under Napoleon, a Tussaud from the family Curtius took over managing the Cabinet, which subsequently was followed by the famous wax cabinet in London. See: Fournel, Victor: *Le Vieux Paris*, Paris 1979, p. 326–331

68 'The divine Restaurant consisted of beef, mutton, veal, capon, pigeon, partridge, onion, root vegetables, and herbs that have been simmered without adding water for five to six hours in a pot sealed with dough. The broth thus created was carefully skimmed of fat and poured over bread slices and eaten with chopped meat.' Andressen, Michael B.: op. cit., p. 118

69 Spang, Rebecca L.: *The Invention of the Restaurant. Paris and Modern Gastronomic Culture*, Cambridge, Mass. and London (2000), 2001, p. 11

70 op.cit., p. 28

71 Andressen, Michael B.: op.cit., p. 118–119

72 Réstif de La Bretonne, Nicolas-Edmé, Les nuits de Paris, Paris 1788. Quoted in: MacDonogh, Giles: op.cit., p. 50–51

73 Steel, Caroline: *Hungry City. How Food Shapes Our Lives*, London 2008, p. 227

74 One standard work on this subject is: Rauers, Friedrich: *Kulturgeschichte der Gaststätte*, 2 volumes, Berlin 1941

75 Nemeitz, Joachim C.: *Séjour de Paris, c'est à dire instructions fidèles pour les voyageurs de condition...*, Leiden 1727, p. 58. Quoted in: Spang, Rebecca L.: op.cit., p. 7

76 See: 'The Cosmos of the Hotel' in this book, pp. 66–130

77 Courtine, Robert: *La vie parisienne. Le ventre de Paris de la Bastille à l'Étoile … des siècles d'appétit*, Paris 1985, p. 247

78 So, for example, the receptions of Octave de Beauvau in *Splendeur et misère des Courtisanes* (1838–1847) or in *Les Illusions perdues* (1837–1844), the supper at Florine's and the dinner arranged by Lucien du Rubempré for his friends at Coralie's. 'Un couvert splendide, des candélabres charges de quarante bougies, les recherches 'Royales' du dessert.' In: Courtine, Robert, op.cit, p. 248

79 Spang, Rebecca L., op.cit., p. 24–25

80 Aron, Jean-Paul, op.cit., p. 22

81 From: Büchner, Georg: *Danton's Death*, act 3, scene 10: Square in front of the judiciary court. Quoted in: Aron, Jean-Paul, op. cit., p. 22

82 Cf. Heuler, Norbert: case study no. 13, Restaurant Moskau, Berlin, in: Bollerey, Franziska and Christoph Grafe: *Restaurants and Dining Rooms*. London/New York 2019

83 Niemeyer, August Hermann: *Beobachtungen auf einer Deportationsreise nach Frankreich im Jahre 1807*, 2 volumes, Halle/Saale 1824-1826. Quoted in: Andressen, Michael B., op.cit., p. 126

84 See Alcock, Joan P., *London in Signs*, Stroud 2007; Lauter, Wolfgang: *Schöne Laden- und Wirtshausschilder*, Dortmund 1980; Anon.: *À la belle enseigne*, exhibition catalogue Paris Musée de la Publicité, ca. 1980. See also: Balzac, Honoré de: *Dictionnaire des enseignes* (1850). In: id., *Oeuvres complètes*, volume 14, Paris 1966, p. 193–285

85 Kleist, Heinrich von: 'Fragment eines Schreibens aus Paris. Den 6. September (probably 1810)' in: Heinrich von Kleist: *Sämtliche Werke. Kleine Schriften*, Munich 1967, p. 954/955

86 MacDonogh, Giles: op.cit., p. 88. Between 1866 and 1874 there were 116 registered businesses in the field of catering, restaurant, and hotel food establishments. op. cit., p. 81

87 See: *London Eats Out*. op.cit.

88 See also: *The Epicure's Yearbook or Calendar of Good Living*, London 1815, op. cit.

89 Ehrmann, Edwina. In: *London Eats Out*, op.cit., p. 80

90 In 1848, traiteur/caterer John Simpson joined forces with

bis van Gogh (Ausstellungskatalog). Darmstadt/Köln 1996, S. 303

66 Klemp, Klaus und Karl Weber (Hg.): *Fragile – Die Tafel der Zaren und das Porzellan der Revolutionäre. Porzellan als Kunst und Instrument in Diplomatie, Wirtschaft und Gesellschaft. Die russische Tafelkultur des 18. bis 20. Jahrhunderts* (Ausstellungskatalog). Bad Homburg 2008, S. 69ff., 190–191

67 Wachsnachbildungen kamen bis zum 18. Jahrhundert vor allem in der Medizin vor, bis ein Deutscher namens Curtius, eigentlich Creutz, mythologische Figuren, internationale Potentaten, Kriminelle, Literaten et cetera in seinen Kabinetten in Paris zeigte. Unter Napoleon führt dann ein Tussaud aus der Familie Curtius das Kabinett, dem das berühmte in London folgte. Vgl.: Fournel, Victor: *Le vieux Paris*. Paris 1979, S. 326–331

68 „Das göttliche ‚Restaurant' bestand aus Rind, Hammel, Kalb, Kapaun, Taube, Rebhuhn, Zwiebel, Wurzelgemüse und Kräutern, die ohne Wasserzusatz in einem mit Teig verschlossenen Topf 5 bis 6 Stunden lang gegart wurden. Die so gewonnene und sorgfältig entfettete Brühe wurde über Brotscheiben gegossen und mit dem geschnittenen Fleisch gegessen." Andressen, Michael B., op. cit., S. 118

69 Spang, Rebecca L.: *The Invention of the Restaurant. Paris and Modern Gastronomic Culture*. Cambridge, Mass./London (2000), 2001, S. 11

70 Ibid., S. 28

71 Andressen, Michael B., op. cit., S. 118–119

72 Réstif de La Bretonne, Nicolas-Edmé: *Les nuits de Paris*. Paris 1788. Zitiert in: MacDonogh, Giles, op. cit., S. 50–51

73 Steel, Caroline: *Hungry City. How Food Shapes Our Lives*. London 2008, S. 227

74 Ein Standardwerk zur Thematik ist: Rauers, Friedrich: *Kulturgeschichte der Gaststätte*, 2 Bde. Berlin 1941

75 Nemeitz, Joachim C.: *Séjour de Paris: oder getreue Anleitung, welchergestalt Reisende von Condition sich zu verhalten haben, wenn sie ihre Zeit und Geld nützlich und wohl zu Paris anwenden wollen; nebst einer zulänglichen Nachricht von dem königl. französischen Hof, Parlement, Universität, Academien, Bibliothequen, Gelehrten, Künstlern u.*, Straßburg 1750, S. 51. Online verfügbar unter: http://reader.digitale-sammlungen.de/de/fs1/object/display/bsb11249288_00069.html

76 Vgl. das Kapitel zur Geschichte des Hotels in diesem Buch

77 Courtine, Robert: *La vie parisienne. Le ventre de Paris de la Bastille à l'Étoile – des siècles d'appétit*. Paris 1985, S. 247

78 So zum Beispiel die Empfänge von Octave de Bauvau in *Splendeur et misère des courtisanes* (1838–1847) oder in *Les illusions perdues* (1837–44) das Souper bei Florine und das von Lucien du Rubempré für seine Freunde bei Coralie ausgerichtete Diner. „Un couvert splendide, des candélabres chargés de quarante bougies, les recherches 'royales' du dessert." In Courtine, Robert, op. cit., S. 248

79 Spang, Rebecca L., op. cit., S. 24–25

80 Aron, Jean-Paul, op. cit., S. 22

81 Aus: Büchner, Georg: *Dantons Tod*, 3. Akt, 10. Aufzug: Platz vor der Justiz. Zitiert in: Aron, Jean-Paul, op. cit., S. 22

82 Vgl. den Beitrag von Norbert Heuler zum Fallbeispiel Restaurant Moskau in Bollerey, Franziska und Christoph Grafe: *Restaurants and Dining Rooms*. London, New York 2019

83 Niemeyer, August Hermann: *Beobachtungen auf einer Deportationsreise nach Frankreich im Jahre 1807*, 2 Bde. Halle/Saale 1824–26. Zitiert in: Andressen, Michael B., op. cit., S. 126

84 Vgl. Alcock, Joan P.: *London in Signs*. Stroud 2007; Lauter, Wolfgang: *Schöne Laden- und Wirtshausschilder*. Dortmund 1980; o. V.: *Á la belle enseigne* (Ausstellungskatalog Paris Musée de la Publicité), ca. 1980. Vgl. hierzu auch: Balzac, Honoré de: „Dictionnaire des enseignes" (1850?). In ders.: *Oeuvres complètes*, Band 14, S. 193–285. Hg. von Le club français du livre, Paris 1966

85 Kleist, Heinrich von: „Fragment eines Schreibens aus Paris. Den 6. September" (wahrscheinlich 1810). In: Heinrich von Kleist:

Samuel Reiss who had been managing the 'Grand Cigar Divan,' since 1828. Simpson's successor Edmund William Catley brought with him the master chef Thomas Davey, who insisted that 'in the restaurant everything should be British'.

91 Ehrmann, Edwina, op.cit. p. 81
92 Täubrich, Hans-Christian: *Zu Gast im alten Berlin. Erinnerungen an die Alt-Berliner Gastlichkeit mit Hotelpalästen, Vergnügungslokalen, Ausflugsgaststätten und Destillen*, Munich 1995, p. 159, p. 170–172
93 Fontane, Theodor: *Der Stechlin*, Berlin 1899. The work was published in sequels in 1897 in the journal 'Über Land und Meer' (Across Land and Sea), a typical way of earning money also for English and French speaking writers
94 Täubrich, Hans-Christian, op.cit., p. 91, p. 110–111
95 The historic wine cellar survived the Second World War. It disappeared in 1965 as a result of the demolition of the old buildings and the replanning of the Fischerinsel. By this time, however, a new restaurant under the same name had already been built in Schlüterstraße in West Berlin.
96 *Berlin für Kenner. Ein Bärenführer bei Tag und Nacht durch die deutsche Reichshauptstadt*, Berlin 1912. Quoted in: Täubrich, Hans-Christian, op.cit., p. 108
97 These buildings survived both World War Two and the GDR. In 1992, the restaurant *Borchardt* was opened anew.
98 See the chapter on 'Genius Loci: The Coffee House' in this book, p. 10–65
99 Theodore Dreiser: *Sister Carrie*, New York 1900, German translation (Vienna 1929) Berlin 1980, p. 43
100 Zischka, Ulrike, Hans Ottomeyer and Susanne Bäumler, op.cit., p. 213
101 Dreiser, Theodore, op.cit., p. 57–59
102 op.cit., p. 292–296
103 Maupassant, Guy de: *Bel ami*, 1885, as a serial novel in *Le Gil Blas*; as book, Paris 1895. English translation, Douglas Parmee, London 1975, p. 349
104 Flaubert, Gustave: *Sentimental Education* (original French: *L'éducation sentimentale*, 1869), English translation, Adrianne Tooke, Ware, UK, 2013, p. 347
105 Ehrenburg, Ilja: „Der Berliner Westen, das Café Schottenhaml und George Grosz". In: Zimmermann, Margarete and Gilda Rodeck: *„Ach, wie gût schmeckt mir Berlin." Französische Passanten im Berlin der zwanziger und frühen dreißiger Jahre*. Berlin 2010, pp. 51–52
106 Kronberger, Michaela, Martin Mosser and Sigrid Czeika: 'Taberna, popina und das älteste Wirtshaus Wiens'. In: Spring, Ulrike, Wolfgang Kos and Wolfgang Freitag (publ.): *Im Wirtshaus*, exhibition catalogue Vienna 2007, p. 68
107 Goethe, Johann Wolfgang von: *Letters from Switzerland: Letters from Italy*, Boston, 1902, p. 22
108 See Wagner, Heinrich. In: *Handbuch der Architektur*, 4th part, 4th half volume, *Gebäude für Erholungs- Beherbergungs- und Vereinszwecke. Schenk- und Speiselokale, Kaffeehäuser und Restaurants*, Darmstadt 1885
109 Canetti, Elias: *Masse und Macht*, Frankfurt am Main 1966, p. 224. Quoted in: Zischka, Ulrike, Hans Ottomeyer and Susanne Bäumler, op.cit.,p. 15
110 Steel, Caroline, op.cit., p. 155–156
111 Gisau, Peter: *Carl Theodor Ottmer (1800-1843) Braunschweiger Hofbaurat zwischen Klassizismus und Historismus*, Berlin 1997, p. 35
112 MacCarthy, Fiona: *William Morris. A Life of Our Time*, London (1994) 1995, p. 212–213, plate no. VII
113 Zola, Emile: *L'Assommoir*, Paris 1877. English translation by Robin Buss: *The Drinking Den*, London 2004.
114 The project was rejected by the Danish landscape protection act. Pedersen, Johan: *Arkitekten Arne Jacobsen*, Copenhagen 1954, p. 27
115 Gantenbein, Köbi: 'Seit zwanzig Jahren lobt und fördert der

Sämtliche Werke. Kleine Schriften. München 1967, S. 954–955
86 MacDonogh, Giles, op. cit., S. 88. Zwischen 1866 und 1874 waren 116 im Catering-, Restaurant- und Hotelrestaurantwesen tätige Betriebe registriert. Op. cit., S. 81
87 Vgl. *London Eats Out*, op. cit.
88 Siehe auch *The Epicure's Yearbook or Calendar of Good Living*, op. cit.
89 Ehrmann, Edwina in: *London Eats Out*, op. cit., S. 80
90 Der Traiteur/Caterer John Simpson liiert sich 1848 mit dem seit 1828 den Grand Cigar Divan führenden Samuel Reiss. Simpsons Nachfolger Edmund William Catley brachte den Meisterkoch Thomas Davey mit, der darauf bestand, dass „in the restaurant everything should be British". Tames, Richard, op. cit., S.145–146
91 Ehrmann, Edwina, op. cit., S. 81
92 Täubrich, Hans-Christian: *Zu Gast im alten Berlin. Erinnerungen an die Alt-Berliner Gastlichkeit mit Hotelpalästen, Vergnügungslokalen, Ausflugsgaststätten und Destillen*. München 1995, S. 159, S. 170–172
93 Fontane, Theodor: *Der Stechlin*. Berlin 1899. Das Werk war bereits 1897 in der Zeitschrift *Über Land und Meer* in Fortsetzungen erschienen, eine auch bei englisch- und französischsprachigen Schriftstellern durchaus übliche Art des Gelderwerbs.
94 Täubrich, Hans-Christian, op. cit., S. 91, S. 110–111
95 Der historische Weinkeller überlebte den Zweiten Weltkrieg. Im Zusammenhang mit dem Abriss der Altbausubstanz und der Neuplanung der Fischerinsel verschwand er 1965. Um diese Zeit war in West-Berlins Schlüterstraße bereits ein neues Restaurant gleichen Namens eröffnet worden.
96 *Berlin für Kenner. Ein Bärenführer bei Tag und Nacht durch die deutsche Reichshauptstadt*. Berlin 1912. Zitiert in: Täubrich, Hans-Christian, op. cit., S. 108
97 Die Räumlichkeiten haben den Zweiten Weltkrieg und die DDR überlebt. 1992 wurde das Restaurant Borchardt neu eröffnet
98 Vgl. das Kapitel zu Kaffeehäusern in diesem Band.
99 Dreiser, Theodore: *Sister Carrie*. New York 1900. Deutsche Übersetzung (Wien 1929) Berlin 1980, S. 43
100 Zischka, Ulrike, Hans Ottomeyer und Susanne Bäumler, op. cit., S. 213
101 Dreiser, Theodore, op. cit., S. 57–59
102 Op. cit., S. 292–296
103 Maupassant, Guy de: *Bel ami*, 1885, als Fortsetzungsroman in: *Le Gil Blas*; als Buch Paris 1895. Deutsche Übersetzung: München 1974, S. 349
104 Flaubert, Gustave: *Lehrjahre des Herzens*. München 1957, S. 431/432 (französisches Original: *L'éducation sentimentale*, 1869)
105 Ehrenburg, Ilja: „Der Berliner Westen, das Café Schottenhaml und George Grosz". In: Zimmermann, Margarete und Gilda Rodeck: *Ach, wie gût schmeckt mir Berlin." Französische Passanten im Berlin der zwanziger und frühen dreißiger Jahre*. Berlin 2010, S. 51–52
106 Kronberger, Michaela, Martin Mosser und Sigrid Czeika: „Taberna, popina und das älteste Wirtshaus Wiens". In: Spring, Ulrike, Wolfgang Kos, und Wolfgang Freitag (Hg.): *Im Wirtshaus* (Ausstellungskatalog). Wien 2007, S. 68
107 Nagel, Joachim: *Zu Gast bei Goethe. Der Dichterfürst als Genießer*. München (1998) 1999, S. 193
108 Vgl. hierzu: Wagner, Heinrich. In: *Handbuch der Architektur*, 4. Teil, 4. Halb-Band, *Gebäude für Erholungs- Beherbergungs- und Vereinszwecke. Schenk- und Speiselokale, Kaffeehäuser und Restaurants*, Darmstadt 1885
109 Canetti, Elias: *Masse und Macht*. Frankfurt am Main 1980, S. 224. Zitiert in: Zischka, Ulrike, Hans Ottomeyer und Susanne Bäumler, op. cit., S. 15
110 Steel, Caroline, op. cit., S. 155–156
111 Gisau, Peter: *Carl Theodor Ottmer (1800–1843). Braunschweiger Hofbaurat zwischen Klassizismus und Historismus*. Berlin 1997, S. 35
112 MacCarthy, Fiona: *William Morris. A Life of Our Time*. London

Solarpreis das Bauen mit und an der Sonne'. In: *Hochparterre*, volume. 9, September 2010, p. 50–53
116 Massaglia, Ait-Ahmed, Marina: *Maurice Braillard. Architect et urbaniste*, Geneva 1991, p. 135–139
117 This is a design that demonstrates mass and balance: 'Anlegestelle und Restaurant, Aufgabenstellung von Nikolai Alexandrowitsch Ladowski'. In: Chan-Magomedow, Selim O.: *Pioniere der sowjetischen Architektur. Der Weg zur neuen sowjetischen Architektur in den 20er und frühen 30er Jahren*, Dresden 1983, p. 114
118 Negro, Francesco dal: *Hotel des Alpes. Storie di alberghi ed albergatori dalla Savoia al Tirolo. Historische Gastlichkeit von Savoyen bis Tirol.* Baden 2007, p. 135–139
119 Pisanik, Sonja, Walter Loos, Fridel Loos, Hermann Loos: *Paraíso Argentino*, Vienna 2006
120 Danesi, Silvia and Luciano Patetta (publ.): *Il razionalismo e l'architettura in Italia durante il fascismo*, exhibition catalogue Biennale di Venezia, Venice 1976
121 Koch, Alexander: *Hotels, Restaurants, Café- und Barräume*, Stuttgart 1951
122 Amberger, Eva-Maria: *Sergius Ruegenberg. Architekt zwischen Mies van der Rohe und Hans Scharoun*, Berlin 2000, p 165
123 Simmen, Jeannot: *Ruinen-Faszination in der Graphik vom 16. Jahrhundert bis in die Gegenwart*, Dortmund 1980, plate 112
124 Bruisson, Michel and Fiona Meadows: 'Ma cantine en ville. Voyages au coeur de la cuisine de rue'. Valorisation de l'innovation dans la meublement. Competition: *Microarchitektur Mini Maousse 5.* exhibition Paris 2012, Galerie VIA. See Tinker, Irene: *Urban Food and Employment in Developing Countries*, Oxford 1997
125 Quoted in: Bollerey, Franziska: *Mythos Metropolis*, op.cit., p. 54
126 Their public appearance goes back to the tradition of the town crier. The corporation of 'crieurs du roi' started in the twelfth century in Paris. Their duty was to call out news and announcements or the hour of night, before the introduction of bulletins and news sheets.
127 Maurenbrecher, C.P.: *Europäische Kaufrufe I. Straßenhändler in graphischen Darstellungen. Mitteleuropa, England, Rußland*, Dortmund 1980, p. 12. See also idem: *Europäische Kaufrufe II. Straßenhändler in graphischen Darstellungen. Paris, Lissabon, Neapel, Rom, Bologna, Mailand, Venedig und Konstantinopel*, Dortmund 1980
128 *New York Times Magazine*, February 7, 1926. Quoted in: Gutman, Richard J.S. and Elliott Kaufman: *American Diner*, New York 1979, p. 6
129 Gutman, J.S., op.cit., p. 4
130 Ibid., p. 2
131 Ibid., p. 3
132 Ibid., p. 11. In 1898, 230,804 meals were served. The initiative was made possible by the support of wealthy New Yorkers. In recognition of these 'restaurants on wheels,' Cornelis Vanderbilt funded a wagon called 'Good Cheer' in 1922, located on the east side of Union Square.
133 Jakle, John A. and Keith A. Sculle: *Fast Food. Roadside Restaurants in the Automobile Age*, Baltimore 1999, p. 36
134 Camus, Dominique: *Paris décors. Art Nouveau—Art Déco…*, Paris 2012, p. 206–207
135 Manzo, Joseph: 'From Pushcart to Modular restaurant. The Diner on the Landscape'. In: *Journal of American Culture*, 13, Autumn 1990, p. 13–21, here p. 19. Quoted in Jakle, John A. and Keith A. Sculle, op.cit., p. 37
136 Jakle, John A. and Keith A. Sculle, op.cit., p. 37
137 Op.cit., p. 36 Ibid., p. 23
138 Ibid., p. 23
139 The diner was built in 1946 by the Fodero Dining Car Company. As 'Arthur's Diner' it was more a shaky type of greasy-spoon restaurant. But after being placed under new management and renamed in 1970, and being close in

(1994) 1995, S. 212–213, Tafel Nr. VII
113 Zola, Emile: *L'Assommoir*. Paris 1877. Deutsche Übersetzung: *Der Totschläger*. Berlin 1880. Später auch als „Die Schnapsbude" und „Die Giftschänke" übersetzt
114 Eine Realisierung scheiterte am Einspruch des dänischen Landschaftsschutzes. Pedersen, Johan: *Arkitekten Arne Jacobsen*. Kopenhagen 1954, S. 27
115 Gantenbein, Köbi: „Seit zwanzig Jahren lobt und fördert der Solarpreis das Bauen mit und an der Sonne". In: *Hochparterre*, Nr. 9, September 2010, S. 50–53
116 Massaglia, Ait-Ahmed, Marina: *Maurice Braillard. Architect et urbaniste*. Genf 1991, S. 135–139
117 Hier handelt es sich um einen Entwurf zur Demonstration der Masse und des Gleichgewichts: Anlegestelle und Restaurant, Aufgabenstellung von Nikolai Alexandrowitsch Ladowski. In: Chan-Magomedow, Selim O.: *Pioniere der sowjetischen Architektur. Der Weg zur neuen sowjetischen Architektur in den 20er und frühen 30er Jahren*. Dresden 1983, S. 114
118 Negro, Francesco dal: *Hotel des Alpes. Storie di alberghi ed albergatori dalla Savoia al Tirolo. Historische Gastlichkeit von Savoyen bis Tirol*. Baden 2007, S. 135–139
119 Pisanik, Sonja: *Walter Loos, Fridel Loos, Hermann Loos. Paraíso Argentino*. Wien 2006
120 Danesi, Silvia und Luciano Patetta (Hg.): *Il rationalismo e l'architettura in Italia durante il fascismo* (Ausstellungskatalog Biennale di Venezia). Venedig 1976
121 Koch, Alexander: *Hotels, Restaurants, Café- und Barräume*. Stuttgart 1951
122 Amberger, Eva-Maria: *Sergius Ruegenberg. Architekt zwischen Mies van der Rohe und Hans Scharoun*. Berlin 2000, S. 165
123 Simmen, Jeannot: *Ruinen-Faszination in der Graphik vom 16. Jahrhundert bis in die Gegenwart*. Dortmund 1980, Abb. 112
124 Bruisson, Michel/Meadows, Fiona: „Ma cantine en ville. Voyages au coeur de la cuisine de rue". Valorisation de l'innovation dans la meublement. Wettbewerb: Microarchitektur: Mini Maousse 5. Ausstellung Paris 2012, Galerie VIA. Vgl.: Tinker, Irene: *Urban Food and Employment in Developing Countries*. Oxford 1997
125 Zitiert in: Bollerey, Franziska: *Mythos Metropolis*, op. cit., S. 54
126 Ihr Auftritt in der Öffentlichkeit geht auf die Tradition der Ausrufer zurück. Seit dem 12. Jahrhundert gab es in Paris die Korporation der „Crieurs du roi", denen es vor der Einführung von Aushängen und Nachrichtenblättern oblag, Bekanntmachungen oder auch die Nachtstunde auszurufen.
127 Maurenbrecher, C. P.: *Europäische Kaufrufe I. Straßenhändler in graphischen Darstellungen. Mitteleuropa, England, Rußland*. Dortmund 1980, S. 12. Siehe auch ders.: *Europäische Kaufrufe II. Straßenhändler in graphischen Darstellungen. Paris, Lissabon, Neapel, Rom, Bologna, Mailand, Venedig und Konstantinopel*. Dortmund 1980
128 *New York Times Magazine*, 7. Februar 1926. Zitiert in: Gutman, Richard J. S. und Elliott Kaufman: *American Diner*. New York 1979, S. 6
129 Gutman, J.S., op. cit., S. 4
130 Ibid., S. 2
131 Ibid., S. 3
132 Ibid., S. 11. Im Jahr 1898 wurden 230.804 Essen ausgegeben. Die Initiative war durch die Unterstützung reicher New Yorker Bürger möglich. Cornelis Vanderbilt finanzierte in Anerkennung dieser „Restaurants on Wheels" 1922 einen „Good Cheer" genannten Wagen mit Standort an der Ostseite des Union Square.
133 Jakle, John A. und Keith A. Sculle: *Fast Food. Roadside Restaurants in the Automobile Age*. Baltimore 1999, S. 36
134 Camus, Dominique: *Paris décors. Art Nouveau – Art Déco ….* Paris 2012, S. 206–207
135 Manzo, Joseph: „From Pushcart to Modular Restaurant. The Diner on the Landscape". In: *Journal of American Culture*, 13, Herbst 1990, S. 13–21, hier S. 19. Zitiert in Jakle, John A. und Keith A. Sculle, op. cit., S. 37

proximity to the legendary 'Chelsea Hotel', it became a popular social hangout. The icon painted by John Baeder was made during this time (1976).

140 Cf. 'Genius Loci: The Coffee House' in this book, pp. 10–65

141 Allen, Frederick: *Secret Formula*, New York 1994

142 Morand, Paul, New York (1930) 1986, p. 228. Quoted in: Fischler, Claude: 'Über den Prozeß der McDonaldisierung'. In: Hürlimann, Annemarie and Alexander Reininghaus: *mäßig und gefräßig*, exhibition catalogue MAK Vienna 1996, p. 255. At the end of the nineteenth century another Frenchman described a similar scene. See: Rousiers, Paul de: *La vie americaine*, Paris 1892

143 Merill, Robert S.: 'Spreads Unjust Criticism of Fountain Lunch'. In: *The Soda Fountain*, 23, June 1924, p. 37. Quoted in: Jakle, John A. and Keith A. Sculle, op.cit., p. 27

144 For example the *Soda Fountain Magazine* and *The Soda Fountain*

145 The bathing and drinking fountain culture developed in ancient Rome still serves the city of Rome today, by means of public fountains with drinking water, the source of life non plus ultra. Noteworthy is the lack of public fountains in the American cityscape. There, it is typical to have water dispensers installed in office or administration buildings.

146 Caradec, François and Jean-Robert Massou: *Guide de Paris mysterieux. Les guides noires*, Paris 1978, p. 282/283 and p. 301

147 An apt characterisation of American eating habits and eating establishments was written by Ilya Ilf and Yevgeny Petrov: *Das eingeschossige Amerika. Eine Reise mit Fotos von Ilja Ilf in schwarz-weiß und Briefen aus Amerika*, (1936/37) Frankfurt am Main 2011.

148 Sinclair, Upton: *Oil!*, New York 1926, p. 18. Quoted in: Jakle, John A. and Keith A. Sculle, op.cit., p. 32

149 In 1888, the 'All Male Exchange Buffet' was opened in New York as a cafeteria. In 1905 Helen Mesher attempted a version for women. Every member, including the cook, was female.

150 Jakle, John A. and Keith A. Sculle, op.cit., p. 33

151 Ibid., p. 34

152 'Presto' von Otto Bauer near the Parisian stock exchange only had 27 dispensers.

153 Lorraine, B. Deal and Marianne Hardart: *The Automat. The History, Recipes and Allure of Horn & Hardart's Masterpiece*, New York 2002

154 Breentjes, Yvonne (ed.): *Piet Zwart. Vorm-ingenieur*. 1885-1977, exhibition catalogue Gemeente Museum Den Haag 2008, here: *Een 'machine à manger' in Parijs*, p. 154

155 Ibid., p. 157

156 Ilf, Ilja and Jewgeni Petrov, op.cit., p. 70

157 Pillsbury, Richard: *From Boarding House to Bistro. The American Restaurant Then and Now*, Boston 1990, p. 46. In 1950, Childs had only fifty-three locations left, and in the 1960s they went into a merger.

158 'Aschinger' real estate strategy was to buy not only the ground floor of a building but the entire building. The upper floors served as housing for their female employees (up to 1914, half of their employees were women). Work and housing rental contract were linked.

159 Allen, Keith R.: *Hungrige Metropole: Essen, Wohlfahrt und Kommerz in Berlin*, Hamburg 2002, p. 95

160 The *Schrippe* is a bread roll made of wheat flour and can be traced back to the baguettes of the Huguenots, who immigrated to Prussia after the decree of Potsdam in 1685. *Hackepeter* is minced pork mixed with onions and in the Rhineland is called *Mett*.

161 Allen, Keith R., op.cit., p. 96

162 Kiaulehn, Walther: *Berlin. Schicksal einer Weltstadt*, München und Berlin 1958. Here, see the chapter: 'Berlin, wie es ißt und trinkt', p. 213-234, p. 222

163 Balzac, Honoré: *Illusions perdues*, drei Teile: *Les deux poètes*, Paris 1837; *Un grand homme de province à Paris*, 1839; *David*, 1844

136 Ibid.

137 Ibid., S. 23

138 Ibid.

139 Der Diner wurde 1946 von der Fodero Dining Car Company gebaut. Als Arthur's Diner war er ein eher schmieriges Restaurant. Mit der Umbenennung und neuen Bewirtschaftung wurde er 1970 in unmittelbarer Nähe des legendären Chelsea Hotel ein Szenetreffpunkt. Aus dieser Zeit (1976) stammt auch die gemalte Ikone von John Baeder.

140 Vgl. das Kapitel zu Kaffeehäusern in diesem Band

141 Allen, Frederick: *Secret Formula*. New York 1994

142 Morand, Paul: *New York*. (1930) 1986, S. 228. Zitiert in Fischler, Claude: „Über den Prozeß der McDonaldisierung". In: Hürlimann, Annemarie und Alexander Reininghaus: *mäßig und gefräßig* (Ausstellungskatalog). Wien 1996, S. 255. Bereits Ende des 19. Jahrhunderts hat ein anderer Franzose Vergleichbares geschildert: Siehe Rousiers, Paul de: *La vie americaine*. Paris 1892

143 Merill, Robert S.: „Spreads Unjust Criticism of Fountain Lunch". In: *The Soda Fountain*, 23. Juni 1924, S. 37. Zitiert in Jakle, John A. und Keith A. Sculle, op. cit., S. 27

144 So zum Beispiel das *Soda Fountain Magazine* und *The Soda Fountain*

145 Die in der römischen Antike entwickelte Bade- und Trinkbrunnenkultur versorgt die Stadt Rom noch heute über alle öffentlichen Brunnen mit Trinkwasser, dem Lebensmittel Nummer Eins. Auffällig ist ein Fehlen öffentlicher Brunnen im amerikanischen Stadtbild. Typisch hingegen sind die vor allem in Büro- und Verwaltungsgebäuden überall installierten *water dispenser*.

146 Caradec, François und Jean Robert Massou *Guide de Paris mysterieux. noires*. Paris 1978, S. 282–283 und S. 301

147 Eine treffende Charakterisierung amerikanischer Essgewohnheiten und -lokalitäten geben Ilja Ilf und Jewgeni Petrow in *Das eingeschossige Amerika. Eine Reise mit Fotos von Ilja Ilf in schwarz-weiß und Briefen aus Amerika*. (1936/37) Frankfurt am Main 2011.

148 Sinclair, Upton: *Oil!* New York 1926, S. 18. Zitiert in Jakle, John A. und Keith A: Sculle, op. cit., S. 32

149 1888 wurde als Cafeteria das All Male Exchange Buffet in New York eröffnet. 1905 unternimmt Helen Mesher den Versuch einer Frauenvariante. Bis hin zu den Köchen war das gesamte Personal weiblich.

150 Jakle, John A.und Keith A. Sculle, op. cit., S. 33

151 Ibid., S. 34

152 Das Presto von Otto Bauer in der Nähe der Pariser Börse hatte nur 27 Fächer.

153 Lorraine, B. Deal und Marianne Hardart: *The Automat. The History, Recipes and Allure of Horn & Hardart's Masterpiece*. New York 2002

154 Breentjes, Yvonne (Hg.): *Piet Zwart. Vorm-ingenieur. 1885–1977* (Ausstellungskatalog Gemeente Museum). Den Haag 2008. Dort: „Een ‚machine à manger' in Parijs", S. 154

155 Ibid., S. 157

156 Ilf, Ilja und Jewgeni Petrow, op. cit., S. 70

157 Pillsbury, Richard: *From Boarding House to Bistro. The American Restaurant Then and Now*. Boston 1990, S. 46. 1950 verfügte Childs nur noch über 53 Standorte, um dann in den 1960er Jahren in Fusionen aufzugehen.

158 Aschingers Immobilienpolitik umfasste nicht nur den Erwerb des Erdgeschosses, sondern ganzer Häuser. In den oberen Geschossen wurden dann für das weibliche Personal – bis 1914 waren die Hälfte aller Beschäftigten Frauen – Wohnungen eingerichtet. Arbeits- und Mietverträge waren gekoppelt.

159 Allen, Keith R.: *Hungrige Metropole. Essen, Wohlfahrt und Kommerz in Berlin*. Hamburg 2002, S. 95

160 Die Schrippe ist ein Weizenmehlbrötchen und geht auf die Baguette der Hugenotten, die nach dem Edikt von Potsdam von 1685 nach Preußen einwanderten, zurück. Hackepeter ist mit

164 On the site of the latter, there was also the central administration of the Aschinger Corporation as well as a dormitory for women. Up to four thousand people were employed in the bread factory. In 1947, after the expropriation, the baking operations were run by a 'VEB' (Volkseigener Betrieb/nationally owned enterprise). After the fall of the Berlin Wall, the company 'Cityback' was based here. After more renovation and modernisation, the factory-like architecture still remains a major structural and aesthetical feature of the complex, which is today used for residential purposes, small businesses, studios, and restaurants. See: Raach, Jörg: *Industriekultur in Berlin: Die 115 wichtigsten Bauten des Industriezeitalters*, Berlin 2008, p. 150–151

165 Döblin, Alfred: *Berlin Alexanderplatz* (Berlin 1929), Munich 1965, p. 146

166 Allen, Keith R., op. cit., p. 95. Acquiring the 'aryanised' company 'Kempinski' in 1936 was the most economically relevant acquisition, which also consolidated the company. Kempinski was a renowned world-class business with more than 1,000 employees. As early as 1905, Aschinger entered the field of exclusive gastronomy through its acquisition of top-notch restaurants and hotels. They bought the wine restaurant 'Rheingold' and the 'Fürstenhof Hotel'. After the First World War came the 'Kaiserhof' Hotel, the 'Baltikum,' 'Esplanade,' 'Bristol,' 'Zentral-,' 'Grand-,' and 'Palast-Hotel,' as well as the Restaurant-Palast 'Haus Vaterland' (named 'Picadilly' before the First World War). Except, for the 'Adlon, 'Continental,' 'Excelsior,' 'Eden,' and 'Kempinski' practically every renowned hotel in Berlin belonged to Aschinger in the 1920s.

167 Nelson, Walter Henry: *The Berliners. Portrait of People and a City*, New York 1969, p. 282f. Quoted in: Allen, Keith R., op.cit., p. 95

168 Ritzer, George: 'Fast Food' in: Biswas, Ramesh Kumar, Siegfried Mattl and Ulrike Davis-Sulikowski (Eds.): *Götterspeisen*, exhibition catalogue Historisches Museum der Stadt Wien, Vienna 1997, p.122 and Ritzer, George: *The McDonaldization of Society*, Thousand Oaks, rev. ed. 1996

169 'Minced chicken meat was mixed with a binder of cereal flour, dry milk, spices, salt, water and vinegar. The whole was covered with a batter of flour, eggs, spices, and cornflake crumbs to give the product an appetising colour while frying. The nugget contains, in addition to thirteen products derived from corn, numerous chemicals including the carcinogen-suspicious polydimenthylsiloxan … or the preservative butylhydroquinone which is derived from petroleum.' Of course, experiments in breeding special chickens were carried out in the interest of profit maximisation. A chicken variety was developed that had a particularly large breast, which would ensure supply. It was baptised 'Mr. McDonalds'. Cf. Haffner, Peter: 'Sushi des Volkes. Das Produkt kennt jeder, seine Schöpfer fast niemand: Robert Baker hat 1963 die Chicken Nuggets erfunden'. In: *Neue Zürcher Zeitung Folio,* 12, 2009, p. 22 and 24

170 Schlosser, Eric: *Fast Food Nation*, New York 2001 p. 139

171 See: Love, John F.: *McDonald's: Behind the Arches*, New York 1986

172 Wallraff, Günter: *Ganz unten*, Köln 1985

173 Ritzer, George, op. cit., p. 129

174 Sullivan, Barbara: 'McDonald's sees India as Golden Opportunity', in: *Chicago Tribune*, April 5, 1995. Quoted in: Ritzer, George, op.cit., p. 126

175 Morin, Edgar : *L'Esprit du temps*, Paris (1962) 1975

176 Ibid., p. 85

177 Fischler, Claude: ‚Über den Prozeß der McDonaldisierung', in: Hürlimann, Annemarie and Alexander Reininghaus, op.cit., p. 259

178 Zola, Emile: *Au Bonheur des dames*, Paris 1883. Eleventh novel of the cycle *Les Rougon Macquart*. Zola perceptively analyses how the enticing offers encourage women's desire to buy, who ultimately buy under an 'urge' to consume but without the need

Zwiebeln vermischtes gehacktes Schweinefleisch, im Rheinland „Mett" genannt.

161 Allen, Keith R., op. cit., S. 96

162 Kiaulehn, Walther: *Berlin. Schicksal einer Weltstadt*. München, Berlin 1958. Hier das Kapitel: „Berlin, wie es ißt und trinkt", S. 213–234, S. 222

163 Balzac, Honoré: *Illusions perdues*. Drei Teile: *Les deux poètes*. Paris 1837; *Un grand homme de province à Paris*. Paris 1839; *David*. Paris 1844

164 Auf dem Gelände letzterer befand sich auch die zentrale Verwaltung des Aschinger-Konzerns sowie ein Wohnheim für Frauen. In der Brotfabrik waren bis zu 4000 Beschäftigte tätig. 1947, nach der Enteignung, backte hier ein VEB. Nach der Wende hatte die Firma Cityback hier ihren Standort. Nach erneuter Sanierung und Modernisierung der nicht in den Hintergrund gedrängten Fabrikarchitektur wird der Komplex nun für Wohnen, Kleingewerbe, Ateliers und Restaurants genutzt. Vgl.: Raach, Jörg: *Industriekultur in Berlin Die 115 wichtigsten Bauten des Industriezeitalters*. Berlin 2008, S.150–151

165 Döblin, Alfred: *Berlin Alexanderplatz*. (Berlin 1929) München 1965, S. 146

166 Allen, Keith R., op. cit., S. 95. Der ökonomisch relevanteste und das Unternehmen konsolidierende Zuerwerb erfolgte 1936 mit der Übernahme des „arisierten" Unternehmens Kempinski, einer renommierten Firma von Weltklasse mit mehr als 1000 Beschäftigten. Bereits 1905 hatte sich Aschinger durch die Übernahme von Nobelrestaurants und Hotels in die gehobene Gastronomie begeben. Erworben wurden das Weinhaus Rheingold und das Hotel Fürstenhof. Nach dem Ersten Weltkrieg folgten die Hotels Kaiserhof, Baltikum, Esplanade, Bristol, Zentral- , Grand- und Palast-Hotel sowie der Restaurantpalast Haus Vaterland (vor dem ersten Weltkrieg Picadilly genannt). Bis auf die Häuser Adlon , Continental , Excelsior , Eden und Kempinski gehörten Ende der 1920er Jahre praktisch alle renommierten Hotels in Berlin Aschinger.

167 Nelson, Walter Henry: *The Berliners. Portrait of People and a City*. New York 1969, S. 282f. Zitiert in: Allen, Keith R., op. cit., S. 95

168 Ritzer, George: „Fast Food". In: Biswas, Ramesh Kumar, Siegried Mattl und Ulrike Davis-Sulikowski (Hg.): *Götterspeisen*. (Ausstellungskatalog). Wien 1997, S.122 und Ritzer, George: *The McDonaldization of Society*. Thousand Oaks rev.ed. 1996

169 „Dem gehackten Hühnerfleisch wurde ein Bindemittel aus Getreidemehl, Trockenmilch, Gewürzen, Salz, Wasser und Essig beigemengt. Das Ganze wurde mit einem Backteig aus Mehl, Eiern, Gewürzen und Cornflakebröseln überzogen, um dem Produkt beim Braten eine appetitliche Farbe zu verleihen. Immer noch finden sich neben dreizehn Produkten aus Mais zahlreiche Chemikalien darunter, wie das als karzinogen verdächtige Polydimenthylsiloxan…oder das aus Petroleum gewonnene Butylhydrochinon, das der Frischhaltung dient, im Nugget". Selbstverständlich wurde unter dem Aspekt der Gewinnmaximierung auch mit Züchtungen experimentiert. Es wurde eine Hühnerrasse mit besonders großer Brust entwickelt, um für Nachschub zu sorgen. Sie wurde auf den Namen „Mr. McDonald's" getauft. Vgl. Haffner, Peter: „Sushi des Volkes. Das Produkt kennt jeder, seine Schöpfer fast niemand: Robert Baker hat 1963 die Chicken Nuggets erfunden". In: *NZZ Folio*, 12, 2009, S. 22 und 24

170 Schlosser, Eric: *Fast Food Nation*, New York 2001. S. 139

171 Vgl. hierzu: Love, John F.: *McDonald's: Behind the Arches*. New York 1986

172 Wallraff, Günter: *Ganz unten*. Köln 1985

173 Ritzer, George, op. cit., S. 129

174 Sullivan, Barbara: „McDonald's sees India as Golden Opportunity". In: *Chicago Tribune*, 5. April, 1995. Zitiert in: Ritzer, George, op. cit., S. 126

175 Morin, Edgar: *L'Esprit du temps*. Paris (1962) 1975

176 Ibid., S. 85

177 Fischler, Claude: „Über den Prozeß der McDonaldisierung".

to do so.
179 In response to the harmful effects of 'junk food,' all chain providers in New York with more than twenty branches were forced to disclose calorie and nutritional information starting in 2008. Restaurants were also ordered to gradually stop using harmful 'transfats'. *Time Magazine*, June 18, 2012
180 'Das Streiflicht'. *Süddeutsche Zeitung*, February 3, 2012
181 Viction:ary (ed.): *Eat me. Appetite for Design. Product, Packaging, Art, Branding, Interior*, Hongkong 2012, p. 138–139
182 Levenstein, Harvey: *Revolution at the Table. The Transformation of the American Diet*, New York 1988, p. 227. Cf: ibid. *Paradox of Plenty—A Social History of Eating in Modern America*, New York 1993. Quoted in: Fischler, Claude, op.cit. p. 255
183 Bravermann, Harry: *Labor and Monopoly Capital: The Degradation of Work in the 20th Century*, New York 1974. Quoted in: Ritzer, George, op.cit., p. 130
184 Graham, Sylvester: *Treatise on Bread and Breadmaking*, Boston 1827. Quoted in: Giedion, Sigfried, op.cit., p. 235
185 Pigott, Sadi: 'Amuse bouche. Kitchen existential'. In: *Time Magazine*, September 6, 2010. In 2010 Osteria Francescana ranked number six of the world's top fifty restaurants.
186 Curnonsky, actually Maurice Edmond Sailland (1872-1956), together with Marcel Rouff (1887-1936), the author of the culinary novel *La vie et la passion de Daudin-Bouffant, gourmet* (1924), published the thirteen volume work entitled *La France gastronomique. Guide des merveilles culinaires et des bonnes auberges Françaises*, Paris 1921–1928, which placed focus on regional products.
187 Abend, Lisa: 'The Starmaker. Andrea Petrini, Paris's tireless culinary networker and cultivator of talent'. *Time Magazine*, November 18, 2013
188 Ibid.
189 Abend, Lisa: 'Would you like chicken … or chicken? The Gelinaz dinner was part meal, part art happening and wholly unforgettable'. *Time Magazine*, July 22, 2013
190 Ibid.
191 Ibid.
192 Marinetti, Filippo Tommaso: *La cucina futurista*, Milan 1932; German translation: F.T. Marinetti. *Die futuristische Küche*, Stuttgart 1983
193 Künstlerverein Malkasten (ed.). Conceived by Robert Hartmann and Andreas Wünkhaus, *eat art. Restaurant spoerri.* Sammlung Carlo Schröter, Düsseldorf 2009
194 Stiftung Museum Haus Moyland (ed.): *Joseph Beuys—'Beethovens Küche.' Eine Dokumentation in Photographien von Brigitte Dannehl*, Bedburg-Hau 2004
195 Anon.: *Restaurant de Paris*, 1993; German translation: *Paris. Die schönsten Restaurants*, Cologne 1994
196 Camus, Dominique: *Paris décor. Art nouveau—art déco…*, Clermont-Ferrand 2012
197 Anon.: *Die schönsten Restaurants*, op.cit. p. 173
198 Sallas, Joan, op.cit., p. 14
199 Oaklander, Mandy: 'Pop chefs' tiny, temporary restaurants are a model with staying power'. *Time Magazine,* vol. 181, February 16, 2015
200 Spring, Ulrike, Wolfgang Kos and Wolfgang Freitag: *Im Wirtshaus. Eine Geschichte der Wiener Geselligkeit*, exhibition catalogue Vienna 2007, p. 53
201 Bajekal, Nana: 'Moveable Feast. Stephen Leguillon brings fine dining home'. In: *Time Magazine,* vol. 181, June 8, 2015
202 *Time Magazine,* vol. 179, November 18, 2013
203 Abend, Lisa: 'Kitchen gods. They start behind the counter and end up in the spotlight. How the phenomenon of the celebrity chef has transformed the restaurant industry and even changed the way we eat.', *Time Magazine,* vol. 176. July 12, 2010, p. 32–25
204 Montgomery-Massingberd, Hugh and David Watkin: *The London Ritz. A social and architectural history*, London 1980, p. 15

In: Hürlimann, Annemarie und Alexander Reininghaus, op. cit., S. 259
178 Zola, Emile: *Au bonheur des dames.* Paris 1883. Elfter Roman des Zyklus *Les Rougon-Macquart.* Scharfsinnig analysiert Zola, wie die verlockenden Angebote die Kauflust der Frauen anfeuerten, die schließlich unter „Konsumzwang" ohne Bedürfnis kaufen.
179 In Reaktion auf die gesundheitsschädigende Wirkung von „*junk food*" hat bereits 2008 New York alle Restaurants mit mehr als 20 Filialen zu Kalorienangaben gezwungen. Auch wurden Restaurants aufgefordert, stufenweise den Gebrauch von schädlichen Transfetten einzustellen. *Time Magazine*, 18. Juni 2012
180 „Das Streiflicht". In: *Süddeutsche Zeitung*, 3. Februar 2012
181 Viction:ary (Hg.): *Eat me. Appetite for Design. Product, Packaging, Art, Branding, Interior.* Hongkong 2012, S. 138–139
182 Levenstein, Harvey: *Revolution at the Table. The Transformation of the American Diet.* New York 1988, S. 227. Vgl. auch ders.: *Paradox of Plenty – A Social History of Eating in Modern America.* New York 1993. Zitiert in Fischler, Claude, op. cit., S. 255
183 Bravermann, Harry: *Labor and Monopoly Capital: The Degradation of Work in the 20th Century.* New York 1974. Zitiert in: Ritzer, George, op. cit., S. 130
184 Graham, Sylvester: *Treatise on Bread and Breadmaking.* Boston 1827, zitiert in: Giedion, Sigfried, op. cit., S. 235
185 Pigott, Sadi: „Amuse bouche. Kitchen existential". In: *Time Magazine*, 6. September 2010. 2010 rangierte die Osteria Francescana an sechster Stelle der weltbesten 50 Restaurants.
186 Curnonsky, eigentlich Maurice Edmond Sailland (1872–1956) veröffentlichte zusammen mit Marcel Rouff (1887–1936), dem Autor des kulinarischen Romans *La vie et la passion de Daudin-Bouffant, gourmet* (1924), das 13-bändige Werk *La France gastronomique. Guide des merveilles culinaires et des bonnes auberges Françaises*, Paris 1921–1928, in dem die regionalen Produkte im Mittelpunkt stehen.
187 Abend, Lisa: „The Starmaker. Andrea Petrini, Paris tireless culinary networker and cultivator of talent." In: *Time Magazine*, 18. November 2013
188 Ibid.
189 Abend, Lisa: „Would you like chicken … or chicken? The Gelinaz dinner was part meal, part art happening and wholly unforgettable." In: *Time Magazine*, 22. July 2013
190 Ibid.
191 Ibid.
192 Marinetti, Filippo Tommaso: *La cucina futurista.* Mailand 1932; deutsche Übersetzung: Marinetti, Filippo Tommaso: *Die futuristische Küche.* Stuttgart 1983
193 Künstlerverein Malkasten (Hg.): Konzeption Robert Hartmann und Andreas Wünkhaus: *eat art. Restaurant spoerri. Sammlung Carlo Schröter.* Düsseldorf 2009
194 Stiftung Museum Haus Moyland (Hg.): *Joseph Beuys „Beethovens Küche". Eine Dokumentation in Photographien von Brigitte Dannehl.* Bedburg-Hau 2004
195 O. V.: *Restaurants de Paris.* 1993; deutsche Übersetzung: *Paris. Die schönsten Restaurants.* Köln 1994
196 Camus, Dominique: *Paris décor. Art nouveau – art déco ….* Clermont-Ferrand 2012
197 O.V.: *Paris. Die schönsten Restaurants*, op. cit., S. 173
198 Sallas, Joan, op. cit., S. 14
199 Oaklander, Mandy: „Pop chefs' tiny, temporary restaurants are a model with staying power". In: *Time Magazine,* vol. 181, 16. Februar 2015
200 Spring, Ulrike, Wolfgang Kos und Wolfgang Freitag: *Im Wirtshaus. Eine Geschichte der Wiener Geselligkeit* (Ausstellungskatalog). Wien 2007, S. 53
201 Bajekal, Nana: „Moveable Feast. Stephen Leguillon brings fine dining home". In: *Time Magazine,* vol. 181, 8. Juni 2015
202 *Time Magazine,* vol. 179, 18. November 2013
203 Abend, Lisa: „Kitchen gods. They start behind the counter and

205 Hong, Dorothy: 'el bullient'. *Financial Times*, May 3, 2014, p. 10–12. Also see: Luscombe, Belinda: '10 questions. Groundbreaking chef Ferran Adrià talks about the weirdness of honey and why everyone is wrong about tomatoes.', *Time Magazine*, June 2, 2014, p. 52
206 Hong, Dorothy, op.cit., p. 12
207 op.cit., p. 10
208 Beusen, Paul and others, op.cit., p. 301
209 The *Guide Gault et Millau* by Henri Gault and Christian Millau was launched in 1977
210 The *Michelin guide pour les chauffeurs et vélocipédistes* appeared for the first time in 1900 in Clermont-Ferrand and contained references to and a descriptive assessment of restaurants and accommodations
211 Abend, Lisa: 'Kitchen Gods', op.cit., p. 35
212 Ibid.
213 Abend, Lisa: 'Top chef. How 34-year-old Danish chef René Redzepi came to lead the latest revolution in European cuisine'. *Time Magazine*, March 26, 2012, p. 35
214 Based on the 'Society for Nutrition Education' founded in 1981, the movement was established around 2000 with the goal of bringing consumers and producers together at local markets.
215 Canetti, Elias: *Masse und Macht*, Frankfurt am Main 1980, p. 224. Quoted in: Ottomeyer, Hans: *Die anständige Lust*, op.cit., p. 15
216 Quoted in: von Vaerst, Eugen, op.cit., first volume, p. 19
217 Abend, Lisa: 'Courses of Nature. The chef who uses his menu as a metaphor of the sea'. In: *Time Magazine*, May 23, 2011 … 'he created a 'food chain' tasting menu that began with a spoonful of green phytoplankton, then moved upward through tiny shrimp served as fritters, to local sardines and spectacular gray mullet, which Léon hung for nine days as if it were game, before serving in a yellow plankton emulsion.'
218 Ibid.
219 Abend, Lisa: 'Kitchen Gods', op.cit., p. 36
220 Hal made a pilgrimage through Morocco for years in search of recipes. She visited hundreds of women as well as the 'dada,' a caste of female cooks on the brink of extinction. She employs only women in the kitchen of her 150-seat restaurant. Some of her dishes are designed to draw attention to forgotten relationships. 'The Sephardic Jewish dafina stew, French cassoulet and North African chick pea hergma are related', Hal points out, being carried to different countries by Jews fleeing the Spanish Inquisition. Iverson, Jeffrey T.: 'The conciliatory chef. Making the world a better place, one dish at a time', *Time Magazine*, October 17, 2011
221 Ibid.
222 Abend, Lisa: 'Kitchen gods', op. cit., p. 33

For footnotes 3, 86, 100, 102, 104, 105, 109, and 114 the quoted pages refer to the German editions used by the author.

end up in the spotlight. How the phenomenon of the celebrity chef has transformed the restaurant industry and even changed the way we eat'. In: *Time Magazine, vol. 176,* 12. Juli 2010, S. 32–25
204 Montgomery-Massingberd, Hugh und David Watkin: *The London Ritz. A social and architectural history*. London 1980, S. 15
205 Hong, Dorothy: „el bullient". In: *how to spend it.* Magazin der *Financial Times*, 3. May 3, 2014, S. 10–12. Siehe auch: Luscombe, Belinda: 10 questions. Groundbreaking chef Ferran Adrià talks about the weirdness of honey and why everyone is wrong about tomatoes. In: *Time Magazine*, June 2, 2014, S. 52
206 Hong, Dorothy, op. cit., S. 10–12
207 Op. cit., S. 10
208 Beusen, Paul u.a., op. cit., S. 301
209 Der von Henri Gault und Christian Millau herausgegebene *Guide Gault et Millau* erscheint seit 1977.
210 1900 erscheint in Clermont-Ferrand zum ersten Mal der *Guide Michelin pour les chauffeurs et vélocipédistes* mit Hinweisen auf und einer beschreibenden Beurteilung von Restaurants und Übernachtungsmöglichkeiten.
211 Abend, Lisa: „Kitchen gods", op. cit., S. 35
212 Ibid.
213 Abend, Lisa: „Top chef. How 34-year old Danish chef René Redzepi came to lead the latest revolution in European cuisine". In: *Time Magazine*, 26. März 2012, S. 35
214 Basierend auf der 1981 gegründeten Society for Nutrition Education hat es sich die Bewegung ab etwa 2000 zum Ziel gesetzt, Konsumenten und Produzenten auf lokalen Märkten einander näher zu bringen.
215 Canetti, Elias: *Masse und Macht*. Frankfurt am Main 1980, S. 224. Zitiert in: Ottomeyer, Hans: *Die anständige Lust*, op. cit., S. 15
216 Zitiert in: von Vaerst, Eugen, op. cit., erster Band, S. 19
217 Abend, Lisa: „Courses of Nature. The chef who uses his menu as a methaphor of the sea". In: *Time Magazine*, 23. Mai 2011: „he created a ‚food chain' tasting menu that began with a spoonful of green phytoplankton, then moved upward through tiny shrimp served as fritters, to local sardines and spectacular gray mullet, which Léon hung for nine days as if it were game, before serving in a yellow plankton emulsion."
218 Ibid.
219 Abend, Lisa: „Kitchen gods", op. cit., S. 36
220 Hal pilgerte auf der Suche nach Rezepten jahrelang durch Marokko. Sie besuchte dabei Hunderte von Frauen und die sogenannten *dada*, eine im Aussterben begriffene Kaste weiblicher Köche. In ihrem 150 Plätze bietenden Restaurant beschäftigt sie in der Küche nur Frauen. Einige ihrer Speisen zielen darauf ab, auf vergessene Beziehungen aufmerksam zu machen. „The Sephardic Jewish *dafina* stew, French cassoulet and North African chick pea *hergma* are related", Hal points out, being carried to different countries by Jews fleeing the Spanish Inquisition. Iverson, Jeffrey T.: „The conciliatory chef. Making the world a better place, one dish at a time". In: *Time Magazine*, 17. Oktober 2011
221 Ibid., S. 23
222 Abend, Lisa: „Kitchen gods", op. cit., S. 33

Bibliography
Bibliografie

Selected Bibliography Cafés and Bars

Albrecht, Peter: *Kaffee. Zur Sozialgeschichte eines Getränkes*, Exhibition catalogue, Braunschweig 1980.

Albrecht, Peter: 'Coffee-Drinking as a Symbol of Social Change in Continental Europe in the Seventeenth and Eighteenth Centuries'. In: *Studies in Eighteenth Century Culture*, 18 (1988), 91–103.

Andreini, Laura (Ed.): *Cafés & Restaurants*, Kempen 2000.

Aslan, Carlo and Line Dru: *Cafés, Restaurants*, Stuttgart 1991.

Ball, Daniela U. (Ed.): *Kaffee im Spiegel europäischer Trinksitten*, Zürich 1991.

Bernart Skarek, Brigitta: 'Konglomerat von alten und neuen Wertvorstellungen. Gaststätten in Japan'. In: *architektur*, 7 (2001), no. 4, 34–37.

Bernier, Georges: 'Paris cafes: their role in the birth of modern art'. November 13–December 20, 1985, New York 1985.

Bersten, Ian: *Coffee Floats, Tea Sinks. Through History and Technology to a Complete Understanding*, Sydney 1993.

Beynet, Agricol: *Les chroniques du Palais-Royal: origine, splendeur et décadence; les ducs et les duchesses, la régence, théâtres, cafés, restaurants, tripots, les galeries de bois, etc.*, Paris 1881.

Binder, Hartmut: *Wo Kafka und seine Freunde zu Gast waren. Prager Kaffeehäuser und Vergnügungsstätten in historischen Bilddokumenten*, Furth im Wald 2000.

Biziere, Jean Maurice: 'Hot beverages and the enterprising spirit in 18th century Europe'. In: *Journal of Psychohistory*, 7 (1979), 135–145.

Blas Vega, José: *Los cafés cantantes de Sevilla*, Madrid 1987.

Bodor, Ferenc: 'Old coffee houses'. In: *Magyar epitömüveszet*. Budapest 1985, no. 4, 58.

Bödecker, Hans Erich: 'Le café allemand au XVIIIe siècle. Une forme de sociabilité éclairée'. In: *Revue d'histoire moderne et contemporaine*, 37 (1990), 570–588.

Boettcher, Jürgen: *Coffee houses of Europe*, photographs by Manfred Hamm, Introduction by George Mikes, London 1980.

Bologne, Jean Claude: *Histoire des cafés et des cafetiers*, Paris 1993.

Borràs, Tomás: 'Los cafés literarios'. In: *Villa de Madrid*, Madrid, 3 (1959), no. 12, 30–35.

Bossio, Jorge Alberto: *Los cafés de Buenos Aires: reportaje a la nostalgia*, Buenos Aires 1995.

Bramah, Edward and Joan Bramah: *Coffee Makers*, London 1989.

Brandstätter, Christian (Ed.): *Das Wiener Kaffeehaus*, Munich/Vienna/Zürich 1978.

Brewster, Pomeroy: *The coffee houses and tea gardens of old London*, Rochester 1888.

Burgert, Helmuth: *Das Wiener Kaffeehaus*. Österreichische Bücherei Nr. 2 (edited by Alfred Missong), Brixlegg, Tirol 1937.

Buß, Georg: 'Kaffee und Kaffeehäuser'. In: *Westermanns Monatshefte*, Braunschweig, vol. 1908.

Caradec, François: *Le café-concert*, Paris 1980.

Christophe, Delphine and Georgina Letourny (Ed.): *Paris et ses Cafés*, Paris 2004.

Clayton, Antony: *London's Coffee Houses. A stimulating story*, London 2003.

Condemi, Concetta: *Les cafés-concerts: histoire d'un divertissement (1849–1914)*, Paris 1992.

Constantin, Marc: *Histoire des Cafes-Concerts et des Cafes de Paris*, Paris 1872.

Coste, René: *Les cafétiers et les cafés dans le monde*, 3 vols, Paris 1955, 1959, 1961.

Courtine, Robert: *La vie parisienne, Vol. 1, Cafés et restaurants des boulevards 1814–1914*, Paris 1984.

Cunow, Heinrich: *Politische Kaffeehäuser. Pariser Silhouetten aus der Grossen Französischen Revolution*, Berlin 1925.

Delvau, Alfred: *Histoire anecdotique des cafés & cabarets de Paris*, Paris 1862.

Depaule, Jean-Charles: 'Conteurs et cafés du caire' [selected texts]. In: *Lectures du roman de Baybars* (2003), 201–208.

Devoto, Alberto: *De los cafés de Buenos Aires*, Buenos Aires 1995.

Diament, Jacques: *Les cafés de philosophie, une forme inédite de socialisation par la philosophie*, Paris 2001.

Dias, Marina Tavares: *Os cafés de Lisboa*, Lisboa 1999.

Díaz y de Ovando, Clementina: *Los cafés en México en el siglo XIX*, México 2000.

Díaz, Lorenzo: *Madrid: tabernas, botillerías y cafés (1476–1991)*, Madrid 1992.

Dru, Line: *Les Cafés*, Milan 1988.

Duis, Perry: *The Saloon – Public Drinking in Chicago and Boston 1880–1920*, Urbana/Chicago 1983.

Ecker, Ludwig: *250 Jahre Wiener Kaffeehaus. Festschrift des Gremiums der Kaffeehausbesitzer in Wien zur Erinnerung an die Gründung des ersten Wiener Kaffeehauses*, Vienna 1933.

Eleb, Monique and Jean-Charles Depaule: *Paris – Société des Cafés*, Paris 2005.

Eleb, Monique: *La Société des Cafés – Los Angeles*, Paris 2004.

Ellis, Ayton: *The Penny Universities*, London 1956.

Ellis, Markman: *The Coffee House, A Cultural History*, London 2004.

Erki, Edit: *Kávéház-sirató: törzshelyek, írók, mhelyek /válogatta és az összeköt szöveget írta*. Budapest 1995. [Budapest Coffee houses of the past as meeting points of literates, actors and artists].

Espinàs, Josep Maria: *Obra completa, Vol. 8, Escrits sobre Catalunya 2, ciutats de Catalunya, cafès de Barcelona*, Barcelona 1994.

Espinàs, Josep Maria: *Quinze anys de cafès de Barcelona, 1959–1974*, Barcelona 1975.

Fitch, Noël Riley: *Die literarischen Cafés von Paris*, Zürich 1993.

Fosca, François: *Histoire des cafés de Paris*, Paris 1934.

Girouard, Mark: *Victorian Pubs*, New Haven/London 1984.

Girveau, Bruno: *La belle époque des cafés et des restaurants*, Paris 1990.

Gomes, Danilo: *Antigos cafés do Rio de Janeiro*, Rio de Janeiro 1989.

Gorham, Maurice: 'The Pub and the People'. In: *The Architectural Review*, October 1949, 213.

Gugitz, Gustav: *Das Wiener Kaffeehaus. Ein Stück Kultur- und Lokalgeschichte*, Vienna 1940.

Haine, W. Scott: *The world of the Paris café: sociability among the French working class*, 1789–1914, Baltimore 1996 .

Hattox, Ralph S.: *Coffee and coffeehouses: the origins of a social beverage in the medieval Near East*, Seattle 1996 (1985), (Near Eastern studies, no. 3).

Hazeu, Wim: *Literaire cafés van Antwerpen*, Amsterdam 1993.

Heering, Kurt-Jürgen (Ed): *Das Wiener Kaffeehaus*, Frankfurt 1993.

Heise, Ulla: *Histoire du café et des cafés les plus célèbres*, Paris 1988.

Heise, Ulla: *Kaffee und Kaffeehaus: eine Kulturgeschichte*, Leipzig 1987. (English edition: *Coffee and coffee houses*, West Chester 1987).

Hess, Alan: *Googie - fifties coffee shop architecture*, San Francisco 1985.

Hoffmann, Paul: 'Aus dem ersten Jahrhundert des Kaffees. Kulturgeschichtliche Streifzüge'. In: *Zeitschrift für Kulturgeschichte*, 8 (1901), 405–441 and 9 (1902), 90–104.

Huddleston, Sisley: *Bohemian literary and social life in Paris : salons, cafés, studios*, London 1928.

Jones, Colin and Rebecca Spang: 'Sans-culottes, sans café, sans tabac: Shifting realms of necessity and luxury in eigtheenth-century France'. In: Berg, Maxine, Helen Clifford (Ed.): *Consumers and luxury. Consumer culture in Europe 1650–1850*, Manchester 1999, 37–62.

Jünger, Wolfgang: *Herr Ober, ein Kaffee! Illustrierte Kulturgeschichte des Kaffeehauses*, Munich 1955.

Kafe-resutoran: 62 outstanding cafes, tearooms, cafe-bars, restaurants,

Tokyo 2002.
Kindblom, Maria and Johan Kondisboken: *Klassiska svenska kaféer och konditorier*, Stockholm 2003.
Koch, Alexander: *Restaurants, Cafés, Bars*, Stuttgart 1959.
Kracauer, Siegfried: 'Caféhaus-Projekte'. In: *Frankfurter Zeitung*, 66, no. 877, 25 November 1921
Kracauer, Siegfried: 'Die Frau vor dem Café'. In: *Frankfurter Zeitung*, 71, no. 682, 13 September 1926.
Kracauer, Siegfried: 'Café im Berliner Westen'. In: *Frankfurter Zeitung*, 76, no. 285–286, 17 April 1932.
Kracauer, Siegfried (G. Hellfried): 'Seminar im Café'. In: *Frankfurter Zeitung*, 77, no. 316–317, 29 April 1933.
Kraus, Karl: 'Die demolirte Litteratur', Vienna 1897 (pre-publication *Wiener Rundschau*, 15 November, 1 December, 15 December 1896 and 1 January 1897).
Krulic, Brigitte: *Europe, lieux communs: cafés, gares, jardins publics ...*, Paris 2004.
Langle, Henry-Melchior de: *Le petit monde des cafés et débits parisiens au XIXe siècle: évolution de la sociabilité citadine*, Paris 1990.
Leclaut, Jean: 'Le Café et les Cafés à Paris (1644-1693)'. In: *Annales*, 6 (1951), 1–13.
Lemaire, Gerard-Georges: *L'Europe des Cafes*, Paris 1991.
Lemaire, Gerard-Georges: *Theoriés des Cafés*. 2 vols : Anthologie et Catalogue, Paris 1997.
Lepage, Auguste: *Les cafés politiques et littéraires de Paris*, Paris 1885.
Lummel, Peter (Ed.): *Kaffee – vom Schmuggelgut zum Lifestyle-Klassiker: drei Jahrhunderte Berliner Kaffeekultur*, Berlin 2002.
Maddox, Adrian: *Classic cafés*, Photographs by Phil Nicholls, London 2003.
Mauro, Frédéric: *Histoire du Café*, Paris 1991.
May, Herbert und Andrea Schulz (Ed): *Gasthäuser. Geschichte und Kultur*, Petersberg 2004.
Michelena, Alejandro: *Los cafés montevideanos*, Montevideo 1986
Moderne Cafés, Restaurants und Vergnügungsstätten: Aussen- u. Innenarchitektur. Berlin 1928.
Nairz, Joerg: 'Das Kaffeehaus. Renaissance einer Institution' In: *architektur aktuell*, 19 (1984), no. 101, 29–30.
Neumann, Petra (Ed.): *Wien und seine Kaffeehäuser. Ein literarischer Streifzug durch die berühmtesten Cafés der Donaumetropole*, Munich 1997.
Oberthür, Mariel: *Cafés and cabarets of Montmartre*. Salt Lake City 1984.
Oldenburg, Ray: *The great good place: cafés, coffee shops, bookstores, bars, hair salons, and other hangouts at the heart of a community*, New York 1999.
Pegler, Martin M. [Ed.]: *Cafés & Coffee Shops*, New York 1995.
Pegler, Martin M. [Ed.]: *Cafés & Coffee Shops No. 2*, New York: 2001.
Peña Muñoz, Manuel: *Los cafés literarios en Chile*, Santiago de Chile 2001.
Peressut, Luca Basso: *L'architettura del caffè: tradizione e progetto in Europa*, Milan 1994.
Polgar, Alfred: 'Theorie des Café Central'. In: Alfred Polgar: *An den Rand geschrieben*, Berlin 1927.
Rauers, Friedrich: *Kulturgeschichte der Gaststätten*, Berlin 1941.
Reinders, Pim and Thera Wijsenbeek: *Koffie in Nederland*, Zutphen 1994.
Roca, Maria Mercè: *La màgia dels cafès*, Barcelona 1992.
Rocca, Pablo: *Montevideo: altillos, cafés, literatura (1849–1986)*, Montevideo 1992.
Roden, Claudia: *Coffee*, London 1977.
Rössner, Michael (Ed.): Literarische Kaffeehäuser, Kaffeehausliteraten, Vienna 1999.
Sampelayo, Juan: 'Noticias y anécdota de los cafés madrileños'. In: *Anales del Istituto de Estudios Madrileños*, Madrid , 6 (1970), 507–527.
Sapparelli, Bruno: *Des bruits, des cafés, des hommes*, Geneva 1983.
Scevola, Annamaria: *New bars, cafés & pubs in Italy*, Milan 2001.
Schivelbusch, Wolfgang: *Das Paradies, der Geschmack und die Vernunft. Eine Geschichte der Genussmittel*. Munich 1980. (English translation: *Tastes of paradise: a social history of spices, stimulants, and intoxicants*, New York 1992)
Schivelbusch, Wolfgang: 'Der Kaffee als bürgerliche Produktivkraft'. In: *Ästhetik und Kommunikation. Beiträge zur politischen Erziehung*, 9 (1978), 5–20.
Schmidt, Karl August: *Geschichte des Pariser Cafégastes*, Berlin 1909.
Smith, Woodruff D.: 'From Coffeehouse to parlour. The consumption of coffee, tea and sugar in north-western Europe in the seventeenth and eighteenth centuries'. In: Goodman, Jordan (Ed.). *Consuming Habits. Drugs in History and Anthropology*, London 1995, 148–164.
Spiel, Hilde: 'Das Kaffeehaus als Weltanschauung'. In: *Wien. Spektrum einer Stadt*, Vienna 1971.
Teply, Karl: *Die Einführung des Kaffees in Wien. Georg Franz Koltschitzky, Johannes Diodato, Isaak de Luca* (Forschungen und Beiträge zur Wiener Stadtgeschichte, vol. 6), Vienna 1980.
Timbs, John: *Clubs and club life. With anecdotes of its famous coffee houses, hostelries and taverns from the seventeenth century up to present time*, London 1898.
Torberg, Friedrich: 'Das Kaffeehaus'. In: *Wien. Vorstadt Europas*, Zürich 1963.
Vernes, Michel: 'Cafes de Paris'. In: *Architecture interieure*. C.R.E.E., (1987), no. 220, 88–95.
Wagner, Heinrich: *Handbuch der Architektur* (general editor: Eduard Schmitt): Teil 4: Entwerfen, Anlage und Einrichtung der Gebäude, Halb-Bd. 4: Gebäude für Erholungs-, Beherbergungs- und Vereinszwecke, Teil: H. 1: Schankstätten und Speisewirtschaften, Kaffeehäuser und Restaurants. Volksküchen und Speiseanstalten für Arbeiter, Volkskaffeehäuser. Öffentliche Vergnügungsstätten. Festhallen. Gasthöfe höheren Ranges. Gasthöfe niederen Ranges, Schlaf- und Herbergshäuser, Stuttgart 1904 (3rd edition).
Welter, Henri: *Essai sur l'histoire du café*, Paris 1868.
Westerfrölke, Hermann: *Englische Kaffeehäuser als Sammelpunkte der literarischen Welt im Zeitalter von Dryden und Addison*, Jena 1924.

Selected Bibliography Hotels

'2000 Meter über dem Meer'. In: Kunst und Architektur in der Schweiz, 3 (1999).
Abraben, E.: *Resort Hotels: Planning and Management*, New York 1965.
Albrecht, Donald: *New Hotels for Global Nomads*, London 2002.
‚Ambassador Hotel', *American Architect*, 5 August 1928, 165.
Baeder, John: *Gas, Food, and Lodging*, New York 1982.
Berens, Carol: *Hotel Bars and Lobbies*, New York 1997.
Bern. *Hotel Bellevue Palace. Dépendance der Macht*. In: *Du. Die Zeitschrift der Kultur*, 8 August 1988.
Binney, Marcus: *The Ritz Hotel London*, London 1999.
Boniface, Priscilla: *Hotels and Restaurants 1830 to the Present Day*, London 1981
Borràs, Montse: Hotel Spaces, Beverly 2008.
Braden, Susan R.: *The Architecture of Leisure: The Florida Resort Hotels of Henry Flagler and Henry Plant*, Florida 2002.
Brucken, Carolyn: 'In the public eye: women and the American luxury hotel', *Winterthur Portfolio*, 31 (4), 1996: 203–20.
Carry, James: *Frank Lloyd Wright's Imperial Hotel*, New York 1989.
Cathcart Borer, Mary: *The British Hotel Through the Ages*, London 1972.
Colby, Reginald: ‚London's Palm Court Hotels', *Country Life*, 16 April 1964, 896.
Curtis, Wayne: ‚The Plaza checks out: converting New York's most famous hotel marks the end of a storied past', *Preservation*, 57 (6), 2005, 22–7.

Davey, Peter: 'Morecambe and modernity: Union North and Avanti Architects help revive Morecambe's Midland Hotel for developer/hotelier, Urban Splash', *Architectural Review*, 224 (1339), 2008, 76–81.
Denby, Elaine: *Grand Hotels: Reality and Illusion: An Architectural and Social History*, London 1998.
Donzel, Catherine, Gregory, Alexis and Walter, Marc: *Grand American Hotels*, London 1989.
D' Ormesson, Jean , David Watkin u.a.: *Grand Hotel. The Golden Age of Palace Hotels. An Architectural and Social History*, New York 1984.
Evans , Nancy Goyne: 'The Sans Souci, a fashionable resort hotel in Ballston Spa', *Winterthur Portfolio*, (6), 1970: 111–26.
Fahrenkamp, Emil: P*arkhotel Haus Rechen, Bochum. Erbaut von E. Fahrenkamp*, Berlin/Leipzig/Wien 1929.
Firebaugh, W. C.: *The Inns of Greece and Rome. And a History of Hospitality from the Dawn of Time to the Middle Ages*, New York (1928), 1972.
Fischer, Bernhard (Bearb.): *Der Badische Hof 1807–1830. Cottas Hotel in Baden-Baden*, Marbach 1997 (Marbacher-Magazin 79/1997).
Flückiger-Seiler, Roland: *Hotelpaläste zwischen Traum und Wirklichkeit. Schweizer Tourismus und Hotelbau 1830–1920*, Zürich (2001) 2003.
Flückiger-Seiler, Roland: *Hotelträume zwischen Gletschern und Palmen. Schweizer Tourismus und Hotelbau. 1830–1920*, Zürich (2001) 2005.
Frishauer, Willi: *The Grand Hotels of Europe*, New York 1965.
Frost, Barbara: *Memories of the Midland*, Manchester 1992.
Garrard Lowe, David: *Beaux Arts New York*, New York 1998.
Gibson, Sarah: 'Accomodating strangers: British hospitality and the asylum hotel debate', *Journal for Cultural Research*, 7 (4), 2003: 367–86.
Glücksmann, Robert: *Das Gaststättenwesen*, Stuttgart 1927.
Hamilton, W.J.: *Promoting New Hotels. When does it pay*, New York/ London 1930.
Gogarty, Amy: ‚New craft in old spaces: artist-designed rooms at Toronto's Gladstone Hotel', In: *Craft, Space and Interior Design, 1855–2005*, Aldershot 2008.
Groth, Paul: *Living Downtown: The History of Residential Hotels in the United States*, California 1994.
Guise, Barry and Brook, Pam: *The Midland Hotel: Morecombe's White Hope*, Lancaster 2008.
'Havana Hilton', *Interiors*, August 1958, 66.
Hayner, Norman S.: *Hotel Life*, Chapel Hill 1936.
Hayner, Norman S.: 'Hotel life and personality', *The American Journal of Sociology*, 33 (5), 1928, 784–95.
'Hotel'. In: Schweiz, Suisse, Svizzera, Switzerland, 3/1981, Vol. 54, Zürich 1981.
'Hotels – Hôtels'. In: *Archithese. Zeitschrift und Schriftenreihe für Architektur*, 2/1988.
'Hotels from grand to fabulous', *Architectural Review*, September 1960, 240.
'Hotels and motels', *Interiors*, November 1958, 86.
Hude, Hermann von der: 'Hotels'. In: *Handbuch der Architektur*. Teil 4, Entwerfen, Anlage und Einrichtung der Gebäude. Gebäude für Erholungs-, Beherbergungs- und Vereinszwecke, Darmstadt 1885.
Ingram, Paul: *The Rise of Hotel Chains in the United States, 1896–1980*, New York/London 1996.
Jen, Leslie: ‚Checking in: the formally downbeat Gladstone Hotel invites the art and design community to give it more than just a facelift', *Canadian Architect*, 50 (9), 2005, 24–9.
Just, Karl Wilhelm: 'Hotels, Restaurants', Leipzig 1933.
Klasen, Ludwig: *Grundriss-Vorbilder von Gasthäusern, Hôtels und Restaurants*, Leipzig 1884 (Grundriss-Vorbilder für Gebäude aller Art, Abth. II).
Klein, Dan: ‚A twenties affair: the Park Lane Hotel', *Connoisseur*, 208 (836), 1981,145–7.
Knapp , Frederic: 'The Sheraton Palace: preserving the past, positioning for the future', *The Cornell Hotel and Restaurant Administration Quarterly*, 32 (4), 1991: 13–23.
Koch, Alexander: *Hotelbauten, Motels, Ferienhäuser*, Stuttgart 1961.
Koprince, Susan: 'Edith Wharton's hotels', *Massachusetts Studies in English*, 10, 1985: 12–23
Künzli, Lis (Hrsg.): *Hotels. Ein literarischer Führer*, Frankfurt am Main 1996.
Lamonaca, Marianne and Jonathan Mogul (Eds.): *Grand Hotels of the Jazz Age: The Architecture of Schultze and Weaver*, New York 2005.
Lapidus, Morris: *An Architecture of Joy*, Miami 1979.
Lapidus, Morris: *Too Much is Never Enough: An Autobiography*, New York 1996.
Leitner, Maria: *Hotel Amerika*, Dresden (1930) 1950.
Limerick, Jeffrey: *America's Grand Resort Hotels*, New York 1979.
London (Illustrated) A Complete Guide to The Places of Amusement, Objects of Interest, Parks, Clubs, Markets, Docks, Principal Railway Routes, Leading Hotels…, London 1881.
Ludy, Robert Borneman: *Historic Hotels of the World*, Philadelphia 1927.
Ludy, Robert: *Historic Hotels of the World*, Philadelphia (1927) 2009.
MacKenzie, Compton: *The Savoy of London*, London/Toronto/ Wellington/Sydney 1953.
Matthias, Bettina: ‚A home away from home? The hotel as space of emancipation in early twentieth century Austrian bourgeois literature', *German Studies Review*, 27 (2), 2004: 325–40.
Matthew, Christopher: *A Different World: Stories of Great Hotels*, London 1974.
McNeill, Donald: ‚The hotel and the city', *Progress in Human Geography*, 32 (3), 2008: 383–98.
Meade, Martin and Anthony Lawrence Joseph Fitchett: *Grand Oriental Hotels*, London 1987.
Montgomery-Massingberd, Hugh and David Watkin (Eds.): *The London Ritz. A Social and Architectural History*, London 1980.
Morecombe Hotel: the L.M.S as Maecenas, *Country Life*, November 1933.
North British Railway Company's Station Hotels. O.O., o. J.
Page, Marion: ‚Hotel Plaza, „Manhattan's proud memento of Edwardian elegance": an historical outline from its inception in 1907', *Interiors*, April 1959: 128-33.
Price, Matlock: ‚Great modern hotels of America, their leadership in architecture and interior decoration: the Los Angeles Biltmore', *Arts and Decoration*, 21, 1924: 25–8.
Raitz, Karl B. and Jones, John Paul: ‚The city hotel as landscape artifact and community symbol', *Journal of Cultural Geography*, 9 (1), 1988: 17–36.
Rätisches Museum (Eds.) *Bündner Hotellerie um 1900 in Bildern*, Chur 1992
Reynolds, Donald Martin: *The Architecture of New York City: Histories and Views of Important Structures, Sites, and Symbols*, New York 1984 .
Rubinstein, Hilary: *Hotels and Inns*, Oxford 1984.
Rucki, Isabelle: *Das Hotel in den Alpen. Die Geschichte der Oberengadiner Hotelarchitektur von 1860 bis 1914*, Zürich 1989.
Saint, Andrew: ‚Evolution of a hotel interior: Claridge's, London II', *Country Life*, 170 (4376), 1981: 36–40.
Sandoval-Strausz , A. K.: *Hotel: An American History*, London 2007.
Saudan, Michel et Sylvia: *De L'Hotel-Palais en Riviera*, Genève 1985.
Schmitt, Michael: *Palast-Hotels. Architektur und Anspruch eines Bautyps. 1870–1920*, Berlin 1982.
Schweizer Heimatschutz (Ed.): *Die schönsten Hotels der Schweiz. Der Schweizer Heimatschutz stellt aussergewöhnliche Gasthäuser vor*, Zürich 2008.
Seger, Cordula: *Grand Hotel. Schauplatz der Literatur*, Köln/Weimar/ Wien 2005.
Seger, Cordula, Reinhard G. Wittmann (Eds.): *Grand Hotel. Bühne der Literatur*, Hamburg 2007.
Sherman, Rachel: *Class Acts: Service and Inequality in Luxury Hotels*,

London 2007.
Shopsin, William C.: *The Villard Houses. Life Story of a Landmark (Hotel Helmsley Palace)*, New York 1980.
'Stadthotels'. In: *Bauwelt*, 24. November (86) 1995, no. 44.
Tang, T. C.: ‚The Shophouse Hotel: vernacular heritage in a creative city', *Urban Studies*, 46 (2), 2009: 341–67.
Taylor, Derek and Bush, David: *The Golden Age of British Hotels*, London: 1974.
'The influence of various styles on the design of a modem apartment hotel', *The American Architect*, 20 January 1928, 109.
Tolles, Bryant Franklin: *Resort Hotels of the Adirondacks: The Architects of a Summer Paradise*, New Hampshire 2003.
'Übernachten – Sleeping out'. In: *Daidalos. Architektur, Kunst, Kultur*, no. 62, Dezember 1996.
Watkins, David: Grand Hotel: *The Golden Age of Palace Hotels, An Architectural and Social History*, London 1984.
Wharton, Annabel Jane: *Building the Cold War: Hilton International Hotels and Modern Architecture*, London . 200[illegible].
White, Arthur: *Palaces of the People: A Social History of Commercial Hospitality*, London 1968.
Wilson , Richard (Ed.): *Victorian Resorts and Hotels: Essays from a Victorian Society Autumn Symposium*, Philadelphia 1982.
Young, Lucie: 'Miami Moderne: funky design innovations have restored the dignity to a clutch of decaying Deco hotels in Miami', *Designer's Journal*, 81, 1992: 22–6.

Selected Bibliography Restaurants

Admji, Morris (Ed.): *Aldo Rossi, architecture: 1981–1991*. New York 1991.
Allen, Keith R.: *Hungrige Metropole: Essen, Wohlfahrt und Kommerz in Berlin*. Hamburg 2002.
Amberger, Eva-Maria: *Sergius Ruegenberg: Architekt zwischen Mies van der Rohe und Hans Scharoun*, Berlin 2000.
André, Jacques: *Essen und Trinken im alten Rom*, Stuttgart 1998.
Andreini, Laura (Ed.): *Cafés & Restaurants*, Kempen 2000.
Andressen, B. Michael: *Barocke Tafelfreuden: Tischkultur an Europas Höfen*, Niedernhausen 2001.
Appetite for Design: Eat Me: Product. Packaging. Art. Branding. Interior, Hong Kong 2011.
Aslan, Carlo and Line Dru: *Cafés, Restaurants*, Stuttgart 1991.
Avermaete, Tom, and Anne Massey (Eds.): *Hotel Lobbies and Lounges: The Architecture of Professional Hospitality*, London 2012.
Bastek, Alexander, Achatz von Müller, Livia Cárdenas and Anna Ahrens (Eds.): *Kunst, Küche und Kalkül: Carl Friedrich von Rumohr (1785–1843) und die Entdeckung der Kulturgeschichte*, Petersberg 2010.
Belli, Gabriella, and Beatrice Avanzi (Eds.): *Depero Pubblicitario: Dall'auto-réclame all'architettura pubblicitaria*, Milan 2007.
Besatsu Shotenkenchiku-Sha: *Excellent Shop Designs* (vol. 28): *Cafés, restaurants, bars*, Tokyo 1986.
Beusen, Paul, Sybille Ebert-Schifferer and Ekkehard Mai (Eds.): *L'art Gourmand: Stilleben für Auge, Kochkunst und Gourmets von Aertsen bis Van Gogh*, Gent 1997.
Beynet, Agricol: *Les chroniques du Palais-Royal: origine, splendeur et décadence: les ducs et les duchesses, la régence, théâtres, cafés, restaurants, tripots, les galeries de bois, etc.*, Paris 1881.
Bird, Peter: *The First Food Empire - The History of J. Lyons and Co.*, Chichester 2000.
Biswas, Ramesh Kumar, Siegfried Mattl and Ulrike Davis-Sulikowski (Eds.): *Götterspeisen*, Wien 1997.
Bock, Sybille, Michael Bachmann, Ines Heim and Thomas Schwarz (Eds.): *Zu Dürers Zeiten: Druckgraphik des 15. und 16. Jahrhunderts aus dem Augustinermuseum Freiburg*, Freiburg i. Br. 1991.
Brillat-Savarin, Jean Anthelme: *Physiologie des Geschmacks oder physiologische Anleitung zum Studium der Tafelgenüsse*, Braunschweig 1865 (reprint 1983)
Brown-Manrique, Gerardo (Ed.): *Rudolf Fränkel and Neues Bauen: Work in Germany, Romania and the United Kingdom*, Tübingen 2009.
Chan-Magomedov, Selim O.: *Pioniere der sowjetischen Architektur: der Weg zur neuen sowjetischen Architektur in den Zwanziger und zu Beginn der dreißiger Jahre*, Dresden 1983.
Christophe, Delphine, and Georgina Letourny (Eds.): *Paris et ses Cafés*, Paris 2004.
Conran, Terence: *Terence Conran on Restaurants*, London 2000.
Courtine, Robert: *Cafés et Restaurants des Boulevards. 1814–1914*, Paris 1984.
Courtine, Robert: *La Rive Gauche*, Paris 1987.
Courtine, Robert: *La Vie Parisienne: Le Ventre de Paris, de la Bastille a l'Étoile... Des Siècles d'appétit*, Paris 1985.
Dalby, Andrew: *Essen und Trinken im alten Griechenland: Von Homer bis zur byzantinischen Zeit* (Original Title: Sirens Feasts. A History of Food and Gastronomy in Greece, London 1996), Stuttgart 1998.
Danesi, Silvia, and Luciano Patetta (Eds.): *Il Razionalismo e l'architettura in Italia durante il Fascismo*, Venice 1976.
de Chantal, Laure (Ed.): *À La Table des Anciens. Guide de Cuisine Antique*, 2nd Ed., Paris 2010.
de Franciscis, Alfonso: *Pompei*, Novara 1967.
Duboy, Philippe: *Edoardo Detti, 1913-1984, Architetto e Urbanista: Dilemma del futuro di Firenze*, Milan 199[illegible].
Ehlert, Trude: *Das Kochbuch des Mittelalters. Rezepte aus alter Zeit*, Düsseldorf 2000.
Ehrman, Edwina (Ed.): *London Eats Out: 500 Years of Capital Dining*, London 1999.
Eleb, Monique, and Jean-Charles Depaule: *Paris – Société des Cafés*, Paris 2005.
Eleb, Monique: *La Société des Cafés – Los Angeles*, Paris 2004.
Foote MacDougall, Alice: *The Secret of Successful Restaurants*, New York/London 1929.
Fournel, Victor: *Le vieux Paris*, Paris 1979.
Galinou, Mireille, and John T. Hayes (Eds.): *London in Paint: Oil Paintings in the Collection at the Museum of London*, London 1996.
Gantenbein, Köbi: 'Seit zwanzig Jahren lobt und fördert der Solarpreis das Bauen mit und an der Sonne', In: *Hochparterre*, September 2010, 50–53.
Gatz, Konrad, and Hugo Kämmerer: *Gaststätten – Anlage, Bau, Ausstattung*, Munich 1951.
Girveau, Bruno: *La belle époque des cafés et des restaurants*, Paris 1990.
Gopnik, Adam: *The Table Comes First: Family, France, and the Meaning of Food*, New York 2011.
Guides Gallimard Restaurants de Paris: *Paris, Die schönsten Restaurants*, Paris 1993.
Gutman, Richard, Elliott Kaufman and David Slovi (Eds.): *American Diner*, New York 1979.
Hartmann, Robert, and Andreas Wünkhaus (Eds.): *Eat Art; Restaurant Spoerri: Sammlung Carlo Schröter: Mit Arbeiten von Arman, Joseph Beuys, Pol Bury, César, Roy Lichtenstein, Richard Lindner, Bernhard Luginbühl, Francois Morellet, Tony Morgan, Dieter Roth, Miralda-Selz, Daniel Spoerri, André Thomkins, Jean Tinguely, Günther Uecker, Günter Weseler*, Düsseldorf 2009.
Hell-Girod, Ginette: *L'esprit des brasseries*, Paris 1995.
Hilberseimer, Ludwig: *Contemporary Architecture: Its Roots and Trends*, Chicago 1964.
Hoffmann, Herbert (Ed.): *Gaststätten, Cafés und Restaurants, Ausflugs- und Tanzlokale, Bars, Trink- und Imbißstuben aus Deutschland und dem Ausland*, Stuttgart 1939.
Hogan, David Gerard: *Selling 'em by the Sack: White Castle and the Creation of American Food*, New York/London 1997.

Hooton-Smith, Eileen: *The restaurants of London*, London 1928.
Jakle, John A., and Keith A. Sculle (Eds.): *Fast Food. Roadside Restaurants in the Automobile Age*, Baltimore 1999.
Koch, Alexander: *Restaurants, Cafés, Bars* (Stuttgart 1959)
Kreis, Barbara (Ed.): *Bruno Taut. Moskauer Briefe 1932–1933: Schönheit, Sachlichkeit und Sozialismus*, Berlin 2006.
Krulic, Brigitte: *Europe, lieux communs: cafés, gares, jardins publics...*, Paris 2004.
Lander, Nicholas: *The Art of the Restaurateur*, London 2012.
Logue, A. W.: *Die Psychologie des Essens und Trinkens* (Original Title: The Psychology of Eating and Drinking, New York 1986, 1991), Heidelberg/Berlin 1995.
MacCarthy, Fiona: *William Morris: A Life for our Time*, New York 1994, 1995.
MacDonogh, Giles: *A Palate in Revolution. Grimond de La Reynière and the Almanac des Gourmands*, London 1987.
Marinetti, Filippo Tommaso: *Die futuristische Küche*, 1931, Klaus M. Rarisch. Stuttgart, 1983.
Massaglia Aït-Ahmed, Marina: *Maurice Braillard: Architecte et Urbaniste*, Geneva 1991.
Maurenbrecher, C. P.: *Europäische Kaufrufe. Strassenhändler in graphischen Darstellungen Paris, Lissabon, Neapel, Rom, Bologna, Mailand, Venedig und Konstantinopel*, Dortmund 1980.
Maurenbrecher, C. P.: *Europäische Kaufrufe. Strassenhändler in graphischen Darstellungen, Mitteleuropa, England, Russland*, Dortmund 1980.
May, Herbert, and Andrea Schilz (Eds.): *Gasthäuser – Geschichte und Kultur*, Petersberg 2004.
Merkert, Jörn, Marga Döpping, Lothar Klünner and Klara Drenker-Nagels (Eds.): *Jeanne Mammen, 1890–1976: Monographie und Werkverzeichnis*, Cologne 1997.
Moderne Cafés, Restaurants und Vergnügungsstätten: Aussen- u. Innenarchitektur, Berlin 1928.
Montgomery-Massingberd, Hugh, and David Watkin (Eds.): *The London Ritz: A Social and Architectural History*, London 1980.
Motels, Hotels, Restaurants and Bars, New York 1953.
Moulin, Leo: *Augenlust und Tafelfreuden. Essen und Trinken in Europa – eine Kulturgeschichte* (Original title: Les Liturgies de la Table, 1988), Steinhagen 1989.
Mullen, Richard, and James Munson: *'The Smell of the Continent' – The British discover Europe*, London 2009.
Museum für Angewandte Kunst Frankfurt (Ed.): *Fragile. Die Tafel der Zaren und das Porzellan der Revolutionäre: Die Russische Tafelkultur des 18. bis 20. Jahrhunderts*, Frankfurt am Main 2008.
Nagel, Joachim: *Zu Gast bei Goethe. Der Dichterfürst als Genießer: Mit 40 Rezepten*, München 1999.
Negro, Francesco dal: *Hotel des Alpes: Storie di Alberghi ed Albergatori dalla Savoia al Tirolo, Historische Gastlichkeit von Savoyen bis Tirol*, Baden 2007.
'Nieuw toprestaurant in het rijksmuseum', *De Volkskrant*, vol. 6, 31 Oct. 2014
Ory, Pascal: *Le discours gastronomique français des origines à nos jours*, Paris 1998.
Ottomeyer, Hans, and Michaela Völkel (Eds.): *Die öffentliche Tafel. Tafelzeremoniell in Europa 1300-1900*, Berlin 2002.
Pedersen, Johan (Ed.): *Arkitekten Arne Jacobsen*, Copenhagen 1954.
Pence, Gregory E.: *The Ethics of Food: A Reader for the Twenty-first Century*, Lanham 2002.
Pfeiffer, Ingrid, and Max Hollein (Eds.): *Esprit Montmartre: die Bohème in Paris um 1900*, Frankfurt 2014.
Pile, John F.: *Interior Design*, New York 1995.
Pile, John F.: *A history of Interior Design*, London 2000.
Pisarik, Sonja (Ed.): *Walter Loos, Fridl Loos, Hermann Loos: Paraíso Argentino*, Vienna 2006.
Rauers, Friedrich: *Kulturgeschichte der Gaststätte*, 2 vols., Berlin 1941.
Russell, Herts B.: *The Art and Business of Interior Decoration*, Boston 1922.
Sala, Teresa M. (Ed.): *Barcelona 1900*, Brussels 2007.
Sallas, Joan: *Tischlein deck dich: Ursprung und Entwicklung des Serviettenbrechens* (Katalog Zur Ausstellung), Salzburg 2008.
Schivelbusch, Wolfgang: *Das Paradies, der Geschmack und die Vernunft. Eine Geschichte der Genussmittel*, Munich 1980, English translation: *Tastes of paradise: a social history of spices, stimulants, and intoxicants*, New York 1992.
Schuyt, Michael, and Joost Elffers (Eds.): *Phantasievolle Ideen für vergnügte Köche: Die Radieschenmaus im Käseloch*, Cologne 1982, 2002.
Simmen, Jeannot: *Ruinenfaszination in der Graphik vom 16. Jahrhundert bis in die Gegenwart*, Dortmund 1980.
Simon, André L., and Peter Hunt (Eds.): *Eating and Drinking. An Anthology for Epicures*, London 1961.
Smith, Andrew F.: *Eating History: Thirty turning points in the Making of American Cuisine*, New York 2011.
Spang, Rebecca L.: *The invention of the restaurant. Paris and modern gastronomic culture*, Cambridge, Mass./London 2000, 2001.
Spring, Ulrike, Wolfgang Kos, and Wolfgang Freitag (Eds.): *Im Wirtshaus. Eine Geschichte der Wiener Geselligkeit*, Vienna 2007.
Steel, Carolyn: *Hungry City. How Food Shapes Our Lives*, London 2008, 2009.
Stern, Robert, Gregory Gilmartin and Thomas Mellis: *New York 1930 – Architecture and Urbanism between the two World Wars*, New York 1987.
Tames, Richard: *Feeding London. A Taste of History*, London 2003.
Täubrich, Hans-Christian: *Zu Gast im alten Berlin. Erinnerungen an die Alt-Berliner Gastlichkeit mit Hotelpalästen, Vergnügungslokalen, Ausflugsgaststätten und Destillen*, Munich 1990.
Thomas, Lately: *The Delmonico's, A Century of Splendor*, Boston 1967.
Tinker, Irene: *Street Foods. Urban Food and Employment in Developing Countries*, New York/Oxford 1997.
Tretter, Sandra (Ed.): *Koloman Moser, 1868–1918*, Munich 2007.
Vatsella, Katerina, and Andreas Pfeiffer (Eds.): *Rodin und die Skulptur im Paris der Jahrhundertwende*, Bremen 2000.
von Peschke, Hans-Peter, and Werner Feldmann (Eds.): *Das Kochbuch der Renaissance*, Düsseldorf 2001.
von Vaerst, Eugen: *Gastrosophie, oder Lehre von den Freuden der Tafel*, 2 vols. (1851), Leipzig (Reprint 1975).
von Wetzlar, Jon. (Ed.): *Urbane Anarchisten: Die Kultur der Imbissbude*, Marburg 2003.
Wagner, Heinrich and Hugo Koch: 'Schankstätten und Speisewirtschaften'. In: Eduard Schmitt et al. (Ed.): *Handbuch der Architektur*, Teil 4/1, *Gebäude für Erholungs- Berherbergungs- und Vereinszwecke*, Stuttgart 1904.
Wagner, Leopold: *More London Inns and Taverns*, London 1925.
Weisberg, Gabriel: *Montmartre and the Making of Mass Culture*, New Brunswick/London 2001.
Whiton, Augustus Sherrill: *Elements Of Interior Design And Decoration*, Philadelphia/New York 1951.
Willy, John: *Ideas for refreshment rooms: hotel, restaurant, lunch room, tea room, coffee shop, cafeteria, dining car, industrial plant, school, club, soda fountain, a ready reference to catering methods, covering a wide range of practice*, Chicago 1923.
Zimmermann, Margarete, and Gilda Rodeck (Eds.): *'Ach, wie gut schmeckt mir Berlin'. Französische Passanten im Berlin der zwanziger und frühen dreißiger Jahre*, Berlin 2010.
Zischka, Ulrike, Hans Ottomeyer, and Susanne Bäumler (Eds.): *Die anständige Lust: Von Esskultur und Tafelsitten*, Munich 1993.

Illustration Credits
Bildnachweis

Cover Illustrations

1 Filmstill 'Hotel Adlon'
2 Café Museum, Adolf Loos, Vienna
3 'Empire Diner', New York
4 'Hotel Kursaal de la Maloja', Engadin
5 Restaurant Wembley Stadion, London

Cafés and Bars

1 Dufour, Sylvestre: *Traitez nouveaux & curieux du café, du thé et du chocolate*, La Haye 1671
2, 4 (left), 9 (top) Kaffeehistorische Sammlungen Tchibo
3 (left) Melling, *Voyage pittoresque de Constantinople*, British Library
3 (right), 9, 11, 14, 16, 18, 20 (top), 21, 22 Jünger Wolfgang: *Herr Ober, ein Kaffee! Illustrierte Kulturgeschichte des Kaffeehauses*, Munich 1955
4 (right) Gastro Communication (Archive), Leipzig
5 (left) Galleria Civica d'Arte Moderna, Milan
5 (right) Archive Caffè Florian, Venice
6 (left) Museum für Kunsthandwerk, Leipzig
6 (centre) Recueil le Hay, *Explications des cents estamps répresentant differents nations du Levant*, British Library, London
6 (right) Renato Danilo, *La bottega del caffè. I caffè veneziani tra il 800 e il 900*, Venice
7 (left) Kunsthalle Hamburg/Museum für Kunsthandwerk, Leipzig
7 (right) Barrier, Janine: *Piranèse*, Paris 1995
8 , 14 (bottom), 17, 23, 24 Musée Carnavalet, Paris
10, 20, 32, 33 Archive Franziska Bollerey
12 Johann Jacobs Museum, Zurich
13 Museo Correr, Venice
15 May, Herbert, Andrea Schilz (Eds.): *Gasthäuser. Geschichte und Kultur*, Petersberg 2004; Klaus Lindow, Berlin
19 Heise, Ulla: *Kaffee und Kaffeehaus: Eine Kulturgeschichte*, Leipzig 1987
25 Postcard, BHVP
26 Jean Cocteau/Éditions Filipacchi
27 Museu da Cidade de Lisboa, Lisbon
28 Stadtgeschichtliches Museum, Leipzig
29 Albertina, Vienna
30 Söhn, Gerhard: *Von Mokka bis Espresso*, Hamburg 1957
31 Weigel, Hans, Christian Brandstätter, Werner J. Schweiger (Eds.): *Das Wiener Kaffeehaus*, Vienna/Munich/Zurich 1978

Hotels

1 Fuchs, Eduard: *Geschichte der erotischen Kunst*, Munich 1908
2, 17 (right), 31 (left), 32 , 36 (bottom right), 37 (right), 39 (bottom), 42 (left) Rucki, Isabelle: *Das Hotel in den Alpen. Die Geschichte der Oberengadiner Hotelarchitektur von 1860 bis 1914*, Zurich 1989
3 (left) Ludy, Robert: *Historic Hotels of the World*, Philadelphia 2009 (1927)
3 (right) Peck, Amelia: *Alexander Jackson Davis. American Architect 1803–1892*, New York 1992.
4 (top right), 10, 12 (bottom left), 13 (top left and centre), 25, 26, 34 (left), 36 (top), 38, 40, 41 (right) Flückiger-Seiler, Roland: *Hotelpaläste zwischen Traum und Wirklichkeit. Schweizer Tourismus und Hotelbau 1830–1920*, Zurich 2003 (2001)
4 (top right), 27 Saudan, Michel and Sylvia: *De L'Hotel-Palais en Riviera*, Geneva 1985
5 Durand, Claude Nicolas Louis: *Recueil et paralleles des edifices de tous genres, anciens et modernes,remarquables par leur beaute,par leur grandeur ou par leur singularite et dessine sur une meme echelle, Atlante, in folio di 92 tavole*, Paris 1800
6, 7 (top left) Montgomery-Massingberd, Hugh and David Watkin: *The London Ritz. A Social and Architectural History*, London 1980
7 (bottom right), 8, 17 (left), 18, 19, 21 (top), 22 (right), 41 (bottom) D'Ormesson, Jean, David Watkin et al: *Grand Hotel. The Golden Age of Palace Hotels. An Architectural and Social History*, New York 1984
7 (bottom left), 33 MacKenzie, Compton: *The Savoy of London,* London/Toronto/Wellington/Sydney 1953
7 (top right) Meade, Martin, Joseph Fitchett, Anthony Lawrence: *Grand Oriental Hotels*, London 1987
9 Horstmann,Theo, Regina Weber (Ed.): *„Hier wirkt Elektrizität". Werbung für Strom 1890–2010*, Essen 2010
11 (left), 15, 16 (bottom right) Just, Karl Wilhelm: *Hotels, Restaurants*, Leipzig 1933 (Handbuch der Architektur, IV., 4. Halbband, no. 1).
11 (right) Pizza, Antonio, Josep Maria M. Rovira (Eds.): I*n Search of Home. Coderch 1940/1964*, Barcelona 2000
12 (right) Klasen, Ludwig: *Grundriss-Vorbilder von Gasthäusern, Hotels und Restaurants*, Leipzig 1884
12 (top left), 14, 16 (left and top right) Hude, Hermann von der: 'Hotels'. In: *Handbuch der Architektur. Vierter Teil, 4. Halbband: Entwerfen, Anlage und Einrichtung der Gebäude. Gebäude für Erholungs-, Beherbergungs- und Vereinszwecke*, Darmstadt 1885
13 (top right), 28, 29 (left), 31 (top right), 34 (right) Flückiger-Seiler, Roland: *Hotelträume zwischen Gletschern und Palmen. Schweizer Tourismus und Hotelbau. 1830–1920*, Zurich 2005 (2001)
13 (bottom left) 'Hotels-Hôtels'. In: *Archithese. Zeitschrift und Schriftenreihe für Architektur*, no. 2, 1988
13 (bottom right), 24 (right) Schmitt, Michael: *Palast-Hotels. Architektur und Anspruch eines Bautyps. 1870–1920*, Berlin 1982
20 Prinzler, Hans Helmut: *Friedrich Wilhelm Murnau. Ein Melancholiker des Films*, Berlin 2003
21 (bottom), 23 'Stadthotels'. In: *Bauwelt*, 86 (1995), no. 44
22 (left) Rota, Italo: *Not only Buildings,* Milan 2000
24 (left) Bollerey, Franziska: Photography July 1998
29 (right) Negro, Francesco dal: *Hotel des Alpes. Historische Gastlichkeit von Savoyen bis Tirol*, Baden 2007
30, 39 (top), 41 (top) Roethlisberger, Marcel, Hans Hartmann: *Die Alpen in der Schweizer Malerei*, Chur 1977
31 (bottom left) Leuzinger, Hans: 1887–1971. *Pragmatisch modern. Dokumente zur Schweizer Architektur*, Zurich 1993
35 Künzli, Lis (Ed.): *Hotels. Ein literarischer Führer*, Frankfurt am Main 1996
37 (top) Rätisches Museum (Ed.): *Bündner Hotellerie um 1900 in Bildern*, Chur 1992

Restaurants

1 Moulin, Leo: *Augenlust und Tafelfreuden. Essen und Trinken in Europa – eine Kulturgeschichte* (Original title: Les Liturgies de la Table, 1988), Steinhagen 1989
2 (left), 11 (left and right) von Vaerst, Eugen: *Gastrosophie, oder Lehre von den Freuden der Tafel*, 2 Vols. (1851) (Leipzig, Reprint 1975)
2 (right), 3 Brillat-Savarin, *Jean Anthelme: Physiologie des Geschmacks oder physiologische Anleitung zum Studium der Tafelgenüsse*, Braunschweig 1965 (Reprint 1983)
4, 8 (top left, top center), 9, 25, 61 (left) BNF, Paris
5, 6, 15, 32 (top left), 36 (top right), 6 (right) Zischka, Ulrike,

Hans Ottomeyer, and Susanne Bäumler (Eds.): *Die anständige Lust: Von Esskultur und Tafelsitten*, München 1993.
7 MacDonogh, Giles, *A Palate in Revolution. Grimond de La Reyniére and the Almanac des Gourmands*, London 1987.
10 Staatsbibliothek I, Berlin.
11 (centre) Bastek, Alexander, Achatz von Müller, Livia Cárdenas, und Anna Ahrens (Eds.): *Kunst, Küche und Kalkül: Carl Friedrich von Rumohr (1785-1843) und die Entdeckung der Kulturgeschichte*, Petersberg 2010.
12 *Guides Gallimard Restaurants de Paris*: Paris, *Die schönsten Restaurants*, Paris 1993.
13, 14, 26 (bottom left), 36 (left), 44, 46 (bottom right), 50, 53 Archive Franziska Bollerey
16, 18, 20 (top left), 21, 23, 28 Ottomeyer, Hans, and Michaela Völkel (Eds.): *Die öffentliche Tafel. Tafelzeremoniell in Europa 1300–1900*, Berlin 2002
Bock, Sybille, Michael Bachmann, Ines Heim, and Thomas Schwarz (Eds.): *Zu Dürers Zeiten: Druckgraphik des 15. und 16. Jahrhunderts. Aus dem Augustinermuseum Freiburg*, Freiburg i. Br. 1991
19, 20 (bottom, right) Sallas, Joan, *Tischlein deck dich: Ursprung und Entwicklung des Serviettenbrechens*, Salzburg 2008
22, 24, 26 (right), 32 (bottom left) Andressen, B. Michael, *Barocke Tafelfreuden: Tischkultur an Europas Höfen*, Niedernhausen 2001
26 (top left) Schuyt, Mike, and Joost Elffers (Eds.): *Phantasievolle Ideen Für Vergnügte Köche: Die Radieschenmaus Im Käseloch*, Köln (o.v. 1982) 2002
27, 46 (centre right) Museum Für Angewandte Kunst Frankfurt (Eds.): *Fragile. Die Tafel der Zaren und das Porzellan der Revolutionäre: Die Russische Tafelkultur des 18. bis 20. Jahrhunderts*, Frankfurt am Main, 2008
29 Fournel, Victor: *Le vieux Paris*, Paris 1979
30 (left), 45 (top left) Simon, André L., and Peter Hunt (Eds.): *Eating and Drinking. An Anthology for Epicures*, London 1961.
30 (right) Tames, Richard: *Feeding London. A Taste of History*, London 2003
31, 34, 52, 54 (top), 55 (bottom), 59 Täubrich, Hans-Christian: *Zu Gast im alten Berlin: Erinnerungen an die Alt-Berliner Gastlichkeit mit Hotelpalästen, Vergnügungslokalen, Ausflugsgaststätten und Destillen*, München, Hugendubel, 1990
32 (top and bottom right), 46 (bottom centre) Pfeiffer, Ingrid, and Max Hollein (Eds.): *Esprit Montmartre: die Bohème in Paris um 1900*, Frankfurt 2014
32 (top left) Beusen, Paul, Sybille Ebert-Schifferer and Ekkehard Mai (Eds.): *L'art Gourmand: Stilleben für Auge, Kochkunst und Gourmets von Aertsen bis Van Gogh*, Gent, 1997
33 (left) Franciscis, Alfonso de: *Pompei*, Novara, Istituto Geografico De Agostini, 1967
33 (centre) Spring, Ulrike, Wolfgang Kos and Wolfgang Freitag (Eds.): *Im Wirtshaus. Eine Geschichte der Wiener Geselligkeit*, Vienna 2007.
33 (right) Nagel, Joachim: *Zu Gast bei Goethe. Der Dichterfürst als Genießer*, München 1999
34 (centre) Brown-Manrique, Gerardo, and Kenneth Frampton (Eds.): *Rudolf Fränkel and Neues Bauen: Work in Germany, Romania and the United Kingdom*, Tübingen 2009
34 (bottom), 42 (right) Koch, Alexander: *Restaurants, Cafés, Bars*, Stuttgart 1959
35 (top) Sala, Teresa M. (ed.): *Barcelona 1900*, Brussels 2007
35 (centre) Tretter, Sandra (ed.): *Koloman Moser, 1868–1918*, Vienna 2007
35 (bottom) Belli, Gabriella, and Beatrice Avanzi: *Depero Pubblicitario: Dall'auto-réclame All'architettura Pubblicitaria*, Milan 2007.
36 (bottom right) Avermaete, Tom, and Anne Massey (Eds.): *Hotel Lobbies and Lounges: The Architecture of Professional Hospitality*, London, Routledge, 2012
37 Kreis, Barbara: *Moskauer Briefe 1932-1933: Schönheit, Sachlichkeit und Sozialismus. Berlin*, Mann, 2006
38 (left) MacCarthy, Fiona: *William Morris: A Life for our Time.* London/New York (1994) 1995
38 (right) 'Nieuw Toprestaurant in het Rijks', *De Volkskrant*, p. 9, 31 Oct. 2014
39 (top) Duboy, Philippe: *Edoardo Detti, 1913-1984, Architetto E Urbanista*, Milan 1993
39 (bottom) Admji, Morris: *Aldo Rossi - Bauten und Projekte*, 1981–1991, Zurich 1997
40 (bottom left) Pedersen, Johan: *Arkitekten Arne Jacobsen*, Copenhagen 1954
40 (top) *Hochparterre*, 2010
40 (top right) Sallstedts Bildbyrå, Stockholm
40 (bottom centre) Massaglia Aït-Ahmed, Marina: *Maurice Braillard: Architecte et Urbaniste*, Geneva 1991
40 (bottom right) Chan-Magomedov, Selim O.: Pioniere Der Sowjetischen Architektur, Dresden 1983
41 (left) Negro, Francesco Dal: *Hotel des Alpes, Storie di Alberghi ed Albergatori dalla Savoia al Tirolo*, Baden 2007.
41 (top right) Pisarik, Sonja (ed.): *Walter Loos, Fridl Loos, Hermann Loos: Paraíso Argentino*, Vienna 2006
41 (bottom right) Danesi, Silvia, and Luciano Patetta (Eds.): *Il Razionalismo e L'architettura in Italia Durante Il Fascismo.* N.p.: La Biennale De Venezia 1976
42 (left) Hoffmann, Herbert: *Gaststätten, Cafés und Restaurants, Ausflugs- und Tanzlokale, Bars, Trink- und Imbisstuben aus Deutschland und dem Ausland*, Stuttgart 1939
43 (top) Amberger, Eva-Maria, and Sergius Ruegenberg (Eds.): *Sergius Ruegenberg: Architekt Zwischen Mies Van Der Rohe und Hans Scharoun*, Berlin 2000
43 (bottom) Simmen, Jeannot: *Ruinenfaszination. In der Graphik vom 16. Jahrhundert bis in die Gegenwart*, Dortmund 1980
45 (top centre) Dalby, Andrew: *Essen und Trinken im alten Griechenland: Von Homer bis zur byzantinischen Zeit* (Original title: *A History of Food and Gastronomy in Greece*, London 1996), Stuttgart 1998
45 (top right, bottom), 46 (top left), 46 (bottom left) Maurenbrecher, C. P.: *Europäische Kaufrufe. Strassenhändler in graphischen Darstellungen Paris, Lissabon, Neapel, Rom, Bologna, Mailand, Venedig und Konstantinopel*, Dortmund 1980
46 (top centre, centre left, centre) Maurenbrecher, C. P.: *Europäische Kaufrufe. Strassenhändler in graphischen Darstellungen, Mitteleuropa, England, Russland*, Dortmund 1980
46 (top right) Galinou, Mireille, and John T. Hayes (Eds.): *London in Paint: Oil Paintings in the Collection at the Museum of London*, London 1996
47, 48, 49, 50 Gutman, Richard, Elliott Kaufman, and David Slovi (Eds.): *American Diner*, New York 1979
51 Jakle, John A., and Keith A. Sculle (Eds.): *Fast Food. Roadside Restaurants in the Automobile Age*, Baltimore 1999
54 (bottom) Allen, Keith R.: *Hungrige Metropole: Essen, Wohlfahrt und Kommerz in Berlin*, Hamburg 2002
55 Merkert, Jörn, Marga Döpping, Lothar Klünner, and Klara Drenker-Nagels (Eds.): *Jeanne Mammen, 1890–1976: Monographie und Werkverzeichnis*, Köln 1997
56 *Appetite for Design: Eat Me: Product. Packaging. Art. Branding. Interior*, Hong Kong 2011
57 Marinetti, Filippo Tommaso: *Die futuristische Küche.* Trans. Klaus M. Rarisch, Stuttgart (1932), 1983
58 Hartmann, Robert, and Andreas Wünkhaus (Eds.): Eat Art; Restaurant Spoerri; Sammlung Carlo Schröter; Mit Arbeiten Von Arman, Joseph Beuys, Pol Bury, César, Roy Lichtenstein, Richard Lindner, Bernhard Luginbühl, Francois Morellet, Tony Morgan, Dieter Roth, Miralda-Selz, Daniel Spoerri, André Thomkins, Jean Tinguely, Günther Uecker, Günter Weseler, Düsseldorf 2009.
60 Montgomery-Massingberd, Hugh, David Watkin, and Keith Collie (Eds.): *The London Ritz: A Social and Architectural History*, London 1980
62 Ory, Pascal: *Le discours gastronomique français des Origines à nos Jours*, Paris 1998

Index

Register of Persons

Register of Places

Register of General Subjects

Register

Personenregister

Ortsregister

Sachregister

IMPRINT
IMPRESSUM

IHAAU
Institute of History of Art, Architecture and Urbanism

Front cover/Vorderseite
'Hotel Adlon', filmstill/Standfoto, 1955.
Film director/Regisseur: Josef von Baky
'Café Museum', Vienna/Wien, 1899.
Architect/Architekt: Adolf Loos
'Empire Diner', New York, 1946.
Fodero Dining Car Company

Back cover/Rückseite
'Hotel Kursaal de la Maloja', Maloja, 1884.
Architect/Architekt: Jules Rau
'Restaurant Wembley Stadion', London, 1921–1924.
Architect/Architekt: Sir Owen Williams

Translation/Übersetzung: Axel Föhl, Laura Bruce
Design and setting/Gestaltung und Satz:
Susanne Rösler, Heiko Niebur, Sogol Nayeri
Lithography/Lithografie: Bild1Druck
Printed in the European Union/
Gedruckt in der Europäischen Union

The Mondriaan Fonds, van Doesburg Huis, supported the research on the chapter 'Restaurants and "Haute Cuisine."'
Der Mondriaan Fonds, van Doesburg Huis, subventionierte die Recherchen zum Kapitel "Restaurants und 'Haute Cuisine'".

Bibliographic information published by the Deutsche Nationalbibliothek
The Deutsche Nationalbibliothek lists this publication in the Deutsche Nationalbibliografie; detailed bibliographic data are available on the Internet at http://dnb.d-nb.de
Bibliografische Information der Deutschen Nationalbibliothek
Die Deutsche Nationalbibliothek verzeichnet diese Publikation in der Deutschen Nationalbibliografie; detaillierte bibliografische Daten sind im Internet über http://dnb.d-nb.de abrufbar.

jovis Verlag GmbH
Kurfürstenstraße 15/16
10785 Berlin

www.jovis.de

jovis books are available worldwide in select bookstores. Please contact your nearest bookseller or visit www.jovis.de for information concerning your local distribution.
jovis-Bücher sind weltweit im ausgewählten Buchhandel erhältlich. Informationen zu unserem internationalen Vertrieb erhalten Sie von Ihrem Buchhändler oder unter www.jovis.de.

ISBN 978-3-86859-483-6